Complete Curriculum

Grade 5

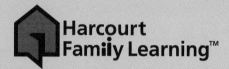

Harcourt
Family Learning™

© 2006 by Flash Kids
Adapted from *Comprehension Skills Complete Classroom Library* by Linda Ward Beech, Tara McCarthy, and Donna Townsend;
© 2001 by Harcourt Achieve. • Adapted from *Steck-Vaughn Spelling: Linking Words to Meaning, Level 5*
by John R. Pescosolido; © 2002 by Harcourt Achieve. • Adapted from *Steck-Vaughn Working with Numbers, Level E*;
© 2001 by Harcourt Achieve. • Adapted from *Language Arts, Grade 5*; © 2003 by Harcourt Achieve. • Adapted from *Experiences with Writing
Styles Grade 5*; © 1998 by Steck-Vaughn Company and *Writing Styles Grade 5*;
© 2003 by Steck-Vaughn Company. • Adapted from *Test Best for Test Prep, Level E*; © 1999 by Harcourt Achieve.
Licensed under special arrangement with Harcourt Achieve.

For more information, please visit www.flashkids.com
Please submit all inquiries to Flashkids@sterlingpublishing.com

ISBN 978-1-4114-9880-8

Manufactured in China

Lot#:
22 24 26 28 30 29 27 25 23 21
12/16

FlashKids

New York

Dear Parent,

Beginning a new grade is a milestone for your child, and each new subject is bound to present some challenges that may require some attention out of the classroom. With this comprehensive fifth-grade workbook at hand, you and your child can work together on any skill that he or she is finding difficult to master. Here to help are hundreds of fun, colorful pages for learning and practicing reading, spelling, math, language arts, writing, and test preparation.

In the reading section, the wide range of high-interest stories will hold your child's attention and help develop his or her proficiency in reading. Each of the six units focuses on a different reading comprehension skill: finding facts, detecting a sequence, learning new vocabulary through context, identifying the main idea, drawing conclusions, and making inferences. Mastering these skills will ensure that your child has the necessary tools for a lifetime love of reading.

Lessons in the spelling section present fifth-grade words in lists grouped by vowel sound, suffix, or related forms, like plurals and contractions. This order will clearly show your child the different ways that similar sounds can be spelled. Your child will learn to sort words, recognize definitions, synonyms, and base words, as well as completing analogies and using capitalization and punctuation. Each lesson also features a short passage containing spelling and grammar mistakes that your child will proofread and correct.

The math section starts by reviewing addition, subtraction, multiplication, and division skills. Next your child learns to add and subtract simple and complex fractions before moving on to decimals, customary and metric units of measure, and geometric concepts such as area and perimeter. Each section begins with clear examples that illustrate new skills, and then practice drills, problem-solving lessons, and unit reviews encourage your child to master each new technique.

More than 100 lessons in the language arts section provide clear examples of and exercises in language skills such as parts of speech, sentences, mechanics, vocabulary and usage, writing, and research skills. Grammar lessons range from using nouns and verbs to constructing better sentences. Writing exercises include the business letter and the research report. These skills will help your child improve his or her communication abilities, excel in all academic areas, and increase his or her scores on standardized tests.

Each of the six units in the writing section focuses on a unique type of writing: personal narrative, how-to writing, story, comparative writing, descriptive writing, and short report. The first half of each unit reinforces writing aspects such as putting ideas in a sequence and using descriptive details, in addition to providing fun, inspirational writing ideas for your child to explore alone or with a friend. In the second half of each unit, your child will read a practice paragraph, analyze it, prepare a writing plan for his or her own paper or paragraph, and then write and revise.

Lastly, the test prep section employs your child's knowledge in reading, math, and language to the basic standardized test formats that your child will encounter throughout his or her school career. Each unit in the first half of this section teaches specific test strategies for areas such as word study skills, reading comprehension, and mathematics. The second half of the section allows your child to apply these test-taking skills in a realistic testing environment that includes a detachable answer sheet. By simulating the experience of taking standardized tests, these practice tests can lessen feelings of intimidation during school tests.

As your child works through the test prep section, help him or her keep in mind these four important principles of test-taking:

1. *Using Time Wisely*

All standardized tests are timed, so your child should learn to work rapidly but comfortably. He or she should not spend too much time on any one question, and mark items to return to if possible. Use any remaining time to review answers. Most importantly, use a watch to keep on track!

2. *Avoiding Errors*

When choosing the correct answers on standardized tests, your child should pay careful attention to directions, determine what is being asked, and mark answers in the appropriate place. He or she should then check all answers and not make stray marks on the answer sheet.

3. *Reasoning*

To think logically toward each answer, your child should read the entire question or passage and all the answer choices before answering a question. It may be helpful to restate questions or answer choices in his or her own words.

4. *Guessing*

When the correct answer is not clear right away, your child should eliminate answers that he or she knows are incorrect. If that is not possible, skip the question. Then your child should compare the remaining answers, restate the question, and then choose the answer that seems most correct.

An answer key at the back of this workbook allows you and your child to check his or her work in any of the subject sections. Remember to give praise and support for each effort. Also, learning at home can be accomplished at any moment—you can ask your child to read the newspaper aloud to you, write grocery lists, keep a journal, or convert the ingredients for a recipe. Use your imagination! With help from you and this workbook, your child is well on the way to completing the fifth grade with flying colors!

TABLE OF CONTENTS

Reading Skills

Spelling Skills

Math Skills

Language Arts

Writing Skills

Test Prep

Answer Key

Reading Skills

What Are Facts?

Facts are sometimes called details. They are small pieces of information. Facts can appear in true stories, such as those in the newspaper. Facts can also appear in legends and other stories that people make up.

How to Read for Facts

You can find facts by asking yourself questions. Ask *who*, and your answer will be a fact about a person. Ask *what*, and your answer will be a fact about a thing. Ask *where*, and your answer will be a fact about a place. Ask *when*, and your answer will be a fact about a time. Ask *how many* or *how much*, and your answer will be a fact about a number or an amount.

Try It!

Read this story and look for facts as you read. Ask yourself *how many* and *what*.

Snakes

If you're afraid of snakes, maybe it's because you don't know much about these interesting animals. There are more than 2,400 different kinds of snakes. They live on every continent of the world except Antarctica. They come in all sizes. The largest snake ever measured was a python that was 32 feet long. One of the smallest is the thread snake, which is only about 4 inches long.

Did you find these facts when you read the paragraph? Write the facts on the lines below.

◆ How many different kinds of snakes are there?

Fact: _____

◆ What is one of the smallest snakes?

Fact: _____

Practice Finding Facts

Below are some practice questions. The first two are already answered. Answer the third one on your own.

B **1.** The thread snake is

    A. 4 feet long   **C.** 32 feet long

    B. 4 inches long   **D.** 32 inches long

Look at the question and answers again. The word *long* is asking for a number. There are many numbers in the paragraph, but you are looking for one that describes the length of the thread snake. Read the paragraph until you find the words *thread snake*. You should find this sentence: "One of the smallest is the thread snake, which is only about 4 inches long." Anwer **B** is the correct answer. Answer **C** is also a fact from the story, but it describes pythons, not thread snakes.

C **2.** The continent that has no snakes is

    A. Africa   **C.** Antarctica

    B. Australia   **D.** America

Look at the question. It asks for the name of a *continent* that has no snakes. Search the story about snakes for the name of a continent. You should find this sentence: "They live on every continent of the world except Antarctica." The words are a little different from the words in the story. The words "except Antarctica" tell you that Antarctica has no snakes, so the answer is **C**.

Now it's your turn to practice. Answer the next question by writing the letter of the correct answer on the line.

3. The largest snake ever measured was

    A. a python   **C.** a thread snake

    B. a continent snake   **D.** an Antarctic snake

Read each story. After each story you will answer questions about the facts in the story. Remember, a fact is something that you know is true.

Hug Someone Else, Please!

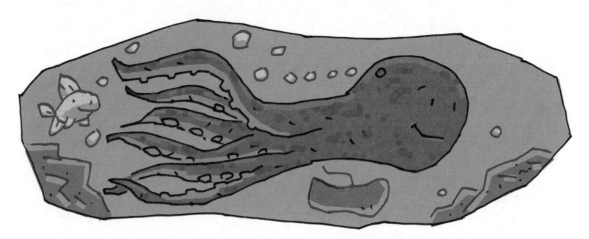

Many people think that an octopus makes a curious sight. It has eight arms coming out of a rounded head. Its name, *octopus*, comes from two Greek words that mean "eight feet."

People once thought that the octopus was a "devilfish" or a "monster of the sea." They thought that an octopus had arms long enough to hug a whole ship. Experts today know that this is not true. These odd sea creatures actually prefer to be left alone. Even the largest type of octopus is too small to hug a ship. Their average length is only about 10 feet. Most kinds of octopus are not any larger than a person's fist. However, an octopus that feels threatened *will* bite, using its sharp, parrotlike beak. Also, every once in a while, an octopus will "hug" a diver.

_____ **1.** An octopus has
    A. six arms   **C.** eight arms
    B. four arms   **D.** two arms

_____ **2.** People once thought that the octopus was a
    A. mammal   **C.** whale
    B. monster   **D.** pet

_____ **3.** The octopus likes to
    A. be left alone   **C.** attack people
    B. play with people   **D.** swim beside boats

_____ **4.** The average length of an octopus is
    A. 12 feet   **C.** 10 feet
    B. 30 feet   **D.** 50 feet

_____ **5.** Octopuses have parrotlike
    A. wings   **C.** eyes
    B. beaks   **D.** tails

Even though it cannot pull ships down into the sea, an octopus can use its arms to move rocks much heavier than itself. Its arms can also handle tiny objects quite well. In one study scientists placed food for an octopus in screw-top jars. The octopus unscrewed the lid and then ate the food from the jar.

An octopus uses its arms mainly to gather food. It eats shellfish, including clams, crabs, and lobsters. It leaves its den at the bottom of the sea at night. When an octopus finds a crab or something else good to eat, it releases poison into the water. This makes the victim easy to catch. For the trip home, the octopus gathers the food into the skin between its arms. This area is called the web. When its web is full, the octopus returns home for a fine meal.

_____ 6. An octopus will use its arms to
- **A.** sink ships
- **B.** attack people
- **C.** poison a crab
- **D.** move large objects

_____ 7. When given a screw-top jar, an octopus will probably
- **A.** break it
- **B.** open it
- **C.** swallow it
- **D.** look at it

_____ 8. An octopus uses its arms mainly to
- **A.** eat
- **B.** fight
- **C.** move rocks
- **D.** carry young

_____ 9. The octopus carries its food in
- **A.** its mouth
- **B.** its beak
- **C.** a layer of skin
- **D.** its gills

_____ 10. The octopus eats its meals
- **A.** above its den
- **B.** in its den
- **C.** away from home
- **D.** while swimming

Cats in History

Cats first became pets long, long ago. This may have happened as early as 3500 B.C. People in early Egypt loved cats. The cats kept homes free of rats, mice, and snakes. Cats also kept pests away from farms and places where grain was stored.

A thousand years later, cats in Egypt had become more important than ever. They were protected by law. Under the law, people who harmed cats could be put to death. Also during this time, cat owners had a special way to express their sadness when a pet cat died. The owners shaved their eyebrows to show how much they had loved their special pet. Cats even became part of the religion in certain areas of Egypt. In those places people prayed to a goddess of love named Bast. Statues of Bast had a cat's head and a woman's body.

_____ 1. Cats became pets as early as
     A. 1000 B.C.   C. 3500 B.C.
     B. 2000 B.C.   D. 5000 B.C.

_____ 2. Cats in early Egypt kept pests away from
     A. farms   C. streets
     B. rats   D. trees

_____ 3. People who harmed cats were sometimes
     A. put in jail   C. given honors
     B. cheered   D. put to death

_____ 4. When cats died, their owners shaved their
     A. heads   C. arms
     B. eyebrows   D. beards

_____ 5. Bast had a cat's
     A. legs   C. body
     B. fur   D. head

People in the Far East also loved cats. They used cats to keep mice from nibbling holy books in temples. Cats also kept mice from eating silkworm cocoons. Silk makers traded silk cloth for other fine goods, so they depended on their cats.

Cats in Europe in the 1300s were not treated as well. People killed them by the thousands because they were a symbol of bad luck. This caused the number of rats to grow. Rats carried diseases. A deadly disease called the Black Death spread, killing one-fourth of all people in Europe.

Over time people once again learned that cats keep many pests away. By the 1600s cats had again become popular. Settlers arriving in the New World brought cats with them. Some of the cats you know today came from those early cats.

_____ **6.** Cats in the Far East kept mice away from
- **A.** water
- **C.** cocoons
- **B.** people
- **D.** Europe

_____ **7.** People in Europe in the 1300s thought cats were
- **A.** cute
- **C.** good
- **B.** fun
- **D.** bad

_____ **8.** With fewer cats the number of rats
- **A.** was larger
- **C.** stayed the same
- **B.** was smaller
- **D.** was unimportant

_____ **9.** One-fourth of the people in Europe
- **A.** moved
- **C.** owned cats
- **B.** died
- **D.** loved cats

_____ **10.** By the 1600s people once again
- **A.** liked cats
- **C.** killed cats
- **B.** saved rats
- **D.** hated cats

Steeplejacks

Do you know what a steeplejack is? First you have to know what a steeple is. A steeple is a tower on a church. A steeplejack is someone who repairs steeples. Steeplejacks may also do painting or cleaning.

There is a family of steeplejacks. They travel around the country finding work as they go. They carry a scrapbook showing the steeples they have repaired. In addition to churches, they work on courthouses and other buildings with towers.

Many of these buildings are old and in need of careful repair. The steeplejacks climb up to look. Often they work with engineers and other experts to decide what to do. Then the family goes to work. Some jobs take a few weeks. Other jobs take months.

_____ 1. A steeple is a church
- **A.** door
- **B.** bell
- **C.** tower
- **D.** window

_____ 2. Steeplejacks do painting and
- **A.** watering
- **B.** waxing
- **C.** preaching
- **D.** cleaning

_____ 3. Besides fixing churches, steeplejacks sometimes work on
- **A.** courthouses
- **B.** churchyards
- **C.** courtyards
- **D.** courtrooms

_____ 4. The first step of a steeplejack's job is to
- **A.** work for weeks
- **B.** look at problems
- **C.** paint the steeple
- **D.** clean the steeple

_____ 5. Steeplejacks often work with
- **A.** engines
- **B.** reporters
- **C.** trains
- **D.** engineers

Many steeples have lovely clocks on them. Sometimes the golden numbers on the clocks have worn out. The steeplejacks replace the worn-out numbers and cover them with thin pieces of gold. Then the clock numbers shine just as they did in the past.

Some steeples have weather vanes on top that need repair. Sometimes the roof of a steeple is worn out. The steeplejacks repair the roofs too. If a steeple is made of metal, then parts of it may have rusted. The steeplejacks replace these parts. If a steeple is made of wood, it may need to be painted. Sometimes steeplejacks paint the inside of a steeple too.

Steeplejacks work in high places and do a lot of climbing. They have to be careful. They don't work in the rain, and they stay home on windy days.

_____ **6.** Sometimes steeplejacks have to replace clock
     A. hands   **C.** alarms
     B. times   **D.** numbers

_____ **7.** Weather vanes on steeples sometimes have to be
     A. turned   **C.** repaired
     B. blown   **D.** finished

_____ **8.** Sometimes steeplejacks repair
     A. roofs   **C.** watches
     B. ladders   **D.** bricks

_____ **9.** Steeplejacks do not work in the
     A. winter   **C.** steeples
     B. clocks   **D.** wind

_____ **10.** In their work steeplejacks need to be very
     A. careful   **C.** careless
     B. stormy   **D.** windy

Please Pass the Drink Fruit

Chimpanzees do not have speech organs that allow them to speak. They can make noises, but they cannot say words. They do have hands with four fingers and a thumb, so some chimps have been able to learn Ameslan, American Sign Language. This is the sign language used by some people who are deaf.

One of the first chimps to learn Ameslan was Washoe. Born in 1965, Washoe began learning to sign words when she was one year old. Like many toddlers, the first "word" she learned was *more*. When she was six, she could use more than 200 signs. Washoe's teachers, Allen and Beatrice Gardner, treated Washoe as their own child. She lived with them in their home, and she did not see other chimpanzees. When she did meet another chimp, she must have thought that it was a strange creature. Her sign for chimp was *bug*.

_____ **1.** Chimpanzees do not have
- **A.** a tongue
- **B.** a throat
- **C.** speech organs
- **D.** teeth

_____ **2.** A sign language used by some deaf people is called
- **A.** English
- **B.** Ameslan
- **C.** Washoe
- **D.** Gardner

_____ **3.** Washoe's first "word" was
- **A.** go
- **B.** bug
- **C.** drink
- **D.** more

_____ **4.** When she was six, Washoe could use more than
- **A.** 200 signs
- **B.** 250 signs
- **C.** 300 signs
- **D.** 1,000 signs

_____ **5.** Washoe probably thought that other chimps were
- **A.** her teachers
- **B.** her friends
- **C.** strange creatures
- **D.** deaf people

Lucy is another chimpanzee that learned sign language. She was born a year after Washoe and lived with another family, the Temerlins. The Temerlins taught her to sign, and she learned quickly. She learned to ask for one of her favorite foods by signing the words for *candy drink fruit*. When Lucy did this, the Temerlins knew that she wanted watermelon. Washoe also made up a word for watermelon. She called it *drink fruit* too.

The Temerlins and the Gardners have found that Lucy and Washoe are like humans in many ways. Sometimes they behave as if they are human. When they are joyful, they clap their hands. When they are angry, they sometimes call their enemies names. They use names they have learned in sign language.

_____ **6.** Lucy was a good
     A. student   **C.** musician
     B. athlete   **D.** teacher

_____ **7.** Both Lucy and Washoe made up a word for
     A. drink   **C.** watermelon
     B. fruit   **D.** candy

_____ **8.** In many ways chimps are like
     A. bugs   **C.** names
     B. people   **D.** their enemies

_____ **9.** When a chimp claps its hands, it is probably
     A. angry   **C.** happy
     B. sad   **D.** thinking

_____ **10.** When a chimp is angry, it might
     A. bite   **C.** call others names
     B. swing its arms   **D.** jump up and down

Sluggers at Work

The wood for baseball bats comes from the ash-tree forests of Pennsylvania. Ash wood is especially strong, so it makes good baseball bats. Ash trees are thin compared to other trees. In a high wind, an ash tree can break and fall. However, in the Pennsylvania forests, thicker kinds of trees grow all around the ash trees. These thick trees keep the ash trees from bending too far in a wind storm.

At Slugger Park workers make baseball bats out of ash trees. Workers and their machines can make an ordinary bat in about eight seconds. It takes longer to make a bat for a major-league player. Many of these players want bats that meet their special needs. Once Ted Williams, a famous baseball player, returned some bats to Slugger Park. "The grips just don't feel right to me," he said. The workers carefully measured the grips. Sure enough, Williams was right! The grips were wrong by just a small fraction of an inch.

_____ 1. Wooden baseball bats are made
    A. in wind storms   **C.** from ash trees
    B. in forests   **D.** from thick trees

_____ 2. Thick trees protect ash trees from
    A. breaking   **C.** playing
    B. growing   **D.** cutting

_____ 3. Workers can make an ordinary bat in about
    A. ten seconds   **C.** twelve seconds
    B. thirty seconds   **D.** eight seconds

_____ 4. Many major-league players want bats that are
    A. special   **C.** stronger
    B. returned   **D.** longer

_____ 5. When Ted Williams didn't like the grips, he
    A. gave the bats away   **C.** measured the grips
    B. sent the bats back   **D.** used the bats anyway

Some players use many bats in a single game. Orlando Cepeda used to throw away a bat after he made a hit with it. He thought that each bat had only a certain number of hits in it. No one could tell how many hits were in a bat. Maybe there was only one. "So why take a chance?" asked Cepeda. When it was his turn to face the pitcher again, he grabbed a brand new Slugger Park bat.

The Slugger Park factory also makes aluminum bats. These are used mostly by college teams and minor-league players. Aluminum bats last longer than wooden ones do. Many baseball fans hope that major-league players will never use these new bats, however. When you hit a ball with one, the sound you hear is a soft *ping*. Fans like to hear the solid *crack* made by a strong wooden bat. Baseball fans don't like the game to change.

_____ **6.** Some players use many bats
     A. over and over   **C.** in a single game
     B. for their fans   **D.** at the same time

_____ **7.** Orlando Cepeda threw away a bat after he
     A. made a hit   **C.** faced the pitcher
     B. took a chance   **D.** had an idea

_____ **8.** Some college teams use
     A. oak bats   **C.** 15 bats
     B. aluminum bats   **D.** fans

_____ **9.** Many baseball fans don't like
     A. college teams   **C.** aluminum bats
     B. pitchers   **D.** major-league players

_____ **10.** Compared to wooden bats, aluminum bats
     A. feel better   **C.** miss balls
     B. break often   **D.** last longer

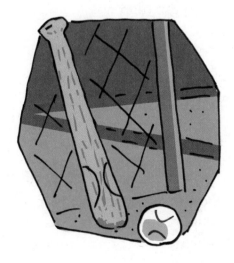

The Midnight Tulip

It was after midnight. A Dutch farmer made one last trip through his greenhouse before going to bed. He walked past rows and rows of tulips. Suddenly he stopped. There, blooming in the early morning hours, was a rare flower. It was a black tulip. In the morning the excited farmer took the tulip to a flower show. By evening the farmer and his prize plant were on television. He was a hero.

Most tulips are red, yellow, white, or pink. A black tulip takes years to develop. The farmer worked on his midnight tulip for seven years. He crossed two dark-purple tulips. They made a seed. The seed took years to grow into a round bulb. Finally a black flower grew from the bulb.

Tulips are a major industry for the Dutch people. Tulip sales bring in millions of dollars.

_____ **1.** The farmer made one last trip through his
    A. grayhouse   **C.** bath house
    B. greenhouse   **D.** pumphouse

_____ **2.** The midnight tulip was
    A. dry   **C.** rare
    B. red   **D.** late

_____ **3.** The farmer crossed tulips that were
    A. pink   **C.** white
    B. black   **D.** purple

_____ **4.** Tulip flowers grow from
    A. leaves   **C.** roots
    B. bulbs   **D.** greenhouses

_____ **5.** For the Dutch people, tulips are a major
    A. import   **C.** industry
    B. million   **D.** problem

The Dutch people first received tulips in the early 1600s. The tulips came from the Far East. The Dutch loved the beautiful flowers, and soon grew their own.

People began trying to produce new kinds of tulips. The results were striped tulips, double tulips, and lily tulips. People grew tulips of many new colors, but black tulips were very rare. Someone grew a black tulip in 1891. Another black tulip bloomed in 1955. It was called Queen of the Night.

Now black tulips grow in ordinary gardens. The Dutch farmer is working on two other unusual tulips. He hopes to grow a tulip that is dark blue. He wants to grow bright green tulips, too. It may take 20 years before they can be sold.

_____ **6.** Tulips were brought to the Dutch people in
     A. 1891   **C.** the 1500s
     B. 1955   **D.** the 1600s

_____ **7.** Tulips first came from
     A. the Far East   **C.** farmers
     B. the Dutch   **D.** queens

_____ **8.** Black tulips bloomed in 1891 and in
     A. 1981   **C.** 1595
     B. 1955   **D.** 1819

_____ **9.** Developing bulbs to sell takes
     A. 16 years   **C.** ordinary gardens
     B. 20 years   **D.** double blooms

_____ **10.** The farmer is working on two other tulips that will be
     A. double   **C.** ordinary
     B. different   **D.** striped

Money Doctors

Have you ever ripped a dollar bill by mistake? If so, perhaps you taped it back together. Sometimes money is damaged in more serious ways. Then it is not as easy to fix. If you cannot repair paper money, you cannot use it. You have to send badly damaged money to a special government office in Washington, D.C.

The people who work in this office sit at long tables under bright lights. Their main tools are magnifying glasses and tweezers. Their job is to piece together the damaged bills. The workers try to find at least half of each bill. Otherwise the government will not pay the owner for it.

This office is very busy. It handles about 30,000 cases per year. People may wait a long time before their case comes up, but it's worth it. The service is free, and you may get your money back.

_____ **1.** If you cannot repair paper money, you cannot
- **A.** buy it
- **B.** use it
- **C.** hide it
- **D.** send it

_____ **2.** You can send badly damaged money to a government
- **A.** bank
- **B.** bill
- **C.** office
- **D.** tool

_____ **3.** The workers' main tools are magnifying glasses and
- **A.** tables
- **B.** tape
- **C.** tweezers
- **D.** lights

_____ **4.** Workers find half of a bill so the government will
- **A.** pay the owner
- **B.** fix the money
- **C.** call the owner
- **D.** take the job

_____ **5.** The services of this office are
- **A.** expensive
- **B.** free
- **C.** early
- **D.** easy

How is money damaged? Sometimes it is damaged in a fire. Then a person may have mostly ashes to send in. Sometimes money is damaged in a flood. Then the bills are faded and stuck together. People have sent money that had gone through the washing machine. Some bills have been chewed by animals. Others somehow got into blenders.

Also some people don't like banks, so they hide their money in unusual places. If bills are buried in cans, they sometimes get moldy. Mice often nibble at money hidden in attics and basements.

Once, a truck carrying money for a bank exploded. There was a big fire. The truck company sent in the remains of the bills. They were worth $2.5 million dollars. Thanks to the government workers, the company got a check for all the money.

_____ **6.** When bills are burned, they turn to
    A. coins   **C.** dust
    B. ashes   **D.** sand

_____ **7.** When bills get wet, they
    A. fade   **C.** fall
    B. burn   **D.** blend

_____ **8.** Some people hide money because they don't like
    A. fires   **C.** mice
    B. checks   **D.** banks

_____ **9.** One time, money carried in a truck was burned in
    A. lightning   **C.** an explosion
    B. a basement   **D.** an airplane

_____**10.** Thanks to the workers, the company was able to
    A. put out the fire   **C.** get the money back
    B. write a check   **D.** buy the money back

Lesson 8

A Life of Art

Frida Kahlo was a famous Mexican painter. Many claim that she is Mexico's greatest artist. As a child she dreamed of becoming a doctor, but a traffic accident changed her entire life. At age 15 Kahlo was riding on a bus in Mexico City. It crashed into a trolley car. Kahlo was seriously hurt and had to stay in the hospital a long time. She felt her dreams of being a doctor were over.

In the hospital Kahlo grew bored. She began to paint to fill her time. She once had taken art lessons from a teacher who thought she had great talent. Kahlo now hoped she could make a living by selling her paintings.

_____ 1. Frida Kahlo was a famous Mexican
         A. painter   **C.** writer
         B. doctor   **D.** singer

_____ 2. Kahlo's life was changed by a
         A. new teacher   **C.** total stranger
         B. traffic accident   **D.** family doctor

_____ 3. Kahlo had once dreamed of being
         A. an artist   **C.** a doctor
         B. an author   **D.** a teacher

_____ 4. In the hospital Kahlo
         A. knitted scarves   **C.** wrote many letters
         B. began to paint   **D.** grew much sicker

_____ 5. A former teacher thought Kahlo
         A. needed classes   **C.** had great talent
         B. had little talent   **D.** should work for him

Most of Kahlo's works were self-portraits. She used bold and harsh colors. They showed the pain that she felt in her body. People praised the art for being so original. Many of her works show symbols from Mexican history as well. She also liked to paint herself in native clothing and jewelry.

At age 22 Kahlo wed Diego Rivera. He was an artist best known for his murals. Many of Kahlo's new paintings showed her feelings about marriage and children.

Sadly, Kahlo's pain never left her. She had 35 operations in her lifetime. Yet she produced many works of art that people still greatly admire.

_____ **6.** Most of Kahlo's paintings were
    A. about buses   **C.** about her husband
    B. done in watercolors   **D.** of herself

_____ **7.** Kahlo's art reflected her
    A. sense of direction   **C.** own feelings
    B. sense of shame   **D.** youth

_____ **8.** Kahlo often painted herself in
    A. dark outfits   **C.** modern jewelry
    B. large hats   **D.** native clothing

_____ **9.** Diego Rivera was Kahlo's
    A. husband   **C.** doctor
    B. art teacher   **D.** neighbor

_____ **10.** People praised Kahlo's art for
    A. being humorous   **C.** its pale colors
    B. being so original   **D.** its high cost

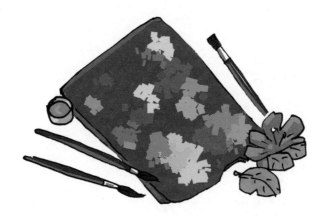

Writing Roundup

Read the story below. Think about the facts. Then answer the questions in complete sentences.

Salt has always been considered a valuable item. In ancient times it was often traded ounce for ounce with gold. In China people once used coins made of salt. In other countries workers were paid with salt cakes or bags of salt. You may have heard the expression, "You are worth your salt." It means you are worth the money you are being paid.

All salt comes from water in seas and lakes. The salty water is called brine. Some salt is also found underground, but even that salt came from sea water that evaporated over time.

1. What was salt often traded for in ancient times?

_____

_____

2. What does the saying "You are worth your salt" mean?

_____

_____

3. What is salty water called?

_____

_____

Prewriting

Think of an idea you might write about, such as a product you use or an important invention. Write the idea in the center of the idea web below. Then fill out the rest of the web with facts.

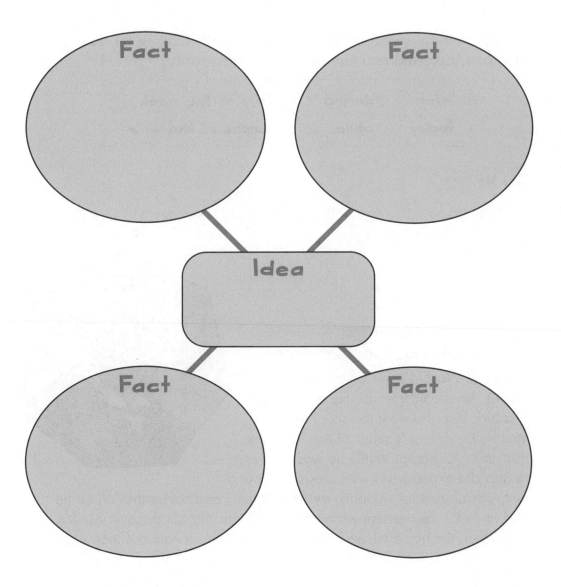

On Your Own

Now use another sheet of paper to write a paragraph about your idea. Use the facts from your idea web.

unit 2

What Is Sequence?

Sequence means time order, or 1-2-3 order. If several things happen in a story, they happen in a sequence. One event happens first, and it is followed by another event.

You can find the sequence of events in a story by looking for time words, such as *first*, *next*, and *last*. Here is a list of time words:

later	during	days of the week
today	while	months of the year

Try It!

This paragraph tells a story. Try to follow the sequence. Circle all the time words.

George Washington Carver

George Washington Carver was a famous American scientist. He was born in Missouri. Later he went to school in Iowa. Then he became a teacher at the Tuskegee Institute in Alabama. While he was teaching, he also did experiments with crops. He found hundreds of uses for peanuts, sweet potatoes, and soybeans. When he died in 1943, he was known all over the world for his discoveries. Ten years later, the home where he was born became a national monument.

Try putting these events in the order that they happened. What happened first? Write the number **1** on the line by that sentence. Then write the number **2** by the sentence that tells what happened next. Write the number **3** by the sentence that tells what happened last.

_____ Carver made many discoveries.

_____ Carver's home became a national monument.

_____ Carver became a teacher at the Tuskegee Institute.

Practice with Sequence

Here are some practice sequence questions. The first two are already answered. You can do the third one on your own.

__C__ **1.** When did Carver do experiments with crops?
   A. before he was in Missouri
   B. after he became famous
   C. while he was teaching

The question has the words, "experiments with crops." Find those words in the story about Carver. You will find them in the sentence, "While he was teaching, he also did experiments with crops." Find the time word in that sentence. The word is *while*. The words, "while he was teaching" are the same as answer **C**, so **C** is correct.

__B__ **2.** Where did Carver go just before he went to Alabama?
   A. Missouri
   B. Iowa
   C. Tuskegee

Look at the question carefully. Notice the time word *before*. Notice also that the word *just* is there. The question is asking where Carver went *just before* he went to Alabama. In the story you will find these sentences: "He was born in Missouri. Later he went to school in Iowa. Then he became a teacher at the Tuskegee Institute in Alabama." Answer **B** is correct. Answer **A** tells where he was born, but not where he was *just before* he went to Alabama. Answer **C** is not correct because it is the name of the place where he went in Alabama.

_____ **3.** When did Carver's home become a national monument?
   A. when he lived in Alabama
   B. after he died
   C. while he was teaching

Read each story. After each story you will answer questions about the sequence of events in the story. Remember, sequence is the order of things.

Remarkable Journey

How does a young dog or cat get to know a new home? The animal uses its nose. Right away it sniffs its new surroundings. Then it makes wider and wider circles, sniffing all the time. Before long it can find its way home very well, even in the dark. It simply follows familiar scents.

Stories exist of animals who found their way across land they had never sniffed before. Take the case of Smoky, the Persian cat. Smoky had a funny tuft of red fur under his chin. One day Smoky and his owner began a long journey. They were moving from Oklahoma to Tennessee. When they were just 18 miles from their Oklahoma home, Smoky jumped out of the car. Somehow he found his way back to the old house. There he wandered around outside for many days. Finally he disappeared.

A year later Smoky meowed at the door of a house in Tennessee. A man opened the door. "Is that you, Smoky?" he whispered. At first he couldn't believe it. Then he recognized the tuft of red fur. It was Smoky!

A dog named Bobby also made a remarkable journey. Bobby lived at a farmhouse in a small town in France. One day Bobby's master decided to take him to Paris, which was 35 miles away. For hours the two wandered through the crowded, noisy city. At the end of the day, when it was time to go home, Bobby's master looked down. The dog had disappeared! The man searched everywhere, but he finally decided that his dog was gone forever, and he sadly went home. Five days later Bobby was barking at the farmhouse door!

Perhaps the most amazing journey of all was made by Prince, a dog who belonged to a British soldier. During World War I, Prince's master was sent to France to fight. After his master left, Prince somehow crossed a wide body of water called the English Channel. Remarkably the dog managed to find his master in the trench where he was fighting.

1. Put these events in the order that they happened. What happened first? Write the number **1** on the line by that sentence. Then write the number **2** by the sentence that tells what happened next. Write the number **3** by the sentence that tells what happened last.

_____ Smoky traveled to Tennessee.

_____ Smoky jumped out of the car.

_____ Smoky went to his old home.

_____ **2.** What is the first thing a pet does in a new place?
  A. travels long distances
  B. explores its surroundings
  C. finds its way in the dark

_____ **3.** When was the man sure the cat was Smoky?
  A. when he saw the tuft of fur
  B. as soon as he opened the door
  C. before he opened the door

_____ **4.** When did the man discover that Bobby was gone?
  A. after 35 miles
  B. five days later
  C. at the end of the day

_____ **5.** What did Prince do just before he found his master?
  A. found the British Army
  B. crossed the English Channel
  C. located a trench

Meat-Eating Plants

Sundews are beautiful little plants. They seem so small and harmless. All around the edges of their leaves are tiny hairs that glisten with a shiny liquid. To an insect this liquid looks like food. The insect lands on the leaf. The liquid is sticky, and the insect cannot get loose. The sundew wraps itself around the insect and eats it.

Many years ago a scientist named Charles Darwin became fascinated with sundews. Would they eat only insects? Darwin put small bits of roast lamb on the sticky leaves. The plant gobbled them up. Darwin next tried drops of milk, bits of egg, and other foods. The sundew loved them all.

Sundews are just one kind of *meat-eating* plant. These plants trap insects in different ways. Some, like the sundew, use their tiny hairs. Others, like the pitcher plant, have bright colors that attract insects. When an insect lands on the colorful petals, the bug starts falling. The insect slides down into the slippery insides of the plant. At the bottom is a pool of liquid. Special chemicals in this liquid turn the insect into food for the flower.

Bladderworts are meat-eating plants that live mostly in water. Bladderworts have trapdoors in their sides. When an insect comes near the tiny hairs on a bladderwort leaf, the trapdoor opens. The insect is pulled inside.

Some plants collect rainwater at their base. When insects go to get the water, they cannot escape. The plants are lined with a powder that makes it impossible for the insects to get away. A scientist named Durland Fish put four of the plants on a fence around a garden. Within eight days these four plants trapped 136 insects.

1. Put these events in the order that they happened. What happened first? Write the number **1** on the line by that sentence. Then write the number **2** by the sentence that tells what happened next. Write the number **3** by the sentence that tells what happened last.

_____ An insect lands on a sundew leaf.

_____ The sundew wraps itself around the bug.

_____ The sundew's hairs glisten.

_____ **2.** When did Darwin become fascinated with sundews?
    A. recently
    B. years ago
    C. within eight days

_____ **3.** What did Darwin feed the plant before he fed it milk?
    A. roast lamb
    B. bits of egg
    C. a drinking straw

_____ **4.** When does the insect slide down into the pitcher plant?
    A. after the insect falls into a pool of liquid
    B. before the plant uses its hairs
    C. after the insect lands on the petals

_____ **5.** When does the bladderwort's trapdoor open?
    A. after the insect is pulled inside
    B. after the insect climbs out
    C. after the insect comes near its hairs

Giraffes

Giraffes are the tallest living animals. Most adult giraffes are tall enough to look into second-story windows. Their long necks help them get leaves and fruit that no other animal can reach. Let's see how a giraffe's life begins.

A female giraffe, or cow, gives birth to a baby 15 months after mating. The mother searches for a safe place to give birth. Both the baby, or calf, and the mother are in a great deal of danger right after the birth. More than half of all baby giraffes are killed by lions, cheetahs, or hyenas minutes after birth.

With a thud, the new baby drops the 5 feet from its mother to the ground. It weighs about 130 pounds and is 6 feet tall. The baby can run and jump 10 hours after it is born, but it cannot outrun an enemy.

The mother hides the calf in tall grass. Then she goes to search for food. The baby is fairly safe as long as it stays still. The cow returns to nurse the baby. The calf stays hidden for about a month.

After a month the mother and baby join a group of four or five other cows with their calves. The calves stay together while their mothers gather food. Sometimes one mother stays with them. The cows return at night to protect the calves. The calves stay in this group until they are about a year old.

By the time they are a year old, the giraffes from 10 to 12 feet tall. They can outrun all of their enemies except the cheetah. A cheetah rarely attacks an animal larger than itself. Giraffes continue to grow until they are seven or eight years old. Adults are between 14 and 18 feet tall.

1. Put these events in the order that they happened. What happened first? Write the number **1** on the line by that sentence. Then write the number **2** by the sentence that tells what happened next. Write the number **3** by the sentence that tells what happened last.

_____ The baby can run and jump.

_____ The baby drops 5 feet to the ground.

_____ The female giraffe looks for a safe place to give birth.

_____ 2. When does a female giraffe give birth?
   A. after she joins a group of other cows
   B. every year
   C. 15 months after mating

_____ 3. When are the mother and baby in danger?
   A. 10 hours after the baby's birth
   B. right after the baby's birth
   C. 15 months after the baby's birth

_____ 4. When do the cow and calf join a group of other females and babies?
   A. about a month after the baby is born
   B. when the calf is a year old
   C. when the calf is seven or eight years old

_____ 5. When do giraffes stop growing?
   A. when they are
      three or four years old
   B. when they are
      seven or eight years old
   C. when they join a
      group of other giraffes

Telltale Prints

Eyewitnesses say Louie stole a necklace. Officer Valdez needs more evidence. She recalls fingerprinting Louie and his brother when they got in trouble last year. If prints at this crime scene are the same as the ones on file, she's got a strong case.

Officer Valdez sprinkles colored powder on a book, jewelry box, shelf, phone, and doorknob. She puts a chemical on cloth items. These treatments show the finger marks left by natural oil from skin. Photos are taken. At the police station, she looks in the computer file for a match. The prints match someone else. The thief was Louie's identical twin, Lester!

This tale shows how fingerprints can be used. In the 1880s, Sir Francis Galton did studies in Great Britain that proved no two people have the same prints. Ten years later, Sir Edward R. Henry made a system to recognize criminals by their prints. Other countries used it. In 1924, the United States set up a print file at the FBI. It has cards with prints of more than 173 million people.

A print is the pattern of ridges on the pad of a finger. These last a lifetime unless they are altered by disease or injury. When Officer Valdez made Louie's prints, she first pressed his finger pad in ink. Then she rolled it on a card from side to side. This was repeated for each finger.

You can create your own prints. Scribble with a pencil on a piece of paper until you have a gray smudge. Rub your finger pad in the smudge. Press a piece of clear tape on your finger. Stick the tape to a card. There's your fingerprint!

1. Put these events in the order that they happened. What happened first? Write the number **1** on the line by that sentence. Then write the number **2** by the sentence that tells what happened next. Write the number **3** by the sentence that tells what happened last.

_____ The United States set up a fingerprint file at the FBI.

_____ Sir Edward Henry set up a system to recognize criminals.

_____ Sir Francis Galton proved people have different prints.

_____ 2. What was the first thing Officer Valdez did to find fingerprints at the scene of the crime?
   A. sprinkled colored powder on a doorknob
   B. looked in the computer files
   C. put on her glasses

_____ 3. When was a system made to recognize criminals by their prints?
   A. in the 1920s
   B. in the 1880s
   C. in the 1890s

_____ 4. What did Officer Valdez do after she pressed Louie's finger in ink?
   A. put a chemical on cloth items
   B. scribbled with a pencil
   C. rolled it on a card

_____ 5. To take your own fingerprint, when do you put tape on your finger?
   A. before you scribble a pencil smudge
   B. before you press it in ink
   C. after you rub your finger in the smudge

Changes in Farming

What job would you have had if you had lived in England in 1540? Chances are you would have been a farmer. Most people were. It took many people to raise enough food. Now just two out of 100 people in England farm. The rest work in towns and cities. This pattern is true in many parts of the world. What allowed so many people to leave the farm?

Several discoveries and inventions caused this change. One of these was rotating, or changing, crops. Farmers had long known that growing the same crop in the same field year after year made the soil poor. For this reason they usually left fields empty part of the time.

In the early 1700s, Charles Townshend found a way to rotate four crops. This way fields could be used all year. For example, four fields would be planted with wheat, clover, barley, and turnips. By rotating the crop grown in each field every year, the soil remained rich. Grasslands that could not be used before could now be farmed. This rotation system allowed farmers to raise much more food, both for themselves and their animals.

Robert Bakewell was an English farmer in the late 1700s. He wanted to raise better farm animals. He produced better horses, cattle, and sheep. He developed a sheep that could be raised for meat as well as for wool.

The invention of new farm tools also led to great change. Around 1700, the seed drill was invented. Before that time seeds were scattered by hand. The seed drill dug trenches in the dirt and planted the seeds. This tool was the first modern farm machine. Crop rotation, better farm animals, and new farm tools made it possible for fewer people to produce a lot of food. Thousands of families moved from farms to the cities.

1. Put these events in the order that they happened. What happened first? Write the number **1** on the line by that sentence. Then write the number **2** by the sentence that tells what happened next. Write the number **3** by the sentence that tells what happened last.

_____ Townshend developed a system of crop rotation.

_____ The seed drill was invented.

_____ Thousand of families moved to cities.

_____ **2.** When were most people farmers?
  A. in the 1980s
  B. after the invention of the seed drill
  C. before the 1700s

_____ **3.** When were seeds scattered by hand?
  A. during the 1900s
  B. before the seed drill was invented
  C. during the winter

_____ **4.** When were better farm animals developed?
  A. during the late 1700s
  B. before Townshend lived
  C. after people moved to the cities

_____ **5.** When was the seed drill invented?
  A. in 1540
  B. after crop rotation was developed
  C. before Bakewell produced better animals

Yellowstone Park on Fire!

The year 1988 will not be forgotten for a long time at Yellowstone National Park. Fires broke out in June and burned fiercely until September. The flames were not put out completely until November. They covered almost half of the huge park. What caused such huge fires? There are several answers to this question.

Lodgepole pines make up 80 percent of the park's forests. These trees grow quickly, but they only live about 200 years. Then many of the pines die and are blown down by high winds. The trees lie on the forest floor for many years. In wet forests they would rot and turn back into soil, but it is too dry for this to happen in Yellowstone. In 1988, dead wood covered the forest floor.

Yellowstone usually gets a lot of snow in the winter. When the snow melts, it provides water for the plants. For six winters in the 1980s, little snow had fallen. Rain also usually falls during the summer months, but 1988 was the driest summer in 116 years.

Several fires started in and near the park in June. Park officials fought the fires caused by human carelessness. They didn't try to put out the fires started by lightning. They knew that fires help clean out the dead wood. When little rain fell in June and July, the fires became larger and larger. More than 17,000 acres had burned by July 21. Park officials decided that it was time to fight all of the roaring fires.

On June 23, strong winds blew the fires into new areas of the park. Firefighters battled the blazes, but they had little success. On August 20, 80 mile-per-hour winds swept through the park. This day became known as Black Saturday. Fires that had almost died out came back to life. No matter how hard the firefighters tried, they couldn't control the flames. Snow and rain began to fall in September. Then the worst of the fires were put out. The remaining fires were put out by heavy snows in November.

1. Put these events in the order that they happened. What happened first? Write the number **1** on the line by that sentence. Then write the number **2** by the sentence that tells what happened next. Write the number **3** by the sentence that tells what happened last.

_____ Yellowstone had the driest summer in 116 years.

_____ The worst of the fires were put out.

_____ Several fires started in the park.

_____ **2.** When did the fires begin in Yellowstone?
    A. when the trees began to die
    B. when the heavy snows fell
    C. before the strong winds blew in

_____ **3.** When did little snow fall in the park?
    A. during the 1980s
    B. in November
    C. 116 years ago

_____ **4.** When did park officials decide to fight all of the fires?
    A. when lightning struck
    B. after 17,000 acres had burned
    C. on Black Saturday

_____ **5.** When was Black Saturday?
    A. when the trees died
    B. one month before the first fires started
    C. when strong winds hit the park

The History of Kites

No one knows when the first kite was made. The first record of a kite was more than 2,000 years ago in China. General Han Hsin was the leader of a rebel army. He wanted to overthrow a cruel king, but he had only a few men. Hsin decided to dig a tunnel into the king's castle. He flew a kite to determine how long the tunnel should be. The men in the tunnel took the kite string with them. When they reached the end of the string, they knew to dig up. They came up in the castle courtyard and defeated the king.

Kites have been flown in Japan for hundreds of years. In the 1700s, kites were flown in the fall to give thanks for a good harvest. Stalks of rice were tied to the kites. Kites were also flown to send good wishes to couples who had had their first son.

Today in Japan kites are often flown as part of a celebration, such as the beginning of a new year. The kites are painted to look like animals, heroes, and gods. Small kites as well as huge ones are made. Kite festivals are held each year in many regions of the country.

Kites have been used for scientific purposes in the western world. Most people have heard of Benjamin Franklin and his kite. Franklin had been studying electricity. He thought that lightning was a form of electricity, but he wasn't sure. In 1752, he tried to find out. He flew a kite in a storm. A key was attached to the kite. When sparks jumped from the key, it proved his idea was correct.

In the 1890s, Lawrence Hargrave invented the box kite. He used this kite to test ideas about flight. From 1898 until 1933, the United States Weather Bureau used box kites to gather weather data. The Wright Brothers also experimented with kites. What they learned helped them make the first airplane flight in 1903.

1. Put these events in the order that they happened. What happened first? Write the number **1** on the line by that sentence. Then write the number **2** by the sentence that tells what happened next. Write the number **3** by the sentence that tells what happened last.

_____ Franklin discovered that lightning was electricity.

_____ Han Hsin used a kite to measure distance.

_____ The Wright brothers experimented with kites.

_____ **2.** When was the first record of a kite?
    A. 100 years ago
    B. before Benjamin Franklin was born
    C. before General Han Hsin was born

_____ **3.** When were kites often flown in Japan?
    A. before a good harvest
    B. after the birth of a first son
    C. during storms

_____ **4.** When did Franklin fly a kite in a storm?
    A. before the cruel king was defeated
    B. before the Wrights experimented with kites
    C. when he studied electricity

_____ **5.** When did the Weather Bureau use kites?
    A. after the invention of the box kite
    B. before the Wright brothers made their first plane
    C. before Benjamin Franklin studied electricity

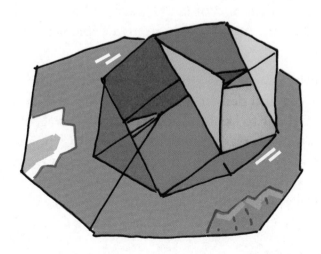

Dolphins

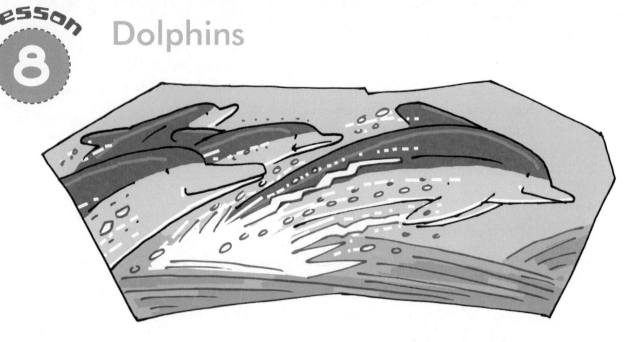

For centuries dolphins have been thought of as special animals. Plutarch, a Greek writer, praised their friendliness 2,000 years ago. Scenes of people riding on dolphins have appeared in the art of many countries.

There are more than 38 kinds of dolphins. Most types live in the ocean. They are related to whales. Dolphins are very smart. They can learn, remember, and solve problems. They are natural entertainers who love to perform. You can see them do tricks at marine amusement parks.

Dolphins travel in herds. They are social animals who like to play. They often toss seaweed and driftwood in the air. Dolphins become very unhappy and lonely if they are separated from their companions. Dolphins mate in the spring. A baby is born a year later. The other dolphins surround the mother while she is giving birth. They do this to protect her from danger. Soon after birth the mother pushes the baby to the surface so that it can breathe. The baby nurses, or drinks the mother's milk, for about 18 months. The mother teaches the baby and protects it from harm.

Many tales have been told of dolphins helping people. One famous dolphin was named Pelorus Jack. Jack lived in Cook's Strait between the North Island and the South Island of New Zealand. From 1888 until the 1920s, Jack guided ships through Cook's Strait. People came from around the world to see him.

In 1978, a small fishing boat was lost off the coast of South Africa. It was caught in a thick fog and dangerous water. The fishermen told of four dolphins who led their boat to shore. Another newspaper account told of a ship that exploded. A woman was injured and thrown overboard. She said three dolphins swam near her and helped her float. They stayed with her until she could climb on a buoy. There are many other stories of dolphins saving drowning people by pushing them to shallow water.

1. Put these events in the order that they happened. What happened first? Write the number **1** on the line by that sentence. Then write the number **2** by the sentence that tells what happened next. Write the number **3** by the sentence that tells what happened last.

_____ The baby nurses for about 18 months.

_____ The mother pushes the baby to the surface.

_____ The other dolphins surround the mother.

_____ **2.** When did Plutarch praise dolphins?
   A. 300 years ago
   B. in 1888
   C. 2,000 years ago

_____ **3.** When do other dolphins surround a mother dolphin?
   A. while the mother dolphin gives birth
   B. while the mother nurses her baby
   C. while the mother pushes her baby to the surface

_____ **4.** When did Pelorus Jack guide ships through Cook's Strait?
   A. before Plutarch died
   B. before four dolphins helped some lost fishermen
   C. before dolphins were thought of as special animals

_____ **5.** When was a small fishing boat lost off the coast of South Africa?
   A. during the time when Pelorus Jack guided ships
   B. when a woman's ship exploded
   C. in 1978

Writing Roundup

Read the paragraph below. Think about the sequence, or time order. Answer the questions in complete sentences.

Andrew talked about how well he shot basketball free throws, so Chris challenged him to a contest. Andrew took his first shot, which bounced off the backboard. Next Andrew threw the ball to Chris. Chris took a shot, and the ball went in the basket. Then Andrew took a second shot, but it rolled off the rim. Chris's second shot went in. Andrew decided to get some tips from Chris.

1. When did Chris challenge Andrew to a free-throw contest?

_____

_____

2. What happened after Andrew took his first shot?

_____

_____

3. When did Chris take his first shot?

_____

_____

4. When did Andrew decide to get tips from Chris?

_____

_____

Prewriting

Think about something that you have done, such as doing your laundry, training to improve your fitness, or tie-dyeing a T-shirt. Write the events in sequence below.

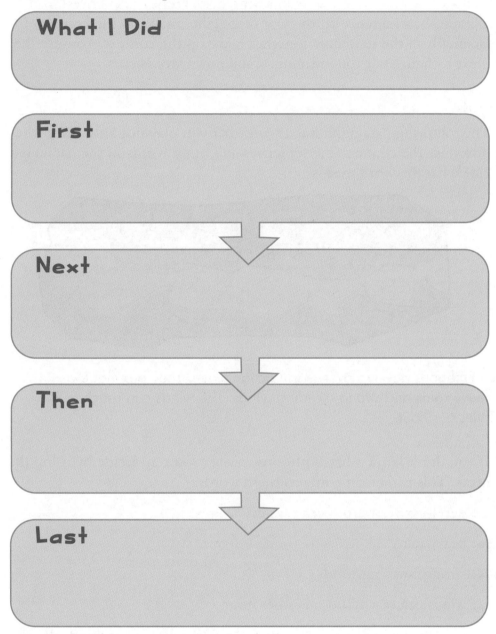

What I Did

First

Next

Then

Last

On Your Own

Now use another sheet of paper to write a paragraph about what you have done. Write the events in the order that they happened. Use time order words.

What Is Context?

Context means all the words in a sentence or all the sentences in a paragraph. In a sentence all the words together make up the context. In a paragraph all the sentences together make up the context. You use the context to figure out the meaning of unknown words.

Try It!

The following paragraph has a word that you may not know. See whether you can use the context (the sentences and other words in the paragraph) to decide what the word means.

Typhoons develop over warm ocean water. They are made of heavy rains and strong, swirling winds. The winds can reach 200 miles per hour.

If you don't know what **typhoons** means, you can decide by using the context. This paragraph contains these words:

Clue: develop over warm ocean water

Clue: heavy rains

Clue: strong, swirling winds

Clue: winds can reach 200 miles per hour

Find these clues in the paragraph and circle them. What words do you think of when you read the clues? You might think of *weather*. What other words do you think of? Write the words below:

_____

Did you write *storm* or *hurricane*? The context clue words tell you that a **typhoon** is a kind of storm like a hurricane.

Working with Context

This unit asks questions that you can answer by using context clues in paragraphs. There are two kinds of paragraphs. The paragraphs in the first part of this unit have blank spaces in them. You can use the context clues in the paragraphs to decide which words should go in each space. Here is an example:

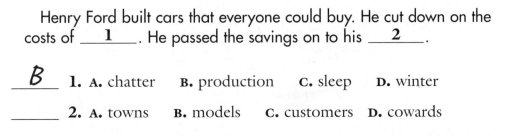

Henry Ford built cars that everyone could buy. He cut down on the costs of ____1____. He passed the savings on to his ____2____.

_**B**___ **1. A.** chatter   **B.** production   **C.** sleep   **D.** winter

_____ **2. A.** towns   **B.** models   **C.** customers   **D.** cowards

Look at the answer choices for question 1. Try putting each choice in the paragraph to see which one makes the most sense. Treat the paragraph as a puzzle. Which pieces don't fit? It doesn't make sense for a car builder to cut down on the costs of *chatter*, *sleep*, or *winter*. You have decided what doesn't fit. The correct answer is *production*, answer **B**. Now try to answer question 2 on your own.

The paragraphs in the second part of this unit are different. For these you figure out the meaning of a word that is printed in **dark letters** in the paragraph. Here is an example:

The scientists studied the volcano carefully. There was a lump on its side. The lump was getting bigger. They knew that the volcano would **erupt** soon. They warned all the people who lived nearby to move before it blew up.

In this paragraph the word in dark type is **erupt**. Find the context clues, and treat the paragraph as a puzzle. Then choose a word that means the same as **erupt**.

_____ **3.** In this paragraph, the word **erupt** means
     A. disappear   **C.** blow up
     B. get bigger   **D.** bring rain

LESSON 1

Read the passages and answer the questions about context. Remember, context is a way to learn new words by thinking about the other words used in a story.

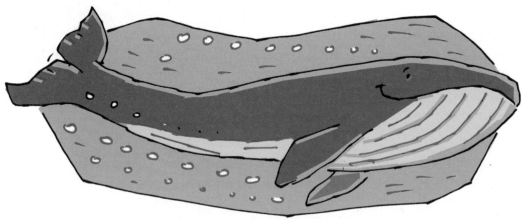

The great blue whale is bigger than the dinosaurs were. A human being could stand up straight inside a whale's ___**1**___ mouth. However, a whale's throat is very tiny. A whale could not ___**2**___ a person.

_____ **1. A.** little   **B.** tremendous   **C.** hungry   **D.** tight

_____ **2. A.** taste   **B.** capture   **C.** swallow   **D.** find

The game of tennis began around 800 hundred years ago. Players in France hit a ball over a net. However, they did not use a ___**3**___ to play the game. They used the ___**4**___ of their hands.

_____ **3. A.** mask   **B.** motor   **C.** trap   **D.** racket

_____ **4. A.** palms   **B.** nets   **C.** riddles   **D.** families

Your fingerprints are unlike those of any other person. Even twins have fingerprints that ___**5**___. Experts say that fingerprints are the best way to ___**6**___ someone. These prints can help solve crimes.

_____ **5. A.** whisk   **B.** vary   **C.** flicker   **D.** advance

_____ **6. A.** huddle   **B.** invite   **C.** grasp   **D.** identify

Scientists say that black holes ___**7**___ in space although they cannot be seen. It is thought that black holes ___**8**___ when huge stars cave in. If the Sun became a black hole, it would be only 4 miles across.

_____ **7. A.** budge   **B.** gust   **C.** exist   **D.** lend

_____ **8. A.** leak   **B.** satisfy   **C.** admire   **D.** develop

Florida is on the southeastern coast of the United States. It has water on three sides. Since the ___9___ is warm, there are many palm trees. There are also many beautiful beaches. For these reasons, many people take ___10___ in Florida.

_____ 9. **A.** climate   **B.** size   **C.** rowboat   **D.** insect

_____10. **A.** water   **B.** tests   **C.** vacations   **D.** lists

The first motion pictures were made in 1887. To see these movies, people looked through a hole in a box. Movies were later shown on a ___11___. Recordings were used for sound. Later, sound was put ___12___ on the movie film.

_____11. **A.** screen   **B.** oven   **C.** hive   **D.** tub

_____12. **A.** sadly   **B.** happily   **C.** directly   **D.** angrily

Artists often use colors to ___13___ feelings. Bright colors show happy feelings. Dark colors show sad feelings. When you look at a painting, you can tell what the artist's ___14___ was.

_____13. **A.** buy   **B.** eat   **C.** shovel   **D.** express

_____14. **A.** height   **B.** mood   **C.** brush   **D.** meal

Nothing lives or grows on the Moon, but scientists have discovered that some plants on Earth grow better if they are ___15___ by the Moon. If moon dust is ___16___ over the plants, they grow much bigger. No one yet knows why.

_____15. **A.** melted   **B.** aided   **C.** wet   **D.** arranged

_____16. **A.** trusted   **B.** curved   **C.** sprinkled   **D.** chosen

Red Jacket was a famous Native American in the 1700s. He helped the British soldiers. He ____1____ the Americans fighting against the British. A British ____2____ gave him a red jacket. That is how he got his name.

_____ 1. **A.** loved   **B.** rewarded   **C.** forgot   **D.** opposed

_____ 2. **A.** tea   **B.** officer   **C.** rifle   **D.** coat

Several things help broken bones get well fast. Young people seem to ____3____ faster than old people do, so the age of the ____4____ counts. It also helps to get the hurt person to a doctor as soon as possible.

_____ 3. **A.** yawn   **B.** level
        C. heal   **D.** bend

_____ 4. **A.** chapter   **B.** sheet
        C. doctor   **D.** patient

When roads were built, people threw dirt from each side of the road to the ____5____. This raised road came to be ____6____ a highway.

_____ 5. **A.** center   **B.** witch   **C.** apron   **D.** contest

_____ 6. **A.** parked   **B.** swept   **C.** showered   **D.** termed

Experts say that swimming is the best exercise. Swimming ____7____ your strength. Pushing your way through the water builds your muscles. This exercise is less ____8____ than most other sports. Swimmers are not hurt as often as are joggers and runners.

_____ 7. **A.** fails   **B.** tickles   **C.** improves   **D.** poisons

_____ 8. **A.** dangerous   **B.** correct   **C.** lazy   **D.** awake

The Statue of Liberty was ____9____ in many separate pieces. The pieces were packed in ____10____. Then they were shipped from France to America. There the pieces were joined to form Miss Liberty.

_____ 9. **A.** whole   **B.** originally   **C.** never   **D.** bent

_____10. **A.** beds   **B.** nickels   **C.** lights   **D.** crates

The first kites were made about 2,500 years ago in China. They were made of large leaves. String had not been ____11____ yet. The kite strings were made of twisted ____12____.

_____11. **A.** shown   **B.** liked   **C.** wanted   **D.** invented

_____12. **A.** vines   **B.** trees   **C.** tops   **D.** rows

Columbus found many ____13____ things to eat in the New World. When he went back to Europe, he carried some of these new foods with him. He gave the king and queen of Spain a ____14____. He offered them corn, peppers, pineapples, pumpkins, and sweet potatoes.

_____13. **A.** hidden   **B.** secret   **C.** short   **D.** delicious

_____14. **A.** banquet   **B.** carpet   **C.** princess   **D.** batter

Some people are ____15____ that mice scare elephants. However, these big beasts do not ____16____ fear when they see a mouse. Elephants will run away from a rabbit or a dog, though!

_____15. **A.** clear   **B.** comfortable   **C.** hopeful   **D.** convinced

_____16. **A.** enjoy   **B.** choose   **C.** exhibit   **D.** challenge

Lesson 3

The first Olympic Games were held in Greece. Boys between the ages of 12 and 17 entered the junior ___1___. At the age of 18, they could enter the ___2___ contests.

_____ 1. **A.** schools   **B.** darkness   **C.** events   **D.** grounds

_____ 2. **A.** small   **B.** championship   **C.** fast   **D.** strange

Some bats have only one baby at a time. When the mother bat flies out at night, she carries her ___3___ along with her. The young one hangs onto the mother as she ___4___ through the dark.

_____ 3. **A.** amount   **B.** sister   **C.** newborn   **D.** enemy

_____ 4. **A.** swoops   **B.** blinks   **C.** motions   **D.** hatches

Plants need light in order to grow, but many plants ___5___ to grow fast in the dark. Corn is one ___6___. It grows most quickly during warm summer nights.

_____ 5. **A.** continue   **B.** burn   **C.** complete   **D.** dip

_____ 6. **A.** flower   **B.** field   **C.** example   **D.** weed

On the ___7___ person's head, there are about 100,000 hairs. When people are young, their hair grows fast. It grows about one-hundredth of an inch per day. This ___8___ growth slows down as people get older. If you never cut your hair in your life, it might grow to be 25 feet long.

_____ 7. **A.** neat   **B.** old   **C.** average   **D.** noisy

_____ 8. **A.** hard   **B.** rapid   **C.** sleepy   **D.** straight

Young Mozart never went to school. His father ___9___ him in music and math at home. By the time he was five, Mozart was writing his own music for the piano. A year later he played his ___10___ for people all over Europe.

_____ **9. A.** tried   **B.** found   **C.** paid   **D.** tutored

_____ **10. A.** compositions   **B.** lanes   **C.** lessons   **D.** ideas

There are 50 states in the United States. Alaska and Hawaii ___11___ no states at all. Maine touches only one other state. Both Missouri and Tennessee are ___12___ by eight other states.

_____ **11. A.** defend   **B.** border   **C.** cross   **D.** show

_____ **12. A.** covered   **B.** owned   **C.** held   **D.** surrounded

On April Fool's Day, some people make ___13___ calls to zoos, so many zoos unplug their telephones. The zoo workers are busy. They can't ___14___ time taking messages for Mr. Fish, Mrs. Bear, and Miss Lion!

_____ **13. A.** helpful   **B.** ridiculous   **C.** beautiful   **D.** new

_____ **14. A.** hurry   **B.** tell   **C.** waste   **D.** count

You have probably heard about people who ___15___ stamps, signs, strings, buttons, or fire hats. You never know what ___16___ and silly things people want to save.

_____ **15. A.** collect   **B.** carve   **C.** manage   **D.** return

_____ **16. A.** tough   **B.** comfortable   **C.** unusual   **D.** lively

Dragons still live. The Komodo dragon in Asia is the largest living ___1___. It grows to be more than 10 feet long. It has a long tail, ___2___ skin, and a wide red mouth.

_____ 1. **A.** western   **B.** visitor   **C.** puppet   **D.** lizard

_____ 2. **A.** thirsty   **B.** sweet   **C.** rough   **D.** private

Exercise can help people live longer. ___3___ say that people who walk or run about half an hour each day stay in better ___4___. Some people say they don't have time to work out. They should take the time. For each hour a person exercises, that person may live an hour longer.

_____ 3. **A.** Owners   **B.** Elephants   **C.** Experts   **D.** Uncles

_____ 4. **A.** sunshine   **B.** order   **C.** matter   **D.** health

A woman said to a friend, "Yesterday I fell over 40 feet." The friend ___5___, "That's just ___6___! Were you hurt?" The first woman said, "No, I was just finding my seat at the movies."

_____ 5. **A.** felt   **B.** exclaimed   **C.** discovered   **D.** bounced

_____ 6. **A.** horrible   **B.** favor   **C.** silent   **D.** aboard

Some gardeners like to ___7___ huge plants. Farmers in Alaska enter contests. They see whose cabbages are largest. A man in New England raised giant ___8___. They weighed 580 pounds each!

_____ 7. **A.** cultivate   **B.** send
        C. ride   **D.** mail

_____ 8. **A.** fields   **B.** feasts
        C. pumpkins   **D.** ants

The unicorn is an imaginary beast. It is supposed to have a __9__ horn that twists out of the middle of its forehead. In pictures it is __10__ as having the head and body of a horse, the beard of a goat, the legs of a deer, and the tail of a lion.

_____ **9.** **A.** spiral   **B.** buffalo   **C.** button   **D.** flat

_____**10.** **A.** born   **B.** portrayed   **C.** divided   **D.** touched

---

A mountain is worn down year by year. Some of the rocks on the mountain have cracks in them. Water goes into the cracks. As the water freezes, it __11__ . This causes the cracks to get larger. Then the rocks are __12__ by wind and more water.

_____**11.** **A.** expands   **B.** replies   **C.** goes   **D.** aims

_____**12.** **A.** dared   **B.** gone   **C.** seen   **D.** weathered

---

Deborah Sampson dressed up as a man. She did this so she could join an army __13__ during the American Revolution. In one battle she was wounded in the __14__ . She removed the bullet herself. That way no one discovered that she was a woman.

_____**13.** **A.** ax   **B.** regiment   **C.** knife   **D.** park

_____**14.** **A.** mitten   **B.** suitcase   **C.** rope   **D.** thigh

---

Seamounts are __15__ cones, or mountains, that rise up from the bottom of the sea. They can be thousands of feet high and still be far below the surface of the water. They are entirely __16__ in the ocean.

_____**15.** **A.** spicy   **B.** awful   **C.** volcanic   **D.** easy

_____**16.** **A.** killed   **B.** proved   **C.** loose   **D.** submerged

The honeysucker, or honey possum, eats the **nectar** found in large flowers. To do this it sticks its long, thin nose into a flower. Then it uses its long, rough tongue to get the sticky food.

_____ **1.** In this paragraph, the word **nectar** means
- **A.** fruit
- **B.** roots
- **C.** sweet liquid
- **D.** green leaves

Long ago, a feast was more than just fancy food on a table. People dressed in fine clothing. Guests were often **entertained** with music, dancing, and juggling.

_____ **2.** In this paragraph, the word **entertained** means
- **A.** starved
- **B.** seated
- **C.** invited
- **D.** amused

People have always feared the blasts of hot lava and ashes from a volcano. The power of a volcano has caused many disasters. In 1991, the explosion of a volcano in the Philippine Islands **demolished** an air force base. The base was completely covered with hot ash.

_____ **3.** In this paragraph, the word **demolished** means
- **A.** built
- **B.** visited
- **C.** destroyed
- **D.** landed

A boomerang is made so that it returns to the person who throws it. A boomerang has two arms and a **curve** in the middle. This shape makes the boomerang spin. This spinning causes the boomerang to circle back to the person who threw it.

_____ **4.** In this paragraph, the word **curve** means
- **A.** leg
- **B.** well
- **C.** belt
- **D.** bend

Some people fear alligators, but there are not many **authentic** cases of alligators attacking people. Most reports have not been backed by facts.

_____ **5.** In this paragraph, the word **authentic** means
- **A.** long
- **B.** thin
- **C.** real
- **D.** lengthy

You will find few birds in the deepest, darkest part of a forest. Birds like a **habitat** near the edge of the forest. There is more food for them there.

_____ **6.** In this paragraph, the word **habitat** means
- **A.** sunshine
- **B.** home
- **C.** cage
- **D.** insect

You know that the "home on the range" is "where the deer and the antelope play." However, no animal in North America fits the true **classification** of antelope.

_____ **7.** In this paragraph, the word **classification** means
- **A.** friendliness
- **B.** kind of music
- **C.** particular group
- **D.** surrounding land

Some people who are good at **archery** like to enter contests. They aim their arrows at a target. It is divided into colored rings. An arrow that hits the center circle is worth 10 points.

_____ **8.** In this paragraph, the word **archery** means
- **A.** running
- **B.** swimming
- **C.** public speaking
- **D.** arrow shooting

When ducks **migrate** south each fall, many of them pass over Stuttgard, Arkansas, so the people there hold a duck-calling contest. As the ducks fly by, the people quack away!

_____ **1.** In this paragraph, the word **migrate** means
  A. locate   **C.** travel
  B. mumble   **D.** honk

Have you ever seen a moonbow? It's like a rainbow, but it's made by the moon. Moonbows **occur** when the moon's light shines through the mist from a waterfall.

_____ **2.** In this paragraph, the word **occur** means
  A. rain   **C.** happen
  B. flow   **D.** disappear

In the middle of Enterprise, Alabama, stands a **monument**. It is shaped like an insect called the boll weevil. This insect once ate all the cotton plants in Enterprise, so people decided to grow peanuts. They earned more money with peanuts. That's why they honored the boll weevil.

_____ **3.** In this paragraph, the word **monument** means
  A. statue   **C.** tree
  B. farm   **D.** plant

Every June **mobs** of people gather at Jensen Beach in Florida to watch for sea turtles. Hundreds of people snap pictures of the turtles as they lay their eggs.

_____ **4.** In this paragraph, the word **mobs** means
  A. crowds   **C.** swimmers
  B. visitors   **D.** couples

Clowns spend much time painting their faces. They don't want people to copy their design. Pictures of the clowns' faces are put in a file as a **permanent** record.

_____ **5.** In this paragraph, the word **permanent** means
- **A.** playing
- **B.** pretty
- **C.** lasting
- **D.** broken

A **typical** American saying is *O.K.* There are many stories about how this saying got started. One story is that some writers in Boston were having fun. They used *O.K.* to stand for "oll korrect," a misspelling of "all correct."

_____ **6.** In this paragraph, the word **typical** means
- **A.** common
- **B.** west
- **C.** wild
- **D.** odd

Shirley Temple won an Oscar award for her **performance** in the movie *Bright Eyes*. She was in this movie when she was only six years old.

_____ **7.** In this paragraph, the word **performance** means
- **A.** youth
- **B.** sewing
- **C.** acting
- **D.** dinner

The town of Young America, Minnesota, **sponsors** a bed-racing contest each year. People line up all sorts of beds on wheels. Then they roll them down the main street toward the finish line.

_____ **8.** In this paragraph, the word **sponsors** means
- **A.** owns
- **B.** wins
- **C.** sells
- **D.** holds

Libraries have **revealed** some interesting facts about books that are returned. One librarian reported that socks were often left in books. Another librarian found a peanut butter sandwich in a returned book!

_____ **1.** In this paragraph, the word **revealed** means
    A. made known   **C.** torn down
    B. kept hidden   **D.** laughed at

A lizard has a forked tongue. The tongue has two **functions**. The lizard both touches and smells with it.

_____ **2.** In this paragraph, the word **functions** means
    A. tests   **C.** teeth
    B. purposes   **D.** leads

Some animals can **resemble** other things. This helps keep them safe from enemies. For instance, the treehopper looks just like a thorn on a rosebush. Birds may like to eat treehoppers, but it's hard for birds to find them.

_____ **3.** In this paragraph, the word **resemble** means
    A. see like   **C.** look like
    B. report to   **D.** differ from

Rain forests grow where it is warm and wet all year. Thick trees and vines form a high **canopy** over the forest. As a result, little sunlight reaches the forest floor.

_____ **4.** In this paragraph, the word **canopy** means
    A. cloud   **C.** capitol
    B. covering   **D.** night

Many people wear black as a sign of **mourning**. In China the color for death is white. People in Turkey wear purple. Everywhere, people follow special customs when someone dies.

_____ **5.** In this paragraph, the word **mourning** means
- **A.** seeing dawn
- **B.** feeling sick
- **C.** showing joy
- **D.** showing sadness

The most common **source** of milk is the cow. The goat also gives milk. Other animals that give milk are the camel, buffalo, yak, reindeer, llama, and zebra.

_____ **6.** In this paragraph, the word **source** means
- **A.** bottle
- **B.** direction
- **C.** drink
- **D.** supply

When Franz Liszt played the piano, he became **violent**. Often the keys would fly off the piano. Sometimes the strings of the piano would snap with the force of his blows.

_____ **7.** In this paragraph, the word **violent** means
- **A.** rough
- **B.** purple
- **C.** gentle
- **D.** large

In 1608, Thomas Coryat brought a new custom to England. He had learned how to eat with a fork. At first the English didn't think this new way to eat was **appropriate**. They did not think it was a good idea. They did not begin to use forks until some time later.

_____ **8.** In this paragraph, the word **appropriate** means
- **A.** fun
- **B.** correct
- **C.** filling
- **D.** magic

Most animals that live in the sea have layers of fat to keep them warm. Sea otters have thick, furry coats instead. Their coats are so **effective** against the cold that they stay warm even in cold water.

_____ 1. In this paragraph, the word **effective** means
   A. chilly
   B. successful
   C. hot
   D. wet

Before airplanes, trains were common. They moved people and freight long distances. As years went by, air and highway travel became easier. Then train use **declined**.

_____ 2. In this paragraph, the word **declined** means
   A. grew   C. rose
   B. dropped   D. rushed

Henry Ford didn't invent the factory, but he improved it. Ford used **conveyors** that brought parts to the workers as they stood in their places.

_____ 3. In this paragraph, the word **conveyors** means
   A. mattresses   C. types of small airplanes
   B. skilled workers   D. means of carrying things

The oldest false teeth are almost 3,000 years old. They were found on the body of a **deceased** person in an old grave. The teeth were strung together with gold wire.

_____ 4. In this paragraph, the word **deceased** means
   A. dead   C. healthy
   B. old   D. rich

Long ago a bride's father gave all her shoes to her new husband. This **indicated** that the father no longer had to care for the bride. Today we recall this custom by tying shoes to a wedding car.

_____ **5.** In this paragraph, the word **indicated** means
- **A.** behaved
- **B.** pained
- **C.** prayed
- **D.** meant

In spite of its name, banana oil isn't **derived** from bananas. It is made from chemicals that are mixed in a laboratory. The smell of the oil is like the smell of a banana.

_____ **6.** In this paragraph, the word **derived** means
- **A.** taken
- **B.** slippery
- **C.** grown
- **D.** pasted

The bits of paper thrown during parades are called confetti. This word means "candy." Once people threw candy during **festive** and merry events. Now we throw paper.

_____ **7.** In this paragraph, the word **festive** means
- **A.** worn
- **B.** tasty
- **C.** smooth
- **D.** jolly

Astronauts have a big problem when traveling in space. In space, water does not pour. Drops of water just float around. Astronauts must use special **methods** for getting clean. They can't take regular baths or showers. They must wash with special equipment.

_____ **8.** In this paragraph, the word **methods** means
- **A.** brushes
- **B.** ideas
- **C.** ways
- **D.** tubs

Writing Roundup

Read each paragraph. Write a word that makes sense on each line.

Darrell was reading a book about an adventure
on a ranch. "I hope this book has an ending that's

(1) _____," he said. "Some adventure

books are **(2)** _____."

Tamika had practiced for weeks, but still she felt

(3) _____ because she had never

played her violin in public. She hoped the audience

would like her **(4)** _____.

What an ice storm we had last winter! The **(5)** _____

was off for several hours. We had to use **(6)** _____ to

light our way around the house.

Read each paragraph. Write a sentence that makes sense on each line.

Ms. Dixon's class was making shoebox models of

a scene at the bottom of the ocean. Akiko wanted to include

seashells, but they didn't have any. What could they use?

(1) _____.

They needed fish, and Leslie had an idea for that.

(2) _____.

Ryan suggested a way to make the scene look more real.

(3) _____.

The parade was coming! Daniel jumped up and down with

excitement. What would he see first as the parade rounded

the corner? **(4)** _____

_____. At last, there it was!

(5) _____.

That was fun to see, but Daniel's favorite part of the parade

turned out to be something else. **(6)** _____

_____.

unit 4

What Is a Main Idea?

The main idea of a paragraph tells what the paragraph is about. All the other sentences are details that add to the main idea. The main idea sentence is often the first or last sentence in the paragraph. You may find the main idea sentence in the middle of the paragraph too.

This example may help you think about main ideas:

3　　+　　4　　+　　5　　=　　　12

detail　+　detail　+　detail　=　main idea

The *3*, *4*, and *5* are like details. They are smaller than their sum, *12*. The *12*, like the main idea, is bigger. It is made up of several smaller parts.

Try It!

Read this story and underline the main idea sentence.

Small dogs usually live longer than big dogs. The tiny Pekingese can live to be 20 years old. The giant Saint Bernard rarely lives as long as 14 years.

The main idea sentence is the first sentence in the story. The other sentences are details about the main idea sentence.

The main idea could come at the end of the paragraph:

The tiny Pekingese can live to be 20 years old. The giant Saint Bernard rarely lives as long as 14 years. Small dogs usually live longer than big dogs.

Practice Finding the Main Idea

This unit asks you to find main ideas of paragraphs. Read the paragraph and answer the question below.

The monarch butterfly makes a long trip south each fall. Some butterflies fly almost 1,800 miles from the northern United States to Mexico. As spring warms the air, the butterflies begin to return. The butterflies lay their eggs and then die. The young return to the north to start the cycle over again.

_____D_____ 1. The story mainly tells
　　　　　　 A. which butterflies make the trip
　　　　　　 B. how far the insects fly
　　　　　　 C. when butterflies lay their eggs
　　　　　　 D. what the monarch's long trip is like

The correct answer is **D**. The first sentence says, "The monarch butterfly makes a long trip south each fall." This is the main idea sentence. The other sentences give details about the trip.

Sometimes a paragraph does not have a main idea sentence. Then it is made up only of details. Read the story below and answer the question. Write the letter of your answer in the blank.

The front part of a newspaper contains important stories of national and local events. The sports pages report scores and give information about players, coaches, and teams. The comics section makes many people laugh.

_____ 2. The story mainly tells
　　　　　　 A. what the front section contains
　　　　　　 B. where you can read about players
　　　　　　 C. about different parts of a newspaper
　　　　　　 D. what makes people laugh

Read each passage. After each passage you will answer a question about the main idea of the passage. Remember, the main idea is the main point in a story.

1. Scientists are teaching gorillas how to talk. The apes' names are Koko and Michael. Although their mouths and throats are not made for speaking, they can talk with their hands. They use Ameslan, which is a sign language some deaf people use. Koko and Michael can say more than 500 words and can understand at least 1,000.

_____ **1.** The story mainly tells
   A. how to use Ameslan
   B. how Koko and Michael talk
   C. how scientists are studying gorillas
   D. how apes are like human children

_____

2. Today there are gyms for people who use wheelchairs. These people can lift weights or do other exercises. Teams of people can get together for a game of basketball. Being in a wheelchair doesn't have to mean just sitting around!

_____ **2.** The story mainly tells
   A. how some people use wheelchairs
   B. where people in wheelchairs can exercise
   C. how to work out for good health
   D. how to lift weights on special machines

3. Sim One is an unusual robot. *Sim* is short for *simulator*, which means "a thing that imitates something real." In this case, Sim One imitates a living human being. It looks like a man. It has teeth, hair, and even blinking eyelids. It has a heart that beats and a chest that moves up and down when it breathes. Everything is controlled by a computer. Doctors use Sim One to teach students how to care for people who are ill.

_____ **3.** The story mainly tells
  A. about the many different kinds of robots
  B. how doctors teach students
  C. what Sim One is like
  D. how computers control breathing

4. Cats are very hard to train, but some people have figured out how to do it. The secret is that a cat's brain is in its stomach. All you need is cat food, a spoon, and plenty of time! Put some food on the spoon and hold it wherever you want the cat to go. The cat will learn to obey your hand motions, even when there isn't any food.

_____ **4.** The story mainly tells
  A. how to teach an old dog new tricks
  B. where the parts of a cat are located
  C. how to train a cat
  D. the differences between cats and dogs

---

5. The sport of logrolling was invented by lumberjacks. Lumberjacks are workers who cut down trees and float the logs down the river to the lumber mills. For fun, these people hold contests. Two lumberjacks stand on a log in the river and try to make each other fall off by rolling the log with their feet.

_____ **5.** The story mainly tells
  A. about the sport of logrolling
  B. where lumberjacks work
  C. how to float logs
  D. where to saw lumber

1. Comic books appeared in 1920. The first ones were only collections of comic strips that had been in the newspaper. Later someone wrote new stories instead of using the old strips. The first all-new comic book was a detective story. It was very popular. In June 1938, the first *Superman* comic book was printed. Comic books quickly became part of the American way of life.

_____ **1.** The story mainly tells
  A. when *Superman* comic books were first printed
  B. how comic strips looked in newspapers
  C. how comic books developed
  D. when a detective story became popular

---

2. Certain facts help people know what the weather will be. For instance, weather patterns move from west to east. This happens because Earth turns to the east, and the wind often blows from the west. Also, Earth tilts on its axis. The part that leans toward the Sun is always warmer than the part that leans away.

_____ **2.** The story mainly tells
  A. how people determine weather patterns
  B. why the Sun is warmer
  C. why the wind blows
  D. why Earth tilts

---

3. "Learning the ropes" comes from the sport of sailing. Some sailboats have so many ropes that they look like spiderwebs. Some of the ropes keep the mast from leaning too much into the wind. Sailors use other ropes to adjust the sails. Sailing is easy, once you learn the ropes!

_____ **3.** The story mainly tells
  A. how to sail
  B. about the ropes on a sailboat
  C. how boats change directions
  D. how the mast works

4. Richard Byrd was a famous explorer. He was the first person to fly over both the North and South Poles. He once spent five months alone in a hut studying Antarctica. The temperature was 70 degrees below zero, and he almost froze to death. However, he lived and continued exploring for many more years.

_____ **4.** The story mainly tells
- **A.** how to explore Antarctica
- **B.** why Richard Byrd is remembered
- **C.** when to fly over the North Pole
- **D.** how to keep from freezing to death

5. Kids have been racing in the Soap Box Derby since 1934. The kids must build their own cars, but they can get help from their parents. The kids get companies to pay for the things they need. In return, the kids paint the company's name on their car. The cars don't have engines. Instead, they roll down a hill.

_____ **5.** The story mainly tells
- **A.** about kids and the Soap Box Derby
- **B.** how the power of gravity moves cars
- **C.** how long the Soap Box Derby is
- **D.** how parents help in the Soap Box Derby

1. Whitcomb Judson won a patent for a device. He called it the "clasp-locker." He showed it at the 1893 World's Fair, but it didn't attract any interest. Twenty years later Gideon Sundback improved the device. He renamed it the "hook-less fastener." Then B. F. Goodrich put the fastener on boots. He named it for the sound it made. Z-i-p! Now everyone calls the device a "zipper." It sounds a lot better than "clasp-locker."

_____ **1.** The story mainly tells
  A. that Judson won a patent
  B. when the World's Fair took place
  C. who Gideon Sundback was
  D. how a device got its name from the sound it made

2. Bees and wasps are alike in many ways, but there are big differences between the two insects. Wasps are slimmer, more brightly colored, and less hairy than bees. A worker bee can sting only once, but a wasp can sting several times. Bees make their nests from wax, while wasps make them out of paper and mud. Bees, not wasps, make honey to feed their young. Although many wasps are meat eating, bees are not. They don't eat spiders, flies, or caterpillars.

_____ **2.** The story mainly tells
  A. about the ways that bees and wasps are alike
  B. how bees and wasps are different
  C. how bees build their nests
  D. why wasps and bees sting

3. A human baby is born without teeth. As an adult he or she will have 32 permanent teeth. A baby grows a set of 20 baby teeth before a set of permanent teeth. One by one, the baby teeth fall out as the permanent teeth begin to appear. By the age of 25, a person has a full set of 32 permanent teeth.

_____ **3.** The story mainly tells
   A. about baby and permanent teeth
   B. what teeth are made of
   C. at what age baby teeth are lost
   D. how long it takes teeth to grow

---

4. The year 1972 was important for Yvonne Burke. It was the year in which she turned 40, got married, and ran for the United States Congress. She was selected Woman of the Year by the _Los Angeles Times_ and the National Association of Black Manufacturers. She was also named as one of America's 200 future leaders by _Time_ magazine.

_____ **4.** The story mainly tells that
   A. 1972 was a difficult year for Burke
   B. Burke won election to the Senate
   C. 1972 was a successful year for Burke
   D. Burke was _Time_ magazine's Woman of the Year

---

5. Sand is made up of millions of tiny, loose, and gritty pieces of rock. The rocks are broken down by wind, rain, frost, or water. The rubbing away of the rocks wears them down into the tiny grains found on the beach. Sand is coarser than dust but finer than gravel. It's made up mostly of quartz, mica, and feldspar.

_____ **5.** The story mainly tells
   A. the many uses of sand
   B. how rocks are worn down into sand
   C. how many rocks it takes to make sand
   D. about the size of a grain of sand

1. Did you know that when a sheep falls down, it cannot get up again by itself? A sheep has a heavy body but delicate legs. When it's lying on its back, it's weighted down by its thick, heavy fleece. Even waving its legs doesn't help. Its legs are too thin and weak to swing its heavy body onto its side. A shepherd has to help the sheep back onto its feet!

_____ **1.** The story mainly tells
A. how a sheep uses its legs to get up
B. that a sheep never falls down
C. why a sheep can't get itself up when it falls down
D. how a sheep uses its fleece to get up

2. Are you one of those people who is bothered by mosquitoes? If you are, there are ways to help prevent mosquitoes from biting. Dark colors and rough textures attract mosquitoes. If you will be outdoors, wear pale, smooth clothing instead of jeans. Some scents attract mosquitoes, so don't wear perfume or aftershave lotion. Be careful about the shampoo you use. Even scented shampoo can attract a bite!

_____ **2.** The story mainly tells
A. why mosquitoes bite
B. why mosquito bites itch
C. how to prevent mosquitoes from biting
D. how mosquitoes are attracted to yellow clothing

3. There is an easy way to find out how far away a thunderstorm is from you. Count the number of seconds between the flash of lightning and the clap of thunder. Then divide this number by five. This will tell you about how many miles away the lightning has struck. If you see the flash and hear the thunder at the same time, the storm is directly overhead.

_____ **3.** The story mainly tells
A. how to find out how far away a thunderstorm is
B. where lightning and thunder come from
C. how to guess when a thunderstorm will end
D. how to figure out the direction of a storm

4. How can bloodhounds pick up and follow the scents of missing people? Bloodhounds have a very keen sense of smell. A person's body sheds about 50 million skin cells a day. It releases about 30 to 50 ounces of moisture in the form of sweat. When bacteria mix with skin cells and sweat, a scent is produced. As a person moves, the scent is left on things such as grass and bushes. Bloodhounds can smell this. They have rescued many people.

_____ **4.** The story mainly tells
   A. how bloodhounds can follow a person's scent
   B. how people sweat every day
   C. that bloodhounds have their own scent
   D. that bloodhounds don't have a sense of smell

---

5. The Cullinan Diamond is the largest diamond ever found. It weighed more than 1 1/4 pounds. It was found in a mine in South Africa. It was sent to King Edward II of England. The Cullinan Diamond was cut into 105 separate diamonds. Among these was the largest stone, the 530-carat Star of Africa. Today it is one of the British crown jewels.

_____ **5.** The story mainly tells
   A. how King Edward II found a large diamond
   B. about the largest diamond ever found
   C. that the diamond is a British crown jewel
   D. that there aren't any diamonds in South Africa

1. In 1823, a man in Ohio checked out a library book, but he forgot to return it. In 1968, the man's great-grandson returned the book to the library. It was 145 years late! Of course, the library did not make the great-grandson pay the fine. The overdue fine would have been $2,264!

_____ **1.** The story mainly tells
   A. about a man who decided to keep a library book
   B. about a library book that was 145 years past due
   C. about a man who paid a library fine
   D. when to return overdue library books

---

2. Daniel Defoe wrote a book called *The Adventures of Robinson Crusoe*. It was about a man who lived on a deserted island. Did you know that there was a real-life Robinson Crusoe, only his name was Alexander Selkirk? Selkirk was a sailor on a ship. One day he had a fight with its captain. He left the ship and stayed on an island off the coast of Chile. Selkirk lived on the deserted island for more than four years. Defoe heard about Selkirk's experience. He used Selkirk's adventures as a model to write his story about Robinson Crusoe.

_____ **2.** The story mainly tells that
   A. Crusoe was a real person
   B. Daniel Defoe met Alexander Selkirk
   C. the story of Crusoe was based on Selkirk's life
   D. Defoe lived on a deserted island

3. Harry S Truman was the president of the United States. When Truman was born, his parents couldn't agree on a middle name. Both of his grandfathers' names began with the letter *S*. Truman's parents couldn't decide on a name, so they used *S*. However, it doesn't have a period after it. The *S* in Harry S Truman is a middle name, not an initial.

_____ **3.** The story mainly tells that
    A. Harry Truman's middle name is S
    B. Harry S Truman was named after his father
    C. Harry S Truman didn't have a middle name
    D. Harry S Truman's parents agreed on everything

---

4. Doctors have found that smiling is good for your health. It puts you in a good mood. It could help keep your immune system strong. Luckily, smiling is very easy to do. It takes only 17 muscles to smile, while it takes 43 to frown.

_____ **4.** The story mainly tells
    A. how smiling is good for your health
    B. what makes a good mood
    C. about the immune system
    D. how muscles work

---

5. What is the most popular street name in the United States? Most people might think it's *Main Street*, but *Main* isn't even in the top three. The U.S. Postal Service claims that *Park* is the most common name. *Washington* is second in popularity. *Maple* is the third most common name in the country.

_____ **5.** The story mainly tells that
    A. *Main* is the least popular street name
    B. nobody knows what the most popular name is
    C. *Maple* is the most popular street name
    D. *Park* is the most popular street name

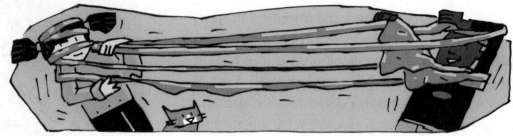

1. James Wright was trying to invent something to replace rubber. He put some acid into a test tube of oil. It produced something that bounced better than a rubber ball. It was stretchable and great fun. It was called Silly Putty and sold better than anything except crayons.

_____ 1. The story mainly tells
   A. how James Wright invented rubber
   B. why Silly Putty is sold in an egg-shaped box
   C. how the first Silly Putty didn't bounce
   D. how Silly Putty was invented

2. When Millard Fillmore was 19, he could hardly read or write. He lived on a farm. He spent more time working than going to school. Later he decided to return to school. Abigail Powers was Fillmore's teacher. They fell in love, and later they were married. Fillmore went on to become a teacher, a lawyer, and the president of the United States!

_____ 2. The story mainly tells that
   A. Fillmore never learned to read and write
   B. Fillmore had a successful life
   C. Fillmore taught Abigail Powers to read
   D. Fillmore never married

3. In 1849, a mapmaker in Alaska was working on a map of the coastline. None of his maps showed a name for one of the capes. A cape is a point of land that juts out into the sea. So he wrote *Name?* on the map and sent it to his mapmaking company in England. A worker at the map company thought the man had written *Nome* on the map. Since then the city on that cape has been known as Nome, Alaska.

_____ 3. The story mainly tells
   A. how maps are made
   B. how Nome, Alaska, got its name
   C. how the mapmaker traveled around Alaska
   D. how Alaska got its name

4. When Katherine Dunham was in college, she went to Haiti. There she studied the country's native dances. When she returned to the United States, she formed a group of African American dancers. They traveled around the world, performing the native dances of different countries. Today Dunham is recognized as one of the pioneers of African American dance.

_____ **4.** The story mainly tells that
    A. Dunham was from Haiti
    B. Dunham was a pioneer in Haiti
    C. Dunham was a pioneer in African American dance
    D. Dunham studied the food of Haiti

5. What does a music conductor do at a concert? The conductor's hands and arms tell the musicians what to do. The right hand keeps the beat. At the same time, movements of the left hand might show the violins when to join in. Musicians watch to see when to play faster or more softly. Sometimes it looks as if the conductor's arms are about to take flight, but that is the special way the conductor creates a musical story.

_____ **5.** The story mainly tells
    A. how a music conductor creates a musical story
    B. which of the conductor's hands keeps the beat
    C. why musicians watch the conductor
    D. when the violins join in

1. Hurricanes and tornadoes can whirl all kinds of creatures in the air and carry them for miles. At one time fish rained down on a town in Scotland. The storm had blown in from the Atlantic. Another time people in England felt bugs and frogs falling from the sky after a big storm.

_____ **1.** The story mainly tells
  A. how fish fell from the sky
  B. what hurricanes and tornadoes can do
  C. what strange things fall from the sky
  D. how England had a big storm

2. Trevor Ferrell was just 13 years old, but he wanted to help homeless people. Trevor took food and clothes to the homeless living in his city. Other people heard what he was doing and wanted to help too. Now people are doing Trevor's work in many cities!

_____ **2.** The story mainly tells
  A. about the problems of the world
  B. how Trevor Ferrell felt
  C. why people are without food, clothes, and shelter
  D. how Trevor Ferrell helped homeless people

3. The Great Salt Lake in Utah is bigger than the whole state of Delaware. Thousands of years ago, it was 10 times bigger than it is today. Over the years, the water has dried up. People at one time thought that the lake would disappear. Now the water is too high. Each spring it floods nearby towns.

_____ **3.** The story mainly tells
  A. why you should visit the state of Utah
  B. how the Great Salt Lake has changed in size
  C. why the Great Salt Lake is salty
  D. how big Delaware is

---

4. Mae Jemison became a doctor to help others. She joined the Peace Corps and brought medical aid to people in poor countries. Later this African American doctor joined the astronaut program. She took part in experiments on the space shuttle *Endeavor*. When Mae Jemison left the space program, she went back to helping people who are poor.

_____ **4.** The story mainly tells
  A. about Mae Jemison's life
  B. when Jemison joined the Peace Corps
  C. how Jemison became an astronaut
  D. which space shuttle Jemison went on

---

5. Some children are full of pep in the morning but get tired after lunch. Others don't even feel awake until two or three o'clock in the afternoon. Studies show that many children learn best during the middle of the afternoon, but that's the time when the school day is over! Perhaps someday children will be able to go to school when their "learning clock" says that the time is right.

_____ **5.** The story mainly tells
  A. how children feel during the day
  B. why children fall asleep in class
  C. why clocks tell time differently
  D. when schools will start in the future

1. Once Native Americans made beads from seashells. They called the beads "wampum." Wampum was used for many things. Wampum belts were special. Native Americans recorded agreements on them. First they cut the beads from shells. Next they drilled holes in the beads and rolled them smooth. Then they wove the beads into a belt that told the story of an agreement. For an important agreement, most of the beads were purple.

_____ **1.** The story mainly tells
   A. how beads were called wampum
   B. how purple beads were used
   C. how fabric was woven
   D. about a particular use for wampum

---

2. Isabella Baumfree was born a slave. When New York outlawed slavery, her master would not set her free, so Baumfree escaped. She changed her name to Sojourner Truth. She chose the name because she hoped to speak out against slavery. Truth traveled all over the North, spreading her message against slavery. Finally Truth lived to see the day in which slavery was outlawed throughout the country.

_____ **2.** The story mainly tells
   A. that Truth lived in New York
   B. that Truth fought to end slavery everywhere
   C. the year in which slavery was outlawed
   D. that Isabella Baumfree was a slave all her life

---

3. Movie stars were the first people to wear sunglasses. Early movie lights were very bright and hurt people's eyes. Actors wore sunglasses to rest their eyes. Today sunglasses are very popular. People wear them to protect their eyes from the sun.

_____ **3.** The story mainly tells
   A. how sunglasses were made
   B. who invented sunglasses
   C. why movie stars wore sunglasses
   D. that movie stars wanted to look mysterious

4. During World War I, the White House gardeners joined the army. To keep the White House lawn from looking uncared for, President Wilson bought a flock of sheep to eat the grass. Mrs. Wilson sold the sheep's wool. She made more than $100,000 and presented it as a gift to the Red Cross.

_____ **4.** The story mainly tells
  A. how a flock of sheep helped the Wilsons
  B. that Mrs. Wilson was a shepherd
  C. that gardeners did not have to serve in the army
  D. that President Wilson spent $100,000 on wool

---

5. During the 1850s, Levi Strauss moved to San Francisco. He sold canvas material used for making tents and covered wagons. Gold miners and railroad workers complained that their pants tore easily or became worn too soon. Strauss used his canvas to make a pair of pants. He called the pants after himself, or Levi's. They sold for 22¢ per pair. Later Strauss made a pair of denim pants and dyed them blue.

_____ **5.** The story mainly tells
  A. why Levi Strauss moved to San Francisco
  B. that Levi Strauss was a gold miner
  C. that the first Levi's were brown
  D. that Levi Strauss invented the first blue jeans

Writing Roundup

Read each paragraph. Think about the main idea. Write the main idea in your own words.

1. One bad taste is bad news for birds. In a test, birds were fed worms that would make them sick. After that the birds wouldn't eat the same type of worm even though there was nothing wrong with it. The birds lost an important food source.

What is the main idea of this paragraph?

_____

_____

2. If you see a live rattlesnake, stay away from it. If you see a dead rattlesnake, stay away from it too. Doctors in Arizona looked at the records of 34 people who had snake bites. Five people were bitten by dead snakes. Snakes can strike and bite for an hour or so after death. In fact, two people were bitten by the snake heads they picked up!

What is the main idea of this paragraph?

_____

_____

3. *Semaphore* is the name for a way of sending messages by flags. The army uses semaphore, and so does the navy. Doctor Albert Myer invented semaphore. The army began to use it in 1858. Doctor Myer credited a Native American tribe for the idea. He got it by watching Comanches in New Mexico signal each other by waving lances.

What is the main idea of this paragraph?

_____

_____

Prewriting

Think of a main idea that you would like to write about, such as your favorite food, a state you would like to visit, or what it would be like to take a trail ride in the desert. Fill in the chart below.

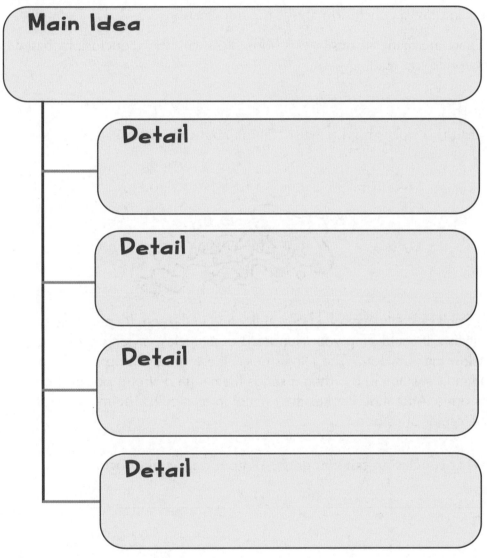

Main Idea

Detail

Detail

Detail

Detail

On Your Own

Now use another sheet of paper to write your paragraph. Underline the sentence that tells the main idea.

What Is a Conclusion?

A conclusion is a decision you make after thinking about all the information you have. In a story the writer may not state all of his or her ideas. When you read, you often have to hunt for clues so that you can understand the whole story. By putting all of the writer's clues together, you can draw a conclusion about the information.

There are many stories in this book. You will draw conclusions based on the stories you read.

Try It!

Read this story about jellyfish. Think about the information it gives you.

Don't touch that colorful balloon floating in the sea. It's probably a jellyfish. It could sting you. Hundreds of tentacles, or long arms, hang below the "balloon." The jellyfish uses these arms to trap small sea animals swimming by. Then it stings them with a strong poison from its arms. After that, it takes the animal to its mouth. The mouth is at the center of its body.

What conclusion can you draw? Write it on the lines below.

_____

_____

You might have written, "Jellyfish can be very colorful." You might have said, "The poison of the jellyfish can hurt people." You might have written, "The arms of the jellyfish have several uses." You can draw these conclusions from the story. The first sentence compares the jellyfish to a colorful balloon. The next sentences tell what the jellyfish can do with its arms. From these clues you can draw the above conclusions.

Using What You Know

Read the stories on this page. Hunt for clues that will help you draw a conclusion about each school subject being described.

This is my favorite subject. I am learning to read maps. I can tell you what the largest bodies of water are called. I can name the seven continents. I can even tell you what percent of Earth is covered by water.

I am studying _____ .

This subject is a great change of pace during the day. Instead of sitting in a classroom, I go outside and get some exercise. Sometimes I run around the track. Other times I jump over hurdles. If it is raining, I play an indoor game like basketball.

I am studying _____ .

This subject is very important. I study nouns, verbs, and all the parts of speech. I learn to put words together in order to make complete sentences. I am learning how to write well.

I am studying _____ .

This is a fun subject for me because I love to draw. I am able to use pencils, charcoal, and all kinds of paint. I like trying out different colors and designs.

I am studying _____ .

Read each passage. After each passage you will answer a question that will require you to draw a conclusion about the story. Remember, a conclusion is a decision you make after putting together all the clues you are given.

1. Why do people sneeze? Scientists aren't sure why, but they know that sneezing can be a sign of illness. The early Romans believed that sneezing helped people make smart decisions. People in Europe thought that sneezing was a symbol of good health. Any patient who sneezed three times was always released from the hospital.

_____ **1.** From this story you can tell that
   A. sneezing has improved through the years
   B. the early Romans were the first to sneeze
   C. ideas about sneezing have changed over time
   D. most people sneeze only three times

2. People in England used to hold many handwriting contests. The winner usually received a gold pen. In one contest the judges could not decide between two men who wrote beautifully. The judges looked at the handwriting samples for days. They found that one of the men had forgotten to dot an _i_. Because of this the other man walked away with the gold pen.

_____ **2.** One man lost the contest because he
   A. did not want the gold pen
   B. could not write beautifully
   C. forgot an important part of a letter
   D. did not follow the rules of the contest

3. When the United States was new, most people lived on farms. About 95 out of every 100 people made their living by growing food. They ate the food they grew and sold whatever was left over to the people in cities. By 1998, fewer than 3 out of every 100 people were farmers.

_____ **3.** Over time, Americans have been
   A. eating less and less
   B. moving away from farms
   C. moving out of towns and cities
   D. buying more farmland

4. People who visit Washington, D.C., often want souvenirs. Many want a flag that has flown over the dome of the Capitol. To fill these requests, a flag crew takes about 300 flags to the dome every day. They run each flag up the flagpole for a few seconds, and then they take the flag down. The flags are folded, stored, and sold to visitors.

_____ **4.** You can tell from the story that
   A. many flags fly over the Capitol every day
   B. most people cannot tell one flag from another
   C. the flag crew does not like its work
   D. everyone has respect for the American flag

5. A famous poet sat down in a restaurant. A man working in the restaurant recognized the poet. "I will put my poems by the poet's plate," thought the worker. Later the poet read the worker's poems. The next day the worker's name was in the newspapers. His name was Langston Hughes.

_____ **5.** You can conclude that the famous poet
   A. liked the restaurant
   B. did not like the worker's poems
   C. ate pizza
   D. liked the worker's poems

1. Jesse Owens was one of the greatest athletes of the twentieth century. He took part in the 1936 Olympics, in which he won four gold medals. He also won an even greater honor there. That year the Olympics were held in Berlin. The German leader was Adolph Hitler, who believed that white Germans were better than everyone else in the world. Because Owens was an African American, he wanted to prove Hitler wrong. With his great talent, Owens did just that.

_____ **1.** From the story you can tell that
   A. Jesse Owens agreed with Adolph Hitler
   B. Adolph Hitler liked Jesse Owens
   C. Jesse Owens had a special reason for winning
   D. Adolph Hitler was an African American

2. Leslie Silko is a modern writer. She was born in New Mexico. She is part Pueblo, part white, and part Mexican. As a child she heard many Native American stories. She liked the legends of her people. She also learned the customs of her tribe. She uses that knowledge to write stories. She wants everyone to know about the history of Native Americans.

_____ **2.** The story suggests that Leslie Silko
   A. was born in New Jersey
   B. writes about fancy cloth
   C. forgot all her childhood stories
   D. takes pride in her Native American background

3. Pickles are made from cucumbers. People have been eating pickles for more than 4,000 years. People in the United States eat more than 1 billion pounds of pickles each year. There is even a time for celebrating pickles. The third week in May is known as Pickle Week.

_____ **3.** You can tell from the story that
   A. Pickle Week is in March
   B. people in the United States like pickles
   C. pickles are a recent invention
   D. cucumbers are made from pickles

4. A gulf is a body of water that is partly enclosed by land. The Gulf of Mexico is the biggest gulf in the world. It is just south of the United States. This gulf covers 700,000 square miles of Earth's surface. It is 1,000 miles wide from east to west. From north to south, the gulf is 800 miles wide.

_____ **4.** You can conclude that
    A. the Gulf of Mexico contains huge amounts of water
    B. a gulf is completely surrounded by land
    C. the Gulf of Mexico is a river
    D. the United States is south of the Gulf of Mexico

---

5. Checkers is one of the oldest board games. It began in Egypt about 4,000 years ago. It has always been a two-player game, and it has always been played on a checkered board. The game was taken up and changed slightly by the Greeks and the Romans. It soon became a popular game for rich leaders.

_____ **5.** From this story you can conclude that
    A. the Greeks and Romans invented checkers
    B. checkers is played only by young people
    C. only rich leaders should play checkers
    D. the Egyptians invented checkers

1. Columns and columns of rock stand along the coast of Ireland. They make up a natural wonder called the Giant's Causeway. An old story says that this bridge was built by a character named Finn MacCool. He was building a bridge so that giants could walk from Ireland to Scotland.

_____ **1.** From this story you can tell that
- **A.** the causeway must be small
- **B.** the causeway must be new
- **C.** MacCool didn't really build the causeway
- **D.** giants still walk across the causeway

2. Many children are familiar with Mother Goose rhymes. Historians aren't sure whether or not Mother Goose was a real person. Some say that her real name was Elizabeth Vergoose. They believe Vergoose is buried in Boston, Massachusetts. Historians think that her son published a book of her songs and rhymes. Such a book has never been found.

_____ **2.** From this story you can tell that
- **A.** Elizabeth Vergoose wrote a book
- **B.** the truth about Mother Goose remains a mystery
- **C.** there was never a real person called Mother Goose
- **D.** no one tells Mother Goose tales anymore

3. The porcupine uses the quills on its tail to defend itself. When an animal comes too close, the porcupine slaps its tail at the enemy. The sharp quills come off easily. They stick into the other creature's skin. Each quill has a hook at the end. This makes the quills very painful to remove.

_____ **3.** If the quills didn't have hooks, they would
- **A.** not stay on the porcupine
- **B.** come out more easily
- **C.** hurt much more
- **D.** shoot through the air

---

4. The U.S. Constitution gives people freedom of speech, but that does not mean that people can say whatever they want. What if someone was in a store and wanted to cause trouble? The person could shout, "Fire!" even if there weren't any fire. Everyone would run out of the store at once, and people could get hurt. In this case the guilty person would not be protected under the freedom-of-speech laws.

_____ **4.** You can conclude that the freedom-of-speech laws
- **A.** are unfair to people
- **B.** cause trouble in stores
- **C.** may not protect people who lie
- **D.** let people say whatever they want

---

5. In the English alphabet, _G_ is the seventh letter. It was the third letter in the alphabet of the ancient Greeks. In addition to its main use in forming words, _G_ is sometimes used to stand for other words and things. If you are measuring weight, small _g_ stands for _gram_. In music, _G_ is the name of the note that follows _F_.

_____ **5.** From this story you <u>cannot</u> tell
- **A.** how to pronounce _G_ in English
- **B.** which things _G_ stands for
- **C.** which place _G_ has in the alphabet
- **D.** what _G_ is mainly used for

1. Rosa gave the gift to her friend Maria. It was wrapped in beautiful, handmade paper. She watched as Maria untied the ribbon. Rosa had spent hours making the wrapping paper. In fact she thought the paper was better than the gift. She held her breath as Maria removed the paper and opened the box.

_____ **1.** From this story you can tell that
   A. Maria will like the gift
   B. Maria will not like the gift
   C. Rosa made the greeting card, too
   D. Rosa took great care in wrapping the gift

2. In 1987, Lorenzo Amato made a huge pizza. In fact, it was the biggest pizza that had ever been made. It weighed more than 18,000 pounds and was topped with more than 1,000 pounds of cheese. After it was baked, it was cut into 60,000 pieces!

_____ **2.** The story suggests that
   A. Amato's pizza fed many people
   B. the pizza was not very heavy
   C. Amato's pizza tasted awful
   D. Amato hated making pizzas

3. Adolfo Esquivel is a great believer in human rights. He lives in Argentina, where he is head of the Peace and Justice Service. This group works hard for the rights of all people. Sometimes the work proves dangerous. For his efforts Esquivel has been jailed and even tortured several times, but he continues his struggle. His work has paid off. He won the Nobel Peace Prize in 1980.

_____ **3.** You can tell from the story that
   A. fighting for human rights is always fun
   B. Esquivel is willing to suffer for his beliefs
   C. Argentina is a state in the United States
   D. Esquivel gave up his struggle after being jailed

4. In Czechoslovakia, children celebrate the end of winter in an unusual way. First they make a straw figure. The figure is a symbol of death called Smrt. The straw is decorated with colored rags and bits of eggshell. Then the children burn the straw figure. Sometimes they throw it into a river. After destroying Smrt the children wear flowers to welcome springtime.

_____ **4.** The story suggests that
    A. the straw figure is a symbol of summer
    B. straw doesn't burn
    C. the flowers are a sign of springtime
    D. the Czech children hate to see winter end

5. William Taft was once president. He was different in many ways. He was the heaviest president ever. He weighed more than 300 pounds. Taft was the first president to play golf. He was the first one to throw a ball to mark the start of baseball season. Taft died in 1930. He was laid to rest in Arlington National Cemetery. He was the first president to be buried there.

_____ **5.** From the story you can tell that
    A. Taft began many presidential customs
    B. tennis was Taft's favorite game
    C. Taft was a small man
    D. President Taft is still alive

1. Juanita was very discouraged about her art. She could hardly draw a tree. One day the art teacher talked to Juanita. "The colors and shapes you use are striking," she said. "I think you have a good chance of winning the art contest this year." The teacher's kind words changed Juanita's attitude.

_____ **1.** This story suggests that
  A. Juanita is not a good artist
  B. color and shape are important art elements
  C. Juanita's teacher cannot draw a tree
  D. Juanita will not enter the art contest

2. Chiang Kai-shek was a famous Chinese leader. As a young man, he gained much power in China. He led the Chinese army against the Japanese in World War II. After the war the Communists tried to take over China. Kai-shek fought bravely against them, but he lost the fight. With his followers he fled to Taiwan. Until his death he continued to fight against the Communist rule of China.

_____ **2.** The story suggests that Chiang Kai-shek
  A. believed that China should remain a free country
  B. is still the leader of China
  C. fled to Japan
  D. was a Communist

3. Seashores experience a daily change in water level. This change is called tide. As the water is pulled from shore, the water level drops. This is known as low tide. As the water returns to shore, the water level rises. This is called high tide. The coming and going of the water is caused by the pull of the Moon's gravity.

_____ **3.** You can tell from the story that
    A. tides are caused by the gravity of the Sun
    B. the water level drops at high tide
    C. the Moon has a strong effect on Earth's seas
    D. a _tide_ is a change in water temperature

4. Carbon dioxide in the atmosphere acts as a blanket. It lets light pass through, but it traps heat. This is called the greenhouse effect. It is rather good, for without it Earth would be much colder. As the carbon dioxide increases, the heat of Earth's surface rises. This isn't good. Carbon dioxide comes from the burning of oil, coal, and gasoline. If we do not limit this burning, the world may suffer as a result.

_____ **4.** From this story you can tell that
    A. carbon dioxide traps light
    B. Earth would be warmer without the greenhouse effect
    C. the greenhouse effect is never good
    D. too much carbon dioxide is bad

5. Have you ever looked up a word in a dictionary? Well, you can thank Noah Webster. He worked almost all his life to make spelling fit a standard in America. He produced two large books of words. The larger one appeared in 1828. Webster's work has been improved many times. His dictionary is still in use today.

_____ **5.** You can conclude that Noah Webster
    A. respected and loved language
    B. didn't know how to spell
    C. liked to write long letters
    D. couldn't read

1. Many cities hold distance races called marathons. Runners gather from around the country. They race through the streets, up and down hills, and over bridges. People who want something different can go run a marathon in Indiana. The runners there dash down the dark passages of the Merengo Cave!

_____ **1.** From this story you can tell that
- **A.** all marathons are alike
- **B.** most runners like cave races
- **C.** Merengo Cave must be pretty long
- **D.** marathons are bicycle races

2. Moths are related to butterflies. However, most moths fly at night. Butterflies fly during the day. When a moth is resting, it folds its wings back over its body. A butterfly, on the other hand, holds its wings upward.

_____ **2.** This story tells
- **A.** how moths and butterflies are alike
- **B.** how moths and butterflies are different
- **C.** why people confuse moths and butterflies
- **D.** why moths are better than butterflies

3. The sidewinder is a snake that lives in the desert. Unlike other snakes the sidewinder does not crawl. Instead, it coils its body into big loops. Then suddenly it unwinds itself. The snake skims over the sand much like a leaf in the wind. It moves forward and slightly sideways at the same time.

_____ **3.** The sidewinder gets its name from
- **A.** the place in which it lives
- **B.** the way in which it moves
- **C.** the fact that it moves easily
- **D.** a group of other snakes

4. Inventors record their inventions with the government. The inventors hope that someone will buy their bright ideas. Some inventions are so strange that no one wants them. Government files show inventions for odd things, such as flying fire escapes and eyeglasses for chickens. There is even an alarm clock that taps the sleeping person on the head with a piece of wood!

_____ **4.** The story tells about inventions that
   A. do not work
   B. were turned down by the government
   C. have been used in many places
   D. no one wants to buy

---

5. White eggs and brown eggs taste exactly the same. In some places, however, people think that brown eggs are better. They are willing to pay more money for them. For example, in Boston brown eggs usually cost more than they do in New York.

_____ **5.** You could conclude that people in New York
   A. don't eat brown eggs
   B. think brown eggs are best
   C. eat more eggs than people eat in Boston
   D. don't think brown eggs are better

1. Some people love a good story. Once every year a group of people get together for a storytelling festival. They take turns entertaining each other by spinning yarns and swapping tales.

_____ **1.** You can tell that
- **A.** storytellers like wool
- **B.** the festival has many activities
- **C.** the festival is dull
- **D.** storytellers like to share stories

---

2. By noting changes, a lie-detector machine shows whether someone is lying. The machine shows changes in heartbeat and breathing. These changes might take place when a person is lying. These changes also take place when a person is nervous. Sometimes a person is lying but doesn't know it. In this case the machine doesn't note any change at all.

_____ **2.** From the story you <u>cannot</u> tell
- **A.** what happens when a person lies
- **B.** what a lie detector shows
- **C.** which changes take place when a person is nervous
- **D.** how a lie detector is used in court

3. In the making of a baseball, machines do most of the work. One machine covers a piece of cork with rubber. Another machine wraps yarn around the ball. The leather used to cover the ball is also cut by a machine. People are still needed to sew the leather covers on the balls by hand.

_____ **3.** You can tell that machines
   A. probably can't sew leather covers on balls
   B. always get tangled up in the yarn
   C. make the cork used for making balls
   D. can't cover cork with rubber

4. The United States once had a state named for Benjamin Franklin. It was at the time that North Carolina gave some land to the new government. The land was later returned to North Carolina. Today that land is part of the state of Tennessee.

_____ **4.** From the story you <u>cannot</u> tell
   A. who Benjamin Franklin was
   B. where the state was located
   C. when we had a state named for Franklin
   D. what happened to the state

5. Many animals shed their outer coverings every year. Then they grow new ones. Birds lose their feathers and grow new, colorful ones. Snakes lose their old skins. New, shiny skin forms underneath the old skin. Some mammals lose part of their hair in warm weather. They grow heavy coats in cold weather.

_____ **5.** Some mammals lose part of their hair
   A. so that they can grow larger
   B. in order to keep cool
   C. when cold weather is on the way
   D. when they are babies

1. The man carefully eyed the painting in the flea market. The picture was torn, but the frame was in good shape. The man decided to pay the asking price of $4. Later when the man removed the picture from the frame, he found an old piece of paper. The man's eyes widened in surprise because he had found an old copy of the Declaration of Independence. It was worth $1 million!

_____ **1.** You can conclude that
    A. the man always had rotten luck
    B. the old piece of paper was a restaurant menu
    C. the man was glad that he bought the painting
    D. the frame was worth $1 million

2. Mary Bacon loved to ride horses, and she turned that love into a job. Being one of the first female jockeys, Mary rode her horses to many wins, but she also experienced many setbacks. One time she was thrown from a horse and broke her back. Another time a horse fell on top of her. Each time she returned to race again. She once said, "You can't quit just because you've been thrown."

_____ **2.** From the story you <u>cannot</u> tell
    A. about Bacon's job
    B. which horse threw Bacon in 1969
    C. if Bacon returned to racing after her accidents
    D. how Bacon broke her back

3. Charles Edensaw was a member of the Haida tribe. He lived in western Canada. Edensaw became a fine artist. He used wood, gold, and silver in his works. He was also a talented crafter of argillite, which is a kind of shale. His art included drawings, sketches, pipes, and totem poles. Many of his works are found in museums.

_____ **3.** From this story you can tell that
    A. Charles Edensaw was a successful artist
    B. all of Edensaw's works are missing today
    C. Edensaw used only crayons in his works
    D. the Haida tribe lived in Kansas

4. Sonja Henie was one of the best ice-skaters of all time. Her first major contest was the 1924 Winter Olympics. Henie was just 12 years old! She won gold medals in the next three Olympics. She even won 10 world titles in a row. Then Henie became a movie star. Her movies often showed her skating. As a result, ice-skating was soon a popular sport around the world.

_____ **4.** From the story you <u>cannot</u> tell
     A. which sport Henie was best at
     B. how many movies Henie made
     C. when Henie's first major contest took place
     D. how many world titles Henie won in a row

5. Estella was looking at ruby rings. She knew that the stone had special meaning, for it was considered the birthstone for July. That was why Estella thought she should have one. Estella had a pearl ring, but she did not have a ruby ring. She hoped that someone would get one for her for her birthday.

_____ **5.** You can conclude from the story that
     A. Estella does not really like rubies
     B. rubies cost a lot of money
     C. the rings Estella saw were made of gold
     D. Estella's birthday is in July

Writing Roundup

Read each paragraph. Think about a conclusion you can draw. Write your conclusion in a complete sentence.

1. Jumping from a plane is a daring act. Imagine how daring it would be if you were the first to do it. Georgia Broadwick was such a person. On June 21, 1913, she jumped from a plane over Los Angeles. She fell 100 feet before her parachute opened. She was the first woman to parachute from a plane. In those days, just going up in a plane was daring enough!

What conclusion can you draw from this paragraph?

_____

_____

2. Have you ever seen a $100,000 bill? These bills were made in 1935. They had a portrait of Woodrow Wilson on them. The bills were not put into public use. They were used only by the government.

What conclusion can you draw from this paragraph?

_____

_____

3. Amalia does not remember who taught her to whistle. She does remember the first bird she learned how to imitate. It was a robin. Since then, Amalia has learned to make the sounds of many birds.

What conclusion can you draw from this paragraph?

_____

_____

Read the paragraph below. What conclusions can you draw? Use the clues in the paragraph to answer the questions in complete sentences.

Jackie Robinson was the first African American to play major-league baseball. He joined the Brooklyn Dodgers in 1947. Another African American joined the Dodgers team later that year. His name was Dan Bankhead. He pitched in four games. He also hit a home run. The next year Bankhead returned to the minor leagues. Robinson was voted into the Baseball Hall of Fame. Still, Bankhead should not be forgotten. It took courage for him to play with the Dodgers in 1947.

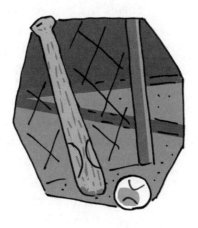

1. Did any African Americans play in the major leagues in 1946? How do you know?

_____

_____

2. In Jackie Robinson's first game with the Dodgers, was he the only African American in the major leagues? How do you know?

_____

_____

3. Was Dan Bankhead a star with the Dodgers? How do you know?

_____

_____

4. Was Jackie Robinson a baseball star? How do you know?

_____

_____

unit 6

What Is an Inference?

An inference is a guess you make after thinking about what you already know. Suppose you are going to the post office. From what you know about the post office, you might infer that you will wait in line at the counter. You can assume that when it is your turn, you will pay the fee for the services you need.

An author does not write every detail in a story. If every detail were included, stories would be long and boring, and the main point would be lost. Suppose an author wrote, "Debra ran along the beach." The writer does not have to tell you what a beach is. You already know that it is a sandy area next to the ocean. From what you know, you might guess that people who go to the beach can swim, build sand castles, or collect seashells. By filling in these missing details, you could infer that Debra was at the beach to swim in the waves with her family. You can infer the missing details from what you know.

Try It!

Read this story about foxes. Think about the facts.

Foxes sleep during the day and hunt at night. They prey on squirrels, rabbits, frogs, and birds. They also eat eggs and berries. Although foxes often live near people, they usually stay hidden. If a person approaches them, they will run away or climb up a tree.

What inference can you make about foxes? Write an inference on the line below.

_____

You might have written something such as: "Foxes are afraid of people." You can make this inference from what the story tells you and what you already know. You know that if an animal hides or runs away, it is not comfortable around people.

Practice Making Inferences

Read each story. Then read the statements that follow. Some of the statements are facts and can be found in the story. Other statements are inferences. You can make these by thinking about what you've read and what you know. Decide whether each statement is a fact or an inference. The first one has been done for you.

Laura had $5.00. Her mother had given the money to her so that she could buy a present for her brother. While Laura was shopping, she saw a book she had been wanting to read. It cost $4.50.

Fact	Inference		
●	○	**1.**	**A.** Laura had $5.00.
●	○		**B.** The book cost $4.50.
○	●		**C.** Laura bought the book she wanted.
○	●		**D.** She didn't have a present to give to her brother.

You can find statements **A** and **B** in the story. They are facts. You can infer that Laura bought the book and that she didn't have a present to give to her brother, but this is not stated in the story. Statements **C** and **D** are inferences.

Juan lives in Madrid, Spain. He teaches at a private school. Juan walks to work every weekday and holds classes from 9:00 until noon. Then he walks home for lunch. His family eats a large meal, and then everyone takes a nap. Juan returns to work at 4:00 and teaches until 9:00 at night.

Fact	Inference		
○	○	**2.**	**A.** Juan teaches at a private school.
○	○		**B.** He walks to work every weekday.
○	○		**C.** Juan's family feels drowsy after lunch.
○	○		**D.** The school is near Juan's home.

Read the passages. Use what you know about inference to answer the questions. Remember, an inference is a guess you make by putting together what you know and what you read or see in the stories.

1. The Lincoln Highway opened in 1913. It was the first paved road in the United States that stretched from coast to coast. The highway started at Times Square in New York City. It ran more than 3,000 miles to California. There it reached its end at Lincoln Park in San Francisco.

Fact	Inference	
○	○	**1.** **A.** The Lincoln Highway opened in 1913.
○	○	**B.** Many people drove on the new highway.
○	○	**C.** The road made cross-country travel easier.
○	○	**D.** The highway was more than 3,000 miles long.

2. Sometimes the Moon passes between the Earth and the Sun and completely blocks the Sun's light. On Earth it looks as if the Sun has disappeared. This is called a total solar eclipse. Stars appear in the sky. Flowers close their petals. Many animals are fooled into going to sleep. As the Moon continues to move, the Sun can be seen again. First it appears as a tiny sliver, then a crescent, then the full Sun. Roosters begin to crow and flowers open back up. Long ago people were afraid that the Sun had been swallowed by a monster. They would beat drums to scare the monster away. Now we know that total solar eclipses happen every 18 months or so. They last just a few minutes. Each eclipse can be seen only from certain places on Earth.

Fact	Inference	
○	○	**2.** **A.** People used to be afraid that the Sun would not reappear.
○	○	**B.** A total solar eclipse is visible only from certain parts of Earth.
○	○	**C.** During an eclipse it is possible to see the stars.
○	○	**D.** A total solar eclipse lasts only a few minutes.

3. Elizabeth Butler was an English painter. She enjoyed painting battle scenes. Butler often worked on a very large canvas in order to capture the whole scene. Her paintings are full of life and interest. Her most famous painting is named *The Roll Call*.

Fact	Inference		
○	○	**3. A.**	Elizabeth Butler was a painter.
○	○	**B.**	Butler felt battle scenes were exciting.
○	○	**C.**	One of Butler's paintings is *The Roll Call*.
○	○	**D.**	Butler visited battle scenes to get ideas.

---

4. Harvest moon is a full moon that comes in late September or early October. At this time of year, the Moon rises slowly. It seems to hang near the horizon for a long time after sunset. Because of this the Moon reflects more light from the Sun. The twilight is brighter, and farmers have extra time to harvest their crops.

Fact	Inference		
○	○	**4. A.**	Farmers can't harvest crops in the dark.
○	○	**B.**	The Moon reflects the Sun's light.
○	○	**C.**	Farmers like the harvest moon.
○	○	**D.**	The harvest moon is a full moon.

---

5. The New York Yankees play baseball in Yankee Stadium. This ballpark opened in 1923. More than 70,000 people crowded in on opening day. They all wanted to see the Yankees play in the new park. That day Babe Ruth hit a home run. It was the first ball hit out of Yankee Stadium.

Fact	Inference		
○	○	**5. A.**	In 1923 baseball was popular in New York.
○	○	**B.**	Yankee Stadium is in New York.
○	○	**C.**	Babe Ruth hit a home run on opening day.
○	○	**D.**	Yankee Stadium opened in 1923.

1. Some animals make long journeys to escape cold or to find food. For example, a gray whale can travel up to 5,600 miles. Bats have been known to travel as far as 1,500 miles, and the record distance traveled by a butterfly is 4,000 miles. For toads the record is 2 miles. This may not seem like much, but that's a lot of hopping!

Fact	Inference		
○	○	**1.** **A.**	A butterfly has traveled 4,000 miles.
○	○	**B.**	Some animals travel to escape cold.
○	○	**C.**	Scientists can track how far an animal travels.
○	○	**D.**	Some bats have traveled 1,500 miles.

---

2. The date was January 10, 1901. Captain Anthony Lucas had his men hard at work in the Spindletop oil field in Texas. Suddenly their equipment began to shake. Then oil gushed from the ground, shooting high into the air. Everything nearby was coated with the thick, black oil. Lucas and his men didn't mind, because they had struck oil! Spindletop soon became one of the highest-producing oil fields in the world.

Fact	Inference		
○	○	**2.** **A.**	The Spindletop oil field was in Texas.
○	○	**B.**	Captain Lucas knew a lot about oil wells.
○	○	**C.**	Lucas and his men found oil.
○	○	**D.**	It was exciting when the men struck oil.

---

3. Have you ever been in a hailstorm? The balls of ice can cause great damage. A hailstone begins as a raindrop that is blown high up into a thundercloud, where it freezes. The lump of ice is blown back up several times, each time gaining more ice. Finally it grows too heavy and falls to Earth.

Fact	Inference		
○	○	**3.** **A.**	Hail can be dangerous.
○	○	**B.**	A hailstone begins as a raindrop.
○	○	**C.**	Winds blow the lump of ice back up.
○	○	**D.**	Hail falls when it grows too heavy.

4. Have you ever heard of a "swan song"? This saying means a farewell appearance or a final act. The saying comes from an ancient legend about swans. It was once thought that a swan would remain silent all its life until it was dying. Then it would sing out in its final minutes. This swan song would be one of great feeling and beauty.

Fact   Inference

○   ○   **4.** **A.** Ancient people thought swans were special.

○   ○   **B.** A "swan song" means a final act.

○   ○   **C.** Swans were supposedly silent until near death.

○   ○   **D.** The swan's final song was supposed to be very beautiful.

---

5. Before 1892, women did not play basketball. Senda Berenson started women's basketball. Many people thought that women should not play sports as rough as basketball. Berenson changed the rules a little to make the game more "ladylike." However, women soon began playing the game just like men.

Fact   Inference

○   ○   **5.** **A.** Berenson changed some of the rules.

○   ○   **B.** Many people thought that women should not play basketball.

○   ○   **C.** Women's basketball began in 1892.

○   ○   **D.** Some people did not like women's basketball.

1. Krakatoa was an island in the Indian Ocean. It lay just west of Java. On the island was a large volcano. In 1883, the volcano blew up. The whole island was destroyed. The noise of the blast was heard thousands of miles away. The blast also formed a giant wave more that 100 feet tall. The wave swept over nearby islands and killed 40,000 people. Ash from the volcano darkened the region for two days. Dust reached the atmosphere and spread over the whole Earth.

Fact	Inference		
○	○	**1.** **A.**	Krakatoa was in the Indian Ocean.
○	○	**B.**	The volcano blew up in 1883.
○	○	**C.**	Every person on Krakatoa was killed.
○	○	**D.**	The giant wave killed 40,000 people.

2. The bell rang sharply in the middle of the night. Missy sat upright in her bed, rubbing her eyes. Again the sharp ringing split the silence. Trying to pull herself together, Missy scrambled for the phone. She had no idea who could be calling at that time of night, but she hoped it was not an emergency. When she answered the phone, a voice at the other end asked for someone named Felix. Disgusted, Missy said that Felix did not live there. Then the person on the other end slammed down the phone.

Fact	Inference		
○	○	**2.** **A.**	Missy was asleep when the phone rang.
○	○	**B.**	The other person dialed a wrong number.
○	○	**C.**	The phone rang in the middle of the night.
○	○	**D.**	The other person did not apologize.

3. In July 1969, a spaceship rushed toward the Moon. The ship was called *Apollo 11*. On board were three men. They were Michael Collins, Neil Armstrong, and Edwin Aldrin Jr. When the spaceship neared the Moon, it began to orbit. Then a smaller craft carried two men to the Moon's surface. Neil Armstrong became the first man to walk on the Moon. He was soon followed by Edwin Aldrin Jr.

Fact	Inference	
◯	◯	**3.** **A.** *Apollo 11* went to the Moon.
◯	◯	**B.** Three men were on *Apollo 11*.
◯	◯	**C.** Armstrong was the first to walk on the Moon.
◯	◯	**D.** Collins remained on the spaceship.

---

4. *Dandelion* was first a French word. It refers to a part of a lion. Long ago the flower was called "lion's tooth" because of the leaf's shape. In French it was known as *dent de lion*, or tooth of the lion. After a while this became the English word *dandelion*.

Fact	Inference	
◯	◯	**4.** **A.** *Dandelion* comes from a French word.
◯	◯	**B.** In French the name meant "lion's tooth."
◯	◯	**C.** Dandelions grow in France.
◯	◯	**D.** People thought the leaf looked like a tooth.

5. Lewis Carroll was a successful British writer. His real name was Charles Dodgson. He wrote about a small girl named Alice. Perhaps you have read his book called *Alice's Adventures in Wonderland*.

Fact	Inference	
◯	◯	**5.** **A.** Carroll was a successful writer.
◯	◯	**B.** Charles Dodgson was Carroll's real name.
◯	◯	**C.** Carroll wrote about a girl named Alice.
◯	◯	**D.** *Alice's Adventures in Wonderland* is a popular book.

1. Mei came to the United States from China when she was two years old. She was adopted by American parents. When she turned 12 years old, her parents took her to China to visit her uncle. Mei learned much about the Chinese culture. From then on, Mei visited China every year. She felt lucky to have family in two different countries.

Fact	Inference	
○	○	**1. A.** Mei lived in China before she moved to America.
○	○	**B.** Mei visited her uncle in China.
○	○	**C.** Mei loved the Chinese culture.
○	○	**D.** Mei was glad that American parents adopted her.

2. Jakob and Wilhelm Grimm lived in Germany. They loved many of the folktales told in their country. The brothers collected the tales and published them in a book. Now many people know of *Grimm's Fairy Tales.* The collection has been translated into many different languages.

Fact	Inference	
○	○	**2. A.** The Grimm brothers lived in Germany.
○	○	**B.** The folktales were first told in German.
○	○	**C.** The brothers loved many German folktales.
○	○	**D.** People in many parts of the world like folktales.

3. Drive-in movies were once a fun family outing. The whole gang would pile into the car and head to the drive-in. Beneath the stars they would munch popcorn and watch a movie. The first drive-in movie opened in New Jersey in 1933. Now there are only a few drive-in movies left.

Fact	Inference	
○	○	**3. A.** Drive-in movies were popular in the past.
○	○	**B.** The first drive-in movie was in New Jersey.
○	○	**C.** People don't go to drive-in movies much now.
○	○	**D.** The first drive-in opened in 1933.

4. Delbert had planned a big party for Saturday. He invited many of his friends from school and even a few old friends from across town. He bought some tasty refreshments and picked out some good music. When the time of the party arrived, the doorbell did not ring. An hour later, as Delbert sat alone munching corn chips in his living room, there was a knock on his door.

Fact	Inference	
◯	◯	**4. A.** Delbert picked out some good music.
◯	◯	**B.** He expected his friends to come to the party.
◯	◯	**C.** Delbert's friends were late to the party.
◯	◯	**D.** Delbert ate his corn chips alone.

---

5. Vampire bats almost never bite humans. Movies have made people think that vampire bats hurt us, but movies are not real. Vampire bats usually bite sleeping cows and then lick up a tiny amount of blood from the wound. The bite is so small and harmless that it does not even wake up the cow. Since vampire bats are wild, some of them may get rabies. Only vampire bats that carry rabies are dangerous.

Fact	Inference	
◯	◯	**5. A.** Healthy vampire bats do not hurt cows.
◯	◯	**B.** Vampire bats with rabies are dangerous.
◯	◯	**C.** Some movies do not tell the truth about bats.
◯	◯	**D.** Vampire bats usually bite cattle.

1. "A package came for you today," Greg's mother said as he walked in. "I think it's from Aunt Ginny." Greg peeled the tape from the box and ripped off the brown paper. He tore off the gift wrap to find a stuffed bear inside. Aunt Ginny never seemed to realize that he was no longer three years old and hadn't been for more than seven years. Then he thought about the trouble Aunt Ginny had gone through to select the present and mail it. Greg sat down at the kitchen table with a pen and paper.

Fact	Inference		
○	○	**1. A.**	The present was a stuffed bear.
○	○	**B.**	Greg did not like the gift.
○	○	**C.**	His aunt doesn't see Greg very often.
○	○	**D.**	Greg is a thoughtful boy.

2. Meg was dyeing a T-shirt for a friend. Her 18-month-old sister Sue was watching. Sue was very interested in the process. Meg filled a big plastic tub with dye. When Meg left the room to get a bucket of water, Sue grabbed onto the wobbly sides of the tub and pulled herself up to look inside.

Fact	Inference		
○	○	**2. A.**	Sue was curious.
○	○	**B.**	Meg was dyeing a shirt.
○	○	**C.**	By leaving Sue alone, Meg acted carelessly.
○	○	**D.**	Sue pulled the tub over.

3. The ostrich is the largest bird in the world. It can grow to more than 9 feet tall. Although ostriches cannot fly, these African birds can run quite fast. Their highest speed is about 40 miles per hour. Ostrich eggs are very large and weigh about 4 pounds. That's 24 times as heavy as a chicken egg!

Fact	Inference		
○	○	**3. A.**	Chicken eggs are much smaller than ostrich eggs.
○	○	**B.**	Ostriches cannot fly.
○	○	**C.**	Nine feet high is very tall for a bird.
○	○	**D.**	Ostriches can run up to 40 miles per hour.

---

4. The nursery rhyme "Humpty Dumpty" might have been written about King Richard III of England. The king had a horse named Wall. When King Richard lost an important battle, he lost his position as king. It is perhaps this event that the rhyme talks about in the line "Humpty Dumpty had a great fall."

Fact	Inference		
○	○	**4. A.**	"Humpty Dumpty" is a rhyme.
○	○	**B.**	It was important for kings to win in battle.
○	○	**C.**	King Richard III had a horse named Wall.
○	○	**D.**	Richard III was once the king of England.

---

5. Burt had played the saxophone for three years. This year he got up the courage to try out for the jazz band. For weeks before the tryout, he practiced every day after school for an hour. On the day of the tryout, he was very nervous and did not do well. When he found out he did not make the jazz band, he was very disappointed. A few weeks later, the music teacher decided another sax was needed, and she asked Burt to join the jazz band.

Fact	Inference		
○	○	**5. A.**	Burt really wanted to be in the jazz band.
○	○	**B.**	Burt plays the saxophone.
○	○	**C.**	Burt was disappointed about not being chosen.
○	○	**D.**	The teacher asked Burt to join the band.

1. Crocodiles lay their eggs in sand. Three months later the eggs are ready to hatch. The baby crocodiles are too weak to dig out of the sand around them, so they start to peep from inside their shells. Their mother, who has never strayed very far away, hears the calls and digs the eggs out.

Fact	Inference	
○	○	**1. A.** The mother stays nearby so she can hear the babies.
○	○	**B.** The babies have loud voices.
○	○	**C.** Sand protects the crocodile eggs.
○	○	**D.** The mother digs the eggs out.

2. Stuart always did very well on science tests, but his friend Kevin had trouble with science. Next week's test on the planets seemed especially difficult to Kevin. The Saturday before the test, Kevin asked Stuart if he would help him study. Although Stuart had planned to play soccer with his friends that afternoon, he decided to change his plans and help Kevin instead.

Fact	Inference	
○	○	**2. A.** Kevin has trouble with science.
○	○	**B.** Stuart changed his plans.
○	○	**C.** Kevin wanted to make better science grades.
○	○	**D.** Stuart is a kind friend.

3. Have you ever thought about how keys open doors? A key is cut a special way so that it matches the pattern of its lock. Inside the lock there is a metal bar. A row of pins holds the bar in place. When the matching key is put into the lock, it raises the pins and allows the bar to move. The bar then slides out of the way and unlocks the door when the key is turned.

Fact	Inference	
○	○	**3. A.** Keys are cut a special way.
○	○	**B.** A metal bar is inside the lock.
○	○	**C.** The bar keeps the door locked.
○	○	**D.** The wrong key won't raise a lock's pins.

4. Although Duke was a dog, the Clark family treated him like a member of the family. They took Duke everywhere with them, even on vacation. Once, on their way home from the mountains, they stopped at a rest area after several hours of driving. Ten minutes later everyone piled into the van to continue the trip. Since they were in a hurry to get home, no one checked to make sure Duke was with them.

Fact	Inference		
○	○	**4. A.**	The Clarks loved their dog.
○	○	**B.**	Duke went everywhere with the Clarks.
○	○	**C.**	The Clarks treated Duke like a family member.
○	○	**D.**	Duke was left behind at the rest area.

5. Ruth's hobby was making radio-controlled airplanes. But even more than making them, she enjoyed flying the planes. Once Ruth spent every weekend for an entire month working with her dad to build an airplane. The next Saturday Ruth decided to try out the plane. When Ruth set up the airplane for takeoff, she didn't notice the tall pine trees standing in its path.

Fact	Inference		
○	○	**5. A.**	Ruth enjoys flying radio-controlled planes.
○	○	**B.**	Tall trees were in the path of the plane.
○	○	**C.**	The airplane crashed in the trees.
○	○	**D.**	Ruth worked with her dad to build a plane.

1. When she was a girl, Marian Anderson dreamed of becoming a famous concert singer. In those days, that dream seemed impossible for someone who was both poor and black. When she was 17, she began studying with a famous voice teacher. Within a year she performed throughout the South in her first concert tour. In the 1930s she sang all over the world. In 1963, President Lyndon Johnson awarded her the Presidential Medal of Freedom.

Fact	Inference	
○	○	**1. A.** Anderson was a talented singer.
○	○	**B.** A famous teacher gave Anderson lessons.
○	○	**C.** Anderson was respected by many people.
○	○	**D.** President Johnson gave Anderson an award.

2. Dean was five years old. He couldn't tie his shoes yet, and they were almost always untied. One day his sister Nancy decided to help him learn to tie his shoes. The first step was easy for him, but he had trouble with the loop. Nancy worked with him patiently for three days. On the third day, Dean proudly showed his parents how he could tie his shoes.

Fact	Inference	
○	○	**2. A.** Dean's shoes were often untied.
○	○	**B.** Nancy is a patient person.
○	○	**C.** Dean's parents were proud of him.
○	○	**D.** Nancy helped Dean learn to tie his shoes.

3. Camels do not need much water. During the cool months in the desert, they usually do not drink water since they get enough from the plants they eat. When the temperature is around 95 degrees, they can go about 15 days without a drink. When the temperature is 104 degrees, camels drink water whenever they can.

Fact	Inference		
○	○	**3.** **A.**	Camels need more water in hotter weather.
○	○	**B.**	Camels can go 15 days without a drink.
○	○	**C.**	Eating plants provides camels with water.
○	○	**D.**	Camels are used to living in dry climates.

---

4. Patty and her mom were very excited to plant their first garden. They looked forward to growing their own vegetables. First they used a hoe to prepare the soil. Then they added peat moss to the soil. They planted tomatoes, lettuce, beans, and peas. Every week Patty spent at least an hour weeding and watering the plants. At the end of the summer, Patty shared the vegetables with her friends.

Fact	Inference		
○	○	**4.** **A.**	Patty planted tomatoes in her garden.
○	○	**B.**	They prepared the soil with a hoe.
○	○	**C.**	Her friends appreciated the vegetables.
○	○	**D.**	Patty is a hard worker.

---

5. Lightning was the cause of many house fires before lightning rods became popular. Lightning rods can prevent such disasters. In 1753, Benjamin Franklin published instructions for making lightning rods. Soon afterwards women in Europe started wearing lightning rods on their hats.

Fact	Inference		
○	○	**5.** **A.**	Hats were in fashion during the 1750s.
○	○	**B.**	European women were afraid of lightning.
○	○	**C.**	Lightning rods can prevent house fires.
○	○	**D.**	Many house fires were caused by lightning.

1. The first pair of roller skates was made in 1760 by Joseph Merlin. Merlin tried to sell his skates in London, but he didn't have much success. One problem was that they didn't have brakes! That problem was soon solved, and more people began trying the new sport. Roller skating became more popular as the result of a play staged in 1849. The actors were supposed to ice skate, but they could not make ice on stage. So the actors used roller skates instead.

Fact	Inference	
○	○	**1. A.** A play made roller skating more popular.
○	○	**B.** At first roller skates were not popular.
○	○	**C.** Merlin made the first roller skates.
○	○	**D.** Skates were dangerous without brakes.

2. John was out of school, and he wished he had something to do. One morning he read in the newspaper that volunteers were needed at the local hospital. That afternoon John called the hospital and offered to help three days a week.

Fact	Inference	
○	○	**2. A.** John was on summer vacation.
○	○	**B.** John was bored.
○	○	**C.** John offered to help.
○	○	**D.** John likes to help people.

3. Charlie Chaplin was one of the first movie actors. Americans loved "The Little Tramp" from London, who lived in the United States. In Chaplin's later movies, he gave his opinions about the United States government. When he left the United States for a vacation, the government would not let him enter the country again. Twenty-three years later, after he was finally allowed to return to the United States, the queen of England made him a knight.

Fact	Inference	
○	○	**3. A.** "The Little Tramp" was Chaplin's nickname.
○	○	**B.** Chaplin was made a knight.
○	○	**C.** The queen enjoyed Chaplin's movies.
○	○	**D.** Chaplin disagreed with the United States government.

4. In some parts of the country in the 1880s, soda fountain owners were not allowed to serve sodas on Sundays. Illinois owners got around the law by serving the syrup on ice cream rather than with fizzy water. The new idea was called a "Sunday soda." The dish later became known as a sundae.

Fact   Inference

○   ○   **4.** **A.** Soda fountains were open on Sundays.

○   ○   **B.** Customers liked the "Sunday sodas."

○   ○   **C.** Sodas are made only with syrup and fizzy water.

○   ○   **D.** The dish became known as a sundae.

---

5. Rhonda was walking 10 miles to raise money for a new cancer center. It was 90 degrees that day, and some of her friends had dropped out after the sixth mile. Now Rhonda was in the final mile, and her throat was dry. As she looked ahead, Rhonda saw her father holding a tall glass of lemonade.

Fact   Inference

○   ○   **5.** **A.** Rhonda didn't want to give up.

○   ○   **B.** It was a 90-degree day.

○   ○   **C.** Rhonda's friends dropped out of the race.

○   ○   **D.** Rhonda felt better when she saw her father.

Writing Roundup

Read each story. Then read the question that follows it. Write your answers on the lines below each question.

1. Carmela opened the brightly colored paper and spread it across the table. Then she positioned the box on the paper. It fit nicely. Next she neatly folded the paper and taped it into place. This was going to be a pleasant surprise for her mother, but it would be better if Carmela could find a bow.

What was Carmela doing?

_____

_____

2. A few green leaves were left on the tree, but they didn't look very good. The tree bark looked bad, too. The sun was shining bright, but this tree needed something else.

What was wrong with the tree?

_____

_____

3. Yoko didn't realize that there were so many different stamps. She didn't know which ones and how many she would need for a letter to her cousin. She could ask when she went to the counter.

Where was Yoko?

_____

_____

Read the paragraph below. Then answer the questions.

The Sun was setting when Bernardo got off his ladder. He had another bucket of cherries to add to his picking for the day. To Bernardo, the picking of cherries was the easiest work on his farm, but after 12 hours, his fingers and arms ached. They had a right to be aching. After all, they'd been working his farm for 40 years. Bernardo had been almost 30 years old when he purchased the farm. He'd believed his children would take over at some time, but they had gone off once they finished school. Now Bernardo was all alone, and keeping up the farm was a struggle.

1. How old is Bernardo?

_____

_____

2. Why did Bernardo need a ladder?

_____

_____

3. What kind of person is Bernardo?

_____

_____

4. Why was keeping up the farm such a struggle for Bernardo?

_____

_____

Spelling
Skills

spelling strategies

What can you do when you aren't sure how to spell a word?

Say the word aloud. Make sure you say it correctly. Listen to the sounds in the word. Think about letters and patterns that might spell the sounds.

Look in the Spelling Table on page 265 to find common spellings for sounds in the word.

Think about related words. They may help you spell the word you're not sure of.

instruction—instruct

Guess the spelling of the word and check it in a dictionary.

Write the word in different ways. Compare the spellings and choose the one that looks correct.

tuch   toch   (touch)   tooch

Think about any spelling rules you know that can help you spell the word.

To form the plural of a singular word ending in a consonant and **y**, change the **y** to **i** and add **-es**.

Listen for a common word part, such as a prefix, a suffix, or an ending.

appoint<u>ment</u>

person<u>al</u>

Break the word into syllables and think about how each syllable might be spelled.

an-i-ma-tion

Create a memory clue to help you remember the spelling of the word.

<u>Cloth</u>ing is made of <u>cloth</u>.

Proofreading Marks

Mark	Meaning	Example
⬭	spell correctly	I (liek) dogs.
⊙	add period	They are my favorite kind of pet ⊙
?	add question mark	What kind of pet do you have ?
≡	capitalize	My dog's name is <u>s</u>cooter.
ℰ	take out	He is a great companion for me and my ~~my~~ family.
⌃	add	We got Scooter when ⌃he⌃ was eight weeks old.
/	make lowercase	My /Uncle came over to take a look at him.
∿	trade places	He watched the puppy run (in around) circles.
⟨⟨ ⟩⟩	add quotation marks	⟨⟨Scooter! That's the perfect name!⟩⟩ I said.
¶	indent paragraph	¶ I love my dog Scooter. He is the best pet I have ever had. Every morning he wakes me with a bark. Every night he sleeps with me.

Words with /ă/

act	sandwich	traffic	magic
chapter	rabbit	snack	rapid
plastic	laughter	calf	program
planet	crash	salad	aunt
factory	magnet	half	crack

Say and Listen

Say each spelling word. Listen for the /ă/ sound you hear in *act*.

Think and Sort

Look at the letters in each word. Think about how /ă/ is spelled. Spell each word aloud.

How many spelling patterns for /ă/ do you see?

1. Write the **eighteen** spelling words that have the *a* pattern, like *act*.

2. Write the **two** spelling words that have the *au* pattern, like *laughter*.

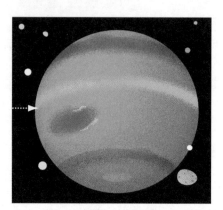

planet

1. a Words

_____   _____   _____
_____   _____   _____
_____   _____   _____
_____   _____   _____
_____   _____   _____
_____   _____   _____

2. au Words

_____   _____

Definitions

Write the spelling word for each definition.
Use a dictionary if you need to.

1. a heavenly body that circles the sun _____
2. a place where things are made _____
3. the movement of cars and trucks _____
4. a young cow or bull _____
5. a sound that shows amusement _____
6. a ceremony or presentation _____
7. a substance made from chemicals _____

Analogies

An analogy states that two words go together in the same way as
two others. Write the spelling word that completes each analogy.

8. *Perform* is to _____ as *exercise* is to *jog*.

9. *Big* is to *large* as *fast* is to _____.

10. A *third* is to *three* as _____ is to *two*.

11. *Bear* is to *honey* as *nail* is to _____.

12. *Feast* is to _____ as *mansion* is to *cottage*.

13. *Correct* is to *right* as *smash* is to _____.

14. *Hire* is to *employ* as *split* is to _____.

15. *Man* is to *woman* as *uncle* is to _____.

16. *Lettuce* is to _____ as *flour* is to *bread*.

17. *Kitty* is to *cat* as *bunny* is to _____.

18. *Room* is to *house* as _____ is to *book*.

19. *Artist* is to *art* as *magician* is to _____.

act	sandwich	traffic	magic
chapter	rabbit	snack	rapid
plastic	laughter	calf	program
planet	crash	salad	aunt
factory	magnet	half	crack

Proofreading

Proofread the e-mail message below.
Use proofreading marks to correct five spelling
mistakes, three capitalization mistakes, and two
punctuation mistakes. See the chart on page 131
to learn how to use the proofreading marks.

Proofreading Marks

◯ spell correctly
= capitalize
⊙ add period

---

e-mail

New	Read	File	Delete	Search

Hi, andy,

This weekend I went skiing with my dad I was coming

down a hill at a rapud speed when a calf ran out in front of

me. I managed to avoid hitting it, but i tripped and landed

with a krash. Nothing was hurt but the egg salad sanwitch

I had brought along as a snak. it was squashed flat in

its plastic wrapper I burst into laugter at the sight! What did

you do this weekend? Let's talk later!

Bailey

Dictionary Skills

Alphabetical Order

Words are listed in alphabetical order in a dictionary.
When two letters are the same, the next letter is used to alphabetize them.

about   **ar**ound   a**b**le   a**b**out   abo**a**rd   abo**u**t

Write each group of words in alphabetical order.

1. traffic   half   rabbit   plastic

_____

_____

_____

_____

2. program   aunt   planet   act

_____

_____

_____

_____

3. chapter   calf   crack   factory

_____

_____

_____

_____

4. salad   sandwich   magic   magnet

_____

_____

_____

_____

5. loose   laughter   library   length

_____

_____

_____

_____

6. raw   raccoon   rabbit   rapid

_____

_____

_____

_____

Words with /ā/

paid	bakery	weight	remain	escape
raise	brain	delay	break	male
snake	weigh	scale	neighbor	container
complain	holiday	explain	parade	female

Say and Listen

Say each spelling word. Listen for the /ā/ sound you hear in *paid*.

Think and Sort

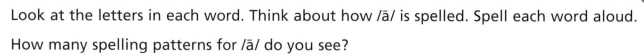

weight

Look at the letters in each word. Think about how /ā/ is spelled. Spell each word aloud.

How many spelling patterns for /ā/ do you see?

1. Write the **six** spelling words that have the *a*-consonant-*e* pattern, like *male*.

2. Write the **one** spelling word that has the *a* pattern.

3. Write the **nine** spelling words that have the *ai* or *ay* pattern, like *paid*.

4. Write the **three** spelling words that have the *eigh* pattern, like *weigh*.

5. Write the **one** spelling word that has the *ea* pattern.

1. a-consonant-e Words

_____   _____   _____

_____   _____   _____

2. a Word

_____

3. ai, ay Words

_____   _____   _____

_____   _____   _____

_____   _____   _____

4. eigh Words

_____   _____   _____

5. ea Word

_____

Clues

Write the spelling word for each clue.

1. This is a kind of reptile. _____

2. People use a scale to do this. _____

3. This word is the opposite of *fix*. _____

4. People do this to tell why. _____

5. This word is the opposite of *leave*. _____

6. A band might march in one of these. _____

7. A jar is one kind of this. _____

8. This word is the opposite of *lower*. _____

9. People may do this when they don't like something. _____

10. This is a special day. _____

Hink Pinks

Hink pinks are pairs of rhyming words that have a funny meaning.
Read each meaning. Write the spelling word that completes each hink pink.

11. a locomotive carrying geniuses _____ train

12. a hotel worker on pay day _____ maid

13. a light-colored weighing device pale _____

14. something that is very heavy great _____

15. a story told by a woman _____ tale

16. what is used to build a community garden _____ labor

17. plastic cakes and pies _____ fakery

18. a story about a man _____ tale

19. why the employees were paid late pay _____

paid	brain	scale	parade
raise	weigh	explain	escape
snake	holiday	remain	male
complain	weight	break	container
bakery	delay	neighbor	female

Proofreading

Proofread the journal entry below. Use proofreading marks to correct five spelling mistakes, three capitalization mistakes, and two punctuation mistakes.

Proofreading Marks

○ spell correctly
≡ capitalize
⊙ add period

March 9

I found out today that our nayber, pete, has a

pet snake. he named the snake Toby Toby is a mayle

garter snake, and he has beautiful stripes on his

back. He sleeps in a cage that Pete made out of a

wooden apple contayner. He spends the rest of his

time watching Pete's pet mice. They look a little

nervous to me.

I like Toby, but I hope he will remane at Pete's

house He had better not excape and decide to visit

my house. having him next door is just fine with me!

Sentences

A sentence begins with a capital letter and ends with a punctuation mark.
A sentence that tells something ends with a period.

> I like chicken soup.

A sentence that asks a question ends with a question mark.

> Do you like chicken soup?

A sentence that shows strong feeling or surprise ends with an exclamation point.

> Don't spill the chicken soup!

The following sentences contain errors in capitalization and punctuation.
Write each sentence correctly.

1. our class planned a holiday vacation

_____

2. mr. Peterson bought fresh bread at the bakery

_____

3. watch out for that snake by your foot

_____

4. what did you do on your break from school

_____

Words with /ĕ/

bench	healthy	thread	intend
invent	wealth	sentence	weather
self	instead	friendly	questions
measure	address	breath	pleasure
checkers	sweater	depth	treasure

Say and Listen

Say each spelling word. Listen for the /ĕ/ sound you hear in *bench*.

Think and Sort

sweater

Look at the letters in each word. Think about how /ĕ/ is spelled. Spell each word aloud.

How many spelling patterns for /ĕ/ do you see?

1. Write the **nine** spelling words that have the *e* pattern, like *bench*.

2. Write the **ten** spelling words that have the *ea* pattern, like *thread*.

3. Write the **one** spelling word that has the *ie* pattern.

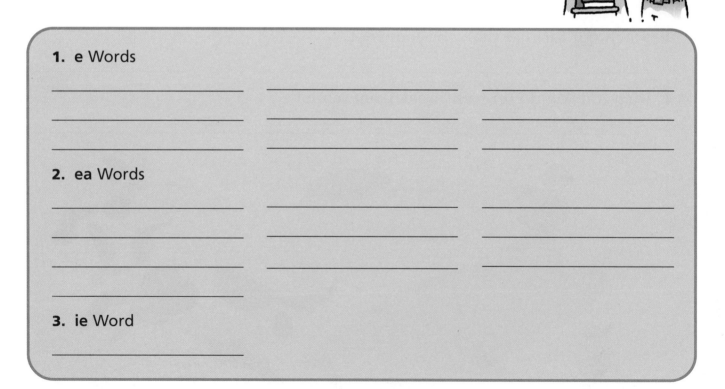

1. e Words

_____ _____ _____

_____ _____ _____

_____ _____ _____

2. ea Words

_____ _____ _____

_____ _____ _____

_____ _____ _____

_____

3. ie Word

_____

Classifying

Write the spelling word that belongs in each group.

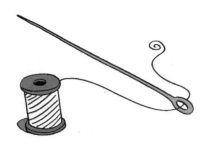

1. coat, jacket, _____

2. pins, needle, _____

3. name, phone number, _____

4. pirate, map, _____

5. width, height, _____

6. well, fit, _____

7. warm, kind, _____

8. statements, exclamations, _____

Rhymes

Write the spelling word that completes each sentence and rhymes with the underlined word.

9. Mr. <u>Beckers</u> and I enjoy playing _____ together.

10. Did you _____ the distance to the hidden <u>treasure</u>?

11. I sat on the _____ to study my <u>French</u>.

12. Good <u>health</u> is better than all the _____ in the world.

13. <u>Heather</u> doesn't like rainy _____.

14. On cold mornings, <u>Seth</u> can see his _____.

15. The sick <u>elf</u> did not feel like her normal _____.

16. Maria and Jonas _____ to <u>send</u> letters to the editor.

17. Henry wants to _____ a lightweight <u>tent</u>.

18. Dave will go with us _____ of <u>Ted</u>.

19. It is impossible to <u>measure</u> my _____.

bench	healthy	thread	intend
invent	wealth	sentence	weather
self	instead	friendly	questions
measure	address	breath	pleasure
checkers	sweater	depth	treasure

Proofreading

Proofread the article below. Use proofreading marks to correct five spelling mistakes, two capitalization mistakes, and three missing words.

Proofreading Marks

◯ spell correctly
≡ capitalize
⋀ add

All the Right Moves

A huge crowd was on hand for annual cheakers tournament last weekend. because the wethar was bad, the contest took place in the school gymnasium insted of at the park. The mood was frendly as players took their places and qestions were answered. Spectators held their breath as they watched play after play. beth Meadows was finally named champion. She will compete in the state meet Memphis next month. The runner-up was Ben Treasure, who also took home trophy.

Dictionary Skills

Guide Words

Guide words are the two words in dark type at the top of each dictionary page. The first guide word is the first word on the page. The second guide word is the last word on the page.

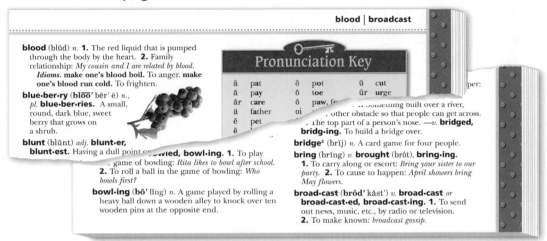

Write the following words in alphabetical order. Then look up each word in a dictionary and write the guide words for the page on which it appears.

| bench | address | measure | intend | sentence | wealth |

Word		Guide Words	
1. _____	_____		_____
2. _____	_____		_____
3. _____	_____		_____
4. _____	_____		_____
5. _____	_____		_____
6. _____	_____		_____

More Words with /ĕ/

else	century	extra	remember
pledge	selfish	petal	exercise
elephant	energy	desert	length
expert	metal	excellent	vegetable
metric	wreck	gentle	special

Say and Listen

Say each spelling word. Listen for the /ĕ/ sound.

Think and Sort

The /ĕ/ sound is spelled e in each of the spelling words. Some of the spelling words have one e. Others have more than one e, but only one is pronounced /ĕ/. Look at the letters in each word. Spell each word aloud.

elephant

1. Write the **nine** spelling words that have one e, like *century*.

2. Write the **eleven** spelling words that have more than one e. Circle the e that has the /ĕ/ sound, like *pl⊙dge*.

1. Words with One **e**

_____ _____ _____

_____ _____ _____

_____ _____ _____

2. Words with More Than One **e**

_____ _____ _____

_____ _____ _____

_____ _____ _____

_____ _____ _____

Analogies

Write the spelling word that completes each analogy.

1. *Pineapple* is to *fruit* as *squash* is to _____.

2. *Wet* is to *dry* as *ocean* is to _____.

3. *Weak* is to *powerful* as _____ is to *generous*.

4. *Annoying* is to *irritating* as *wonderful* is to _____.

5. *Branch* is to *tree* as _____ is to *rose*.

6. *Construct* is to *build* as _____ is to *destroy*.

7. *Penny* is to *dollar* as *year* is to _____.

8. *Width* is to *wide* as _____ is to *long*.

9. *Recall* is to _____ as *border* is to *edge*.

10. *Oak* is to *wood* as *copper* is to _____.

Definitions

Write the spelling word for each definition.

11. relating to the system of weights and measures based on meters and grams   _____

12. mild   _____

13. more than what is usual or expected   _____

14. besides; in addition   _____

15. different from others   _____

16. physical activity that improves the body   _____

17. ability to do work   _____

18. a serious promise   _____

19. someone with special skill or knowledge   _____

else	century	extra	remember
pledge	selfish	petal	exercise
elephant	energy	desert	length
expert	metal	excellent	vegetable
metric	wreck	gentle	special

Proofreading

Proofread the news article below. Use proofreading marks to correct five spelling mistakes, two punctuation mistakes, and three unnecessary words.

Proofreading Marks

◯ spell correctly
⊙ add period
ℓ take out

Master of the Air

Anna Chung is is an expurt circus acrobat visiting Cedar Rapids this month. In an interview for the *Daily News*, Ms. Chung told us about her work

"I remeber to practice every day. I also get plenty of of rest and exerize. If I didn't, I wouldn't have the enerjy to give a an excellant performance."

To see Chung in a performance this

weekend, call 555-6262

Nouns

A noun is a word that names a person, a place, a thing, or an idea.
Proper nouns are capitalized. Common nouns are not.

Person	Place	Thing	Idea
teenager	desert	pumpkin	happiness
Cody	Utah	Lee Street	

Unscramble each sentence and write it correctly. Then circle the nouns.

1. drove desert week We the last through.

_____

2. the down swam wreck The to divers.

_____

3. Elephants Africa large are from animals.

_____

4. ran field length Andy the of the.

_____

5. vegetable Jill on ate plate every her.

_____

6. pen can't where I remember put and I paper my.

_____

7. globe to circle Explorers the seventeenth began century the in.

_____

Capitalized Words

October	December	Sunday	August	November
Monday	Thursday	May	July	September
June	March	January	Saturday	Friday
Tuesday	Wednesday	April	February	St.

Say and Listen

Say each spelling word. Listen for the vowel sounds.

Think and Sort

October

A **syllable** is a word part or a word with one vowel sound. *Thursday* has two syllables. *October* has three syllables.

Look at the letters in each word. Think about the number of syllables in the word. Spell each word aloud.

1. Write the **three** spelling words that have one syllable, like *March*.

2. Write the **nine** spelling words that have two syllables, like *A-pril*.

3. Write the **five** spelling words that have three syllables, like *Oc-to-ber*.

4. Write the **two** spelling words that have four syllables, like *Jan-u-ar-y*.

5. Write the **one** spelling word that is an abbreviation for *Street* and *Saint*.

1. One-syllable Words

_____ _____ _____

2. Two-syllable Words

_____ _____ _____

_____ _____ _____

_____ _____ _____

3. Three-syllable Words

_____ _____ _____

_____ _____

4. Four-syllable Words   **5.** Abbreviation

_____ _____ _____

Hink Pinks

Read each meaning. Write the spelling word that completes each hink pink.

1. a doorway to spring _____ arch

2. a song sung in a summer month _____ tune

3. a day in the fifth month _____ day

4. to recall the first month of fall remember _____

Clues

Write the spelling word for each clue.

5. the first day of the school week _____

6. the day after Monday _____

7. the day after Saturday _____

8. a short way of writing *Street* _____

9. the month in which many people celebrate the new year _____

10. the last day of the school week _____

11. the eleventh month of the year _____

12. the day before Friday _____

13. the month after September _____

14. the fourth month of the year _____

15. the day before Sunday _____

16. the day that begins with *W* _____

17. the shortest month of the year _____

18. the last month of the year _____

19. the month that is the middle of summer _____

October	Thursday	January	February
Monday	March	April	November
June	Wednesday	August	September
Tuesday	Sunday	July	Friday
December	May	Saturday	St.

Proofreading

Proofread the letter below. Use proofreading marks to correct five spelling mistakes, three capitalization mistakes, and two punctuation mistakes.

Proofreading Marks

⬭ spell correctly
≡ capitalize
⊙ add period

dear Grandma,

Thank you so much for the new flute! It sounds great

Every Wednesday I take lessons at mr. han's house on

Forest Ste. On Munday, Octobre 10, I give my first

recital. Our school band will play for the Veterans Day

parade on Teusday, Novumber 11 Will you come to hear

me play?

Love,

Jeremy

Using the Spelling Table

If you need to look up a word in a dictionary but aren't sure how to spell it, a spelling table can help. A spelling table lists common spellings for sounds. Suppose you are not sure how the first vowel sound in *August* is spelled. First, look in the table to find the pronunciation symbol for the sound. Then read the first spelling listed for /ô/, and look up *Agust* in a dictionary. Look for each spelling in the dictionary until you find the correct one.

Sound	Spellings	Example Words
/ô/	a au aw o ough o_e ou oa	already, autumn, raw, often, thought, score, court, roar

The following words contain boldfaced letters that represent sounds. Write each word correctly, using a dictionary and the Spelling Table on page 265.

1. rec**e**d _____

2. **a**lment _____

3. **e**sel _____

4. b**i**lt _____

5. myster**e** _____

6. l**a**ghter _____

7. l**oo**nar _____

8. **k**omet _____

9. cu**s**in _____

10. breth _____

11. fr**e**ndly _____

12. bu**s**e _____

13. bri**j** _____

14. r**i**lax _____

15. sk**e** _____

16. **g**ide _____

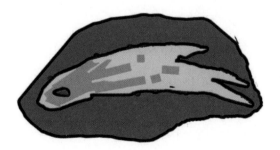

unit 1 Review
LESSONS 1-5

LESSON 1

sandwich
factory
half
laughter

Words with /ă/

Write the spelling word for each clue.

1. Two fourths of something equals this.

_____

2. This is where workers and machines make things.

_____

3. This has meat between two slices of bread.

_____

4. When people respond to a funny joke, you hear this.

_____

LESSON 2

escape
parade
bakery
holiday
container
neighbor
break

Words with /ā/

Write the spelling word for each definition.

5. a public event for a special occasion _____

6. a place where bread is sold _____

7. a person who lives nearby _____

8. a day such as Thanksgiving _____

9. to break loose or get away _____

10. a gap or an opening _____

11. a box, a jar, or a can used to hold something

_____

LESSON 3

depth
wealth
breath
treasure
friendly

Words with /ĕ/

Write the spelling word that completes each analogy.

12. *Sociable* is to _____ as
bashful is to *shy*.

13. *Brain* is to *thought* as *lung* is to

_____.

14. *Cookie* is to *jar* as _____ is to *chest.*

15. *Riches* is to _____ as *story* is to *tale.*

16. *Mountain* is to *ocean* as *height* is to _____.

LESSON 5

length
special
exercise
excellent
vegetable

More Words with /ĕ/

Write the spelling word that belongs in each group.

17. fruit, grain, _____

18. outstanding, wonderful, _____

19. width, height, _____

20. different, unique, _____

21. diet, rest, _____

LESSON 6

Tuesday
Saturday
January
February

Capitalized Words

Write the spelling word that completes each sentence.

22. The month of _____ is the shortest month of all.

23. Ling went to bed late Monday night and overslept _____ morning.

24. This weekend I have plans for _____, but not Sunday.

25. The new year for many people begins in the month of _____.

Words with /ē/

hobby	believe	compete	delivery
angry	evening	tardy	fancy
trapeze	athlete	merry	pretty
penalty	ugly	theme	liberty
empty	shady	busy	complete

Say and Listen

Say each spelling word. Listen for the /ē/ sound you hear in *hobby*.

Think and Sort

Look at the letters in each word. Think about how /ē/ is spelled. Spell each word aloud.

How many spelling patterns for /ē/ do you see?

athlete

1. Write the **thirteen** spelling words that have the *y* pattern, like *hobby*.

2. Write the **six** spelling words that have the *e*-consonant-*e* pattern, like *complete*.

3. Write the **one** spelling word that has the *ie* pattern.

---

1. y Words

_____   _____   _____

_____   _____   _____

_____   _____   _____

_____   _____   _____

_____

2. e-consonant-e Words

_____   _____   _____

_____   _____   _____

3. ie Word

_____

Classifying

Write the spelling word that belongs in each group.

1. swing, acrobat, _____

2. topic, subject, _____

3. displeasing, bad-looking, _____

4. vacant, hollow, _____

5. activity, interest, _____

6. think, suppose, _____

7. shadowy, dark, _____

8. morning, afternoon, _____

9. punishment, fine, _____

10. shipment, distribution, _____

Trading Places

Complete each sentence by writing the spelling word that
can take the place of the underlined word or words.

11. Our country has many symbols of _____. freedom

12. We sent some _____ flowers to our aunt. lovely

13. I was _____ that I fell down and skinned my knee! furious

14. Matthew was _____ this morning. late

15. Mom wore a _____ gown to the party. elaborate

16. The little man had a _____ laugh. happy

17. Tran leads a _____ life. active

18. This Canadian stamp makes my collection _____. whole

19. Ray will _____ in the race this Saturday. take part

hobby	believe	compete	delivery
angry	evening	tardy	fancy
trapeze	athlete	merry	pretty
penalty	ugly	theme	liberty
empty	shady	busy	complete

Proofreading

Proofread this paragraph from the back of a book.
Use proofreading marks to correct five spelling mistakes,
two capitalization mistakes, and two missing words.

Proofreading Marks

◯ spell correctly

☰ capitalize

∧ add

A Martian in the Library

It is friday evning. Daniel and Jasmine sit at a
table in the library. They are buzy doing a report
about life other planets. to their surprise,
Martian sits down in the emty seat next to them.
The Martian is not only uggly but very angry.
Readers won't beleive what happens next in this
intergalactic tale of loyalty, liberty, and
friendship written by the award-winning
author of fiction for young adults, Lisa Lowry.

Dictionary Skills

Multiple Meanings

When you look up the meaning of a word in a sentence, you will often find that the word has several meanings. To know which one the writer intends, you must know the word's part of speech in the sentence. Then you can use other words in the sentence to decide on the correct meaning of the word.

> **com·plete** (kəm plēt′) *adj.* **1.** Whole: *a complete set of the encyclopedia.* **2.** Finished; ended: *My report is complete.* **3.** Fully equipped: *a new car complete with power steering.* —*v.* **com·plet·ed, com·plet·ing.** To finish.

> **emp·ty** (ĕmp′ tē) *adj.* **1.** Containing nothing. **2.** Without meaning: *empty promises.* —*v.* **emp·tied, emp·ty·ing, emp·ties.** To remove the contents of.

Use the dictionary entries above to write the part of speech and the definition for *empty* or *complete* in each of the following sentences.

	Part of Speech	Definition
1. Dad bought a sailboat **complete** with sails and motor.	_____	_____
2. My Saturday chore is to **empty** the trash cans.	_____	_____
3. I must **complete** my homework by six o'clock.	_____	_____
4. I wanted some juice, but the pitcher was **empty**.	_____	_____
5. Ashley has a **complete** set of the books you want.	_____	_____
6. The man's **empty** welcome made us feel uneasy.	_____	_____

More Words with /ē/

greet	pizza	weak	breathe
freeze	piano	speech	asleep
increase	peace	ski	defeat
reason	needle	steep	sheet
wheat	agree	degree	beneath

Say and Listen

Say each spelling word. Listen for the /ē/ sound.

Think and Sort

Look at the letters in each word. Think about how /ē/ is spelled. Spell each word aloud.

How many spelling patterns for /ē/ do you see?

pizza

1. Write the **eight** spelling words that have the *ea* pattern, like *weak*.

2. Write the **nine** spelling words that have the *ee* pattern, like *greet*.

3. Write the **three** spelling words that have the *i* pattern, like *pizza*.

1. ea Words

_____   _____   _____

_____   _____   _____

_____   _____

2. ee Words

_____   _____   _____

_____   _____   _____

_____   _____   _____

3. i Words

_____   _____   _____

Classifying

Write the spelling word that belongs in each group.

1. thread, pins, _____
2. sled, skate, _____
3. inhale, exhale, _____
4. enlarge, grow, _____
5. beat, win, _____
6. under, below, _____
7. corn, oats, _____
8. spaghetti, ravioli, _____
9. ounce, watt, _____
10. guitar, violin, _____
11. pillow, blanket, _____
12. quiet, silence, _____

Rhymes

Write the spelling word that completes each sentence
and rhymes with the underlined word.

13. <u>Each</u> student had to give a _____.
14. After the race, the winner was too _____ to <u>speak</u>.
15. The raccoons <u>creep</u> up the _____ hill to our house.
16. Snow is the _____ I like the winter <u>season</u>.
17. When you <u>meet</u> them, _____ them with a smile.
18. <u>Please</u> give me my gloves before my hands _____.
19. The tired <u>sheep</u> were _____ in the meadow.

greet	pizza	weak	breathe
freeze	piano	speech	asleep
increase	peace	ski	defeat
reason	needle	steep	sheet
wheat	agree	degree	beneath

Proofreading

Proofread the paragraph below. Use proofreading marks to correct five spelling mistakes, three capitalization mistakes, and two unnecessary words.

Proofreading Marks

◯ spell correctly

≡ capitalize

ℓ take out

A Baker's Life

Uncle Al gets up early and is open for business when I go to school. Sometimes I stop in, and we eat hot doughnuts together. When i enter to his bakery and breeth in, lovely aromas greet me. that is one reazon why I am want to be a baker. I also like to help Uncle Al toss the wheet dough for pitza or roll it into balls for rolls. I enjoy taking baked cookies off the big cookie sheat, too. a baker's life is the life for me!

Language Connection

Predicates

Every sentence has two main parts, the complete subject and the complete predicate. The complete subject includes all the words that tell whom or what the sentence is about. The complete predicate includes all the words that tell what the subject does or is.

> **Complete Subject**
> The little gray kitten
>
> **Complete Predicate**
> followed me all the way to the fair.

Use the words in the boxes to complete each sentence below. Then circle the complete predicate.

1. The team from Smallville is difficult to _____.
2. We will _____ down these snowy mountains every winter.
3. All the students listened to the principal's farewell _____.
4. That mountain is much too _____ to climb.
5. The pond behind our barn began to _____ at midnight.
6. We all _____ on the date for Maria's surprise party.
7. Ling can _____ him at the door.

Words with /ĭ/

wrist	guitar	expect	chimney
riddle	bridge	guilty	enough
since	disease	except	equipment
built	quit	quickly	relax
review	different	discuss	divide

Say and Listen

Say each spelling word. Listen for the /ĭ/ sound you hear in *wrist*.

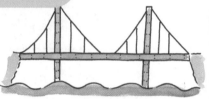

bridge

Think and Sort

Look at the letters in each word. Think about how /ĭ/ is spelled. Spell each word aloud.

How many spelling patterns for /ĭ/ do you see?

1. Write the **eleven** spelling words that have the *i* pattern, like *wrist*.

2. Write the **five** spelling words that have the *e* pattern, like *expect*.

3. Write the **one** spelling word that has both the *i* and *e* patterns.

4. Write the **three** spelling words that have the *ui* pattern after a consonant other than *q*, like *built*.

1. i Words

_____ _____ _____

_____ _____ _____

_____ _____ _____

_____ _____

2. e Words

_____ _____

_____ _____

3. i and e Word

_____

4. ui Words

_____ _____ _____ _____

Analogies

Write the spelling word that completes each analogy.

1. *Under* is to *tunnel* as *over* is to _____.
2. *Ankle* is to *leg* as _____ is to *arm*.
3. *Add* is to *subtract* as *multiply* is to _____.
4. *Wrong* is to *right* as _____ is to *innocent*.
5. *Water* is to *faucet* as *smoke* is to _____.
6. *Stop* is to _____ as *start* is to *begin*.
7. *Walk* is to *slowly* as *run* is to _____.
8. *Same* is to *like* as _____ is to *unlike*.
9. *Jog* is to *exercise* as *nap* is to _____.
10. *Before* is to *preview* as *after* is to _____.

Clues

Write the spelling word for each clue.

11. You have this if you have as much as you need.   _____
12. You did this if you made a house.   _____
13. Baseball bats, balls, and gloves are this.   _____
14. You play this by strumming its strings.   _____
15. This kind of joke asks a question.   _____
16. This is another word for *because*.   _____
17. You do this when you think a thing will happen.   _____
18. You do this when you talk with other people
    about something.   _____
19. You might use this word instead of *but*.   _____

wrist	guitar	expect	chimney
riddle	bridge	guilty	enough
since	disease	except	equipment
built	quit	quickly	relax
review	different	discuss	divide

Proofreading

Proofread the letter below. Use proofreading marks to correct five spelling mistakes, three capitalization mistakes, and two punctuation mistakes.

Proofreading Marks

◯ spell correctly
≡ capitalize
⊙ add period

14th Street SW

Calgary, AB

Canada T2T 3Y9

May 7, 2004

Dear Marty,

 you asked how I learned to play the keyboard

It's been a year sinse I started lessons There are so

many diferent things to learn, and i wanted to learn

everything quikly. The best thing I learned is to relaax.

I just remember to take it slowly and never qwit.

Your friend,

ted

Capitalization

Capitalize the names of days and months.

> Sally was born on a **F**riday in **D**ecember.

The following scrambled sentences contain errors in capitalization and spelling. Unscramble each sentence and write it correctly.

1. my april broke last I rist.

_____

2. our sinse february had We've trampoline.

_____

3. field discus june Let's go where our on trip in we'll.

_____

4. chimley september built Dad our a house new last on.

_____

5. and july expeck can really august weather We hot in.

_____

6. before to I tuesday our test riview need my notes on.

_____

7. theater saturday go diffrent We'll to move a next.

_____

More Words with /ĭ/

business	system	package	skill
chicken	mystery	arithmetic	film
message	picnic	kitchen	damage
village	sixth	garbage	pitch
insect	cottage	insist	timid

Say and Listen

Say each spelling word. Listen for the /ĭ/ sound.

Think and Sort

cottage

Look at the letters in each word. Think about how /ĭ/ is spelled. Spell each word aloud.

How many spelling patterns for /ĭ/ do you see?

1. Write the **eleven** spelling words that have the *i* pattern, like *film*.

2. Write the **two** spelling words that have the *y* pattern, like *mystery*.

3. Write the **five** spelling words that have the *a* pattern, like *cottage*.

4. Write the **one** spelling word that has the *i* and *a* patterns.

5. Write the **one** spelling word that has the *u* pattern.

1. i Words

_____ _____ _____

_____ _____ _____

_____ _____ _____

_____ _____

2. y Words

_____ _____

3. a Words

_____ _____ _____

_____ _____

4. i and **a** Word   **5. u** Word

_____   _____

Making Connections

Write the spelling word that relates to each person listed below.

1. a farmer _____

2. a baseball player _____

3. a movie director _____

4. a math teacher _____

5. a chef _____

6. a mail carrier _____

Definitions

Write the spelling word for each definition.
Use a dictionary if you need to.

7. a group of related things that make up a whole _____

8. a meal eaten outside _____

9. a small group of houses and businesses _____

10. trash _____

11. a small house _____

12. one of six equal parts _____

13. shy or lacking in self-confidence _____

14. news sent from one person to another _____

15. injury or harm _____

16. the ability to do something well _____

17. to take a stand or demand strongly _____

18. a small creature with wings and six legs _____

19. what a person does to earn a living _____

business	system	package	skill
chicken	mystery	arithmetic	film
message	picnic	kitchen	damage
village	sixth	garbage	pitch
insect	cottage	insist	timid

Proofreading

Proofread this paragraph. Use proofreading marks to correct five spelling mistakes, three capitalization mistakes, and two punctuation mistakes.

Proofreading Marks
⬭ spell correctly
☰ capitalize
⊙ add period

Bees in our House!

We had bees in our kytchen, but not for long. My dad is good at catching them. he showed me how he does it. First, he lowers a glass carefully over the bee. Next, he slips a postcard under the glass Then, he takes the whole thing outside and lets the bee go. i tried to catch one of the bees in our kitchen, but I couldn't get the glass over it because the bee scared me A bee is not a timud insec. Last year I was stung near a garbige can at a picnec. Since then I've never cared much for picnics—or bees.

Language Connection

Commas

A series is a list of three or more items. The items can be single words or groups of words. A comma is used to separate the items in a series.

> Bill had a sandwich, a piece of pie, and a glass of milk.
> Then he gathered up his baseball glove, bat, and ball.

Write the following sentences correctly, adding commas where they are needed and correcting the misspelled words.

1. I need a pencil an eraser and some paper to do my arithmatick.

_____

2. Chikcen can be fried broiled or baked.

_____

3. We saw tulips roses and daisies outside the cottige.

_____

4. The villaje had a bakery a post office and a town hall.

_____

5. Lynn wanted to study history bizness and medicine.

_____

6. The timmid elephant was afraid of mice, snakes, and his own shadow!

_____

Plural Words

stories	speeches	penalties	neighbors	athletes
calves	wives	crashes	degrees	hobbies
parties	sandwiches	benches	wishes	vegetables
exercises	companies	branches	skis	businesses

Say and Listen

Say the spelling words. Notice the ending sounds and letters.

Think and Sort

sandwiches

A **plural** is a word that names more than one thing. A **base word** is a word to which suffixes, prefixes, and endings can be added. All of the spelling words are plurals. Most plurals are formed by adding -s to a base word. Other plurals are formed by adding -es.

The spelling of some base words changes when -es is added. A final *y* is often changed to *i*. An *f* is often changed to *v*.

Look at the spelling words. Think about how each plural is formed. Spell each word aloud.

1. Write the **six** spelling words formed by adding -s to the base word, like *skis*.

2. Write the **seven** -es spelling words that have no changes in the base word, like *branches*.

3. Write the **seven** -es spelling words that have changes in the spelling of the base word, like *wives*.

---

1. -s Plurals

_____ _____ _____

_____ _____ _____

2. -es Plurals with No Base Word Changes

_____ _____ _____

_____ _____ _____

_____

3. -es Plurals with Base Word Changes

_____ _____ _____

_____ _____ _____

Clues

Write the spelling word for each clue.

1. Corn and spinach are kinds of these. _____
2. You can use these to slide over snow. _____
3. You make these with bread and a filling. _____
4. These are very young cows. _____
5. These people live next door to you. _____
6. These women have husbands. _____
7. These reach out from tree trunks. _____
8. You sit on these in a park. _____
9. These happen when cars hit other cars. _____
10. Collecting stamps is an example of these. _____
11. Doing these can make you stronger. _____
12. Runners and gymnasts are these. _____
13. These can be about real or made-up events. _____
14. Referees give these to rule-breakers. _____
15. These places make things to sell. _____

Rhymes

Write the spelling word that completes each sentence and rhymes with the underlined word.

16. The workers put their <u>wrenches</u> on the _____.
17. When it was twenty _____, my nose began to <u>freeze</u>!
18. Ms. Lowe <u>teaches</u> us how to give _____.
19. Everyone loves to go to <u>Artie's</u> birthday _____.

stories	wives	benches	skis
calves	sandwiches	branches	athletes
parties	companies	neighbors	hobbies
exercises	penalties	degrees	vegetables
speeches	crashes	wishes	businesses

Proofreading

Proofread the paragraph below. Use proofreading marks to correct five spelling mistakes, three capitalization mistakes, and two punctuation mistakes.

Proofreading Marks

◯ spell correctly

≡ capitalize

⊙ add period

Up and Away

I learned about model airplanes from my neighbors, Victor

and melinda Last Saturday we sat on the benchs in their yard,

ate sandwitches, and talked about planes. They showed me

their models and told storyes about each one Victor's favorite

model is one that his great-grandfather gave him. It's a

Spitfire, an airplane used by the Royal Air Force in World

War II. Victor's great-grandfather flew a Spitfire in that

war. i decided to build my own models. Victor said that of all

the hobies, building model airplanes is his favorite. now it's mine,

too. My father is helping me build a Spitfire and a Hornet.

Language Connection

Subject-Verb Agreement

The subject and the verb of a sentence must "agree" in number. A plural subject must have a plural verb. A singular subject must have a singular verb.

> **Singular Subject**
> This **story** is about a zookeeper.
>
> **Plural Subject**
> **All** of the stories are interesting.

The subject of each of the following sentences appears in dark type.
Choose the correct verb for the subject. Then write the sentence correctly.

1. My **neighbor** (was, were) upset about losing her parrot.

_____

2. The **vegetables** in our garden (is, are) ready to be picked.

_____

3. The mayor's **speech** (seem, seems) too long and too serious.

_____

4. These cucumber **sandwiches** really (does, do) taste good.

_____

5. Our **calves** (spends, spend) most of the day playing.

_____

6. The **benches** at the city park (need, needs) to be replaced.

_____

7. His father's **company** (build, builds) parts for computers.

_____

unit 2 Review
Lessons 6-10

LESSON 6

delivery
empty
athlete
evening
believe

Words with /ē/

Write the spelling word that completes each sentence.

1. The _____ trained every day.
2. Every _____ after dinner, we play a word game.
3. Tell the truth so that people will always _____ you.
4. Joe's Pizza Place has free _____ service.
5. I spent all my money, so my wallet is _____.

LESSON 7

weak
reason
breathe
speech
piano

More Words with /ē/

Write the spelling word for each clue.

6. This is a musical instrument with keys. _____
7. If something is not strong, then it's this. _____
8. Humans do this to get air. _____
9. This tells why something is the way it is.
   _____
10. You give one of these when you give a talk.
    _____

LESSON 8

different
chimney
except
enough
guilty

Words with /ĭ/

Write the spelling word for each definition.

11. a tall structure through which smoke can flow _____
12. feeling that one has done something wrong _____

174 SPELLING SKILLS

13. outside of or apart from _____

14. not the same as _____

15. as much as is needed _____

kitchen
mystery
garbage
message
business

More Words with /ĭ/

Write the spelling word that completes each analogy.

16. *Trash* is to _____ as *bag* is to *sack*.

17. *Store* is to _____ as *cottage* is to *house*.

18. *Passage* is to *hall* as *letter* is to _____.

19. *Piece* is to *puzzle* as *clue* is to _____.

20. *Bedroom* is to *sleep* as _____ is to *cook*.

skis
businesses
companies
calves
wives

Plural Words

Write the spelling word that answers each question.

21. What are baby cows called? _____

22. What is another word for *businesses*? _____

23. What do people use to go down a snowy mountain?

_____

24. What do husbands have? _____

25. What can you see on the main streets of small towns?

_____

Words with /ī/

mild	library	science	guide
idea	quite	awhile	ninth
pirate	polite	tried	decide
remind	revise	island	grind
knife	climb	invite	blind

island

Say and Listen

Say each spelling word. Listen for the /ī/ sound you hear in *mild*.

Think and Sort

Look at the letters in each word. Think about how /ī/ is spelled. Spell each word aloud.

How many spelling patterns for /ī/ do you see?

1. Write the **seven** spelling words that have the *i*-consonant-*e* pattern, like *quite*.

2. Write the **eleven** spelling words that have the *i* pattern, like *mild*.

3. Write the **one** spelling word that has the *ie* pattern.

4. Write the **one** spelling word that has the *ui* pattern after a consonant other than *q*.

1. i-consonant-e Words

_____   _____   _____

_____   _____   _____

_____

2. i Words

_____   _____   _____

_____   _____   _____

_____   _____   _____

_____   _____

3. ie Word   **4. ui Word**

_____   _____

Classifying

Write the spelling word that belongs in each group.

1. mathematics, reading, _____
2. lead, direct, _____
3. robber, thief, _____
4. chop, crush, _____
5. change, edit, _____
6. spear, dagger, _____
7. tested, attempted, _____
8. thought, opinion, _____
9. calm, gentle, _____
10. seventh, eighth, _____

Definitions

Write the spelling word for each definition.
Use a dictionary if you need to.

11. to go or move up _____
12. to come to a conclusion _____
13. unable to see _____
14. completely or very _____
15. to ask someone to go somewhere _____
16. for a brief period of time _____
17. a place with books and reference materials _____
18. to make a person remember _____
19. a piece of land completely surrounded by water _____

mild	library	science	guide
idea	quite	awhile	ninth
pirate	polite	tried	decide
remind	revise	island	grind
knife	climb	invite	blind

Proofreading

Proofread this paragraph from a short story. Use proofreading marks to correct five spelling mistakes, two punctuation mistakes, and three unnecessary words.

Proofreading Marks

◯ spell correctly

? add question mark

↪ take out

The Decision

The sailor depended on the stars that twinkled in the black night sky to giude him along his course. Tonight, however, a thick fog had stolen in and a covered everything in a thick, wet blanket. The sailor had no iddea where he was, and he couldn't deside what to do. Should he drop it the ship's anchor and wait for awile Would the that just invite a pyrate attack The choice that he made in this moment could change the rest of his life.

Direct Quotations

Quotation marks are placed around the exact words of a speaker. The first word in a direct quotation begins with a capital letter. If the quotation falls at the end of a sentence, the end punctuation is placed inside the final quotation mark. A comma is usually used to set off the quotation from the rest of the sentence. Notice the capitalization and punctuation in the following examples.

> Lisa asked, "Will you come to the parade with us?"
>
> "I would love to go with you," said Bob.
>
> "Can you bring some chairs?" asked Lisa.

The following sentences contain errors in capitalization and punctuation. Write each sentence correctly.

1. Mr. Perry said my workload is easing up quite a bit

_____

2. why don't you decide to take a vacation asked Mrs. Perry

_____

_____

3. Mr. Perry answered i'd like to climb a high mountain

_____

_____

4. we should take a guide so that we won't get lost added Mr. Perry

_____

_____

Words with /ŏ/

dollar	honor	collar	closet
common	lobster	quantity	hospital
solid	copper	wander	problem
object	comma	watch	bother
bottom	shock	honest	promise

Say and Listen

Say each spelling word. Listen for the /ŏ/ sound you hear in *dollar*.

Think and Sort

Look at the letters in each word. Think about how /ŏ/ is spelled. Spell each word aloud.

How many spelling patterns for /ŏ/ do you see?

1. Write the **seventeen** spelling words that have the *o* pattern, like *dollar*.

2. Write the **three** spelling words that have the *a* pattern, like *watch*.

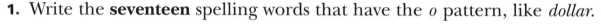

dollar

1. o Words

_____ _____ _____

_____ _____ _____

_____ _____ _____

_____ _____ _____

_____ _____ _____

_____ _____

2. a Words

_____ _____ _____

Synonyms

Write the spelling word that is a synonym for each word below.

1. clinic   _____

2. annoy   _____

3. difficulty   _____

4. usual   _____

5. firm   _____

6. lowest   _____

7. thing   _____

8. respect   _____

9. amount   _____

10. vow   _____

11. roam   _____

Clues

Write the spelling word for each clue.

12. This word describes a truthful person.   _____

13. This is a metal that turns green as it ages.   _____

14. This is a very sudden surprise.   _____

15. This is one hundred cents.   _____

16. This is a shellfish with two large front claws.   _____

17. This part of a shirt goes around the neck.   _____

18. This is where clothes are kept.   _____

19. This is worn on the wrist.   _____

dollar	honor	collar	closet
common	lobster	quantity	hospital
solid	copper	wander	problem
object	comma	watch	bother
bottom	shock	honest	promise

Proofreading

Proofread the e-mail below. Use proofreading marks to correct five spelling mistakes, three capitalization mistakes, and two unnecessary words.

Proofreading Marks

◯ spell correctly

≡ capitalize

✍ take out

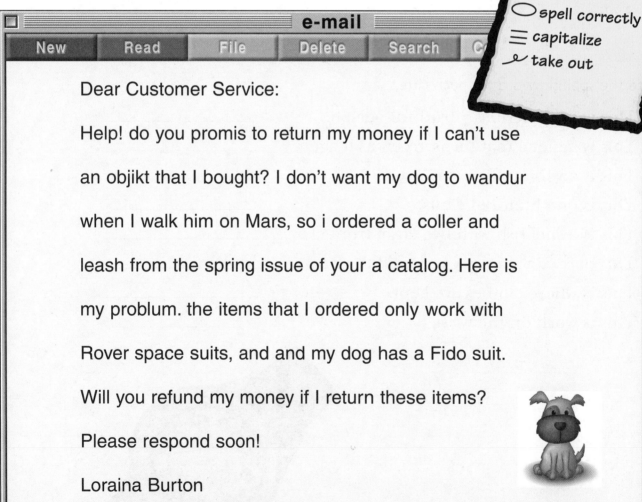

e-mail

New	Read	File	Delete	Search	C

Dear Customer Service:

Help! do you promis to return my money if I can't use

an objikt that I bought? I don't want my dog to wandur

when I walk him on Mars, so i ordered a coller and

leash from the spring issue of your a catalog. Here is

my problum. the items that I ordered only work with

Rover space suits, and and my dog has a Fido suit.

Will you refund my money if I return these items?

Please respond soon!

Loraina Burton

Simple Subjects

The simple subject of a sentence tells who or what is doing the action of the verb or is being talked about. The simple subject is the main word of the complete subject. In the following sentence, the complete subject is underlined. The simple subject appears in dark type.

> The **boy** in the blue shirt won the race.

Write the simple subject of each sentence below.

1. The local hospital was a busy place on Saturday. _____
2. Fresh lobster is a tasty meat. _____
3. A comma is a punctuation mark. _____
4. The closet in your room is a mess. _____
5. A dollar is worth ten dimes. _____
6. My new gold watch is broken. _____
7. A promise should not be broken. _____
8. The bottom of the page is empty. _____
9. The soldier's honor was at stake. _____
10. Copper is a reddish-brown metal. _____
11. The object of the game is simple. _____
12. Dina saw the deer through the trees. _____
13. The dog's collar was lying in the mud. _____
14. The engine problem can easily be solved. _____

Words with /ō/

vote	zone	known	follow
alone	microscope	arrow	grown
borrow	swallow	tomorrow	telephone
code	suppose	chose	sew
throw	bowl	owe	elbow

Say and Listen

Say each spelling word. Listen for the /ō/ sound you hear in *vote*.

telephone

Think and Sort

Look at the letters in each word. Think about how /ō/ is spelled. Spell each word aloud.

How many spelling patterns for /ō/ do you see?

1. Write the **nine** spelling words that have the *o*-consonant-*e* pattern, like *vote*.

2. Write the **ten** spelling words that have the *ow* pattern, like *arrow*.

3. Write the **one** word that has the *ew* pattern.

---

1. o-consonant-e Words

_____   _____   _____

_____   _____   _____

_____   _____   _____

2. ow Words

_____   _____   _____

_____   _____   _____

_____   _____   _____

_____

3. ew Word

_____

Classifying

Write the spelling word that belongs in each group.

1. pitch, hurl, _____

2. plate, cup, _____

3. yesterday, today, _____

4. grow, grew, _____

5. mend, stitch, _____

6. imagine, expect, _____

7. know, knew, _____

8. area, district, _____

9. dart, spear, _____

10. telescope, kaleidoscope, _____

11. picked, selected, _____

12. puzzle, signal, _____

What's Missing?

Write the missing spelling word.

13. Leave me _____!

14. Answer the _____, please.

15. _____ the leader.

16. The pill was hard to _____.

17. You _____ me a favor.

18. May I _____ your pencil?

19. Let's _____ on it.

vote	zone	known	follow
alone	microscope	arrow	grown
borrow	swallow	tomorrow	telephone
code	suppose	chose	sew
throw	bowl	owe	elbow

Proofreading

Proofread the journal entry below. Use proofreading marks to correct five spelling mistakes, three capitalization mistakes, and two mistakes in word order.

Proofreading Marks
◯ spell correctly
≡ capitalize
∿ trade places

april 8

Tommorrow I give will my science report. It's called "The Amazing microscope." I choze the microscope as a topic because have I grone very interested in tiny living things. The only way to see them is to view them through a microscope. without this important invention, we would never have knoan why people get typhoid fever and food poisoning. I suppows that we wouldn't be able to see what a flea or a mite really looks like, either. I hope everyone likes my report. I've tried to make it fun and interesting.

Verbs

The complete predicate is the part of a sentence that tells what the subject does or is. The verb is the main word or words in the predicate. In the sentences below, *Chelsey* is the subject, and the words in dark type are the verbs.

> Chelsey **will jog** to school today.
> Chelsey **is** a very good athlete.

Write each of the following sentences, correcting the spelling errors and underlining the verbs.

1. I oew Jo Anne a dollar.

_____

2. Noah can borow my bike.

_____

3. I soe my own clothes.

_____

4. Tyler and Cody folloe directions well.

_____

5. Zoey answered the telefone.

_____

6. Rosie put the slide under the microskope.

_____

More Words with /ō/

oak	hotel	coach	notice
dough	yolk	boast	poem
groan	echo	float	control
tornado	hero	coast	though
throat	clothing	scold	roast

tornado

Say and Listen

Say each spelling word. Listen for the /ō/ sound.

Think and Sort

Look at the letters in each word. Think about how /ō/ is spelled. Spell each word aloud.

How many spelling patterns for /ō/ do you see?

1. Write the **ten** spelling words that have the *o* pattern, like *yolk*.

2. Write the **eight** spelling words that have the *oa* pattern, like *oak*.

3. Write the **two** spelling words that have the *ough* pattern, like *though*.

---

1. o Words

_____ _____ _____

_____ _____ _____

_____ _____

_____

2. oa Words

_____ _____ _____

_____ _____ _____

_____

3. ough Words

_____ _____

Classifying

Write the spelling word that belongs in each group.

1. hats, shoes, _____
2. egg white, eggshell, egg _____
3. resound, repeat, _____
4. elm, birch, _____
5. ear, nose, _____
6. since, however, _____
7. direct, operate, _____
8. lecture, yell, _____
9. crust, batter, _____
10. manager, trainer, _____
11. motel, inn, _____
12. see, observe, _____
13. drift, bob, _____

Synonyms

Complete each sentence by writing the spelling word that is a synonym for the underlined word.

14. The <u>champion</u> of the chess match was our _____.
15. This _____ is <u>verse</u> that doesn't rhyme.
16. Sail along the _____ and stop near the <u>shore</u>.
17. A stomachache can make you <u>moan</u> and _____.
18. Some people <u>brag</u> and _____ when they win a game.
19. Should I <u>bake</u> the chicken and _____ the corn?

oak	hotel	coach	notice
dough	yolk	boast	poem
groan	echo	float	control
tornado	hero	coast	though
throat	clothing	scold	roast

Proofreading

Proofread the diary entry below.
Use proofreading marks to correct five
spelling mistakes, three capitalization
mistakes, and two punctuation mistakes.

Proofreading Marks

◯ spell correctly

/ make lowercase

⊙ add period

Dear Diary,

Last night a tornadoe hit our Town. I've never been so scared

in all my life. I woke up around Midnight when our house began

to grone. I looked outside and saw lawn chairs and branches

flying through the air. Dad said we had to get somewhere in the

middle of the house, so we gathered in the hall Soon we heard

nothing but the roaring wind spinning out of controle. This

morning we saw that the roof of the hotell next door was gone.

The oke tree in our yard had been pulled up by the roots.

I'm grateful that We are all unharmed

Dictionary Skills

Parts of Speech

The parts of speech include noun *(n.)*, verb *(v.)*, adverb *(adv.)*, and preposition *(prep.)*. Some words can be used as more than one part of speech. The parts of speech for those words are usually listed within one dictionary entry.

> **coast** (kōst) *n.* The edge of land along the sea. —*v.* **coast·ed, coast·ing.** To move without power or effort: *coast down a hill.*

> **con·trol** (kən trōl′) *v.* **con·trolled, con·trol·ling.** To have power over: *control a country; control a car.* —*n.* **1.** Authority or power: *the athlete's control over his body.* **2. controls.** Instruments for operating a machine.

Both *coast* and *control* can be used as a noun and a verb. Use the words to complete the sentences below. Then write *noun* or *verb* after each to tell how it is used in each sentence.

1. Joan couldn't _____ the frisky pony.

_____

2. I like to _____ down the hill on my skateboard.

_____

3. We rented a house on the _____ of Florida.

_____

4. Gymnasts have remarkable _____ over their body.

_____

5. The hotel guests' fear seemed out of _____.

_____

6. We drove along the _____ today.

_____

Media Words

graphics	animation	columnist	byline
studio	earphones	producer	commercial
recorder	video	network	camera
newspaper	director	television	editorial
headline	musician	masthead	broadcast

musician

Say and Listen

Say each spelling word. Listen for the number of syllables in each word.

Think and Sort

Look at the letters in each word. Think about the number of syllables in the word. Spell each word aloud.

1. Write the **seven** spelling words that have two syllables, like *graphics*. Draw dashes between the syllables, like *graph-ics*.

2. Write the **ten** spelling words that have three syllables, like *director*. Draw dashes between the syllables.

3. Write the **three** spelling words that have more than three syllables, like *animation*. Draw dashes between the syllables.

1. Words with Two Syllables

_____   _____   _____

_____   _____   _____

_____

2. Words with Three Syllables

_____   _____   _____

_____   _____   _____

_____   _____   _____

_____

3. Words with More than Three Syllables

_____   _____   _____

Compound Words

Write the spelling word that is made from the two underlined words in each sentence.

1. The <u>phones</u> were close to my right <u>ear</u>. _____

2. The horse's <u>head</u> has a white <u>line</u> on it. _____

3. We walked <u>by</u> the <u>line</u> for the movie. _____

4. Lee <u>cast</u> a glance over the <u>broad</u> meadow. _____

5. I bumped my <u>head</u> on the sailboat's <u>mast</u>. _____

6. Will this <u>net</u> <u>work</u> in the river? _____

7. The reporter read the <u>news</u> from a sheet of <u>paper</u>. _____

Clues

Write the spelling word for each clue.

8. an ad on TV _____

9. someone who plays a musical instrument _____

10. a person who writes a daily or weekly feature _____

11. a newspaper column that tells the writer's opinion _____

12. a movie put on tape for viewing on television _____

13. a device for taking pictures _____

14. a way to bring drawings to life _____

15. a person who instructs movie actors and crew _____

16. a place where TV shows and movies are filmed _____

17. the person who manages the making of a TV show _____

18. a device that saves sounds on magnetic tape _____

19. artwork in a video game _____

graphics	animation	columnist	byline
studio	earphones	producer	commercial
recorder	video	network	camera
newspaper	director	television	editorial
headline	musician	masthead	broadcast

Proofreading

Proofread the help-wanted ad below. Use proofreading marks to correct five spelling mistakes, three capitalization mistakes, and two mistakes in word order.

Proofreading Marks

◯ spell correctly

≡ capitalize

∿ trade places

Help Wanted!

KNBE, the most popular network in North America, is seeking a praducer and a director for its new telavision show. the show about is a newspaper columist and a musician who are roommates. job requirements include a bachelor's degree in theater arts or radio/TV, three years' experience working on similar small-screen projects, camara knowledge, and a stable work history. if are you interested, contact the KNBE stewdio at 555-3054 for an application. KNBE is an equal opportunity employer.

Capitalization

Names of cities, states, countries, bodies of water, mountains, and streets are capitalized.

> Larry visited **S**an **F**rancisco, **C**alifornia, last summer.
> He saw the **P**acific **O**cean.

The following scrambled sentences contain errors in capitalization.
Unscramble each sentence and write it correctly.

1. broadcast came The new york from.

_____

2. the was commercial rocky mountains The filmed in.

_____

3. mentioned The washington, d.c., headline virginia and.

_____

4. was arctic ocean The about newspaper the article.

_____

5. a hollywood We studio visited.

_____

6. lives director paris in The of that film.

_____

7. The show atlantic ocean television was about the.

_____

unit 3 review
Lessons 11–15

Lesson 11

decide
island
library
ninth
science
guide

Words with /ī/

Write the spelling word that completes each analogy.

1. *Cloud* is to *sky* as _____ is to *sea*.
2. *Reside* is to *residence* as _____ is to *decision*.
3. *Eight* is to *eighth* as *nine* is to _____.
4. *Scientist* is to _____ as *historian* is to *history*.
5. *Leader* is to _____ as *path* is to *trail*.
6. *Teacher* is to *classroom* as *librarian* is to _____.

Lesson 12

collar
common
hospital
promise
wander

Words with /ŏ/

Write the spelling word that belongs in each group.

7. waistband, cuff, _____
8. doctor's office, clinic, _____
9. usual, ordinary, _____
10. guarantee, oath, _____
11. roam, drift, _____

Lesson 13

telephone
owe
borrow
sew

Words with /ō/

Write the spelling word that answers each question.

12. What can you use to call a friend? _____
13. What can you do if you forget your pencil? _____
14. How do you attach a missing button to a coat?
_____

15. What word has the meaning "to be in debt"?
_____

LESSON 14

echo
notice
yolk
groan
throat
though

More Words with /ō/

Write the spelling word for each definition.

16. a repeating or bouncing sound

_____

17. a narrow passage or entryway _____

18. even if; in spite of the fact that _____

19. a printed announcement _____

20. to moan deeply or sadly _____

21. the yellow part of an egg _____

LESSON 15

musician
camera
commercial
graphics

Media Words

Write the spelling word that completes each sentence.

22. The girl was a brilliant _____ .

23. Kayla liked the _____ on her computer screen.

24. My new _____ has a zoom lens.

25. The new pizza _____ features a singing parrot.

Words with /ŭ/

crush	judge	rough	husband	tongue
pumpkin	monkey	onion	touch	hundred
jungle	compass	blood	among	knuckle
flood	instruct	country	dozen	wonderful

Say and Listen

Say each spelling word. Listen for the /ŭ/ sound you hear in *crush*.

pumpkin

Think and Sort

Look at the letters in each word. Think about how /ŭ/ is spelled.
Spell each word aloud.

How many spelling patterns for /ŭ/ do you see?

1. Write the **eight** spelling words that have the *u* pattern, like *crush*.

2. Write the **seven** spelling words that have the *o* pattern, like *among*.

3. Write the **three** spelling words that have the *ou* pattern, like *touch*.

4. Write the **two** spelling words that have the *oo* pattern, like *flood*.

1. u Words

_____   _____   _____

_____   _____   _____

_____   _____

2. o Words

_____   _____   _____

_____   _____   _____

_____

3. ou Words

_____   _____   _____

4. oo Words

_____   _____

Classifying

Write the spelling word that belongs in each group.

1. courtroom, lawyer, _____

2. pepper, garlic, _____

3. desert, plains, _____

4. teeth, gums, _____

5. map, backpack, _____

6. hand, finger, _____

Clues

Write the spelling word for each clue.

7. If you pound ice into pieces, you do this. _____

8. This red liquid is pumped through the body. _____

9. This is a married man. _____

10. This is a group of twelve. _____

11. This word means "excellent." _____

12. A wagon bounces over this kind of road. _____

13. If you teach, you do this. _____

14. This is ten times ten. _____

15. This is another word for *nation*. _____

16. When you have a lot of rain, you might get this. _____

17. This word means "in the company of." _____

18. This is what you don't do to a hot stove. _____

19. This animal has hands with thumbs. _____

crush	judge	rough	husband
tongue	pumpkin	monkey	onion
touch	hundred	jungle	compass
blood	among	knuckle	flood
instruct	country	dozen	wonderful

Proofreading

Proofread the advertisement below.
Use proofreading marks to correct five spelling mistakes, two punctuation mistakes, and three missing words.

Proofreading Marks

◯ spell correctly

? add question mark

∧ add

Try No-Cry!

Do you cry when peel an uniun Have you tried chilling it, peeling it underwater, or shutting your eyes As you know, these old-fashioned remedies don't work, but we have a new one does. Now is the time to try No-Cry!

Just place two No-Cry pills on your tung. No tears will stream down your face. Your eyes will not sting.

No store in the countre sells these pills, so order a bottle now. In fact, order two. Each bottle contains a dozan pills.

They wonderfull!

Dictionary Skills

Homographs

Some words are spelled exactly like other words but have different meanings and different origins. Some are also pronounced differently. These words are called homographs. *Homo* means "same," and *graph* means "write." Homographs appear as separate entry words in dictionaries, and they are numbered.

> **bowl¹** (bōl) *n.* **1.** A round dish used to hold things. **2.** Something shaped like a bowl.
> **bowl²** (bōl) *v.* **bowled, bowl·ing. 1.** To play the game of bowling: *Rita likes to bowl after school.* **2.** To roll a ball in the game of bowling: *Who bowls first?*

> **des·ert¹** (dĕz' ərt) *n.* A dry, sandy region.
> **de·sert²** (dĭ zûrt') *v.* **de·sert·ed, de·sert·ing.** To forsake; abandon: *She did not desert her friends when they needed her.*

Complete each sentence with one of the homographs above. Then write the entry number for the homograph.

1. May I have a _____ of soup?   _____

2. I like to _____ with my team

on Saturdays.   _____

3. I hope I _____ a few strikes.   _____

4. The _____ had not seen rain

in two years.   _____

5. The students walked down into the rocky

_____ left by the meteorite.   _____

6. Don't _____ a person in need.   _____

Words with /ô/

dawn	wrong	already	daughter	automobile
thought	raw	taught	bought	all right
fought	fault	autumn	often	brought
caught	straw	lawn	crawl	awful

Say and Listen

Say each spelling word. Listen for the /ô/ sound you hear in *dawn*.

Think and Sort

daughter

Look at the letters in each word. Think about how /ô/ is spelled. Spell each word aloud.

How many spelling patterns for /ô/ do you see?

1. Write the **two** spelling words that have the *a* pattern, like *already*.
2. Write the **two** spelling words that have the *o* pattern, like *wrong*.
3. Write the **three** spelling words that have the *au* pattern, like *fault*.
4. Write the **six** spelling words that have the *aw* pattern, like *dawn*.
5. Write the **seven** spelling words that have the *augh* or *ough* pattern, like *taught*.

1. a Words

_____   _____

2. o Words

_____   _____

3. au Words

_____   _____   _____

4. aw Words

_____   _____   _____

_____   _____   _____

5. augh, ough Words

_____   _____   _____

_____   _____   _____

_____

Antonyms

Antonyms are words that have opposite meanings.
Write the spelling word that is an antonym of each word below.

1. dusk   _____
2. sold   _____
3. right   _____
4. seldom   _____
5. wonderful   _____
6. cooked   _____
7. unsatisfactory _____
8. learned   _____

Analogies

Write the spelling word that completes each analogy.

9. *Spring* is to *warm* as _____ is to *cool.*

10. *Tell* is to *told* as *catch* is to _____ .

11. *Grass* is to _____ as *leaves* are to *tree.*

12. *Fast* is to *run* as *slow* is to _____ .

13. *Fight* is to _____ as *sing* is to *sang.*

14. _____ is to *past* as *right away* is to *soon.*

15. *Eat* is to *ate* as *think* is to _____ .

16. *Mother* is to _____ as *father* is to *son.*

17. *Pillow* is to *feather* as *scarecrow* is to _____ .

18. *Asked* is to *ask* as _____ is to *bring.*

19. *Find* is to *locate* as *mistake* is to _____ .

dawn	raw	autumn	crawl
thought	fault	lawn	automobile
fought	straw	daughter	all right
caught	already	bought	brought
wrong	taught	often	awful

Proofreading

Proofread the e-mail below. Use proofreading marks to correct five spelling mistakes, three capitalization mistakes, and two punctuation mistakes.

Proofreading Marks

◯ spell correctly
≡ capitalize
⊙ add period

---

e-mail

New	Read	File	Delete	Se...

Hi, Aunt sylvia!

Did you have a good summer? I did, except for one problem. I was supposed to mow mrs. Hu's laun each week until she returned in the awtumn. She taght me how to start her mower, and I thought I had caught on. I was rong

After ten days, her yard looked auful. I finally asked a neighbor what to do. he showed me how to start the mower, and everything was fine I hope I can do it again next summer.

Raymond

Apostrophes

A contraction is a shortened form of two or more words in which one or more letters are left out. An apostrophe shows where the letters have been left out.

> had + not hadn't

A possessive noun is a noun form that shows ownership. An apostrophe and -*s* are used to form the possessive of a singular noun. An apostrophe and -*s* are also used to form the possessive of a plural noun that does not end in -*s*. If a plural noun ends in -*s*, only an apostrophe is used.

> **Singular Possessives**   **Plural Possessives**
> the dog**'s** house   the mice**'s** cage
>   the girls**'** dresses

The following sentences contain spelling errors and apostrophe errors. Write each sentence correctly.

1. Mom: Ive brawt you a surprise.

_____

2. Stuart: I thawt youd forgotten my birthday.

_____

3. Mom: Its all boys favorite means of transportation.

_____

4. Stuart: You bougt me a car like Dads!

_____

5. Mom: Youre rong, silly boy. Its a bicycle.

_____

Words with /ōō/

choose	loose	lose	rooster
balloon	shampoo	improve	clue
kangaroo	fruit	proof	prove
truth	foolish	shoe	whom
juice	whose	raccoon	glue

Say and Listen

Say each spelling word. Listen for the /ōō/ sound you hear in *choose*.

Think and Sort

Look at the letters in each word. Think about how /ōō/ is spelled. Spell each word aloud.

kangaroo

How many spelling patterns for /ōō/ do you see?

1. Write the **nine** spelling words that have the *oo* pattern, like *choose*.

2. Write the **five** spelling words that have the *u, ue,* or *ui* pattern, like *truth*.

3. Write the **six** spelling words that have the *o-consonant-e, oe,* or *o* pattern, like *whom*.

1. oo Words

_____ _____ _____

_____ _____ _____

_____ _____ _____

2. u, ue, ui Words

_____ _____ _____

_____ _____

3. o-consonant-e, oe, o Words

_____ _____ _____

_____ _____ _____

Hink Pinks

Write the spelling word that completes each hink pink.

1. colored paste   blue _____

2. song sung by a masked animal   _____ tune

3. drink for large animal with antlers   moose _____

4. an unattached train car   _____ caboose

5. honesty from a ten-year-old   youth _____

6. what puppies make from footwear   _____ chew

Clues

Write the spelling word for each clue.

7. This is a form of *who*.   _____

8. An apple is this kind of food.   _____

9. You do this when you show a thing is true.   _____

10. This word is a homophone for *who's*.   _____

11. People use this to wash their hair.   _____

12. A lawyer presents this to a jury.   _____

13. This is the opposite of *wise*.   _____

14. This animal crows in the morning.   _____

15. People fill this with air.   _____

16. This is the opposite of *find*.   _____

17. You do this when you pick something.   _____

18. You practice so that you will do this.   _____

19. A detective looks for this.   _____

choose	loose	lose	rooster
balloon	shampoo	improve	clue
kangaroo	fruit	proof	prove
truth	foolish	shoe	whom
juice	whose	raccoon	glue

Proofreading

Proofread the paragraph below from a book report. Use proofreading marks to correct five spelling mistakes, three capitalization mistakes, and two punctuation mistakes.

Proofreading Marks

◯ spell correctly

╱ make lowercase

⊙ add period

Jeremy Garza   Benton Middle School

Fourth Period   January 5, 2003

"The Grape Mystery"

"The Grape Mystery" is a short Story by Anna Heglin

The main character is a detective named Reba Barberra.

Reba needs to solve a mystery about a Missing diamond

necklace. Reba suspects the next door neighbor, whooz wife

is going on a long voyage. Reba's clew is a spot on the floor

Someone has stepped on a grape and smashed it. Now she

has to find a shoo with Smashed fruite on the bottom of

it. Will that be enough for Reba to proove this person is

the thief?

Dictionary Skills

Pronunciation

A dictionary lists the pronunciation for each entry word. The pronunciation is written in special symbols. To know what sound each of the symbols stands for, you must refer to the pronunciation key. It lists the symbols and gives examples of words that have the sounds of the symbols.

Write the word for each pronunciation below.
Check your answers in a dictionary.

1. (ră ko͞on′) _____

2. (jo͞os) _____

3. (bə lo͞on′) _____

4. (tro͞oth) _____

5. (ĭm pro͞ov′) _____

6. (pro͞of) _____

7. (lo͞os) _____

8. (ro͞o′ stər) _____

9. (shăm po͞o′) _____

10. (fo͞o′ lĭsh) _____

11. (lo͞oz) _____

12. (glo͞o) _____

ă	pat	ŏ	pot	ŭ	cut	
ā	pay	ō	toe	ûr	urge	
âr	care	ô	paw, for	ə	about,	
ä	father	oi	noise		item,	
ĕ	pet	o͝o	took		edible,	
ē	bee	o͞o	boot		gallop,	
ĭ	pit	ou	out		circus	
ī	pie	th	thin	ər	butter	
îr	deer	*th*	this			

Pronunciation Key

Words with /oi/

noise	destroy	annoy	enjoy
choice	appoint	moisture	employment
boiler	oyster	coin	loyal
avoid	loyalty	voice	voyage
royal	broil	employ	appointment

Say and Listen

Say each spelling word. Listen for the /oi/ sound you hear in *noise*.

Think and Sort

Look at the letters in each word. Think about how /oi/ is spelled.
Spell each word aloud.

How many spelling patterns for /oi/ do you see?

1. Write the **ten** spelling words that have the *oy* pattern, like *loyal*.

2. Write the **ten** spelling words that have the *oi* pattern, like *noise*.

coin

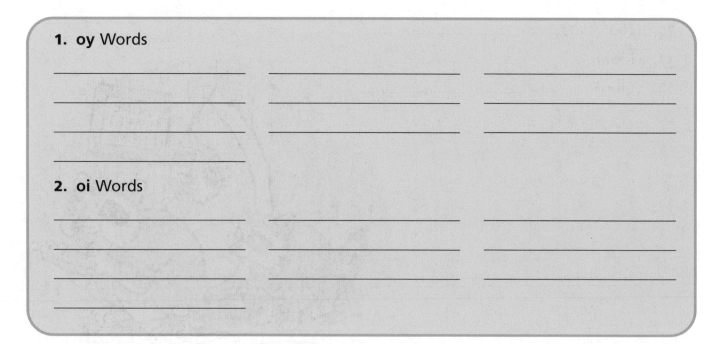

1. oy Words

_____   _____   _____

_____   _____   _____

_____   _____   _____

_____

2. oi Words

_____   _____   _____

_____   _____   _____

_____   _____   _____

_____

What's the Answer?

Write the spelling word that answers each question.

1. An opera singer uses what to make music? _____

2. A diver might find a pearl in what? _____

3. What do you need in order to see the doctor? _____

4. What do you want if you're looking for a job? _____

5. What do you feel when you walk barefoot on damp grass? _____

6. What is a trip on a ship called? _____

7. Where does the steam to power a steamboat come from? _____

8. You do what when you name someone to do something? _____

9. What word describes the palace of a king? _____

Synonyms

Complete each sentence by writing the spelling word that is a synonym for the underlined word.

10. Pele knew the rain would <u>wreck</u> his sand castle. _____

11. The coat with the hood is my <u>selection</u>. _____

12. Mr. Bander will <u>grill</u> hamburgers and chicken. _____

13. A dog can be a <u>faithful</u> friend. _____

14. Students who talk out of turn <u>bother</u> Mrs. Reyna. _____

15. The department store will <u>hire</u> ten new clerks. _____

16. Sam showed his <u>faithfulness</u> by keeping Ann's secret. _____

17. Jordan will do anything to <u>escape</u> yardwork. _____

18. A loud, frightening <u>sound</u> blared from the foghorn. _____

19. Ping and Sara really <u>like</u> opera music. _____

noise	destroy	annoy	enjoy
choice	appoint	moisture	employment
boiler	oyster	coin	loyal
avoid	loyalty	voice	voyage
royal	broil	employ	appointment

Proofreading

Proofread the journal entry below. Use proofreading marks to correct five spelling mistakes, two capitalization mistakes, and three unnecessary words.

Proofreading Marks

◯ spell correctly
≡ capitalize
ℓ take out

April 5

maria wants to be a doctor, and Rita hopes to be

a a ballet dancer. But I enjoye so many things that

it's hard to decide on just one career. Each day i

have a new idea and make a new choyce.

I'd like to to avoid being a singer, because my voyce

sounds more like noyze than music! I love horses, so

maybe I could work with with them. Maybe someone

would employe me to train and ride their horses.

Dictionary Skills

Syllables and Accent Marks

A syllable is a word part or a word with one vowel sound. An accent mark (′) tells which syllable in a word is spoken with more force, or stress. The pronunciations in a dictionary show the accented syllables in words.

> **loyal** (loi′əl)   **annoy** (ə noi′)

Find each word in a dictionary. Write the pronunciation of each word. Circle the accented syllable.

1. destroy _____
2. royal _____
3. moisture _____
4. appoint _____
5. oyster _____
6. avoid _____
7. loyalty _____
8. voyage _____
9. annoy _____
10. enjoy _____
11. employment _____
12. boiler _____
13. appointment _____
14. employ _____

Sports Words

cycling	track	soccer	football
professional	basketball	skin diving	skiing
Olympics	champion	volleyball	bowling
skating	golf	baseball	amateur
swimming	tennis	hockey	competition

soccer

Say and Listen

Say each spelling word. Listen for the number of syllables.

Think and Sort

Look at the syllables in each word. Think about how each syllable is spelled.
Spell each word aloud.

1. Write the **one** spelling word that is a two-word compound.

2. Write the **two** spelling words that have one syllable, like *track*.

3. Write the **ten** spelling words that have two syllables, like *cy-cling*.

4. Write the **five** spelling words that have three syllables, like *bas-ket-ball*.

5. Write the **two** spelling words that have four syllables, like *pro-fes-sion-al*.

1. Two-word Compound   **2. One-syllable Words**
_____   _____   _____

3. Two-syllable Words
_____   _____   _____
_____   _____   _____
_____   _____   _____
_____

4. Three-syllable Words
_____   _____   _____
_____   _____

5. Four-syllable Words
_____   _____

Classifying

Write the spelling word that belongs in each group.

1. blades, wheels, ice, rink, _____
2. mitt, mound, bat, bases, _____
3. snow, poles, lifts, slopes, _____
4. tee, course, hole, caddy, _____
5. puck, stick, goalie, ice, _____
6. racket, court, net, serve, _____
7. ocean, mask, fin, snorkel, _____
8. pins, strike, lanes, gutter, _____
9. race, bicycle, water bottle, helmet, _____
10. kick, goalie, ball, net, _____
11. hoop, backboard, basket, court, _____

Definitions

Write the spelling word for each definition. Use a dictionary if you need to.

12. a path or a trail _____
13. a game in which two teams hit a large ball across a net _____
14. an oval leather ball _____
15. someone who does something for pleasure, not money _____
16. someone who is paid to play a sport _____
17. moving through water by moving one's arms and legs _____
18. a person who wins first place in a contest _____
19. a contest _____

cycling	track	soccer	football
professional	basketball	skin diving	skiing
Olympics	champion	volleyball	bowling
skating	golf	baseball	amateur
swimming	tennis	hockey	competition

Proofreading

Proofread the letter below. Use proofreading marks to correct five spelling mistakes, three capitalization mistakes, and two missing words.

Proofreading Marks

○ spell correctly

≡ capitalize

∧ add

9820 Hardy trail

Englewood, CO 80155

Dear Nadia,

I am so glad we have become pen pals! There is much I want

to tell you about my family and our life in louisiana. Everyone in

my family is an athlete. Dad plays gollf and basball. Mom loves

sking. I play socer, and my sister ana the star of her trak

team. Maybe one of us will become a professional some day!

Maybe one of us will even be in the Olympics!

What does your family like do? I hope you write back soon!

Sincerely,

Sydney

Language Connection

Commas

Use commas in a friendly letter

- to separate the city from the state in the heading
- to separate the day from the year in the heading
- after the person's name in the greeting
- after the last word in the closing.

> Casper, WY
> February 4, 2003
> Dear Bob,
> Yours truly,

The friendly letter below contains comma errors and spelling errors. Use proofreading marks to add commas where they are needed and to correct the misspelled words.

1722 W. River Rd.

Chicago IL 60657

May 5 2004

Dear Alicia

    I'm so pleased that you're coming to visit. We can certainly plan lots of time for sports. Swiming and skatting have always been my favorites. My brother is going to become a profesional baskitball player. Right now he's just an amatuer. See you soon!

                Sincerely

                Marta

unit 4 review
LESSONS 16–20

judge
tongue
rough
flood

Words with /ŭ/

Write the spelling word that completes each sentence and rhymes with the underlined word.

1. The mouse in the movie pretended to be _____ and <u>tough</u>.

2. Who will _____ the <u>fudge</u> at the cooking contest?

3. The _____ left behind <u>mud</u> in all the houses.

4. When Victor bit his _____, he <u>hung</u> up the phone.

LESSON 17

all right
often
fault
awful
daughter
fought

Words with /ô/

Write the spelling word that completes each sentence.

5. It was my _____ that the dish broke.

6. The man's only child was not a son but a _____.

7. A flu virus can make you feel _____.

8. When I looked outside, everything seemed _____.

9. I like to read, so I go to the library _____.

10. Doctors have _____ long and hard to wipe out diseases.

raccoon
truth
clue
juice
whose
shoe
whom

Words with /o͞o/

Write the spelling word that completes each analogy.

11. *Glove* is to *hand* as _____ is to *foot*.

12. *Mammal* is to _____ as *reptile* is to *snake*.

13. *Dark* is to *light* as *lie* is to _____.

14. *It's* is to *its* as *who's* is to _____.

15. *Flour* is to *wheat* as _____ is to *orange*.

16. *Scarlet* is to *red* as *hint* is to _____.

17. *Pencil* is to *what* as *person* is to _____.

annoy
destroy
appointment
avoid
choice

Words with /oi/

Write the spelling word for each definition. Use a dictionary if you need to.

18. something that is chosen _____

19. to bother _____

20. to make useless _____

21. to stay away from _____

22. an arrangement to meet at a specific time and place _____

cycling
amateur
champion

Sports Words

Write the spelling word that answers each question.

23. What do you call someone who plays a sport for fun?

_____

24. What sport involves riding a bike? _____

25. What do you call someone who wins first prize in a contest? _____

More Words with /ô/

score	quarrel	court	adore	roar
shore	before	reward	course	board
wore	warn	tore	export	toward
perform	fortunate	orchard	import	important

Say and Listen

Say each spelling word. Listen for the /ô/ sound you hear in *score*.

Think and Sort

orchard

Look at the letters in each word. Think about how /ô/ is spelled. Spell each word aloud.

How many spelling patterns for /ô/ do you see?

1. Write the **six** spelling words that have the *o*-consonant-*e* pattern, like *score*.
2. Write the **six** spelling words that have the *o* pattern, like *perform*.
3. Write the **four** spelling words that have the *a* pattern, like *warn*.
4. Write the **two** spelling words that have the *ou* pattern, like *court*.
5. Write the **two** spelling words that have the *oa* pattern, like *roar*.

1. o-consonant-e Words

_____   _____   _____

_____   _____   _____

2. o Words

_____   _____   _____

_____   _____   _____

3. a Words

_____   _____   _____

_____

4. ou Words

_____   _____

5. oa Words

_____   _____

Synonyms

Write the spelling word that is a synonym for each word below.

1. act   _____
2. love   _____
3. plank   _____
4. caution   _____
5. direction   _____
6. ripped   _____
7. argue   _____
8. earlier   _____
9. to   _____

Clues

Write the spelling word for each clue.

10. the past tense of *wear*   _____
11. where people play tennis   _____
12. what is often offered for finding a lost pet   _____
13. the number of points in a game   _____
14. where sand castles are found   _____
15. what a lucky person is   _____
16. the place to find apples   _____
17. worth noticing   _____
18. what lions and tigers do   _____
19. what people do in selling goods to another country   _____

score	quarrel	court	adore
roar	shore	before	reward
course	board	wore	warn
tore	export	toward	perform
fortunate	orchard	import	important

Proofreading

Proofread the part of a newspaper article below. Use proofreading marks to correct five spelling mistakes, three capitalization mistakes, and two punctuation mistakes.

Proofreading Marks

◯ spell correctly
≡ capitalize
⊙ add period

A Heady Discovery

In a press conference on thursday, Dr. G.Y. Nott announced an importent discovery Standing befour reporters in a derby hat with a large feather, he read the findings of a four-year study. according to Dr. Nott, the people in his study who woar funny hats usually didn't kwarrel with one another Dr. Nott added that these findings made him feel very fortunat. he himself adores funny hats.

Dictionary Skills

Multiple Pronunciations

Some words may be pronounced in more than one way. A dictionary gives all the acceptable pronunciations for these words, but the one listed first is usually the most common or the preferred.

Look at the pronunciations for *quarrel* given in the entry below. Notice that only the syllable that is pronounced in a different way is given in the second pronunciation. Say *quarrel* to yourself and see which pronunciation you use.

> **quar·rel** (**kwôr′** əl) *or* (**kwŏr′-**) *n.* A fight with words; an argument. —*v.* **quar·reled, quar·rel·ing.** To have a fight with words.

Each of the following words has more than one pronunciation. Look up each word in a dictionary. Write the complete pronunciation that you use.

1. course _____   **2.** score _____

3. export _____   **4.** import _____

5. toward _____   **6.** aunt _____

7. aurora _____   **8.** chorus _____

9. closet _____   **10.** compass _____

11. perfume _____   **12.** program _____

13. absurd _____   **14.** meteor _____

15. pumpkin _____   **16.** story _____

Words with /ûr/

skirt	purpose	earn	certain
dirty	service	furnish	early
thirteen	perfect	permit	firm
hurt	furniture	learning	heard
perfume	third	pearl	personal

dirty

Say and Listen

Say each spelling word. Listen for the /ûr/ sound you hear in *skirt*.

Think and Sort

Look at the letters in each word. Think about how /ûr/ is spelled. Spell each word aloud.

How many spelling patterns for /ûr/ do you see?

1. Write the **six** spelling words that have the *er* pattern, like *permit*.
2. Write the **five** spelling words that have the *ir* pattern, like *skirt*.
3. Write the **four** spelling words that have the *ur* pattern, like *hurt*.
4. Write the **five** spelling words that have the *ear* pattern, like *pearl*.

1. **er** Words
_____ _____ _____
_____ _____ _____

2. **ir** Words
_____ _____ _____
_____ _____

3. **ur** Words
_____ _____ _____
_____

4. **ear** Words
_____ _____ _____
_____ _____

Classifying

Write the spelling word that belongs in each group.

1. fragrance, scent, _____

2. sure, positive, _____

3. spotless, flawless, _____

4. eleven, twelve, _____

5. private, inner, _____

6. late, on time, _____

7. researching, studying, _____

8. curtains, rugs, _____

9. supply, provide, _____

10. allow, let, _____

11. assistance, help, _____

12. aim, goal, _____

13. solid, hard, _____

Rhymes

Write the spelling word that completes each sentence and rhymes with the underlined word.

14. There are <u>thirty</u> _____ shirts in the laundry.

15. I need to <u>learn</u> some ways to _____ money.

16. We _____ a <u>bird</u> singing in a tree.

17. Carmen wore a yellow <u>shirt</u> that matched her _____.

18. The <u>girl</u> found a huge white _____ in the oyster.

19. Mr. <u>Byrd</u> lives in the _____ house on the left.

skirt	purpose	earn	certain
dirty	service	furnish	early
thirteen	perfect	permit	firm
hurt	furniture	learning	heard
perfume	third	pearl	personal

Proofreading

Proofread the letter below. Use proofreading marks to correct five spelling mistakes, two punctuation mistakes, and three unnecessary words.

Proofreading Marks

◯ spell correctly
⊙ add period
℘ take out

295 Hill Drive

Billings, MT 59102

September 9, 2004

Dear Aunt Libby,

Mom told me that when you were thurteen, you did extra

chores for money She said your perpose was to to buy Grandma

Dora a sertain kind of pirfume. The day you you bought it,

Uncle Benny spilled the whole bottle on Grandma's skurt What

a smell it must have made!

I'm trying to earn money to buy a gift for Mom. Do you you

have any ideas for me?

Love,

Madison

Language Connection

Adjectives

An adjective describes a noun or pronoun by telling which one, what kind, or how many.

> A **colorful** bird was singing in the **old** tree.
>
> A **big fat** cat scared it away.

The following sentences contain adjectives and misspelled words. Write the sentences, spelling the misspelled words correctly and underlining the adjectives.

1. We made new ferniture for the treehouse.

_____

2. I herd there is a fantastic movie downtown.

_____

3. The urly bird catches the worm.

_____

4. I'd like to fernish my room with large green plants.

_____

5. I hert my foot when I dropped the heavy suitcase.

_____

6. Jennifer wants a perl necklace for her birthday.

_____

Words with /âr/ or /är/

share	charge	discharge	aware
harvest	prepare	fare	alarm
farther	stare	carefully	starve
margin	depart	declare	compare
square	marbles	apartment	bare

marbles

Say and Listen

Say each spelling word. Listen for the /âr/ sounds you hear in *share* and the /är/ sounds you hear in *charge*.

Think and Sort

Look at the letters in each word. Think about how /âr/ or /är/ is spelled. Spell each word aloud.

How many spelling patterns for /âr/ and /är/ do you see?

1. Write the **ten** spelling words that have /âr/, like *share*. Circle the letters that spell /âr/.

2. Write the **ten** spelling words that have /är/, like *charge*. Circle the letters that spell /är/.

1. **/âr/ Words**

_____ _____ _____

_____ _____ _____

_____ _____ _____

_____

2. **/är/ Words**

_____ _____ _____

_____ _____ _____

_____ _____ _____

_____

Making Connections

Complete each sentence with the spelling word that goes with the underlined group of people.

1. <u>Firefighters</u> respond to a fire _____.

2. <u>Children</u> often play the game of _____.

3. <u>Doctors</u> _____ well hospital patients.

4. <u>Bus drivers</u> collect a _____ from each passenger.

5. <u>Math teachers</u> teach about the triangle and the _____.

Clues

Write the spelling word for each clue.

6. This word describes feet without shoes or socks. _____

7. People do this with their eyes. _____

8. Without food, people and animals do this. _____

9. It's good to do this for a test. _____

10. This is how you should handle sharp things. _____

11. People do this to see how things are alike. _____

12. This is the outer edge of paper. _____

13. People do this when they take part of something. _____

14. This word is the opposite of *nearer.* _____

15. If you know there is danger ahead, you are this. _____

16. This is a type of home. _____

17. A bull does this when it sees a waving cape. _____

18. Trains do this when they leave the station. _____

19. If you announce, you do this. _____

share	charge	discharge	aware
harvest	prepare	fare	alarm
farther	stare	carefully	starve
margin	depart	declare	compare
square	marbles	apartment	bare

Proofreading

Proofread this paragraph from a travel article. Use proofreading marks to correct five spelling mistakes, three capitalization mistakes, and two unnecessary words.

Proofreading Marks

◯ spell correctly
≡ capitalize
ℓ take out

Sonoran Scenes

a trip through the Sonoran Desert in arizona is an amazing experience. You don't have to travel far into this national treasure to become awair of its beauty. Nothing can compair to to the rich colors and gorgeous sunsets. The the flat landscape spreads farthur than the eye can see. although the land appears baer, it does have a variety of plant and animal life. But it is hot. You must prepaar for the dry and scorching heat. Tour guides constantly remind visitors to bring lots of water.

Dictionary Skills

Multiple Meanings

Some words can be used as different parts of speech and may have more than one meaning. The dictionary entries for these words list the parts of speech and different definitions.

Study the dictionary entry below.

> **a·larm** (ə lärm') *n.* **1.** Sudden fear caused by a feeling of danger: *The animals ran away in alarm.* **2.** A warning that danger is near. **3.** A warning signal, such as a bell: *The alarm woke me up too early.* —*v.* **a·larmed, a·larm·ing.** To frighten.

Use a dictionary to identify the part of speech for the underlined word in each sentence. Then write the number of the definition.

1. The fire <u>alarm</u> rang out in the night. _____ _____

2. The club asked Maria to be in <u>charge</u> of fundraising. _____ _____

3. The town <u>square</u> is filled with beautiful green trees. _____ _____

4. Please <u>share</u> the cookies with all the children. _____ _____

5. The farmers had an early <u>harvest</u> last year. _____ _____

6. The train will <u>depart</u> at noon. _____ _____

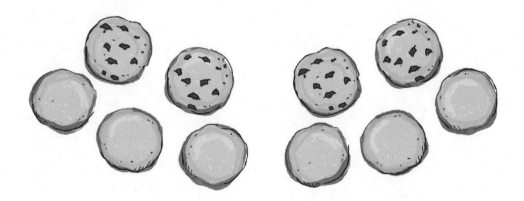

Compound Words

thunderstorm	strawberry	birthday	sailboat
cheeseburger	hallway	nightmare	notebook
upset	cartwheel	flashlight	chalkboard
grasshopper	suitcase	sawdust	uproar
weekend	homework	blueberry	breakfast

Say and Listen

Remember that a syllable is a word part or a word with one vowel sound. Say each spelling word. Listen for the number of syllables.

sailboat

Think and Sort

Each of the spelling words is a **compound word**. Because a compound word is made from two words, it has at least two syllables.

Look at the syllables in each word. Think about how each syllable is spelled. Spell each word aloud.

1. Write the **fifteen** spelling words that have two syllables, like *up-set*.

2. Write the **five** spelling words that have three syllables, like *grass-hop-per*.

1. Two-syllable Words

_____   _____   _____

_____   _____   _____

_____   _____   _____

_____   _____   _____

_____   _____   _____

2. Three-syllable Words

_____   _____   _____

_____   _____

Definitions

Write the spelling word for each definition.

1. the first meal of the day _____
2. a surface to write on with chalk _____
3. a hamburger with cheese _____
4. loud noise _____
5. bits of wood left over after sawing _____
6. a passageway, a walkway, or a corridor _____
7. a small red fruit with many seeds _____
8. a storm that includes lightning and thunder _____
9. a boat powered by wind _____
10. to cause someone to be worried or disturbed _____
11. schoolwork done at home or away from school _____
12. a very small blue fruit that grows on bushes _____

Compound Words

Write the spelling word that is made from the two underlined words in each sentence.

13. Sam's <u>book</u> has a <u>note</u> in it. _____
14. Dad's black <u>case</u> holds a <u>suit</u> and six pairs of jeans. _____
15. The insect in the <u>grass</u> was a <u>hopper</u>, not a crawler. _____
16. What is the <u>day</u> of your <u>birth</u>? _____
17. At the <u>end</u> of next <u>week</u>, we are going on a camping trip. _____
18. The <u>mare</u> whinnied loudly all <u>night</u>. _____
19. The clown hopped over the <u>wheel</u> of the popcorn <u>cart</u>. _____

thunderstorm	*strawberry*	*birthday*	*sailboat*
cheeseburger	*hallway*	*nightmare*	*notebook*
upset	*cartwheel*	*flashlight*	*chalkboard*
grasshopper	*suitcase*	*sawdust*	*uproar*
weekend	*homework*	*blueberry*	*breakfast*

Proofreading

Proofread this excerpt from a restaurant review. Use proofreading marks to correct five spelling mistakes, three capitalization mistakes, and two punctuation mistakes.

Proofreading Marks
◯ spell correctly
≡ capitalize
⊙ add period

Restaurant Review

The Dew drop Inn is a wonderful place to eat Several friends suggested that I eat there and try the bluerry pancakes. Last wekend was my birthday, so my mother and I ate brekkfast there. The pancakes were melt-in-your-mouth moist, and the strawbury jam was delicious. just as I was jotting my thoughts in my noetbook, the waiters came out and sang "Happy birthday" to me This restaurant is a good place to go for both food and fun!

Language Connection

Possessive Nouns

A possessive noun is a noun that shows possession, or ownership. To form the possessive of a singular noun, add -'s. To form the possessive of a plural noun that ends in s, add only an apostrophe. If a plural noun does not end in s, add -'s to form the possessive.

Singular Possessive Nouns	Plural Possessive Nouns
Sam's notebook	the boys' homework
the mouse's fur	the women's sailboat

The sentences below contain apostrophe errors and spelling errors. Write each sentence correctly.

1. Lings flashlite was lying by the door.

_____

2. The mens' chessburgers came quickly.

_____

3. The childrens pet grasshoper was in a cage.

_____

4. Mrs. Sperrys' chalkbored was clean.

_____

5. The six performers cartwheals were magnificent.

_____

Space Words

shuttle	celestial	astronomy	revolution
comet	galaxy	axis	orbit
meteors	motion	universe	light-year
solar	rotation	telescope	asteroids
eclipse	satellite	constellation	lunar

Say and Listen

Say each spelling word. Listen for the number of syllables.

comet

Think and Sort

Look at the syllables in each word. Think about how each syllable is spelled. Spell each word aloud.

How many syllables does each word have?

1. Write the **nine** spelling words that have two syllables, like *so-lar.*

2. Write the **eight** spelling words that have three syllables, like *u-ni-verse.*

3. Write the **three** spelling words that have four syllables, like *as-tron-o-my.*

1. Two-syllable Words

_____ _____ _____

_____ _____ _____

_____ _____ _____

2. Three-syllable Words

_____ _____ _____

_____ _____ _____

_____ _____ _____

3. Four-syllable Words

_____ _____ _____

Classifying

Write the spelling word that belongs in each group.

1. meteor, asteroid, _____
2. mathematics, geology, _____
3. rotation, single turn, _____
4. rocket, spaceship, _____
5. microscope, gyroscope, _____

Clues

Write the spelling word for each clue.

6. the turning of Earth _____
7. a measure of distance in space _____
8. a straight line around which Earth turns _____
9. having to do with the sun _____
10. having to do with the moon _____
11. a kind of star formation _____
12. the path a planet travels around the sun _____
13. a man-made object that orbits Earth _____
14. shooting stars _____
15. relating to the heavens or skies _____
16. the Milky Way _____
17. Earth, space, and all things in it _____
18. occurs when light from the sun is cut off _____
19. a synonym for *movement* _____

shuttle	celestial	astronomy	revolution
comet	galaxy	axis	orbit
meteors	motion	universe	light-year
solar	rotation	telescope	asteroids
eclipse	satellite	constellation	lunar

Proofreading

Proofread this paragraph from an essay. Use proofreading marks to correct five spelling mistakes, three capitalization mistakes, and two punctuation mistakes.

Proofreading Marks

⟠ spell correctly
≡ capitalize
? add question mark

Space travel Far from Earth

Did you ever wonder if we could really reach other solur systems Other stars are at least a liteyear away. a space shuttel traveling to another star would face many problems. it could crash into astoroids. It might not be able to carry enough fuel for the trip. But perhaps it could reach another galixy. What kinds of great discoveries might we make Perhaps we would find new planets with different types of animals and plants.

Language Connection

Greek and Latin Word Parts

Many English words come from Greek and Latin word parts. For example, *telescope* comes from the Greek word *tele.* Complete the chart below by writing the missing words.

Word Part	Meaning	Word	Meaning
tele	distant; far away	telescope	an instrument for viewing faraway things
uni	one	_____	everything in existence; Earth, the heavens, and all of space
		_____	an imaginary animal that looks like a white horse with a single horn on its forehead
		_____	a vehicle with one wheel
		_____	a special set of clothes that identifies the wearer as a member of one group
		_____	to make one; combine
ast	star	_____	the many small rocky bodies revolving around the sun, mainly between Mars and Jupiter
		_____	the science that deals with the sun, moon, stars, planets, and other heavenly bodies
		_____	a person who travels in a spacecraft to outer space
		_____	a star-shaped garden flower

unit 5 Review
LESSONS 21-25

LESSON 21

perform
fortunate
orchard
quarrel
course
board

More Words with /ô/

Write the spelling word that matches each definition.

1. a flat piece of lumber _____
2. lucky _____
3. a path or direction _____
4. to do something _____
5. to argue _____
6. an area where fruit trees grow _____

LESSON 22

certain
service
perfect
firm
furniture
pearl

Words with /ûr/

Write the spelling word for each clue.

7. People can sleep or sit on this. _____

8. People are this when they are really sure.

   _____

9. This describes something that is hard or solid.

   _____

10. This can be found inside some oysters.

    _____

11. This is the kind of score students like to get on a test.

    _____

12. When someone does something useful, he or she
    provides this. _____

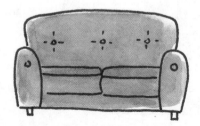

Lesson 23

prepare
carefully
declare
compare
marbles
apartment
starve
margin

Lesson 24

suitcase
nightmare

Lesson 25

celestial
meteors
astronomy

Words with /âr/ and /är/

Write the spelling word that completes each analogy.

13. *Rehearse* is to *play* as _____ is to *dinner*.

14. *Quickly* is to *slowly* as *carelessly* is to _____.

15. *Ask* is to *question* as _____ is to *statement*.

16. *Shoot* is to _____ as *throw* is to *darts*.

17. *Stuff* is to _____ as *swell* is to *shrink*.

18. *Middle* is to *center* as *edge* is to _____.

19. *Stall* is to *horse* as _____ is to *person*.

20. *Different* is to *similar* as *contrast* is to _____.

Compound Words

Write the spelling word that completes each sentence.

21. Beth's _____ was the worst dream she'd ever had.

22. Jason forgot his black _____ at the airport.

Space Words

Write the spelling word that answers each question.

23. What might you see falling toward Earth from outer space? _____

24. The moon and the stars are what kind of bodies? _____

25. What is the science of the sun, moon, and planets? _____

Words with /ə/

season	beautiful	perhaps	dangerous	again
citrus	ocean	canoe	banana	against
approve	chorus	qualify	mosquito	surprise
industry	cousin	government	memory	comfort

Say and Listen

Say the spelling words. Listen for the unstressed syllables with the weak vowel sound you hear at the end of *season*.

citrus

Think and Sort

The weak vowel sound in unstressed syllables is shown as /ə/. It is called **schwa**. Some words have one /ə/; others have more than one.

Look at the letters in each word. Think about how /ə/ is spelled. Spell each word aloud.

1. **Four** spelling words have two /ə/ sounds, like *banana*. Write these words and circle the letter or letters that spell each /ə/ sound.

2. Write the **five** words with /ə/ spelled *a*, like *again*.

3. Write the **one** word with /ə/ spelled *e*.

4. Write the **two** words with /ə/ spelled *i*, like *cousin*.

5. Write the **four** words with /ə/ spelled *o*, like *season*.

6. Write the **four** words with /ə/ spelled *u*, like *citrus*.

1. Two /ə/ Sounds

_____   _____   _____

_____

2. /ə/ Words with a

_____   _____   _____

_____   _____

3. /ə/ Word with e   4. /ə/ Words with i

_____   _____   _____

5. /ə/ Words with o

_____   _____   _____

_____

6. /ə/ Words with u

_____   _____   _____

_____

Synonyms

Write the spelling word that is a synonym for each word below.

1. choir   _____

2. maybe   _____

3. risky   _____

4. shock   _____

5. pretty   _____

6. soothe   _____

7. authorize   _____

Definitions

Write the spelling word for each definition.
Use a dictionary if you need to.

8. a large body of salt water   _____

9. once more   _____

10. the group of people who rule a city, state, or country   _____

11. a long yellow fruit   _____

12. to show enough ability or skill in   _____

13. the ability to remember   _____

14. a small flying insect with long legs   _____

15. one of the four parts of a year   _____

16. a daughter or a son of an aunt or an uncle   _____

17. belonging to orange or lemon trees   _____

18. in an opposite direction   _____

19. business, trade, and manufacturing   _____

season	ocean	qualify	memory
citrus	chorus	government	again
approve	cousin	dangerous	against
industry	perhaps	banana	surprise
beautiful	canoe	mosquito	comfort

Proofreading

Proofread this paragraph from a tourist brochure. Use proofreading marks to correct five spelling mistakes, two words that are out of order, and one unnecessary word.

Proofreading Marks

○ spell correctly
∼ trade places
℮ take out

Maine a is beautyful state in any seasen, but fall is a truly spectacular time of year. Although the state has been given the nickname "the Pine Tree State," Maine is home to many trees whose leaves turn color every autumn. Drive along tree-lined streets and gaze in wunder at the brilliant colors the of foliage. Stand along the edge of the ocian and watch the waves crash agenst the shore. Maine will delight and surprise you. Come see why Maine is the the jewel of the Northeast.

Language Connection

Titles

Capitalize the first word, the last word, and all other important words in a title. Underline titles of books, movies, magazines, television programs, and newspapers. Put quotation marks around titles of short works such as book chapters, stories, poems, songs, and magazine articles.

> <u>James and the Giant Peach</u>   "How to Get Organized"

The words in parentheses after each title tell what kind of title it is. Write each title correctly.

1. a beautiful memory (book chapter)

_____

2. highlights (magazine)

_____

3. chicago tribune (newspaper)

_____

4. the canoe (book)

_____

5. computer tips for kids (magazine article)

_____

6. industry and the canadian government (book)

_____

7. stopping by woods on a snowy evening (poem)

_____

Words with /əl/

nickel	whistle	general	simple
animal	final	pickles	trouble
double	puzzle	natural	tumble
barrel	tremble	musical	example
sample	wrinkle	couple	signal

Say and Listen

Say each spelling word. Listen for the /əl/ sounds you hear at the end of *nickel*.

nickel

Think and Sort

Look at the letters in each word. Think about how /əl/ is spelled. Spell each word aloud. How many spelling patterns for /əl/ do you see?

1. Write the **six** spelling words that have /əl/ spelled *al*, like *final*.

2. Write the **two** spelling words that have /əl/ spelled *el*, like *nickel*.

3. Write the **twelve** spelling words that have /əl/ spelled *le*, like *double*.

1. /əl/ Words with **al**

_____   _____   _____

_____   _____   _____

2. /əl/ Words with **el**

_____   _____

3. /əl/ Words with **le**

_____   _____   _____

_____   _____   _____

_____   _____   _____

_____   _____   _____

Clues

Write the spelling word for each clue.

1. small cucumbers   _____
2. something to copy or imitate   _____
3. a sign   _____
4. twice as much of something   _____
5. a game or a riddle to solve   _____
6. to try a small piece   _____
7. a sound made by blowing air out   _____
8. a movie with songs   _____
9. not specific   _____
10. not fake   _____
11. a five-cent coin   _____

Synonyms

Write the spelling word that is a synonym for the underlined word.

12. We watched the book <u>fall</u> down the stairs.   _____
13. One <u>creature</u> at the zoo was very strange.   _____
14. Jamal could not answer the <u>last</u> question.   _____
15. The pioneer collected rainwater in a large <u>keg</u>.   _____
16. Jack and Jill are a well-known <u>pair</u>.   _____
17. Most people think playing checkers is <u>easy</u>.   _____
18. My dad had a lot of <u>difficulty</u> changing the flat tire.   _____
19. The cold weather made the crossing guard <u>shiver</u>.   _____

nickel	whistle	general	simple
animal	final	pickles	trouble
double	puzzle	natural	tumble
barrel	tremble	musical	example
sample	wrinkle	couple	signal

Proofreading

Proofread the newspaper article below. Use proofreading marks to correct five spelling mistakes, three capitalization errors, and two words that are out of order.

Proofreading Marks

⬭ spell correctly
☰ capitalize
∿ trade places

Marbletown Tribune

Friday, october 13, 2004

The Marbletown police responded to a call late Thursday night from the manager the at generel store on bank Street. The manager reported that a couple things of had been stolen—a jar of pickles and a jigsaw puzzel. This was not the first time the manager had reported trubble at the store. Last week a dog collar and a wistle were taken from the pet display. Marbletown Police Chief marvin Cates stated that this was not a simpal case that could be solved quickly.

Adverbs

An adverb is a part of speech that tells how, when, where, or in what way. Adverbs tell more about verbs, adjectives, and other adverbs.

> Lauren skates **gracefully.**   Her brother dances **beautifully.**

Write the sentences below, underlining the adverbs.

1. We tremble excitedly.

_____

2. All of the animals wait obediently.

_____

3. A couple of people busily sell souvenirs.

_____

4. Suddenly the signal is given.

_____

5. Each animal steps quickly.

_____

6. The circus parade marches noisily.

_____

7. Two tall clowns dance happily.

_____

Words with /ər/

teacher	similar	actor	center
toaster	calendar	rather	character
humor	whether	discover	answer
another	silver	cellar	gather
member	polar	master	sugar

Say and Listen

Say each spelling word. Listen for the /ər/ sound you hear at the end of *teacher*.

discover

Think and Sort

Look at the letters in each word. Think about how /ər/ is spelled. Spell each word aloud. How many spelling patterns for /ər/ do you see?

1. Write the **thirteen** spelling words that have /ər/ spelled *er*, like *teacher*.

2. Write the **two** spelling words that have /ər/ spelled *or*, like *humor*.

3. Write the **five** spelling words that have /ər/ spelled *ar*, like *sugar*.

---

1. /ər/ Words with er

_____   _____   _____

_____   _____   _____

_____   _____   _____

_____   _____   _____

_____

2. /ər/ Words with or

_____   _____

3. /ər/ Words with ar

_____   _____   _____

_____   _____

Classifying

Write the spelling word that belongs in each group.

1. salt, flour, _____

2. alike, same, _____

3. funniness, comedy, _____

4. gold, copper, _____

5. middle, core, _____

6. some other, one more, _____

7. reply, response, _____

8. plot, setting, _____

Analogies

Write the spelling word that completes each analogy.

9. *Basement* is to _____ as *car* is to *automobile.*

10. *Driver* is to *drive* as _____ is to *teach.*

11. *Violinist* is to *orchestra* as _____ is to *play.*

12. *Student* is to *learner* as *expert* is to _____.

13. *If* is to _____ as *comment* is to *remark.*

14. *Hot* is to *tropical* as *cold* is to _____.

15. *Bird* is to *flock* as _____ is to *club.*

16. *Heat* is to _____ as *chill* is to *refrigerator.*

17. *Recover* is to *recovery* as _____ is to *discovery.*

18. *Lake* is to *rake* as *lather* is to _____.

19. *Collect* is to _____ as *scatter* is to *spread.*

teacher	similar	actor	center
toaster	calendar	rather	character
humor	whether	discover	answer
another	silver	cellar	gather
member	polar	master	sugar

Proofreading

Proofread the e-mail below. Use proofreading marks to correct five spelling mistakes, three capitalization mistakes, and two punctuation mistakes.

Proofreading Marks

◯ spell correctly

≡ capitalize

⊙ add period

---

e-mail

New	Read	File	Delete	Search	Contacts	Check

hi, Jenny,

Guess what! I am taking dance lessons! For a long time, I didn't know wether I wanted to be an actor or a dancer The careers are similur because in both you perform for an audience. I finally decided I would rathur dance, even though ballet is hard to mastor. my mother found me a good ballet teacher. i take lessons three days a week at the ballet centur

Maria

Dictionary Skills

Idioms

An idiom is a phrase that cannot be understood by using the meanings of its individual words. In a dictionary, an idiom is sometimes listed at the end of the entry for the main word in the idiom. For example, the idiom in the following sentence is defined in the entry for *blood*.

You **make my blood boil** when you say things like that!

blood (blŭd) *n.* **1.** The red liquid that is pumped through the body by the heart. **2.** Family relationship: *My cousin and I are related by blood.* *Idioms.* **make one's blood boil.** To anger. **make one's blood run cold.** To frighten.

Each of the following sentences contains an idiom in dark type. Try to guess the meaning of each. Use a dictionary to help you.

1. I am **racking my brains** for the name of that movie.

_____

2. John won't answer me because he's feeling **under the weather**.

_____

3. I know he'll help me **right away** when he feels better.

_____

4. Mom says I need to **set an example** for my little brother.

_____

Words with /shən/

action	information	education	location
nation	inspection	vacation	pollution
invention	population	section	election
direction	collection	transportation	instruction
fraction	selection	mention	station

Say and Listen

Say each spelling word. Listen for the /shən/ sounds
you hear in the second syllable of *action*.

Think and Sort

fraction

$\frac{1}{6}$

Look at the letters in each word. Think about how /shən/
is spelled. Spell each word aloud.

1. Many words end in /shən/. The /shən/ sounds are
   almost always spelled *tion*. Write the **eleven** spelling words that have a
   consonant before /shən/, like *action*.

2. Many words have a vowel sound before /shən/. Write the **nine** spelling words
   that have a vowel sound before /shən/, like *information*.

---

1. Consonant + /shən/ Words

_____   _____   _____

_____   _____   _____

_____   _____   _____

_____   _____

2. Vowel + /shən/ Words

_____   _____   _____

_____   _____   _____

_____

Definitions

Write the spelling word for each definition.

1. a stop on a bus or train route _____
2. rest time from school or work _____
3. the number of people living in a given place _____
4. an independent country _____
5. part of a whole _____
6. to briefly speak about _____
7. the act of choosing from a group _____
8. facts about a specific subject _____
9. a separated part _____
10. the means of moving from place to place _____

Base-Word Clues

Complete each sentence by writing the spelling word
that is formed from the base word in dark type.

11. Electricity was a great _____. **invent**
12. Going to college continues your _____. **educate**
13. Ming has stamps from Italy in his _____. **collect**
14. Some rivers and lakes have been spoiled by _____. **pollute**
15. The soldiers stood at attention during _____. **inspect**
16. The science fiction movie was packed with _____. **act**
17. Elena's tutor gave her extra _____. **instruct**
18. No one knows the _____ of the treasure. **locate**
19. In which _____ should we walk? **direct**

action	information	education	location
nation	inspection	vacation	pollution
invention	population	section	election
direction	collection	transportation	instruction
fraction	selection	mention	station

Proofreading

Proofread the announcement below. Use proofreading marks to correct five spelling mistakes, three capitalization mistakes, and two unnecessary words.

Proofreading Marks

◯ spell correctly
≡ capitalize
⌿ take out

Pollution Solution Meeting Tonight

Tonight at City Hall, mayor Jim Bond will discuss polution in in our city. Interested citizens are invited to attend. the mayor will mension plans to provide better clean-environment educasion for the entire popullation. School Superintendent Cliff Clayton and several school principals will outline the details. Anyone with ideas for further acttion that will ensure a cleaner, healthier environment is welcome to to speak. the meeting will be held from 7:00 to 8:00 P.M. A panel discussion hosted by the Sierra Club will follow.

Colons

Use a colon between the hour and the minutes in expressions of time. Also use a colon after a word that introduces a series, or a list.

> The bus will leave the station at 9:30 A.M.
>
> The bus will stop in the following cities: Omaha, Wahoo, and Lincoln.

Write each time correctly.

1. 630 _____   **2.** 1210 _____

3. 245 _____   **4.** 905 _____

Write the sentences below, using colons correctly.

5. Some of the world's best inventions include the following the wheel, the gasoline engine, the telephone, and pizza.

_____

_____

6. Three candidates are running for election Mayor Hibbs, Mrs. Gold, and Mr. Santos.

_____

_____

7. Three topics will be covered on our test pollution, transportation, and population.

_____

_____

Homophones

road	waist	right	its
hole	whole	write	plain
waste	threw	plane	their
to	it's	there	through
too	rode	they're	two

plane

Say and Listen

Say each spelling word. Listen for the words that sound alike.

Think and Sort

All of the spelling words in this lesson are homophones. **Homophones** are words that sound alike but have different meanings.

Look at the letters in each word. Think about how the word is spelled. Spell each word aloud.

1. Write the **fourteen** spelling words that are homophone pairs, like *road* and *rode*.

2. Write the **six** spelling words that are homophone triplets, like *their*, *there* and *they're*.

1. Homophone Pairs

_____   _____   _____

_____   _____   _____

_____   _____   _____

_____   _____   _____

_____

2. Homophone Triplets

_____   _____   _____

_____   _____   _____

Clues

Write the spelling word for each clue.

1. A doughnut has this in the middle. _____

2. This word is another word for *street*. _____

3. This word is the opposite of *caught*. _____

4. This word is the possessive form of *it*. _____

5. You do this with a pen or a pencil. _____

6. This word is the opposite of *wrong*. _____

7. You can use *also* instead of this word. _____

8. If you have a pair, you have this many. _____

9. This word is a contraction for *they are*. _____

10. This word is the possessive form of *they*. _____

11. Belts go around this part of the body. _____

12. Something that is simple is this. _____

13. This word is a contraction for *it is*. _____

14. This is a large machine that flies through the air. _____

Rhymes

Write the spelling word that completes each sentence and rhymes
with the underlined word.

15. The _____ <u>bowl</u> was filled with pretzels.

16. Our <u>crew</u> was the first to paddle _____ the tunnel.

17. He _____ away after he <u>showed</u> us his new bike.

18. Do not go _____ the <u>zoo</u> without me!

19. Tracey got her <u>hair</u> cut over _____.

road	waist	right	its
hole	whole	write	plain
waste	threw	plane	their
to	it's	there	through
too	rode	they're	two

Proofreading

Proofread the book review below. Use proofreading marks to correct five homophone mistakes, three capitalization mistakes, and two words that are out of order.

Proofreading Marks

◯ spell correctly
≡ capitalize
∼ trade places

Wise Words of Warning

In there new book called <u>It's Not Too late</u>, Jarod Marks and emily Davis right that the future the of hole world depends our on stopping the waist of natural resources.

Marks and Davis list hundreds of actions people can take every day to help. for example, turning off the water while we brush our teeth can save millions of gallons of water per day. Marks and Davis say they're is still time to save our planet. Read <u>It's Not Too Late</u>. It can change your life and the world we live in.

Dictionary Skills

Using the Spelling Table

A spelling table can help you find the spelling of a word in a dictionary. Suppose you are not sure how the vowel sound in *prove* is spelled. You can use a spelling table to find the different spellings for the sound. First, find the pronunciation symbol for the sound. Then read the first spelling listed for /o͞o/, and look up *proo* words in a dictionary. Look for each spelling in the dictionary until you find the correct one.

Sound	Spellings	Examples
/o͞o/	oo ew u u_e ue o o_e oe ou ui	loose, grew, truth, presume, clue, whom, prove, shoe, soup, fruit

Write the correct spelling for each word. Use the Spelling Table on page 265 and a dictionary.

1. /gŏlf/ _____
2. /klo͞o/ _____
3. /dĭ **stroi′**/ _____
4. /ûrn/ _____
5. /pə **līt′**/ _____
6. /sēj/ _____
7. /pĭ **kän′**/ _____
8. /ē′ zəl/ _____
9. /fyo͞od/ _____
10. /kōd/ _____

unit 6 Review
Lessons 26-30

LESSON 26 — Words with /ə/

ocean
against
surprise
mosquito
beautiful
dangerous

Write the spelling word that completes each sentence.

1. We ended our day at the beach by watching a _____ sunset.
2. My birthday party was a complete _____ .
3. Driving in a blizzard can be very _____ .
4. A _____ buzzed in my ear all night long.
5. If you want to go deep-sea fishing, you must travel out on the _____ .
6. Push firmly _____ the door to open it.

LESSON 27 — Words with /əl/

general
natural
barrel
couple
example

Write the spelling word for each definition.

7. a large, round wooden container _____
8. made by nature _____
9. two of a kind; a pair _____
10. common to most people _____
11. a sample or a model _____

LESSON 28 — Words with /ər/

character
whether
humor
similar
calendar

Write the spelling word for each clue.

12. This word means "like something else." _____
13. Comedians use this to entertain an audience.

    _____
14. This can help you keep track of the date. _____

15. This is a person in a book, movie, or play.

_____

16. _If_ is a synonym for this word. _____

LESSON 29

invention
direction
collection
education

Words with /shən/

Write the spelling word that completes each analogy.

17. _Collect_ is to _____ as _select_ is to _selection_.

18. _College_ is to _____ as _hospital_ is to _operation_.

19. _Eight_ is to _number_ as _north_ is to _____ .

20. _Planet_ is to _discovery_ as _light bulb_ is to _____ .

LESSON 30

its
it's
their
there
they're

Homophones

Write the spelling word that belongs in each group.

21. we're, you're, _____

22. she's, he's, _____

23. our, your, _____

24. his, hers, _____

25. where, here, _____

commonly misspelled words

again	except	other	through
a lot	exciting	outside	today
always	family	people	together
another	favorite	piece	tomorrow
beautiful	finally	please	too
because	first	pretty	tried
been	friend	probably	until
before	friends	read	upon
beginning	getting	really	usually
believe	goes	right	vacation
birthday	guess	said	very
bought	happened	scared	want
buy	heard	school	weird
children	himself	sent	were
clothes	hospital	should	we're
come	house	since	when
cousin	into	some	where
decided	it's	sometimes	which
different	know	surprise	whole
doesn't	little	their	would
eighth	many	there	write
enough	might	they	writing
especially	morning	they're	wrote
every	myself	though	your
everyone	once	threw	you're

spelling Table

Sound	Spellings	Examples	Sound	Spellings	Examples
/ă/	a ai au	rapid, plaid, aunt	/ŏ/	o a	shock, watch
/ā/	a a_e ai ay ea eigh ey	bakery, snake, brain, delay, break, weigh, surveyor	/ō/	o o_e oa oe ou ough ow ew	hero, code, boast, toe, boulder, dough, throw, sew
/ä/	a	pecan	/oi/	oi oy	coin, enjoy
/âr/	are air ere eir	aware, fair, there, their	/ô/	a au aw o ough o_e ou oa	already, autumn, raw, often, thought, score, court, roar
/b/	b bb	bench, hobby			
/ch/	ch tch t	orchard, watch, amateur	/o͝o/	oo o ou u	rookie, wolf, could, education
/d/	d dd	dawn, meddle			
/ĕ/	e ea a ai ie ue	bench, health, many, again, friend, guess	/o͞o/	oo ew u u_e ue o o_e oe ou ui	loose, grew, truth, presume, clue, whom, prove, shoe, soup, fruit
/ē/	e e_e ea ee ei eo ey i ie y	female, theme, weak, greet, deceive, people, monkey, ski, believe, tardy	/ou/	ou ow	ours, towel
			/p/	p pp	party, grasshopper
/f/	f ff gh ph	film, different, laugh, elephant	/r/	r rr wr	raw, tomorrow, wrong
			/s/	s ss c	solid, message, century
/g/	g gg	golf, jogging	/sh/	sh s ce ci	wishes, sugar, ocean, special
/h/	h wh	here, whole			
/ĭ/	i a e ee u ui y	riddle, damage, relax, been, business, build, mystery	/shən/	tion	competition
			/t/	t tt ed	too, bottom, thanked
			/th/	th	though
/ī/	i i_e ie igh uy y eye	climb, quite, die, right, buy, recycle, eye	/th/	th	think
			/ŭ/	u o o_e oe oo ou	crush, dozen, become, does, blood, touch
/îr/	er ear eer eir ere yr	periodical, hear, cheer, weird, here, lyrics	/ûr/	ear er ere ir or our ur	earn, certain, were, firm, world, flourish, curve
/j/	j g dg	jot, gentle, pledge			
/k/	k c ck ch	kitchen, canoe, chicken, character	/v/	v f	vote, of
			/w/	w wh o	wish, wheat, once
/ks/	x	expert	/y/	y	yolk
/kw/	qu	quick	/yo͞o/	eau eu u u_e	beautiful, feud, mutual, use
/l/	l ll	library, pollution			
/m/	m mb mm mn	male, comb, common, condemn	/z/	z zz s	zone, quizzical, busy
			/zh/	s	treasure
/n/	n kn nn	needle, knife, pinnacle	/ə/	a e i o u	against, elephant, furniture, actor, beautiful
/ng/	n ng	wrinkle, skating			

Math
Skills

unit 1
whole numbers

Place Value

A **place-value chart** can help you understand **whole numbers**.
Each **digit** in a number has a value based on its place in the number.

The 7 is in the millions place.
Its value is 7 millions or 7,000,000.
The 5 is in the ten-thousands place.
Its value is 5 ten thousands or 50,000.
The 3 is in the hundreds place.
Its value is 3 hundreds or 300.

hundred millions	ten millions	millions	hundred thousands	ten thousands	thousands	hundreds	tens	ones
		7,	6	5	4,	3	2	1

Write each number in the place-value chart.

1. 366,789,302

2. 2,304,361

3. 19,076,541

4. 8,854,632

5. 97,065

6. 8,005,002

	hundred millions	ten millions	millions	hundred thousands	ten thousands	thousands	hundreds	tens	ones
1.	3	6	6,	7	8	9,	3	0	2
2.			2,	3	0	4,	3	6	1
3.		1	9,	0	7	6,	5	4	1
4.		1	8,	8	5	4,	6	3	2
5.					9,	7	0	6	5
6.			8,	0	0	5,	0	0	2

Write the place name for the 5 in each number.

           a

7. 362,050 _____ tens _____   2,250,876 _____ ten thousands _____

8. 219,572,080 _____ hundred thousands _____   5,712,309 _____ Millions _____

9. 876,529 _____ hundreds _____   1,804,075 _____ Ones _____

10. 15,782 _____ thousands _____   53,047,260 _____ ten Millions _____

Write the value of the underlined digit.

           a   b

11. 1,390,526 _____ 0 thousands _____   207,389 _____

12. 983,576,091 _____ 8 hundred millions _____   4,523,551 _____

13. 450,086 _____ 4 Hundred thousands _____   232,875 _____

14. 172,034,056 _____ 1 hundred Millions _____   67,043 _____

Reading and Writing Numbers

Comiskey Park and Wrigley Field are baseball stadiums in Chicago. The two stadiums together hold about 81,960 people.

We read and write this number as:
eighty-one thousand, nine hundred sixty.

The digit 8 means 8 ten thousands, or 80,000.
The digit 1 means 1 thousand, or 1,000.
The digit 9 means 9 hundreds, or 900.
The digit 6 means 6 tens, or 60.
The digit 0 means 0 ones, or 0.

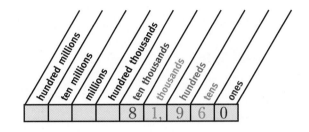

Notice that commas are used to separate the digits into groups of three called **periods**. This helps make larger numbers easier to read.

Rewrite each number. Insert commas where needed.

	a	b	c
1.	758493 _758,493_	6473829 _____	868582 _____
2.	2030200 _____	5000400 _____	6050407 _____
3.	30782 _____	406702 _____	3908454 _____

Write each number using digits. Insert commas where needed.

4. seven hundred twenty thousand, four hundred sixty-two _____ _720,462_ _____

5. twenty-five thousand, two hundred one _____

6. one hundred eighty-four thousand, thirty-nine _____

7. one hundred million, two hundred forty-three thousand _____

Write each number in words. Insert commas where needed.

8. 16,349 _____ _sixteen thousand, three hundred forty-nine_ _____

9. 776 _____

10. 123,456 _____

Addition

To add, start with the digits in the ones place. **Regroup** as needed.

Find: 796 + 304

Add the ones. Regroup.	Add the tens. Regroup.	Add the hundreds. Regroup.
Th H T O — 7 9 6 + 3 0 4 = _ _ _ 0	Th H T O — 7 9 6 + 3 0 4 = _ _ 0 0	Th H T O — 7 9 6 + 3 0 4 = 1,1 0 0

Add.

	a	b	c	d
1.	450 + 394 = 844	251 + 366 = 617	558 + 645 = 1203	712 + 678 = 1390
2.	394 + 759 = 1153	654 + 506 = 1160	431 + 687 = 1118	750 + 947 = 1697
3.	639 + 82 = 721	46 + 567 = 613	826 + 79 = 905	35 + 806 = 841
4.	97 + 344 = 441	532 + 19 = 551	605 + 56 = 661	493 + 28 = 521

Add.

	a	b	c	d	e
5.	¹ ¹ ¹ 5,6 4 6 +2,3 8 7 **8 0 3 3**	¹ ¹ 4,4 8 3 +1,9 3 0 **6 4 1 3**	¹ ¹ ¹ 2,5 5 7 +4,9 6 3 **7 5 2 0**	¹ 2,9 0 4 +6,3 2 5 **9 2 2 9**	¹ ¹ 1,6 6 3 + 9 7 5 **2 6 3 8**
6.	5 2 1 +9,0 3 1 **9 5 5 2**	¹ 7,6 6 2 +1,5 1 7 **9 1 7 9**	¹ 8,6 0 5 + 8 7 **8 6 9 2**	¹ ¹ 6,5 5 4 +2,6 7 1 **9 2 2 5**	¹ 8 6 3 +7,5 0 6 **8 3 6 9**
7.	5,2 1 1 +3,6 8 7 **8 8 9 8**	¹ ¹ 3,0 5 1 +5,2 8 9 **8 3 4 0**	¹ ¹ 6,5 8 4 + 6 2 0 **7 2 0 4**	¹ ¹ ¹ 9 9 9 +1,1 1 1 **2 1 1 0**	¹ 6,5 1 3 +2,9 7 6 **9 4 8 9**

Line up the digits. Then find the sums.

8.
a. 3,697 + 840 = __4537__

¹ ¹
3,697
+ 840
4537

b. 4,305 + 5,224 = __9529__

4305
+ 5224
9529

c. 7,981 + 375 = __8356__

¹ ¹
7981
+ 375
8356

9. 5,208 + 3,114 = __8322__

5208
+3114
8322

8,372 + 609 = __8981__

8372
+ 609
8981

2,584 + 2,639 = ____

¹ ¹
2584
+ 2639
5 2 2 3

Math Club

Problem-Solving Method: Make a Graph

Carlos has a meeting with his boss next week. He wants to show her that sales have increased since he became manager of the store in January. What would be a good way for him to present the sales data in this table?

Month	Jan.	Feb.	Mar.	Apr.	May	June
TVs Sold	27	32	29	30	35	40

Understand the problem.

- **What do you want to know?**
  a good way to present the sales data

- **What information is given?**
  the sales from January to June

Plan how to solve it.

- **What method can you use?**
  You can make a line graph to show how the sales have increased over time.

Solve it.

- **How can you use this method to solve the problem?**
  Make a graph with the months listed along the bottom and the sales along the side. Make a dot where each month meets its sales number. Then connect the dots with a line.

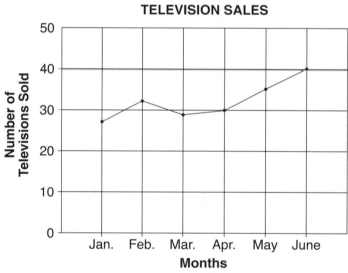

- **What is the answer?**
  A line graph is a good way to display the data.

Look back and check your answer.

- **Is your answer reasonable?**
  Since the line on the graph slants up and to the right, it shows that sales are increasing.

  The answer is reasonable.

Make a line graph to display the data in each table.

1. **Games Won by Houston Astros**

Year	1995	1996	1997	1998	1999
Wins	76	82	84	102	97

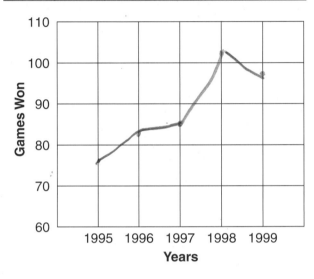

2. **Average Temperature
Rapid City, South Dakota**

Month	Apr.	May	June	July	Aug.
Temp.	45°	55°	65°	72°	71°

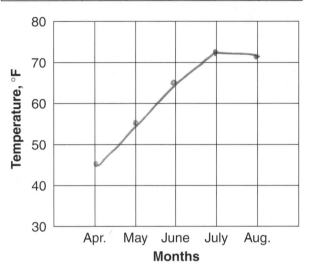

Addition of Three or More Numbers

To add three or more numbers, use the same steps as when adding two numbers.

Find: 949 + 753 + 531

Add the ones. Regroup.	Add the tens. Regroup.	Add the hundreds. Regroup.

Th H T O
      _1_
  9 4 9
  7 5 3
+ 5 3 1
      3
	Th H T O
	  _1_ _1_
	  9 4 9
	  7 5 3
	+ 5 3 1
	   3 3
		Th H T O
		 _2_ _1_ _1_
		  9 4 9
		  7 5 3
		+ 5 3 1
		2, 2 3 3

Add.

	a	b	c	d	e

1.	_1 2_
	2 5 6
	2 4 9
	+1 5 7
	6 6 2
		_2_
		4 1 9
		6 1 7
		+3 1 4
		1 3 5 0
			_1 2_
			  9 8
			1 0 6
			+3 0 7
			5 1 1
				_1 1_
				  2 5
				  9 0
				+2 0 8
				3 2 3
					_1_
					1 0 5
					  6 2
					+ 7
					1 7 4

2.	_1_ 2 1 3 1 1 7 2 3 4 +5 2 5 **1 0 8 9**	_1 2_ 5 5 9 3 0 4 2 0 5 +1 9 8 **1 2 6 6**	_1 2_ 4 3 8 1 6 0 6 3 8 +1 0 6 **1 3 4 2**	_1 1_ 7 1 8 1 6 4 1 3 0 +6 0 7 **1 6 1 9**	_2 2_ 2 6 5 3 2 2 6 7 4 +4 3 9 **1 7 0 0**

Line up the digits. Then find the sums.

3. a. 149 + 753 + 531 = __1433__

    _1 1_
    149
    753
  +531
  14 33

b. 489 + 189 + 78 = __746__

    _2 1_
    489
 + 189
     78
  7 4 6

Addition and Subtraction of Larger Numbers

To add or subtract larger numbers, start with the ones digits.
Regroup as needed.

Add.

	a	b	c	d

1.

a)
```
  1 1 1 1
  3 8,9 1 7
+6 1,1 9 7
─────────
1 0 0,1 1 4
```

b)
```
  1 1 1 1
  5 6,4 5 9
+4 6,5 5 4
─────────
1 0 3 0 1 3
```

c)
```
   1 1 1
  6 7,9 4 3
+9 0,4 9 8
─────────
1 5 8 4 4 1
```

d)
```
   1 1 1 1
    6,7 5 8
 +6 3,2 8 4
─────────
  7 0 0 4 2
```

2.

a)
```
  1 1 1 1
1 9,7 8 9
+    2 1 9
─────────
2 0 0 0 8
```

b)
```
    1 1
9 4,3 8 7
+    5 8 9
─────────
9 4 9 7 6
```

c)
```
1 7,0 0 0
+  2,0 0 0
─────────
1 9 0 0 0
```

d)
```
   1 1 1
1 8,5 5 4
+      4 4 6
─────────
1 9 0 0 0
```

Subtract.

	a	b	c	d

3.

a)
```
      15 12 11
   3 5 2 1 15
   4 6,3 2 5
 -1 7,8 5 8
 ─────────
   2 8,4 6 7
```

b)
```
      15   14
  4 5 6,4 5 2 12
  -2 7,5 6 4
 ─────────
    2 8 9 8 8
```

c)
```
      14 12 17
  3 4 5,3 8 4 14
  -1 7,5 9 6
 ─────────
    2 7 7 8 8
```

d)
```
      12 12 12
  5 6 3,3 3 8 18
  -2 7,9 4 9
 ─────────
    3 0 3 8 9
```

4.

a)
```
     9 18 9
  6 10 8 10 13
  7 0,9 0 3
 -  5,9 9 4
 ─────────
  6 4 9 0 9
```

b)
```
  2 10
  3 0,0 0 0
 -   4,0 0 0
 ─────────
  2 6 0 0 0
```

c)
```
      12 11
   3 2 1 16
  5 3,3 2 6
 -    9 4 7
 ─────────
  5 2 3 7 9
```

d)
```
      12 12
  6 6 7 7
  6 7,3 3 4 14
 -   3,5 5 8
 ─────────
  6 3 7 7 6
```

Line up the digits. Then add or subtract.

	a	b

5. 27,002 − 13,849 = _____   62,525 + 13,475 = _____

```
 27,002
-13,849
───────
```

Estimation of Sums and Differences

To **estimate** a sum or difference, first **round** each number to the same place value. Then add or subtract the rounded numbers.

Estimate: 765 + 321

Round each number to the same place value. Add.

$$765 \rightarrow 800$$
$$+321 \rightarrow +300$$
$$\overline{\qquad 1,100}$$

Estimate: 2,694 − 743

Round each number to the same place value. Subtract.

$$2,694 \rightarrow 2,700$$
$$-\ 743 \rightarrow -\ 700$$
$$\overline{\qquad 2,000}$$

Estimate the sums.

	a	b	c	d
1.	$248 \rightarrow 200$ $+381 \rightarrow +400$ $\overline{\qquad 600}$	$264 \rightarrow$ $+395 \rightarrow$	$293 \rightarrow$ $+346 \rightarrow$	$274 \rightarrow$ $+242 \rightarrow$
2.	$638 \rightarrow$ $+291 \rightarrow$	$543 \rightarrow$ $+376 \rightarrow$	$254 \rightarrow$ $+403 \rightarrow$	$181 \rightarrow$ $+475 \rightarrow$

Estimate the differences.

	a	b	c	d
3.	$911 \rightarrow 900$ $-779 \rightarrow -800$ $\overline{\qquad 100}$	$933 \rightarrow$ $-426 \rightarrow$	$622 \rightarrow$ $-189 \rightarrow$	$511 \rightarrow$ $-134 \rightarrow$
4.	$1,199 \rightarrow$ $-\ 619 \rightarrow$	$1,041 \rightarrow$ $-\ 717 \rightarrow$	$1,491 \rightarrow$ $-\ 888 \rightarrow$	$1,292 \rightarrow$ $-\ 418 \rightarrow$

Estimate the sums or differences.

	a	b	c	d

5.

$$\begin{array}{r} 2\ 7\ 5 \rightarrow \\ +3\ 2\ 6 \rightarrow \end{array}$$
$$\begin{array}{r} 4\ 2\ 1 \rightarrow \\ +1\ 6\ 4 \rightarrow \end{array}$$
$$\begin{array}{r} 8\ 4\ 7 \rightarrow \\ -1\ 2\ 5 \rightarrow \end{array}$$
$$\begin{array}{r} 5\ 0\ 9 \rightarrow \\ +3\ 8\ 7 \rightarrow \end{array}$$

6.

$$\begin{array}{r} 4\ 7\ 9 \rightarrow \\ -2\ 1\ 6 \rightarrow \end{array}$$
$$\begin{array}{r} 6\ 5\ 2 \rightarrow \\ -1\ 5\ 0 \rightarrow \end{array}$$
$$\begin{array}{r} 1\ 2\ 4 \rightarrow \\ +3\ 6\ 9 \rightarrow \end{array}$$
$$\begin{array}{r} 8\ 0\ 6 \rightarrow \\ +2\ 2\ 4 \rightarrow \end{array}$$

7.

$$\begin{array}{r} 1{,}3\ 5\ 7 \rightarrow \\ -\ \ \ 2\ 5\ 3 \rightarrow \end{array}$$
$$\begin{array}{r} 6{,}5\ 4\ 3 \rightarrow \\ +\ \ \ 3\ 1\ 6 \rightarrow \end{array}$$
$$\begin{array}{r} 4{,}7\ 2\ 5 \rightarrow \\ -\ \ \ 1\ 4\ 8 \rightarrow \end{array}$$
$$\begin{array}{r} 5\ 6\ 3 \rightarrow \\ +3{,}7\ 8\ 2 \rightarrow \end{array}$$

8.

$$\begin{array}{r} 4\ 9\ 9 \rightarrow \\ +3{,}2\ 4\ 3 \rightarrow \end{array}$$
$$\begin{array}{r} 9{,}3\ 2\ 7 \rightarrow \\ -\ \ \ 1\ 7\ 5 \rightarrow \end{array}$$
$$\begin{array}{r} 7{,}6\ 0\ 4 \rightarrow \\ -\ \ \ 5\ 9\ 3 \rightarrow \end{array}$$
$$\begin{array}{r} 6{,}2\ 2\ 1 \rightarrow \\ +\ \ \ 6\ 5\ 4 \rightarrow \end{array}$$

9.

$$\begin{array}{r} 8{,}5\ 5\ 7 \rightarrow \\ -2{,}8\ 0\ 6 \rightarrow \end{array}$$
$$\begin{array}{r} 3{,}2\ 1\ 5 \rightarrow \\ +5{,}4\ 2\ 7 \rightarrow \end{array}$$
$$\begin{array}{r} 6{,}9\ 8\ 6 \rightarrow \\ -5{,}7\ 9\ 5 \rightarrow \end{array}$$
$$\begin{array}{r} 4{,}0\ 9\ 8 \rightarrow \\ +4{,}9\ 0\ 8 \rightarrow \end{array}$$

Problem-Solving Method: Work Backwards

Ted has 125 baseball cards. Lucia has 130 baseball cards. Last week, Ted traded 12 cards to Lucia for 9 of her cards. How many cards did Lucia have before the trade?

Understand the problem.

- **What do you want to know?**
  how many cards Lucia had before the trade

- **What information is given?**
  Ted has 125 cards now and Lucia has 130 cards now.
  Ted gave 12 cards to Lucia.
  Lucia gave 9 cards to Ted.

Plan how to solve it.

- **What method can you use?**
  Since you know how many cards Lucia has now, you can work backwards to find how many she started with.

Solve it.

- **How can you use this method to solve the problem?**
  Addition and subtraction are opposite operations. So, add the cards she gave and subtract the cards she got.

  ```
    130  ← Lucia has 130 cards now.
  -  12  ← Ted gave her 12 cards. Subtract 12 cards.
  -----
    118
  +   9  ← Lucia gave 9 cards to Ted. Add back 9 cards.
  -----
    127
  ```

- **What is the answer?**
  Before the trade, Lucia had 127 baseball cards.

Look back and check your answer.

- **Is your answer reasonable?**
  You can check by working forwards from the number of cards she had before the trade.

  ```
    127  ← Lucia had 127 cards.
  -   9  ← She gave 9 cards to Ted.
  -----
    118
  +  12  ← Ted gave Lucia 12 cards.
  -----
    130  ← Lucia has 130 cards now.
  ```

  The number of cards she has now matches.
  The answer is reasonable.

1. A farmer planted 86 acres of soybeans and 65 acres of corn. Last year, 20 of the acres now used for corn were used for soybeans. How many acres of corn did the farmer have last year?

Answer _____

2. Jan spent $45 for two new shirts and $60 for a pair of jeans. She has $7 left over. How much money did Jan take shopping?

Answer _____

3. Shameeka sold her hamsters to a pet store. This doubled the number of hamsters in the store. Then the store got 6 more hamsters. If the pet store has 46 hamsters now, how many did Shameeka sell to the store?

Answer _____

4. Wong's flight left at 7:00. It took him one and a half hours to check in at the airport. His house is an hour drive from the airport. At what time did Wong leave his house to get to the airport?

Answer _____

5. The club treasury ended the week with $76. On Friday, the treasurer had received $35 in club dues. On Tuesday, she had paid a bill of $15. How much money was in the treasury at the beginning of the week?

Answer _____

Problem Solving

Solve.

1. At 3,212 feet, Angel Falls in Venezuela is the tallest waterfall in the world. Yosemite Falls in California is 2,425 feet tall. How much taller is Angel Falls than Yosemite Falls?

   Answer_____

2. The United States, Britain, and Germany are top Nobel Prize–winning countries. If the U.S. won 241, Britain 98, and Germany 73, how many Nobel Prizes have the three countries won altogether?

   Answer_____

3. *Apollo 8* flew 550,000 miles on its trip around the moon. *Apollo 9* flew 3,700,000 miles. How far did the two *Apollo* missions fly altogether?

   Answer_____

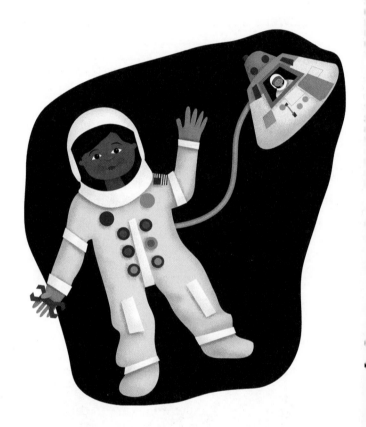

4. The area of North Carolina is 52,672 square miles. South Carolina covers 31,189 square miles. What is the combined area of the Carolinas?

   Answer_____

5. Emily drove from Washington, D.C., to Boston, stopping once in New York. It is about 233 miles from Washington to New York and then about 206 miles from New York to Boston. Estimate how far Emily drove in all.

   Answer_____

6. In 2000, there were 854 endangered species of animals in the United States and 247 in Mexico. Estimate how many more endangered species there were in the U.S. than in Mexico.

   Answer_____

UNIT 1 Review

Write the place name for the 4 in each number.

            a   *b*

1. 3,470,981 _____ 3,504,972 _____

2. 4,168,953 _____ 1,040,831 _____

3. 8,031,142 _____ 831,429 _____

Write the value of the underlined digit.

            a   *b*

4. 16,0<u>3</u>5 _____ 214,20<u>3</u> _____

5. <u>9</u>68,137 _____ 13,641,2<u>5</u>4 _____

6. <u>6</u>,899 _____ <u>1</u>34,618,349 _____

Write each number using digits. Insert commas where needed.

7. seventy-two thousand, eighty-five _____

8. two million, forty thousand, five hundred six _____

9. seventeen million, five hundred thousand, eighteen _____

Write each number in words. Insert commas where needed.

10. 21,106 _____

11. 403,872 _____

12. 1,720,564 _____

Add.

	a	b	c	d
13.	4 2 8 +2 2 9	1 6 7 + 9 2	4 0 5 5 4 0 +7 6 4	1 1 2 4 8 5 +3 6 8

	a	b	c	d
14.	1 3 2 2 7 8 4 0 2 +3 5 8	2 9,2 7 4 +1 3,2 9 6	6 4,3 5 7 +3 5,7 6 4	2 7,8 0 9 + 2,1 9 5

Line up the digits. Then find the sums.

a

15. 449 + 223 + 720 = _____

b

8,629 + 6,587 = _____

Subtract.

	a	b	c	d
16.	5 3,6 4 7 −2 8,6 5 8	3 7,8 5 3 − 7,8 6 5	6 2,5 0 3 −4 7,1 2 3	6 4,9 7 1 −1 4,9 2 1

Line up the digits. Then find the differences.

a

17. 795 − 658 = _____

b

9,235 − 479 = _____

Estimate the sums or differences.

	a	b	c	d
18.	8 5 4 → −1 6 5 →	2 5 4 → +5 2 9 →	7 4 5 → −2 8 6 →	2 4 4 → +3 9 8 →

UNIT 1 Review

Make a line graph to display the data in each table.

19. **Baltimore Orioles Games Won**

Year	1995	1996	1997	1998	1999
Wins	71	88	98	79	78

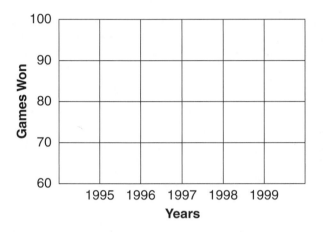

20. **Average Temperature Omaha, Nebraska**

Month	Apr.	May	June	July	Aug.
Temp.	52°	62°	72°	77°	74°

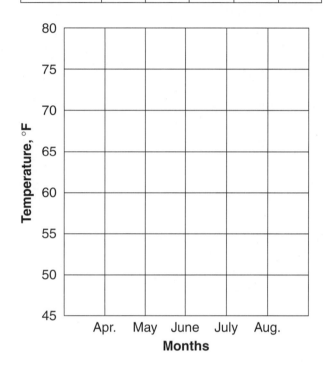

Work backwards to solve each problem.

21. Kelly has 47 model cars. Jamal has 58 model cars. Yesterday, Jamal traded 8 model cars to Kelly for 14 of her cars. How many cars did Kelly have before the trade?

Answer_____

22. Anita had $15 left after going shopping for the party. She bought food and drinks for $58. Then she spent $27 for decorations. How much money did Anita take shopping?

Answer_____

unit 2
multiplication

Multiplication of One-digit Numbers

To multiply by one-digit numbers, use your basic multiplication facts.

Find: 6×325

Multiply 5 by 6 ones.	Multiply 2 tens by 6 ones.	Multiply 3 hundreds by 6 ones.
Regroup.	Regroup.	

	Th	H	T	O
			3	
		3	2	5
×				6
				0

	Th	H	T	O
		1	*3*	
		3	2	5
×				6
			5	0

	Th	H	T	O
		1	*3*	
		3	2	5
×				6
	1,	9	5	0

Multiply.

1.

a

	H	T	O
		1	
		3	2
×			7
	2	2	4

b

	H	T	O
		1	
		4	5
×			3
	1	3	5

c

	H	T	O
		1	
		8	7
×			2
	1	7	4

d

	H	T	O
		4	
		5	6
×			8
	4	6	8

e

	H	T	O
		1	
		4	2
×			7
	2	9	4

2.

	H	T	O
	4		
	8	6	
×		8	
6	8	8	

	H	T	O
	5		
	6	6	
×		9	
5	9	4	

	H	T	O
	4		
	3	7	
×		6	
		2	

	H	T	O
	2		
	5	6	
×		4	
2	2	4	

	H	T	O
2		*3*	
	6	8	
×		4	
6	7	2	

3.

a

	Th	H	T	O
		7	3	9
×				3

b

	Th	H	T	O
		2	6	5
×				7

c

	Th	H	T	O
		4	3	1
×				9

d

	Th	H	T	O
		5	7	3
×				5

Multiplying Two-digit Numbers by Two-digit Numbers

To multiply two-digit numbers by two-digit numbers, line up the digits. Multiply the ones, then the tens. Write zeros as place holders. Add the partial products.

Find: 36 × 46

Multiply by 6 ones. Regroup.

Th	H	T	O
		3	
		4	6
×		3	6
	2	7	6

Write a zero place holder. Multiply by 3 tens. Regroup.

Th	H	T	O
		1	
		4	6
×		3	6
	2	7	6
1,	3	8	0

zero place holder

Add the partial products.

Th	H	T	O
		4	6
×		3	6
	2	7	6
+1,	3	8	0
1,	6	5	6

Multiply.

	a	b	c	d
1.	1 4 × 1 3 = 4 2 + 1 4 0 = 1 8 2	4 1 × 2 2	2 7 × 5 4	3 2 × 6 7
2.	2 8 × 1 5	5 8 × 2 1	6 5 × 4 2	8 4 × 7 3
3.	3 9 × 2 6	5 1 × 1 9	6 3 × 8 1	9 2 × 5 5

Multiplying Three-digit Numbers by Two-digit Numbers

Multiply three-digit numbers the same way you multiply two-digit numbers.

Find: 69 × 618

Multiply by 9 ones. Regroup.	Write a zero place holder. Multiply by 6 tens. Regroup.	Add the partial products.

TTh Th H T O
  1 7
  6 1 8
× 6 9
5,5 6 2
	TTh Th H T O
	  1 4
	  6 1 8
	× 6 9
	5,5 6 2
	3 7,0 8 0
		TTh Th H T O
		  6 1 8
		× 6 9
		5,5 6 2
		+ 3 7,0 8 0
		4 2,6 4 2

Multiply.

	a	b	c	d
1.	7 4 1 × 2 5 3,7 0 5 +1 4,8 2 0 1 8,5 2 5	9 1 2 × 1 9	1 5 8 × 2 9	2 2 6 × 1 6
2.	3 4 5 × 3 2	1 2 8 × 4 2	5 1 2 × 3 4	4 1 4 × 4 8

Line up the digits. Then find the products.

	a	b
3.	362 × 76 = _____ 362 × 76	847 × 54 = _____

Zeros in Multiplication

Remember,
- the product of o and any number is o.
- the sum of o and any number is that number.

Find: 27 × 608

Multiply by 7 ones.
Regroup.

TTh	Th	H	T	O
			5	
		6	0	8
×			2	7
	4,	2	5	6

Write a zero place holder.
Multiply by 2 tens. Regroup.

TTh	Th	H	T	O
			1	
		6	0	8
×			2	7
	4,	2	5	6
1	2,	1	6	0

Add the partial products.

TTh	Th	H	T	O
		6	0	8
×			2	7
	4,	2	5	6
+ 1	2,	1	6	0
1	6,	4	1	6

Multiply.

	a	b	c	d	e
1.	30 × 3 9 0	20 × 6 120	10 × 7 7 0	60 × 4 240	40 × 6 240
2.	709 × 82	304 × 49	55 × 70	48 × 20	14 × 30
3.	507 × 20	806 × 40	390 × 60	204 × 90	100 × 20

Problem-Solving Method: Solve Multi-Step Problems

Many people think that one "dog year" is equal to seven "human years."
But according to veterinarians, the first two years of a dog's life are equal to
35 human years. Every year after that is equal to three human years.
Max is a dog. He is eight years old. How old is Max in human years?

Understand the problem.

- **What do you want to know?**
  Max's age in human years

- **What information is given?**
  First 2 dog years = 35 human years
  Every year after that = 3 human years
  Max is 8 years old.

Plan how to solve it.

- **What method can you use?**
  You can separate the problem into steps.

Solve it.

- **How can you use this method to solve the problem?**
  Subtract the first 2 years from his age. Multiply the
  remaining years by 3. Then add 35 years.

Step 1 Subtract	Step 2 Multiply	Step 3 Add
8 ← Max's age −2 ← first 2 years **6 years**	6 ← dog years ×3 ← human years **18 years**	35 ← first 2 years +18 ← remaining 6 years **53 years**

- **What is the answer?**
  Max is 53 years old in human years.

Look back and check your answer.

- **Is your answer reasonable?**
  You can add to check your multiplication.

  35 + 3 + 3 + 3+ 3 + 3 + 3 = 53

  The answer matches the sum.
  The answer is reasonable.

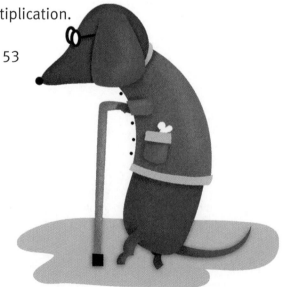

Separate each problem into steps to solve.

1. One egg has 75 calories. One slice of bacon has 38 calories. How many calories are in a breakfast of 2 eggs and 4 slices of bacon?

Answer_____

2. A bushel of apples weighs about 42 pounds. Bill's truck can carry 7,000 pounds. If he loads 150 bushels of apples, how many more pounds can the truck carry?

Answer_____

3. The football team needs $600 for new equipment. They washed 38 cars on Saturday for $15 each car. How much more money do they need?

Answer_____

4. In an ordinary year, there are 365 days. In a leap year, there are 366 days. There are 24 hours in a day. How many more hours are there in one leap year than in one ordinary year?

Answer_____

5. A dolphin can swim 30 miles per hour. A sea lion can swim 25 miles per hour. If both animals swim for 5 hours, how much farther will the dolphin go?

Answer_____

Estimation of Products

To estimate products, round each **factor**. Then multiply the rounded factors.

Find: 28 × 44

Round each factor to the greatest place value. Multiply.

$$
\begin{array}{r}
4\ 4 \rightarrow\quad 4\ 0 \\
\times 2\ 8 \rightarrow\quad \times 3\ 0 \leftarrow \text{2 zeros} \\
\hline
1{,}2\ 0\ 0 \leftarrow \text{2 zeros}
\end{array}
$$

Estimate the products.

	a	b	c	d

1.
$$
\begin{array}{r}
3\ 2 \rightarrow\ 30 \\
\times 5\ 7 \rightarrow \times 60 \\
\hline
1{,}800
\end{array}
\qquad
\begin{array}{r}
1\ 8 \rightarrow \\
\times 2\ 9 \rightarrow \\
\hline
\end{array}
\qquad
\begin{array}{r}
4\ 6 \rightarrow \\
\times 1\ 3 \rightarrow \\
\hline
\end{array}
\qquad
\begin{array}{r}
6\ 5 \rightarrow \\
\times 2\ 1 \rightarrow \\
\hline
\end{array}
$$

2.
$$
\begin{array}{r}
7\ 3 \rightarrow \\
\times 2\ 8 \rightarrow \\
\hline
\end{array}
\qquad
\begin{array}{r}
8\ 4 \rightarrow \\
\times 6\ 6 \rightarrow \\
\hline
\end{array}
\qquad
\begin{array}{r}
5\ 7 \rightarrow \\
\times 3\ 9 \rightarrow \\
\hline
\end{array}
\qquad
\begin{array}{r}
4\ 3 \rightarrow \\
\times 2\ 2 \rightarrow \\
\hline
\end{array}
$$

3.
$$
\begin{array}{r}
9\ 4 \rightarrow \\
\times 3\ 5 \rightarrow \\
\hline
\end{array}
\qquad
\begin{array}{r}
7\ 9 \rightarrow \\
\times 1\ 8 \rightarrow \\
\hline
\end{array}
\qquad
\begin{array}{r}
5\ 2 \rightarrow \\
\times 3\ 9 \rightarrow \\
\hline
\end{array}
\qquad
\begin{array}{r}
8\ 1 \rightarrow \\
\times 2\ 4 \rightarrow \\
\hline
\end{array}
$$

Line up the digits. Then estimate the products.

	a	b	c

4. 27 × 55 _____   86 × 12 _____   48 × 33 _____

$$
\begin{array}{r}
27 \rightarrow\ 30 \\
\times 55 \rightarrow \times 60 \\
\hline
\end{array}
$$

Multiplying Three-digit Numbers by Three-digit Numbers

To multiply three-digit numbers by three-digit numbers, line up the digits.
Multiply, starting with the ones digits. Write zeros as place holders.
Add the three partial products.

Find: 342 × 576

Multiply by 2 ones. Regroup.	Write one zero. Multiply by 4 tens. Regroup.	Write two zeros. Multiply by 3 hundreds. Regroup.	Add.

Multiply by 2 ones. Regroup.

Th	H	T	O
	1	1	
	5	7	6
×	3	4	2
1,	1	5	2

Write one zero. Multiply by 4 tens. Regroup.

TTh	Th	H	T	O
		3	2	
		5	7	6
×		3	4	2
	1,	1	5	2
2	3,	0	4	0

Write two zeros. Multiply by 3 hundreds. Regroup.

HTh	TTh	Th	H	T	O
			2	1	
			5	7	6
×			3	4	2
		1,	1	5	2
	2	3,	0	4	0
1	7	2,	8	0	0

Add.

HTh	TTh	Th	H	T	O
			5	7	6
×			3	4	2
		1,	1	5	2
	2	3,	0	4	0
+ 1	7	2,	8	0	0
1	9	6,	9	9	2

Multiply.

	a	b	c	d

1.

a)
TTh	Th	H	T	O
		4	2	4
×		1	2	2
		8	4	8
	8,	4	8	0
+ 4	2,	4	0	0
5	1,	7	2	8

b)
HTh	TTh	Th	H	T	O
			2	5	0
×			4	3	6

c)
HTh	TTh	Th	H	T	O
			5	0	9
×			2	6	7

d)
HTh	TTh	Th	H	T	O
			7	4	6
×			8	9	1

2.

a)
TTh	Th	H	T	O
		2	3	2
×		2	3	2

b)
HTh	TTh	Th	H	T	O
			5	4	0
×			4	3	2

c)
HTh	TTh	Th	H	T	O
			7	1	4
×			3	6	9

d)
HTh	TTh	Th	H	T	O
			9	1	3
×			5	4	0

Multiplication of Large Numbers

To multiply large numbers, use the same steps you use to multiply smaller numbers.

Study these examples.

Multiply by 6 ones.	Multiply by 6 ones, 2 tens. Then add.	Multiply by 2 ones, 3 tens. Then add.

Multiply by 6 ones.

	HTh	TTh	Th	H	T	O
		2	3	1	1	
	2	4,	6	3	2	
×						6
1	4	7,	7	9	2	

Multiply by 6 ones, 2 tens. Then add.

	HTh	TTh	Th	H	T	O
			4,	6	7	1
×					2	6
		2	8,	0	2	6 ✓
+		9	3,	4	2	0
	1	2	1,	4	4	6

Multiply by 2 ones, 3 tens. Then add.

	M	HTh	TTh	Th	H	T	O
			5	0,	0	0	0
×						3	2
		1	0	0,	0	0	0
+	1,	5	0	0,	0	0	0 ✓
	1,	6	0	0,	0	0	0

Multiply.

	a	b	c	d
1.	5 5 3 7,8 9 6 × 6 —————— 4 7,3 7 6	4,6 8 7 × 4	2,4 6 8 × 7	5,0 0 0 × 8
2.	2,3 9 2 × 5 4	3,0 0 0 × 9 0	5 3,4 0 4 × 1 6	4 2,0 0 0 × 1 9

Line up the digits. Then find the products.

	a	b	c
3.	2 × 4,653 = _____	9 × 38,641 = _____	14 × 5,207 = _____

4,653
×   2
—————

Problem-Solving Method: Identify Extra Information

Niagara Falls is on the border between the United States and Canada, with about 85 percent of the water on the Canadian side. Every second, 2,830 cubic meters of water pour over Niagara Falls. The energy from the water is used to power 13 generators in New York. How much water goes over the falls every minute?

Understand the problem.

- **What do you want to know?**
  how much water goes over Niagara Falls every minute (60 seconds)

Plan how to solve it.

- **What method can you use?**
  You can identify extra information that is not needed to solve the problem.

Solve it.

- **How can you use this method to solve the problem?**
  Reread the problem. Cross out any unnecessary words. Then you can focus on the facts needed to solve the problem.

> ~~Niagara Falls is on the border between the United States and Canada, with about 85 percent of the water on the Canadian side~~. Every second, 2,830 cubic meters of water pour over Niagara Falls. ~~The energy from the water is used to power 13 generators in New York~~. How much water goes over the falls every minute?

- **What is the answer?**

  2,830 × 60 = 169,800

  Every minute, 169,800 cubic meters of water pour over Niagara Falls.

Look back and check your answer.

- **Is your answer reasonable?**
  You can estimate to check your answer.

  $$
  \begin{array}{r}
  2,830 \\
  \times\ \ 60 \\
  \hline
  \end{array}
  \longrightarrow
  \begin{array}{r}
  3,000 \\
  \times\ \ 60 \\
  \hline
  180,000
  \end{array}
  $$

  The estimate is close to the answer.
  The answer is reasonable.

In each problem, cross out the extra information. Then solve the problem.

1. Cheetahs are found in Africa and Asia. They are the fastest animals in the world, reaching up to 70 miles per hour. Cheetahs are usually less than 3 feet tall and weigh about 110 pounds. How far can a cheetah run in 5 hours?

   Answer _____

2. Each square inch of human skin has 19 million cells, 60 hairs, 90 oil glands, 19 feet of blood vessels, and 625 sweat glands. If the palm of your hand covers 16 square inches, how many sweat glands are in your palm?

   Answer _____

3. One honeybee would have to visit over 2,000,000 flowers and travel 55,000 miles to collect enough nectar to produce 1 pound of honey. How many miles would a honeybee have to fly for 3 pounds of honey?

   Answer _____

4. One million dollars in $1 bills would weigh about one ton, or 2,000 pounds. Placed in a pile, it would be 360 feet high—as tall as 60 average adults standing on top of each other. How many pounds would $5,000,000 in $1 bills weigh?

   Answer _____

5. A mile on the ocean and a mile on land are not the same distance. On the ocean, a nautical mile measures 6,080 feet. A land mile is 5,280 feet. If a cruise ship sails 75 nautical miles, how many feet does it travel?

   Answer _____

Problem Solving

Solve.

1. People dream an average of 5 times a night. How many times do you dream in 1 year? (365 days)

    Answer_____

2. Greenland is the largest island in the world—about 21 times the size of Iceland. Iceland covers 39,800 square miles. About how many square miles does Greenland cover?

    Answer_____

3. Craig drove 12 hours at an average speed of 55 miles per hour. Estimate how many miles he traveled.

    Answer_____

4. From 1997 to 2000, people making minimum wage and working 40 hours a week earned $10,712 a year. How much did they earn in the 3 years altogether?

    Answer_____

5. The theater seats 375 people. There will be 428 shows this year. How many people can see a show this year?

    Answer_____

6. Noah Webster spent 36 years writing his dictionary. There are 12 months in a year. How many months did Webster spend writing the dictionary?

    Answer_____

7. The Concord jet flies 2,222 kilometers per hour. How far can the Concord travel in 8 hours?

    Answer_____

Multiply.

	a	b	c	d
1.	6 0 × 7	9 0 × 4	7 0 0 ×2 0 0	8 3 0 ×4 6 3
2.	2,6 0 5 × 4	4,8 9 1 × 3 6	2,0 0 5 × 8 7	1 1,8 4 7 × 4 2

Line up the digits. Then find the products.

	a	b	c
3.	$427 \times 906 =$ _____	$313 \times 211 =$ _____	$128 \times 975 =$ _____
4.	$3 \times 46,168 =$ _____	$4 \times 21,741 =$ _____	$20 \times 2,403 =$ _____

Estimate the products.

	a	b	c	d
5.	6 2 → ×1 7 →	9 3 → ×4 2 →	3 8 → ×2 6 →	3 5 → ×4 6 →
6.	2 5 → ×3 8 →	8 7 → ×1 4 →	6 4 → ×7 1 →	4 7 → ×8 2 →

Separate each problem into steps to solve.

7. A whippet can run 36 miles per hour. A greyhound can run 40 miles per hour. If both dogs run for 3 hours, how much farther will the greyhound go?

Answer_____

8. Every day there are 36 flights to Paris and 22 flights to New York from Heathrow Airport in London. Each plane holds about 130 passengers. How many people can fly to Paris or New York from Heathrow each day?

Answer_____

9. The Empire State Building in New York is hit by lightning about 100 times a year. The building opened in 1931. About how many times was it hit by lightning by the year 2000? (69 years)

Answer_____

In each problem, cross out the extra information. Then solve the problem.

10. The gray kangaroo is the largest kangaroo in the world. It stands 7 feet tall and weighs 200 pounds. Gray kangaroos can reach speeds of 43 miles per hour and cover 29 feet with each hop. How many feet can a gray kangaroo cover in 25 hops?

Answer_____

11. During World War II, the United States Navy built the world's first floating ice cream parlor. While cruising the Pacific Ocean, this ship was capable of making 85 gallons of ice cream every minute. How many gallons of ice cream could they make every hour?
(1 hour = 60 minutes)

Answer_____

unit 3
division

One-digit Divisors

To divide by a one-digit divisor, first decide on a **trial quotient**.
Then multiply and subtract.

**Remember, if your trial quotient is too large or too small,
try another number.**

Find: 378 ÷ 6

Divide.

```
      H | T | O
6 ) 3 | 7 | 8
```

3 < 6

6 does not
go into 3.

Move to the next
place value.

Multiply and subtract.

```
      H | T | O
          6 |
6 ) 3 | 7 | 8
  - 3 | 6
      | 1 | 8
```

6)37 is about 6.

Multiply and subtract.

```
quotient →    H | T | O
                  6 | 3
divisor → 6 ) 3 | 7 | 8
            - 3 | 6
                | 1 | 8
              - | 1 | 8
                |   | 0
```
6)18 = 3

Check:

Multiply the
quotient by
the divisor.

```
   63
 ×  6
  378
```

Divide.

	a	b	c	d	e

1.

a.
```
   T | O
   1 | 2
8 ) 9 | 6
 - 8 |↓
   1 | 6
 - 1 | 6
     | 0
```

b.
```
   T | O
4 ) 7 | 6
```

c.
```
   T | O
3 ) 8 | 1
```

d.
```
   H | T | O
2 ) 9 | 4 | 6
```

e.
```
   H | T | O
8 ) 9 | 6 | 8
```

2.

a.
```
   H | T | O
2 ) 1 | 9 | 6
```

b.
```
   H | T | O
6 ) 3 | 3 | 6
```

c.
```
   H | T | O
7 ) 1 | 5 | 4
```

d.
```
   H | T | O
9 ) 8 | 3 | 7
```

e.
```
   H | T | O
3 ) 4 | 2 | 3
```

One-digit Divisors with Remainders

To divide, first decide on a trial quotient. Multiply and subtract.
Then write the **remainder** in the quotient.

Find: 749 ÷ 5

Multiply and
subtract.

```
  H|T|O
  1
5)7 4 9
 -5↓
  2 4
```
5)7 is about 1.

Multiply and
subtract.

```
  H|T|O
  1 4
5)7 4 9
 -5
  2 4
 -2 0↓
    4 9
```
5)24 is about 4.

Multiply and subtract.
Write the remainder in
the quotient.

```
  H|T|O
  1 4 9  R 4
5)7 4 9
 -5
  2 4
 -2 0
    4 9
   -4 5
      4
```
5)49 is about 9.

Check:

Multiply the quotient
by the divisor.

Add the remainder.

```
   149
 ×   5
   745
 +   4
   749
```

Divide.

	a	b	c	d

1.

a)
```
  T|O
  1 1  R 1
6)6 7
 -6↓
   7
  -6
   1
```

b)
```
  T|O
    1 4  R2
3)4 4
 -3↓
   1 4
  -1 2
     2
```

c)
```
  T|O
  1 5  R1
5)7 6
 -5↓
  2 6
 -2 5
    1
```

d)
```
  T|O
7)8 8
```

2.

a)
```
  T|O
8)1 0
```

b)
```
  H|T|O
4)1 3 9
```

c)
```
  Th|H|T|O
8)6,9 1 1
```

d)
```
  Th|H|T|O
7)1,0 1 3
```

Zeros in Quotients

To divide, decide on a trial quotient. Then multiply and subtract.
Remember to divide every time you bring down a number.
When you cannot divide, write a zero in the quotient as a
place holder.

Find: 325 ÷ 3

Multiply and subtract.

```
    H | T | O
        1
  3 ) 3 | 2 | 5
   -3  ↓
    0 | 2                1
                        3)3
```

Multiply and subtract.

```
    H | T | O
        1   0  ← Write a zero in the
  3 ) 3 | 2 | 5    quotient as a place
   -3              holder.
        2   ↓
       -0   ↓          0
        2   5         3)2
```

Multiply and subtract.

```
    H | T | O
        1   0   8  R1
  3 ) 3 | 2 | 5  ↑
   -3
        2
       -0                3)25 is
        2   5            about 8.
       -2   4
            1
```

Divide.

	a	*b*	*c*	*d*

1.

```
    1 0 9 R4
  5)5 4 9  ↑
  -5  ↓ │ │
     4  ↓ │
    -0  ↓ │
     4 9  │
    -4 5 ╱
       4
```

b   2)8 1 5

c   7)7 3 8

d   3)9 2 3

2.

3)1 5 0   5)2 0 2   9)7,2 3 4   8)4,8 3 2

Two-digit Divisors: Multiples of 10

To divide by multiples of ten, choose a trial quotient.
Then multiply and subtract.

Find: 760 ÷ 60

Multiply and subtract.	Multiply and subtract.	Check:
$$\begin{array}{r} 1 \\ 60\overline{)760} \\ -60\downarrow \\ \hline 160 \end{array}$$	$$\begin{array}{r} 1\ 2 \text{ R}40 \\ 60\overline{)760} \\ -60\downarrow \\ \hline 160 \\ -120 \\ \hline 40 \end{array}$$	$$\begin{array}{r} 12 \\ \times\ 60 \\ \hline 720 \\ +\ 40 \\ \hline 760 \end{array}$$

Think: 6)7̄ is about 1.
So, 60)76̄ is about 1.
Put the 1 above the 6.

Think: 6)16̄ is about 2.
So, 60)160̄ is about 2.

Divide.

	a	b	c	d
1.	$$\begin{array}{r} 1\ 8 \text{ R}37 \\ 50\overline{)937} \\ -50\downarrow \\ \hline 437 \\ -400 \\ \hline 37 \end{array}$$	$30\overline{)978}$	$20\overline{)860}$	$40\overline{)885}$
2.	$80\overline{)1,040}$	$70\overline{)2,620}$	$60\overline{)1,560}$	$90\overline{)4,430}$

Set up the problems. Then find the quotients.

	a	b	c
3.	$1{,}285 \div 20 =$ _____	$1{,}670 \div 60 =$ _____	$3{,}760 \div 80 =$ _____
	$20\overline{)1,285}$		

Problem-Solving Method: Choose an Operation

Every week, 847 tons of dust from outer space enter Earth's atmosphere. If the dust could be shoveled into one pile, it would be as big as a 14-story building. How many tons of dust from outer space enter the atmosphere every day?

Understand the problem.

- **What do you want to know?**
  how much dust enters the atmosphere every day

- **What information do you know?**
  847 tons enter every week.
  There are 7 days in a week.

Plan how to solve it.

- **What method can you use?**
  You can choose the operation needed to solve the problem.

	Unequal Groups	Equal Groups
	Add to combine unequal groups.	**Multiply** to combine equal groups.
	Subtract to separate into unequal groups.	**Divide** to separate into equal groups.

Solve it.

- **How can you use this method to solve the problem?**
  Since you need to separate the total, 847 tons, into 7 equal groups, you can divide to find how many tons will be in each group.

$$\begin{array}{r} 121 \\ 7\overline{)847} \\ -7 \\ \hline 14 \\ -14 \\ \hline 07 \\ -7 \\ \hline 0 \end{array}$$

- **What is the answer?**
  Every day, 121 tons of dust enter Earth's atmosphere.

Look back and check your answer.

- **Is your answer reasonable?**
  You can check division with multiplication.

$$\begin{array}{r} 121 \\ \times 7 \\ \hline 847 \end{array}$$

The product matches the dividend.
The answer is reasonable.

Choose an operation to solve each problem. Then solve the problem.

1. Tuna swim at a steady speed of 9 miles per hour. They never stop during their entire lives. How many hours does it take a tuna to swim 216 miles?

Operation_____

Answer_____

2. Zippers were invented in 1891. Velcro was invented in 1948. How many years passed between the two inventions?

Operation_____

Answer_____

3. An ant can lift 50 times its own weight. Ted weighs 165 pounds. If Ted were as strong as an ant, how much could he lift?

Operation_____

Answer_____

4. The average two-year-old learns 112 new words a week. How many words does a two-year-old learn each day? (1 week = 7 days)

Operation_____

Answer_____

5. Pluto is the slowest planet. It travels around the sun at a speed of 10,600 miles per hour. How far does Pluto travel in 8 hours?

Operation_____

Answer_____

Estimating Quotients

To estimate quotients, use rounded numbers.

Estimate: 345 ÷ 5

Round the dividend until you can use a basic fact. Divide.

$$5\overline{)3\ 4\ 5} \qquad\qquad 345 \div 5$$

Think: $35 \div 5 = 7$ $\qquad\qquad 350 \div 5 = 70$

Estimate: 828 ÷ 23

Round the dividend and the divisor until you can use a basic fact. Divide.

$$2\ 3\overline{)8\ 2\ 8} \qquad\qquad 828 \div 23$$

Think: $8 \div 2 = 4$ $\qquad\qquad 800 \div 20 = 40$

Round the dividends to estimate the quotients.

a	b	c

1. $272 \div 3$ $\qquad\qquad$ $419 \div 7$ $\qquad\qquad$ $363 \div 9$

$270 \div 3 = 90$

2. $\qquad\qquad\qquad 80$

$5\overline{)4\ 1\ 8} \rightarrow 5\overline{)400} \qquad\qquad 3\overline{)1\ 6\ 7} \rightarrow \qquad\qquad 6\overline{)2\ 3\ 3} \rightarrow$

Round the dividends and the divisors to estimate the quotients.

a	b	c

3. $756 \div 36$ $\qquad\qquad$ $924 \div 28$ $\qquad\qquad$ $578 \div 17$

$800 \div 40 = 20$

4.

$5\ 2\overline{)9\ 8\ 8} \rightarrow \qquad\qquad 3\ 1\overline{)8\ 9\ 9} \rightarrow \qquad\qquad 4\ 3\overline{)7\ 7\ 4} \rightarrow$

Trial Quotients

When you divide, you may have to try several quotients. Estimate to choose a **trial quotient**. Then multiply and subtract. If it is too large or too small, try again.

Find: 928 ÷ 32

Estimate to choose a trial quotient.	Multiply and subtract.	Try a smaller number. Multiply and subtract.	Finish the problem.
$32\overline{)928}$	$\begin{array}{r} 3 \\ 32\overline{)928} \\ -96 \end{array}$	$\begin{array}{r} 2 \\ 32\overline{)928} \\ -64 \\ \hline 28 \end{array}$	$\begin{array}{r} 29 \\ 32\overline{)928} \\ -64\downarrow \\ \hline 288 \\ -288 \\ \hline 0 \end{array}$
Think: 32 rounds to 30. $\dfrac{3}{3\overline{)9}}$ So, $32\overline{)92}$ is about 3.	Since 96 > 92, 3 is too large.	Since 28 < 32, 2 is correct.	

Write *too large*, *too small*, or *correct* for each trial quotient. Then write the correct trial quotient.

a   b

1. $\begin{array}{r} 4 \\ 22\overline{)858} \\ -88 \end{array}$ *too large*   3 $\begin{array}{r} 2 \\ 26\overline{)795} \\ -52 \end{array}$ _____

2. $\begin{array}{r} 3 \\ 31\overline{)907} \end{array}$ _____ $\begin{array}{r} 7 \\ 51\overline{)3,542} \end{array}$ _____

3. $\begin{array}{r} 7 \\ 45\overline{)3,688} \end{array}$ _____ $\begin{array}{r} 5 \\ 87\overline{)4,241} \end{array}$ _____

Trial Quotients

Write *too large, too small,* or *correct* for each trial quotient.
Then write the correct trial quotient.

a   b

1.
$$\begin{array}{r} 2 \\ 2\,4\,\overline{)4\,3\,2} \end{array}$$
_____
_____

$$\begin{array}{r} 7 \\ 2\,9\,\overline{)2\,3\,2} \end{array}$$
_____
_____

2.
$$\begin{array}{r} 2 \\ 4\,4\,\overline{)8\,3\,6} \end{array}$$
_____
_____

$$\begin{array}{r} 6 \\ 6\,7\,\overline{)4\,6\,9} \end{array}$$
_____
_____

3.
$$\begin{array}{r} 6 \\ 3\,2\,\overline{)1,8\,2\,4} \end{array}$$
_____
_____

$$\begin{array}{r} 4 \\ 1\,3\,\overline{)4,0\,5\,6} \end{array}$$
_____
_____

4.
$$\begin{array}{r} 6 \\ 5\,5\,\overline{)3,8\,5\,0} \end{array}$$
_____
_____

$$\begin{array}{r} 7 \\ 2\,5\,\overline{)2,1\,7\,5} \end{array}$$
_____
_____

5.
$$\begin{array}{r} 4 \\ 4\,4\,\overline{)1\,6,8\,0\,8} \end{array}$$
_____
_____

$$\begin{array}{r} 5 \\ 8\,5\,\overline{)5\,1,9\,3\,5} \end{array}$$
_____
_____

TOO SMALL!

Two-digit Divisors

To divide by a two-digit divisor, decide on a trial quotient.
Multiply and subtract. Write the remainder in the quotient.

Find: 569 ÷ 43

Choose a trial quotient.	Multiply and subtract.	Multiply and subtract.	Check:

Choose a trial quotient.

```
    H T O
  4 3 ) 5 6 9
```
Think:
4)5 is about 1.
So, 43)56 is about 1.

Multiply and subtract.

```
          1
  4 3 ) 5 6 9
      − 4 3 ↓
        1 3 9
```
Think:
4)13 is about 3.
So, 43)139 is about 3.

Multiply and subtract.

```
        1 3 R 10
  4 3 ) 5 6 9
      − 4 3 ↓
        1 3 9
      − 1 2 9
          1 0
```

Check:
```
      13
    × 43
     559
    + 10
     569
```

Divide.

1.

a
```
        H T O
          1 4 R 27
  4 5 ) 6 5 7
      − 4 5 ↓
        2 0 7
      − 1 8 0
          2 7
```

b
```
        H T O
  3 8 ) 8 3 6
```

c
```
        H T O
  6 1 ) 9 5 4
```

2.

```
        H T O
  7 5 ) 7 3 5
```

```
        H T O
  5 2 ) 1 2 6
```

```
        H T O
  9 1 ) 3 8 2
```

3.

```
   TTh Th H T O
  3 6 ) 1 1,6 6 9
```

```
   TTh Th H T O
  5 3 ) 2 2,1 6 1
```

```
   TTh Th H T O
  1 7 ) 1 1,4 8 3
```

Two-digit Divisors

Divide.

	a	*b*	*c*	*d*

1. $1\,2\,\overline{)\,8\,8}$ $\qquad$ $1\,3\,\overline{)\,6\,5}$ $\qquad$ $1\,6\,\overline{)\,9\,6}$ $\qquad$ $1\,7\,\overline{)\,5\,4}$

2. $1\,5\,\overline{)\,4\,6\,5}$ $\qquad$ $3\,2\,\overline{)\,6\,7\,2}$ $\qquad$ $4\,1\,\overline{)\,8\,3\,9}$ $\qquad$ $2\,4\,\overline{)\,9\,4\,4}$

3. $8\,2\,\overline{)\,1,3\,1\,2}$ $\qquad$ $4\,3\,\overline{)\,2,2\,0\,0}$ $\qquad$ $2\,6\,\overline{)\,1,8\,9\,8}$ $\qquad$ $1\,7\,\overline{)\,5,1\,7\,6}$

4. $5\,5\,\overline{)\,1\,7,2\,7\,0}$ $\qquad$ $3\,8\,\overline{)\,1\,9,9\,2\,7}$ $\qquad$ $7\,4\,\overline{)\,3\,0,3\,1\,3}$ $\qquad$ $6\,3\,\overline{)\,1\,0,5\,8\,4}$

Set up the problems. Then find the quotients.

	a	*b*	*c*

5. $38 \div 12 = $ _____ $\qquad$ $882 \div 42 = $ _____ $\qquad$ $931 \div 71 = $ _____

$12\overline{)38}$

Problem-Solving Method: Write a Number Sentence

In 1999, *Orbiter 3* became the first balloon to travel around the entire world. The journey, which began in Switzerland, lasted 19 days and covered a distance of 26,600 miles. On average, how many miles a day did the balloon fly?

Understand the problem.

- **What do you want to know?**
  the average number of miles the balloon flew each day

- **What information is given?**
  The balloon flew a total of 26,600 miles in 19 days.

Plan how to solve it.

- **What method can you use?**
  You can write a number sentence to model the problem.

Solve it.

- **How can you use this method to solve the problem?**
  You want to separate the total miles into 19 even groups. So, write a division number sentence.

$$26,600 \div 19 = \underline{\hspace{2cm}}$$

total miles / number of days / miles per day

$$
\begin{array}{r}
1,400 \\
19\overline{)26,600} \\
-19 \\
\hline
76 \\
-76 \\
\hline
000
\end{array}
$$

- **What is the answer?**
  The balloon flew an average of 1,400 miles each day.

Look back and check your answer.

- **Is your answer reasonable?**
  You can check division with multiplication.

$$
\begin{array}{r}
1,400 \\
\times 19 \\
\hline
12,600 \\
+14,000 \\
\hline
26,600
\end{array}
$$

The product matches the dividend.
The answer is reasonable.

Write a number sentence to solve each problem.

1. Mexico City is one of the fastest growing cities in the world. If the population there increased by 15,183 people every week, how many more people would be in Mexico City every day?
(1 week = 7 days)

Answer _____

2. A sheepdog's sense of smell is 44 times better than a human's. If a person can smell a hamburger cooking from 12 feet away, how far away can the sheepdog be and still smell it?

Answer _____

3. China has more school days than any other nation. Students there go to school 251 days a year. Japan is second, with 243 school days. How many more days a year do students in China go to school than students in Japan?

Answer _____

4. The highest mountain on Earth, Mount Everest, is 29,035 feet tall. K2 is the world's second highest mountain. It is 28,250 feet tall. What is the difference between the two mountains?

Answer _____

5. The average human heart rate is 70 beats per minute. How many times does a human heart beat per hour?
(1 hour = 60 minutes)

Answer _____

UNIT 3 Review

Divide.

	a	b	c	d
1.	4$\overline{)9\ 2}$	8$\overline{)6\ 0\ 0}$	5$\overline{)2\ 9\ 5}$	9$\overline{)1\ 0\ 8}$
2.	3$\overline{)5\ 0}$	6$\overline{)5\ 6\ 1}$	7$\overline{)4\ 2\ 5}$	2$\overline{)1,0\ 1\ 4}$
3.	7$\overline{)1,5\ 0\ 2}$	4$\overline{)3,6\ 8\ 5}$	8$\overline{)2,4\ 3\ 9}$	5$\overline{)7,6\ 2\ 1}$
4.	2 0$\overline{)8\ 4\ 0}$	3 0$\overline{)1,0\ 5\ 0}$	7 0$\overline{)6,3\ 5\ 0}$	8 0$\overline{)1,6\ 0\ 8}$

Set up the problems. Then find the quotients.

	a	b	c
5.	$84 \div 4 =$ _____	$695 \div 5 =$ _____	$368 \div 8 =$ _____
6.	$46 \div 7 =$ _____	$1,465 \div 30 =$ _____	$2,690 \div 50 =$ _____

UNIT 3 Review

Round the dividends to estimate the quotients.

	a	*b*	*c*
7.	$8\overline{)4\ 5\ 0}$	$7\overline{)2\ 0\ 5}$	$9\overline{)3\ 4\ 2}$

Round the dividends and the divisors to estimate the quotients.

	a	*b*	*c*
8.	$5\ 7\overline{)6\ 2\ 4}$	$4\ 7\overline{)9\ 7\ 2}$	$2\ 3\overline{)6\ 4\ 2}$

**Write *too large, too small,* or *correct* for each trial quotient.
Then write the correct trial quotient.**

	a		*b*	
9.	$7\ 2\overline{)5,1\ 0\ 9}^{\quad 7}$	_____	$4\ 2\overline{)3,2\ 8\ 7}^{\quad 8}$	_____
		_____		_____
10.	$3\ 1\overline{)2,5\ 2\ 7}^{\quad 7}$	_____	$5\ 1\overline{)1,6\ 2\ 4}^{\quad 4}$	_____
		_____		_____

Divide.

	a	*b*	*c*	*d*
11.	$3\ 8\overline{)9\ 8\ 8}$	$6\ 4\overline{)1,3\ 4\ 4}$	$4\ 2\overline{)1,6\ 0\ 0}$	$5\ 7\overline{)3,6\ 7\ 3}$

Set up the problems. Then find the quotients.

	a	*b*	*c*
12. $65 \div 13 =$ _____		$649 \div 31 =$ _____	$823 \div 47 =$ _____

Choose an operation to solve each problem.
Then solve the problem.

13. It takes about 4 pounds of worms to eat a pound of garbage. How many pounds of worms are needed to eat 500 pounds of garbage?

Operation_____

Answer_____

14. An adult's small intestine is about 300 inches long. How long is that in feet? (1 foot = 12 inches)

Operation_____

Answer_____

Write a number sentence to solve each problem.

15. Every week, about 1,162 square miles of tropical rain forests are cut down. How many square miles are cut down every day?

Answer_____

16. One hour of bicycling burns about 210 calories. Steve rode his bike for 3 hours. About how many calories did he burn?

Answer_____

17. There are 167 steps from ground level to the top of the Statue of Liberty's pedestal. There are 168 steps from the pedestal to her head. How many steps are there from the ground to the Statue of Liberty's head?

Answer_____

unit 4

Meaning of Fractions

A **fraction** names part of a whole. This circle has 3 equal parts. Each part is $\frac{1}{3}$ of the circle.
Two of the three equal parts are shaded green.

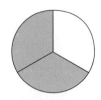

numerator   ⟶   <u>**2** — **two green parts**</u>
denominator ⟶   **3** — **three parts in all**

We read $\frac{2}{3}$ as two-thirds.

A fraction also names part of a group.
Three of the five flowers are red.

$$\frac{3 - \textbf{three red flowers}}{5 - \textbf{five flowers in all}}$$

Three-fifths are red.

Write the fraction and the word name for the part that is shaded.

        a   *b*   *c*

1.

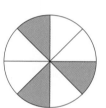

  $\frac{1}{5}$ or   one-fifth   3/8 or three eighiths   _____ or _____

Write the fraction for the word name.

        a   *b*   *c*

2. two-sevenths _____$\frac{2}{7}$_____   three-fourths _____   six-ninths _____

Write the word name for the fraction.

        a   *b*   *c*

3. $\frac{5}{8}$ _____ five-eighths _____ $\frac{4}{7}$ _____ $\frac{1}{4}$ _____

Write the fraction and the word name for the part that is shaded.

            a   *b*   *c*

4.   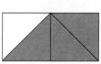

_____ or _____   _____ or _____   _____ or _____

Write the fraction for the word name.

            a   *b*   *c*

5. nine-tenths _____   six-sixths _____   two-eighths _____

6. five-sevenths _____   ten-twelfths _____   four-ninths _____

Write the word name for the fraction.

            a   *b*   *c*

7. $\frac{1}{3}$ _____ $\frac{7}{9}$ _____ $\frac{5}{5}$ _____

8. $\frac{6}{7}$ _____ $\frac{3}{10}$ _____ $\frac{9}{12}$ _____

There are 7 days in a week. Each day is $\frac{1}{7}$ week. Write the following as a fraction of a week. Write the word name for the fraction.

            a   *b*   *c*

9. 4 days = ___$\frac{4}{7}$___ week   5 days = _____ week   2 days = _____ week

_____*four-sevenths*_____   _____   _____

There are 20 nickels in a dollar. Each nickel is $\frac{1}{20}$ dollar. Write the following as a fraction of a dollar. Write the word name for the fraction.

            a   *b*   *c*

10. 6 nickels = ___$\frac{6}{20}$___ dollar   11 nickels = _____ dollar   8 nickels = _____ dollar

_____*six-twentieths*_____   _____   _____

Equivalent Fractions

Equivalent fractions have the same value. Compare the circles. The shaded part of one circle is equal to the shaded part of the other circle. What part of each circle is shaded?

$\frac{1}{2}$ of the circle is shaded. $\frac{3}{6}$ of the circle is shaded.

$\frac{1}{2}$ and $\frac{3}{6}$ are equivalent fractions. $\frac{1}{2} = \frac{3}{6}$

**The pizza at the right is divided into 8 equal parts.
Each part is $\frac{1}{8}$ of the figure.
Write the equivalent fractions.**

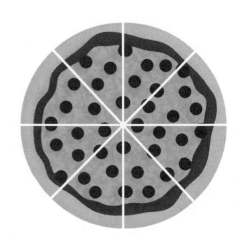

1. How many $\frac{1}{8}$ parts are in $\frac{1}{4}$ of the figure? ___2___ $\frac{1}{4} = \frac{2}{8}$

2. How many $\frac{1}{8}$ parts are in $\frac{1}{2}$ of the figure? _____ $\frac{1}{2} = \frac{}{8}$

3. How many $\frac{1}{8}$ parts are in $\frac{3}{4}$ of the figure? _____ $\frac{3}{4} = \frac{}{8}$

4. How many $\frac{1}{8}$ parts are in $\frac{2}{4}$ of the figure? _____ $\frac{2}{4} = \frac{}{8}$

Write two equivalent fractions for the shaded part of each figure.

a   *b*

5.

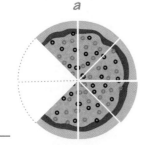

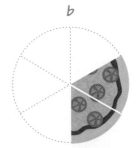

$\frac{3}{4} = \frac{6}{8}$

_____   _____

6.

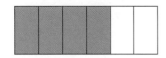

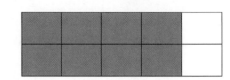

_____   _____

Compare and Order Fractions

Number lines can be used to compare and order fractions.
On a number line, the fractions become greater as you move
from the left to the right.

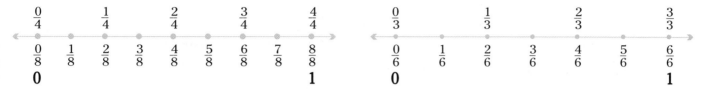

Compare $\frac{1}{8}$ **and** $\frac{3}{8}$.

Find $\frac{1}{8}$ and $\frac{3}{8}$ on the number line. Since $\frac{1}{8}$ is farther to the left, it is less than $\frac{3}{8}$.
$$\frac{1}{8} < \frac{3}{8}$$

Compare $\frac{4}{4}$ **and** $\frac{8}{8}$.

Find $\frac{4}{4}$ and $\frac{8}{8}$ on the number line. They name the same mark on the line.
$$\frac{4}{4} = \frac{8}{8} = 1$$

Compare $\frac{2}{3}$ **and** $\frac{2}{6}$.

Find $\frac{2}{3}$ and $\frac{2}{6}$ on the number line. Since $\frac{2}{3}$ is farther to the right, it is greater than $\frac{2}{6}$.
$$\frac{2}{3} > \frac{2}{6}$$

Use the number lines above to compare these fractions. Write <, >, or =.

	a	b	c	d
1.	$\frac{7}{8}$ > $\frac{2}{8}$	$\frac{3}{3}$ = $\frac{6}{6}$	$\frac{3}{6}$ < $\frac{5}{6}$	$\frac{1}{3}$ = $\frac{2}{6}$
2.	$\frac{1}{4}$ < $\frac{2}{4}$	$\frac{1}{4}$ = $\frac{2}{8}$	$\frac{5}{8}$ < $\frac{7}{8}$	$\frac{1}{6}$ < $\frac{2}{3}$

Write the fractions in order from least to greatest.

	a	b
3.	$\frac{7}{8}$ $\frac{3}{4}$ $\frac{3}{8}$ $\frac{3}{8}$ $\frac{3}{4}$ $\frac{7}{8}$	$\frac{1}{3}$ $\frac{3}{6}$ $\frac{1}{6}$
4.	$\frac{3}{8}$ $\frac{1}{8}$ $\frac{3}{4}$ $\frac{1}{8}$ $\frac{3}{8}$ $\frac{3}{4}$	$\frac{2}{3}$ $\frac{1}{3}$ $\frac{3}{6}$
5.	$\frac{2}{6}$ $\frac{2}{3}$ $\frac{1}{6}$ $\frac{1}{6}$ $\frac{2}{6}$ $\frac{2}{3}$	$\frac{7}{8}$ $\frac{1}{4}$ $\frac{4}{8}$

Equivalent Fractions in Higher Terms

To add or subtract fractions, you might need to change a fraction to an equivalent form. To change a fraction to an equivalent fraction in **higher terms**, multiply the numerator and the denominator by the same non-zero number.

Rewrite $\frac{1}{2}$ with 6 as the denominator.

Compare the denominators.

$$\frac{1}{2} = \frac{}{6} \quad \text{Think: } 2 \times 3 = 6$$

Multiply the numerator and the denominator by 3.

$$\frac{1}{2} = \frac{1 \times 3}{2 \times 3} = \frac{3}{6}$$

Multiply to write each fraction as an equivalent fraction in higher terms.

	a		b

1. $\frac{1}{3} = \frac{1 \times 4}{3 \times 4} = \frac{4}{12}$ 　　　　 $\frac{2}{5} = \frac{2 \times}{5 \times} = \frac{}{15}$

2. $\frac{3}{8} = \frac{3 \times}{8 \times} = \frac{}{16}$ 　　　　 $\frac{2}{3} = \frac{2 \times}{3 \times} = \frac{}{9}$

3. $\frac{3}{4} = \frac{3 \times}{4 \times} = \frac{}{12}$ 　　　　 $\frac{5}{8} = \frac{5 \times}{8 \times} = \frac{}{16}$

4. $\frac{2}{3} = \frac{2 \times}{3 \times} = \frac{}{12}$ 　　　　 $\frac{2}{5} = \frac{2 \times}{5 \times} = \frac{}{10}$

Write each fraction as an equivalent fraction in higher terms.

	a		b		c

5. $\frac{4}{5} = \frac{8}{10}$ 　　 $\frac{1}{4} = \frac{}{12}$ 　　 $\frac{7}{8} = \frac{}{16}$

6. $\frac{1}{3} = \frac{}{15}$ 　　 $\frac{5}{6} = \frac{}{12}$ 　　 $\frac{3}{5} = \frac{}{15}$

7. $\frac{1}{2} = \frac{}{12}$ 　　 $\frac{3}{4} = \frac{}{20}$ 　　 $\frac{3}{10} = \frac{}{20}$

8. $\frac{1}{5} = \frac{}{25}$ 　　 $\frac{2}{3} = \frac{}{15}$ 　　 $\frac{1}{2} = \frac{}{8}$

9. $\frac{1}{2} = \frac{}{10}$ 　　 $\frac{5}{9} = \frac{}{18}$ 　　 $\frac{2}{7} = \frac{}{14}$

$$\frac{1}{6}$$

$$=$$

$$\frac{2}{12}$$

Equivalent Fractions in Simplest Terms

Sometimes you might need to change a fraction to an equivalent fraction in **simplest terms**. To change a fraction to an equivalent fraction in simplest terms, divide the numerator and denominator by the same greatest number possible.

Rewrite $\frac{6}{8}$ in simplest terms.

Consider the numerator and denominator.

$\frac{6}{8} =$ **Think:** 8 can be divided evenly by 4, but 6 cannot.

6 can be divided evenly by 3, but 8 cannot.

Both 8 and 6 can be divided evenly by 2.

Divide the numerator and the denominator by 2.
$$\frac{6}{8} = \frac{6 \div 2}{8 \div 2} = \frac{3}{4}$$

A fraction is in simplest terms when 1 is the only number that divides both the numerator and the denominator evenly.

The fraction $\frac{3}{4}$ is in simplest terms.

Divide to write each fraction as an equivalent fraction in simplest terms.

	a	b	c
1.	$\frac{5}{15} = \frac{5 \div 5}{15 \div 5} = \frac{1}{3}$	$\frac{8}{10} = \frac{8 \div}{10 \div} =$	$\frac{9}{12} = \frac{9 \div}{12 \div} =$
2.	$\frac{4}{6} = \frac{4 \div}{6 \div} =$	$\frac{14}{16} = \frac{14 \div}{16 \div} =$	$\frac{10}{25} = \frac{10 \div}{25 \div} =$
3.	$\frac{8}{16} = \frac{8 \div}{16 \div} =$	$\frac{2}{16} = \frac{2 \div}{16 \div} =$	$\frac{2}{4} = \frac{2 \div}{4 \div} =$

Write each fraction as an equivalent fraction in simplest terms.

	a	b	c
4.	$\frac{12}{16} = \frac{3}{4}$	$\frac{2}{6} = $ _____	$\frac{4}{12} = $ _____
5.	$\frac{4}{16} = $ _____	$\frac{6}{10} = $ _____	$\frac{6}{9} = $ _____
6.	$\frac{8}{14} = $ _____	$\frac{5}{25} = $ _____	$\frac{10}{18} = $ _____
7.	$\frac{15}{18} = $ _____	$\frac{3}{12} = $ _____	$\frac{4}{14} = $ _____
8.	$\frac{5}{10} = $ _____	$\frac{8}{18} = $ _____	$\frac{4}{10} = $ _____

Improper Fractions and Mixed Numbers

An **improper fraction** is a fraction with a numerator that is greater than or equal to the denominator.

$$\frac{4}{4}, \frac{14}{2}, \text{ and } \frac{7}{4} \text{ are improper fractions.}$$

An improper fraction can be written as a whole or mixed number.

A **mixed number** is a whole number and a fraction.

$$2\frac{1}{3} \text{ is a mixed number.}$$

A mixed number can be written as an improper fraction.

Write $\frac{4}{4}$ and $\frac{14}{2}$ as whole numbers.

Divide the numerator by denominator.

$$4\overline{)4}^{\,1} \qquad \frac{4}{4} = 1$$

$$4\overline{)12}^{\,3} \qquad \frac{12}{4} = 3$$

Write $\frac{7}{4}$ as a mixed number.

Divide the numerator by the denominator. Write the remainder as a fraction by writing the remainder over the divisor.

$$\begin{array}{r} 1\frac{3}{4} \\ 4\overline{)7} \\ -4 \\ \hline 3 \end{array} \qquad \frac{7}{4} = 1\frac{3}{4}$$

Write $2\frac{1}{3}$ as an improper fraction.

Multiply the whole number and the denominator. Add this product to the numerator. Then write the sum over the denominator.

$$2\frac{1}{3} = \frac{2 \times 3 + 1}{3} = \frac{6+1}{3} = \frac{7}{3}$$

$$2\frac{1}{3} = \frac{7}{3}$$

Write as a whole number.

	a	b
1.	$\frac{20}{5} = \underline{\quad 4 \quad}$	$\frac{16}{8} = \underline{\qquad}$
2.	$\frac{56}{4} = \underline{\qquad}$	$\frac{14}{14} = \underline{\qquad}$

Write as a mixed number.

3.	$\frac{13}{12} = \underline{\quad 1\frac{1}{12} \quad}$	$\frac{18}{7} = \underline{\qquad}$
4.	$\frac{15}{8} = \underline{\qquad}$	$\frac{12}{11} = \underline{\qquad}$

Write as an improper fraction.

5.	$1\frac{4}{5} = \underline{\quad \frac{9}{5} \quad}$	$4\frac{3}{7} = \underline{\qquad}$
6.	$5\frac{1}{4} = \underline{\qquad}$	$2\frac{2}{5} = \underline{\qquad}$

Write as a mixed number or whole number. Simplify.

	a	*b*	*c*	*d*
7.	$\frac{6}{5} = $ _____	$\frac{5}{3} = $ _____	$\frac{32}{6} = $ _____	$\frac{18}{12} = $ _____
8.	$\frac{12}{5} = $ _____	$\frac{16}{3} = $ _____	$\frac{12}{9} = $ _____	$\frac{19}{4} = $ _____
9.	$\frac{21}{12} = $ _____	$\frac{23}{6} = $ _____	$\frac{13}{2} = $ _____	$\frac{20}{8} = $ _____
10.	$\frac{36}{9} = $ _____	$\frac{12}{12} = $ _____	$\frac{16}{8} = $ _____	$\frac{54}{6} = $ _____

Write as an improper fraction.

	a	*b*	*c*	*d*
11.	$4\frac{1}{4} = $ _____	$3\frac{2}{3} = $ _____	$4\frac{1}{2} = $ _____	$1\frac{1}{6} = $ _____
12.	$2\frac{1}{4} = $ _____	$1\frac{7}{8} = $ _____	$4\frac{1}{3} = $ _____	$3\frac{4}{5} = $ _____
13.	$4\frac{2}{3} = $ _____	$1\frac{1}{10} = $ _____	$2\frac{3}{5} = $ _____	$2\frac{5}{7} = $ _____
14.	$2\frac{2}{9} = $ _____	$4\frac{2}{5} = $ _____	$5\frac{1}{2} = $ _____	$4\frac{1}{6} = $ _____

Addition and Subtraction of Fractions with Like Denominators

To add or subtract fractions with like denominators, add or
subtract the numerators. Use the same denominator. Simplify the answer.

Remember,
- to simplify an improper fraction, write it as a whole
  number or a mixed number.
- to simplify a proper fraction, write it in simplest terms.

Find: $\frac{4}{5} + \frac{3}{5}$

Add the numerators.	Use the same denominator.
$\frac{3}{5}$ $+\frac{4}{5}$ $\overline{7}$	$\frac{3}{5}$ $+\frac{4}{5}$ $\overline{\frac{7}{5}} = 1\frac{2}{5}$
	Simplify the answer.

Find: $\frac{7}{8} - \frac{3}{8}$

Subtract the numerators.	Use the same denominator.
$\frac{7}{8}$ $-\frac{3}{8}$ $\overline{4}$	$\frac{7}{8}$ $-\frac{3}{8}$ $\overline{\frac{4}{8}} = \frac{1}{2}$
	Simplify the answer.

Add. Simplify.

	a	b	c	d	e
1.	$\frac{5}{12}$ $+\frac{3}{12}$ $\overline{\frac{8}{12}} = \frac{2}{3}$	$\frac{4}{9}$ $+\frac{2}{9}$	$\frac{3}{7}$ $+\frac{1}{7}$	$\frac{3}{8}$ $+\frac{1}{8}$	$\frac{4}{9}$ $+\frac{3}{9}$
2.	$\frac{3}{5}$ $+\frac{3}{5}$	$\frac{4}{5}$ $+\frac{3}{5}$	$\frac{3}{8}$ $+\frac{6}{8}$	$\frac{2}{3}$ $+\frac{2}{3}$	$\frac{7}{8}$ $+\frac{1}{8}$

Subtract. Simplify.

	a	b	c	d	e
3.	$\frac{5}{8}$ $-\frac{1}{8}$ $\overline{\frac{4}{8}} = \frac{1}{2}$	$\frac{6}{6}$ $-\frac{4}{6}$	$\frac{5}{8}$ $-\frac{3}{8}$	$\frac{5}{6}$ $-\frac{2}{6}$	$\frac{5}{9}$ $-\frac{2}{9}$

Addition and Subtraction of Mixed Numbers with Like Denominators

To add or subtract mixed numbers with like denominators, first add or subtract the fractions. Then add or subtract the whole numbers and simplify.

Find: $1\frac{1}{8} + 2\frac{5}{8}$

Add the fractions.	Add the whole numbers. Simplify.
$1\frac{1}{8}$ $+2\frac{5}{8}$ $\overline{\frac{6}{8}}$	$1\frac{1}{8}$ $+2\frac{5}{8}$ $\overline{3\frac{6}{8} = 3\frac{3}{4}}$

Find: $8\frac{5}{9} - 4\frac{2}{9}$

Subtract the fractions.	Subtract the whole numbers. Simplify.
$8\frac{5}{9}$ $-4\frac{2}{9}$ $\overline{\frac{3}{9}}$	$8\frac{5}{9}$ $-4\frac{2}{9}$ $\overline{4\frac{3}{9} = 4\frac{1}{3}}$

Add. Simplify.

	a	b	c	d	e
1.	$2\frac{1}{4}$ $+3\frac{1}{4}$ $\overline{5\frac{2}{4} = 5\frac{1}{2}}$	$3\frac{2}{4}$ $+6\frac{1}{4}$	$9\frac{3}{5}$ $+5\frac{1}{5}$	$6\frac{1}{8}$ $+\;2\frac{3}{8}$	$4\frac{3}{10}$ $+\;5\frac{3}{10}$
2.	$8\frac{1}{5}$ $+9\frac{3}{5}$	$6\frac{1}{4}$ $+9\frac{2}{4}$	$6\frac{1}{3}$ $+5\frac{1}{3}$	$12\frac{2}{5}$ $+\;9\frac{1}{5}$	$12\frac{2}{9}$ $+\;4\frac{4}{9}$

Subtract. Simplify.

	a	b	c	d	e
3.	$4\frac{11}{12}$ $-2\frac{1}{12}$ $\overline{2\frac{10}{12} = 2\frac{5}{6}}$	$3\frac{7}{8}$ $-2\frac{3}{8}$	$6\frac{7}{12}$ $-2\frac{5}{12}$	$5\frac{9}{10}$ $-3\frac{7}{10}$	$7\frac{5}{6}$ $-2\frac{1}{6}$
4.	$7\frac{6}{8}$ $-4\frac{4}{8}$	$6\frac{3}{8}$ $-1\frac{1}{8}$	$8\frac{4}{5}$ $-3\frac{2}{5}$	$5\frac{5}{12}$ $-4\frac{1}{12}$	$8\frac{7}{10}$ $-4\frac{3}{10}$

Problem-Solving Method: Use Logic

Recycling Times reported the aluminum can recycling statistics for 1990, 1995, and 1999. In those years, $\frac{3}{5}$, $\frac{2}{3}$, and $\frac{3}{7}$ of all the cans collected were recycled. The fraction for 1999 has an even numerator. More cans were recycled in 1995 than in 1990. What were the aluminum can recycling statistics for 1990, 1995, and 1999?

Understand the problem.

- **What do you want to know?**
  the can recycling statistics for 1990, 1995, and 1999

- **What information are you given?**
  In those years, $\frac{3}{5}$, $\frac{2}{3}$, and $\frac{3}{7}$ of all the cans collected were recycled.

  Clue 1: The fraction for 1999 has an even numerator.
  Clue 2: More cans were recycled in 1995 than in 1990.

Plan how to solve it.

- **What method can you use?**
  You can organize all the possibilities in a table.
  Then you can use logic to match the clues to the possibilities.

Solve it.

- **How can you use this method to solve the problem?**
  Since each of the years has one statistic, there can only be one YES in each row and column. You can use a number line to compare the fractions for 1995 and 1990.

	$\frac{3}{5}$	$\frac{2}{3}$	$\frac{3}{7}$
1990	no	no	**YES**
1995	**YES**	no	no
1999	no	**YES**	no

- **What is the answer?**

  In 1990, $\frac{3}{7}$ of all the aluminum cans were recycled.

  In 1995, $\frac{3}{5}$ of all the aluminum cans were recycled.

  In 1999, $\frac{2}{3}$ of all the aluminum cans were recycled.

  Check:
  In $\frac{2}{3}$, 2 is even.
  $\frac{3}{5} > \frac{3}{7}$

Look back and check your answer.

- **Is your answer reasonable?**

  Clue 1: The fraction for 1999 has an even numerator.
  Clue 2: More cans were recycled in 1995 than in 1990.

  The answer matches the clues.
  The answer is reasonable.

Use logic to solve each problem.

1. In 1998, New York, Cleveland, and Boston had the best records in American League baseball. They won $\frac{7}{10}$, $\frac{5}{9}$, and $\frac{1}{2}$ of their games. New York had the best record. Cleveland won fewer games than Boston. What fraction of their games did each team win?

   New York_____

   Cleveland_____

   Boston_____

2. In the United States, petroleum, natural gas, and coal are used more than any other sources of energy. They make up $\frac{1}{5}$, $\frac{1}{4}$, and $\frac{2}{5}$ of all the energy used. Coal is used the least. More petroleum is used than natural gas. What fraction is each energy source?

   petroleum_____

   natural gas_____

   coal_____

3. The smallest mammal in the world is a Kitti's hognosed bat. The next two smallest bats are the proboscis bat and the banana bat. Their weights are $\frac{11}{10}$, $\frac{7}{10}$, and $\frac{9}{10}$ of an ounce. The banana bat weighs less than the proboscis bat. What are the weights of the three smallest bats?

   Kitti's hognosed bat_____

   proboscis bat_____

   banana bat_____

Estimate Fractions

Use these rules to **round** fractions.

When the numerator is:	Round to:
much less than the denominator	0
about $\frac{1}{2}$ the denominator	$\frac{1}{2}$
about the same as the denominator	1

To **estimate** fraction sums or differences, round the fractions. Then add or subtract.

Find: $\frac{3}{8} + \frac{1}{5}$

Round the fractions.

$$\frac{3}{8} \rightarrow \frac{1}{2}$$
$$+\frac{1}{5} \rightarrow +0$$

Add.

$$\frac{1}{2}$$
$$+0$$
$$\frac{1}{2}$$

Round the fractions. Write about 0, about $\frac{1}{2}$, or about 1.

	a		b

1. $\frac{6}{10}$ _____ about $\frac{1}{2}$ _____ $\frac{3}{4}$ _____

2. $\frac{1}{7}$ _____ $\frac{2}{11}$ _____

3. $\frac{7}{8}$ _____ $\frac{5}{9}$ _____

Estimate the sums or differences.

a

4. $\frac{6}{7} \rightarrow 1$
   $-\frac{1}{10} \rightarrow -0$
   _____
   1

5. $\frac{5}{6} \rightarrow$
   $-\frac{2}{3} \rightarrow$
   _____

6. $\frac{1}{4} \rightarrow$
   $+\frac{6}{7} \rightarrow$
   _____

b

4. $\frac{4}{9} \rightarrow$
   $+\frac{4}{7} \rightarrow$
   _____

5. $\frac{11}{12} \rightarrow$
   $-\frac{1}{9} \rightarrow$
   _____

6. $\frac{7}{8} \rightarrow$
   $-\frac{4}{9} \rightarrow$
   _____

c

4. $\frac{1}{6} \rightarrow$
   $+\frac{7}{8} \rightarrow$
   _____

5. $\frac{3}{5} \rightarrow$
   $+\frac{1}{6} \rightarrow$
   _____

6. $\frac{5}{9} \rightarrow$
   $+\frac{2}{5} \rightarrow$
   _____

Addition of Fractions with Different Denominators

To add fractions with different denominators, first rewrite the fractions as equivalent fractions with like denominators. Then add and simplify the answer.

Find: $\frac{1}{3} + \frac{5}{6}$

Write equivalent fractions with like denominators.

$\frac{1}{3} = \frac{2}{6}$

$+\frac{5}{6} = \frac{5}{6}$

Remember: $\frac{1}{3} = \frac{1 \times 2}{3 \times 2} = \frac{2}{6}$

Add the numerators.
Use the same denominator.

$\frac{1}{3} = \frac{2}{6}$

$+\frac{5}{6} = \frac{5}{6}$ Simplify the answer.

$\frac{7}{6} = 1\frac{1}{6}$

Add. Simplify.

	a	b	c	d

1.

a: $\frac{1}{6} = \frac{1}{6}$; $+\frac{1}{3} = \frac{2}{6}$; $\frac{3}{6} = \frac{1}{2}$

b: $\frac{3}{10} = \frac{}{10}$; $+\frac{1}{2} = \frac{}{10}$

c: $\frac{1}{8} = \frac{}{8}$; $+\frac{3}{4} = \frac{}{8}$

d: $\frac{1}{2} = \frac{}{6}$; $+\frac{1}{6} = \frac{}{6}$

2.

a: $\frac{3}{5} = \frac{}{10}$; $+\frac{7}{10} = \frac{}{10}$

b: $\frac{6}{7} = \frac{}{14}$; $+\frac{5}{14} = \frac{}{14}$

c: $\frac{8}{9} = \frac{}{9}$; $+\frac{2}{3} = \frac{}{9}$

d: $\frac{10}{12} = \frac{}{12}$; $+\frac{3}{4} = \frac{}{12}$

3.

a: $\frac{1}{8}$; $+\frac{1}{4}$

b: $\frac{1}{5}$; $+\frac{3}{10}$

c: $\frac{3}{10}$; $+\frac{1}{2}$

d: $\frac{3}{4}$; $+\frac{1}{8}$

Subtraction of Fractions with Different Denominators

To subtract fractions with different denominators, first rewrite the fractions as equivalent fractions with like denominators. Then subtract and simplify the answer.

Find: $\frac{9}{10} - \frac{1}{2}$

Write equivalent fractions with like denominators.

$$\frac{9}{10} = \frac{9}{10}$$
$$-\frac{1}{2} = \frac{5}{10}$$

Remember: $\frac{1}{2} = \frac{1 \times 5}{2 \times 5} = \frac{5}{10}$

Subtract the numerators. Use the same denominator.

$$\frac{9}{10} = \frac{9}{10}$$
$$-\frac{1}{2} = \frac{5}{10}$$ Simplify the answer.
$$\frac{4}{10} = \frac{2}{5}$$

Subtract. Simplify.

	a	b	c	d

1.

a.
$$\frac{1}{2} = \frac{4}{8}$$
$$-\frac{1}{8} = \frac{1}{8}$$
$$\frac{3}{8}$$

b.
$$\frac{1}{3} = \frac{}{6}$$
$$-\frac{1}{6} = \frac{}{6}$$

c.
$$\frac{3}{4} = \frac{}{4}$$
$$-\frac{1}{2} = \frac{}{4}$$

d.
$$\frac{5}{6} = \frac{}{6}$$
$$-\frac{2}{3} = \frac{}{6}$$

2.

a.
$$\frac{13}{14} = \frac{}{14}$$
$$-\frac{3}{7} = \frac{}{14}$$

b.
$$\frac{1}{2} = \frac{}{6}$$
$$-\frac{1}{6} = \frac{}{6}$$

c.
$$\frac{4}{5} = \frac{}{10}$$
$$-\frac{3}{10} = \frac{}{10}$$

d.
$$\frac{7}{20} = \frac{}{20}$$
$$-\frac{1}{4} = \frac{}{20}$$

Addition of Mixed Numbers with Different Denominators

To add mixed numbers with different denominators, write the
mixed numbers with like denominators. Add the fractions.
Then add the whole numbers and simplify.

Find: $3\frac{5}{12} + 5\frac{1}{3}$

Write the mixed numbers with like denominators.	Add the fractions.	Add the whole numbers.	Simplify.
$3\frac{5}{12} = 3\frac{5}{12}$	$3\frac{5}{12} = 3\frac{5}{12}$	$3\frac{5}{12} = 3\frac{5}{12}$	$8\frac{9}{12} = 8\frac{3}{4}$
$+5\frac{1}{3} = 5\frac{4}{12}$	$+5\frac{1}{3} = 5\frac{4}{12}$	$+5\frac{1}{3} = 5\frac{4}{12}$	
	$\frac{9}{12}$	$8\frac{9}{12}$	

Remember: $5\frac{1}{3} = 5\frac{4}{12}$
They are equivalent fractions.

Add. Simplify.

	a	b	c	d
1.	$3\frac{1}{8} = 3\frac{1}{8}$	$9\frac{2}{3} = 9\frac{}{6}$	$4\frac{1}{2} = 4\frac{}{12}$	$2\frac{5}{8} = 2\frac{5}{8}$
	$+6\frac{3}{4} = 6\frac{6}{8}$	$+1\frac{1}{6} = 1\frac{1}{6}$	$+1\frac{5}{12} = 1\frac{5}{12}$	$+6\frac{1}{4} = 6\frac{}{8}$
	$9\frac{7}{8}$			

2.	$12\frac{3}{4} =$	$5\frac{3}{8} =$	$8\frac{2}{3} =$	$7\frac{1}{10} =$
	$+\ \ 4\frac{1}{8} =$	$+15\frac{1}{2} =$	$+3\frac{1}{9} =$	$+6\frac{3}{5} =$

3.	$5\frac{5}{8} =$	$15\frac{5}{12} =$	$6\frac{3}{10} =$	$9\frac{2}{3} =$
	$+4\frac{1}{4} =$	$+\ \ 8\frac{1}{3} =$	$+10\frac{1}{5} =$	$+8\frac{2}{9} =$

Addition of Mixed Numbers with Regrouping

When adding mixed numbers, sometimes your sum will contain an improper fraction. To regroup a sum that contains an improper fraction, first write the improper fraction as a mixed number. Then add and simplify.

Find: $6\frac{2}{3} + 2\frac{5}{6}$

Write the fractions with like denominators. Add the mixed numbers.

$$6\frac{2}{3} = 6\frac{4}{6}$$
$$+2\frac{5}{6} = 2\frac{5}{6}$$
$$\overline{\hspace{1em}8\frac{9}{6}}$$

The sum, $8\frac{9}{6}$, contains an improper fraction. To regroup, write the improper fraction as a mixed number.

$$\frac{9}{6} = 1\frac{3}{6}$$

Then add the whole numbers.

$$8\frac{9}{6} = 8 + 1\frac{3}{6} = 9\frac{3}{6}$$

Simplify.

$$9\frac{3}{6} = 9\frac{1}{2}$$

Regroup. Simplify.

	a	b	c	d
1.	$3\frac{5}{3}$ $\frac{5}{3} = 1\frac{2}{3}$ $3 + 1\frac{2}{3} = 4\frac{2}{3}$	$6\frac{13}{10}$	$9\frac{9}{8}$	$12\frac{7}{4}$
2.	$4\frac{8}{6}$	$8\frac{12}{9}$	$7\frac{18}{12}$	$10\frac{14}{8}$

Add. Regroup. Simplify.

	a	b	c
3.	$2\frac{3}{4} = 2\frac{3}{4}$ $+1\frac{1}{2} = 1\frac{2}{4}$ $\overline{3\frac{5}{4} = 3 + 1\frac{1}{4} = 4\frac{1}{4}}$	$4\frac{5}{8} =$ $+2\frac{3}{4} =$	$5\frac{9}{10} =$ $+3\frac{2}{5} =$
4.	$4\frac{2}{3} =$ $+8\frac{7}{12} =$	$3\frac{7}{10} =$ $+3\frac{4}{5} =$	$6\frac{11}{18} =$ $+2\frac{5}{9} =$

Subtraction of Mixed Numbers with Different Denominators

To subtract mixed numbers with different denominators, write the mixed numbers with like denominators. Subtract the fractions. Subtract the whole numbers. Simplify.

Find: $9\frac{11}{12} - 2\frac{1}{4}$

Write the mixed numbers with like denominators.	Subtract the fractions.	Subtract the whole numbers.	Simplify.
$9\frac{11}{12} = 9\frac{11}{12}$ $-2\frac{1}{4} = 2\frac{3}{12}$	$9\frac{11}{12} = 9\frac{11}{12}$ $-2\frac{1}{4} = 2\frac{3}{12}$ $\frac{8}{12}$	$9\frac{11}{12} = 9\frac{11}{12}$ $-2\frac{1}{4} = 2\frac{3}{12}$ $7\frac{8}{12}$	$7\frac{8}{12} = 7\frac{2}{3}$

Subtract. Simplify.

a b c d

1.
$8\frac{5}{6} = 8\frac{5}{6}$
$-2\frac{1}{3} = 2\frac{2}{6}$
$6\frac{3}{6} = 6\frac{1}{2}$

$5\frac{3}{4} = 5\frac{3}{4}$
$-3\frac{1}{2} = 3\frac{}{4}$

$9\frac{5}{8} = 9\frac{5}{8}$
$-3\frac{1}{4} = 3\frac{}{8}$

$8\frac{7}{10} = 8\frac{7}{10}$
$-1\frac{1}{2} = 1\frac{}{10}$

2.
$15\frac{3}{4} =$
$-\ 8\frac{3}{8} =$

$16\frac{5}{6} =$
$-10\frac{1}{2} =$

$9\frac{5}{6} =$
$-6\frac{2}{3} =$

$12\frac{5}{8} =$
$-\ 7\frac{1}{4} =$

3.
$3\frac{4}{9} =$
$-1\frac{1}{3} =$

$5\frac{6}{7} =$
$-2\frac{1}{14} =$

$4\frac{5}{12} =$
$-3\frac{1}{4} =$

$9\frac{7}{18} =$
$-6\frac{2}{9} =$

Subtraction of Fractions and Mixed Numbers from Whole Numbers

Sometimes you will need to subtract a fraction from a whole number.
To subtract from a whole number, write the whole number as a mixed number
with a like denominator. Then subtract the fractions. Subtract the whole numbers.

Find: $6 - 4\frac{2}{3}$

To subtract, you need two fractions with like denominators.	Write 6 as a mixed number with 3 as the denominator.	Subtract the fractions.	Subtract the whole numbers.
6 $-4\frac{2}{3}$	$6 = 5 + \frac{3}{3} = 5\frac{3}{3}$ Remember: $\frac{3}{3} = 1$	$6 = 5\frac{3}{3}$ $-4\frac{2}{3} = 4\frac{2}{3}$ <hr> $\frac{1}{3}$	$6 = 5\frac{3}{3}$ $-4\frac{2}{3} = 4\frac{2}{3}$ <hr> $1\frac{1}{3}$

Write each whole number as a mixed number.

	a	b	c
1.	$4 = 3 + \frac{6}{6} = 3\frac{6}{6}$	$6 = 5 + \frac{8}{} =$	$2 = 1 + \frac{}{3} =$
2.	$10 = 9 + \frac{}{5} =$	$14 = 13 + \frac{}{3} =$	$9 = 8 + \frac{}{6} =$

Subtract.

	a	b	c	d
3.	$9 = 8\frac{4}{4}$ $-2\frac{3}{4} = 2\frac{3}{4}$ <hr> $6\frac{1}{4}$	$12 = 11\frac{3}{3}$ $-5\frac{1}{3} = 5\frac{1}{3}$	$9 = 8\frac{}{4}$ $-3\frac{1}{4} = 3\frac{1}{4}$	$20 = 19\frac{}{10}$ $-3\frac{7}{10} = 3\frac{7}{10}$
4.	$17 =$ $-5\frac{2}{15} =$	$5 =$ $-\frac{1}{6} =$	$13 =$ $-\frac{4}{9} =$	$9 =$ $-\frac{3}{7} =$

Subtraction of Mixed Numbers with Regrouping

When subtracting mixed numbers, it may be necessary to regroup first. To regroup a mixed number for subtraction, write the whole number part as a mixed number. Add the mixed number and the fraction. Then subtract and simplify.

Find: $6\frac{5}{12} - 2\frac{3}{4}$

Write the fractions with like denominators. Compare the numerators.	$\frac{9}{12}$ is greater than $\frac{5}{12}$. You can't subtract the fractions.	Add the mixed number and the fraction.	Subtract and simplify.
$6\frac{5}{12} = 6\frac{5}{12}$ $-2\frac{3}{4} = 2\frac{9}{12}$	To regroup $6\frac{5}{12}$, write 6 as a mixed number. $6 = 5\frac{12}{12}$	$6\frac{5}{12} = 5\frac{12}{12} + \frac{5}{12} = 5\frac{17}{12}$ Note: $\frac{17}{12}$ is an improper fraction.	$6\frac{5}{12} = 5\frac{17}{12}$ $-2\frac{3}{4} = 2\frac{9}{12}$ $\overline{\qquad 3\frac{8}{12} = 3\frac{2}{3}}$

Regroup each mixed number.

a	b	c
1. $6\frac{1}{3} = 5\frac{3}{3} + \frac{1}{3} = 5\frac{4}{3}$	$8\frac{7}{8} = 7\frac{}{8}$	$9\frac{1}{6} = 8\frac{}{6}$
2. $3\frac{6}{8} = 2\frac{}{8}$	$5\frac{9}{12} = 4\frac{}{12}$	$14\frac{8}{10} = 13\frac{}{10}$

Regroup. Subtract. Simplify.

a	b	c
3. $\quad 9\frac{3}{8} = 9\frac{3}{8} = 8\frac{11}{8}$ $\quad -4\frac{3}{4} = 4\frac{6}{8} = 4\frac{6}{8}$ $\overline{\qquad\qquad\qquad\quad 4\frac{5}{8}}$	$7\frac{1}{3} = 7\frac{}{6}$ $-2\frac{5}{6} = 2\frac{5}{6}$	$9\frac{1}{5} = 9\frac{}{10}$ $-2\frac{3}{10} = 2\frac{3}{10}$
4. $\quad 6\frac{3}{10}$ $\quad -4\frac{2}{5}$	$13\frac{1}{4}$ $-\ 6\frac{5}{8}$	$12\frac{5}{12}$ $-\ 7\frac{2}{3}$

Problem-Solving Method: Make a Model

Brent sewed two pieces of cloth end to end to make a flag. The first piece was yellow and $\frac{1}{2}$ yard long. The second piece was $\frac{1}{3}$ yard long and blue. How long was the flag that Brent sewed?

Understand the problem.

- **What do you want to know?**
  the length of the flag

- **What information is given?**
  He sewed $\frac{1}{2}$ yard of yellow cloth to $\frac{1}{3}$ yard of blue cloth.

Plan how to solve it.

- **What method can you use?**
  You can make a model of the flag.

Solve it.

- **How can you use this method to solve the problem?**
  Use fraction strips to model the sum of $\frac{1}{2}$ yard and $\frac{1}{3}$ yard.

Place one $\frac{1}{2}$ strip and one $\frac{1}{3}$ strip end to end under a 1-whole fraction strip.

1	
$\frac{1}{2}$	$\frac{1}{3}$

Find equal size fraction strips that fit exactly under $\frac{1}{2}$ and $\frac{1}{3}$.

1				
$\frac{1}{2}$			$\frac{1}{3}$	
$\frac{1}{6}$	$\frac{1}{6}$	$\frac{1}{6}$	$\frac{1}{6}$	$\frac{1}{6}$

- **What is the answer?**
  The flag was $\frac{5}{6}$ yard long.

Look back and check your answer.

- **Is your answer reasonable?**
  You can check your model with addition.

$$\frac{1}{2} = \frac{3}{6}$$
$$+\frac{1}{3} = \frac{2}{6}$$
$$\overline{\phantom{+\frac{1}{3} = } \frac{5}{6}}$$

The model and the sum are the same.
The answer is reasonable.

Make a model to solve each problem.

1. Kendra walked $\frac{1}{4}$ mile from school to the store. Then she walked $\frac{2}{3}$ mile from the store to home. How far did Kendra walk in all?

1										
$\frac{1}{4}$			$\frac{1}{3}$				$\frac{1}{3}$			
$\frac{1}{12}$	$\frac{1}{12}$	$\frac{1}{12}$	$\frac{1}{12}$	$\frac{1}{12}$	$\frac{1}{12}$	$\frac{1}{12}$	$\frac{1}{12}$	$\frac{1}{12}$	$\frac{1}{12}$	$\frac{1}{12}$

Answer _____

2. Jack grew $\frac{1}{2}$ inch in May and $\frac{2}{5}$ inch in June. How many inches did he grow in the two months altogether?

Answer _____

3. An average bark beetle is $\frac{1}{8}$ inch long. Carpenter ants are usually $\frac{1}{2}$ inch longer than a bark beetle. How long is an average carpenter ant?

Answer _____

4. Amy used $\frac{1}{4}$ yard of lace for curtains. Then she used $\frac{1}{3}$ yard of lace for a table cloth. How many yards of lace did Amy use in all?

Answer _____

5. José used $\frac{1}{2}$ cup of white flour and $\frac{1}{4}$ cup of whole-wheat flour to make bread. How much flour did he use in all?

Answer _____

Problem Solving

Solve. Simplify.

1. Ruby and Chung work together. Ruby lives $13\frac{1}{2}$ miles from work. Chung lives $2\frac{1}{6}$ miles beyond Ruby. How far from work does Chung live?

   Answer_____

2. Anne is $64\frac{1}{2}$ inches tall. Shaneeka is $61\frac{1}{4}$ inches tall. How much taller is Anne than Shaneeka?

   Answer_____

3. Fred used $1\frac{1}{6}$ cups of raisins and $3\frac{1}{3}$ cups of nuts to make his trail mix. How many cups of the mix did he make?

   Answer_____

4. The world's biggest pineapple weighed $17\frac{3}{4}$ pounds. The world's biggest apple weighed $3\frac{11}{16}$ pounds. How much more did the pineapple weigh than the apple?

   Answer_____

5. The largest butterfly in North America is the giant swallowtail. Its wingspan is 5 inches wide. The smallest is the pygmy blue. Its wingspan is only $\frac{1}{2}$ inch. How much larger is a giant swallowtail than a pygmy blue?

   Answer_____

6. An average car uses $1\frac{3}{5}$ ounces of gasoline for one minute of sitting still with the engine on. If a car waits at a traffic light for 2 minutes, how much gasoline will it use?

   Answer_____

7. Inez caught two fish. One weighed $3\frac{1}{2}$ pounds. The second fish weighed $4\frac{1}{4}$ pounds. How many pounds of fish did she catch?

   Answer_____

UNIT 4 Review

Write the fraction for the word name.

                  a   *b*   *c*

1. three-fifths _____   four-ninths _____   one-sixth _____

Write the fractions in order from least to greatest.

                               a   *b*

2. $\frac{3}{9}$ $\frac{2}{3}$ $\frac{1}{9}$ _____ $\frac{4}{5}$ $\frac{3}{10}$ $\frac{3}{5}$ _____

Write each fraction as an equivalent fraction in simplest terms.

        a   *b*   *c*   *d*

3. $\frac{9}{12}=$ _____ $\frac{6}{10}=$ _____ $\frac{4}{6}=$ _____ $\frac{4}{8}=$ _____

Rewrite each fraction as an equivalent fraction in higher terms.

       a   *b*   *c*   *d*

4. $\frac{2}{3}=\frac{}{9}$ $\frac{1}{6}=\frac{}{12}$ $\frac{3}{5}=\frac{}{15}$ $\frac{1}{2}=\frac{}{10}$

Add. Simplify.

      a   *b*   *c*   *d*

5. $\begin{array}{r} \frac{3}{9} \\ +\frac{4}{9} \\ \hline \end{array}$ $\begin{array}{r} \frac{4}{7} \\ +\frac{3}{7} \\ \hline \end{array}$ $\begin{array}{r} \frac{1}{8} \\ +\frac{4}{8} \\ \hline \end{array}$ $\begin{array}{r} \frac{3}{10} \\ +\frac{3}{10} \\ \hline \end{array}$

6. $\begin{array}{r} \frac{3}{8} \\ +\frac{1}{4} \\ \hline \end{array}$ $\begin{array}{r} \frac{1}{3} \\ +\frac{7}{9} \\ \hline \end{array}$ $\begin{array}{r} \frac{3}{5} \\ +\frac{3}{10} \\ \hline \end{array}$ $\begin{array}{r} \frac{1}{2} \\ +\frac{1}{16} \\ \hline \end{array}$

7. $\begin{array}{r} 7\frac{1}{3} \\ +3\frac{4}{9} \\ \hline \end{array}$ $\begin{array}{r} 6\frac{3}{4} \\ +4\frac{5}{12} \\ \hline \end{array}$ $\begin{array}{r} 9\frac{1}{2} \\ +1\frac{3}{8} \\ \hline \end{array}$ $\begin{array}{r} 5\frac{1}{5} \\ +2\frac{4}{15} \\ \hline \end{array}$

UNIT 4 Review

Write as a mixed number or whole number.

	a	b	c	d
8.	$\frac{31}{8} =$ _____	$\frac{13}{6} =$ _____	$\frac{25}{5} =$ _____	$\frac{19}{4} =$ _____

Write as an improper fraction.

	a	b	c	d
9.	$4\frac{1}{3} =$ _____	$8\frac{2}{5} =$ _____	$2\frac{1}{8} =$ _____	$5\frac{3}{10} =$ _____

Write each whole number as a mixed number.

	a	b	c	d
10.	$5 = 4 + \frac{}{2} =$	$8 = 7 + \frac{5}{} =$	$12 = 11 + \frac{}{9} =$	$16 = 15 + \frac{7}{} =$

Subtract. Simplify.

	a	b	c	d
11.	$\begin{array}{r} \frac{7}{10} \\ -\frac{3}{10} \\ \hline \end{array}$	$\begin{array}{r} \frac{4}{7} \\ -\frac{2}{7} \\ \hline \end{array}$	$\begin{array}{r} \frac{11}{12} \\ -\frac{7}{12} \\ \hline \end{array}$	$\begin{array}{r} \frac{5}{6} \\ -\frac{2}{6} \\ \hline \end{array}$
12.	$\begin{array}{r} 7\frac{2}{3} \\ -2\frac{1}{3} \\ \hline \end{array}$	$\begin{array}{r} 5\frac{5}{6} \\ -3\frac{1}{6} \\ \hline \end{array}$	$\begin{array}{r} 8\frac{9}{10} \\ -4\frac{3}{10} \\ \hline \end{array}$	$\begin{array}{r} 9\frac{7}{8} \\ -1\frac{1}{8} \\ \hline \end{array}$
13.	$\begin{array}{r} 9\frac{1}{6} \\ -3\frac{2}{3} \\ \hline \end{array}$	$\begin{array}{r} 6\frac{1}{2} \\ -4\frac{3}{4} \\ \hline \end{array}$	$\begin{array}{r} 5\frac{1}{5} \\ -1\frac{3}{10} \\ \hline \end{array}$	$\begin{array}{r} 8 \\ -3\frac{4}{9} \\ \hline \end{array}$

Estimate the sums or differences.

	a	b	c
14.	$\begin{array}{r} \frac{1}{5} \rightarrow \\ +\frac{4}{9} \rightarrow \\ \hline \end{array}$	$\begin{array}{r} \frac{7}{8} \rightarrow \\ -\frac{1}{3} \rightarrow \\ \hline \end{array}$	$\begin{array}{r} \frac{3}{10} \rightarrow \\ +\frac{4}{5} \rightarrow \\ \hline \end{array}$

Use logic to solve each problem.

15. In 1998, Atlanta, Philadelphia, and New York had the best records in the Eastern division of National League baseball. They won about $\frac{4}{9}$, $\frac{2}{3}$, and $\frac{5}{9}$ of their games. The denominator for Atlanta's record is not a 9. New York won more of its games than Philadelphia. About what fraction of its games did each team win?

Atlanta_____

Philadelphia_____

New York_____

16. The three largest butterflies in the world are the Goliath, the Queen Alexandra, and the African swallowtail. Their wingspans are $9\frac{1}{10}$, $8\frac{3}{10}$, and 11 inches. The Queen Alexandra is the largest. The African swallowtail is larger than the Goliath. What are the wingspans of the three largest butterflies?

Goliath_____

Queen Alexandra_____

African swallowtail_____

Make a model to solve each problem.

17. The track at the gym is $\frac{1}{3}$ mile long. The high school's track is $\frac{1}{12}$ mile longer than the gym's. How long is the high school track?

Answer_____

18. Nando mixed $\frac{1}{4}$ gallon of red paint with $\frac{3}{8}$ gallon of white paint to make pink. How much pink paint did Nando mix?

Answer_____

Meaning of Decimals

Like fractions, **decimals** show parts of a whole. The shaded portion of each square can be written as a fraction or as a decimal.

 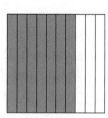 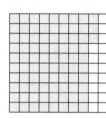 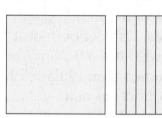

$\frac{1}{1}$ or 1	$\frac{7}{10}$ or 0.7	$\frac{83}{100}$ or 0.83	$1\frac{5}{10}$ or 1.5
Read: one	**seven-tenths**	**eighty-three hundredths**	**one and five-tenths**

Remember,

- a *decimal point* separates a whole number and its decimal parts.
- a whole number has a decimal point, but it is usually not written. 2 is the same as 2.0.
- a decimal point is read as *and*.

Write the decimal shown by the shaded part of each figure.

         a   *b*   *c*

1.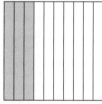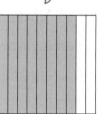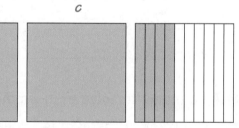

_____   _____   _____

2.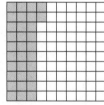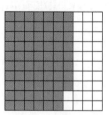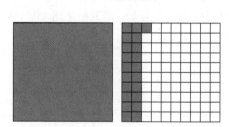

_____   _____   _____

Write each money amount with a dollar sign and a decimal point.

                  a   *b*

3.   one dollar _____*$1.00*_____   ten cents _____*$0.10*_____

4.   twelve dollars _____   three dimes _____

Decimal Place Value

You can use a place-value chart to help you understand decimal places.
The digits to the right of the decimal point show decimals.
The digits to the left of the decimal point show whole numbers.

The **2** is in the tens place.
Its value is 20 or **2** tens.

The **8** is in the ones place.
Its value is 8 or **8** ones.

The **6** is in the tenths place.
Its value is 0.6 or **6** tenths.

The **0** is in the hundredths place.
Its value is 0 or **0** hundredths.

The **3** is in the thousandths place.
Its value is 0.003 or **3** thousandths.

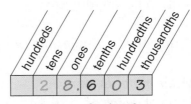

whole numbers . decimals

Write each number in the place-value chart.

1. 29.01
2. 0.485
3. 3.782
4. 67.567
5. 10.0
6. 142.04

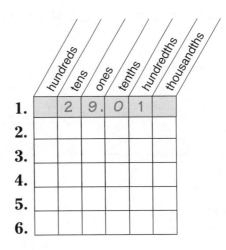

Write the place name for the 7 in each number.

	a	b	c
7.	2.73 _____tenths_____	8.076 _____	12.687 _____
8.	0.017 _____	7.019 _____	6.007 _____
9.	10.47 _____	70.480 _____	0.760 _____

Write the value of the underlined digit.

	a	b	c
10.	0.22<u>3</u> __3 thousandths__	0.1<u>9</u>4 _____	0.60<u>4</u> _____
11.	1.9<u>5</u> _____	<u>3</u>.008 _____	0.1<u>8</u> _____
12.	6<u>4</u>.5 _____	4.67<u>8</u> _____	16.9<u>6</u> _____

Reading and Writing Decimals

A place-value chart can help you understand how to read and write decimals.

To read a decimal, read it as a whole number. Then name the place value of the last digit.

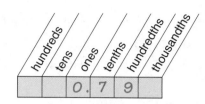

Read 0.79 as seventy-nine hundredths.

To read a decimal that has a whole number part,

- read the whole number part.
- read the decimal point as *and*.
- read the decimal part as a whole number and then name the place value of the last digit.

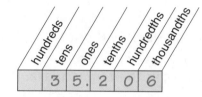

Read 35.206 as thirty-five and two-hundred six thousandths.

Write the place value of the last digit of the number.

	a	*b*	*c*
1.	3.09 _____hundredths_____	89.065 _____	0.4 _____
2.	12.1 _____	2.63 _____	4.002 _____
3.	0.4 _____	64.002 _____	640.20 _____

Write as a decimal.

	a	*b*
4.	four tenths _____0.4_____	four hundredths _____
5.	four thousandths _____	five hundred four thousandths _____
6.	sixteen thousandths _____	sixteen hundredths _____
7.	ten and thirteen hundredths _____	fifty-four and one hundredth _____

Write each decimal in words.

8. 0.048 _____*forty-eight thousandths*_____

9. 0.64 _____

10. 9.4 _____

Write as a decimal.

a   b

11. five tenths _____ eighty-nine hundredths _____

12. three and four thousandths _____ sixty-three hundredths _____

13. four and seven tenths _____ eight and five hundredths _____

14. thirty-one hundredths _____ twenty-eight thousandths _____

15. seventeen thousandths _____ eight and nine thousandths _____

16. nine and nine hundredths _____ twenty-three hundredths _____

17. seventy and one tenth _____ seventy-one hundredths _____

Write each decimal in words.

18. 0.23 _____

19. 0.8 _____

20. 4.53 _____

21. 6.009 _____

22. 9.802 _____

23. 18.04 _____

24. 0.18 _____

Compare and Order Decimals

To compare two decimal numbers, begin at the left.

Compare the digits in each place value.

The symbol > means *is greater than*.   **1.9 > 1.2**
The symbol < means *is less than*.   **3.1 < 3.5**
The symbol = means *is equal to*.   **2.7 = 2.70**

Compare: 1.5 and 1.4

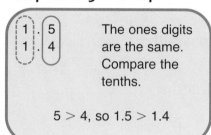

| 1 . 5 |
| 1 . 4 |

The ones digits are the same. Compare the tenths.

5 > 4, so 1.5 > 1.4

Compare: $0.06 and $0.31

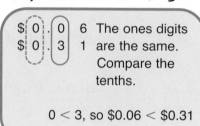

| $ 0 . 0 | 6 |
| $ 0 . 3 | 1 |

The ones digits are the same. Compare the tenths.

0 < 3, so $0.06 < $0.31

Compare: 0.2 and 0.29

| 0 . 2 | 0 |
| 0 . 2 | 9 |

Write a zero. The ones and tenths digits are the same. Compare the hundredths.

0 < 9, so 0.2 < 0.29

Compare. Write <, >, or =.

  a   b   c

1. 1.5 ___<___ 1.9   1.3 _____ 1.8   3.5 _____ 3.3

| 1 . 5 | 1 . 3   3 . 5
| 1 . 9 | 1 . 8   3 . 3

2. $1.76 _____ $1.92 $0.38 _____ $0.56 $8.62 _____ $8.27

3. 0.49 _____ 0.490   0.890 _____ 0.089   0.134 _____ 0.143

Write in order from least to greatest.

             a   b

4. 14.0   1.4   140 ____1.4   14.0   140____   0.7   0.007   0.07

    1 4 . 0
        1 . 4
1 4 0

5. 345   3.45   34.5 _____   0.80   0.79   0.81
_____

Compare. Write <, >, or =.

	a	b	c
6.	6.210 _____ 6.201	$19.78 _____ $19.87	58.9 _____ 59.0
7.	117.8 _____ 171.8	0.609 _____ 0.61	44.8 _____ 44.80
8.	6 _____ 6.0	27.9 _____ 2.79	15.34 _____ 5.434
9.	0.89 _____ 0.009	0.9 _____ 0.89	$0.09 _____ $0.89
10.	61.4 _____ 61.40	6.315 _____ 6.31	200.0 _____ 200
11.	165 _____ 165.001	12.385 _____ 12.3	2.428 _____ 2.43

Write in order from least to greatest.

	a	b
12.	$17.0 $1.70 $170 _____	0.06 0.60 0.066 _____
13.	5.6 5.06 5.602 _____	0.3 0.003 0.03 _____
14.	1.2 21 2.1 _____	0.090 0.8 0.007 _____

"HE WAS LESS THAN SPOT OR SCRUFFY, BUT GREATER THAN FLUFFY OR PEPE."

Fraction and Decimal Equivalents

Sometimes you will need to either change a decimal to a fraction or a fraction to a decimal.

To write a decimal as a fraction, identify the value of the last place in the decimal. Use this place value to write the denominator.

Decimal		Fraction or Mixed Number
0.7	=	$\frac{7}{10}$
0.59	=	$\frac{59}{100}$
0.005	=	$\frac{5}{1,000}$
3.47	=	$3\frac{47}{100}$ or $\frac{347}{100}$

To write a fraction that has a denominator of 10, 100, or 1,000 as a decimal, write the digits from the numerator. Then write the decimal point.

Fraction or Mixed Number		Decimal
$\frac{3}{10}$	=	0.3
$\frac{43}{100}$	=	0.43
$\frac{529}{1,000}$	=	0.529
$\frac{618}{100}$ or $6\frac{18}{100}$	=	6.18

Write each decimal as a fraction.

	a	b	c	d
1.	0.3 $\frac{3}{10}$	0.7 _____	0.9 _____	0.1 _____
2.	0.03 _____	0.07 _____	0.09 _____	0.01 _____

Write each decimal as a mixed number.

	a	b	c	d
3.	2.3 $2\frac{3}{10}$	6.9 _____	3.7 _____	8.1 _____
4.	9.88 _____	5.07 _____	4.90 _____	2.25 _____

Write each fraction as a decimal.

	a	b	c	d
5.	$\frac{4}{10}$ 0.4	$\frac{8}{10}$ _____	$\frac{6}{10}$ _____	$\frac{2}{10}$ _____
6.	$\frac{23}{100}$ _____	$\frac{97}{100}$ _____	$\frac{246}{1,000}$ _____	$\frac{810}{1,000}$ _____
7.	$\frac{306}{100}$ _____	$\frac{901}{100}$ _____	$\frac{8,825}{1,000}$ _____	$\frac{6,975}{1,000}$ _____

Fraction and Decimal Equivalents

Not all fractions can be changed to decimal form easily. To write fractions that have denominators other than 10, 100, or 1,000 as decimals, first write an equivalent fraction that has a denominator of 10, 100, or 1,000. Then write the equivalent fraction as a decimal.

Remember, not all fractions have simple decimal equivalents.

Examples: $\frac{1}{3} = 0.333\ldots$ $\frac{1}{6} = 0.166\ldots$

Write $\frac{1}{2}$ as a decimal.

Write $\frac{1}{2}$ with 10 as the denominator.	Write the fraction as a decimal.
$\frac{1}{2} = \frac{1 \times 5}{2 \times 5} = \frac{5}{10}$	$= 0.5$

Write $3\frac{1}{4}$ as a decimal.

Write $3\frac{1}{4}$ as an improper fraction.	Write the new fraction with 100 as the denominator.	Write the fraction as a decimal.
$3\frac{1}{4} = \frac{13}{4}$	$\frac{13}{4} = \frac{13 \times 25}{4 \times 25} = \frac{325}{100}$	$= 3.25$

Write each fraction as a decimal.

	a	b	c
1.	$\frac{3}{4} = \frac{3 \times 25}{4 \times 25} = \frac{75}{100} = 0.75$	$\frac{1}{5} = $ _____	$\frac{24}{25} = $ _____
2.	$\frac{4}{5} = $ _____	$\frac{7}{20} = $ _____	$\frac{3}{20} = $ _____
3.	$\frac{6}{25} = $ _____	$\frac{10}{20} = $ _____	$\frac{13}{25} = $ _____
4.	$\frac{17}{5} = $ _____	$\frac{9}{2} = $ _____	$\frac{51}{20} = $ _____
5.	$\frac{68}{25} = $ _____	$\frac{33}{4} = $ _____	$\frac{34}{5} = $ _____

Write each mixed number as a decimal.

	a	b
6.	$4\frac{3}{20} = \frac{83}{20} = \frac{83 \times 5}{20 \times 5} = \frac{415}{100} = 4.15$	$20\frac{1}{5} = $ _____
7.	$3\frac{2}{25} = $ _____	$5\frac{22}{25} = $ _____

Problem-Solving Method: Find a Pattern

Linda grew a plant for her science fair project. She measured and recorded the plant's height every week to track its growth. How fast did the plant grow?

Week 1	Week 2	Week 3	Week 4	Week 5
$1\frac{1}{10}$ inches	$1\frac{1}{5}$ inches	$1\frac{3}{10}$ inches	$1\frac{2}{5}$ inches	$1\frac{1}{2}$ inches

Understand the problem.

- **What do you want to know?**
  how fast the plant grew

- **What information is given?**
  measurements for five weeks

Plan how to solve it.

- **What method can you use?**
  You can find a pattern.

Solve it.

- **How can you use this method to solve the problem?**
  Write each measurement as a decimal. Then look for a pattern between each week's height.

> **Week 1** $1\frac{1}{10}$ inch   =   1.1
>
> **Week 2** $1\frac{1}{5}$ inch   =   1.2   ← Each week the plant
>
> **Week 3** $1\frac{3}{10}$ inch   =   1.3   was 0.1 inch taller.
>
> **Week 4** $1\frac{2}{5}$ inch   =   1.4
>
> **Week 5** $1\frac{1}{2}$ inch   =   1.5

- **What is the answer?**
  The plant grew 0.1 inch, or $\frac{1}{10}$ inch, a week.

Look back and check your answer.

- **Is your answer reasonable?**
  You can check the pattern by adding $\frac{1}{10}$ inch to each week's height.

  $1\frac{1}{10} + \frac{1}{10} = 1\frac{2}{10} = 1\frac{1}{5}$ inch

  $1\frac{1}{5} + \frac{1}{10} = 1\frac{3}{10}$ inch

  $1\frac{3}{10} + \frac{1}{10} = 1\frac{4}{10} = 1\frac{2}{5}$ inch

  $1\frac{2}{5}$ inch $+ \frac{1}{10} = 1\frac{5}{10} = 1\frac{1}{2}$ inch

  The sums match the growth pattern.
  The answer is reasonable.

Find a pattern to solve each problem.

1. The African sharp-nosed frog is one of the best jumpers in the world. Complete the pattern below to find how far the frog would travel by the fourth jump.

Jump 1	Jump 2	Jump 3	Jump 4
$4\frac{1}{2}$ in.	9 in.	$13\frac{1}{2}$ in.	?

Answer _____

Write the number pattern. Then answer the question.

2. What is the next number in the pattern?

   $\frac{9}{10}$, $\frac{4}{5}$, $\frac{7}{10}$, $\cdots$

   Pattern _____

   Answer _____

3. What is the next number in the pattern?

   8.72, 8.52, 8.32, . . .

   Pattern _____

   Answer _____

4. A square can be made with 4 toothpicks. It takes 7 toothpicks to make two squares side by side. Three squares in a row can be made with 10 toothpicks. How many toothpicks would you need to make four squares in a row?

   Pattern _____

   Answer _____

5. The first five multiples of 11 are 11, 22, 33, 44, 55. Write the number pattern for the sum of the digits in each multiple. What would be the next number in this pattern?

   Pattern _____

   Answer _____

Rounding Decimals

Rounding decimals can be used to tell **approximately** how many. You can use a number line to round decimals.

Remember, when a number is halfway, always round up.

Round 42.3 to the nearest one.

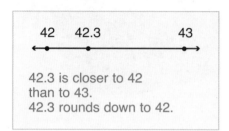

42.3 is closer to 42 than to 43.
42.3 rounds down to 42.

Round $5.78 to the nearest dollar.

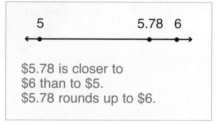

$5.78 is closer to $6 than to $5.
$5.78 rounds up to $6.

Round 7.25 to the nearest tenth.

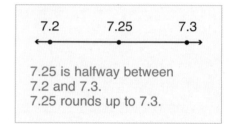

7.25 is halfway between 7.2 and 7.3.
7.25 rounds up to 7.3.

Round to the nearest one.

	a	b	c	d
1.	3.8 ___4___	2.5 _____	1.9 _____	7.3 _____
2.	39.6 _____	82.3 _____	78.9 _____	50.5 _____

Round each amount to the nearest dollar.

	a	b	c	d
3.	$9.15 ___$9.00___	$3.67 _____	$1.42 _____	$73.07 _____
4.	$0.98 _____	$3.49 _____	$10.10 _____	$25.50 _____

Round to the nearest tenth.

	a	b	c	d
5.	0.36 ___0.4___	0.72 _____	0.83 _____	0.45 _____
6.	82.78 _____	29.93 _____	85.54 _____	60.04 _____

Addition of Decimals

To add decimals, line up the decimal points. Write zeros as needed. Then add as with whole numbers. Write a decimal point in the sum.

Find: 5.7 + 6.84

Write a zero.	Add the hundredths.	Add the tenths. Regroup. Write a decimal point in the sum.	Add the ones.

T | O | Ts | Hs
 	
  5 .7 0
+ 6 .8 4
―――――
	T | O | Ts | Hs
	
	  5 .7 0
	+ 6 .8 4
	―――――
	        4
		T | O | Ts | Hs
		     1
		  5 .7 0
		+ 6 .8 4
		―――――
		     .5 4
			T | O | Ts | Hs
			     1
			  5 .7 0
			+ 6 .8 4
			―――――
			  1 2 .5 4

Add. Write zeros as needed.

	a	b	c	d

1.

a)
```
 T | O | Ts
     1
   1 2 .7
 + 1 3 .8
 ―――――――
   2 6 .5
```

b)
```
 T | O | Ts
   4 9 .5
 + 2 7 .3
 ―――――――
```

c)
```
 T | O | Ts
   3 4 .6
 + 5 6 .9
 ―――――――
```

d)
```
 T | O | Ts
   6 2 .7
 + 1 4 .5
 ―――――――
```

2.

a)
```
 O | Ts | Hs | Ths
 1 .2  4  5
+7 .5  6  8
―――――――――
```

b)
```
 O | Ts | Hs | Ths
 3 .5  1  8
+2 .3  6  4
―――――――――
```

c)
```
 O | Ts | Hs | Ths
 7 .0  0  5
+2 .9  8  6
―――――――――
```

d)
```
 T | O | Ts | Hs | Ths
 1 6 .1  3  6
+4 8 .0  5  4
――――――――――――
```

3.

a)
```
 T | O | Ts | Hs
   2 .7  1
   4 .3  6
 + 3 .0  8
 ――――――――
```

b)
```
 O | Ts | Hs
 5 .0  3
 3 .6  1
+0 .9  5
――――――――
```

c)
```
 T | O | Ts | Hs
   1 .5
   7 .3  9
 + 6 .8
 ――――――――
```

d)
```
 T | O | Ts | Hs
   6 .4  7
   2 .8  9
   3 .1  5
 + 1 .2  4
 ――――――――
```

Add. Write zeros as needed.

	a	*b*	*c*
1.	$\begin{array}{r} 5.7 \\ +0.2 \\ \hline \end{array}$	$\begin{array}{r} 4.4 \\ +2.8 \\ \hline \end{array}$	$\begin{array}{r} 4\,2.9 \\ +3\,3.5 \\ \hline \end{array}$
2.	$\begin{array}{r} 1.3\,1 \\ +6.0\,2 \\ \hline \end{array}$	$\begin{array}{r} 2.3\,2 \\ +1.9\,6 \\ \hline \end{array}$	$\begin{array}{r} 2\,4.2\,7 \\ +1\,3.6\,4 \\ \hline \end{array}$
3.	$\begin{array}{r} \$3\,2.5\,1 \\ +\$1\,8.7\,5 \\ \hline \end{array}$	$\begin{array}{r} \$6.3\,2 \\ +\$3.4\,2 \\ \hline \end{array}$	$\begin{array}{r} \$5\,7.9\,4 \\ +\$2\,1.5\,7 \\ \hline \end{array}$
4.	$\begin{array}{r} 1\,6\,5.3 \\ +1\,2\,8.9 \\ \hline \end{array}$	$\begin{array}{r} 8\,0.0\,7 \\ +1\,8.6 \\ \hline \end{array}$	$\begin{array}{r} 0.8\,9 \\ +0.3\,6 \\ \hline \end{array}$

Line up the digits. Then find the sums. Write zeros as needed.

	a	*b*	*c*
5.	$0.9 + 0.6 = $ _____	$1.7 + 2.8 = $ _____	$54.3 + 41.5 = $ _____
	$\begin{array}{r} 0.9 \\ +0.6 \\ \hline \end{array}$		
6.	$\$6.37 + \$4.21 = $ _____	$\$0.23 + \$8.76 = $ _____	$\$67.95 + \$22.05 = $ _____
7.	$8.815 + 0.173 = $ _____	$4.321 + 9.876 = $ _____	$2.843 + 1.562 = $ _____
8.	$9.5 + 2 = $ _____	$14 + 3.2 = $ _____	$0.6 + 16 = $ _____

Estimation of Decimal Sums

To estimate a decimal sum, first round the decimals to the same
place value. Then add the rounded numbers.

Estimate: $5.28 + $3.63

> Round each decimal to the nearest one.
> Add.
>
> $5.28 → $5
> +$3.63 → + 4
> ―――――――
> $9

Estimate: 5.28 + 3.63

> Round each decimal to the nearest tenth.
> Add.
>
> 5.28 → 5.3
> +3.63 → +3.6
> ―――――――
> 8.9

Estimate each sum by rounding to the nearest one.

	a	b	c	d
1.	2.4 → 2 +6.8 → +7 ――――― 9	$5.0 2 → + 8.1 1 →	$7 2.6 → + 3 5.9 →	$4 8.3 5 → + 3 7.6 6 →
2.	7.8 9 → +8.9 →	9 6.5 4 → +2 2.1 8 →	4.2 7 3 → +3.7 9 →	2 1.1 0 9 → +1 8.3 8 1 →

Estimate each sum by rounding to the nearest tenth.

	a	b	c	d
3.	0.9 3 → 0.9 +0.2 8 → +0.3 ―――――― 1.2	2.3 1 → +4.5 3 →	9.8 8 → +7.4 3 →	$1 2.6 9 → + 8 6.7 6 →
4.	3 8.5 2 → +1 4.6 2 →	0.3 8 5 → +0.7 6 9 →	3.2 6 9 → +1.4 1 →	5.7 3 → +0.8 9 8 →

Subtraction of Decimals

To subtract decimals, line up the decimal points. Write zeros as needed.
Then subtract as with whole numbers. Write a decimal point in the difference.

Find: 28.3 − 14.95

Write a zero. Regroup. Subtract the hundredths.	Regroup. Subtract the tenths. Write a decimal point in the difference.	Subtract the ones.	Subtract the tens.
T O Ts Hs 2 10 2 8 . 3 0 − 1 4 . 9 5 5	T O Ts Hs 12 7 2 10 2 8 . 3 0 − 1 4 . 9 5 . 3 5	T O Ts Hs 12 7 2 10 2 8 . 3 0 − 1 4 . 9 5 3 . 3 5	T O Ts Hs 12 7 2 10 2 8 . 3 0 − 1 4 . 9 5 1 3 . 3 5

Subtract. Write zeros as needed.

	a	b	c	d

1.

a)
T	O	Ts
5	12	
6	2	.7
− 1	4	.2
4	8	.5

b)
T	O	Ts
8	3	.8
− 7	5	.4

c)
T	O	Ts	Hs
$5	3	.8	2
−$1	0	.1	1

d)
T	O	Ts	Hs
$3	7	.4	3
−$2	9	.5	2

2.

a)
O	Ts	Hs
8	.0	0
− 6	.1	2

b)
O	Ts	Hs
8	.6	
− 4	.2	9

c)
T	O	Ts	Hs
2	3	.5	4
− 1	2	.6	

d)
T	O	Ts	Hs
8	6	.2	8
− 5	4		

3.

a)
O	Ts	Hs	Ths
9	.2	1	0
− 0	.8	4	7

b)
O	Ts	Hs	Ths
7	.5	1	6
− 5	.2	8	

c)
O	Ts	Hs	Ths
1	.9		
− 0	.6	7	4

d)
T	O	Ts	Hs	Ths
1	9	.0	0	5
− 1	4	.5		

Subtract. Write zeros as needed.

	a	b	c	d
4.	4.2 −2.4	1 6.5 −1 3.9	7.3 −0.8	9 −5.6
5.	5.4 5 −0.1 6	0.9 6 −0.3 8	2 2.7 7 −1 1.8 8	7.0 2 −1.8
6.	$6.2 8 −$2.6 4	$3.4 2 −$0.7 8	$1 7.6 3 −$1 3.4 5	$3 0.0 0 −$1 9.2 5

Line up the digits. Then find the differences. Write zeros as needed.

	a	b	c
7.	9.6 − 3.7 = _____	7.02 − 1.86 = _____	4.007 − 2.628 = _____
	9.6 −3.7		
8.	13.7 − 11.99 = _____	9.976 − 2.18 = _____	8.5 − 3.725 = _____

Estimation of Decimal Differences

To estimate a decimal difference, first round the decimals to the same place value. Then subtract the rounded numbers.

Estimate: $8.93 – $6.29

Round each decimal to the nearest one. Subtract.

$$\$8.93 \rightarrow \quad \$9$$
$$-\ 6.29 \rightarrow -\ 6$$
$$\overline{\qquad\qquad \$3}$$

Estimate: 8.93 – 6.29

Round each decimal to the nearest tenth. Subtract.

$$8.93 \rightarrow \quad 8.9$$
$$-6.29 \rightarrow -6.3$$
$$\overline{\qquad\qquad 2.6}$$

Estimate each difference by rounding to the nearest one.

	a	b	c	d
1.	$6.1 \rightarrow 6$ $-2.8 \rightarrow -3$ $\overline{3}$	$\$9.0\ 7 \rightarrow$ $-\$5.3\ 5 \rightarrow$	$1\ 5.9 \rightarrow$ $-1\ 1.2 \rightarrow$	$\$4\ 2.5\ 7 \rightarrow$ $-\$2\ 7.8\ 3 \rightarrow$
2.	$7.4 \rightarrow$ $-6.3\ 4 \rightarrow -$	$3.9\ 4\ 4 \rightarrow$ $1.3\ 5\ 1 \rightarrow$	$1\ 6.1\ 7 \rightarrow$ $-1\ 0.6\ 8\ 2 \rightarrow$	$3\ 8.9 \rightarrow$ $-1\ 3.6\ 6\ 7 \rightarrow$

Estimate each difference by rounding to the nearest tenth.

	a	b	c	d
3.	$0.8\ 2 \rightarrow 0.8$ $-0.3\ 9 \rightarrow -0.4$ $\overline{0.4}$	$4.6\ 4 \rightarrow$ $-2.1\ 3 \rightarrow$	$2\ 5.2\ 7 \rightarrow$ $-1\ 6.5\ 1 \rightarrow$	$3\ 2.0\ 8 \rightarrow$ $-1\ 9.7\ 5 \rightarrow$
4.	$4\ 7.0\ 2\ 3 \rightarrow$ $-3\ 9.3\ 4\ 5 \rightarrow$	$5.3\ 7 \rightarrow$ $4.6 \rightarrow$	$6\ 3.8\ 7 \rightarrow$ $-1\ 0.1\ 5\ 4 \rightarrow$	$9.2 \rightarrow$ $-7.5\ 9\ 5 \rightarrow$

Problem-Solving Method: Use Estimation

Evan has $100.00 to buy art supplies. He wants to buy an easel for $46.75, a canvas for $31.99, and a new brush for $11.50. Does he have enough money to buy all the supplies?

Understand the problem.

- **What do you want to know?**
  if Evan has enough money for the art supplies

- **What information is given?**
  He has $100.00.
  The easel is $46.75, the canvas is $31.99, and the brush is $11.50.

Plan how to solve it.

- **What method can you use?**
  Since the problem is not asking for an exact answer, you can use estimation to find the sum of the art supply prices.

Solve it.

- **How can you use this method to solve the problem?**
  Round the prices to the nearest whole dollar. Then add.

$$
\begin{array}{rcr}
\$46.75 & \rightarrow & \$47 \\
31.99 & \rightarrow & 32 \\
+\ 11.50 & \rightarrow & +\ 12 \\
\hline
& & \$91
\end{array}
$$

- **What is the answer?**
  Yes, $100.00 is enough to buy all the art supplies.

Look back and check your answer.

- **Is your answer reasonable?**
  You can check your estimate by finding the exact answer.

$$
\begin{array}{r}
\$46.75 \\
31.99 \\
+\ 11.50 \\
\hline
\$90.24
\end{array}
$$

The exact answer is less than $100.00 and close to the estimate. The estimate is reasonable.

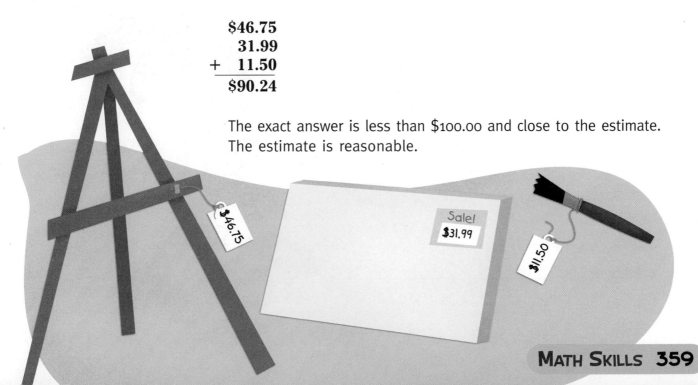

Use estimation to solve each problem.

1. Tyler bought a tennis racket for $54.99, a can of tennis balls for $8.53, and a new hat for $7.63. About how much did he spend in all at the sporting goods store that day?

Answer _____

2. The average blue whale is 33.5 meters long. The average pilot whale is 6.4 meters long. About how much longer is a blue whale than a pilot whale?

Answer _____

3. Blue Canyon, California, gets about 240.8 inches of snow every year. Marquette, Michigan, gets 129.2 inches and Sault Ste. Marie, Michigan, gets 116.1 inches each year. It snows in these three cities more than anywhere else in the United States. About how much snow do they get each year altogether?

Answer _____

4. The world's largest ice cream sundae was made in 1988. It used 18.38 tons of ice cream and 4.25 tons of syrup and toppings. About how many whole tons did the sundae weigh altogether?

Answer _____

5. It takes Jupiter 11.9 years to orbit, or go around, the sun. Saturn takes 17.6 more years than Jupiter to orbit the sun. About how long does it take Saturn to orbit the sun?

Answer _____

UNIT 5 Review

Write the place name for the 8 in each number.

	a	b	c
1.	0.583 _____	6.038 _____	7.82 _____

Write the value of the underlined digit.

	a	b	c
2.	0.3_14 _____	0.6_02 _____	0.079_ _____

Write as a decimal.

	a	b
3.	fourteen thousandths _____	seven hundredths _____

Write each decimal in words.

4. 8.52 _____

5. 12.023 _____

Compare. Write <, >, or =.

	a	b	c
6.	0.3 _____ 0.6	2.95 _____ 2.59	0.246 _____ 0.426

Write in order from least to greatest.

	a	b
7.	0.53 0.32 0.42 _____	0.33 0.033 0.303 _____

Write each fraction as a decimal.

	a	b	c	d
8.	$\frac{7}{10}$ _____	$\frac{82}{100}$ _____	$\frac{2}{5}$ _____	$\frac{29}{2}$ _____

Write each mixed number as a decimal.

	a	b	c
9.	$2\frac{7}{10}$ _____	$12\frac{4}{5}$ _____	$8\frac{7}{20}$ _____

UNIT 5 Review

Write each decimal as a fraction or mixed number.

	a	*b*	*c*	*d*
10.	0.41 _____	0.063 _____	0.8 _____	3.17 _____

Round to the nearest tenth.

	a	*b*	*c*	*d*
11.	0.43 _____	0.75 _____	0.86 _____	0.98 _____

Round to the nearest one.

	a	*b*	*c*	*d*
12.	14.6 _____	6.5 _____	19.8 _____	$13.44 _____

Add or subtract. Write zeros as needed.

	a	*b*	*c*	*d*	*e*
13.	7.2 +5.3	6.4 7 +1.0 9	7 5.3 4 4 +1 2.9 5 1	3.2 7.4 +2.6	5.3 2 1.9 7 +1.7 2

	a	*b*	*c*	*d*	*e*
14.	6.3 −4.7	3.7 1 2 −2.1 2 3	1 6.8 0 − 7.1 7	9.0 5 3 −8.4 4 3	7.1 3 6 −4.9 0 1

Estimate by rounding to the nearest one.

	a	*b*	*c*	*d*
15.	8.6 → +4.3 →	$7.6 5 → − 3.1 4 →	6 9.7 5 → +2 4.3 1 →	1 1.2 0 → − 4.1 9 →

Estimate by rounding to the nearest tenth.

	a	*b*	*c*	*d*
16.	3.7 5 → −2.1 7 → −	3 9.3 3 → 6.8 8 →	2.3 2 3 → +1.0 1 0 →	1 6.4 9 → + 2 3.4 1 →

Find a pattern to solve each problem.

17. Kurt measured and recorded the corn plant's height every week to track its growth. How fast did the corn grow?

Week 1	Week 2	Week 3	Week 4
6 in.	$7\frac{1}{4}$ in.	$8\frac{1}{2}$ in.	$9\frac{3}{4}$ in.

Answer_____

18. Maggie kept a running journal for four months. She wrote down her total miles for each month. By how many miles did she increase her work-outs each month?

Jan.	Feb.	March	April
31.4	35.6	39.8	44

Answer_____

Use estimation to solve each problem.

19. In 1900 in the United States, the life expectancy for women was 48.7 years. In 1999, the life expectancy for women was 76.1 years. About how much longer could a woman in the U.S. expect to live in 1999 than in 1900?

Answer_____

20. A black vulture has a wingspan 3.1 meters wide. A great bustard is the heaviest bird that can fly. Its wingspan is 2.7 meters. About how many meters wider is a black vulture's wingspan than a great bustard's?

Answer_____

21. It takes Neptune 164.8 years to orbit the sun. Pluto takes 82.9 more years than Neptune to orbit the sun. About how long does it take Pluto to orbit the sun?

Answer_____

unit 6
measurement

Customary Length

The customary units that are used to measure length
are **inch, foot, yard,** and **mile**.
The chart gives the relationship of one unit to another.

- A business envelope is about 10 inches long.
- A basketball hoop is about 10 feet high.

1 foot (ft.) = 12 inches (in.)
1 yard (yd.)= 3 ft.
= 36 in.
1 mile (mi.)= 1,760 yd.
= 5,280 ft.

You can multiply or divide to change units of
measurement.

Find: 5 yd. = _____ ft.

> To change larger units to smaller units, multiply.
>
> $$1 \text{ yd.} = 3 \text{ ft.}$$
> $$5 \times 3 = 15$$
> $$5 \text{ yd.} = 15 \text{ ft.}$$

Find: 18 in. = _____ ft.

> To change smaller units to larger units, divide.
>
> $$12 \text{ in.} = 1 \text{ ft.}$$
> $$18 \div 12 = 1\frac{6}{12} \text{ or } 1\frac{1}{2}$$
> $$18 \text{ in.} = 1\frac{1}{2} \text{ ft.}$$

Choose the most appropriate unit of measure. Write *in., ft.,* **or** *mi.*

a

1. length of a new pencil _____ *in.* _____

b

height of a telephone pole _____

Use the chart to complete the following.

a

2. 36 in. = ___ 1 ___ yd.

3. 1,760 yd. = _____ mi.

b

12 in. = _____ ft.

1 yd. = _____ in.

Change each measurement to the smaller unit.

a

4. 7 ft. = ___ 84 ___ in.

5. 6 yd. = _____ in.

b

15 yd. = _____ ft.

2 mi. = _____ ft.

Change each measurement to the larger unit.

a

6. 42 in. = ___ $3\frac{1}{2}$ ___ ft.

7. 35 in. = _____ ft.

b

72 in. = _____ yd.

17 ft. = _____ yd.

Customary Weight

The customary units that are used to measure weight are **ounce, pound,** and **ton.**
The chart shows the relationship of one unit to another.

- A stick of margarine weighs 4 ounces.
- A small loaf of bread weighs about 1 pound.
- An elephant weighs about 7 tons.

> **1 pound (lb.) = 16 ounces (oz.)**
> **1 ton (T.) = 2,000 pounds**

Find: 3 lb. = _____ oz.

To change larger units to smaller units, multiply.

$$1 \text{ lb.} = 16 \text{ oz.}$$
$$3 \times 16 = 48$$
$$3 \text{ lb.} = 48 \text{ oz.}$$

Find: 5,000 lb. = _____ T.

To change smaller units to larger units, divide.

$$2,000 \text{ lb.} = 1 \text{ T.}$$
$$5,000 \div 2,000 = 2\frac{1}{2}$$
$$5,000 \text{ lb.} = 2\frac{1}{2} \text{ T.}$$

Choose the most appropriate unit of measure. Write _oz._, _lb._, or _T._

	a	b
1.	weight of a cat _____*lb.*_____	weight of a pick-up truck _____
2.	weight of a tennis ball _____	weight of a tiger _____

Use the chart to complete the following.

	a	b	c
3.	16 oz. = ___*1*___ lb.	2,000 lb. = _____ T.	1 lb. = _____ oz.

Change each measurement to the smaller unit.

	a	b	c
4.	5 lb. = ___*80*___ oz.	2 T. = _____ lb.	2 lb. = _____ oz.

Change each measurement to the larger unit.

	a	b	c
5.	24 oz. = ___$1\frac{1}{2}$___ lb.	6,000 lb. = _____ T.	3,000 lb. = _____ T.
6.	36 oz. = _____ lb.	92 oz. = _____ lb.	50 oz. = _____ lb.

Customary Capacity

The customary units that are used to measure
capacity are **cup, pint, quart,** and **gallon**.
The chart shows the relationship of one unit to another.

- A drinking glass holds 1 cup of liquid.
- A small pan for cooking holds 1 quart.
- A large water pitcher holds 1 gallon.

1 pint (pt.) = 2 cups (c.)
1 quart (qt.) = 2 pt.
= 4 c.
1 gallon (gal.) = 4 qt.
= 8 pt.
= 16 c.

Find: 7 qt. = _____ pt.

> To change larger units to smaller units, multiply.
>
> $$1 \text{ qt.} = 2 \text{ pt.}$$
> $$7 \times 2 = 14$$
> $$7 \text{ qt.} = 14 \text{ pt.}$$

Find: 10 pt. = _____ gal.

> To change smaller units to larger units, divide.
>
> $$8 \text{ pt.} = 1 \text{ gal.}$$
> $$10 \div 8 = 1\frac{2}{8} \text{ or } 1\frac{1}{4}$$
> $$10 \text{ pt.} = 1\frac{1}{4} \text{ gal.}$$

Choose the most appropriate unit of measure. Write *c., pt., qt.,* or *gal.*

        a   *b*

1. capacity of a cereal bowl _____   capacity of a fish tank _____

Use the chart to complete the following.

     a   *b*   *c*

2. 2 c. = _____ pt.   2 pt. = _____ qt.   4 qt. = _____ gal.

Change each measurement to the smaller unit.

     a   *b*   *c*

3. 7 qt. = _____ c.   3 gal. = _____ c.   8 pt. = _____ c.

4. 16 pt. = _____ c   25 qt. = _____ c.   50 gal. = _____ c.

Change each measurement to the larger unit.

     a   *b*   *c*

5. 24 c. = _____ gal.   12 c. = _____ qt.   8 pt. = _____ gal.

6. 10 c. = _____ qt.   15 pt. = _____ gal.   28 c. = _____ gal.

Comparing Customary Units

To compare two measurements, first change them to the same unit.

Remember, to change larger units to smaller units, multiply.

Compare: 2 ft. to 30 in.

> **Think:** 1 ft. = 12 in.
> 2 ft. = 2 × 12 = 24 in.
>
> 24 in. _is less than_ 30 in.
>
> 2 ft. _<_ 30 in.

Compare: 20 qt. to 4 gal.

> **Think:** 1 gal. = 4 qt.
> 4 gal. = 4 × 4 = 16 qt.
>
> 20 qt. _is greater than_ 16 qt.
>
> 20 qt. _>_ 4 gal.

Compare. Write <, >, or =.

                    a   *b*

1. 48 oz. _____=_____ 3 lb.   36 c. _____ 2 qt.

  1 lb. = 16 oz.
  3 lb. = 3 × 16 = 48 oz.

2. 3 mi. _____ 2,000 yd.   3 T. _____ 6,000 lb.

3. 24 ft. _____ 6 yd.   6 pt. _____ 10 c.

4. 2 mi. _____ 5,280 ft.   6 lb. _____ 100 oz.

5. 10 yd. _____ 40 ft.   5 T. _____ 9,000 lb.

6. 40 qt. _____ 6 gal.   12 ft. _____ 144 in.

Metric Length: Meter and Kilometer

The **meter** (m) is the basic metric unit of length. A baseball bat is about 1 meter long.

A **kilometer** (km) is one thousand meters. (**Kilo** means 1,000.) The kilometer is used to measure long distances. The distance from New York City to Chicago is 1,140 km.

1 km = 1,000 m
1 m = 0.001 km

Find: 8 km = _____ m

> To change larger units to smaller units, multiply.
>
> $$1 \text{ km} = 1,000 \text{ m}$$
> $$8 \times 1,000 = 8,000$$
> $$8 \text{ km} = 8,000 \text{ m}$$

Find: 6,000 m = _____ km

> To change smaller units to larger units, divide.
>
> $$1,000 \text{ m} = 1 \text{ km}$$
> $$6,000 \div 1,000 = 6$$
> $$6,000 \text{ m} = 6 \text{ km}$$

Choose the most appropriate unit of measure. Write *m* or *km*.

a

1. distance between cities _____

b

height of a jogger _____

2. length of a city block _____

distance to the moon _____

Circle the best measurement.

a

3. distance between airports
   125 m   125 km

b

height of a ceiling
2.8 m   2.8 km

4. length of six automobiles
   30 m   30 km

distance walked in one hour
6 m   5 km

Change each measurement to the smaller unit.

a

5. 7 km = __7,000__ m

b

3 km = _____ m

c

57 km = _____ m

Change each measurement to the larger unit.

a

6. 2,000 m = ___2___ km

b

6,000 m = _____ km

c

10,000 m = _____ km

Metric Length: Centimeter and Millimeter

A meter (m) can be measured with a **meter stick**.

A **centimeter** (cm) is one hundredth of a meter. (**Centi** means 0.01.) The centimeter is used to measure small lengths. The length of a pencil is about 18 cm.

A **millimeter** (mm) is one thousandth of a meter. (**Milli** means 0.001.) The millimeter is used to measure very small lengths. The width of a housefly is about 5 mm.

⊢────⌒ 1 cm
ₕ ⌒ 1 mm

```
1 m = 100 cm
    = 1,000 mm
1 cm = 0.01 m
     = 10 mm
1 mm = 0.1 cm
     = 0.001 m
```

Choose the most appropriate unit of measure. Write *m, cm,* or *mm*.

a

1. width of your book _____

2. height of a honeybee _____

3. length of a basketball court _____

b

length of a safety pin _____

length of your shoe _____

thickness of a penny _____

Circle the best measurement.

a

4. width of your fingernail

   1 cm   1 m

5. width of a couch

   3 m   3 mm

b

length of a football field

   100 m   100 cm

length of a notebook

   25 cm   25 m

Change each measurement to the smaller unit.

a

6. 5 cm = _____ mm

b

12 m = _____ cm

Change each measurement to the larger unit.

a

7. 20 mm = _____ cm

b

500 cm = _____ m

Metric Mass

The **mass** of an object is not often measured outside the field of science. Mass measures the amount of matter in an object.

The **gram** (g) is the basic unit of mass. The gram is used to measure the mass of very light objects. A paper clip equals about 1 gram.

1 kg = 1,000 g
1 g = 0.001 kg

The **kilogram** (kg) is one thousand grams. It is used to measure the mass of heavier objects. A baseball bat equals about 1 kg. Remember, **kilo** means 1,000.

Find: 5 kg = _____ g

To change larger units to smaller units, multiply.

$$1 \text{ kg} = 1,000 \text{ g}$$
$$5 \times 1,000 = 5,000$$
$$5 \text{ kg} = 5,000 \text{ g}$$

Find: 4,000 g = _____ kg

To change smaller units to larger units, divide.

$$1,000 \text{ g} = 1 \text{ kg}$$
$$4,000 \div 1,000 = 4$$
$$4,000 \text{ g} = 4 \text{ kg}$$

Choose the most appropriate unit of measure. Write _g_ or _kg_.

a	*b*
1. mass of a textbook _____	mass of a nickel _____
2. mass of a football _____	mass of a television _____

Circle the best measurement.

a	*b*
3. mass of a dog	mass of a spoonful of salt
9 g 9 kg	1 kg 1 g
4. mass of a loaf of bread	mass of a bicycle
500 g 500 kg	18 g 18 kg

Change each measurement to the smaller unit.

a	*b*	*c*
5. 9 kg = _9,000_ g	7 kg = _____ g	13 kg = _____ g

Change each measurement to the larger unit.

a	*b*	*c*
6. 4,000 g = _4_ kg	2,000 g = _____ kg	15,000 g = _____ kg

Metric Capacity

The **liter** (L) is the basic metric unit of capacity.
A liter of liquid will fill a box 10 centimeters on each side.
A large bottle of soda holds about 2 liters.

1 L = 1,000 mL
1 mL = 0.001 L

A **milliliter** (mL) is one thousandth of a liter.
It is used to measure very small amounts of liquid. A milliliter of liquid will fill a box
1 centimeter on each side. An eyedropper holds about 2 mL.

Remember, *milli* means 0.001.

Choose the most appropriate unit of measure. Write *L* or *mL*.

a

1. capacity of a tablespoon _____

2. capacity of a bathtub _____

b

capacity of a water jug _____

capacity of a test tube _____

Circle the best measurement.

a

3. capacity of a swimming pool
   5,000 mL   5,000 L

4. capacity of a teapot
   700 mL   700 L

b

capacity of a jug of apple cider
4 mL   4 L

capacity of a bowl
180 mL   180 L

Change each measurement to the smaller unit.

a

5. 10 L = _10,000_ mL

b

4 L = _____ mL

c

250 L = _____ mL

Change each measurement to the larger unit.

a

6. 5,000 mL = __5__ L

b

6,000 mL = _____ L

c

30,000 mL = _____ L

Relating Units

The basic metric units are meter (m), liter (L), and gram (g). They are used with **prefixes** to form larger and smaller units.

larger

Prefix	Symbol	Meaning
kilo-	k	1,000
base unit	m, L, g	1
centi-	c	0.01
milli-	m	0.001

smaller

Examples:

- **Kilo-** plus **gram** is kilogram (kg).
  Since kg means 1,000 g, kg is larger than g.
- **Centi-** plus **meter** is centimeter (cm).
  Since cm mean 0.01 m, cm is smaller than m.
- **Milli-** plus **liter** is milliliter (mL).
  Since mL means 0.001 L, mL is smaller than L.

Decide whether the following units are larger or smaller than the base unit. Then write < or >.

	a		b		c
1. kL __>__ L		km _____ m		cg _____ g	
2. cm _____ m		cL _____ L		mg _____ g	
3. kg _____ g		mm _____ m		mL _____ L	

Give the value of each unit. Use the values in the table.

	a		b		c
4. kL = __1,000__ L		cg = _____ g		cL = _____ L	
5. cm = _____ m		mm = _____ m		mg = _____ g	

Decide which is larger or smaller. Then write < or >.

	a		b		c
6. kL __>__ mL		mL _____ cL		cg _____ kg	
7. mg _____ cg		km _____ cm		cm _____ mm	

Comparing Metric Units

To compare two measurements, first change them to the same unit.

Remember, to change larger units to smaller units, multiply.

Compare: 3 m to 400 cm

> **Think:** 1 m = 100 cm
> 3 m = 3 × 100 = 300 cm
>
> 300 cm   *is less than*   400 cm
>
> 3 m   <   400 cm

Compare: 7,500 mL to 6 L

> **Think:** 1 L = 1,000 mL
> 6 L = 6 × 1,000 = 6,000 mL
>
> 7,500 mL   *is greater than*   6,000 mL
>
> 7,500 mL   >   6 L

Compare. Write <, >, or =.

	a		b
1. 3 kg ___=___ 3,000 g		5 km _____ 4,500 m	

1 kg = 1,000 g
3 kg = 3 × 1,000 = 3,000 g

2. 32 cm _____ 300 mm   62 L _____ 6,000 mL

3. 5 m _____ 5,000 mm   25 km _____ 25,000 m

4. 600 cm _____ 6 m   29,456 g _____ 2 kg

5. 5,500 mL _____ 5 L   54 m _____ 54,000 cm

6. 40 kg _____ 685 g   250 cm _____ 25,000 mm

Problem-Solving Method: Guess and Check

Every day, a vampire bat drinks half of its own body weight in blood. A mosquito can drink about $\frac{1}{10}$ the amount of blood a vampire bat drinks. Together, the mosquito and bat drink 33 milliliters of blood. How much blood does a vampire bat drink every day?

Understand the problem.

- **What do you want to know?**
  how much blood a vampire bat drinks each day

- **What information is given?**
  Clue 1: $\frac{1}{10}$ of bat's meal = mosquito's meal
  Clue 2: bat's meal + mosquito's meal = 33 mL

Plan how to solve it.

- **What method can you use?**
  You can guess an answer that satisfies one clue.
  Then check to see if your answer satisfies the other clue.

Solve it.

- **How can you use this method to solve the problem?**
  Try to guess in an organized way so that each of your guesses gets closer to the exact answer. Use a table.
  (Remember, to find $\frac{1}{2}$ of 8, divide 8 by 2. $\frac{1}{2}$ of 8 = 8 ÷ 2 = 4)

Guess Bat Drink	Check		Evaluate the Guess
	Clue 1	Clue 2	
10 mL	$\frac{1}{10}$ of 10 = 1	10 + 1 = 11	too low
50 mL	$\frac{1}{10}$ of 50 = 5	50 + 5 = 55	too high
40 mL	$\frac{1}{10}$ of 40 = 4	40 + 4 = 44	too high
30 mL	$\frac{1}{10}$ of 30 = 3	30 + 3 = 33	satisfies both clues

- **What is the answer?**
  A vampire bat drinks 30 mL of blood every day.

Look back and check your answer.

- **Is your answer reasonable?**
  You can check division with multiplication and addition with subtraction.

  $10 \times 3 = 30$
  $33 - 3 = 30$

  The amount satisfies both clues.
  The answer is reasonable.

Use guess and check to solve each problem.

1. Kendra is twice as old as Tim. In 10 years, Kendra will be four years older than Tim. How old are Kendra and Tim now?

Answer _____

2. Rita has five United States coins. Their total value is 31 cents. What coins and how many of each does she have?

Answer _____

3. A gray whale usually weighs 3 times as much as a baird's whale. The sum of their weights is 48 tons. How much does each whale usually weigh?

Answer _____

4. Vatican City and Monaco are the two smallest countries. Together, they only cover about 2.3 square kilometers. Monaco is 1.3 square km bigger than Vatican City. How big is each country?

Answer _____

5. A hot dog has about $\frac{1}{4}$ the amount of protein as 3 ounces of hamburger. Together, they have about 25 grams of protein. How many grams of protein are in a 3-oz. hamburger?

Answer _____

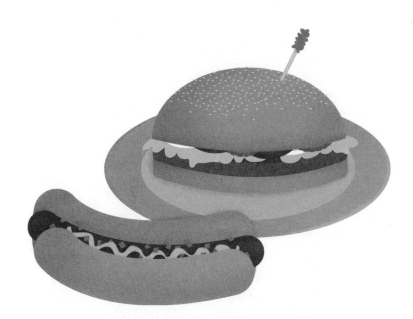

Choose the most appropriate unit of measure.
Write *in., ft., mi., c., qt., pt., gal., oz., lb.,* or *T.*

a   *b*

1. width of a kitchen table _____   capacity of a swimming pool _____

2. weight of a bag of potatoes _____   length of your thumb _____

Circle the best measurement.

a   *b*

3. capacity of a baby bottle   capacity of a milk carton
   2 L   200 mL   20 mL   1 L

4. distance between your eyes   mass of a notebook
   10 cm   25 mm   100 g   1 kg

Change each measurement to the smaller unit.

a   *b*   *c*

5. 2 gal. = _____ pt.   5 kg = _____ g   3 T. = _____ lb.

Change each measurement to the larger unit.

a   *b*   *c*

6. 70,000 mm = _____ m   8 pt. = _____ gal.   4,000 g = _____ kg

Compare. Write <, >, or =.

a   *b*

7. 450 cm _____ 45 m   24 c. _____ 2 qt.

8. 4 ft. _____ 50 in.   1,900 mL _____ 2 L

9. 2 mi. _____ 16,000 ft.   48 km _____ 5,000 m

Guess and check to solve each problem.

10. Jane has 43 cents. She has 8 coins. Find the coins and the number of each that Jane has.

Answer _____

11. The playground director has a total of 24 basketballs and footballs. He has 6 more footballs than basketballs. How many of each does he have?

Answer _____

12. Jeremy stores his baseball cards in two boxes. He has 36 cards altogether. If one box holds twice as many cards as the other, how many cards are in each box?

Answer _____

13. Caroline and Ron have 11 goldfish in all. Caroline has three more than Ron. How many fish do they each have?

Answer _____

14. The ostrich and the emu are the two largest birds. An emu is usually $\frac{1}{2}$ the size of an ostrich. The sum of their heights is 150 inches. How tall is the average ostrich?

Answer _____

unit 7
Geometry

Angles

A **ray** is an endless straight path starting at one point.

Say: ray BG

Write: $\overrightarrow{BG}$

An **angle** is two rays with a common endpoint.

Say: angle ABC or angle CBA

Write: ∠ABC or ∠CBA
or ∠B

Angles are measured in *degrees* (°).

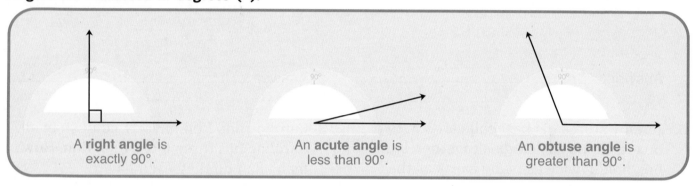

A **right angle** is exactly 90°.

An **acute angle** is less than 90°.

An **obtuse angle** is greater than 90°.

Name each angle using symbols.

     a   *b*   *c*   *d*

1.

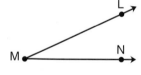

∠LMN or∠NML or∠M

Name each angle. Write *right angle*, *acute angle*, or *obtuse angle*.

     a   *b*   *c*   *d*

2.

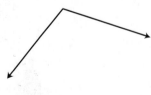

obtuse angle

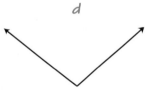
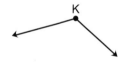

Perimeter

Perimeter is the distance around a figure.

To find the perimeter of a figure, count the number of units around the figure.

Find the perimeter of this rectangle by counting units.

Start at point A. Move clockwise and count the units from A to B (4), to C (6), to D (10), to A (12).

The perimeter of this rectangle is 12 units.

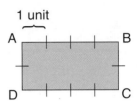

Find the perimeter of each rectangle.

	a	*b*	*c*

1.

_____8 units_____   _____   _____

2.

      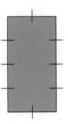

_____   _____   _____

3.

   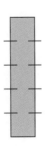   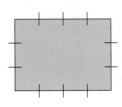

_____   _____   _____

Formula for Perimeter of a Rectangle

To find the perimeter of a rectangle, you can also use a **formula**.

Rectangles

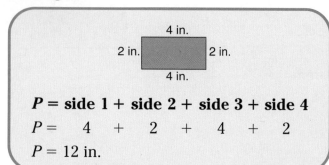

P = side 1 + side 2 + side 3 + side 4

P =   4   +   2   +   4   +   2

P = 12 in.

Squares (rectangles with four equal sides)

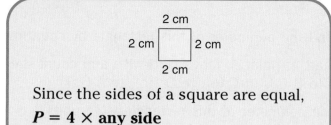

Since the sides of a square are equal,

$P = 4 \times$ **any side**

$P = 4 \times 2 = 8$ cm

Find the perimeter of each figure by using one of the formulas.

a

1.

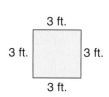

3 ft.

3 ft.   3 ft.

3 ft.

_____ *12 feet* _____

b

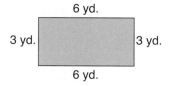

5 m

2 m   2 m

5 m

_____

2.

6 yd.

3 yd.   3 yd.

6 yd.

_____

8 in.

8 in.   8 in.

8 in.

_____

3.

10 in.

10 in.   10 in.

10 in.

_____

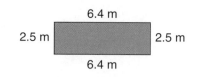

6.4 m

2.5 m   2.5 m

6.4 m

_____

Area

The **area** of a figure is the number of square units that cover its surface.

This is 1 square unit.

Count the number of square units to find the area of a figure.

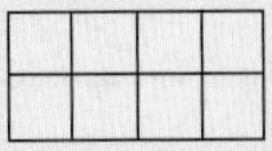

The area of this figure
is 8 square units.

Find the area of each figure.

a

b

1.

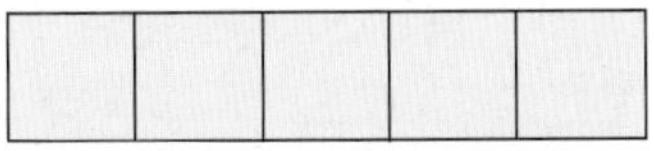

5 square units

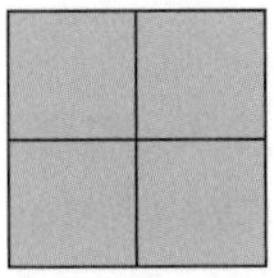

2.

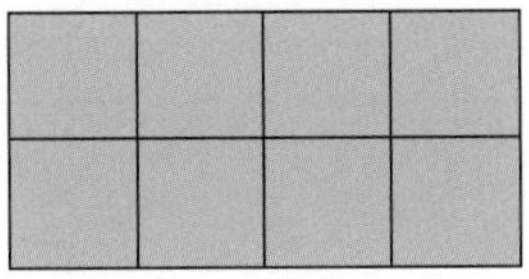

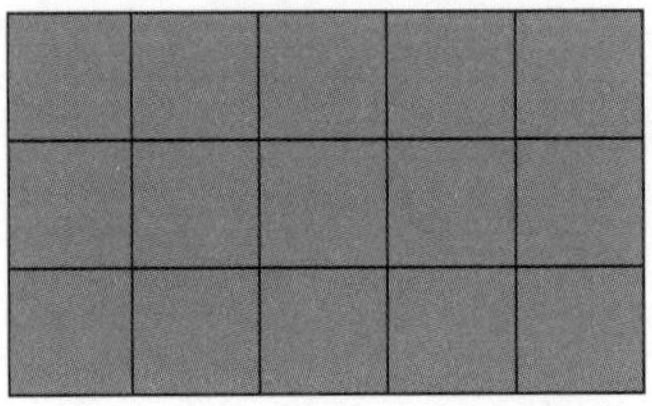

3.

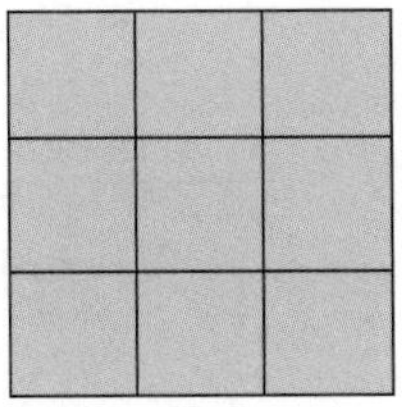

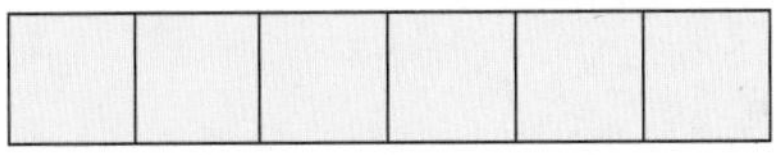

Formula for Area of a Rectangle

To find the area of a rectangle, you can also use a formula.

The formula, **A = l × w,** means the area of a rectangle equals the length times the width.

Remember, write your answer in *square* units.

A = length × width

A =   5   ×   2

A = 10 square inches

Find the area of each rectangle by using the formula.

a $\qquad\qquad\qquad\qquad\qquad\qquad\qquad$ b

1.

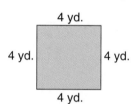

4 yd.

4 yd.   4 yd.

4 yd.

_____ *16 square yards* _____

1 ft.

3 ft.   3 ft.

1 ft.

_____

2.

2 cm

2 cm   2 cm

2 cm

6 in.

2 in.   2 in.

6 in.

_____   _____

3.

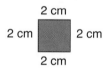

10 m

4 m   4 m

10 m

12 mm

12 mm   12 mm

12 mm

_____   _____

Problem-Solving Method: Use a Formula

Carla needs to replace the pad covering her dining room table. Her table is 7 feet long and 4 feet wide. How much padding does she need?

Understand the problem.

- **What do you want to know?**
  how much padding Carla needs to cover her table

- **What information do you know?**
  The tabletop is 7 feet long and 4 feet wide.
  The table is a rectangle.

Plan how to solve it.

- **What method can you use?**
  You can use a formula.

Solve it.

- **How can you use this method to solve the problem?**
  Since you want to know how much material will cover the surface of the table, you can use the formula for the area of a rectangle.

$$A = l \times w$$
$$A = 7 \times 4$$
$$A = 28$$

- **What is the answer?**
  Carla needs 28 square feet of padding.

Look back and check your answer.

- **Is your answer reasonable?**
  You can check by drawing the top of the table and dividing it into square units. Then count the units.

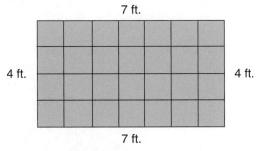

There are 28 squares.
The answer is reasonable.

Use a formula for area or perimeter to solve each problem.

1. Sam wants to put a fence around his garden. The garden is 6 yards long and 4 yards wide. How many yards of fencing should he order?

Answer _____

2. The floor of Kim's room measures 13 feet in length and 11 feet in width. How many square feet of carpet does she need to cover her floor?

Answer _____

3. Emily wants to put trim around a square window that measures 3 feet on each side. How many feet of trim does she need?

Answer _____

4. One acre is equal to 4,840 square yards. Jamal's backyard is 121 yards long and 40 yards wide. How big is Jamal's backyard in acres?

Answer _____

5. A professional soccer field is 75 meters wide and 110 meters long. If you run all the way around the soccer field, how far do you go?

Answer _____

Name each angle using symbols.

1.

a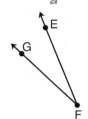

b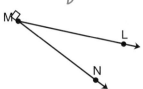

c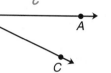

d

_____   _____   _____   _____

Name each angle. Write *right angle, acute angle,* or *obtuse angle*.

2.

a

b

c

d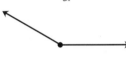

_____   _____   _____   _____

Find the perimeter of each figure.

3.

a

b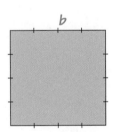

c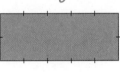

_____   _____   _____

Find the area of each figure.

4.

a

b

c

_____   _____   _____

Use a formula to solve each problem.

5. The class bulletin board is 4 feet long and 6 feet wide. How many feet of border does Mr. Chow need to surround the bulletin board?

Answer _____

6. The school yard is twice as long as it is wide. The width is 23 yards. How much fencing is needed to enclose the school yard?

Answer _____

7. The park is 3 miles long and 2 miles wide. Manuel walked around the park two times. How many miles did he walk in all?

Answer _____

8. A National Hockey League ice rink is 58 meters long and 26 meters wide. How many square meters of ice cover the rink's surface?

Answer _____

9. Andy had wood flooring installed in his living room for $12 a square foot. The room measures 9 feet by 12 feet. What did the wood flooring cost?

Answer _____

Language
Arts

Nouns

A **noun** is a word that names a person, a place, a thing, or an idea.
Use exact nouns to make clear pictures.
Examples:
person = girl   place = park   thing = door   idea = freedom

DIRECTIONS > Read each sentence. Write the nouns. Write *person, place, thing,* or *idea* after each noun to tell what the noun names.

1. Our sense of smell is located in the nose.

_____

2. Most people like the smell of delicious food, mowed grass, and clean rain.

_____

3. People get a lot of enjoyment from these special odors.

_____

4. Rotten eggs produce an unpleasant odor.

_____

5. The sense of smell can protect a person from danger.

_____

DIRECTIONS > Rewrite each sentence. Replace the underlined nouns with more exact words.

6. José likes the smells of <u>meat</u> cooking and <u>dessert</u> baking.

_____

_____

7. José and Frank sat in the <u>room</u> waiting for their <u>meal</u>.

_____

_____

Common Nouns and Proper Nouns

A **common noun** names any person, place, or thing. It begins with a lowercase letter.
Examples:

writer   state   month

A **proper noun** names a particular person, place, or thing. Each important word of a proper noun begins with a capital letter.
Examples:

Fred Gipson   Hawaii   February

DIRECTIONS Read the sentences. Underline each common noun and circle each proper noun. Rewrite each sentence, replacing the common and proper nouns with different ones.

1. The young scientist was born in Maryland.

_____

2. Many friends helped Benjamin Banneker.

_____

3. People throughout the United States still recall his accomplishments.

_____

_____

4. Banneker helped design Washington, D.C.

_____

5. This man had an unusually good memory.

_____

6. The astronomer spent many nights watching the stars and planets.

_____

7. Now, scientists are exploring Mars, Jupiter, and other planets.

_____

_____

8. What would Banneker think of the changes in his country?

_____

Singular and Plural Nouns

A **singular noun** names one person, place, thing, or idea.
Examples:

| hog | blouse | fox | liberty |

A **plural noun** names more than one person, place, thing, or idea. Make most nouns plural by adding *s* or *es*.
Examples:

| hogs | blouses | foxes | liberties |

DIRECTIONS ▸ Write each underlined noun. Then, write *singular* or *plural* to tell what kind of noun it is.

1. A <u>tornado</u> does not last as long as a <u>hurricane</u> does.

_____

2. A tornado usually lasts only <u>minutes,</u> or at the most a few <u>hours.</u>

_____

3. Its <u>winds</u> are much stronger than a hurricane's.

_____

4. The hot <u>air</u> from a large forest <u>fire</u> can cause a tornado.

_____

5. Certain weather <u>conditions</u> are warning <u>signs</u> for a tornado.

_____

DIRECTIONS ▸ Rewrite each sentence. Change each underlined singular noun to a plural noun. Make any other changes that are necessary.

6. The <u>girl</u> ate her <u>lunch</u> on the school <u>bench.</u>

_____

7. The young <u>lady</u> looked at the dark <u>cloud</u> overhead.

_____

8. A strong <u>wind</u> picked up a <u>box</u> of books by the library <u>door.</u>

_____

_____

Special Plural Nouns

Some nouns change spelling in the plural form. Other nouns have the same spelling in the singular and plural form.
Examples:

Change Spelling	Same Singular and Plural
woman–women	salmon
child–children	elk
tooth–teeth	deer
goose–geese	trout
hoof–hooves	sheep

DIRECTIONS ▷ **Complete each sentence by writing the plural form of the noun in ( ).**

1. Lisa caught four special _____ in that stream.
(trout)

2. These _____ told Lisa a story.
(fish)

3. They said that they were really _____.
(hero)

4. Two of them were really _____.
(woman)

5. The other two were really _____.
(man)

6. They had chased out all the _____ from their village.
(mouse)

7. This went against the _____ of the other people in the village.
(belief)

8. The village people thought that mice protected them from _____.
(wolf)

9. For a while, there had been four _____ in a field.
(ox)

10. Then, they had been turned into _____ in a barnyard.
(calf)

11. All the _____ in the village made fun of them.
(child)

12. Finally, their _____ were turned into fins.
(foot)

13. If they could eat bread, their _____ would return to normal.
(life)

Singular Possessive Nouns

A **singular possessive noun** shows ownership by one person or thing.
Add an apostrophe (') and *s* to most singular nouns to show possession.
Examples:

     Natoh's cat   the cat's whiskers

DIRECTIONS   Write each sentence. Change the underlined words to form a singular possessive noun.

1. The mother of my friend had a baby yesterday.

_____

2. The teeth of the baby are not in yet.

_____

3. The head of the child is still soft.

_____

4. The tie of the bib is torn.

_____

5. The sheets of the crib are pink.

_____

6. The smile of the uncle is happy.

_____

7. The gift of the grandmother is a new blanket.

_____

8. The pleasure of the father is easy to see.

_____

9. The eyes of the infant are blue.

_____

10. The life of my friend will be different now.

_____

Plural Possessive Nouns

A **plural possessive noun** shows ownership by more than one person or thing.
To form the possessive of a plural noun ending in *s* or *es*, add only an apostrophe (').
To form the possessive of a plural noun that does not end in *s*, add an apostrophe and *s* ('*s*).
Examples:

trucks' tires   foxes' lair   children's lunches

DIRECTIONS   Write each sentence. Change the underlined words to form a plural possessive noun.

1. Imagine the <u>surprise of the children</u>!

_____

2. They found the <u>baby of the robins</u> on the sidewalk.

_____

3. They returned it to the <u>nest of the parents</u>.

_____

4. They watched the <u>activities of the adult birds</u> for a while.

_____

5. The <u>fear of the birds</u> was apparent.

_____

6. The <u>odor of the humans</u> was on the baby bird.

_____

7. The bird was now the <u>responsibility of the young people</u>.

_____

8. The <u>job of the students</u> was to find a shoe box.

_____

9. The <u>job of the parents</u> was to find some soft lining.

_____

Pronouns

A **pronoun** is a word that takes the place of one or more nouns.
Use pronouns to avoid repeating words.
A **singular pronoun** replaces a singular noun. The words *I, me, you, he, she, him, her,* and *it* are singular pronouns. Always capitalize the pronoun *I*.
A **plural pronoun** replaces a plural noun. The words *we, you, they, us,* and *them* are plural pronouns.
Examples:

The woman thought that *she* should go to the store.
She takes the place of *the woman*.

The travelers searched for a place *they* could spend the night.
They takes the place of *the travelers*.

DIRECTIONS Read each pair of sentences. Draw a line under the pronoun in the second sentence. Circle the word or words in the first sentence that the pronoun replaces.

1. Explorers came to Australia.

They were amazed by the strange native animals and plants.

2. An animal the size of a greyhound lived there.

It could leap like a grasshopper.

3. These animals are now known as kangaroos.

Some of them can cover 27 feet in one jump.

4. Two interesting birds of Australia are emus and cassowaries.

They cannot fly.

5. The early explorers told about the platypus.

It is a mammal that lays eggs.

6. Scientists of the time did not believe the stories.

They thought the stories were lies.

7. The coolabah of Western Australia is an interesting tree.

It can survive frost as well as 120 degree heat.

8. The official flower of Western Australia is called the kangaroo paw.

It looks like a paw and is even furry to the touch.

Subject Pronouns

A **subject pronoun** takes the place of one or more nouns in the subject of a sentence. The words *I, you, he, she, it, we,* and *they* are subject pronouns.
Examples:

He brought a rat to school.
We do not like rats.
You can pet the rat.

DIRECTIONS ➤ **Rewrite each sentence. Replace the underlined word or words with a subject pronoun.**

1. <u>My brother and I</u> read about the Wrights last week.

_____

2. It was <u>my brother</u> who found the book.

_____

3. <u>Wilbur and Orville Wright</u> grew up in Dayton, Ohio.

_____

4. <u>Their father</u> was a bishop there.

_____

5. <u>Their older sister, Katharine,</u> helped care for them.

_____

6. <u>A toy bicycle</u> was a gift from their father.

_____

7. <u>Wilbur Wright</u> was four years older than Orville.

_____

8. On December 17, 1903, <u>the world's first airplane flight</u> took place.

_____

9. <u>The first flight</u> lasted 12 seconds.

_____

10. <u>The next three flights</u> were 13 seconds, 15 seconds, and 59 seconds.

_____

Object Pronouns

An **object pronoun** follows an action verb, such as *see* or *tell*, or a word such as *about, at, for, from, near, of, to,* or *with.*
The words *me, you, him, her, it, us,* and *them* are object pronouns.
Examples:

        Chen took *it* to school.
        Grandpa had a gift for *me.*
        My cousin saw *you.*

DIRECTIONS ▷ Rewrite each sentence. Replace the underlined word or words with an object pronoun.

1. Darkness covered <u>the pine woods, the swamp, and the game wardens</u>.

_____

2. The game wardens noticed <u>the light</u>.

_____

3. Then, the game wardens saw <u>the alligator poachers</u>.

_____

4. Two men and a woman were searching <u>the lake</u> for alligators.

_____

5. The game wardens pushed <u>their boat</u> out of the brush.

_____

6. The wardens raced toward <u>the poachers</u>.

_____

7. The powerful engine moved <u>the boat</u> quickly over the water.

_____

8. The poachers quickly dumped <u>two alligators</u> back into the water.

_____

9. The wardens searched the inside of <u>the poachers' boat</u>.

_____

Subject or Object Pronoun?

Remember that pronouns can be subjects or objects in sentences.

ⓞ ⓞⓞ ⓞ ⓞⓞ ⓞⓞⓞ ⓞⓞ ⓞⓞ ⓞ ⓞⓞⓞ ⓞⓞ ⓞⓞ ⓞ ⓞⓞ ⓞ ⓞⓞⓞ ⓞⓞ ⓞⓞ ⓞ ⓞⓞ ⓞⓞ ⓞ

DIRECTIONS ▷ **Choose the pronoun in ( ) that correctly completes each sentence. Write it on the line. Then, circle *subject pronoun* or *object pronoun*.**

1. _____ has studied kung fu for years.
   (He, Him)
   subject pronoun   *object pronoun*

2. The history of the martial arts is interesting to _____.
   (he, him)
   subject pronoun   *object pronoun*

3. _____ know about many great warriors.
   (We, Us)
   subject pronoun   *object pronoun*

4. One of _____ was a 13-year-old girl named Shuen Guan.
   (they, them)
   subject pronoun   *object pronoun*

5. _____ lived during the Jinn Dynasty, over 1600 years ago.
   (She, Her)
   subject pronoun   *object pronoun*

6. Her people had a nickname for _____.
   (she, her)
   subject pronoun   *object pronoun*

7. _____ called her "Little Tigress."
   (They, Them)
   subject pronoun   *object pronoun*

8. When her town was attacked by bandits, no one would fight _____.
   (they, them)
   subject pronoun   *object pronoun*

9. _____ was the only one brave enough.
   (She, Her)
   subject pronoun   *object pronoun*

10. Shuen Guan fought her way through _____ and went for help.
    (they, them)
    subject pronoun   *object pronoun*

Reflexive Pronouns

A **reflexive pronoun** refers to the subject of a sentence. The words *myself, yourself, himself, herself,* and *itself* are singular reflexive pronouns. *Ourselves, yourselves,* and *themselves* are plural reflexive pronouns.

DIRECTIONS ▶ Choose the reflexive pronoun in ( ) that correctly completes each sentence. Write the pronoun on the line.

1. I will help _____ enjoy this vacation.
(myself, ourselves)

2. Last year Jerry bought _____ a book about Australia.
(himself, yourself)

3. The book concerned _____ with the history of the land.
(itself, themselves)

4. Jerry's sister Joan made _____ read the book.
(herself, ourselves)

5. "Jerry and Joan, teach _____ about Australia before our vacation,"
(yourself, yourselves)
their mother said.

6. "That way, we can all enjoy _____ more," she continued.
(myself, ourselves)

7. "Joan, buy _____ a good pair
(yourself, yourselves)
of walking shoes before the trip," said her father.

DIRECTIONS ▶ Write a reflexive pronoun on each line to complete the sentence.

8. My sister and I will be treating _____ to a trip.

9. She still has to buy _____ a ticket.

10. I have bought _____ some new clothes for the trip.

11. Susan, our travel agent, taught _____ the travel business.

12. Her partner, Mark, talked _____ into learning it, too.

Possessive Pronouns

A **possessive pronoun** shows ownership. Some possessive pronouns come before a noun. Some stand alone. Some possessive pronouns are *my, your, his, her, its, our,* and *their.*
Examples:

Joe lost *his* glove.
He lost it in *your* barn.
The new car is *ours.*

DIRECTIONS ➤ Underline the possessive pronoun in each sentence. Then, write *before a noun* or *stands alone* to tell the kind of possessive pronoun used.

1. The members of the Dallas club wanted to send their team to the Olympic trials.

   _____

2. Its membership included just one person. _____

3. Babe Didrikson was proud that the position would be hers. _____

4. Her teammates were proud of Didrikson, too. _____

5. They knew that, at the end of the trials, the championship would be theirs.

   _____

6. "All our fans will be supporting you," they told Didrikson. _____

DIRECTIONS ➤ Write the pronoun in ( ) that correctly completes each sentence.

7. Didrikson's fans were always impressed by the range of _____
   (her, hers)
   athletic abilities.

8. Two gold medals were _____ at the end of the 1932 Olympic Games.
   (her, hers)

9. Many fans followed her varied career, and she appreciated all _____
   (their, theirs)
   attention.

10. Of all the sports in which she competed, _____ favorite is swimming.
    (your, yours)

Agreement of Pronouns

A pronoun is a word that takes the place of one or more nouns. Pronouns show number and gender. The number tells whether a pronoun is singular or plural. The gender tells whether the pronoun is masculine, feminine, or neutral. The **antecedent** of a pronoun is the noun or nouns to which the pronoun refers. A pronoun should agree with its antecedent in number and gender.

DIRECTIONS ➤ Write the pronoun that correctly completes the second sentence in each pair. Then, circle the pronoun's antecedent in the first sentence.

1. Mr. Les Harsten did an experiment with plants. _____ investigated with sound.

2. The man used two banana plants. He exposed _____ to the same amount of light.

3. Les also gave both plants the same amount of warmth and water. _____ did, however, change one thing.

4. One of the plants was exposed to a special sound for an hour a day. _____ was a high-pitched hum.

5. That plant grew faster. In fact, _____ was 70 percent taller than the other plant.

6. All sounds won't work this way. Some of _____ can harm plants.

7. A recording of Harsten's sound is being sold. _____ is used by some plant growers.

8. Classical music works just as well with plants. _____ seem to thrive on it.

9. Hard rock music, however, does not work. _____ can stunt their growth.

10. You may want to play music for your plants. _____ may like it.

Adjectives

An **adjective** is a word that describes a noun or pronoun.
Adjectives can tell how many, what color, or what size or
shape. They can also describe how something feels,
sounds, tastes, or smells.
You usually separate two adjectives with a comma.
Use vivid adjectives to paint clear word pictures.
Examples:
>*Two* eggs were in the nest.
>The *blue* stone was in a *small* box.
>The *fat* cat has *soft* fur.

DIRECTIONS ▸ Write each adjective that describes the underlined nouns. Then, write *what kind* or *how many* to identify what the adjective tells about the noun.

1. The azalea is a spectacular <u>plant</u>.

_____

2. It has superb, beautiful <u>flowers</u>.

_____

3. It will grow wherever winter <u>temperatures</u> are not too low.

_____

4. There are many different <u>types</u> of azaleas.

_____

5. You can find azaleas with red, pink, violet, or white <u>flowers</u>.

_____

6. Azaleas do best in spongy, acid <u>soil</u>.

_____

7. They should be fed three or four <u>times</u> between the end of the flowering <u>season</u> and September.

_____

_____

8. Bright, colorful <u>flowers</u> make the azalea a special <u>plant</u>.

_____

Proper Adjectives

A **proper adjective** is formed from a proper noun.
Capitalize each important word in a proper adjective.

⊚⊚⊚⊚⊚⊚⊚⊚⊚⊚⊚⊚⊚⊚⊚⊚⊚⊚⊚⊚⊚⊚⊚⊚⊚⊚⊚⊚⊚

DIRECTIONS ▷ Underline the proper adjective in each sentence.
On the line, write the proper noun from which
it is formed. Use a dictionary if you need help.

1. Our modern Olympics come from an ancient Greek tradition.

_____

2. The chariot races were often won by Spartan men.

_____

3. An Athenian racer won three times in a row, starting in 536 B.C.

_____

4. After 146 B.C., Roman athletes also competed in the games.

_____

5. The 1988 Olympics took place in the Korean city of Seoul.

_____

6. In 1976, a young Romanian girl, Nadia Comaneci, had seven perfect scores in gymnastics.

_____

DIRECTIONS ▷ Complete each sentence by writing a proper adjective on the line. Form
the proper adjective from the proper noun in ( ).

7. Gertrude Ederle was the first woman to swim the _____ Channel.
(England)

8. Sonja Henie was a famous _____ ice skater.
(Norway)

9. Barbara Ann Scott was a _____ ice skater.
(Canada)

10. Several _____ skaters have won awards in international competition.
(America)

Predicate Adjectives

An adjective is a word that describes a noun. A **predicate adjective** follows a linking verb such as *is, seems,* or *looks.* When an adjective follows a linking verb, it can describe the subject of the sentence.

In some sentences, different adjectives in different positions describe the same noun or pronoun.

Examples:

Sam is *young* and *bold.*

That snake looks *scary.*

DIRECTIONS ▸ Circle the adjective following the linking verb in each sentence. Write the noun or pronoun the adjective describes.

1. These peanuts are crunchy. _____

2. They taste very salty. _____

3. The skin on the peanut is red. _____

4. Those pumpkin seeds look delicious. _____

5. Pumpkin seeds once seemed inedible. _____

6. They have grown popular lately. _____

7. Some quick snacks are healthful. _____

8. Green apples are sometimes sour. _____

9. This common fruit is crisp and juicy. _____

10. A crispy vegetable can be noisy if you eat it. _____

DIRECTIONS ▸ Write two adjectives to complete each sentence.

11. Bananas are _____.

12. Pickles taste _____.

13. Candy canes usually look _____.

14. During the summer, watermelons become _____.

15. With enough rain, pole beans will grow _____.

Articles and Demonstrative Adjectives

The words *a, an,* and *the* are called **articles**. Use *a* before a word that begins with a consonant sound. Use *an* before a word that begins with a vowel sound. Use *the* before a word that begins with a consonant or a vowel.

This, that, these, and *those* are called **demonstrative adjectives**.

Examples:

Have you ever seen *an* owl?
The owl is *a* nocturnal animal.
That owl scared *those* people.

DIRECTIONS > **Choose the adjective in ( ) that best completes each sentence. Write it on the line.**

1. Many people have _____ strange idea about naturalists.
   (a, an)

2. _____ people regard naturalists as weird.
   (This, These)

3. They think naturalists wander around in forests, eating roots and berries along

   _____ way.
   (an, the)

4. Not all naturalists fit _____ description.
   (this, those)

5. You could be _____ naturalist yourself.
   (a, an)

6. You could learn _____ names of trees.
   (a, the)

7. You could also know when _____ chestnut is ready for roasting.
   (a, an)

8. You could tell whether _____ clay is better than that clay.
   (this, these)

9. You could learn all _____ things easily.
   (this, these)

10. You could become one of _____ weird naturalists, too!
    (that, those)

Adjectives That Compare

Add *er* to most short adjectives to compare two nouns or pronouns. Add *est* to most short adjectives to compare more than two nouns or pronouns. Change the *y* to *i* before adding *er* or *est* to adjectives that end in a consonant and *y*.
Use *more* with some adjectives to compare two nouns or pronouns. Use *most* with some adjectives to compare more than two nouns or pronouns.
Examples:
This building is *taller* than that one.
The whale is the *largest* of all animals.
Diving is *more interesting* to watch than golf.
It may be the *most difficult* of all sports.

> **DIRECTIONS** Write the correct form of the adjective in ( ) to complete each sentence.

1. Our trip to New Mexico was even (wonderful) than I expected. _____

2. The mountains there are the (beautiful) I have ever seen. _____

3. We saw Wheeler Peak, the (high) point in the state. _____

4. We visited a mine shaft that was (deep) than a mile. _____

5. Mining is one of the (big) industries in New Mexico. _____

6. Santa Fe, the state capital, is not the (large) city in New Mexico. _____

7. It is not the (easy) city to reach by plane. _____

8. The (unusual) place we saw was Carlsbad Caverns. _____

9. We had never seen (strange) rocks than those. _____

10. My brother was (excited) about seeing some bats than I was. _____

11. To me, the (interesting) place of all was Santa Fe. _____

12. It is one of the (old) cities in North America. _____

Special Forms of Adjectives That Compare

Some adjectives have special forms for comparing.
Examples:
   Trixi has a *good* story.
   Chad's story is *better* than Trixi's.
   Teena's story is the *best* of all.

Adjective	Comparing Two Things	Comparing More Than Two Things
good	better	best
bad	worse	worst
little	less	least
much	more	most
many	more	most

DIRECTIONS ▶ **Complete each sentence by choosing the correct form of the adjective in ( ). Write it on the line.**

1. Hunger brought the Irish to America for a _____ life.
(better, best)

2. About half of Ireland's farms had _____ than three acres of land.
(less, least)

3. They had had the _____ potato crop in years.
(worse, worst)

4. Each day _____ people were starving than the day before.
(many, more)

5. Queen Victoria was told that the situation was becoming _____ every day.
(worse, worst)

6. She visited Ireland and said that she saw _____ ragged and wretched
(more, most)
people than she had seen anywhere else.

7. _____ Irish people chose Boston as their new home.
(Many, Much)

8. Boston was the _____ convenient city for them because many ships
(more, most)
stopped there first.

Action Verbs and Linking Verbs

A **verb** expresses action or being.

An **action verb** is a word or group of words that expresses an action. An action verb is often the key word in the predicate. It tells what the subject does.

A **linking verb** connects the subject of a sentence with a word or words in the predicate. The most common linking verb is *be*. Some forms of *be* are *am, is, are, was,* and *were.* Here are other common linking verbs: *become, feel, seem, look, grow, taste, appear,* and *smell.*

Examples:
> King Uther *ruled* England a long time ago. (action)
> The name of his baby boy *was* Arthur. (linking)
> In time, Sir Ector *became* Arthur's guardian. (linking)

DIRECTIONS — Read each sentence. Underline each action verb. Circle each linking verb.

1. Young Arthur felt very nervous.

2. Sir Kay left his sword at the inn.

3. He needed his sword for the tournament that day.

4. Arthur looked all over the village for a replacement.

5. Suddenly, Arthur saw a sword in a stone.

6. He ran over to the stone and studied the strange sword.

7. It appeared very secure in its stony sheath.

8. Arthur pulled it, and it moved.

9. The sword slid from the stone easily!

10. Arthur hurried back to the tournament with his prize.

11. Sir Ector bowed deeply to his foster son.

12. The sword was the sign of the next king of England.

Main Verbs and Helping Verbs

Sometimes a simple predicate is made up of two or more verbs. The **main verb** is the most important verb in the predicate. It comes last in a group of verbs.
A **helping verb** can work with the main verb to tell about an action. The helping verb always comes before the main verb. These words are often used as helping verbs: *am, is, are, was, were, has, have, had,* and *will.*
Sometimes another word comes between a main verb and a helping verb.

DIRECTIONS Choose the correct form of the verb in ( ) to complete each sentence. Write the word in the sentence. Then, write *main verb* or *helping verb*.

1. Inez has _____ Greek legends to children for many years.
(tell, told, telling)

_____

2. The children were _____ forward to the next story.
(look, looked, looking)

_____

3. "I shall _____ the children the legend of Narcissus," she thought.
(tell, told, telling)

_____

4. Narcissus _____ hunting one day.
(shall, have, was)

_____

5. He had _____ over a mountain pool for a drink.
(lean, leaned, leaning)

_____

6. He _____ gazing at his own reflection in the water.
(are, was, were)

_____

7. Narcissus had _____ in love with his own face.
(fall, fallen, falling)

_____

8. The next moment, a flower_____ growing where
Narcissus had stood.
(am, are, was)

_____

Present-Tense Verbs

A **present-tense verb** tells about actions that are happening now.
Add *s* or *es* to most present-tense verbs when the subject of the sentence is *he*, *she*, *it*, or a singular noun.
Do not add *s* or *es* to a present-tense verb when the subject is *I, you, we, they,* or a plural noun.
Examples:

    Dougal Dixon *writes* books that stretch the reader's imagination.
    His ideas *mix* science and fiction in an exciting way.
    The neck of the lank *reach*es high into the air like a giraffe's.
    The harridan *flies* with wings that fold up when it walks.

DIRECTIONS Write the present-tense form of the verb in ( ) that correctly completes each sentence.

1. Cathy _____ the flower shop down the street.
   (like)

2. She _____ it about once a week.
   (visit)

3. She _____ home with armfuls of flowers.
   (come)

4. Her sisters _____ attractive arrangements.
   (fix)

5. Sometimes Cathy _____ carnations, roses, and irises in her vases.
   (mix)

6. Her sister Gladys _____ pictures of the flowers.
   (take)

7. They _____ the pictures to the owners of the shop.
   (show)

8. Cathy _____ for a job at the shop.
   (wish)

9. The owner of the shop _____ about the business.
   (worry)

10. She _____ her costs very closely.
    (watch)

11. The shop _____ a good profit.
    (make)

12. Maybe the owner _____ to hire Cathy.
    (need)

Past-Tense Verbs

A **past-tense verb** tells about actions that happened in the past.
Add *ed* or *d* to most present-tense verbs to make them show past tense. You may have to drop an *e*, double a final consonant, or change a *y* to an *i*.
Examples:

When Mr. King was a boy, he *lived* on a farm.
He always *carried* his lunch to school.
He *dipped* water from a nearby spring.

DIRECTIONS ▷ Write the past-tense form of each verb in ( ) to complete each sentence.

1. We _____ to the food fair.
(walk)

2. I _____ many different foods.
(sample)

3. Indian curry _____ both spicy
(seem)
and sweet.

4. Colorful signs _____ the unusual treats.
(describe)

5. A Greek restaurant _____ baklava made
(serve)
from nuts, honey, and flaky pastry.

6. My friend _____ a glass of African root beer.
(sip)

7. A woman _____ spring rolls made of shrimp and vegetables.
(fry)

8. I _____ many tasty foods that day.
(try)

9. One chef _____ me a red carnation.
(pass)

10. I _____ the flower onto my shirt.
(pin)

11. All of the meals _____ fresh vegetables and fruit.
(feature)

12. We _____ many unusual ones.
(taste)

Future-Tense Verbs

A **future-tense verb** expresses action that will happen in the future.
To form the future tense of a verb, use the helping verb *will* with the main verb.
Examples:

      Sam *will live* in the woods all year.
      He *will learn* about many things.

Sometimes other words appear between the helping verb and the main verb.
Examples:

      Sam *will* not *go* back to his home.
      Will he *have* a hard time in the winter?

DIRECTIONS ▸ Complete each sentence. Write the future tense of the verb in ( ).

1. What _____ _____ to Sam in the next few months?
   (happen)

2. He _____ _____ for game.
   (hunt)

3. He _____ _____ food at harvest time.
   (gather)

4. _____ Sam _____ his family?
   (miss)

5. _____ they _____ for him in the woods?
   (search)

6. They probably _____ not _____ him.
   (find)

7. Sam _____ _____ David, his friend.
   (remember)

8. Perhaps Sam _____ _____ something different.
   (cook)

9. Maybe Sam _____ _____ down the river on his new raft.
   (float)

10. No matter what, Sam _____ _____.
    (hide)

11. No one _____ _____ him.
    (notice)

12. _____ Sam _____ the woods?
    (leave)

Which Tense Is It?

Remember that a present-tense verb tells about actions that are happening now. A past-tense verb tells about actions that happened in the past. A future-tense verb shows action that will happen in the future.

ⓘⓘⓘⓘⓘⓘⓘⓘⓘⓘⓘⓘⓘⓘⓘⓘⓘⓘⓘⓘⓘⓘⓘⓘⓘⓘⓘ

DIRECTIONS ▷ Underline the verb in each sentence. Then write *present, past,* or *future* to identify the tense.

1. Lizards look different from snakes. _____

2. For one thing, they have legs. _____

3. A gecko lizard climbs across a ceiling. _____

4. Suction cups on its feet make this possible. _____

5. That lizard climbed the hill. _____

6. That other lizard jumps very high. _____

7. Samuel will see many lizards at the zoo. _____

8. He will go to the zoo on Tuesday. _____

9. We will ride to the zoo on a bus. _____

10. The zoo guide will tell us all about lizards. _____

DIRECTIONS ▷ Change each present-tense verb to the correct future-tense form. Rewrite the sentence on the line.

11. Sam sees ten lizards.

_____

12. I see only four.

_____

13. Some lizards change colors.

_____

Irregular Verbs

An **irregular verb** is a verb that does not end with *ed* to show past tense. Some irregular verbs show past tense by using a different form of the main verb with *have, has,* or *had.*
Examples:

Present	Past	Past with Helping Verb
do, does	did	(have, has, had) done
come, comes	came	(have, has, had) come
run, runs	ran	(have, has, had) run
go, goes	went	(have, has, had) gone

DIRECTIONS ▶ **Write the past-tense form of the verb in ( ) that correctly completes each sentence.**

1. Allison has _____ a report on chameleons.
(do)

2. She _____ a bus to the zoo to do research.
(ride)

3. She _____ some change to the bus driver.
(give)

4. At the zoo, Allison _____ from the entrance to the lizard area.
(run)

5. The chameleons had _____ out into the sunlight.
(come)

6. She _____ her lunch and watched the lizards.
(eat)

7. She _____ several chameleons, each a different color.
(see)

8. The guide had _____ hello to her.
(say)

9. Allison _____ twelve photos of the reptiles for her report.
(take)

10. She had _____ about her report for weeks.
(think)

11. She had _____ a rough draft already.
(write)

12. That afternoon, she _____ home and worked on the report.
(go)

Direct Objects

A **direct object** is a noun or pronoun that receives the action of the verb.
Use object pronouns such as *me, you, him, her, it, us,* and *them* as direct objects.
Examples:

The country of France gave the *Statue of Liberty* to the United States.
The French government shipped *her* in pieces to the United States.

DIRECTIONS > Read each sentence. Underline the direct object.

1. A team of engineers and laborers constructed her.

2. The Statue of Liberty greeted many immigrants.

3. She carries a torch in her upraised hand.

4. To immigrants, she represents hope and freedom.

5. Ships full of immigrants passed the statue before arriving in America.

DIRECTIONS > Think of a direct object to complete each sentence. Write it in the blank.

6. Millions of immigrants gave up _____ to come to America.

7. Immigrants sought _____ in America.

8. They first visited _____.

9. The immigration agents at Ellis Island questioned the _____.

10. The immigration agents processed _____ slowly.

11. Many immigrants could not speak _____.

12. Starting over in a new country required _____.

13. They faced many _____.

14. Immigrants found _____ in big cities.

15. Big cities also offered _____.

16. Immigrants who spoke the same language established _____.

Adverbs

An **adverb** is a word that describes a verb.

An adverb may tell how, when, or where an action happens. Many adverbs that tell how end in *ly*.

Use adverbs to make your writing vivid. Vary your sentences by moving the adverbs.

Examples:

Kristen visited the Science Museum *yesterday*.

She saw an exhibit of holograms *upstairs*.

She *finally* learned why holograms look so real.

DIRECTIONS Circle the adverb that describes the underlined verb. Then, circle *where, when,* or *how* to indicate what the adverb tells.

1. Daedalus carefully <u>built</u> two pairs of wings.   *where*   *when*   *how*

2. First, he <u>collected</u> the feathers of birds.   *where*   *when*   *how*

3. Next, he <u>constructed</u> frames of wax.   *where*   *when*   *how*

4. Then, he <u>attached</u> the feathers to the frames.   *where*   *when*   *how*

5. Finally, he <u>put</u> the wings on himself and on his son, Icarus.   *where*   *when*   *how*

6. Daedalus firmly <u>warned</u> Icarus about the Sun.   *where*   *when*   *how*

7. The warmth of the Sun would surely <u>melt</u> the wax.   *where*   *when*   *how*

8. The father and son <u>flew</u> joyfully in the sky.   *where*   *when*   *how*

9. Icarus <u>flew</u> higher.   *where*   *when*   *how*

10. Soon, the Sun <u>melted</u> all the wax.   *where*   *when*   *how*

11. Icarus <u>fell</u> down into the sea.   *where*   *when*   *how*

DIRECTIONS Add an adverb to make each sentence more vivid. Write the new sentence.

12. Daedalus looked at the surface of the sea.

_____

13. Feathers drifted on the waves.

_____

Adverbs That Compare

Adverbs can be used to compare two or more actions.
When you compare two actions, add *er* to most short adverbs. When you compare more than two actions, add *est* to most short adverbs.
Use *more* and *most* before most adverbs that have two or more syllables. When you compare two actions, use *more*. When you compare more than two, use *most*.
The adverbs *well* and *badly* have special forms of comparison: *well, better, best; badly, worse, worst.*
Examples:

Autumn comes *sooner* in Maine than in Virginia.
You must drive *more carefully* in wet weather than in dry weather.
This snowblower works *better* with dry snow than with wet snow.

DIRECTIONS ▷ **Write the correct form of the adverb in ( ) to complete each sentence.**

1. On August 3, 1492, the sailors aboard three small ships waited _____ (eagerly) than they ever had.

2. Their captain had argued _____ (strongly) than anyone else that the world was round.

3. Of all the rulers at that time, Queen Isabella of Portugal acted _____ (courageously).

4. She believed, _____ (completely) than King Ferdinand did, that this was a good idea.

5. Columbus appealed to the queen _____ (often) than another explorer did.

6. Of all the explorers at court, Columbus had stated his case _____ (convincingly).

DIRECTIONS ▷ **Complete each sentence with the correct form of *well* or *badly*.**

7. Columbus did _____ (well) than he ever thought possible.

8. At times, his crew thought they were doing _____ (badly) than any other crew in the history of the world.

9. Columbus had prepared _____ (well) for this trip than for any other trip.

10. The three ships were equipped _____ (well) for the journey.

Adverbs Before Adjectives and Other Adverbs

An adverb can be used to describe a verb. An adverb can also be used to describe an adjective or another adverb.
Example:
> Sheri did a *fairly good* job.
> She thought *very long* about the question.

 DIRECTIONS ▶ Circle the adverb that describes the underlined adjective or adverb.

1. Reiko was sitting very <u>quietly</u> at her desk.

2. She felt extremely <u>interested</u> in the book.

3. The book was about carefully <u>planned</u> Japanese gardens.

4. Reiko quite <u>suddenly</u> decided to make one.

5. She knew her garden couldn't be too <u>big</u>.

6. She had a fairly <u>small</u> yard.

7. It was certainly <u>difficult</u> to choose a type of garden.

8. She considered the rather <u>complicated</u> job of making a garden with a pond.

9. Her yard was much <u>too</u> small for that.

 **DIRECTIONS** ▶ Draw an arrow from the underlined adverb to the adjective, other adverb, or verb it describes.

10. A teahouse garden is <u>particularly</u> charming.

11. It <u>gently</u> suggests an approach to a mountain temple.

12. The builder <u>skillfully</u> uses rocks and stones to suggest mountains and valleys.

13. Reiko didn't think this would work <u>effectively</u> in her yard.

14. She <u>finally</u> decided on a dry landscape garden.

15. A dry landscape garden is <u>much</u> less expensive than a teahouse garden to create.

Adverb or Adjective?

Use an adverb to describe a verb. Use an adjective to describe a noun or pronoun. Use *good* as an adjective. Use *well* as an adverb or as an adjective to mean "healthy."

DIRECTIONS > Complete each sentence by writing the correct word in ( ).

1. Have you ever brushed up _____ against a stinging nettle?
   (gentle, gently)

2. Were you surprised by the _____ number of stinging sensations?
   (great, greatly)

3. When this happens to you, you might _____ lift up a leaf.
   (careful, carefully)

4. Notice that the underside is _____ covered with sharp bristles.
   (complete, completely)

5. These are _____ attached to sacs of formic acid, the same acid you
   (firm, firmly)
   get from an ant sting.

6. Nettle stings are not _____.
   (serious, seriously)

7. The pain will go away _____ quickly.
   (fair, fairly)

8. You can dab the _____ area with
   (entire, entirely)
   rubbing alcohol to soothe the pain.

DIRECTIONS > Complete each sentence with *good* or *well.*

9. Tina and Ted went for a _____, long walk in the woods.

10. Tina had not been feeling _____ for a few days.

11. Tina and Ted both walk _____.

12. They had packed a _____ lunch of sandwiches and apples.

Prepositions

A **preposition** is a word that relates a noun or pronoun to other words in the sentence. The **object of the preposition** is the noun or pronoun that follows the preposition. Some commonly used prepositions are in the box below.
Example:

I went *to* the store.

A prepositional phrase is a group of words made up of a preposition, its object, and all the words that come between them. Prepositional phrases often tell where, what kind, when, or how.
Example:

At night she guided her canoe *through the waves*.

above	below	from	through	after	between	into	around
by	of	under	at	during	off	until	before
except	on	up	behind	for	over	without	

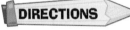 **DIRECTIONS** Read each sentence. Underline each prepositional phrase. Circle the object of the preposition.

1. The girl returned to her island.

2. A leaking boat had nearly taken her below the waves.

3. She had traveled without any means of navigation except the stars.

4. For many centuries, sailors have found their position by the stars.

5. New developments in the 1700s made navigation easier.

6. However, even modern travelers on the sea use the ancient method of celestial navigation.

7. Navigators take the bearing of a star.

8. A sextant measures a star's angle above the horizon.

9. Sailors can tell their position from that reading.

10. Without this information, navigation would be a hard task.

Prepositional Phrases

Remember that a prepositional phrase is made up of a preposition, the object of the preposition, and all the words in between.

DIRECTIONS ▷ Underline each prepositional phrase. Circle the preposition.

1. Did you ever feel seasick in a car?

2. When you are seasick, you are not really sick from the sea.

3. You are sick from the motion of the waves.

4. In this same way, you can get sick in the back of a car.

5. Your sense of balance has been upset.

6. Deep inside your ears are semicircular canals.

7. These canals are filled with a fluid and are lined with special hairs.

8. These hairs pick up the sense of movement when you change position.

9. Usually, the fluid lies still in the bottom of the canals.

10. Quick, violent motions make the fluid move around the canals.

11. This can cause a sick feeling in your stomach.

DIRECTIONS ▷ Add a prepositional phrase to each sentence. Write the new sentence on the line.

12. Lying down may help you feel better.

_____

13. There is less motion in the front seat, so you might move.

_____

_____

14. Reading can make motion sickness worse, so don't ever read.

_____

_____

Preposition or Adverb?

Some words can be used as prepositions or adverbs.
Examples:
    The cat climbed *up* the tree.   We looked *up*.

DIRECTIONS ▷ Circle *preposition* or *adverb* to identify the underlined word in each sentence.

1. The Morgans were driving <u>down</u> the highway.

   preposition   *adverb*

2. Suddenly, the youngest child cried <u>out</u>.

   preposition   *adverb*

3. "Don't drive <u>through</u> the lake, Mom!" he shouted.

   preposition   *adverb*

4. The family looked <u>around</u>.

   preposition   *adverb*

5. <u>On</u> the road they saw shimmering patches of water.

   preposition   *adverb*

6. "It's just a mirage, David," his sister Camille said, looking <u>outside</u>.

   preposition   *adverb*

7. "No matter how far we drive, we will never even get <u>near</u> it," Camille explained.

   preposition   *adverb*

8. "On a day like this, a hot layer of air is <u>above</u> the road," said David's mother.

   preposition   *adverb*

9. "The hot layer of air is bending the light, as if <u>through</u> a prism," continued Camille.

   preposition   *adverb*

DIRECTIONS ▷ Add a prepositional phrase to each sentence.

10. The family continued to drive _____.

11. _____ they decided to stop.

12. They got out _____.

13. They looked _____.

Conjunctions

A **conjunction** is a word that joins words or groups of words.
Conjunctions may be used in several ways. The conjunction *and* is used to mean "together." The conjunction *but* is used to show contrast. The conjunction *or* is used to show choice.

Examples:

    Patrick *and* the twins looked at their new home.
    His mother felt sad, *but* Patrick was excited.
    Might this old house hold mysteries *or* treasures?

DIRECTIONS Complete each sentence, using the conjunction that has the meaning in ( ).

1. The house looked bare _____ gloomy.
(together)

2. The twins began to cry, _____ Patrick cheered them up.
(contrast)

3. Patrick walked from room to room _____ looked for trapdoors.
(together)

4. He did not find any trapdoors _____ mysterious stairways.
(choice)

5. Patrick was disappointed, _____ his parents were glad.
(contrast)

6. They did not want a house with ghosts _____ goblins in it.
(choice)

7. Patrick told them there might be treasure _____ gold instead.
(together)

8. His mother _____ father thought he was being silly.
(together)

9. The treasure could be in the cellar _____ in the backyard.
(choice)

10. He found a coin in the backyard near the cellar door, _____ he knew
(together)
that he was right.

11. People were coming to work on the house, _____ Patrick was afraid
(together)
they would find the treasure first.

12. His parents might think it was silly, _____ Patrick would not stop
(contrast)
searching.

Interjections

An **interjection** is a word or a group of words that expresses strong feeling.
Examples:
>   *Help*! I hurt my foot!
>   *Wow*! How did you do that?

DIRECTIONS ▷ Circle the interjection in each item.

1. Gee! The baby is so tiny.

2. Wow! Her hands are so dainty.

3. She seems to be unhappy. Oh, dear!

4. Oh, my! What can we do to make her stop crying?

5. Good grief! That doesn't work.

6. Dad, where are you? Oops!

7. Great! Here comes Dad.

8. Alas! We cannot calm the baby. Can you help, Dad?

9. Of course! I'll show you what to do.

DIRECTIONS ▷ Add an interjection to each exercise to express strong feeling. Punctuate correctly.

10. _____ She smiled at me!

11. _____ I knew she recognized me. I'm her brother, after all.

12. _____ I think the baby is going to sneeze.

13. She already did. _____

14. _____ I just dropped the rattle.

15. _____ I hope she doesn't start crying again.

16. _____ I can't stand all this noise!

17. _____ When will we get some peace and quiet around here?

18. That will happen after she leaves for college. _____

What Is a Sentence?

A **sentence** is a group of words that expresses a complete thought. It always begins with a capital letter. It always ends with a punctuation mark.
Every sentence has two parts. The **subject** is the part about which something is being said. The **predicate** tells about the subject.

Subject
My fifth-grade class

Predicate
is going on a field trip.

The **complete subject** is all the words that make up the subject. A **simple subject** is the key word or words in the subject of a sentence. The simple subject tells whom or what the sentence is about.
The **complete predicate** is a word or group of words that tells something about the subject. The **simple predicate** is the key word or words in the complete predicate. The simple predicate is an action verb or a linking verb, together with any helping verbs.
Examples:

A long, yellow school bus is taking us to New York. (complete subject)
A long, yellow school bus is taking us to New York. (simple subject)
Our teacher sat up front. (complete predicate)
Our teacher sat up front. (simple predicate)

▶ **DIRECTIONS** Add a complete subject or a complete predicate to each sentence.

1. Mr. and Mrs. Brown _____.

2. _____ got off the bus in New York.

3. Tall buildings _____.

4. Some students _____.

5. The field trip _____.

6. _____ wants to go again soon.

7. Next time, the adults _____.

8. Before the second trip, they _____.

9. _____ will make the trip a success.

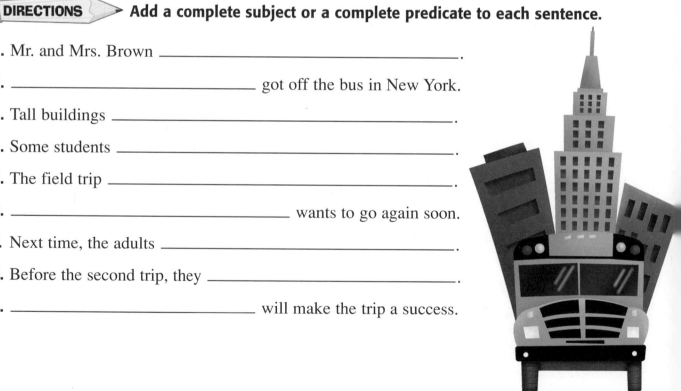

Is It a Sentence?

Remember that a sentence is a group of words that expresses a complete thought. It always begins with a capital letter. It always ends with a punctuation mark.
Example:
The capital of Illinois is Springfield.

DIRECTIONS ➤ **If the group of words is a sentence, write it correctly. Capitalize the first word, and end the sentence with a period. If the group is not a sentence, write *not a sentence*.**

1. we memorized the capitals of all of the states

   _____

2. everyone knew the capital of Arkansas

   _____

3. the capital is not always the largest city in the state

   _____

4. you should picture the map in your mind

   _____

5. the left side is the west side

   _____

6. right through the middle of the country

   _____

7. that river empties into the Gulf of Mexico

   _____

8. the Hudson River valley in New York

   _____

9. three people found Delaware right away

   _____

10. a map of the thirteen original colonies

   _____

Subjects and Predicates

Be sure your sentences have two parts, a **subject** and a **predicate**. The subject is the part about which something is being said. The predicate tells about the subject.

Subject
My whole family

Predicate
went to the mall.

DIRECTIONS Which sentence part is missing? Write *subject* or *predicate* on the line.

1. Your eyes _____.

2. Your other sense organs _____.

3. _____ pick up sounds.

4. _____ feel hot and cold.

5. The tongue _____.

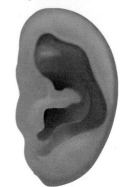

DIRECTIONS Read each sentence. Underline the subject. Circle the predicate.

6. The eye is made of many parts.

7. The pupil is the round, black center of the eye.

8. The outer, colored part is called the iris.

9. The iris is made of a ring of muscle.

10. Too much light can damage the eye.

11. The iris closes up in bright light.

12. Some people are colorblind.

13. They cannot see shades of red and green.

14. A nearsighted person cannot see distant things well.

15. Close objects are blurry to a farsighted person.

16. People who need glasses to read are farsighted.

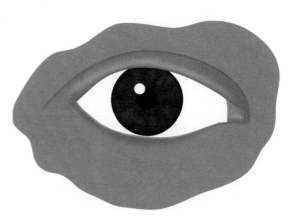

Simple Subjects and Complete Subjects

Remember that the simple subject is the main word or words in the complete subject of a sentence. The complete subject includes all the words that tell whom or what the sentence is about.

Examples:

The county's <u>fair</u> was the best ever this year. (simple subject)

<u>The games on the midway</u> had good prizes. (complete subject)

DIRECTIONS ▶ Read each sentence. Underline the complete subject. Then, write the simple subject on the line.

1. Two young men were on their way from Dallas to Waco, Texas. _____

2. A raging tornado was also on its way to Waco. _____

3. Two square miles of the city would soon be twisted and destroyed. _____

4. An odd roaring noise began with the rain. _____

5. The strong wind tore buildings apart. _____

6. Giant walls fell into the street. _____

7. One side of a street was destroyed in Waco. _____

8. The other side had not been touched. _____

9. Some people were picked up by the wind. _____

10. A tornado will sometimes set a person down gently. _____

11. This lucky person may even be unhurt. _____

12. Unlucky people may be set down violently by a tornado. _____

13. Dorothy was among the lucky ones. _____

14. She was set down safely in Oz. _____

15. A ride in a tornado would be quite an experience. _____

Compound Subjects

A **compound subject** is two or more simple subjects that have the same predicate. Join the two or more simple subjects in a compound subject with *and* or *or*.
Examples:

Sun *and* sand make Hawaii a popular vacation spot.
Surfing *or* swimming can be done on the famous beaches.

DIRECTIONS ▷ Read each sentence. Write the compound subject and the joining word. In your answer, add commas if they are needed.

1. Sally and John like to take care of their garden.

   _____

2. Roses daisies and violets are their favorite flowers.

   _____

3. Jim and Meg came over for lunch in the garden.

   _____

4. Sally John Jim and Meg sat under the big apple tree.

   _____

5. A picnic basket and a jug of lemonade were placed on the blanket.

   _____

6. The four friends and their two dogs had a wonderful afternoon.

   _____

7. Apples peaches and plums were served for dessert.

   _____

8. Frankie and Joanne brought some movies over later.

   _____

9. The six friends the two dogs and a few cats went inside after sunset.

   _____

Simple Predicates and Complete Predicates

The **simple predicate** is the main word or words in the complete predicate of a sentence.

The **complete predicate** includes all the words that tell what the subject of the sentence is or does.

To locate the simple predicate, find the key word in the complete predicate.

Examples:

Tall, snowcapped mountains <u>reach</u> high into the sky. (simple predicate)

Tall, snowcapped mountains <u>reach high into the sky</u>. (complete predicate)

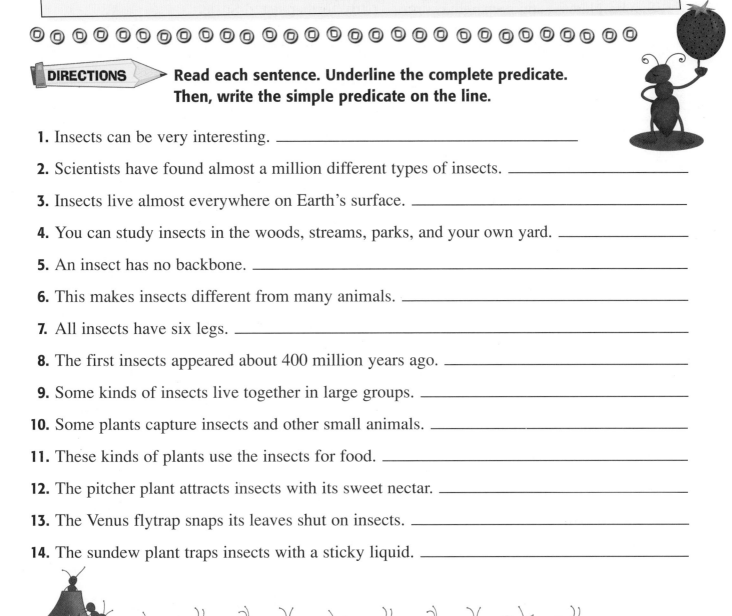

DIRECTIONS ▷ **Read each sentence. Underline the complete predicate. Then, write the simple predicate on the line.**

1. Insects can be very interesting. _____

2. Scientists have found almost a million different types of insects. _____

3. Insects live almost everywhere on Earth's surface. _____

4. You can study insects in the woods, streams, parks, and your own yard. _____

5. An insect has no backbone. _____

6. This makes insects different from many animals. _____

7. All insects have six legs. _____

8. The first insects appeared about 400 million years ago. _____

9. Some kinds of insects live together in large groups. _____

10. Some plants capture insects and other small animals. _____

11. These kinds of plants use the insects for food. _____

12. The pitcher plant attracts insects with its sweet nectar. _____

13. The Venus flytrap snaps its leaves shut on insects. _____

14. The sundew plant traps insects with a sticky liquid. _____

Compound Predicates

A **compound predicate** is two or more predicates that have the same subject. The simple predicates in a compound predicate are usually joined by *and* or *or*. *Examples:*

A leopard <u>sprawls</u> along a limb *and* <u>relaxes</u> in a tree.
Bears <u>chase</u> *or* <u>injure</u> sheep sometimes.

DIRECTIONS → Read each sentence. Write the compound predicate and the joining word. In your answer, add commas if they are needed.

1. Sandra planned and prepared a surprise party for her sister, Susie.

_____

2. She shopped cleaned and cooked the day before the party.

_____

3. She hired a clown and bought some balloons about a week ahead of time.

_____

4. Four days before the party, Sandra ordered a cake and borrowed extra plates.

_____

5. The guests wore party hats and played party games.

_____

6. Everyone ate laughed and danced.

_____

7. Some of the children cleared the table and helped with the dishes.

_____

8. After the party, the guests walked ran or rode home.

_____

9. After the party, Sandra sat and rested.

_____

Complete and Simple Subjects and Predicates

Remember that the complete subject includes all the words that tell whom or what the sentence is about. The simple subject is the main word or words in the complete subject.

The complete predicate includes all the words that tell what the subject of the sentence is or does. The simple predicate is the main word or words in the complete predicate.

DIRECTIONS > Underline each complete subject, and circle each complete predicate. Then, write the simple subject and the simple predicate.

1. Our favorite coach cheers during the race.

_____

2. My youngest sister swims ahead of the others.

_____

3. Her strokes cut through the water.

_____

4. Ripples splash at the edge of the pool.

_____

5. The exciting race ends with a surprise.

_____

6. My sister's team finishes first.

_____

7. The people in the bleachers cheer wildly.

_____

8. The team holds the silver trophy for a school photograph.

_____

9. The team members hug each other happily.

_____

10. Everyone in my family goes for an ice-cream cone.

_____

Simple and Compound Sentences

A sentence that expresses only one complete thought is a **simple sentence**.
A **compound sentence** is made up of two or more simple sentences joined by a conjunction such as *and, or,* or *but*. Use a comma (,) before a conjunction that joins two sentences.

Examples:
      The family moved to Ohio. (simple sentence)
      Patrick liked his new house, and he decided to explore. (compound sentence)

DIRECTIONS ▷ Read each sentence. Underline each simple subject. Circle each simple predicate. Then, write whether each sentence is a *simple sentence* or a *compound sentence*.

1. Once the house was part of the Underground Railroad, and it had many hiding places.

_____

2. Between 1830 and 1860, the Underground Railroad brought about 50,000 slaves to freedom.

_____

3. Farm wagons were the "trains" on this railroad.

_____

4. Often, the "train rides" were long walks between stations.

_____

5. Runaway slaves stopped at "stations" along the way, but they rarely stayed for long.

_____

6. The home of Frederick Douglass was one "station" on the track to freedom.

_____

7. Levi Coffin was a "conductor" in Indiana, and he earned the title "President of the Underground Railroad."

_____

8. Dies Drear was also a "conductor," but he lived in Ohio.

_____

9. Allan Pinkerton made barrels in Illinois, but he also hid slaves in his shop.

_____

10. Harriet Tubman led slaves to the North, and sometimes she took them to Canada.

_____

Kinds of Sentences

A **declarative sentence** makes a statement or tells something. It ends with a period (.).

An **interrogative sentence** asks a question. It ends with a question mark (?).

An **imperative sentence** makes a request or gives a command. It ends with a period (.). *You* is always the subject of an imperative sentence. Often, the word *you* does not appear in the sentence. It is said to be "understood".

An **exclamatory sentence** shows strong feeling or surprise. It ends with an exclamation point (!).

Examples:

We are going to see the Statue of Liberty. (declarative)
Have you ever seen it? (interrogative)
Come see it with me. (imperative)
It must be very heavy! (exclamatory)

> **DIRECTIONS** End each sentence with the correct punctuation mark. Then, write whether the sentence is *declarative, interrogative, imperative,* or *exclamatory.*

1. We are going to New York to see the Statue of Liberty _____

2. We have studied about it in school _____

3. Have you ever seen the Statue of Liberty _____

4. What a feeling it is to be close to her _____

5. Stand over there, and I will take your picture _____

6. It is difficult to imagine that she was a gift _____

7. Can you imagine getting such a large gift _____

8. It would take many mail trucks to deliver it _____

9. We enjoyed our trip to New York this year _____

10. You must go if you get the chance _____

11. Did you know that many New Yorkers have never visited the statue _____

_____

12. Don't be one of those people _____

Subjects in Imperative Sentences

Remember that in an imperative sentence, *you* is always the subject. Often, the word *you* does not appear in the sentence. It is said to be "understood."
Example:
 (*You*) Read the directions carefully.

DIRECTIONS ▶ **Read each sentence. Circle each imperative sentence. On the line, write the simple subject of each sentence.**

1. Trash is one of our biggest problems. _____

2. Be very careful with empty cans and bottles. _____

3. Don't just toss them out. _____

4. Put cans and bottles in separate bags. _____

5. The trash problem can be solved. _____

6. Take old newspapers to recycling centers. _____

7. Never toss plastic trash on the ground. _____

8. Pieces of plastic can kill animals. _____

DIRECTIONS ▶ **Change each declarative sentence to an imperative sentence. Write the new sentence on the line.**

9. Packages with too much wrapping should be avoided.

_____

10. People should buy the largest sizes of products.

_____

11. Old T-shirts can be used as wiping rags.

_____

12. Both sides of writing paper can be used.

_____

Agreement of Subjects and Verbs

A verb must agree with its subject in number. Use
a singular verb with a singular subject. Use a plural
verb with a plural or compound subject.
Examples:
> *Chad finds* a magic carpet.
> *It grants* him wishes.
> The *wishes come* true only for Chad.

DIRECTIONS Underline the simple subject of each sentence. Then, complete each
sentence correctly by circling the form of each verb in ( ) that
agrees with the subject.

1. Chad and his friends (look, looks) around in the old house.

2. Chad (find, finds) an old rug rolled up in a corner.

3. He (pull, pulls) it out and unrolls it.

4. The rug (take, takes) Chad for a ride around the room.

5. Chad's friends (come, comes) into the room as the carpet lands.

6. They (stand, stands) staring with their mouths open.

7. Then, Chad (explain, explains) that the rug has told him he has three wishes.

8. The rug also (tell, tells) Chad that it will take him wherever he wants to go.

9. Chad and his friends (go, goes) for a long ride on the rug.

10. They (fly, flies) over the town and the river.

11. Chad (wish, wishes) that his aunt could come home from the hospital.

12. When Chad gets home, he (hear, hears) his mother talking on the phone.

13. She (says, say) that his aunt can leave the hospital now.

14. In his room, Chad (thank, thanks) the rug and (think, thinks) about his next wishes.

Combining Sentences with the Same Subject or Predicate

A good writer combines two or more sentences that have the same subject or predicate. The conjunctions *and, but,* and *or* are often used to combine sentence parts.

When two sentences have the same predicate, the subjects can be combined.
Example:

> Theseus was angry. King Minos was angry.
> Theseus *and* King Minos were angry.

When two sentences have the same subject, the predicates can be combined.
Example:

> Theseus found the ring. Theseus returned it.
> Theseus found the ring *and* returned it.

How to Combine Sentences with the Same Subjects or Predicates
1. Find two or more sentences that have the same subject or predicate.
2. Combine the subjects or the predicates with the joining word that most clearly expresses your meaning to the audience.
3. If you combine subjects, make sure you use the plural form of the verb.

 **DIRECTIONS** ▷ **Rewrite this paragraph. Combine sentences with the same subjects or predicates to make it more interesting to read.**

Each year, King Minos demanded a human sacrifice from the people of Athens. Seven boys would enter the Labyrinth. Seven girls would enter the Labyrinth. The Labyrinth was the home of the Minotaur. The Minotaur was half man. The Minotaur was half beast.

_____

_____

_____

_____

_____

_____

_____

Combining Adjectives and Adverbs in Sentences

To avoid short, choppy sentences, a writer often combines two or more sentences that describe the same subject. Sentences that describe the same subject with different adjectives can sometimes be combined.
Example:
> Joanie was *diligent*. She was also *courageous*.
> Joanie was *diligent and courageous*.

Sentences that describe the same verb with different adverbs can also be combined.
Example:
> Joanie studied *eagerly*. She studied *carefully*.
> Joanie studied *eagerly and carefully*.

How to Combine Sentences with Adjectives and Adverbs
1. Look for different adjectives or adverbs that describe the same subject or verb.
2. Use an appropriate conjunction (*and*, *but*, or *or*) to combine the adjectives or the adverbs.
3. If you combine three or more adjectives or adverbs in one sentence, use commas to separate them.

 **DIRECTIONS** Combine each set of sentences to make one sentence. Then, tell whether you combined adjectives or adverbs.

1. Joanie waited patiently. She waited quietly. _____

_____

2. She had felt disappointed before. She had felt rejected before. _____

_____

3. She really wanted to be a scientist. She truly wanted to be a scientist. _____

_____

4. Joanie read the letter slowly. She read the letter calmly. _____

_____

Joining Sentences

A writer can join two short, choppy sentences into one that is more interesting to read. The result is a compound sentence.

Use the conjunction *and* to join two sentences that show addition or similarity.
Example:

> Patrick saw the house. He decided it was haunted.
> Patrick saw the house, *and* he decided it was haunted.

Use the conjunction *but* to join two sentences that show contrast.
Example:

> Patrick ran up the steps. He stopped at the door.
> Patrick ran up the steps, *but* he stopped at the door.

Use the conjunction *or* to join two sentences that show choice.
Example:

> Should he go inside? Should he explore outside?
> Should he go inside, *or* should he explore outside?

How to Combine Sentences
1. Choose two short sentences you want to combine.
2. Select the appropriate conjunction to combine them.
3. Be sure the conjunction makes the meaning of the combined sentence clear.
4. Put a comma before the conjunction.

DIRECTIONS ▷ **Join each pair of sentences. Use the conjunctions *and, but,* or *or*.**

1. Patrick studied the wall. He found a hidden button.

_____

2. Patrick pushed the button. The bookcase moved.

_____

3. Patrick could wait. He could explore the path.

_____

4. He wasn't afraid. He wasn't comfortable, either.

_____

Sentence Variety

To add variety to sentences, a writer sometimes changes the order of the words. Usually, the subject comes before the verb. This is called **natural order**.
Example:

Margaret led Danny down a twisting path.

Sometimes the subject and the verb can be reversed. This is called **inverted order**.
Example:

At the end of the path was a small shack.

How to Vary Word Order in Sentences
1. Choose a sentence you have written in which the subject and the verb can be reversed.
2. Write the sentence in inverted order. Be sure the meaning of the sentence does not change.

 **DIRECTIONS** ➤ **Write each sentence, changing the word order whenever it would not change the meaning. Tell which sentences cannot be changed and explain why.**

1. On the little door shone the sunlight.

_____

2. Margaret and Danny walked into the shack.

_____

3. Inside the shack was a large wooden table.

_____

4. On the table lay a black cat.

_____

5. Margaret reached out to the cat.

_____

6. At work in the shack was a witch's magic!

_____

7. Margaret told Danny to follow her out.

_____

Avoiding Sentence Fragments and Run-on Sentences

To avoid writing **sentence fragments**, be sure each sentence has a subject and a predicate and expresses a complete thought.

To avoid writing **run-on sentences**, be sure you join two complete sentences with a comma and a conjunction. You may also write them as two separate sentences.

DIRECTIONS Read each group of words. If it is a simple sentence, write *simple sentence* on the line. If it is a sentence fragment or a run-on sentence, rewrite it correctly.

1. A box turtle is a reptile it lives in woods and fields.

_____

2. The box turtle has a hinged lower shell.

_____

3. Can pull its legs, head, and tail inside its shell and get "boxed in."

_____

4. Many kinds of turtles on land and in the water.

_____

5. Belong to the same family as lizards, snakes, alligators, and crocodiles.

_____

_____

6. Box turtles will eat earthworms, insects, berries, and green leafy vegetables.

_____

_____

7. Painted turtles eat meal worms, earthworms, minnows, and insects the musk turtle finds food along the bottoms of ponds or streams.

_____

_____

8. Painted turtles get their name from the red and yellow patterns on their shells they also have yellow lines on their heads.

_____

_____

Correcting Run-on Sentences

Good writers avoid run-on sentences. Run-on sentences may be rewritten as simple sentences or as compound sentences.

DIRECTIONS ▶ **Read each run-on sentence. Fix it in two ways. Write two simple sentences, and write one compound sentence.**

1. You'll need 101 index cards you'll need a colored marker.

   a. _____

   b. _____

2. Print the name of a state or a state capital on each index card print the rules on the last index card.

   a. _____

   _____

   b. _____

   _____

3. Put the marker away put all the cards in an envelope.

   a. _____

   b. _____

4. This game is for small groups up to three students may play.

   a. _____

   b. _____

5. Players mix up the cards they lay the cards face down.

   a. _____

   b. _____

Capitalization of Names and Titles of People and Pets

Begin each part of the name of a person with a capital letter. Capitalize an initial used in a name.

Begin a title of a person, such as *Ms., Mrs., Mr.,* or *Dr.,* with a capital letter. Always capitalize the word *I.*

Examples:

Pete P. Pelky

Mrs. Morrow

Michael Mixx and I went camping.

DIRECTIONS ▷ **Read each sentence. Circle the letters that should be capital letters.**

1. i was going camping with my friend michael.

2. We met mr. carl g. carbur at the camping supply store.

3. michael and i decided that we needed a new tent.

4. mrs. albright showed us many different tents.

5. we chose one just like dr. pelky's.

6. michael's mother, mrs. mixx, gave us a ride to the campsite.

7. After we set up the tent, i walked down the road.

8. dr. pelky was at the next site!

9. Dr. pelky was camping with mario j. moreno.

10. mario showed michael and me a great place to fish.

11. i caught some trout, and michael caught a bass.

12. michael and i ate supper at dr. pelky's camp.

Capitalization of Proper Nouns and Proper Adjectives

Remember that a proper noun names a particular place, holiday, day of the week, or month. A proper adjective is formed from a proper noun.

Capitalize the first letter of each important word in a proper noun or proper adjective.

Examples:

Canada   Fourth of July   Wednesday   German shepherd

DIRECTIONS ▶ **Rewrite each sentence, using capital letters where needed.**

1. My best friends and i plan to tour the united states.

_____

2. My friend sandy is very excited because she has never been to california.

_____

_____

3. She has never tasted any mexican food, either.

_____

4. She will be coming from new york and meeting jane in philadelphia.

_____

5. Then, the two of them will pick up roxanne in phoenix, arizona.

_____

6. When they get to san francisco, i plan to take them out for chinese food.

_____

_____

7. If we go to green's restaurant for vegetarian food, even jane will like the brussels sprouts.

_____

_____

8. Sometimes i think that july will never get here.

_____

9. I received a letter from sandy last tuesday.

_____

Using Capital Letters

Use a capital letter to begin the first word of a sentence.
Begin each important word in the name of a town, city, state, province, and country with a capital letter.
Begin each important word in the names of streets and their abbreviations with capital letters.
Begin the name of a day of the week or its abbreviation with a capital letter.
Begin the name of a month or its abbreviation with a capital letter.

Examples:

Detroit, Michigan
Athens, Greece
Golden Gate Avenue or Ave.
Saturday or Sat.
November or Nov.

DIRECTIONS Rewrite each sentence. Add capital letters where they are needed.

1. i found a book of rhymes at the library in milwaukee.

_____

2. the book was published in london, england.

_____

3. the book contained rhymes from the countries of kenya, ecuador, and even new zealand.

_____

_____

4. my favorite poem told of a crocodile that lived at the corner of cricket court and bee boulevard.

_____

_____

5. we started driving across the painted desert wednesday.

_____

6. thursday morning we saw a beautiful sunrise.

_____

7. we decided to drive to the rocky mountains on sunday.

_____

8. we finally reached el paso, texas, on tuesday.

_____

Periods

Use a **period (.)** at the end of a declarative or imperative sentence.
Use a period after an abbreviation.
Use a period after an initial.
Use a period after the numeral in a main topic and after the capital letter in a subtopic of an outline.
Examples:

    Arithmetic adds up to answers.
    U.S.   Fri.   Jan.   Dr.   Blvd.
    Capt. Chou A. Hak-Tak

    I. How to Master Multiplication
        A. Learn multiplication tables
        B. Practice doing multiplication problems

DIRECTIONS ▷ **Correct each item. Add periods where they are needed.**

1. Last week our class visited a Chinese exhibit

2. I thought the pen-and-brush pictures were beautiful

3. I was also impressed with the carved jade ships

4. Our teacher, Ms Garrett, showed us a book about Chinese painting in the museum gift shop

5. The book was written by Dr Chun B Fong.

6. Dr Fong included a chapter about wood-block prints.

7. Our guide, T R Adams, knew all about Chinese art

8. J B Barnard asked several questions.

9. The museum is located on N Clark St

10. I   Crafts from China

    A   Silk painting

    B   Porcelain

Abbreviations and Initials

An **abbreviation** is a short way of writing a word or words.
Begin abbreviations with a capital letter. End most abbreviations with a period.
An **initial** is an abbreviation of a name. The initial is the first letter of the name.
Use capital letters and periods to write an initial.
Examples:

Doctor = *Dr.*	Road = *Rd.*	Tuesday = *Tues.*
August = *Aug.*	Tina Devers = *T. Devers*	

DIRECTIONS ➤ **Rewrite each item. Use the correct abbreviations and initials for the underlined words.**

1. My name is <u>Chester Michael</u> Dooley. I live at 4338 Market <u>Boulevard</u> in Alabaster, Alabama. My birthday is on <u>October</u> 27.

   _____

   _____

2. Suzy <u>Elizabeth</u> Ziegler requests the pleasure of your company at a party in honor of her friend, Maryanne <u>Margaret</u> Marbles. Please come to the country club at 23 Country Club <u>Drive</u> at 4:00 on <u>Tuesday</u>, <u>April</u> 14.

   _____

   _____

   _____

3. The <u>James</u> Harold Calabases take great pride in announcing the birth of their twins, Heather <u>Holly</u> Calabas and <u>James</u> Harold Calabas, <u>Junior</u>. This happy event took place on <u>Monday</u>, <u>August</u> 23, at 3:00.

   _____

   _____

   _____

4. <u>Fortunato Augustus</u> Jones has been appointed assistant to the president of Bags and Boxes, <u>Incorporated</u>. This store is located at 45 Ninety-ninth <u>Avenue</u>.

   _____

   _____

Using Commas in Sentences

Use a **comma (,)** after the words *yes* and *no* when they begin a statement.
Use commas to separate three or more words in a series.
Use a comma before the word *and, but,* or *or* when two sentences are combined.
Use a comma to separate a word used in direct address from a sentence.
Use a comma between a quotation and the rest of the sentence.
Examples:

Yes, the boys should join their father.
The boys ran *quickly, silently, and anxiously*.
Josh felt tired, *but* he continued to run.
"*Andy*, I need to rest for a minute."
"*We are almost there*," said Andy.

DIRECTIONS ▷ **Rewrite each sentence, adding commas where they are needed.**

1. Three plants to avoid are poison ivy poison oak and poison sumac.

2. "Steven I see that you have some poison oak growing in your yard."

3. "Your dog cat or rabbit can pick it up on its fur and rub against you" Wesley said.

4. Yes it will make your skin burn itch and swell.

5. Dana put his clothes in a hamper and his mother got a rash from touching the clothes.

DIRECTIONS ▷ **Cross out any commas that are incorrect. Rewrite the sentence on the line, adding any commas that are needed.**

6. Poison ivy looks like, a shrub a vine, or a small plant.

7. Poison ivy, has green leaves in clusters of three and so does poison oak.

Using Commas in Sentences, page 2

> Use a comma before the words *and, but,* and *or* in a compound sentence.
> Use a comma after time-order words, such as *first, next, then,* and *last.*
> Use a comma after introductory words and phrases.
> Use a comma to separate three or more words in a series.
> *Examples:*
> > The old house was big, *and* it also looked mysterious.
> > *First,* I decided to explore the house.
> > *Before I had explored very long,* I found a tunnel.
> > The tunnel was *dark, damp, and long.*

DIRECTIONS > **Correct each sentence. Put commas where they are needed.**

1. The old house looked interesting but it also looked frightening.

2. I inspected the upstairs and I looked in the backyard.

3. The cellar door was open and I decided to look inside.

4. I could look around in one room or I could go to another room.

5. First I was worried that there was something in the cellar.

6. Next I thought I heard voices coming from the other room.

7. After a while I decided I had better get out of the cellar.

8. In addition I began to remember the stories my mother had told me.

9. I thought of all the other people who had lived played and worked in this house.

10. I imagined that I heard footsteps whispers and singing.

11. I ran out of the cellar and I closed the door behind me.

12. Soon I decided I wanted to explore the upstairs of the house.

More Uses for Commas

Use a comma in an address to separate the city and the state or the city and the country.
Use a comma between the day and the year.
Use a comma after the greeting of a friendly letter and after the closing of any letter.
Examples:

Albuquerque, New Mexico	Lima, Peru
April 30, 2005	Monday, January 27, 2005
Dear Uncle Ernie,	
Yours truly,	

DIRECTIONS Correct each letter. Add commas where they are needed.

732 Cactus Road
Albuquerque NM 87107
April 22 2005

Dear Ernest
    I need to show Father that I am old enough to go on the summer trail drive. Please help me by reminding Father that I have helped you do many things this year. I will appreciate any help that you can give me.

Your friend

David Ortez

441 Scorpion Trail
Albuquerque NM 87112
May 3 2005

Dear David
    You have helped me a great deal during this past year. I will speak to your father. Remember that your father is a fair man, and he will reward you when he thinks you are ready.

Sincerely

Ernest

Question Marks and Exclamation Points

Use a **question mark (?)** at the end of an interrogative sentence.
Use an **exclamation point (!)** at the end of an exclamatory sentence.
Examples:
    Did Mika know what was in the box?
    What a surprise she received when she reached inside!

DIRECTIONS ▷ Finish each sentence with a question mark or exclamation point.

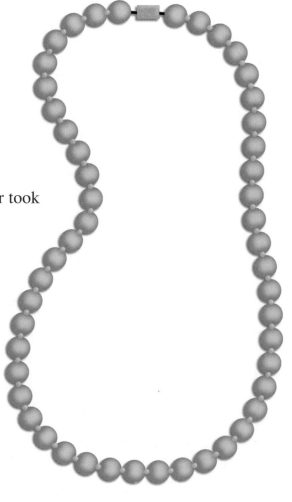

1. Did you know that our teacher, Mr. Holder, visited China last month

2. What a great adventure he had

3. Look at the wonderful postcards he sent our class

4. Do you know where he stayed

5. When did Mr. Holder return

6. Could you tell us about his trip

7. He found a pearl in an oyster shell

8. That was a lucky find

9. You should see the beautiful photographs Mr. Holder took

10. What kind of camera did he use

11. It really is a good one

12. What did he bring back

13. What a beautiful necklace that is

14. Did you know that jade is very expensive

15. Mrs. Holder will certainly be surprised

16. Did Mr. Holder visit the Great Wall of China

17. Of course he did

18. What an awesome sight that must have been

Apostrophes and Colons

Use an **apostrophe (')** to show that one or more letters have been left out in a contraction.
To form a singular possessive noun, add an apostrophe and *s* to singular nouns.
To form a plural possessive noun, add an apostrophe to a plural noun that ends in *s*.
Add an apostrophe and *s* to plural nouns that do not end in *s* to show possession.
Use a **colon (:)** between the hour and the minute in the time of day.
Use a colon after the greeting in a business letter.
Examples:

was not = *wasn't*	could not = *couldn't*
Jane's father	the *pig's* tail
guests' laughter	the *maids'* voices
the *children's* adventure	the *men's* story
2:25 P.M.	5:13 A.M.
Dear Ms. Parker:	Dear Sir or Madam:

DIRECTIONS ▷ **Add apostrophes to the following items as needed.**

1. Uncle Chens problem was difficult to explain.

2. The childrens faces lit up when they saw him flying.

3. The boys smiles made Jane laugh.

4. "I cant stop laughing," Jane said.

5. "Wont you join us, Ms. Parker?" Jane asked.

DIRECTIONS ▷ **Add colons to these items as needed.**

6. "It's only 3 30 in the afternoon," Michel said.

7. "We can stay until 6 00," Meri replied.

8. The movie starts at 7 15.

9. Dear Ms. Parker

   Your application for employment has been received.

Contractions

A **contraction** is a short way of writing two words together. Some of the letters are left out. An apostrophe takes the place of the missing letters.
Examples:

        she + will = *she'll*
        had + not = *hadn't*
        I + would = *I'd*

DIRECTIONS ➤ **Rewrite each sentence. Replace the underlined words with a contraction.**

1. <u>You are</u> getting very hot in this summer weather.

   _____

2. Do you think <u>you would</u> like a water slide?

   _____

3. <u>You will</u> need some plastic at least ten feet long.

   _____

4. <u>It is</u> best to get heavy plastic.

   _____

5. That way, it <u>will not</u> tear too easily.

   _____

6. Place the plastic on a grassy spot where there <u>are not</u> any bumps.

   _____

   _____

7. You can use stones to hold the plastic down, but they <u>must not</u> be sharp.

   _____

   _____

8. If you <u>do not</u> have a sprinkler, get one.

   _____

9. You <u>should not</u> put the sprinkler too far from the plastic.

   _____

10. You <u>must not</u> let the plastic get dry.

    _____

Direct Quotations and Dialogue

Use a **direct quotation** to tell a speaker's exact words.
Use **quotation marks (" ")** before and after the words a speaker says.
Begin the first word a speaker says with a capital letter. Put end punctuation before the ending quotation marks. Begin a new paragraph each time the speaker changes.
If the quotation is interrupted by other words, place quotation marks around the exact spoken words only.
Examples:

       Dad asked, "Where have you been?"
       "I went to the store," Vic said. "Then, I went to the library."

 **DIRECTIONS** ➤ **Write quotation marks where they are needed in the following sentences.**

1. Have you heard of the Nobel Peace Prize? asked Emi.

2. Yes. Mother Teresa and Nelson Mandela have won it, replied Jan.

3. But do you know who Nobel was? Emi asked.

4. Jan responded, No, I guess I don't.

5. He invented dynamite, stated Emi.

6. It seems weird, said Jan, to name a peace prize for the inventor of dynamite.

7. In fact, Emi said, dynamite was once called Nobel's Safety Blasting Powder.

8. Nobel patented the blasting powder in 1867, Emi continued.

9. He did not want dynamite used for war, he said.

10. He added, Nobel once said that war is the horror of horrors and the greatest of all crimes.

11. How did the Nobel Prizes get started? asked Jan.

12. Emi said, In his will, Nobel said that his money should be used to establish prizes in five areas: physics, chemistry, medicine, literature, and peace.

13. Sometimes a prize is shared by two or three people, he continued.

14. I'd like to know more about some of the winners, Jan said.

15. Jimmy Carter, the 39th president of the United States, won the Nobel Peace Prize in 2002, replied Emi.

Titles

Underline the titles of books, newspapers, magazines, movies, and television shows. If you are using a computer to write, replace underlining with italics.

Use quotation marks around the titles of stories, magazine articles, essays, songs, or poems.

Begin the first word, last word, and all other important words in a title with a capital letter.

Examples:

<u>I Like Frogs</u> (book)

<u>Shrek</u> (movie)

"Wind in the Treetops" (story)

"The Bells" (poem)

DIRECTIONS Write each title. Use capital letters correctly. Underline or use quotation marks as needed.

1. a wrinkle in time (book) _____

2. camping in the mountains (magazine article) _____

3. it's not easy being green (song) _____

4. sounder (movie) _____

5. the new york times (newspaper) _____

6. humpty dumpty (magazine) _____

7. the little house (story) _____

8. why i like gymnastics (essay) _____

9. the little prince (book) _____

10. the owl and the pussycat (poem) _____

DIRECTIONS Rewrite each sentence correctly.

11. The sixth chapter in that book is called Animal Language.

_____

12. A book I really like is If I Were in Charge of the World by Judith Viorst.

_____

_____

Compound Words

> A **compound word** consists of two or more words used as a single word.
> A **closed compound** is a compound made of two words written together as one.
> *Examples:*
> runway   bookmark   rainbow
>
> An **open compound** is a compound in which the words are written separately.
> *Examples:*
> dead end   punching bag   bean sprout
>
> A **hyphenated compound** is a compound connected by hyphens.
> *Examples:*
> father-in-law   half-truth   narrow-minded

DIRECTIONS There are eighteen compounds in the following sentences, but all of them are spelled incorrectly. Identify each compound, and spell it correctly. Use a dictionary if necessary. Then, write each word correctly.

1. My cousin Danielle had her wisdom-teeth pulled. _wisdom teeth_

2. As she sat in an arm chair in the sun-shine, she thought about an old family story. _armchair_

3. Isaac, a ten year-old boy, had escaped from slavery. _____

4. His spirits soared skyhigh as he left his birth place. _____

5. The slavedriver went after him with blood-hounds. _____

6. Isaac hid in a stormcellar and a smoke house as he headed north to freedom.

_____

7. For three weeks he lived handtomouth, but he avoided any run ins with his former master.

_____

8. Danielle, a folk-singer of sorts, reached for her note book.

_____

9. "This is no run of the mill story," she thought as she gazed at the wall-paper.

_____

10. "This old story from our familytree will make a terrific song or even a best selling novel!"

_____

Synonyms and Antonyms

A **synonym** is a word that has almost the same meaning as another word.
When a word has several synonyms, use the one that works best in the sentence.
An **antonym** is a word that means the opposite of another word.
When a word has more than one antonym, use the one that expresses your meaning exactly.
Examples:

> *Jobs* is a synonym of *tasks*.
> *Short* is an antonym of *tall*.

DIRECTIONS ▸ Read each sentence. Study the underlined words. Then, write *synonyms* or *antonyms* to describe the two words.

1. As Tio and Nicole approached the <u>forest</u>, they saw a path leading into the <u>woods</u>.

   _____

2. The trees were dripping with moisture, and soon Tio's and Nicole's <u>dry</u> clothes were <u>soaked</u>.

   _____

3. Within the forest, the <u>upper</u> branches kept the light from reaching the <u>lower</u> levels.

   _____

4. As they walked along the muddy <u>path</u>, Tio and Nicole saw rotting leaves on the <u>trail</u>.

   _____

5. They <u>continued</u> along the trail and then <u>halted</u> suddenly in their tracks.

   _____

6. The <u>low</u> sound of a <u>soft</u> chirping had caused them to stop.

   _____

7. As they moved <u>quietly</u> through the forest, they heard a monkey <u>loudly</u> calling to other monkeys.

   _____

8. The <u>younger</u> monkeys were eating leaves of bamboo trees while the <u>older</u> ones watched.

   _____

9. One monkey was <u>curious</u> and looked at Tio and Nicole, but the others were <u>indifferent</u>.

   _____

More Synonyms and Antonyms

Remember that a synonym is a word that has almost the same meaning as another word. An antonym is a word that means the opposite of another word.
Examples:
   Start is a synonym of *begin*.
   Hard is an antonym of *soft*.

DIRECTIONS ▷ **Read each sentence. Identify the two words or two phrases from the sentence that are antonyms, and write them on the lines.**

1. Barbra had always been a success at school, but now she felt like a failure.

   _____   _____

2. T. J. had been left back once because he wasn't mature enough to be promoted.

   _____   _____

3. Barbra saw only one solution to her problem—she had to get rid of her report card.

   _____   _____

4. Barbra had a burning feeling in her stomach that even ice-cold milk couldn't get rid of.

   _____   _____

DIRECTIONS ▷ **Fill in the columns of the chart with a synonym and an antonym for each of the words in the first column.**

Word	Synonym	Antonym
end	_____	_____
fast	_____	_____
simple	_____	_____
gloomy	_____	_____
concealed	_____	_____
unsure	_____	_____

Prefixes

A **prefix** is a letter or group of letters added to the beginning of a base word. A **base word** is the simplest form of a word.
Adding a prefix to a word changes the word's meaning.
Examples:

dis + like = dislike
The boys said they *like* being in the cave.
They *dislike* the cold rocks.

 **DIRECTIONS** ▷ **Find the word in each sentence that begins with a prefix. Draw a line under the prefix. Then, write a definition of the word.**

1. There may be gold in the Black Mountains, waiting to be unearthed.

   _____

2. Many people say this gold is nonexistent.

   _____

3. Others say it's there, but they are unable to find it.

   _____

4. Many searches for the gold have had to be discontinued.

   _____

5. It is improbable that any gold is there.

   _____

6. Our inability to find any probably means there is none.

   _____

DIRECTIONS ▷ **On the line, write a word with the meaning given in ( ). Use one of the prefixes in the box, and use the underlined word as a base word.**

dis	mis	pre	re	un	non	in	im

7. I bought it last week, but I will _____ (<u>sell</u> again) it to you.

8. I have never been _____ (not <u>sincere</u>) with you.

9. I sense some _____ (opposite of <u>comfort</u>) in you.

10. Have you ever known me to _____ (<u>lead</u> incorrectly) you?

11. You don't even have to _____ (<u>pay</u> before) me for the map.

12. I'm a little _____ (not <u>organized</u>) now, but I'll get the map to you tomorrow.

Suffixes

A **suffix** is a letter or group of letters added to the ending of a base word.
A **base word** is a word to which other word parts may be added.
A suffix changes the meaning of a word.
Example:

Do you get *enjoyment* from reading Greek myths, or do they *frighten* you?

Sometimes spelling changes are made when suffixes are added to base words. Drop the *e* at the end of a base word before adding a suffix that begins with a vowel.
Examples:

contribute—contributor   love—lovable

Noun-forming Suffixes		Adjective-forming Suffixes		Verb-forming Suffix	
Suffix	Example	Suffix	Example	Suffix	Example
er	singer	able	laughable	en	brighten
or	director	ful	careful		
ness	gentleness	ible	flexible	**Adverb-forming Suffix**	
ment	appointment	ish	selfish	Suffix	Example
		less	careless	ly	quickly
		y	stormy		

> **DIRECTIONS** Add the kind of suffix given in ( ) to each word. Then, on a separate sheet of paper, write a sentence with each word you have formed.

1. sail (noun) _____

2. fear (adjective) _____

3. kind (noun) _____

4. might (adjective) _____

5. happy (noun) _____

6. light (verb) _____

7. cloud (adjective) _____

8. sudden (adverb) _____

9. quiet (adverb) _____

10. play (noun, adjective) _____

11. wonder (adjective) _____

12. teach (noun) _____

Homophones and Homographs

Homophones are words that sound alike but are spelled differently and have different meanings.
Example:
>   The girl *read* the *red* sign.

Homographs are words that have the same spelling but different meanings. Some homographs are pronounced differently.
Examples:
>   Some animals *live* on land and water.
>   *Live* plants are not allowed in this building.

DIRECTIONS Read each sentence. Circle the homophone in ( ) that correctly completes the sentence.

1. Leaves need (air, heir) in order to breathe.

2. If plants can't breathe, then neither can (ewe, you).

3. Of (coarse, course), if we keep cutting down trees, we'll have less oxygen.

4. It (wood, would) be a mistake to put a plant right next to a heater.

5. Most plants (need, knead) the temperature to be kept even.

6. The (main, mane) enemy of most plants is dry heat.

7. You should spray your plants with a fine (missed, mist) of warm water every day.

DIRECTIONS Use one of the following homographs to complete each sentence.

object	can	present	spring

8. If you mix your own plant food, you _____ do it in a _____.

9. If you _____ to putting a plant in a bigger pot, remember the _____ of replanting.

10. To give your crowded plant a nice _____, _____ it with a bigger pot.

11. In the _____, many plants grow by the _____ in the forest.

More on Homophones

Remember that homophones are words that sound alike. They are spelled differently and have different meanings.
Example:

Brandon spent *four* days thinking about a gift *for* his friend Cara.

DIRECTIONS ▸ **Complete each sentence. Choose the correct homophone in ( ). Write it on the line.**

1. At the end of the _____week_____, Brandon chose a plan.
   (week, weak)

2. He made his _____way_____ to the bus station and traveled downtown.
   (way, weigh)

3. The sporting goods store was easy to _____find_____.
   (fined, find)

4. Brandon thought, "I _____know_____ what Cara would like."
   (know, no)

5. "This is what I have to _____do_____."
   (dew, do)

6. Could he get _____through_____ the line to get an autograph?
   (threw, through)

7. Brandon could _____see_____ his hero.
   (see, sea)

8. His heart _____beat_____ faster.
   (beet, beat)

9. Cara would get _____one_____ special baseball from Brandon.
   (won, one)

DIRECTIONS ▸ **Write one homophone for each of the following words. Then, use five pairs of homophones correctly in sentences. Spell each homophone correctly. Use a separate sheet of paper.**

10. pail _____

11. son _____sun_____

12. flea _____

13. strait _____

14. two _____to too_____

15. meet _____meat_____

16. led _____

17. sighed _____

18. blew _____

19. hymn _____

20. pane _____

21. hoarse _____

Words with Multiple Meanings

Some words have more than one meaning. When you read something, you need to be sure you know which meaning the writer intends.

◎◎◎◎◎◎◎◎◎◎◎◎◎◎◎◎◎◎◎◎◎◎◎◎◎◎◎◎◎◎◎

DIRECTIONS ▷ **Look at the words and their meanings in the chart. Then, read each sentence below, and select the appropriate meaning for the underlined word. Write it in the space provided.**

Word	Meanings	
sail	a. cloth that catches wind to move a boat	b. to move in a boat
craft	a. a skill or an occupation	b. a ship, boat, or aircraft
mission	a. something a person sets out to do	b. a religious outpost
passed	a. moved past or went by	b. voted in favor of, approved
named	a. appointed to a job or an office	b. gave a name to
reached	a. stretched one's hand or arm out	b. arrived at or came to
completed	a. made whole with nothing missing	b. ended or finished

1. Ferdinand Magellan was the first explorer to <u>sail</u> around the world.

In this sentence, *sail* means _____.

2. His <u>craft</u> had to travel from Spain across the Atlantic to South America.

In this sentence, *craft* means _____.

3. From there his <u>mission</u> was to sail along the eastern shore until he reached the southernmost tip.

In this sentence, *mission* means _____.

4. Magellan <u>passed</u> through a strait now named for him and found a great ocean.

In this sentence, *passed* means _____.

5. He <u>named</u> this great ocean the Pacific Ocean, which means "peaceful ocean."

In this sentence, *named* means _____.

6. Magellan continued sailing across the Pacific Ocean and <u>reached</u> the Philippine Islands.

In this sentence, *reached* means _____.

7. After Magellan's death, his crew sailed on and <u>completed</u> the historic voyage around the world.

In this sentence, *completed* means _____.

Troublesome Words

Use *too* when you mean "very" or "also." Use *to* when you mean "in the direction of." Use *two* when you mean the numeral 2.

Use *it's* when you mean "it is." Use *its* when you mean "belonging to it."

Use *their* when you mean "belonging to them." Use *there* when you mean "in that place." Use *they're* when you mean "they are."

Use *your* when you mean "belonging to you." Use *you're* when you mean "you are."

The word *good* is an adjective. Use *good* to describe a noun. Use *well* as an adjective when you mean "healthy." Use *well* as an adverb when you tell how something is done.

DIRECTIONS ▷ Circle the word in ( ) that correctly completes each sentence.

1. We went (to, too, two) the aquarium.

2. Len stayed home because he did not feel (good, well).

3. (Its, It's) a great place to visit.

4. You forgot to bring (you're, your) lunch.

5. (To, Too, Two) beluga whales were (there, their, they're).

6. One whale had a cute spot on (its, it's) face.

7. (You're, Your) the first person I told about our trip.

8. I wish you had been able to come, (to, too, two).

9. It was a (good, well) idea to take the trip.

10. (There, Their, They're) very happy to have students visit them.

11. The fish and other sea animals are taken care of (good, well).

12. We saw the sea otters eat (there, their, they're) meal.

13. I think (its, it's) worthwhile to go again.

14. Did you see the (to, too, two) walruses?

15. (There, Their, They're) sea lions, not walruses.

Negatives

A **negative** is a word that means "no" or "not."
The words *never, no, nobody, none, not, nothing,* and *nowhere* are negatives.
The negative word *not* is often used in contractions.
Do not use two negatives in the same sentence. This is called a double negative.
Examples:

> Jack had *never* worked in a store before.
> *Nobody* there knew him.
> He *didn't* know at first what he should do.

DIRECTIONS ▷ Complete each sentence by choosing the correct word in ( ). Avoid using two negatives in the same sentence.

1. Most people ___*will*___ never get a snakebite.
(will, won't)

2. If you do get bitten, don't go into ___*a*___ panic.
(a, no)

3. Remember that not all snakes ___*aren't*___ poisonous.
(are, aren't)

4. It's best not to do ___*anything*___ that will speed the spread of the poison.
(anything, nothing)

5. Didn't ___*anybody*___ in our group ever study this before?
(anybody, nobody)

6. If you must go for help, don't ___*ever*___ run.
(ever, never)

7. When in snake country, don't take ___*any*___ chances.
(any, no)

DIRECTIONS ▷ Each sentence contains a double negative. Cut or replace at least one of the negatives. Write the sentence correctly.

8. There aren't no more than four kinds of poisonous snakes in North America.
There aren't Anymore than four kinds of poisonous snakes in North America.

9. It won't do no good to try to run away from a rattlesnake.
It won't do any good to try and Run away from the rattlesnake.

Avoiding Wordy Language

Good writers say what they mean in as few words as possible. When you revise, cross out words that don't add to the meaning.

Example:

Mari was putting on her clothes and getting ready for Chet's party. (wordy)

Mari was dressing for Chet's party. (better)

DIRECTIONS ▷ Rewrite each sentence. Replace the words in ( ) with fewer words.

1. Our family was (putting clothes and other items in) suitcases.

   Our family was putting their things in suitcases.

2. Everyone was looking forward to (the vacation that we take every year).

   Everyone was looking forward to our yearly vacation.

3. When all the suitcases were packed, Mom (put all the suitcases in) the trunk.

   When all the suitcases were packed Mom put them in the trunk

4. We (pulled out of the driveway) at noon on Saturday.

   We left the house at noon on Saturday.

5. We (made our way through the streets) to the freeway.

   We drove all the way to the freeway.

6. We (ended up stopping every little while) because my little brother was (not feeling very well).

   We didn't shop long while because my little brother was feeling sick

7. The first day of travel seemed (to go pretty well), though.

   The first day of travel seemed to go great

8. The second day we (stopped off and went to see the sights of) historical places.

   The second day we stopped to see all the historical places

9. Everyone (really had a good time on) the rest of the trip, too.

   Everyone really liked the rest of the trip, too.

10. (Each one of our neighbors) welcomed us back.

    All of our neighbors welcomed us back

Using Sensory Images

Good writers use sensory words that appeal to some or all of the five senses.
Example:

> Cold, white snow blanketed the *green pine trees* in the *quiet valley*.

⊚ ⊚

DIRECTIONS ▷ **Read each sentence. On the line, write each underlined word and tell the sense or senses to which it most appeals as it is used in the sentence.**

1. The young swimmer was wearing a <u>blue</u> suit.

_____

2. She dove cleanly into the <u>cool</u> water.

_____

3. The judges wrote the scores in <u>large</u> black letters.

_____

4. The audience let out a <u>loud</u> cheer.

_____

5. She had been practicing so long that her hair had the odor of <u>chlorine</u>.

_____

6. One tile on the practice pool was rough and <u>jagged</u>.

_____

7. The <u>rough</u> edge had cut her foot, and she had yelled, "Ouch!"

_____

8. Her coach had put a <u>soft</u> bandage on it, and it was fine now.

_____

9. The sweatshirt she put on was <u>warm</u> and soft.

_____

10. After practice, she had a <u>delicious</u> sandwich.

_____

Denotation and Connotation

The **denotation** of a word is its exact meaning as stated in a dictionary. Denotations use literal language.

The **connotation** of a word is a second, suggested meaning of a word. This added meaning often suggests something positive or negative. Connotations use figurative language.

Examples:

> *Skinny* suggests "too thin." *Skinny* has a negative connotation.
> *Slender* suggests "attractively thin." *Slender* has a positive connotation.

Some words are neutral. They do not suggest either good or bad meanings. For example, *hat, seventeen,* and *yearly* are neutral words.

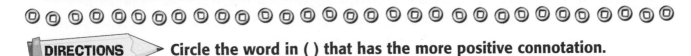

DIRECTIONS ▷ **Circle the word in ( ) that has the more positive connotation.**

1. Our trip to the amusement park was (good, wonderful).

2. (Brave, foolhardy) people rode on the roller coaster.

3. We saw (fascinating, weird) animals in the animal house.

4. Some of the monkeys made (hilarious, goofy) faces.

5. Everyone's face wore a (smile, smirk) on the way home.

DIRECTIONS ▷ **Circle the word in ( ) that has the more negative connotation.**

6. We bought (cheap, inexpensive) souvenirs at the park.

7. I ate a (soggy, moist) sandwich.

8. Mike (nagged, reminded) us to go to the fun house.

9. He was very (determined, stubborn) about going.

10. The fun house was (comical, silly).

DIRECTIONS ▷ **Answer the following questions.**

11. Which is more serious, a <u>problem</u> or a <u>disaster</u>?

_____

12. Which is worth more, something <u>old</u> or something <u>antique</u>?

_____

Denotation and Connotation, page 2

Remember, the denotation of a word is its exact meaning as stated in a dictionary. The connotation of a word is an added meaning that suggests something positive or negative.

Some words, such as *hat, seventeen,* or *yearly,* are neutral. They do not suggest either good or bad meanings.

Examples:

The denotation of *stingy* is "not generous" or "miserly."
Stingy suggests "selfish." *Stingy* has a negative connotation.

DIRECTIONS Read each sentence. Write *negative* if the underlined word has a negative connotation. Write *positive* if it has a positive connotation. Write *neutral* if the word is neutral.

_____ 1. This is my <u>house</u>.

_____ 2. This is my <u>home</u>.

_____ 3. Darren's friends <u>discussed</u> his problem.

_____ 4. Darren's friends <u>gossiped</u> about his problem.

_____ 5. Our dog is <u>sick</u>.

_____ 6. Our dog is <u>diseased</u>.

_____ 7. The play was <u>boring</u>.

_____ 8. The play was <u>fantastic</u>.

_____ 9. Angie was <u>stubborn</u>.

_____ 10. Angie was <u>determined</u>.

DIRECTIONS Complete each sentence with a word that suggests the connotation given.

11. The gift from my aunt was _____. (positive)

12. The gift from my aunt was _____. (negative)

13. The gift from my aunt was _____. (neutral)

Using Figurative Language

Writers often use **figurative language** to compare unlike things. Figurative language uses figures of speech such as similes, metaphors, and personification. Figurative language gives a meaning that is not exactly that of the words used. Figurative language tries to create a clearer word picture for the reader.

Writers can create vivid word pictures by comparing two things that are not usually thought of as being alike. When *like* or *as* is used to compare two things, the comparison is called a **simile**. A **metaphor** makes a comparison by speaking of one thing as if it were another.

Sometimes a writer will give human characteristics to nonhuman things. Objects, ideas, places, or animals may be given human qualities. They may perform human actions. This kind of language is called **personification**.
Examples:
> *His feet* smelled <u>like</u> *dead fish.* (simile)
> *Paul Bunyan* was as big <u>as</u> a *tree.* (simile)
> The deep *lake* was a *golden mirror* reflecting the setting Sun. (metaphor)
> The old tree moaned with pain in the cold wind. (personification)

DIRECTIONS The sentences below include figurative language. Rewrite each sentence. Express the same idea without using figurative language.

1. I was as jumpy as a cat in a roomful of rocking chairs.

_____

2. As I looked out over the audience, my heart was a brick in my chest.

_____

3. I touched the piano keys, and my fingers were like fence posts.

_____

4. Luckily for me, the performance was as smooth as silk.

_____

5. The last notes whispered, "You did just fine!"

_____

DIRECTIONS Complete each sentence below by using figurative language.

6. The deserted old house was as dark as _____.

7. When I opened the squeaky front door, it creaked _____.

Using Figurative Language, page 2

Remember that writers often use figurative language to compare unlike things. Figurative language uses figures of speech such as similes, metaphors, and personification. Figurative language gives a meaning that is not exactly that of the words used.

DIRECTIONS ▸ **Read the paragraph below. Notice how the author uses figurative language to help you visualize the events and descriptions. Then, answer the questions.**

Riding as fast as the wind, Sir Garland spurred his horse toward the castle. When he dashed across the open field, his shadow rode beside him like a good friend. When he galloped through the forest, the leaves whispered, "Hurry! Hurry!" The branches were enemies that caught at his sleeves. Sir Garland rounded a bend, and there before him was the castle, its glistening walls shining more brightly than the sun. "I must see the king!" Sir Garland shouted to the guards. "I bring the most important news in all the world!"

1. What comparison shows how fast Sir Garland was riding?

_____

2. What human characteristic did the author give to the leaves?

_____

3. What simile describes Sir Garland's shadow?

_____

4. What metaphor describes the branches?

_____

DIRECTIONS ▸ **Write three sentences using figurative language.**

5. _____

6. _____

7. _____

Paragraphs

A **paragraph** is a group of sentences that tells about one main idea. The first line of a paragraph is indented. This means the first word is moved in a little from the left margin.

The **topic sentence** expresses the main idea of the paragraph. It tells what all the other sentences in the paragraph are about. The topic sentence is often the first sentence in a paragraph.

The other sentences in a paragraph are **detail sentences.** Detail sentences add information about the topic sentence. They help the audience understand more about the main idea.

Example:

      Optical illusions occur when your eyes and brain give you the wrong idea about the way something looks. In one kind of optical illusion, the brain compares the images you see to images in your memory. Then, your brain makes the wrong interpretation about the new image. Another optical illusion takes place when the brain cannot choose between equally possible interpretations. In yet another, the brain works perfectly well. However, the bending of light through the atmosphere creates mirages that fool your eyes.

How to Write a Paragraph
1. Write a topic sentence that clearly tells the main idea of your paragraph.
2. Indent the first line.
3. Write detail sentences that tell about the main idea.

DIRECTIONS > Complete this chart with details from the example paragraph.

Main Idea: _____

Detail: _____

Detail: _____

Detail: _____

Keeping to the Topic

Good writers keep to the point when they give information. Good writers make sure that each paragraph has a topic sentence and that every other sentence in the paragraph is about the topic sentence. Good writers plan a paragraph so that it gives details about one main idea.

 **DIRECTIONS** ▷ **Circle the letter of the sentence that keeps to the topic in the numbered sentence.**

1. Indira Gandhi was an important leader in India during this century.

   a. John Kennedy was an important leader in the United States.

   b. In 1980, she was elected prime minister of India for the third time.

2. Indira Gandhi believed strongly in women's rights.

   a. She once said, "If a woman has the qualifications and ability for any profession, she should be in it."

   b. Her second son, Sanjay, was born in 1946.

3. When Indira was 12 years old, she organized other children in the "Monkey Brigade."

   a. Indira's father was Jawaharlal Nehru.

   b. The Monkey Brigade was very helpful to the Congress.

4. The Monkey Brigade took over many kinds of tasks from the Congress.

   a. They became good at cooking and serving food, making flags, and stuffing envelopes.

   b. Indira Gandhi lived for almost 67 years.

DIRECTIONS ▷ **Draw a line through any sentences that are not about the topic sentence (the first sentence in the paragraph).**

India's famous "March to the Sea" or "Salt March" was led by Mohandas K. Gandhi. My mother went to India last year. At that time, the British did not allow Indians to make their own salt. Not only that, they had to buy their salt from British merchants. Cinnamon and ginger come from India. To defy this unfair law, Gandhi marched 200 miles to the sea, picking up thousands of Indians along the way. The Ganges is a river in India. Once there, Gandhi took a handful of salt from the beach. From that day onward, people all over India began to gather salt themselves.

Connecting a Main Idea and Details

In an **expository paragraph**, good writers express the main idea in a well-focused topic sentence. They connect the details and examples in the paragraph to the topic sentence and to each other.

ⓞⓞⓞⓞⓞⓞⓞⓞⓞⓞⓞⓞⓞⓞⓞⓞⓞⓞⓞⓞⓞⓞⓞⓞⓞⓞⓞⓞⓞⓞⓞⓞ

DIRECTIONS ▷ **These four sentences can be arranged as a paragraph. Write *M* for main idea or *D* for detail to identify each sentence.**

_____ **1.** September 7 is Brazil's Independence Day.

_____ **2.** This holiday celebrates Brazil's independence from Portugal.

_____ **3.** The green and yellow colors of Brazil's flag are everywhere.

_____ **4.** People wear green and yellow T-shirts.

DIRECTIONS ▷ **Read the sentences. Use the graphic organizer to arrange the main idea and the details.**

Other products of these new factories include shoes, textiles, construction equipment, and leather products. Some of these manufacturing plants produce cars, trucks, and farm equipment. Many large factories have been built in southern Brazil. Many of the goods produced in the factories of southern Brazil are shipped to the United States.

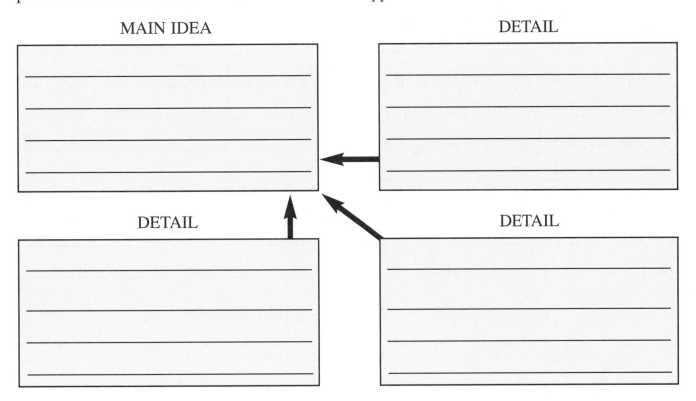

MAIN IDEA

DETAIL

DETAIL

DETAIL

Using Details to Explain

Good writers include details that give causes and effects. They tell their feelings in response to certain causes.

DIRECTIONS The numbered sentences tell about events. After each numbered sentence, write the detail sentence from the box that helps explain that event.

> He was already an expert rider.
> The Crow Indians had stolen some Sioux horses.
> Slow had jabbed the Crow with his stick.
> He no longer seemed so slow and serious.
> He had a slow and serious nature.
> It was considered braver to push an enemy
>   off a horse than to shoot an arrow from far away.
> Slow had acted bravely.
> They had won the battle.

1. When Sitting Bull was a child, he was named Slow. _____

_____

2. At the age of ten, Slow was given his own pony. _____

_____

3. When Slow was fourteen, he and other Sioux fought some Crow Indians. _____

_____

4. Slow was armed only with a stick. _____

_____

5. One Crow Indian fell from his horse. _____

_____

6. The Sioux held a victory party. _____

_____

Narrative

A **narrative** is a story. It tells about real or made-up events. A narrative tells about one main idea. A narrative should have a beginning, a middle, and an end. Most narratives have **dialogue**. A writer uses dialogue to show how characters speak to one another.

Example:

A Gleam in the Dust

Marc Haynes sadly waved good-bye to his friend Thomas and began to walk home. As he was walking, he saw something gleaming in the dirt. He bent over and picked up a coin. Then he read the date, and his eyes opened wide. The date on the coin was 1789!

Marc took the coin to Mr. Ortiz at the coin shop. "Well, Marc," Mr. Ortiz said, "this is a rare coin you've found. It was stolen from a private collection. I know that the owner is offering a reward of fifty dollars for the return of this coin."

Marc ran all the way home. "Wow!" he thought to himself. "I don't even have to leave town like Thomas did to have an adventure!"

How to Write a Story and Dialogue

1. Write an interesting beginning to present the main character and the setting.
2. Tell about a problem that the main character has to solve in the middle. Tell about what happens in order.
3. Write an ending. Tell how the main character solves the problem or meets the challenge.
4. Write a title for your story.
5. Place quotation marks before and after a speaker's exact words.
6. Use a comma to separate a quotation from the rest of the sentence unless a question mark or exclamation point is needed.
7. Begin a new paragraph each time the speaker changes.
8. Be sure the conversation sounds like real people talking. Use words that tell exactly how the character speaks.

Narrative, page 2

DIRECTIONS ➤ Read the example narrative at the top of page 475. Then, answer the questions.

1. What is the problem in the narrative?

_____

_____

2. How is the problem solved?

_____

_____

3. Which two characters have dialogue?

_____

_____

DIRECTIONS ➤ Think about a story that you would like to tell. Use the graphic organizer to plan your narrative.

WRITING PLAN

Beginning	Middle	End
Characters: Setting:	Problem:	Solution:

Narrative, page 3

Tips for Writing a Narrative
- Think about an exciting story to tell your reader.
- Create a realistic setting and at least three characters.
- Organize your ideas into a beginning, a middle, and an end.
- Write an interesting introduction that "grabs" your readers.
- Write a believable ending for your story.

DIRECTIONS Think about a story you would like to tell the readers. Use your writing plan as a guide for writing your narrative.

_____

_____

_____

_____

_____

_____

_____

_____

_____

_____

_____

_____

_____

_____

_____

_____

Descriptive Paragraph

In a **descriptive paragraph**, a writer describes a person, place, thing, or event. A good description lets the reader see, feel, hear, and sometimes taste or smell what is being described.
Example:

> Thanksgiving has to be my favorite holiday. The delicious aromas of turkey roasting and pumpkin pies baking fill the house. The lovely autumn colors of orange, gold, red, and brown can be seen in the special flower arrangements for the table. The sound of children laughing as they play games outside mixes with the music being played inside. The sights, smells, and sounds are very important to me.

How to Write a Descriptive Paragraph
1. Write a topic sentence that clearly tells what the paragraph is about.
2. Add detail sentences that give exact information about your topic.
3. Use colorful and lively words to describe the topic. Make an exact picture for the reader with the words you choose.

> **DIRECTIONS** Complete this paragraph. Add descriptive words that appeal to your senses. Then, in the ( ), tell to what sense each descriptive word appeals.

One _____ (_____) night we went to Loch Ness to see Nessie. We all wore _____ (_____) sweaters and gloves because of the _____ (_____) air. The sun set beyond the Loch, dropping like an _____ (_____) ball. _____ (_____) chirps interrupted the quiet. A _____ (_____) fog settled around us and made our clothes seem _____ (_____). Before we knew it, the _____ (_____) sun had appeared, but we had not seen Nessie.

Descriptive Paragraph, page 2

DIRECTIONS ▷ Read the example description at the top of page 478. Then, answer the questions.

1. What is the writer describing in the paragraph?

_____

2. What is the topic sentence?

_____

3. What are some words the writer uses that appeal to your senses?

_____

_____

_____

DIRECTIONS ▷ Think about something that you would like to describe. It could be a thing, a person you know, or something that has happened to you. Write it in the circle. Then, write words on the lines that describe your topic. Use the graphic organizer to plan your descriptive paragraph.

WRITING PLAN

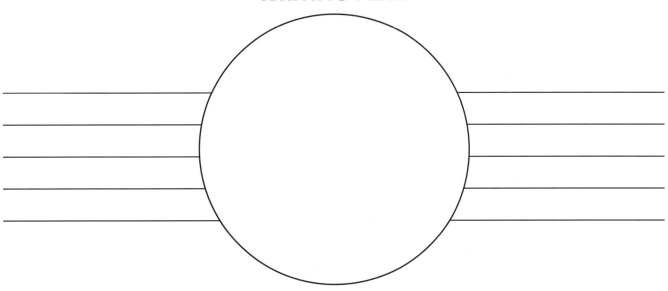

Descriptive Paragraph, page 3

Tips for Writing a Descriptive Paragraph
- Describe a person, a place, an object, or an event.
- Paint a picture using words.
- Use words that appeal to the reader's senses. Let the reader see, smell, taste, feel, and hear what you are writing about.
- Include a sentence that introduces your topic.
- Write detail sentences that use descriptive words.

DIRECTIONS Think about something that you would like to describe. Introduce your topic in your first sentence. Then, use the words that you wrote in the graphic organizer to describe it. Be sure to appeal to the reader's senses.

_____

_____

_____

_____

_____

_____

_____

_____

_____

_____

_____

_____

_____

_____

_____

_____

_____

_____

Business Letter

In a **business letter,** a writer usually writes to someone he or she does not know. One purpose of a business letter is to ask for information or to place an order for something.

A friendly letter has five parts: a heading, a greeting, a body, a closing, and a signature. In addition to the five parts of a friendly letter, a business letter has an inside address. It is the receiver's address.

Example:

heading —
1492 Nakajama Road
Franklin, TN 37064
October 16, 2005

Felicia T. Azar, President
Department of Parks and Recreation — **inside address**
1633 Alberta Place
Franklin, TN 37064

greeting — Dear Ms. Azar:

body —
    I am writing to suggest that the soft-drink machines in the park be removed. In their place, I recommend that fresh fruit machines be installed. There are two reasons I think this is a good idea. First, soft drinks have too much sugar in them, and they have no nutritional value. Second, with soft-drink machines, the city has the problem of cleaning up the empty cans that are sometimes left in the park.

    I urge you to consider this idea seriously. It is for the good of all.

closing — Sincerely,

signature — Hester A. Martin

How to Write a Business Letter
1. Write the heading in the upper-right corner.
2. Write the inside address at the left margin.
3. Write the greeting under the inside address. Put a colon (:) after the greeting.
4. Write the body in paragraph form. Tell why you are writing to the person or business. Use a polite tone.
5. Write the closing in line with the heading. In a business letter, the closing is *Yours truly* or *Sincerely*.
6. Write your signature under the closing. Sign your full name. Then, print your name.

Business Letter, page 2

DIRECTIONS ▷ Read the example business letter on page 481. Then, answer the questions.

1. What is the topic of this letter? _____

_____

2. Is the writer for or against the topic?

_____

3. What are two reasons the writer gives to support this opinion?

_____

_____

4. How would you describe the closing of the letter?

_____

DIRECTIONS ▷ Think about a business letter that you would like to write. You can write to ask for information about a product, to complain about a product or service, or to praise a product or service. Fill in the chart below. Use the graphic organizer to plan your business letter.

To whom am I writing?	
What is my purpose?	
What tone should I use?	
What facts do I want to include?	

Business Letter, page 3

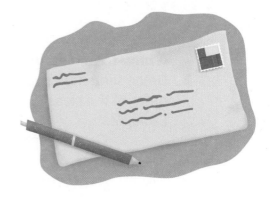

heading _____

_____

_____

_____ inside address

_____

_____

_____

_____ greeting

body _____

_____

_____

_____

_____

_____

closing _____

signature _____

How-to Paragraph

A **how-to paragraph** gives directions or explains how to do something. Detail sentences in a how-to paragraph use time-order words to show the correct order of the steps.

Example:

Popping Popcorn in a Microwave Oven

Before you begin, be sure that you have popcorn that is especially packaged for microwave popping. Of course, you will need a microwave oven. Remove the plastic overwrap from the bag, and place it in the center of the microwave. Be very careful not to puncture or open the special bag the popcorn is in. You should set the microwave for full or 100 percent power. Then, set the timer for five minutes, and push the button to start. Stop the microwave when popping time slows to two to three seconds between pops. Remove the hot bag from the oven. You should shake the bag before opening it to increase flavor and to distribute the salt.

How to Write a How-to Paragraph
1. Write a topic sentence that names the process you are describing.
2. Add a detail sentence that tells what materials are needed.
3. Write detail sentences that tell the steps in the order they need to be done.
4. Use time-order words such as *first, next, then*, and *finally* to show the order of the steps.

How-to Paragraph, page 2

DIRECTIONS ▷ **Read the example how-to paragraph on page 484. Then, answer the questions.**

1. What does this paragraph tell you how to do?

   _____

2. How many items are listed as materials, and what are they?

   _____

3. What is the first thing you must do?

   _____

4. What is the next thing you do?

   _____

5. What happens next?

   _____

6. What do you do last?

   _____

DIRECTIONS ▷ **Think about something you want to tell others how to do. Use this writing plan to help you.**

WRITING PLAN

1. What will you tell others how to do?

2. What materials are needed?

3. What steps must the reader follow? Number the steps.

4. What time-order words will you use?

How-to Paragraph, page 3

Tips for Writing a How-to Paragraph
• Choose one thing to teach someone.
• Think of all the materials that are needed.
• Think of all the steps someone should follow.
• Be sure to write about the steps in the order they must be done.
• Use time-order words to help the reader follow the steps.
• Tell the reader any additional tips that will make the process easier to do.

DIRECTIONS Think about something you want to tell others how to do. Use your writing plan as a guide for writing your how-to paragraph.

_____

_____

_____

_____

_____

_____

_____

_____

_____

_____

_____

_____

_____

_____

_____

_____

_____

Information Paragraph

An **information paragraph** gives facts about one topic.
It has a topic sentence that tells the main idea. Detail sentences give facts about the main idea.
Examples:

Food in Cans — **title**

The idea of storing food in tin cans was developed in — **topic sentence**
England in 1810. A British merchant named Peter Durand is
responsible for this idea. It is interesting that no one invented
a can opener until fifty years later. British soldiers in 1812 tore — **detail sentences**
open canned rations with bayonets and pocket knives. They
were even known to shoot the cans open.

The Modern Can Opener — **title**

The can opener that we use today was invented — **topic sentence**
about 1870. It was invented by an American inventor
named William W. Lyman. It has a cutting wheel that rotates
around the can's edge. It was immediately popular, and it has — **detail sentences**
been changed only once. In 1925, a special wheel was added.
This was called the "feed wheel," and it made the can rotate
against the cutting wheel.

How to Write an Information Paragraph
1. Write a topic sentence that tells your main idea.
2. Write at least three detail sentences that give information about your main idea.
3. Think of a title for your information paragraph.

Information Paragraph, page 2

DIRECTIONS ▸ Read the example information paragraphs on page 487. Then, answer the questions.

1. What is the main idea of the first information paragraph?

_____

_____

2. What are two supporting details in the first information paragraph?

_____

_____

3. What is the topic sentence of the second information paragraph?

_____

_____

4. What are two supporting details in the second information paragraph?

_____

_____

DIRECTIONS ▸ Think about an informative topic you would like to write about. Use this writing plan to help you.

WRITING PLAN

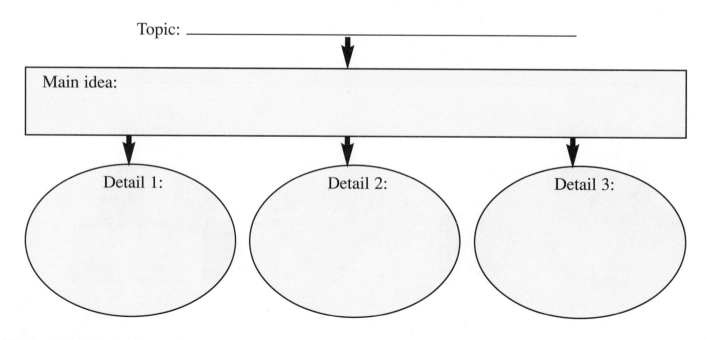

Topic: _____

Main idea:

Detail 1:

Detail 2:

Detail 3:

Information Paragraph, page 3

Tips for Writing an Information Paragraph
- Choose one topic to write about.
- Write a title for your paragraph.
- Write a topic sentence that tells your main idea.
- Write at least three detail sentences that tell facts about the main idea.
- Be sure your facts are correct and complete.

DIRECTIONS > Choose a topic you would like to write about. Use your writing plan as a guide for writing your information paragraph.

_____

_____

_____

_____

_____

_____

_____

_____

_____

_____

_____

_____

_____

_____

_____

_____

_____

Compare and Contrast Paragraph

In a **compare and contrast paragraph**, a writer shows how two people, places, things, or ideas are alike or different. To compare means to show how two things are similar. To contrast means to show how two things are different.

Example:

      The Tasady tribe and the Ik tribe are two examples of people still living in the Stone Age. Neither tribe knew anything about the outside world until recently. The Tasady live in the mountain caves of the Philippine rain forests. The Ik live in the mountains of Uganda, and they build grass huts for shelter. There is plenty of food in the Philippine rain forests, so the Tasady are comfortable and fairly well off. The Ik, however, face a constant lack of food. Ik usually eat any food they find right away. The Tasady have a good chance of surviving; the Ik, on the other hand, face an uncertain future.

How to Write a Compare and Contrast Paragraph

1. Write a topic sentence that names the subjects and tells briefly how they are alike and different.
2. Give examples in the detail sentences that clearly tell how the subjects are alike and different.
3. Write about the likenesses or the differences in the same order you named them in the topic sentence.
4. Try to have at least three ways in which the subjects are alike or different.

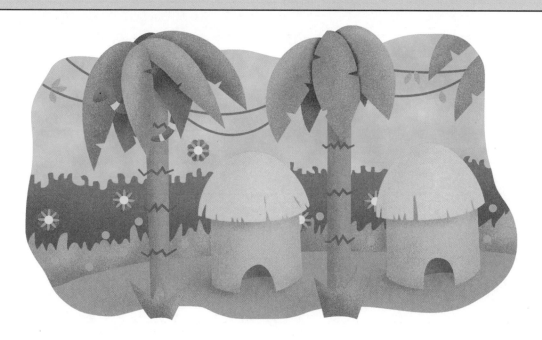

Compare and Contrast Paragraph, page 2

DIRECTIONS ▷ Read the example compare and contrast paragraph on page 490. Then, answer the questions.

1. What is the topic sentence of the paragraph? _____

_____

2. What two subjects are being compared? _____

_____

3. What are three things that are similar about the two subjects?

_____

_____

4. What are three things that are different about the two subjects?

_____

_____

5. Does the last sentence of the paragraph compare or contrast the survival of the tribes?

_____

DIRECTIONS ▷ Choose two things you want to write about. Then, use the Venn diagram to help you plan your writing. List what is true only about A in the A circle. List what is true only about B in the B circle. List what is true about both A and B where the circles overlap.

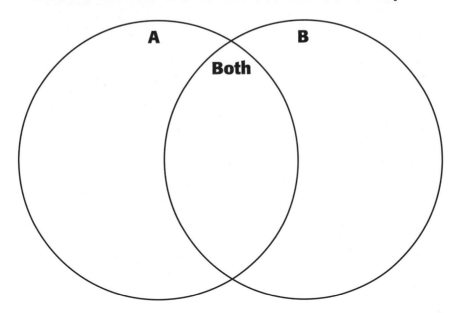

Tips for Writing a Compare and Contrast Paragraph
• Think about your two subjects.
• Decide how the two subjects are alike and different. Choose at least three important similarities and differences.
• Write a topic sentence that tells how the two subjects are alike and different.
• Explain how the two subjects are alike.
• Explain how the two subjects are different.
• Write about the likenesses or the differences in the same order you named them in the topic sentence.

DIRECTIONS Choose two subjects you would like to compare and contrast. Use your Venn diagram to write your compare and contrast paragraph.

_____

_____

_____

_____

_____

_____

_____

_____

_____

_____

_____

_____

_____

_____

_____

_____

_____

Cause and Effect Paragraph

A cause is an event that makes something else happen. An effect is something that happens as a result of a cause. One cause may have several effects. One effect may have several causes.

In a **cause and effect paragraph**, a writer focuses on a cause that results in certain effects or an effect that can be traced back to its causes. This type of paragraph can begin with either the cause or the effect.

Example:

> In the story "The Tournament," a girl named Katharine goes back in time. If Merlin had not reversed Katharine's wish in the story, history would have been very different. First of all, Katharine would have been the champion of the jousting tournament instead of Sir Lancelot. As a result, Sir Lancelot would have been dismissed from the Queen's order of knights. Furthermore, King Arthur's Round Table would have been dissolved and never heard of again.

How to Write a Cause and Effect Paragraph

1. Begin paragraphs of effect with a cause. Write a topic sentence that tells what happened. The detail sentences should all discuss effects.
2. Begin paragraphs of cause with an effect. Write a topic sentence that tells a result. The detail sentences should all discuss causes.
3. Write detail sentences in the order in which the effects or the causes happened.

Cause and Effect Paragraph, page 2

DIRECTIONS ▷ Read the example cause and effect paragraph on page 493. Then, answer the questions.

1. What caused history to be in danger of change?

_____

_____

2. What caused history not to be changed?

_____

_____

3. What would be three effects if history had been changed?

_____

_____

_____

_____

DIRECTIONS ▷ Think of something that happened. What caused it to happen? What were the effects? Use the chart to organize your ideas.

WRITING PLAN

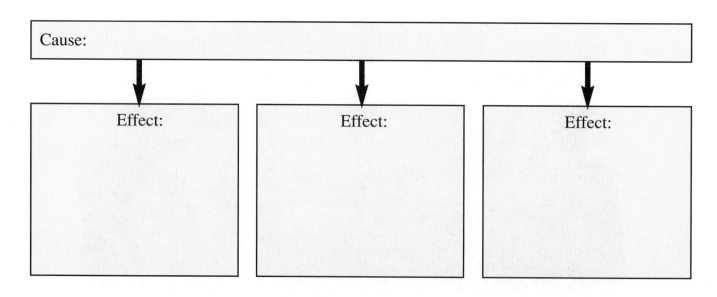

Cause:

Effect: Effect: Effect:

Cause and Effect Paragraph, page 3

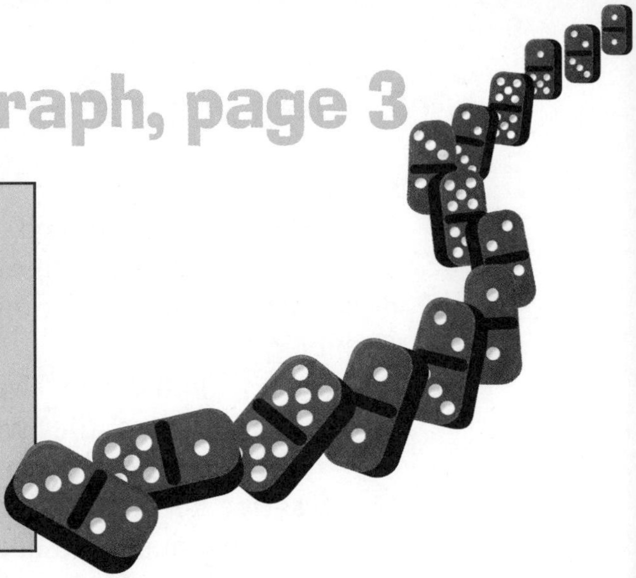

Tips for Writing a Cause and Effect Paragraph
- Think of something that happened.
- In your topic sentence, identify a cause or an effect.
- Clearly explain the cause that made something happen.
- Clearly explain the effect that happened because of something else.
- Try to include an end result or effect.

DIRECTIONS **Choose an event you would like to write about. Use your writing plan as a guide for writing your cause and effect paragraph.**

Evaluation Paragraph

In an **evaluation paragraph**, a writer judges a subject or idea. Then, the writer provides reasons or examples to support this judgment. A writer might like or dislike something. A writer might also judge that something is good or bad. *Example:*

> In the story "Two of Everything," Mr. and Mrs. Hak-Tak made doubles of themselves. They were very clever to make their doubles their neighbors. First, the Hak-Taks could not send their doubles away without telling the secret. Keeping them nearby was a clever way of protecting themselves. Second, building a house next door for their doubles gave Mr. and Mrs. Hak-Tak extra help around the farm. Most important, their doubles became Mr. and Mrs. Hak-Tak's best friends. This was the cleverest outcome of all.

How to Write an Evaluation Paragraph
1. In the topic sentence, state whom or what you will evaluate and your judgment about it.
2. Keep your audience in mind as you write.
3. Provide reasons or strong examples to support your judgment.
4. Write a concluding sentence that summarizes your judgment.

 **DIRECTIONS** > **Read the judgment and the three supporting reasons. Write *1* next to the most important reason, *2* next to the second most important reason, and *3* next to the least important reason.**

Athletic contests between schools are a bad idea.

_____ Such contests lead to bad feelings between schools, and sometimes violent behavior is the result.

_____ It is too expensive to transport students from one place to another.

_____ Athletes spend too much time practicing, and their schoolwork suffers.

Evaluation Paragraph, page 2

DIRECTIONS ▸ Read the example evaluation paragraph on page 496. Then, answer the questions.

1. What is being evaluated in the paragraph?

_____

2. What judgment does the writer make about the Hak-Tak's creating doubles?

_____

3. What is the least important example the writer gives to support the judgment?

_____

_____

4. What is the second most important example the writer gives to support the judgment?

_____

_____

5. What is the most important example the writer gives to support the judgment?

_____

_____

DIRECTIONS ▸ Think of a subject or an idea that you would like to evaluate. Then, use this writing plan to organize your evaluation paragraph.

WRITING PLAN

Topic Sentence: _____

_____

Example: _____

Example: _____

Example: _____

Evaluation Paragraph, page 3

Tips for Writing an Evaluation Paragraph
- Choose one subject or idea to evaluate.
- Decide what your judgment will be.
- Identify your subject and your judgment in your topic sentence.
- Include at least three reasons or examples for your judgment.
- Put your least important reason first in your paragraph.
- Put your most important reason last in our paragraph.

DIRECTIONS Choose a subject or an idea you would like to evaluate. Use your writing plan as a guide for writing your evaluation paragraph.

_____

_____

_____

_____

_____

_____

_____

_____

_____

_____

_____

_____

_____

_____

_____

_____

_____

Persuasive Paragraph

In a **persuasive paragraph**, a writer tries to make readers agree with his or her opinion on an issue.

Example:

Wisconsin should have a "Caddie Woodlawn Day" to celebrate the trust between Caddie and her Native American friends. This trust prevented a massacre and led to the peace between the two groups. "Caddie Woodlawn Day" would remind us to settle problems by peaceful means. In addition, this holiday would give us a reason to practice our ancestors' customs. Then, we would be reminded to appreciate their way of life. Because this holiday would help us to remember Caddie Woodlawn, the state legislature should vote in favor of this idea.

opinion in topic sentence

reasons and facts

strongest reason last

restated opinion or call for action

How to Write a Persuasive Paragraph

1. Write a topic sentence that states the issue and your opinion about it.
2. Keep in mind the audience that you want to convince.
2. Give at least three reasons that will convince your audience to agree with you. Include these reasons in the detail sentences.
3. Explain each reason with one or more examples.
4. Save your strongest reason for last.
5. At the end of your paragraph, tell your opinion again. Ask your reader to feel the same way.

Persuasive Paragraph, page 2

DIRECTIONS Read the example persuasive paragraph on page 499. Then, answer the questions.

1. What is the writer's main idea in this paragraph?

_____

_____

2. What are two reasons the writer gives to support the main idea?

_____

_____

_____

3. What call for action does the writer have in the last sentence?

_____

_____

DIRECTIONS Think of something you feel strongly about. Then, use this writing plan to organize your persuasive paragraph.

WRITING PLAN

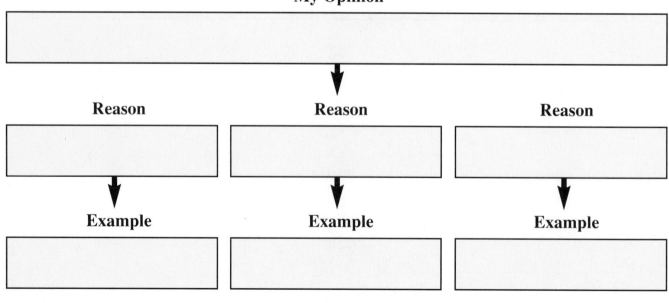

Persuasive Paragraph, page 3

Tips for Writing a Persuasive Paragraph
- Choose a topic that you feel strongly about.
- State your opinion in your topic sentence.
- Write good reasons to support your opinion.
- Try to have at least three good reasons.
- Save your strongest reason for last.
- Try to give an example for each reason.
- At the end of your paragraph, restate your opinion.
  Tell the reader to take some action.

DIRECTIONS Choose a topic that you have an opinion about. Use your writing plan as a guide for writing your persuasive paragraph.

_____

_____

_____

_____

_____

_____

_____

_____

_____

_____

_____

_____

_____

_____

Writing for a Test

Many tests have sections that require you to demonstrate your writing skills. You are usually given a topic and a time limit. The writing process can help you adapt your writing style to meet this challenge. Here are some tips for writing better on a test.

PREWRITING

Analyzing a Topic
• Do I understand the question?
• Am I being asked to compare, contrast, give an opinion, explain, or describe?
• What form of writing will be most effective?

Gathering Information
• Am I allowed to look in books while I write?
• Would it help to make a rough outline before I write?

DRAFTING

• Can I focus my writing by beginning with a clear topic sentence?
• How much time do I have for this assignment?

RESPONDING AND REVISING

• Have I answered the question completely?
• Should I add any additional information?
• Are there any incorrect statements that I should change?
• Have I checked the spelling of every word?
• Have I checked for mistakes in grammar?

FINAL DRAFT

• Do I have time to make a neater copy?
• If not, are there any sloppy sections I should write on another page?

Writing for a Test, page 2

TIMED WRITING

You have probably taken timed tests before. What are some ways to do well during a timed writing test? Follow these tips to make a timed test go more smoothly:

- Stay calm. Don't panic. Take a deep breath and relax.
- For a writing test, remember to check your task and your purpose. (Unless you are told otherwise, your audience is the person who will read the test.)
- Plan how you will use your time. If this is a writing test, decide how much time you need to spend prewriting, drafting, revising, proofreading, and writing the final draft.
- Use your time wisely once you start writing.
- If you begin to run out of time, decide if you can combine some steps. Your goal is to finish.

WRITTEN PROMPTS

A written prompt is a statement or a question that asks you to complete a writing task.

- A narrative prompt asks you to tell a story.
- A persuasive prompt asks you to convince the reader.
- An expository prompt asks you to inform or explain.
- A descriptive prompt asks you to describe something.
- An evaluative prompt asks you to judge something.
- A comparison-contrast prompt asks you to discuss the similarities and the differences between two things.

PICTURE PROMPTS

A picture prompt is a statement or question about a picture. It asks you to tell something about the picture. The prompt also tells the purpose for writing. Study the picture carefully before you begin writing.

Using a Dictionary

The order of letters from *A* to *Z* is called **alphabetical order**. Words in a dictionary are listed in alphabetical order.

There are two **guide words** at the top of every dictionary page. The word on the left is the first word on the page. The word on the right is the last word. All the other words on the page are in alphabetical order between the guide words.

Each word that is defined in the dictionary is an **entry word**. An entry word usually appears in dark print. Each entry word appears in alphabetical order and is divided into syllables.

An **entry** is all the information about an entry word.

A **definition** is the meaning of a word. Many words have more than one definition. Each definition is numbered.

The **part of speech** tells whether a word is a noun, a verb, or some other part of speech. The parts of speech in a dictionary entry usually are abbreviated this way.

noun—n.   verb—v.   adjective—adj.   adverb—adv.   pronoun—pron.

A definition is often followed by an **example** that shows how to use the word.

float [flōt] **1** *v.* To rest or cause to rest on the surface of a liquid, such as water, without sinking: A life preserver *floats*. **2** *n.* An object that floats or holds up something else in a liquid, as an anchored raft at a beach or a piece of cork attached to a fishing line. **3** *v.* To be carried along gently on the surface of a liquid or through the air; drift: Fog *floated* over the city. **4** *v.* To move lightly and without effort: The skater *floated* across the ice. **5** *n.* A wheeled platform or truck on which an exhibit is carried in a parade.

DIRECTIONS ▸ Use the example entry to answer the following questions.

1. How many definitions are given for *float*? _____

2. Which part of speech is the first definition of *float*? _____

3. As what other part of speech can *float* be used? _____

4. Which definition tells the meaning of *float* in the following sentences?

The balloon <u>floated</u> up to the ceiling. _____

Have you ever ridden a <u>float</u> in a parade? _____

Using a Dictionary, page 2

A **syllable** is a word part that has only one vowel sound. Each entry word in the dictionary is divided into syllables.

A **pronunciation** follows each entry word. Letters and symbols show how the word is pronounced. It also shows the number of syllables in the word.

Example:

> **il • lu • sion** [i • lōō´ zhen] *n.* **1** A false, mistaken idea or belief: to lose childish *illusions*. **2** A deceiving appearance or the false impression it gives: an optical *illusion*.

In a word with two or more syllables, the **accent mark** (´) in the pronunciation shows which syllable is said with the most force.

A **pronunciation key** explaining the pronunciation marks usually appears at the beginning of a dictionary. A brief key like the one below is often found at the bottom of dictionary pages.

a	add	i	it	ŏŏ	took	oi	oil
ā	ace	ī	ice	ōō	pool	ou	pout
â	care	o	odd	u	up	ng	ring
ä	palm	ō	open	û	burn	th	thin
e	end	ô	order	yōō	fuse	th	this
ē	equal					zh	vision

ə = { a in *above*, e in *sicken*, i in *possible*, o in *melon*, u in *circus* }

DIRECTIONS ▷ **Write the word shown in each dictionary respelling. Then, use each word in a sentence. Use the dictionary if you need help with pronunciations or definitions.**

1. [op´ ti · kəl] _____

_____

2. [ri · flek´ shən] _____

_____

3. [mə · jish´ ən] _____

_____

4. [nā´ chər] _____

_____

Using a Thesaurus

A **thesaurus** is a book that lists synonyms, words that have nearly the same meaning, and antonyms, words that mean the opposite of a word. Many thesauruses are like dictionaries. The entry words are listed in dark print in alphabetical order. Guide words at the top of the page tell which words can be found on the page. Good writers use a thesaurus to find vivid and exact words to make their writing more interesting.

DIRECTIONS > Replace each underlined word or words with words that express the meaning in a more exact and vivid way. You may want to refer to a thesaurus.

1. When Harvey was growing up, his family was <u>very large</u>. _____

2. At one time Harvey counted <u>about</u> sixty cousins. _____

3. They all lived on a large farm, <u>taking care of</u> animals and crops. _____

4. Everyone <u>worked hard</u>. _____

5. In the 1930s, the family lost the land they had <u>worked</u> for so long. _____

6. Things became very <u>hard</u> for the family. _____

7. Harvey's parents found jobs in the <u>shops</u> in town. _____

8. Harvey, an <u>ambitious</u> young man, decided that he would have his own store someday.

_____

9. Thirty years later, Harvey owned one of the largest chains of stores in the <u>country</u>.

_____

DIRECTIONS > Write sentences using exact, vivid synonyms of the words in parentheses.

10. (small) _____

_____

11. (house) _____

_____

12. (walk) _____

_____

Using an Encyclopedia

An **encyclopedia** is a set of books that contains information on many subjects. The articles are arranged in alphabetical order in different books, called volumes. Guide words at the top of the page show the first subject on the page. Looking up some subjects may be difficult, though. The names of people and some cities may have two words. How do you know which word to use to find information in an encyclopedia?

How To Use an Encyclopedia
1. Always look up the last name of a person.
   Example: To find an article on Babe Ruth, look under *Ruth*.
2. Always look up the first name of a city, state, or country.
   Example: To find an article on New York City, look under *New*.
3. Always look up the most important word in the name of a general topic.
   Example: To find an article on the brown bear, look under *bear*.

DIRECTIONS Write the word you would look under to find an article on each of these subjects.

1. Susan B. Anthony _____

2. salt water _____

3. New Mexico _____

4. lakes in Scotland _____

5. Rio de Janeiro _____

6. United Kingdom _____

7. modern literature _____

8. breeds of horses _____

9. Gila monster _____

10. Robert Frost _____

11. Industrial Revolution _____

12. Queen Victoria _____

Using an Encyclopedia, page 2

Remember that an encyclopedia is a set of books that contains information on many subjects. Each book in an encyclopedia is called a **volume**. The volumes are arranged in alphabetical order. Each article in an encyclopedia is called an **entry**. Each volume is labeled on its spine with the beginning letter or letters of its first and last entries.

Many encyclopedias have a separate **index**. The index is usually the last volume in the encyclopedia. The index lists all the entries in alphabetical order. Next to the entry are the volume and page numbers.

Underground Railroad
>United States History **U 275** *with map*
>>*See also* Slavery *in this index.*
>Abolitionists **A 87**
>Civil War (Origins) **C 160**
>Tubman, Harriet **T 232**
>>*See also the list of Related Readings in the* Black Americans *article.*

>**DIRECTIONS** ▶ **Use the encyclopedia index above to answer the following questions.**

1. In how many volumes might you find information on the Underground Railroad?

_____

2. To what volume and page would you turn to find an article on Harriet Tubman?

_____

3. Which entry also contains a map?

_____

4. Which entry refers the reader to another entry in the index?

_____

5. In what section of the Civil War entry would you find information on the Underground Railroad?

_____

6. Under what entry might you find related readings about Harriet Tubman?

_____

Using the Internet

The computer is a powerful research tool. The **Internet**, a system using telephone and cable lines to send signals, helps you to find almost any information in the blink of an eye. You can communicate instantly with other people by sending electronic mail. Some computers let you see the people as you talk. The key to using the computer as a research tool is knowing what keywords to use to start the Internet search. It takes some practice, but you never know what interesting place you can visit or what information you can find. Here are some hints to speed up the search.

How to Use the Internet
1. Make a list of keywords or names.
2. Choose a search engine that has a directory to narrow the topic.
3. Type in two or three keywords.
4. Type in different combinations of keywords until the topic titles focus on the information you need.

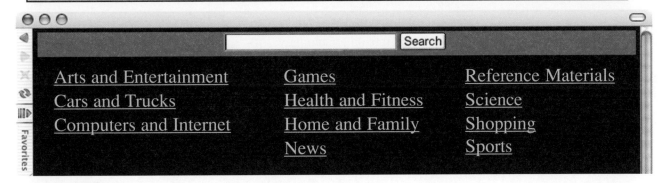

Arts and Entertainment	Games	Reference Materials
Cars and Trucks	Health and Fitness	Science
Computers and Internet	Home and Family	Shopping
	News	Sports

DIRECTIONS ▷ **Use the example Internet directory to choose the category you would search for these subjects.**

1. bicycle champion Lance Armstrong _____

2. how to multiply fractions _____

3. the events at a local museum _____

4. buying a new pair of shoes _____

5. download a new game _____

6. author Shel Silverstein _____

7. astronaut Sally Ride _____

8. which Native American groups lived in your area _____

Parts of a Book

The **title page** tells the name of a book and the name of the author. It also gives the name of the publisher and the city of publication.

The **copyright page** tells when the book was published. It sometimes lists the titles of other books from which material was reprinted by permission. This is the acknowledgments section.

The **table of contents** comes after the title page. It lists each unit, chapter, story, or section in the order in which it appears in the book. A table of contents usually lists the page on which each part of the book begins.

Many nonfiction books also have an **index**. An index is an alphabetical list of all the topics in a book. Indexes include the page or pages on which each topic appears.

Giants **In Myth and Legend** by Gloria Kim KING PRESS, INC. New York Chicago	Copyright © 1983 by King Press, Inc. **Acknowledgments** Ace Publishing Company: from *Giants* by Val Meyer. Copyright © 1981 by Val Meyer. All rights reserved. Printed in the United States of America.	**CONTENTS** The Greek Titans.....................1 The Greek Cyclopes ....17 Jack and the Beanstalk...........21 Jack the Giant-Killer..............35 The Iroquois Stone Giants .....45 Paul Bunyan........................51 Glossary ....65 Index 73
title page	copyright page	table of contents

DIRECTIONS ▸ Use the example pages to answer the following questions.

1. What is the title of this book? _____

2. Which company published the book? _____

3. When and where was the book printed? _____

4. How many chapters are there? _____

5. How many chapters tell of giants that are Greek? _____

6. On what page could you begin to read about Paul Bunyan? _____

7. On what page does the index begin? _____

8. Which is the first page on which you might read about Polyphemus, one of the Cyclopes?

_____

Reading for Information

Skimming is a quick reading method. To skim is to look at material in order to note its general subject, its divisions, and its major headings.

Scanning is also a quick reading method. To scan is to look quickly at a particular passage, searching for key words.

DIRECTIONS ▸ Skim the table of contents of this book to answer questions 1–3. Scan the page from the book to answer questions 4–6.

Bring in all objects that are usually left outside, such as lawn furniture or garbage cans. If you cannot bring them inside, tie them down securely. Board up your windows so that they will not be broken by objects carried by the wind. When the hurricane hits, stay inside and listen to your radio for information. Do not go outside until the authorities announce that it is safe.

1. How many general subjects will this book cover? _____

What are they? _____

2. What does Chapter 1 of each part explain? _____

3. What do Chapters 2 and 3 of each part explain? _____

_____

4. What should you do with lawn furniture if you cannot bring it inside?

_____

5. Why should you board up your windows? _____

_____

6. When can you go outside again? _____

_____

Taking Notes

Good writers take notes to remember the facts they find when doing research for a report.

It is often helpful to write notes on cards. When preparing to write a report, the writer can put the cards in order according to the topic.

Example:

> The Mythological Zoo by Elizabeth Dixon, pages 20–29
> Which Greek and Roman gods had "pet" birds?
>   Zeus: eagle
>   Hera: peacock
>   Apollo: crow

How to Take Notes
1. Record the name of the book or magazine from which you are taking the information.
2. List the main topic of the material.
3. Write the most important facts and details.
4. Use key words and phrases. You need not write complete sentences.
5. Be sure your notes are accurate and readable.

 **DIRECTIONS**   **Read this information taken from page 21 of The Mythological Zoo. Write notes that answer the question, "What are the symbols of Zeus?"**

The Greeks and the Romans both had many gods. However, each of these ancient peoples had one god whom they considered to be the most important. Jupiter was considered the king of the Roman gods. Zeus held the same position for the Greeks. Jupiter's symbols were the king's scepter and the thunderbolt. Zeus was known by these two symbols, as well as by the oak tree and the eagle.

_____

_____

_____

_____

_____

Taking Notes, page 2

When taking notes, remember to write down the name of your source. You should also write down the most important information in the source. Take notes only on the material you will use in your essay or report.

DIRECTIONS > **Read the following paragraph. As you read, take notes on the lines below. Remember to focus on key points and to use abbreviations.**

One of the hottest and driest places in North America is Death Valley, in California. An average of only about one and one half inches of rain falls each year in Death Valley, and in some years it does not rain at all. The valley is the bottom of a lake that dried up in prehistoric times, leaving clay and salt in the center of the valley and sand dunes to the north. Near Badwater is the lowest spot in North America. It is 282 feet below sea level!

My Notes: _____

_____

_____

_____

_____

DIRECTIONS > **Now read over the notes you took. Use your notes to answer the questions.**

1. How did you choose the points to include in your notes?

_____

2. What abbreviations did you use in your notes?

_____

3. Why is it important to take good notes?

_____

Summary

A **summary** is a short sentence or paragraph that tells the main idea and the details in a story or selection. To summarize any writing, you must pay attention to the details. Using the question words *who, what, where, when,* and *why* can help you find the important details to include in a summary. There are some things you leave out of a summary. That is because they are less important than the main idea and the details. They may make the story more interesting, but you can summarize the story or selection without them. A summary table can help you organize the information to write a summary.

DIRECTIONS ▷ **Read the paragraph. Then, complete the summary table.**

Florida is a popular state for tourists. Millions of Americans from colder climates visit there every year. These visitors, often called "snowbirds" by people who live year-round in Florida, show up when snow is on the ground in the northern part of the United States. The northerners think that Florida's beautiful beaches and tourist attractions make it the best place to visit in the winter.

Who:	Summary:
What:	
Where:	
When:	
Why:	

Paraphrasing

Paraphrasing means to restate an idea in your own words. For example, you read a paragraph by another writer. How would you tell the information in the paragraph? You should not copy what the other writer has written. Instead, you would tell the information in your own words. When you do, you paraphrase what the other writer has written.

Example:

Writer's words: Maureen could hardly believe she was going to be in fifth grade this year. She was very excited. But she was nervous, too. The fifth grade was in a different school. The students in her class would be the youngest students in the school. She wondered if the older students would make fun of the younger ones. At the same time, Maureen thought it would be fun to be in a new school with older students. Her stomach was full of butterflies!

Your paraphrased version: Maureen had mixed feelings about going into the fifth grade.

 **DIRECTIONS** Read each paragraph. Then write, in your own words, a sentence or two to tell what the paragraph is about.

Greg was furious. A group of boys had invited Greg to go to the movies with them, but Greg's mother had said that he couldn't go. She did not like the idea of boys his age going to a movie without an adult. Greg sat in his room all night and thought about how angry he was at his mother. He also thought about how embarrassed he would feel when he saw his friends again.

1. In your own words, what is this paragraph about?

_____

_____

The next day, Greg found out that the boys who had gone to the movie had not had a very good time. One of them had begun a popcorn fight in the theater. People had complained, and the boys had to leave the movie. They had all gotten into trouble with their parents. Greg couldn't help feeling glad that he had not gone after all.

2. In your own words, what is this paragraph about?

_____

_____

Using Quotations

Good writers use **quotations** from oral and written sources. Quotations are the exact words that are in a book or that a speaker says. Quotations are enclosed in quotation marks (" ").

DIRECTIONS Each numbered sentence below is the topic sentence of a paragraph in a research report about whales. The box contains sentences with quotations that might be used in the report. Before each topic sentence, write the letter of the quotation sentence that should be included in that paragraph.

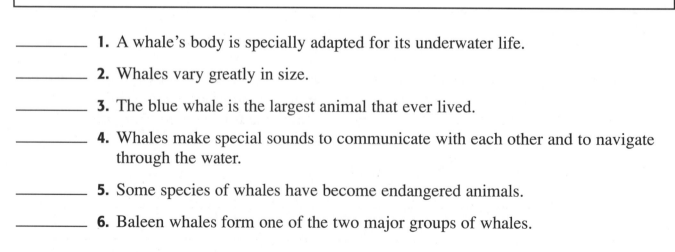

a. "These magnificent creatures are even larger than the famous dinosaurs that died out so long ago," commented Dr. Romley.

b. Said Dr. Schultz, "Although international laws ban hunting, some species of whales are still in danger of extinction."

c. Mr. Walters explained, "The whale's nostrils, located on top of its head, can be tightly closed so that no water leaks in."

d. "I am still thrilled every time I hear these whales 'talking' to each other," said Mr. Clark.

e. "Though we often think of whales as huge animals," said Ms. Kwong, "some species are barely four feet long."

f. "A baleen whale has no teeth. Instead, it has thin plates, called baleen, in its mouth," added Mr. Walters.

_____ **1.** A whale's body is specially adapted for its underwater life.

_____ **2.** Whales vary greatly in size.

_____ **3.** The blue whale is the largest animal that ever lived.

_____ **4.** Whales make special sounds to communicate with each other and to navigate through the water.

_____ **5.** Some species of whales have become endangered animals.

_____ **6.** Baleen whales form one of the two major groups of whales.

Outline

A writer uses an **outline** to organize the information he or she has gathered for a research report.
Example:

    Bird Myths and Mysteries
     I. Birds in Myth and Legend
        A. Birds of the Greek gods
        B. Birdlike monsters

     II. Birds as Modern Symbols
        A. Of people's characteristics
        B. Of political points of view

How to Write an Outline
1. Write a title that tells the subject of your report. Capitalize each important word in the title.
2. Write the main topics. Use a Roman numeral and a period before each topic.
3. Capitalize each important word in a main topic.
4. Write subtopics under each main topic. Use a capital letter followed by a period for each subtopic. Begin each subtopic with a capital letter.
5. Do not write a *I* without a *II* or an *A* without a *B*.
6. Plan one paragraph for each main topic in your outline.

 **DIRECTIONS** ▷ **Read each line of the outline. If the line is correct, write *correct*. If not, rewrite the line correctly.**

the job of a Mother bird   _____

  I. Find a good place for a nest   _____
    A. Dry enough   _____
    b. warm enough   _____
    c out of reach of cats   _____

  II. make the nest   _____
    a big enough   _____
    B. Snug enough   _____
    c. sides tall enough   _____
    d. inside Soft enough   _____

  III. Take care of eggs   _____
    a. Sit on them   _____
    b. keep them warm   _____

Outline, page 2

In an outline, remember to use a Roman numeral and a period before each main topic. Indent each subtopic. Use a capital letter and a period before each subtopic. Capitalize the first word in each topic and subtopic. Capitalize each important word in the outline's title.

DIRECTIONS ▶ **Read the following paragraphs. Then, complete the outline below.**

The smallest living parts of your body are cells. Although they are the building blocks of your body, you cannot see them unless you use a microscope. There are many different kinds of cells, such as bone cells and skin cells.

Tissues are groups of cells working together. Just as there are different kinds of cells, there are different kinds of tissues. Two kinds are fat tissue and muscle tissue. Each kind has a different function in your body.

When groups of tissues work together, organs are formed. Each organ does a different job; however, all of your organs need to work together for your body to operate successfully.

I. Cells

   A. _____

   B. _____

   C. _____

      1. _____

      2. _____

II. _____

   A. _____

   B. _____

      1. _____

      2. _____

   C. _____

III. _____

   A. _____

   B. _____

   C. _____

Rough Draft

A writer quickly puts all of his or her ideas on paper in a **rough draft**.

How to Write a Rough Draft
1. Read your outline and notes. Keep them near you as you write.
2. Follow your outline to write a rough draft. Do not add anything that is not on your outline. Do not leave out anything.
3. Write one paragraph for each Roman numeral in your outline.
4. Write freely. Do not worry about mistakes now. You will revise later.
5. Read over your rough draft. Make notes on changes you want to make.

 DIRECTIONS Choose one of the partial outlines below. Then, write a topic sentence and two detail sentences based upon the points in the outline.

1. I. Dodo Bird Is Extinct
   A. Could not fly
   B. Had short, stubby legs

2. I. Family Life of Birds
   A. Selecting a territory
   B. Building a nest

3. I. Bird Migration
   A. Why birds migrate
   B. Where birds migrate

Topic sentence: _____

_____

Detail sentence 1: _____

_____

Detail sentence 2: _____

_____

Bibliography

A **bibliography** lists all the information a writer uses in a research report. The bibliography gives credit to the authors of the information used. A bibliography is also known as a "works cited" list.

How to Write a Bibliography

1. List the sources in alphabetical order by the author's last name or by the title if there is no author given.
2. After the author's name, write the title of the book or magazine source. Then, write the name of the publisher and the date of publication.
3. An Internet resource lists two dates. The first date tells the day the article was published. The second date is the day you found the article online.

Magazine Article
Bonfield, J. E. "Bird Clothes." Owl, November 1986: 26–29.

Book
Dixon, Elizabeth. The Mythological Zoo. New York: Bendix Books, 1986.

Encyclopedia
"Owls." Collier's Encyclopedia. Vol. 18. 1999 edition.

Internet
Smith, Donald. "On Silent Wings." May 2001. Online. 24 March 2005
        <www.owltime.net>.

DIRECTIONS ▷ Use the model bibliography to answer these questions.

1. Who wrote The Mythological Zoo? _____

2. In which volume of the encyclopedia was "Owls" found? _____

3. In which magazine issue does "Bird Clothes" appear? _____

4. At which Internet site can "On Silent Wings" be found? _____

5. When was the article "On Silent Wings" found online by the student?

_____

Analyzing a Research Report

A **research report** gives information about a topic. It draws facts from various sources. It has a title, an introduction, a body, and a conclusion.

DIRECTIONS ▷ Read the research report. Answer the questions that follow.

Many of our superstitions came to us from very ancient sources. The idea that one should knock on wood for good luck, for example, is a 4,000-year-old custom that began with some Native American tribes of North America. Noticing that the oak was struck often by lightning, members of the tribe thought that it must be the dwelling place of a sky god. They also thought that boasting of a future personal deed was bad luck and meant the thing would never happen. Knocking on an oak tree was a way of contacting the sky god and being forgiven for boasting.

Another interesting superstition is that it is bad luck to open an umbrella indoors. In eighteenth-century England, umbrellas had stiff springs and very strong metal spokes. Opening one indoors could indeed cause an accident. It could injure someone or break a fragile object. This superstition came about for practical reasons.

1. What would be a good title for this research report?

_____

2. What is the topic of the first paragraph?

_____

3. What is the topic of the second paragraph?

_____

4. What are three details from the first paragraph?

_____

_____

_____

_____

Research Report

After making the changes to the rough draft, the writer can complete the final copy of the research report.

Example:

Bird Myths and Mysteries

Birds have always been part of myths and legends. In ancient Greece, many birds were special to the gods. The eagle was a symbol of Zeus. The peacock symbolized Hera, and the crow stood for Apollo. Stories tell of birdlike monsters called Harpies and of a huge, terrible bird called a roe.

Birds are still used as symbols today. Many expressions compare people to birds. A person may be "wise as an owl" or "proud as a peacock." Names of birds can also be found in the world of politics. Senators are often described as hawks or doves, depending on their political point of view.

Scientists have solved some of the mysteries about birds, but many others remain. How do the ptarmigan's feathers act as a camouflage? Why does the arctic tern migrate from the Arctic to the Antarctic? These and other mysteries are sure to keep people fascinated by birds.

How to Write a Research Report
1. Read over your rough draft. Add any material you might have forgotten.
2. Make all revising and editing changes.
3. Write the title of your report.
4. Write the report from your rough draft and your notes.
5. Indent the first sentence of each paragraph.
6. Complete your bibliography.

DIRECTIONS ▷ **Read the example research report on this page. Then, choose a topic that interests you, and write your own report. Remember to take notes, make an outline, write a rough draft, complete a bibliography, and then write your report. Save all your notes to turn in with your report. Your report should be at least three paragraphs long and should have a title.**

Writing
Skills

UNIT 1: Personal Narrative

HOW MUCH DO YOU KNOW?

Read the paragraph. Then answer the questions.

  I planned and prepared a surprise party for my sister Susie. I hired a clown and bought some balloons about a week ahead of time. Three days before the party, I ordered a chocolate cake and borrowed extra plates. I shopped, cleaned, and cooked the day before the party.

  The guests hid in the basement. When Susie came in, they jumped out and yelled "Surprise!" Susie laughed and danced around in a circle. We wore polka-dot party hats and played Susie's favorite music. Everyone ate, laughed, and danced.

  Some of the guests helped clear the table and wash the dishes. I sat and rested.

1. Who is the narrator of the story?

  _____

2. What does the writer tell about in the first paragraph?

  _____

3. What caused Susie to dance around in a circle?

  _____

4. List two details that tell what happened at the party.

  _____

  _____

Analyzing a Personal Narrative

> **A PERSONAL NARRATIVE**
>
> - is a true story the writer tells about himself or herself
> - is written in the first person
> - reveals a writer's feelings about an event or events
> - usually presents events in time order

Read the personal narrative. Answer the questions that follow.

On Saturday afternoon I went to the new barbershop that opened in our neighborhood. I told the barber how I wanted my hair to be cut. Twenty minutes later I walked out with the Mohawk I had always wanted.

When my mom saw my haircut, she almost fainted. She asked, "Why did you do that to yourself?" I told her that I thought she would think it was an original and interesting hairstyle. She said she thought it was an original and terrible hairstyle.

On Monday my teacher made a funny face when he saw my hair. He said, "I hope that's a wig." He was concerned because I was the prince in the school play. A prince with a Mohawk would look pretty strange.

As it turned out, I had to wear a wig for the play. On opening night the wig fell off. When the people in the audience saw the Mohawk, they laughed.

1. What is the topic of this personal narrative?

_____

2. What does the writer tell about in the first paragraph?

_____

3. What does the writer tell about in the second paragraph?

_____

4. What does the writer tell about in the third paragraph?

_____

5. What does the writer tell about in the fourth paragraph?

_____

Connecting Cause and Effect

TO WRITE A PERSONAL NARRATIVE, GOOD WRITERS
- tell what happened
- tell the causes or the effects of the major events

Read each sentence. Circle the part that tells the cause. Draw a line under the part that tells the effect. If the sentence does not show cause and effect, write *none* on the line.

1. In April 1805 Captain Meriwether Lewis and one of his hunters were hiking in what is now Montana.

2. Two grizzly bears suddenly appeared, and the men were immediately frightened.

3. The men fired, and one bear was wounded.

4. The other bear was not hurt, so it ran away.

5. The wounded bear was very angry, so it charged Captain Lewis.

6. Because Lewis still had time to reload, he lived to tell the tale.

7. In the months that followed, Lewis and Clark saw many grizzly bears.

8. If you bother or frighten a grizzly, it will attack.

9. Usually, it goes its own way, and a person avoids trouble.

10. Because these bears do not climb trees, many people have escaped angry grizzlies.

Using Details to Explain

> **GOOD WRITERS**
> - include details that give causes and effects
> - give their feelings in response to certain causes

He was already an expert rider.

Slow had jabbed the Crow with his stick.

He had a slow and serious nature.

Slow had acted bravely.

They had won the battle.

The Crow Indians had stolen some Sioux horses.

He no longer seemed so slow and serious.

It was considered braver to push an enemy off a horse than to shoot an arrow from far away.

The numbered sentences below tell about events. After each numbered sentence, write the detail sentence from the box that helps explain that event.

1. When Sitting Bull was a child, he was named Slow.

   _____

2. At the age of ten, Slow was given his own pony.

   _____

3. When Slow was fourteen, he and other Sioux fought some Crow Indians.

   _____

4. Slow was armed only with a stick.

   _____

5. One Crow Indian fell from his horse.

   _____

6. The Sioux held a victory party.

   _____

Using a Thesaurus

> **Good writers use a thesaurus to find synonyms that will make their writing interesting and give it variety.**

A. Replace each underlined word or words with words that express the meaning in a more exact and vivid way. You may want to refer to a thesaurus.

1. When Harvey was growing up, his family was <u>very large</u>.

   _____

2. At one time Harvey counted <u>about</u> sixty cousins.

   _____

3. They all lived on a large farm, <u>taking care of</u> animals and crops.

   _____

4. Everyone <u>worked hard</u>. _____

5. In the 1930s the family lost the land they had <u>worked</u> for so long.

   _____

6. <u>Things</u> became very <u>hard</u> for the family. _____

7. Harvey's parents found jobs in the <u>shops</u> in town.

   _____

8. Harvey, an <u>ambitious</u> young man, decided that he would have his own store someday. _____

9. <u>Thirty years</u> later, Harvey owned one of the largest chains of stores in the <u>country</u>. _____

B. Write sentences using exact, vivid synonyms of the words in parentheses.

10. (small) _____

11. (house) _____

12. (walk) _____

Proofreading a Personal Narrative

Proofread the beginning of the personal narrative, paying special attention to spelling. Use the Proofreading Marks to correct at least seven errors.

Last weekend I traveled more than a hunderd years back in time. No, I didn't find a time machine—I went to the Dickens Fair in San Francisco. The fare was held on Pier 45 at the famuos Fisherman's Wharf. The whole wharf was crowded with people, and everyone seemed to be having a grate time!

The people who worked at the Dickens Fair were all dressed the way people dressed in Engaland when Charles

PROOFREADING MARKS

⬯	spell correctly
⊙	add period
?	add question mark
≡	capitalize
℘	take out
∧	add
/	make lowercase
∿	switch
⩓	add comma
⩒ ⩒	add quotation marks
¶	indent paragraph

See the chart on p. 643 to learn how to use these marks.

Dickens was alive. The women wore long dresses, and most of the men had fancy hats. These people all spoke with English accents and used special phrases. My parents especially liked being greeted by people who said, "Hello, fair lady" and "Good day, kind sir."

there were some special booths at the dickens Fair. My older sister spent ours looking at the jewlry. Finally, she chose a pare of earrings. I had fun looking at all the booths, but I didn't by anything.

Make a Cause and Effect Chain

Write a series of causes and effects that tells a story. Write each sentence on a strip below.

Write about the Weather

Write an account of a recent weather event. Include details that give causes and effects. Include your feelings about what happened.

_____

_____

_____

_____

_____

_____

_____

_____

_____

_____

_____

_____

_____

Write a Garden Journal

Imagine that you have a garden. Illustrate it in the garden plot provided. Plan and write a journal entry about a day of working with your plants and flowers. Revise and proofread your journal entry.

Write from a Special Point of View

Pretend that you are a fork, a knife, a plate, a glass, or something else that is used at a table. With a friend, discuss how a meal would appear from your point of view. Together, write the story of a meal from that angle.

_____

_____

_____

_____

_____

_____

_____

_____

_____

_____

_____

_____

A Practice Personal Paper

THE MYSTERIOUS ATLANTIC OCEAN FISH

I'm Benny, and here's my story. There's this kid, Sammy, who lives in the apartment across the hall. We don't have much to do with each other for one good reason. He's seven going on eight, and I'm ten going on eleven. He can do everything I like to do, but he's such a little kid. So I don't ask him to play ball with my friends, which is what I like to do most, because they wouldn't want a little kid on the team. Now you understand why we never get together.

One day last summer, my dad was talking to Sammy's dad. The next thing you know we're taking Sammy to the beach. "But my friends are coming over, Dad. We're going to play ball," I say. Then he says that I play ball every day and wouldn't I like to try something new for a change? I'm thinking no, but I don't say it. And before you know it, I'm on my way to the beach.

Sammy rolls his wheelchair into the crowded subway. My dad and I squeeze in, too. It seems like everyone in the city is going to the beach today. Wouldn't you know it? Well, we finally get off the train at Coney Island and go down to the beach with about one million other people. It takes forever before we find a place where we can put down our towels.

We've only been on our towels about 30 seconds before Sammy starts to smile. Pretty soon, he's laughing and having a great time. He finds a tide pool. It's a little pool of water the tide left when it went out. Anyhow, Sammy sees a small fish. After he watches it swim around a little, he scoops it up and plops it into his bucket. That's fine, except when it's time to leave, he wants to take the fish home. I tell him that's a terrible idea. How's an Atlantic Ocean fish going to live in a New York City apartment?

"We'll buy one of those big glass bowls," Sammy says.

"Wait," I say. "You don't get it. This is an Atlantic Ocean fish. It can only live in Atlantic Ocean water."

"So bring some Atlantic Ocean home with us," Sammy says.

Would you believe a smart guy like me actually lets a seven-going-on-eight kid talk him into filling two big buckets with water and dragging those buckets home on the subway? It's embarrassing.

So we buy a bowl and we fill it with Atlantic Ocean water. For about a week, the fish is swimming around pretty well. But as time passes, the fish isn't looking too terrific. Sammy says, "Benny, do something, do something," as if I'm a fish doctor or something. Hey, I can hardly keep my breakfast down when I see the guy at the fish store cleaning a fish. But Sammy won't leave me alone. He just keeps checking out his fish and calling me up with health reports about every 30 seconds.

Finally, he wears me down and I go have a look. You don't have to be a rocket scientist to figure out the problem is the water. At least half the Atlantic Ocean water I carried back in those buckets has evaporated.

Now we've got a real problem because there is no way I'm going back to the beach for more water. Besides, by the time I get out there and back, that fish will be in fish heaven. "Which is not a bad place," I tell Sammy, but that makes him cry.

Obviously, I need to take extreme measures. So I do the only thing I can do in an emergency like this. I fill a pitcher with New York City tap water and I dump the water into the bowl. I slush the tap water around so it mixes with the Atlantic Ocean water. Then I send out lots of good thoughts.

Sammy and I stare at the fish. By now, that fish is too sick to do anything except stare back. And that's the way we are for about a minute. We stare at the fish, and the fish stares back, and we get sadder and sadder, and the fish gets weaker and weaker.

I start making funeral plans. Then an amazing thing happens. Suddenly, the fish is swimming around the tank like it just got some really good news. It swims up, it swims down. It swims this way and that way. It practically does everything except somersault. I have to tell you. It was one amazing sight.

Now do you know why this story is called "The Mysterious Atlantic Ocean Fish"? Well, here's the mystery.

All winter I keep adding New York City water to the bowl. So after a while, with natural evaporation and all, it's clear there's no Atlantic Ocean water left. That saltwater fish is living and swimming in freshwater just as if it had been born in a sink. Is that amazing or what?

The other thing that's amazing is that Sammy and I got, well, you know, real close. Now we trade books, and we play video games. We do lots of stuff together. We even play ball with my other friends. As a matter of fact, Sammy decided that the next time we go to the beach, we'll take the whole team with us. I'm not sure that's a good idea. Can you imagine what he'll want us to help him bring back this time?

Respond to the Practice Paper

Write your answers to the following questions or directions.

1. Why did Benny write this story?

   _____

   _____

2. How did Benny feel in the beginning of the story? How do you know?

   _____

   _____

3. How did Benny feel at the end of the story? How do you know?

   _____

   _____

4. Write a paragraph to summarize the story. Use these questions to help you write your summary:

   - Who is the story about?
   - What are the main ideas in the story?
   - How does the story end?

   _____

   _____

   _____

   _____

   _____

   _____

   _____

   _____

Analyze the Practice Paper

Read "The Mysterious Atlantic Ocean Fish" again. As you read, think about how the writer wrote the story. Write your answers to the following questions.

1. How do you know that this is a personal narrative?

_____

_____

_____

2. What is Benny's problem?

_____

_____

_____

3. How does Benny solve his problem?

_____

_____

_____

4. How does Benny keep your interest in the story?

_____

_____

_____

5. How are the first paragraph and the last paragraph alike?

_____

_____

_____

Writing Assignment

As people grow and change, they may have many best friends. Think about the best friend in your life now. Write a personal narrative that tells about your best friend. Use examples and details to show why this person is your best friend. Use this writing plan to help you write a first draft on the next page.

Name your friend:

▼

Tell how you and your friend became friends.

▼

Give examples to show why this person is your <u>best</u> friend.

First Draft

TIPS FOR WRITING A PERSONAL NARRATIVE:

- Write from your point of view. Use the words *I, me,* and *my* to show your readers that this is your story.

- Think about what you want to tell your reader.

- Organize your ideas into a beginning, middle, and end.

- Write an interesting introduction that "grabs" your readers.

- Write an ending for your story. Write it from your point of view.

Use your writing plan as a guide for writing your first draft of a personal narrative. Include a catchy title.

_____

_____

_____

_____

_____

_____

_____

_____

(Continue on your own paper.)

Revise the Draft

Use the chart below to help you revise your draft. Check YES or NO to answer each question in the chart. If you answer NO, make notes to remind yourself how you can revise, or change, your writing to improve it.

Question	YES ✔	NO ✔	If the answer is NO, what will you do to improve your writing?
Does your story describe your best friend?			
Do you introduce your friend in the first paragraph?			
Do you describe events in the order they happened?			
Do you give examples to show why this person is your best friend?			
Do you include important details?			
Do you tell your story from your point of view? That is, do you use words such as *I, my,* and *me* to tell your story?			
Does your conclusion summarize your story in a new way?			
Have you corrected mistakes in spelling, grammar, and punctuation?			

Use the notes in your chart and your writing plan to revise your draft.

Writing Report Card

Read your revised draft again or ask someone else to read it. Have the person who reads your paper complete the following Report Card. Revise your paper until you have no less than a Very Good Score for each item.

Title of paper: _____

Purpose of paper: _*This is a personal narrative. It tells about*_

*my best friend.*

Person who scores the paper: _____

Score	Writing Goals
	Does the story have a strong beginning, or introduction?
	Are the story's main ideas organized into paragraphs?
	Are there details to support each main idea?
	Are the paragraphs organized in a way that makes sense?
	Are there different kinds of sentences that help make the story interesting?
	Is there a strong ending, or conclusion?
	Does the writer make it clear why the friend in this narrative is the writer's best friend?
	Are the story's grammar, spelling, and punctuation correct?

☺ Excellent Score   ☆ Very Good Score   + Good Score
✔ Acceptable Score   − Needs Improvement

UNIT 2: How-to Writing

HOW MUCH DO YOU KNOW?

These sentences from a how-to paragraph are out of order. Rewrite them in order in a paragraph, adding words and phrases from the box to make the order clear. Then answer the questions that follow.

Tie a knot in the balloon.
Stretch the balloon several times.
Hang it from the ribbon.
Pick out your favorite color of balloon.
Blow it up slowly.
Tie a ribbon around the knot.

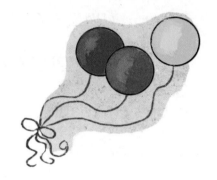

first	then	last
second	after that	the last thing
next	finally	the next thing you do
third	at the end	before you begin
at last	in the first place	

_____

_____

_____

_____

_____

1. What does this paragraph tell you how to do?

_____

2. What is the first thing you must do?

_____

Analyzing a How-to Paragraph

A HOW-TO PARAGRAPH

- gives instructions for making or doing something
- has a topic sentence, a list of materials, and step-by-step instructions with time-order words

Read the how-to paragraph. Answer the questions that follow.

Popping Popcorn in a Microwave Oven

Before you begin, make sure that you have popcorn that is especially packaged for microwave popping. Of course, you will need a microwave oven. Remove the plastic overwrap from the bag and place it in the center of the microwave. Be very careful not to puncture or open the special bag the popcorn is in. You should set the microwave for full, or 100 percent, power. Then set the timer for five minutes and push the button to start. Stop the microwave when popping time slows to two or three seconds between pops. Remove the hot bag from the oven. You should shake the bag before opening it to increase flavor and to distribute the salt.

1. How many items are listed as materials, and what are they?

   _____

2. What is the first thing you must do to make your microwave popcorn?

   _____

3. What is the next thing you do?

   _____

4. What happens next?

   _____

5. What do you do last?

   _____

Visualizing Steps in a Process

In a how-to paragraph, good writers picture the steps of an activity before writing directions for it.

These sentences from a how-to paragraph are out of order. Rewrite them in order in a paragraph, adding words and phrases from the box to make the order clear.

Get a bucket.

Dry the car.

To wash your family car, there are six steps you should follow.

Fill the bucket with soapy water.

Hose down the car to get it wet.

Shine the windows and any chrome trim.

Wash the car, using the soapy water and a soft cloth or sponge.

first
last
next
then
after that
finally
third
second
the last thing
the next thing you do
at the end
at last
before you begin
in the first place

_____

_____

_____

_____

_____

Writing for an Audience and a Purpose

> **GOOD WRITERS**
> - keep the intended audience in mind
> - remember their purpose as they write

Read each version of a how-to paragraph below. Answer the questions that follow.

A. You will need an onion, a sharp knife, and a cutting board. First, peel the onion. Then, slice it in half lengthwise. Then, lay half of the onion cut-side down on the cutting board. Next, cut many lengthwise slices in it, being careful not to cut all the way through to the cutting board. Turn the onion around and cut crosswise slices in the opposite direction of the slices you just made. As you do this, the onion will break into small pieces.

B. You will need an onion, a sharp knife, and a cutting board. First, peel the onion and slice it in half. Next, cut lengthwise slices, and then cut crosswise slices in it. As you do this, the onion will break into small pieces.

1. Which version do you think is for a younger audience? Why?

_____

2. Which version do you think is for an older audience? Why?

_____

3. If Version A were for even younger readers, what information might be added?

_____

Correcting Run-on Sentences

- Good writers avoid run-on sentences.
- Run-on sentences may be rewritten as simple sentences or as compound sentences.

Read each run-on sentence. Fix it in two ways. First write two simple sentences. Then write one compound sentence.

1. You'll need 101 index cards you'll need a colored marker.

    a. _____

    b. _____

2. Print the name of a state or a state capital on each index card print the rules on the last index card.

    a. _____

    b. _____

3. Put the marker away put all the cards in an envelope.

    a. _____

    b. _____

4. This game is for small groups up to three students may play.

    a. _____

    b. _____

5. Players mix up the cards they lay the cards face down.

    a. _____

    b. _____

Proofreading a How-to Paragraph

Proofread the how-to paragraphs, paying special attention to punctuation marks at the end of sentences. Use the Proofreading Marks to correct at least seven errors.

PROOFREADING MARKS	
⬭	spell correctly
⊙	add period
?	add question mark
≡	capitalize
℘	take out
∧	add
/	make lowercase
∿	switch
∧	add comma
⌄ ⌄	add quotation marks
¶	indent paragraph

Do you have a little brother or sister

Do you sometimes help take care of little

children? If so, you might want to make a

set of special building blocks. These blocks

are large and light enough for even a two-

year-old to handle easaly. They are sturdy

and colorful, and they can be lots of fun

To make a set of blocks, you need as many half-gallon milk cartons you can collect. you also need sheets of colorful paper and some glue.

For each block, use two of your milk cartons Cut the tops off both cartons Then wash them thoroughly and let them dry Be sure your cartons are completely clean.

When both cartons are dry, push the open end of one cartoon into the other carton Press the two cartons together as far as possible. You should end up with a block that is the size of a single carton, with both ends closed and with extra-strong sides. Then cover each block, using glue and the paper you have chosen

Write about a Hobby

With a friend or two, make a list of hobbies you all enjoy. Choose one hobby you are familiar with. Plan and write a how-to paragraph about that hobby.

1. _____   2. _____

3. _____   4. _____

5. _____   6. _____

_____

_____

_____

_____

_____

_____

_____

_____

_____

_____

_____

_____

_____

_____

Write about a Terrarium

With a friend or two, plan a terrarium. If necessary, do some library research to find out how to set it up. Write a how-to paragraph, and be sure to include each step needed to make the terrarium.

Write Pointers for Babysitters

With a friend or two, discuss what would be needed in a how-to manual for babysitters. Choose one area from your discussion and write about it. Illustrate your directions. Revise and proofread your work.

Write about Recycling

Think of ways you might recycle the items on the list into a how-to project. Write your ideas next to each item. Choose one idea and write a how-to paragraph about changing trash into a recycled treasure.

corks and bottle caps

_____

_____

worn-out sock

_____

_____

scraps of wrapping paper

_____

_____

_____

_____

_____

_____

_____

_____

A Practice How-to Paper

HOW TO DECORATE A T-SHIRT

Decorating a T-shirt is easy to do, and you'll be proud to wear it. However, before you begin to work, you have some decisions to make.

First, where are you going to wear your T-shirt? Do you want to wear it to school? Do you want to make a T-shirt for a special occasion like a party? Do you want to make one to wear on a holiday like Valentine's Day?

Second, what do you want to put on your T-shirt? This question may be hard to answer because you have so many choices. All kinds of things go on T-shirts: names, sayings, cars, airplanes, trees, birds, people, rainbows. In fact, someone has probably drawn or printed almost anything you can think of on a T-shirt.

If you can't decide what to put on your T-shirt, think about your favorite foods. A big strawberry ice cream cone or a hot dog covered with chili and cheese would look great on a T-shirt.

If you don't want to wear your food, you might prefer to think about other favorite things, such as animals or flowers. You might draw a scene from your favorite book.

Maybe you don't want to draw anything at all. Perhaps you would prefer to make unusual designs. No matter what choice you make, a T-shirt can become a great painting.

The last thing you will need to think about is the colors you want to use. It's probably not a good idea to use too many colors. Otherwise, people will have to wear sunglasses to look at you.

By the time you have made your decisions, you are ready to

paint. Let's start with the materials you'll need.

Materials:

1 white T-shirt

8 in. x 8 in. piece of drawing paper

pen or pencil

2 safety pins

transfer paper (Note: Transfer paper comes in a roll like waxed paper, so you can share a roll with your friends.)

3 or 4 felt-tipped pens in different colors (Note: Felt-tipped pens come with different-sized tips. Use one with a thin tip to make outlines. Use pens with wider tips to fill in large spaces.)

Below are the steps you will follow.

1. Use a pen or pencil to draw your picture, design, or letters on the piece of drawing paper. Your drawing should be an outline. Do not fill it in. If you are printing letters, make sure they are in a straight line.

2. Now place your T-shirt on a hard surface. Make sure the front is smooth. Then lay a piece of transfer paper where you want your drawing to go. Make sure the piece of transfer paper is as big or bigger than the drawing paper.

3. Place your drawing over the transfer paper. Put one safety pin through the top of the drawing paper, the transfer paper, and the T-shirt. Put a second safety pin through the bottom of the drawing paper, the transfer paper, and the T-shirt. The pins will keep the two papers from moving.

4. Use the thin-tipped pen to go over the outline of your drawing or letters. Press firmly.

5. Remove the safety pins and drawing paper. You will see the outline of your drawing on the T-shirt. If the drawing isn't dark enough, trace over it again.

6. Use the colored felt-tipped pens to add color and details. The last step is the most fun. Enjoy wearing your new T-shirt!

Respond to the Practice Paper

Write your answers to the following questions or directions.

1. What does this how-to paper teach you to do?

   _____

2. What materials do you need?

   _____

   _____

   _____

3. What is the first decision you must make?

   _____

   _____

4. What is the second decision you must make?

   _____

   _____

5. What is the third decision you must make?

   _____

   _____

6. Write a paragraph to describe a T-shirt you would like to make. On a separate piece of paper, draw a picture to go with your paragraph.

   _____

   _____

   _____

   _____

   _____

Analyze the Practice Paper

Read "How to Decorate a T-Shirt" again. As you read, think about why the writer wrote this paper. What did the writer do to help explain how to decorate a T-shirt? Write your answers to the following questions or directions.

1. Why is this a good example of a how-to paper?

   _____

   _____

2. Why does the writer use words like *now*, *first*, and *second*?

   _____

   _____

3. Why does the writer list the materials you need to decorate a T-shirt?

   _____

   _____

4. Why does the writer list the steps you must follow to decorate a T-shirt?

   _____

   _____

5. Draw pictures to show the steps in decorating a T-shirt. Label each step.

Writing Assignment

Think about something you want to tell others how to do. Use this writing plan to help you write a first draft on the next page.

Tell what you want to tell others how to do.

List the materials you will need.

Write the steps someone should follow in order. Number the steps.

Write some sequence words that help the reader know what to do.

First Draft

TIPS FOR WRITING A HOW-TO PAPER:

- Choose one thing to teach someone.
- Focus on a plan.
  1. Think of all the materials someone will need.
  2. Think of all the steps someone will follow.
- Use sequence words in your directions.

Use your writing plan as a guide for writing your first draft of a how-to paper. Include a catchy title.

_____

_____

_____

_____

_____

_____

_____

_____

(Continue on your own paper.)

Revise the Draft

Use the chart below to help you revise your draft. Check YES or NO to answer each question in the chart. If you answer NO, make notes to remind yourself how you can revise, or change, your writing to improve it.

Question	YES ✔	NO ✔	If the answer is NO, what will you do to improve your writing?
Does your paper teach how to do something?			
Do you use the first paragraph to introduce the project?			
Do you include the materials someone needs for this project?			
Do you describe all of the steps someone needs to follow?			
Do you write the steps in the order they should happen?			
Is each step written clearly to make it easy to follow?			
Do you use sequence words to make the directions easy to follow?			
Have you corrected mistakes in spelling, grammar, and punctuation?			

Use the notes in your chart and your writing plan to revise your draft.

Writing Report Card

Read your revised draft again or ask someone else to read it. Have the person who reads your paper complete the following Report Card. Revise your paper until you have no less than a Very Good Score for each item.

Title of paper: _____

Purpose of paper: ___*This paper explains how to do something.*_____

Person who scores the paper: _____

Score	Writing Goals
	Does the paper teach how to do something specific?
	Does the first paragraph explain what the paper will be about?
	Does the writer include the materials needed to do this task or project?
	Are the steps in order?
	Are there sequence words and/or numbers that make the directions easy to follow?
	Are there enough details for the reader to follow each step independently?
	Are the paper's grammar, spelling, and punctuation correct?

☺ Excellent Score ☆ Very Good Score + Good Score
✔ Acceptable Score − Needs Improvement

UNIT 3: Story

HOW MUCH DO YOU KNOW?

Read the story. Answer the questions that follow.

Paul Bunyan's helper, Juan, stared up at him and shook his head. "How will we ever get all this hot food to the tables?" Juan asked. "The dining hall is so big that the food gets cold before we can serve it."

"Why, that's easy," answered Paul. "We'll just put roller skates on the ponies. Then the ponies can skate in quickly and deliver the food before it gets cold."

"What a great idea!" cried Juan.

The next night, however, Paul and Juan discovered that Paul's idea wasn't great after all. The ponies weren't good roller skaters. They spilled most of the food, and then they stopped to eat the spilled food.

"What a mess!" exclaimed Paul.

"What will we do?" asked Juan.

"Well," said Paul, "first we'll have to clean up the dining hall. Then, I think we should build tracks between the rows of tables. We can use freight trains to deliver the food."

1. Who are the characters in the story?

   _____

2. What happens in the beginning?

   _____

   _____

3. What information does the writer give about Juan?

   a. _____

   _____

   b. _____

   _____

Analyzing a Humorous Story

> **A HUMOROUS STORY**
>
> - has a beginning, a middle, and an ending
> - achieves humor through language as well as through the characters and the plot

Read the story. Answer the questions that follow.

Once there was a man who thought his wife never did anything right. In fact, he didn't even think she could sneeze correctly. He criticized everything she did. One day the wife got so tired of listening to him that she suggested they trade jobs. The husband quickly agreed, saying it was the only good idea she had ever had.

The next morning the wife went out to the field to do the mowing. She worked very hard outside all morning, while the husband stayed at home to take care of the baby. By noon, the wife was hungry and was listening for the lunch bell.

Meanwhile, the husband was trying his best to bathe the baby. The water in the baby's bathtub ended up on the floor, and the husband used all the towels in the house to soak it up. He had no towels left to dry the baby, so he used diapers. He finally used the last diaper to put on the baby, but he couldn't get it to stay on. The last diaper ended up on the baby's head.

1. Who are the characters in the story?

   _____

2. What is the setting?

   _____

3. What is the general plot?

_____

4. What happens in the beginning?

_____

5. What happens in the end?

_____

_____

Using Details and Dialogue to Create Good Characters

> **GOOD WRITERS**
> - tell what the character says
> - tell what other characters say about the character
> - provide details of action

Read the story. How does the writer give information about Sal? Write each example below.

Aunt Susie looked all around for her nephew Sal. "Where has that boy gone?" she wondered. "He's always into some mischief, but I know he's a good boy deep down." Just then, she heard a sound from the other room. Sal ran out, wearing his bathing suit.

"Now, Sal," said Aunt Susie, "slow down. Where are you going in such a hurry? You know you have some chores to do. This Saturday will be different from last Saturday. You'll finish your work before you play."

"Oh, Aunt Susie," said Sal, looking at the floor. "You know I'll be sure to do it later. The sun is nice and hot now. This is the best time of day for a swim. Besides, all my friends are already at the lake."

After his swim, Sal fell asleep. When he woke up, he had forgotten his promise.

1. What the character says:

    a. _____

    b. _____

2. Details of action:

    a. _____

    b. _____

3. What other characters say about the character:

    a. _____

    b. _____

Expanding Sentences

> **GOOD WRITERS**
> - use lots of details to make their writing interesting
> - expand their sentences by adding prepositional phrases

Expand each sentence by adding at least one prepositional phrase. Begin your phrases with prepositions such as *above, after, before, between, during, for, from, in, on, of, over, through, under, up,* and *without.*

1. Gabrielle had a bad toothache.

    _____

2. Her mother drove her.

    _____

3. Gabrielle did not have to wait.

    _____

4. The dentist's assistant had her sit.

    _____

5. The assistant took an X-ray.

    _____

6. The dentist looked at the X-ray.

    _____

Proofreading a Tall Tale

Proofread the beginning of the tall tale, paying special attention to paragraph indents. Use the Proofreading Marks to correct at least seven errors.

PROOFREADING MARKS

Mark	Meaning
⬭	spell correctly
⊙	add period
?	add question mark
≡	capitalize
ℓ	take out
∧	add
/	make lowercase
∿	switch
⋏	add comma
ᵛ ᵛ	add quotation marks
¶	indent paragraph

One of Paul Bunyan's helpers stared up at Paul and shook his head. "How will we ever get all this hot food two the tables?" he asked. The dining hall is so big that the food gets cold before we can serve it"

"Why, that's easy," answered Paul

"We'll just put roller skates on the ponies. Then the ponies can skate in quickly and deliver the food before it gets cold."

"What a great idea!" cried Paul Bunyan's helpers.

The next night, however, Paul and his helpers discovered that his idea wasn't great after all. The ponies weren't good roller-skaters. They spilled most of the food, and then they stopped to eat the spilled food.

"What a mess!" exclaimed Paul.

"What will we do?" asked his helpers.

Well, said Paul, "first, we'll have to clean up the dining hall. Then, I think we should build tracks between the rose of tables. We can use freight trains to deliver the food."

Write about Flying

Imagine that you can fly like a bird. With a friend or two, plan and write a humorous story about your imaginary flight. Include details and dialogue in your story.

(Continue on your own paper.)

Write an Amazing Explanation

Many tall tales explain how something in nature was created or formed. One amazing explanation shown below is from a Paul Bunyan tale. Choose one of the natural events and write an amazing explanation for it.

Natural Event	Amazing Explanation
an earthquake	Each time Paul Bunyan's cook dropped one of his biscuits, an earthquake occurred.
a volcanic eruption	_____
	_____
	_____
a hurricane	_____
	_____
	_____
Niagara Falls	_____
	_____
	_____

Write about People

With a friend, complete each of the following sentences. Use exaggeration to describe what each character does. The first one is done as an example. Then, decide which sentence you like best and develop it into a tall tale.

I know a <u>sailor</u> from <u>Monterey</u> who is so big that <u>he can wade across Monterey Bay</u>.

I know _____ from _____

who is so strong that _____.

I know _____ from _____

who is so tall that _____.

A TALL TALE

_____

_____

_____

_____

_____

_____

_____

_____

_____

A Practice Fantasy Story

SEND THE CLONE

Tanisha stood with her hands on her hips. "How can I help you, Jemma, if you won't sit still?" Jemma sat on the edge of her bed. Her left leg stuck straight out. The lower half was wrapped in a thin sheet of metal. Tanisha tried to attach the top half.

"Sorry, Tanisha, I just hate wearing this thing. It makes my leg so stiff I can't move," answered Jemma.

"I think that's the point," Tanisha said as she stopped to look at Jemma. She shook her head. "It could have been a lot worse, you know. How many times has Coach warned you about playing in the anti-gravity chamber when she's not there?"

"Yeah, yeah, Tanisha. Gosh, you're as bad as my parents. I've already listened to all of their warnings. I think they're glad to see me wearing this. It means there's no chance I'll go in the chamber for a while."

"It also means you won't be able to practice for the physical fitness test," said Tanisha. "And you know what that means, don't you?" Tanisha stopped fastening the cast to look at Jemma again. Every year the fifth-grade class took a trip together. This year they were going to Mars.

"I know, I know. You have to be healthy to go. That means no broken bones. If I don't get out of this cast, I can't get in shape for the trip. And if I don't get in shape enough to pass the fitness test, then I don't get to go on the class trip. I thought of that, too. We practice the orbital launch test this week. How will I ever pass that if I don't practice first?" Jemma looked at Tanisha as though she had an answer. Actually, she did have an answer, but it wasn't the one Jemma wanted.

"You should have thought about that sooner. Now the only thing you can do is send your clone. Let her practice. Then you can download at night."

Jemma looked disappointed. "Tanisha, we both know what happens in a reverse download test. Do you remember what happened when I had to go to the dentist and sent my clone to take my French test?"

Tanisha laughed and slapped her hand on Jemma's cast. Jemma jumped. "That was a scream," Tanisha said, still laughing. "Who knew that French verbs could do that to electrical wiring? Madame Dejas had to hose her down to put out the fire. How many days did you stay after school that time?"

"Thanks for the reminder. Now get serious, Tanisha. What am I going to do?"

"I mean it," Tanisha said softly as she wiped the tears from her laughing eyes. "Send your clone. It's the only thing you can do. Then download after class each day. It's risky, but what choice do you have? If she crashes, you can re-program her."

"Right, but then I lose everything. It takes days of downloading to restore my clone's memory. I'm already twelve, you know. I've stored twelve years of information in my brain."

"Well, it's up to you. But the way I see it, you don't have a choice. It's either send the clone or miss the class trip," said Tanisha.

"Tanisha, if I miss the trip, you wouldn't go without me, would you?" Jemma asked. Jemma's eyes were wide. Surely, her friend wouldn't go without her. Jemma didn't have to wait long for an answer.

"Are you kidding? Do you know how long I've waited for fifth grade just so I could go on this trip?"

Once again, Jemma looked disappointed. It looked as if she'd end up spending spring break at home with her clone. Tanisha saw the sad look on Jemma's face. "Don't give up, Jemma. Let's try my plan. If it doesn't work, well, I'll send you a postcard."

Jemma looked disgusted. "Some friend you are. Help me get her ready, would you?"

Tanisha turned on the clone to let her warm up. "She seems to be working fine this morning," she said. "The lights are on. The battery check is fine. This could work, you know," she said to Jemma. "Hey, I have another idea."

"If it's better than your first idea, tell me," said Jemma. For a moment, Jemma was hopeful.

"Well, if your clone passes the fitness test, she can go on the trip instead. Then you can download the entire experience." Tanisha started laughing again.

"Very funny," Jemma said as she tried not to laugh. She stood awkwardly and smoothed her school uniform. "Let's get going. My clone and I have to be at the launch pad when first period starts."

Respond to the Practice Paper

Write your answers to the following questions or directions.

1. A fantasy is a kind of imaginative story. It takes the reader into a world that isn't real. Explain why this story is an example of a fantasy.

   _____

   _____

2. What is the setting for this story?

   _____

   _____

3. What is the main character's problem in this story?

   _____

   _____

4. How is the main character's problem solved?

   _____

   _____

5. Write a paragraph to summarize the story. Use these questions to help you write your summary:
   • What is the story about?
   • What happens first? Second? Third?
   • How does the story end?

   _____

   _____

   _____

   _____

   _____

Analyze the Practice Paper

Read "Send the Clone" again. As you read, think about how the writer wrote the story. Answer the following questions or directions.

1. What did the writer do to make this story seem believable?

_____

_____

_____

2. What did the writer do to make this story seem unbelievable?

_____

_____

_____

3. Why do you think the writer uses mostly dialogue, or conversation, to tell this story?

_____

_____

_____

4. What mood, or feeling, does the writer create in this story? Give an example to support your answer.

_____

_____

_____

Writing Assignment

Writing stories lets us use our imaginations. Use your imagination to write a fantasy story. Think about the answers to the questions below. Use this writing plan to help you write a first draft on the next page.

Where will your story take place?

▼

What characters will you use?

▼

How will you make the story believable?

▼

How will you make the story unbelievable?

▼

What problem will the characters have? How will they solve it? List and number the steps in the story.

First Draft

Use your writing plan as a guide for writing your first draft of a fantasy. Include a catchy title.

_____

(Continue on your own paper.)

Revise the Draft

Use the chart below to help you revise your draft. Check YES or NO to answer each question in the chart. If you answer NO, make notes to remind yourself how you can revise, or change, your writing to improve it.

Question	YES ✔	NO ✔	If the answer is NO, what will you do to improve your writing?
Does your story happen in a world that isn't real?			
Is your story believable?			
Do you use an interesting plot to keep the reader's attention?			
Are your characters interesting?			
Do your characters have a problem?			
Do your characters solve their problem?			
Do you describe what happens in order?			
Is the story imaginative?			
Have you corrected mistakes in spelling, grammar, and punctuation?			

Use the notes in your chart and your writing plan to revise your draft.

Writing Report Card

Read your revised draft again or ask someone else to read it. Have the person who reads your paper complete the following Report Card. Revise your paper until you have no less than a Very Good Score for each item.

Title of paper: _____

Purpose of paper: _____*This story is a fantasy.*_____

Person who scores the paper: _____

Score	Writing Goals
	Does the story happen in a world that isn't real?
	Is the story believable?
	Does the story have an interesting setting?
	Are the characters interesting?
	Do the characters have a problem they must solve?
	Do the characters solve their problem?
	Do things happen in the story in order?
	Does the story keep your interest?
	Is the story imaginative?
	Are the story's grammar, spelling, and punctuation correct?

☺ Excellent Score   ☆ Very Good Score   + Good Score
✔ Acceptable Score   − Needs Improvement

UNIT 4: Comparative Writing

HOW MUCH DO YOU KNOW?

Read the paragraph of comparison and contrast. Answer the questions that follow.

    The first time LeAnn went to visit her friend Vanessa, she noticed how much Vanessa's furniture was like her own. The dresser in Vanessa's room was made of pine, just like LeAnn's dresser. Vanessa's aunt had chosen the dresser, just as LeAnn's aunt had chosen LeAnn's. LeAnn also noticed the desk in Vanessa's room. Vanessa said that it had been her grandfather's desk. LeAnn remembered that the desk in her own room had once belonged to her grandmother.

    As LeAnn looked at Vanessa's desk, she pictured her own desk in her mind. LeAnn's desk was a graceful old rolltop. Vanessa's desk, on the other hand, was dark and heavy with a huge flat surface. LeAnn realized that she would rather have a desk like Vanessa's. The flat top was much better for holding a computer screen and keyboard. As soon as LeAnn got a computer, she decided, she would put her grandmother's desk into her brother's room.

1. What is the topic sentence of the first paragraph?

   _____

   _____

2. List two ways in which the dressers are alike.

   _____

   _____

3. List one way in which the desks are different.

   _____

   _____

Analyzing Paragraphs of Comparison and Contrast

> A paragraph of comparison
> compares things (shows their similarities).
>
> A paragraph of comparison
> contrasts things (shows their differences).

Read the paragraph of comparison and contrast. Answer the questions that follow.

The Tasady tribe and the Ik tribe are two examples of people still living in the Stone Age. Neither tribe knew anything about the outside world until recently. The Tasady live in the mountain caves of the Philippine rain forests. The Ik live in the mountains of Uganda, and they build grass huts for shelter. There is plenty of food in the Philippine rain forests, so the Tasady are comfortable and fairly well off. The Ik, however, face a constant lack of food. Ik usually eat any food they find right away. The Tasady have a good chance of surviving; the Ik, on the other hand, face an uncertain future.

1. What two things are being compared?

   _____

2. What are three things that are alike in each?

   _____

   _____

3. What are three things that are different?

   _____

   _____

4. Does the last sentence of the paragraph compare or contrast the survival of the tribes?

   _____

Evaluating to Compare and Contrast

> **BEFORE COMPARING OR CONTRASTING TWO THINGS, GOOD WRITERS**
>
> - observe how they are alike and how they are different
> - evaluate them in terms of some of their important qualities

Think about each pair of things. List two ways in which the things are alike and two ways in which they are different.

LIKENESSES	DIFFERENCES

1. a cloud and a kite

   a. _____   a. _____

   b. _____   b. _____

2. a book and a movie

   a. _____   a. _____

   b. _____   b. _____

3. rain and snow

   a. _____   a. _____

   b. _____   b. _____

4. morning and evening

   a. _____   a. _____

   b. _____   b. _____

5. basketball and baseball

   a. _____   a. _____

   b. _____   b. _____

6. broccoli and cauliflower

   a. _____   a. _____

   b. _____   b. _____

Using Formal and Informal Language

GOOD WRITERS CHANGE THEIR WRITING TO USE

- formal language to communicate in an official way
- informal language to communicate in a casual way

Read each sentence. Write *formal* or *informal* to describe the tone of each sentence.

1. At an early age Kit Carson learned how to work with leather. _____

2. "This notion of working in a leather shop is for the birds," young Kit said to himself. _____

3. "I'm getting out of here the first chance I get!" he vowed.
_____

4. Kit Carson's real ambition was to be a mountain man.
_____

5. He wanted to choose his own company and go where he pleased.
_____

6. "I figure if we march west from here, we'll soon hit California," said one of the men. _____

7. The mountain men started their westward push.
_____

8. Kit Carson was the youngest man in the group.
_____

9. They could not carry much water with them.
_____

10. "It's going to be a long dry spell," thought Kit.
_____

11. They continued to look for signs of water. _____

Making Compound Sentences

Good writers show their audience the connection between ideas by joining two related sentences with a conjunction and a comma.

Use a comma and the word *and* to join each pair of sentences. Write the new sentence.

1. The Pygmies live in the forest in Africa. They hunt there.

   _____

   _____

2. Pygmy men are about four and a half feet tall. The women are even smaller.

   _____

   _____

3. They are the smallest people in the world. Their small size helps them to hide.

   _____

   _____

4. Children the same age call boys "brother." They call girls "sister."

   _____

   _____

5. Pygmies look at a broken branch. They can tell which animal has been there.

   _____

   _____

6. Pygmies know a lot about plants. They can tell which are good to eat.

   _____

   _____

Proofreading Paragraphs that Compare and Contrast

> ## PROOFREADING HINT
>
> To be a good proofreader, look for one type of error at a time. For example, proofread once for capitalization errors, once for punctuation errors, and once for spelling errors.

PROOFREADING MARKS

⬭	spell correctly
⊙	add period
?	add question mark
≡	capitalize
ℛ	take out
∧	add
/	make lowercase
∿	switch
⋏	add comma
⌄ ⌄	add quotation marks
¶	indent paragraph

Proofread the paragraphs that compare and contrast, paying special attention to apostrophes in possessive nouns. Use the Proofreading Marks to correct at least seven errors.

The first time Lee went visit his friend Vladimir, he noticed how much Vlad's furniture was like his own. He saw that the desk in Vlads room was made of pine, just like Lees desk. Vlad's mom had chosen the desk, just as lee's mom had chosen Lee's. Lee also noticed the bed in Vlads room. Vlad explained that it had been his grandfathers bed.

Lee remembered that the bed in his own room had once belonged to his

dad's dad

As Lee looked at Vlads bed, he pictured his own bed in his mind. Lee's

bed was made of brass and steel. It had been made in England more then

100 years ago. Vlad's desk, on the other hand, was dark wood with a tall

hedboard It had been made in Russia about 60 years ago. Lee realized

that he would rather have a bed like Vlads. The headboard was good for

holding books.

Make Comparisons

Work with two friends. Discuss how each of you is similar to and different from the others. Together, write a paragraph comparing and contrasting your similarities and differences. Revise and proofread your work.

_____

_____

_____

_____

_____

_____

_____

_____

_____

_____

_____

_____

_____

_____

_____

_____

Write a Diary Entry

Imagine that you must leave your country to go to another. Plan and write a diary entry comparing and contrasting your present country with the new country. Revise and proofread your work.

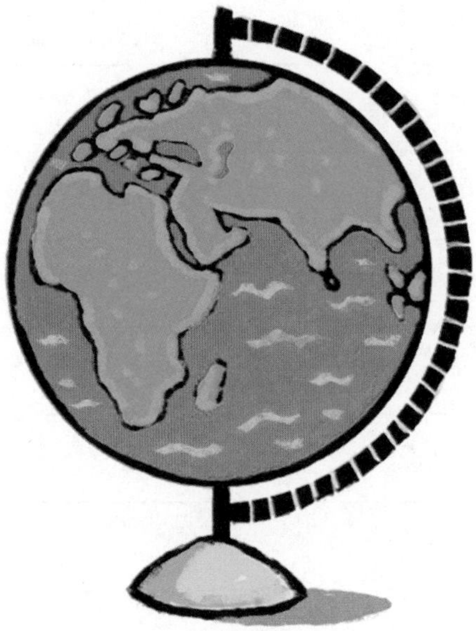

_____

_____

_____

_____

_____

_____

_____

_____

_____

_____

_____

_____

_____

_____

_____

_____

Compare Wildlife

Make a list of wildlife for each category below. Research two animals from one category. Write a paragraph of comparison and contrast using the information you learned.

LAND ANIMALS	BIRDS	INSECTS
_____	_____	_____
_____	_____	_____
_____	_____	_____
_____	_____	_____

_____

_____

_____

_____

_____

_____

_____

A Practice Compare-and-Contrast Paper

THE AMERICAN BLACK BEAR AND THE POLAR BEAR

The most famous bear in the world may be the teddy bear. Almost 100 years ago, President Theodore, or Teddy, Roosevelt was hunting bears in the Mississippi woods. The only bear he found was old, and the president wouldn't shoot it. A newspaper reporter drew a cartoon showing this event. Many people saw it. One of these people was Morris Michtom. He was a shopkeeper whose wife made stuffed bears. Morris got permission from the president to call the stuffed bears "teddy bears." A tradition was born.

The next best-known North American bear is the American black bear. But perhaps the most popular bear at zoos is the polar bear. Both bears are alike in some ways, and different, too. Let's look at them more closely.

American black bears live in most states and throughout Canada. They live in forests that have lots of undergrowth, or low-lying plants. Polar bears live along the northern coasts of Canada, Greenland, and Siberia. They are also on islands in the Arctic Ocean. Polar bears like plenty of ice.

An adult male black bear stands between 3 and 4 feet tall. It weighs between 135 and 350 pounds. An adult male polar bear stands 8 to 11 feet tall. That's probably higher than the ceiling in your classroom. Some male polar bears weigh more than 1,000 pounds. A polar bear is a real heavyweight.

You won't be surprised to learn that many black bears have black fur coats. However, they can be other colors, too. They can be chocolate brown, cinnamon, blond, and silver gray.

Polar bears have thick fur that looks white or yellow, but it isn't. Each hair is a clear, hollow tube. The tube lets the sun's rays reach the bear's skin. The sunlight and seal oil can make the fur look yellow.

Both black bears and polar bears have a good sense of smell. As many visitors to U.S. national parks can tell you, black bears are good at finding food. They can find food in any campsite, even when the food is hidden. They also learn to recognize the containers food comes in. That's why they open car doors, ice chests, and coolers.

Polar bears can smell food that is as far as 10 miles away. They can also sniff out seal dens that are covered by thick layers of snow and ice.

Black bears and polar bears use their sense of smell to find different things to eat. Black bears like berries, nuts, grass, and other plants. They may also eat small animals and fish. Sometimes they'll eat dead animals left by other animals, such as cougars. In the fall, black bears eat a lot. They may gain as many as 30 pounds each week. The extra pounds come from fat stored in their bodies. The bears use this fat for energy while they hibernate, or nap, through the winter.

Polar bears are meat-eaters. They feed mainly on small seals called ringed seals. They eat the seal's skin and fat, and leave the meat for other animals. Polar bears need to eat at least 1 pound of fat each day for energy. Sometimes polar bears eat walruses or the remains of dead animals, such as whales. Their sense of smell helps them find remains that are many miles away.

Male and female black bears hibernate in the winter. They spend 5 to 7 months napping. Only pregnant female polar bears hibernate. The other females and males are active all year, even during the winter.

Black bears are usually born in January or February. Twins are common, and the cubs are born blind and small. Each cub weighs less than 1 pound, but it grows fast. Female polar bears usually have twin cubs, too. They are often born in December or January. Polar bear cubs are also born blind and small. Each cub weighs about $1\frac{1}{2}$ pounds. Like black bear cubs, polar bear cubs grow fast.

Today there are far fewer black bears than there were when colonists came to America. Colonists in the East hunted the bears almost to extinction. That means the bears almost disappeared entirely. In the last 30 years, scientists have learned much more about black bears. The number of black bears is growing again, but the bears are still in danger.

Polar bears are also in danger of disappearing. According to scientists, there are about 28,000 polar bears in the world. To protect them, the United States works with Canada and other countries in the world.

American black bears and polar bears are alike in many ways. They are large, smart animals with sharp senses. They have small babies that grow fast. They are also wonderful models for the stuffed bears we love so much.

Respond to the Practice Paper

Summarize the paper by making a chart. Use the chart below to list ways American black bears and polar bears are alike and different.

AN ALIKE AND DIFFERENT CHART FOR AMERICAN BLACK BEARS AND POLAR BEARS

How American Black Bears and Polar Bears Are Alike	How American Black Bears and Polar Bears Are Different

Analyze the Practice Paper

Read "The American Black Bear and the Polar Bear" again. As you read, think about how the writer achieved his or her purpose for writing. Write your answers to the following questions.

1. Why do you think the writer begins this paper by talking about teddy bears?

   _____

   _____

2. How did the writer relate teddy bears to the real bears described in this paper?

   _____

   _____

3. What main idea is discussed in the fifth and sixth paragraphs?

   _____

   _____

4. Read the ninth paragraph again. How does the writer let you know what this paragraph and the tenth paragraph will be about?

   _____

   _____

5. The writer uses the last paragraph to summarize the main ideas in the paper. What else does the writer do in the last paragraph?

   _____

   _____

   _____

   _____

Writing Assignment

Think about two animals you would like to write about. Write about how they are alike and how they are different. Use this writing plan to help you write a first draft on page 600.

Choose two animals you want to write about. Call them A and B.

A = _____   B = _____

Use reference materials or the Internet to learn more about A and B. Learn about these main ideas: 1. how the animals look, 2. where the animals live, and 3. what the animals eat. For each main idea, list what is true only about A in the A circle. List what is true only about B in the B circle. List what is true about both A and B where the two circles overlap. If you have more than three main ideas, draw and label more diagrams on a separate sheet of paper.

MAIN IDEA:
How the animals look

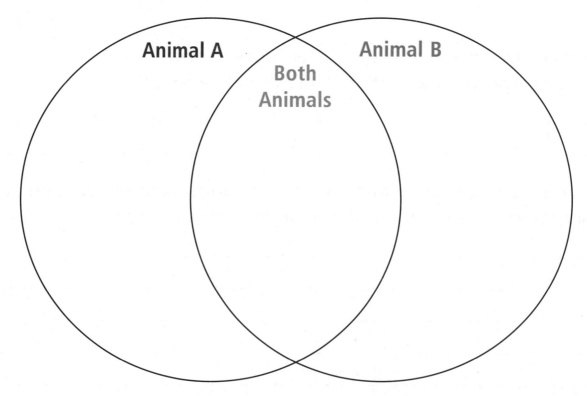

MAIN IDEA:
Where the animals live

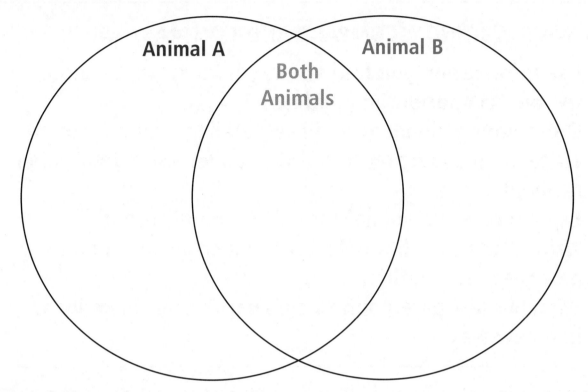

Animal A

Both Animals

Animal B

MAIN IDEA:
What the animals eat

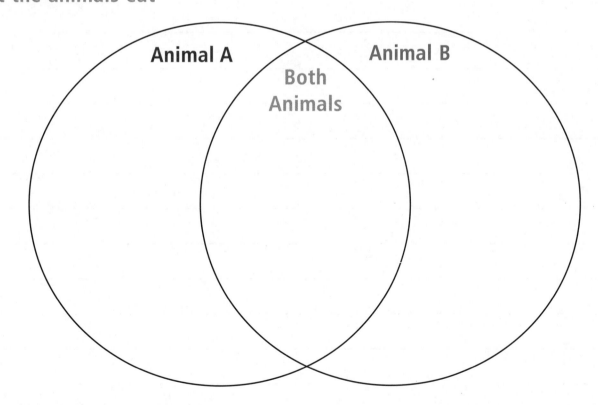

Animal A

Both Animals

Animal B

First Draft

TIPS FOR WRITING A COMPARE-AND-CONTRAST PAPER:

- Use information you find about your animals to choose the most important main ideas.
- Order your main ideas and use details to support them.
- Write an introduction to tell the reader what your paper is about.
- Explain how the animals are alike and different.
- Write sentences that help your reader move from one paragraph to another.
- Use your last paragraph to summarize your main ideas in a new way.

Use your writing plan as a guide for writing your first draft of a compare-and-contrast paper. Include a catchy title.

____

____

____

____

____

____

____

____

____

____

____

(Continue on your own paper.)

Revise the Draft

Use the chart below to help you revise your draft. Check YES or NO to answer each question in the chart. If you answer NO, make notes to remind yourself how you can revise, or change, your writing to improve it.

Question	YES ✔	NO ✔	If the answer is NO, what will you do to improve your writing?
Do you introduce the animals you will write about in your first paragraph?			
Does your paper tell how the two animals are alike?			
Does your paper tell how the two animals are different?			
Do you have more than one main idea?			
Do you organize the main ideas into paragraphs?			
Do you use details to support each main idea?			
Do you use the last paragraph to summarize the main ideas of your paper in a new way?			
Do you tie the first and last paragraphs together?			
Have you corrected mistakes in spelling, grammar, and punctuation?			

Use the notes in your chart and your writing plan to revise your draft.

Writing Report Card

Read your revised draft again or ask someone else to read it. Have the person who reads your paper complete the following Report Card. Revise your paper until you have no less than a Very Good Score for each item.

Title of paper: _____

Purpose of paper: ___*This paper tells how two animals are*___

___*alike and different.*___

Person who scores the paper: _____

Score	Writing Goals
	Does the first paragraph tell what the paper is about?
	Does the paper tell how two animals are alike?
	Does the paper tell how two animals are different?
	Is there more than one main idea?
	Are the main ideas organized into paragraphs?
	Are there enough details to support each main idea?
	Are the paragraphs in an order that makes sense?
	Does the last paragraph summarize what the paper is about?
	Are the paper's grammar, spelling, and punctuation correct?

☺ Excellent Score ☆ Very Good Score + Good Score
✔ Acceptable Score — Needs Improvement

UNIT 5: Descriptive Writing

HOW MUCH DO YOU KNOW?

Read the paragraph. Answer the questions that follow.

A box turtle is a reptile that lives in woods and fields. The box turtle has a hinged lower shell. It can pull its legs, head, and tail inside its shell and get "boxed in." Box turtles eat earthworms, insects, berries, and green leafy vegetables. There are many kinds of turtles on land and in the water. Turtles belong to the same family as lizards, snakes, alligators, and crocodiles.

1. What is being described?

   _____

   _____

2. What are three details?

   a. _____

   _____

   b. _____

   _____

   c. _____

   _____

Read each sentence. On the line, write each underlined word and tell the sense or senses to which it most appeals as it is used in the sentence.

3. I picked up the <u>smooth</u>, <u>hard</u> turtle shell.

   _____

4. There was a <u>rustle</u> of leaves before a <u>loud</u> splash, so I knew the turtle had gone into the lake.

   _____

Analyzing a Descriptive Paragraph

> **A DESCRIPTIVE PARAGRAPH**
> - describes someone or something
> - has a topic sentence that tells what is being described
> - gives sensory details that offer specific information about the subject

Read each paragraph. Answer the questions that follow. You need not write the whole sentence when listing the details.

Thanksgiving has to be my favorite holiday. The delicious aromas of turkey roasting and pumpkin pies baking fill the house. The lovely autumn colors of orange, gold, red, and brown can be seen in the special flower arrangements for the table. The sound of children laughing as they play games outside mixes with the music being played inside. The sights, smells, and sounds are very important to me.

1. What is being described? _____

2. What is the topic sentence? _____

3. What are three details?

   a. _____

   b. _____

   c. _____

Did you ever walk into the kitchen of a good cook just before a special feast? "Here, sample this. What do you think?" the cook might say as you walk in. Then you are treated to a sweet taste of a dessert sauce, a tasty sample of rich gravy, or a yummy mouthful of fresh beets just steamed. Maybe you'll get to taste some fresh, warm bread. You might be full before dinner is even ready!

4. What is being described?

5. What is the topic sentence?

Observing Details in Spatial Order

A. Read each description. Write *left to right, back to front*, or *top to bottom* to tell how the writer organized the details.

1. The judges watched as the runners warmed up for the race. Over on the left, Bobby Malone from Bingham Elementary was touching his toes. Next to him, Mario Gilbert from Stratford Grade School was stretching. On the right, Stuart Meyers from the Drayer School for the Hearing Impaired was bending and stretching.

   _____

2. Of the three runners, Stu Meyers had the best chance of winning. From the short-cropped hair on his head to his slim torso and long legs, he seemed to be in the best physical shape.

   _____

B. Write short descriptions of the item below. Use each of the methods for organizing details in space order.

3. YOUR CLASSROOM

   left to right: _____

   _____

4. back to front: _____

   _____

5. top to bottom: _____

   _____

Using Sensory Images

Good writers use sensory words that appeal to some or all of the five senses.

Read each sentence. On the line, write each underlined word and tell the sense or senses to which it most appeals as it is used in the sentence.

1. The young swimmer was wearing a <u>blue</u> <u>suit</u>.

_____

2. She dove cleanly into the <u>cool</u> <u>water</u>.

_____

3. The judges wrote the scores in <u>large</u> <u>black</u> letters.

_____

4. The audience let out a <u>loud</u> cheer.

_____

5. She had been practicing so long, her <u>hair</u> had the odor of <u>chlorine</u>.

_____

6. One tile on her practice pool was <u>rough</u> and <u>jagged</u>.

_____

7. The rough edge had cut her <u>foot</u>, and she had <u>yelled</u>, "Ouch!"

_____

8. Her coach had put a <u>soft</u> <u>bandage</u> on it, and it was fine now.

_____

9. The sweatshirt she put on was <u>warm</u> and <u>soft</u>.

_____

10. After practice, she had had a <u>delicious</u> <u>sandwich</u>.

_____

Combining Subjects and Predicates

GOOD WRITERS

- write concisely, avoiding unnecessary repetition
- combine subjects and predicates to make their writing smoother and more direct

Rewrite each of the following sentence pairs. Combine subjects and predicates to make sentences that are more concise.

1. Young Soren rolled in the grass under a tree. Young Soren watched the sailboats.

   _____

   _____

2. Some ships were going to Baltimore. Some ships were sailing out to sea.

   _____

   _____

3. Young Soren did not know what a geography book was. Young Soren did not know what an arithmetic book was.

   _____

   _____

4. He had never been to school. He had never learned how to read.

   _____

   _____

5. The hill was a good place to stand. The hill was a good place to watch the boats.

   _____

   _____

6. Soren visited his grandmother in the summer. Soren visited his uncle in the winter.

   _____

   _____

Proofreading a Descriptive Paragraph

Proofread the descriptive paragraphs, paying special attention to capital letters in proper nouns. Use the Proofreading Marks to correct at least seven errors.

PROOFREADING MARKS	
⬭	spell correctly
⊙	add period
?	add question mark
≡	capitalize
℘	take out
∧	add
/	make lowercase
∽	switch
∧	add comma
⌄ ⌄	add quotation marks
¶	indent paragraph

Aunt jane said she would have a

surprise for us last saturday, but she refused

to give us any hints. Just after breakfast, we

heard a low humming sound in our driveway.

It was followed by an unusual, squeaky car

horn. A car! A car!" my Sister shouted.

"Aunt Jane's surprise is a Car!"

We all rushed out to see Aunt Jane's new car, and what a surprise it

was! Her "new" car was more than 50 years old. It was a beautiful 1938

whippet. Its bright green surface shimmered in the sunlight. Its long hood stretched forward elegantly, and its whitewall tires gleamed on our dusty driveway

"Oh, jane," said mom. "What a great car! May we get in?"

"Of course," laughed Aunt Jane, and she clicked the front door open for us. The inside of the car was dark and cool and filled with the soft smell of old lether.

"Let's go for a drive," suggested dad. "Who wants to ride out to Lake barton?"

Describe an Unusual Animal

Plan and write a description of an unusual animal. Draw a picture to go with your description. Revise and proofread your work.

Make a Sense Poster

Look at the boxes below labeled *smell*, *sight*, and *hearing*. Using old magazines, cut out one picture that appeals to each sense. Paste each picture in a section and write three sentences to describe the item as related to that sense.

SMELL

SIGHT

HEARING

Describe the Same Scene in Different Ways

With a friend, draft a description of an athletic event from two different points of view: from the field or court and from the spectator stands. Compare the descriptions.

From the field or court

_____

_____

_____

_____

_____

_____

_____

From the spectator stands

_____

_____

_____

_____

_____

_____

_____

Describe a Natural Event

Choose a common natural event, such as a sunset, a rainstorm, or the growth of a tree. Write a description of that natural event. Remember to use sensory details.

_____

_____

_____

_____

_____

_____

_____

_____

_____

_____

_____

_____

_____

_____

A Practice Descriptive Story

THE TRAVELING GONZALEZ FAMILY

The Gonzalez family loved to travel. Every year they sat down and decided where they wanted to go on their vacation. Usually, they agreed on one place. But this year everyone had a different idea.

"I want to go to California and see the Pacific Ocean," Miguel said.

"Who cares what you want?" said Angela. "You're only eight. I'm eleven and I get to decide. I want to see the White House."

"How about me?" said Mrs. Gonzalez. "I want to go to Arizona and see a rodeo."

"That sounds interesting," said Mr. Gonzalez, "but I would rather go to Yellowstone National Park. Old Faithful, the geyser, is there."

"We have a problem," everyone said. They all looked at each other. "What shall we do?" asked Miguel.

"I have an idea," said Mrs. Gonzalez. "I think I know how we can see all those places."

"Impossible," everyone said. But they agreed to give Mrs. Gonzalez a chance.

The next day they found themselves in front of a very large building. "Now hang onto each other and follow the person in front of you," said Mrs. Gonzalez. "And," she added, "keep your eyes closed until I say open."

The family walked and walked. Finally, Mrs. Gonzalez said, "Open your eyes." There in front of them was the beautiful Pacific Ocean. Its deep, blue-green water looked as smooth as silk. In the distance, two fishers stood in a small fishing boat. They were pulling in a net filled with slick, squirming fish. A flock of gulls soared above the boat. Their feathers reflected the setting sun, making them shine with red and gold light. They swooped and dived toward the boat, waiting for the fishers to throw unwanted fish back into the water.

"This is the most beautiful ocean in the world," Miguel said. Everyone agreed.

"Now close your eyes again," Mrs. Gonzalez said. "We're off to the rodeo."

When everyone opened their eyes, the first thing the family saw was a cowgirl. She and her horse were racing around huge, wooden barrels. The girl's hat sat over her eyes to shade them from the sun. One of her hands gripped the front of the saddle. The other hand waved high in the air. Her horse leaned from side to side. It moved quickly around the first of three barrels, raising a cloud of dirt and pebbles. Behind the horse and rider, the crowd was on its feet, cheering her on. "The rider who races around the three barrels the fastest wins," Mrs. Gonzalez explained.

"I never saw anything so exciting," said Angela. "This is fun!"

"When are we going to Yellowstone Park?" asked Mr. Gonzalez.

"That's our next stop," said Mrs. Gonzalez. "Close your eyes."

When Mrs. Gonzalez said open, everyone whispered, "Ooooh." There in front of them was Yellowstone Canyon. Great splashes of yellow, red, white, orange, and brown peeked through the green of the forest.

"Where's Old Faithful Geyser?" Angela asked.

"Over here," said Mr. Gonzalez. Mr. Gonzalez pointed to the

right. Everyone's eyes turned with his finger. There was Old Faithful Geyser sending a silvery shower of steaming water high into the air. "That spout is as high as a fifteen-story building," Mr. Gonzalez said.

"Speaking of big buildings," Angela said. "When are we going to Washington, D.C.?"

"Next stop, the capital," said Mrs. Gonzalez. Soon the family was in the middle of gardens, parks, and monuments. In the distance, the White House shimmered in the light. A huge flag flapped quietly in a gentle breeze. There were people everywhere. Angela could tell they were on vacation, too. They carried cameras and backpacks. Some had brought picnics and sat in the parks. Someone nearby munched a delicious-looking sandwich.

"I can't go any farther. I'm hungry," Miguel said.

"Well, we can take care of that," said Mr. Gonzalez.

Later that evening, when they were finishing supper, Mrs. Gonzalez said, "Do you know where I took you today?"

"I know," said Miguel.

"I know," said Mr. Gonzalez.

"Me, too," said Angela. "It was my first trip to an art museum. I'm going to take vacations more often. The museum is free on Sunday afternoon. I thought I'd go again this weekend. Who wants to go with me?" Everyone raised a hand.

Respond to the Practice Paper

Write your answers to the following questions or directions.

1. What does the writer describe in this story?

_____

_____

2. What was the problem Mrs. Gonzalez had to solve?

_____

_____

3. Where did each person in the family want to go?

_____

_____

4. How did Mrs. Gonzalez solve her family's problem?

_____

_____

5. Write a paragraph to summarize the story. Use these questions to help you write your summary.

   - What are the main ideas of this story?
   - What happens first? Second? Third?
   - How does the story end?

_____

_____

_____

_____

_____

Analyze the Practice Paper

Read "The Traveling Gonzalez Family" again. As you read, think about how the writer achieved his or her purpose for writing. Write your answers to the following questions or directions.

1. What are some exciting action words the writer uses?

   _____

   _____

2. What are some descriptions the writer uses to help you imagine what the family is seeing?

   _____

   _____

3. In the tenth paragraph, the writer describes seagulls. The writer says, "Their feathers reflected the setting sun, making them shine with red and gold light." What is another way the writer could describe the gulls' feathers?

   _____

   _____

4. The writer has Mr. Gonzalez say that when Old Faithful spouts, it is as "high as a fifteen-story building." What is another way the writer could have described how high the geyser spouts?

   _____

   _____

5. This story has a surprise ending. What would another good surprise ending for this story be?

   _____

   _____

Writing Assignment

To describe something, a writer tells what he or she sees, hears, feels, tastes, and smells. The writer also compares things to other things, like a geyser to a silvery shower. Write about an experience that you would like to describe. Pay special attention to the words you choose. Use this writing plan to help you write a first draft on the next page.

What experience would you like to describe? Write it in the circle. Then write words and comparisons that describe the experience on the lines.

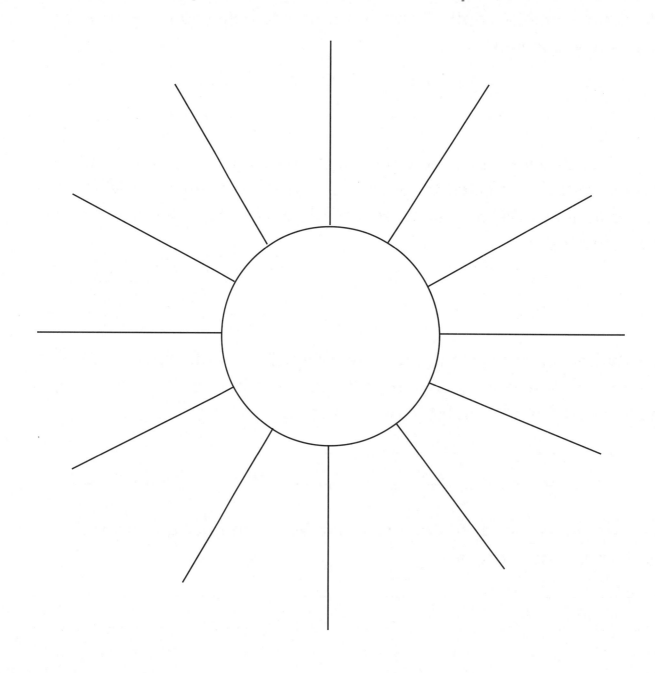

First Draft

TIPS FOR WRITING A DESCRIPTIVE STORY:

- Use your voice when you write. That means you should use your special way of expressing yourself.
- Help your reader see, smell, taste, feel, and hear what you are writing about.
- Use interesting words, similes, and metaphors to help describe your experience.

Use your writing plan as a guide as you write your first draft of a descriptive story. Include a catchy title.

(Continue on your own paper.)

Revise the Draft

Use the chart below to help you revise your draft. Check YES or NO to answer each question in the chart. If you answer NO, make notes to remind yourself how you can revise, or change, your writing to improve it.

Question	YES ✔	NO ✔	If the answer is NO, what will you do to improve your writing?
Does your story describe a specific experience?			
Do you use descriptive language, or words that will help your readers see, hear, taste, feel, and smell?			
Do you use action words to describe what happens?			
Do you compare things in your story to other things to help readers imagine what you are describing?			
Do you organize the main ideas of your story into paragraphs?			
Do you use important details to support each main idea?			
Does your story have a beginning, middle, and end?			
Have you corrected mistakes in spelling, grammar, and punctuation?			

Use the notes in your chart and your writing plan to revise your draft.

Writing Report Card

Read your revised draft again or ask someone else to read it. Have the person who reads your paper complete the following Report Card. Revise your paper until you have no less than a Very Good Score for each item.

Title of paper: _____

Purpose of paper: _____*This is a descriptive story.*_____

_____*It describes something that happened to me.*_____

Person who scores the paper: _____

Score	Writing Goals
	Does the story describe a specific experience?
	Does the story have a strong beginning, or introduction?
	Does the story describe what the writer sees, hears, tastes, smells, and feels?
	Does the story have action words?
	Does the writer compare things to other things to help you imagine what he or she is describing?
	Are main ideas in the story presented in the order that they happened?
	Are there enough details to support each main idea?
	Is there a strong ending, or conclusion?
	Are the story's grammar, spelling, and punctuation correct?

☺ Excellent Score ☆ Very Good Score + Good Score
✔ Acceptable Score − Needs Improvement

UNIT 6: Short Report

HOW MUCH DO YOU KNOW?

Read the short report. Answer the questions that follow.

Air, dust, and clouds make a blanket for the earth. This blanket helps protect us from the sun, but it is not enough. Ultraviolet rays, which are harmful and burning, still get through. Melanin is a substance in skin that gives some protection, but not everybody has enough of it. Melanin makes the skin darker, and it soaks up ultraviolet light.

If you tend to burn in the sun, you can make your own suntan lotion. This lotion can help protect light-skinned people from ultraviolet light. You mix oil and tea in a special way. Add the tea to the oil, then blend or beat until well mixed. Tea contains tannins that provide a sunscreen, and this mixture can block up to 50 percent of the sun's burning rays. This mixture will keep well in a bottle, but you must shake it well before using.

1. What would be a good title for this short report?

   _____

2. What is the topic of the first paragraph?

   _____

3. What is the topic of the second paragraph?

   _____

4. Which of these notes would be used to write this short report?

   _____

   a. Some of the best beaches in the United States are found in Florida.
   b. A lotion with an SPF of 30 provides 30 times your natural sunburn protection.
   c. Apply sunscreen generously and evenly to all exposed areas 30 minutes before sun exposure.
   d. Overexposure to the sun can cause premature skin aging, skin wrinkling, and skin cancer.

Analyzing a Short Report

Read the short report. Answer the questions that follow.

Many of our superstitions came to us from very ancient sources. The idea that one should knock on wood for good luck, for example, is a 4,000-year-old custom that began with some Indian tribes of North America. Noticing that the oak was struck often by lightning, the Indians thought that it must be the dwelling place of a sky god. They also thought that boasting of a future personal deed was bad luck and meant the thing would never happen. Knocking on an oak tree was a way of contacting the sky god and being forgiven for boasting.

Another interesting superstition is that it is bad luck to open an umbrella indoors. In eighteenth-century England, umbrellas had stiff springs and very strong metal spokes. Opening one indoors could indeed cause an accident. It could injure someone or break a fragile object. This superstition came about for practical reasons.

1. What would be a good title for this short report?

_____

2. What is the topic of the first paragraph?

_____

3. What is the topic of the second paragraph?

_____

4. What is one detail from the first paragraph?

_____

Summarizing to Organize Notes

> **IN ORGANIZING NOTES FOR A SHORT REPORT, GOOD WRITERS**
> - use note cards and keep them organized
> - summarize statements that have common ideas into one statement

A. Organize these note cards by writing the letter of the subject to which each one applies. Use these subjects: a. mountain heights; b. people who climbed mountains; c. special mountain-climbing words.

1. _____ Mount Roraima in South America is 9,092 feet high.

2. _____ Miriam O'Brien Underhill was the first woman to climb the Matterhorn, the Grepon, and other famous peaks without any help from men.

3. _____ Asia's Minya Konka is 24,900 feet high.

4. _____ Annapurna in Asia is 26,504 feet high.

5. _____ A *piton* is a metal spike used in mountain climbing to hold ropes in the side of the mountain.

6. _____ James W. Whitaker reached the top of Mt. Everest in 1963, along with Thomas F. Hombein, William F. Unsoeld, Luther G. Jerstad, and Barry C. Bishop.

7. _____ To *rappel* means to go down a cliff or a mountain, using a rope.

B. Read the group of note cards. Organize them into one note card.

8. a. In August 1980, Reinhold Messner climbed Mt. Everest alone.

   b. He was the first to climb Everest without any bottled oxygen.

   c. Messner did not even use a ladder or a rope.

   d. Messner carried no radio that might have kept him in touch with other people.

NEW CARD: _____

_____

Using Quotations

> Good writers use quotations from oral and written sources.

Each numbered sentence below the box is the topic sentence of a paragraph in a short report about whales. The box contains sentences with quotations that might be used in the report. After each topic sentence, write the letter of the quotation sentence that should be included in that paragraph.

---

a. "These magnificent creatures are even larger than the famous dinosaurs that died out so long ago," commented Dr. Romley.

b. Dr. Schultz said, "Although international laws ban hunting, some species of whales are still in danger of extinction."

c. Mr. Walters explained, "The whale's nostrils, located on top of its head, can be tightly closed so that no water leaks in."

d. "I am still thrilled every time I hear these whales 'talking' to each other," said Mr. Clark.

e. "Though we often think of whales as huge animals," said Ms. Kwong, "some species are barely four feet long."

f. "A baleen whale has no teeth. Instead, it has thin plates, called baleen, in its mouth," added Mr. Walters.

---

1. A whale's body is specially adapted for its underwater life. _____

2. Whales vary greatly in size. _____

3. The blue whale is the largest animal that ever lived. _____

4. Whales make special sounds to communicate with each other and to navigate through the water. _____

5. Some species of whales have become endangered animals. _____

6. Baleen whales form one of the two major groups of whales. _____

Giving Your Sentences More Variety

> Good writers avoid using the same sentence pattern all the time.

Rewrite each sentence. Move a word or phrase to the beginning of the sentence so that it no longer starts with the sentence subject. You may have to reword other parts of the sentence, too.

1. Did you read about the Boston Tea Party for homework?

   _____

2. Patriots threw tea into Boston Harbor on December 16, 1773.

   _____

3. The tide was going out when the dumping occurred.

   _____

4. The chests were lined with lead.

   _____

5. They looked beautiful, painted with Chinese lacquer.

   _____

6. These were all simple wooden boxes, except for about 50 of the crates.

   _____

7. These 50 were large boxes of an ornate Chinese design.

   _____

8. An explorer plans to look for the boxes in Boston Harbor.

   _____

9. The tide has probably moved the chests farther out into the harbor.

   _____

Proofreading a Short Report

Proofread the beginning of the short report, paying special attention to capital letters in titles. Use the Proofreading Marks to correct at least eight errors.

PROOFREADING MARKS	
◯	spell correctly
⊙	add period
?	add question mark
=	capitalize
℘	take out
∧	add
/	make lowercase
∿	switch
∧	add comma
⌄ ⌄	add quotation marks
¶	indent paragraph

The Saltiest Lake in the World

The Dead Sea is the world's saltyest

body of water. Usually, sea water has a salt

content of 3.5 percent. The Dead sea is 28

percent salt, or eight times as salty as the

oceans. By comparison, the Great Salt Lake

in utah is six times as salty as Sea water. The water of the Dead Sea is so

salty that salt columns come up out of the water in strange formations.

Many people say these salt formations look like oddly formed, discolored icebergs

the salt in the Dead Sea helped give the huge lake its name. The salt in the water kills almost every form of life that is swept into the Dead Sea. The salt is also the cause of the Dead Seas most well-known quality: its buoyancy. According to Rupert o. Matthews in his book <u>The atlas of natural Wonders,</u> "Sinking and diving are impossible, but it is far easier to swim here than in any other stretch of water."

Write about Japanese Culture

With a friend, look up information on Japanese flower arranging (*ikebana*), dwarf trees (*bonsai*), or anything else about Japanese culture that interests you. Write a short report about what you learn.

_____

_____

_____

_____

_____

_____

_____

_____

_____

_____

_____

_____

_____

_____

_____

_____

_____

Write about a Musical Figure

With a friend, choose a musical figure you both admire. Go to the library to read about him or her. You may wish to have the librarian show you how to find articles in magazines. List three quotations from the musician or about the musician. Write a report on the musician using the quotations in your report.

THREE QUOTATIONS:

_____

_____

_____

Interview Questions

Imagine that you and a friend have met a little baby who can talk. Write five questions you would ask the baby about his or her impressions of the world. Then write what the baby might say in answer to each of your questions.

Questions

1. _____

2. _____

3. _____

4. _____

5. _____

Baby Answers

1. _____

2. _____

3. _____

4. _____

5. _____

A Practice Short Report

LEFT-HANDED OR RIGHT-HANDED

You walk into a new class and see rows of empty desks. It's good that you're the first one here, because there's a problem. These aren't the big square desks you like best. These are what you call the half desks. The desks are made to let you slide into the seat. Then the desk sits under your arm. The problem is that all but one desk in the room is for right-handed people, and you're a leftie. You've done the math before. If there are thirty students in this class, at least three more people will want the same desk. It's a good thing you're here first.

This is a common problem. No one knows why more people are right-handed than left-handed. Scientists ask questions, but so far, they haven't found clear answers. There are a few things they do know. For example, if both parents are right-handed, then almost all of their children will be right-handed. If one of the parents is left-handed, the chances of having left-handed children go up. Now this might make you think that left-handed parents have left-handed children. But when both parents are left-handed, about half their children are right-handed. Puzzling, isn't it?

Some scientists report that 13 percent of people in the world are left-handed. Others report that as many as 30 percent of people are left-handed. There is a simple test you can do to determine which hand you use most. Sit comfortably and fold your hands together. Which thumb is on top? If you are right-handed, it's probably your left thumb. If you're left-handed, the thumb is reversed.

This test doesn't always work. You might want to ask yourself a few questions instead. For example, which hand do you use to do the following things?

- turn on the lights
- brush your teeth
- brush your hair
- pick up something from the ground
- throw a ball
- get your teacher's attention

Whichever answer you give most tells whether you're right-handed or left-handed.

Scientists aren't sure what causes people to use one hand more than the other. Some think that genes determine which hand we use more. Genes are the hereditary information we get from our parents. Some scientists explain that the gene for being right-handed is dominant. Dominant means that if you have this gene, you're right-handed. If you don't, you're left-handed. However, no scientist has found the gene. Plus, studies of identical twins tell us that genes may not be the answer. Identical twins have the same genes, but almost 20 percent of them have different handedness.

While some scientists try to find genes, other scientists look for different clues. Some scientists study how humans act and live. They have found tools made by people who lived during the Stone Age. Some of those tools are millions of years old. Some are only ten thousand years old. These tools tell scientists that the number of left-handed and right-handed people used to be about equal. Does this information leave you scratching your

FAMOUS LEFT-HANDED PEOPLE		
Historical Figures	Entertainers	Musicians
Alexander the Great	Charlie Chaplin	Ludwig van Beethoven
Julius Caesar	Marilyn Monroe	Ringo Starr
Napoleon Bonaparte	Oprah Winfrey	Paul McCartney
Athletes	Artists	Members of the British Royal Family
Monica Seles	Michelangelo	Queen Elizabeth II
Terry Labonte	Leonardo da Vinci	Prince Charles
Larry Bird	Pablo Picasso	Prince William

head? Which hand are you using? As you can see, scientists have more work to do.

Some people claim that most geniuses are left-handed. Benjamin Franklin was a leftie. So was Albert Einstein. So were Leonardo da Vinci and Michelangelo. One newspaper reported that one out of every three American presidents has been a leftie. There are plenty of famous lefties in the world. They work everywhere, including in science, art, music, and sports. Read the chart above to find a few familiar names.

Today there are fewer left-handed people than there are right-handed people. That means that it's hard for a leftie to find a pair of scissors or a desk. It's also hard to find bowling balls and boomerangs. However, things are changing. Lefties are speaking up. Now they have their own sports equipment and musical instruments. They have their own clubs and magazines. There's even an international holiday that celebrates lefties. Next year, you might want to join them.

Respond to the Practice Paper

Write your answers to the following questions or directions.

1. What is the problem in this report?

   _____

   _____

2. Why aren't scientists sure if genes are the reason we use one hand more
   than the other?

   _____

   _____

3. What have scientists learned about Stone Age people?

   _____

   _____

4. Write a paragraph to summarize this report. Use these questions to help
   you write your summary:
   • What is the report about?
   • What explanations does the writer give?
   • How is life changing for lefties?

   _____

   _____

   _____

   _____

   _____

   _____

   _____

Analyze the Practice Paper

Read "Left-Handed or Right-Handed" again. As you read, think about the main ideas the writer discusses. Write your answers to the following questions.

1. Read the first paragraph again. Why do you think the writer began the report this way?

    _____

    _____

2. Why do you think the writer ends the second paragraph with a question?

    _____

    _____

3. The writer uses some special words like *genes* and *dominant*. How does the writer make it easier for the reader to understand these words?

    _____

    _____

4. Why do you think the writer includes the work of scientists in this report?

    _____

    _____

5. Why is the last paragraph important? What makes it different from the other paragraphs?

    _____

    _____

    _____

    _____

Writing Assignment

In a short report, writers write about one topic, or subject. They research the topic to find important main ideas. They also find important details to support the main ideas. Write a short report about a science topic that interests you. Use this writing plan to help you write a first draft on the next page.

The topic of this paper is:

_____

Main Idea of Paragraph 1: _____

Detail: _____

Detail: _____

Detail: _____

Main Idea of Paragraph 2: _____

Detail: _____

Detail: _____

Detail: _____

Main Idea of Paragraph 3: _____

Detail: _____

Detail: _____

Detail: _____

First Draft

TIPS FOR WRITING A SHORT REPORT:

- Use reference materials to collect information about your science topic.

- Take notes about important main ideas.
- Take notes about important details that support each main idea.
- Introduce the topic, or subject, of your report in the first paragraph.
- Organize the main ideas into separate paragraphs.
- Organize the paragraphs in logical order.
- Summarize your report in the last paragraph.

Use your writing plan as a guide as you write your first draft of a short report. Include a catchy title.

_____

_____

_____

_____

_____

_____

_____

_____

_____

_____

(Continue on your own paper.)

Revise the Draft

Use the chart below to help you revise your draft. Check YES or NO to answer each question in the chart. If you answer NO, make notes to remind yourself how you can revise, or change, your writing to improve it.

Question	YES ✔	NO ✔	If the answer is NO, what will you do to improve your writing?
Do you write about one science topic in your report?			
Do you introduce your topic in the first paragraph?			
Do you have more than one main idea?			
Do you organize your main ideas into paragraphs?			
Do you include details to support each main idea?			
Do you summarize your report in the last paragraph?			
Have you corrected mistakes in spelling, grammar, and punctuation?			

Use the notes in your chart and your writing plan to revise your draft.

Writing Report Card

Read your revised draft again or ask someone else to read it. Have the person who reads your paper complete the following Report Card. Revise your paper until you have no less than a Very Good Score for each item.

Title of paper: _____

Purpose of paper: _*This is a short report.*_____

Person who scores the paper: _____

Score	Writing Goals
	Is this paper an example of a short report?
	Does the writer talk about a specific topic, or subject?
	Does the report introduce the topic in the first paragraph?
	Does the report have more than one main idea?
	Are the main ideas organized into paragraphs?
	Does the way the paragraphs are organized make sense?
	Are there details to support each main idea?
	Does the writer summarize the report in the last paragraph?
	Does the writer "stick" to the topic throughout the report?
	Are the report's grammar, spelling, and punctuation correct?

☺ Excellent Score　　☆ Very Good Score　　+ Good Score
✔ Acceptable Score　　— Needs Improvement

Proofreading Marks

Use the following symbols to help make proofreading faster.

MARK	MEANING	EXAMPLE
◯	spell correctly	I (*liek*) dogs. *like*
⊙	add period	They are my favorite kind of pet⊙
?	add question mark	Are you lucky enough to have a dog?
⹀	capitalize	My dog's name is scooter.
℘	take out	He is a great companion for me and my ~~my~~ family.
∧	add	We got Scooter when *he* was eight weeks old.
/	make lowercase	My /Uncle came over to take a look at him.
∽	switch	He watched the puppy run in around circles.
∧	add comma	"Jack that dog is a real scooter!" he told me.
∨ ∨	add quotation marks	Scooter! That's the perfect name! I said.
¶	indent paragraph	¶ Scooter is my best friend in the whole world. He is not only happy and loving but also the smartest dog in the world. Every morning at six o'clock, he jumps on my bed and wakes me with a bark. Then he brings me my toothbrush.

Test
Prep

WHAT ARE STANDARDIZED TESTS?

You will take many different tests while at school. A standardized test is a special test that your state gives to every student in your grade. These tests are designed to find out how much you know about subjects like reading and math. They may not be fun, but they do not have to be a nightmare. This workbook can help you prepare!

WHAT CAN YOU EXPECT ON A STANDARDIZED TEST?

All standardized tests are different, but they do have some things in common.

- **Multiple-Choice Questions**
  Most of these tests use multiple-choice questions. You have to pick the best answer from four or five choices. You usually indicate your choice on an answer sheet by filling in or darkening a circle next to the correct answer.

- **Time Limits**
  Standardized tests all have time limits. It is best to answer as many questions as possible before you run out of time. But do not let the time limit make you nervous. Use it to help you keep going at a good pace.

- **Short Answers and Essays**
  Some standardized tests have questions that require writing an answer. Sometimes the answer is a word or a sentence. Other times you will write a paragraph or an essay. Always read directions carefully to find out how much writing is required.

HOW CAN THIS BOOK HELP?

Everyone gets a little nervous when taking a test. This book can make test-taking easier by providing helpful tips and practice tests. You will learn strategies that will help you find the best answers. You will also review math, reading, and grammar skills that are commonly needed on standardized tests. Here are some hints for using this book.

- Work in a quiet place. When you take a test at school, the room is very quiet. Try to copy that feeling at home. Sit in a chair at a desk or table, just as you would in school.

- Finish one test at a time. Do not try to finish all of the tests in this book in one session. It is better to complete just one activity at a time. You will learn more if you stop at the end of a practice test to think about the completed questions.

- Ask questions. Talk with a family member or a friend if you find a question you do not understand. These practice tests give you the chance to check your own answers.

Look for the Test Tips throughout this workbook. They provide hints and ideas to help you find the best answers.

HOW TO BE TEST SMART

A test-smart student knows what to do when it is test-taking time. You might not know all the answers, but you will feel relaxed and focused when you take tests. Your test scores will be accurate. They will provide a snapshot of what you have learned during the school year. Here is how you can become test-smart!

THINGS YOU CAN DO ALL YEAR

The best way to get ready for tests is to pay attention in school every day. Do your homework. Be curious about the world around you. Learning takes place all the time, no matter where you are! When test day rolls around, you will be ready to show what you know. Here are some ways you can become a year-round learner.

- Do your schoolwork. Standardized tests measure how much you have learned. If you keep up with your schoolwork, your test scores will reflect all the things you have learned.

- Practice smart study habits. Most people study best when they work in a quiet, clean area. Keep your study area neat. Make sure you have a calculator, dictionary, paper, and pencils nearby.

- Read a wide variety of materials, including all sorts of fiction and nonfiction. Your school or local librarian can suggest books you might not have considered reading. Read newspapers and magazines to find out about current events.

- Practice. This book is a great start to help you get ready for test day. It provides practice for all the important skills on the tests.

HOW TO DO YOUR BEST ON TEST DAY

Your teacher will announce a standardized test day in advance. Follow these tips to help you succeed on the big day.

- Plan a quiet night before a test. Trying to study or memorize facts at this point might make you nervous. Enjoy a relaxing evening instead.

- Go to bed on time. You need to be well rested before the test.

- Eat a balanced breakfast. Your body needs fuel to keep your energy high during a test. Eat foods that provide long-term energy, like eggs, yogurt, or fruit. Skip the sugary cereals—the energy they give does not last very long.

- Wear comfortable clothes. Choose a comfortable outfit that you like.

- Do not worry about the other students or your friends. Everyone works at different speeds. Pay attention to answering the questions in a steady fashion. It does not matter when someone else finishes the test.

- Relax. Take a few deep breaths to help you relax. Hold your pencil comfortably and do not squeeze it. Take a break every so often to wiggle your fingers and stretch your hand.

TEST-TAKING TIPS

Here are some hints and strategies to help you feel comfortable with any test. Remember these ideas while taking the tests in this book.

READ THE DIRECTIONS

This sounds obvious, but every year students lose points because they assume they know the right thing to do—and they are wrong! Make sure you read and understand the directions for every test. Always read the directions first. They will focus your attention on finding the right answers.

READ THE ANSWERS

Read the answers—ALL the answers—for a multiple-choice question, even if you think the first one is correct. Test writers sometimes include tricky answers that seem right when you first read them.

PREVIEW THE QUESTIONS

Scan each section. This will give you information about the questions. You also can see how many questions there are in the section. Do not spend too much time doing this. A quick glance will provide helpful information without making you nervous.

USE YOUR TIME WISELY

Always follow test rules. On most standardized tests, you can work on only one section at a time. Do not skip ahead or return to another section. If you finish early, go back and check your answers in that section.

- Before the test begins, find out if you can write in the test booklet. If so, add a small circle or star next to those questions that you find difficult. If time allows, come back to these questions before time is up for that section.

- Try not to spend too much time on one question. Skip a difficult question and try to answer it later. Be careful, though! You need to skip that question's number on your answer sheet. When you answer the next question, make sure you carefully fill in or darken the circle for the correct question.

- When finishing a section, look at your answer sheet. Did you answer every question for the section? Erase any extra marks on your answer sheet. Make sure you did not mark two answers for one question.

MAKE AN EDUCATED GUESS

Most standardized tests take away points for wrong answers. It might be wise to skip a question if you have no idea about the answer. Leave the answer blank and move on to the next question. But if you can eliminate one or more of the answers, guessing can be a great strategy. Remember, smart guessing can improve your test scores!

- Read every answer choice.

- Cross out every answer you know is wrong.

- Try rereading or restating the question to find the best answer.

THINK BEFORE YOU SWITCH

When you check your answers, you might be tempted to change one or more of them. In most cases, your first answer is probably the best choice. Ask yourself why you want to make a change. If you have a good reason, go ahead and pick a new answer. For example, you might have misread the question. If you cannot think of a specific reason, it is probably best to stick with your first answer.

FILL IN THE BLANKS

Many tests include fill-in-the-blank questions. The blank is usually in the middle or at the end of a sentence. Use these steps to answer a fill-in-the-blank question.

- Begin with the first answer choice. Read the sentence with that word or group of words in place of the blank. Ask yourself, "Does this answer make sense?"

- Then try filling in the blank with each of the other answer choices. Also, use the other words in the sentence as clues to help you decide the correct choice.

- Choose the best answer.

LOOK FOR CLUE WORDS

When you read test questions, watch for *clue words* that provide important information. Here are some words that make a difference.

- NOT: Many questions ask you to find the answer that is not true. These questions can be tricky. Slow down and think about the meaning of the question. Then pick the one answer that is not true.

- ALWAYS, NEVER, ALL, NONE, ONLY: These words limit a statement. They often make a generally true statement into a false one.

- SOMETIMES, SOME, MOST, MANY, OFTEN, GENERALLY: These words make a statement more believable. You will find them in many correct answers.

- BEST, MOST LIKELY, SAME, OPPOSITE, PROBABLY: These words change the meaning of a sentence. You often can use them to eliminate choices.

RESTATE THE QUESTION

Short answer or essay questions require writing an answer. Your response must answer the question. Restate the question to make sure your answer stays on target. For example, if the question is "What causes lightning?" your answer should begin with the words "Lightning is caused by . . ."

TEST TIP

Be sure to look for the Test Tips throughout this workbook. They will give you more test-taking strategies and specific help with certain subject areas.

SIX READING SKILLS

Prefixes and suffixes are parts of some words. A prefix appears at the beginning of a word. A suffix appears at the end of a word. Both prefixes and suffixes affect the meaning of words. You can use them to help figure out the meaning of a word.

Mount Mazama is a volcano in Oregon. It has been <u>inactive</u> for years. The edges of the crater have fallen in. The crater has filled up with water. It is now known as Crater Lake.

1   In this paragraph, the word <u>inactive</u> means —

    A upset.

    B quiet.

    C alive.

    D stubborn.

Hint: "In-" is a prefix. It means not.

The porcupine fish can make itself look very odd. If it senses danger, it takes a breath of air and puffs out its body. Then it looks like a spine-covered ball. When the danger passes, the fish <u>deflates</u> itself.

2   What happens when a balloon <u>deflates</u>?

_____

_____

_____

_____

Hint: "De-" is a prefix. It means to reverse the action of, *or* to undo.

The Maya Indians once built great cities. They lived in an area that stretched from southern Mexico to Central America. Then the Maya began to <u>evacuate</u> the large cities. They moved to farms or small towns. The reason they left the cities is still unknown.

3   In this paragraph, the word <u>evacuate</u> means —

    F sweep.

    G build.

    H join.

    J leave.

Hint: "E-" is a prefix. It means out.

When John found the stray cat, its fur was so wet and dirty that he could see its ribs. He tried to give it some milk, but it was too sick to drink any. He could not bear to watch it <u>suffering</u> and took it to the animal shelter.

4   In this paragraph, the word <u>suffering</u> means —

    A drooling.

    B experiencing pain.

    C having stitches.

    D experiencing pleasure.

Hint: The suffix "-ing" means the act of.

GO ON ▶

Answers

1 Ⓐ Ⓑ Ⓒ Ⓓ   **3** Ⓕ Ⓖ Ⓗ Ⓙ   **4** Ⓐ Ⓑ Ⓒ Ⓓ

Sometimes you can figure out the meaning of a new or difficult word by using the words around it as clues.

Have you ever seen a sea monster? People in northern Scotland believe a sea monster lives in Loch Ness, a nearby lake. Many people have reported seeing the creature. Observers say that it has flippers, a hump, and a long, thin neck.

5 **In this paragraph, the word observers means —**

F   police.

G   watchers.

H   campers.

J   doctors.

Hint: You get a clue about what the word means by reading sentences 3 and 4.

Bedrich Smetana wrote music. When he was fifty years old, he became totally deaf. But he did not let this check his interest in music. He wrote some of his finest pieces after going deaf.

6 **In this paragraph, the word check means —**

A   mark.

B   nail.

C   stop.

D   open.

Hint: You get a clue about what the word means by reading sentences 3 and 4.

The space shuttle needs extra power to be launched. To get this power, the shuttle is connected to a large fuel reservoir and two rocket boosters. These fall off as the shuttle climbs into space.

7 **What is a fuel reservoir?**

_____

_____

_____

_____

Hint: You get a clue about what the word reservoir means by reading sentences 1 and 2.

Many plants grow in places that do not have the minerals they need. The plants must adapt to their surroundings. One of these plants is the pitcher plant. It traps and eats insects for the minerals it needs to grow properly.

8 **In this paragraph, the word adapt means —**

F   enjoy.

G   answer.

H   adjust.

J   hatch.

Hint: You get a clue about what the word adapt means by reading sentences 1 and 2.

GO ON ➡

Answers
5 Ⓕ Ⓖ Ⓗ Ⓙ   6 Ⓐ Ⓑ Ⓒ Ⓓ   8 Ⓕ Ⓖ Ⓗ Ⓙ

Specialized or technical words are words used in specific subjects, such as science and social studies. You can use all the other information in the text to help determine the meaning of these words.

Most animals use some kind of respiration to stay alive. A water spider gets air from large bubbles in the water. Whales, however, must come to the surface of the water to get air for their lungs.

9   In this paragraph the word respiration means —

A   food.

B   breathing.

C   water.

D   trick.

Hint: The word respiration is a technical word. You get a clue about what it means by reading the entire paragraph.

Plants can be attacked by insects or destroyed by bad weather. Sometimes plants are struck by an epidemic. Then many plants get sick and die.

10   What is an epidemic?

_____

_____

_____

_____

Hint: Epidemic is a technical word. You get a clue about what it means by reading the entire paragraph.

The moon appears to change its shape over a period of about thirty days. For that reason the moon can be used to measure the passing of time. That's why people long ago developed lunar calendars.

11   In this paragraph the word lunar means —

F   of the time.

G   of long ago.

H   of the moon.

J   of the people.

Hint: Lunar is a technical word. You get a clue about what it means by reading the entire paragraph.

TEST TIP

Remember that many words have more than one meaning. Technical words have special meanings in certain subject areas. For example, the word *work* has a technical meaning in science. *Work* is "the energy used when a force moves an object."

When you read test passages, take a moment to identify the subject area. If it is a science or social studies topic, slow down and be alert for this kind of technical term.

GO ON

Answers
9 Ⓐ Ⓑ Ⓒ Ⓓ   **11** Ⓕ Ⓖ Ⓗ Ⓙ

On July 11, 1991, the people in Hawaii had a thrilling experience. The Earth, moon, and sun lined up. This made the sun seem to disappear. This eclipse of the sun lasted over seven minutes.

12 **In this paragraph the word eclipse means —**

    A darkening.

    B coloring.

    C brightness.

    D heat.

Hint: The word eclipse is a technical term. You get a clue about what eclipse means by reading sentences 2 and 3.

Richard Leakey was born in Kenya, Africa, in 1944. He has found many important fossils of early humans. He discovered some skulls that are thought to be over one million years old!

13 **In this paragraph the word fossils means —**

    F bones.

    G dinosaurs.

    H tribes.

    J photographs.

Hint: The word fossils is a technical term. You get a clue about what fossils means by reading sentences 2 and 3.

When ducks migrate south each fall, many of them pass over Stuttgart, Arkansas. So the people there hold a duck-calling contest. As the ducks fly by, the people quack away!

14 **What does the word migrate mean in this paragraph?**

_____

_____

_____

_____

Hint: The word migrate is a technical term. You get a clue about what the word migrate means by reading the entire paragraph.

TEST TIP

When you have to provide a short answer, choose your words carefully. Try to write an answer that gets right to the point. You do not need to impress people with fancy words. Simply give your answer as directly and completely as possible.

STOP

Answers
12 Ⓐ Ⓑ Ⓒ Ⓓ   **13** Ⓕ Ⓖ Ⓗ Ⓙ

Facts or details are important. By noticing and remembering them, you will know what the passage is about.

Do you think that the North Pole and the South Pole are alike? Most people do. But in fact the two areas are quite different. The North Pole is in the Arctic Ocean. The South Pole lies near the center of Antarctica. Antarctica is colder than the Arctic. In fact, Antarctica is by far the coldest region on earth.

One reason for Antarctica's very cold climate is that it has mountains high above sea level. Summers there rarely get above freezing. Ice and snow cover almost all of Antarctica throughout the entire year.

The Arctic region includes lands around the Arctic Ocean. The Arctic region is mostly at or near sea level. In parts of the Arctic, summers can be as warm as those in Boston. They just do not last as long. Most of the Arctic lands have no snow or ice in the summer.

1   **The Arctic is mostly —**

   A   in Boston.

   B   at sea level.

   C   above sea level.

   D   below sea level.

   Hint: Look at paragraph 3.

2   **Antarctica has —**

   F   rivers.

   G   sand.

   H   mountains.

   J   jungles.

   Hint: The fact is in the story.

3   **The North Pole is —**

   A   on land.

   B   on a mountain.

   C   in the Arctic Ocean.

   D   in Antarctica.

   Hint: Look at sentence 4.

Antarctica has most of the world's permanent ice. The ice rests on land. Its average thickness is 8,000 feet. But ice in the Arctic rests on water. Its thickness varies from 10 to 65 feet.

If you traveled to the Arctic, you would see reindeer, polar bears, seals, birds, and insects. If your stay lasted through all the seasons, you might see over a thousand types of plants. You might also meet some of the people who live there. These people have learned to live in the cold climate quite well. They have been able to use the plants and animals there. Most of the people live near the sea, where they catch fish.

If you visited Antarctica, you would see ice and more ice. Very few animals and plants can live there. Most animals live on the coast. The largest animal that can live on the mainland is a small fly. And you would not see people at all, unless you ran into an explorer or scientist.

4   **What does the Arctic ice rest on?**

   _____

   _____

   _____

   _____

   Hint: Look for the sentence about Arctic ice.

GO ON

Answers
1 Ⓐ Ⓑ Ⓒ Ⓓ   2 Ⓕ Ⓖ Ⓗ Ⓙ   3 Ⓐ Ⓑ Ⓒ Ⓓ

Sometimes it is helpful to arrange events in the order they happened. This may help you to understand a passage better.

Giraffes are the tallest living animals. Most adult giraffes are tall enough to look into second-story windows. Their long necks help them get leaves and fruit that no other animal can reach. Let's see how a giraffe's life begins.

A female giraffe, or cow, gives birth to a baby 15 months after mating. The mother searches for a safe place to give birth. Both the baby, or calf, and the mother are in a great deal of danger right after the birth. More than half of all baby giraffes are killed by lions, cheetahs, or hyenas minutes after they are born.

The new baby drops the 5 feet from its mother to the ground with a thud. It weighs about 130 pounds and is 6 feet tall. The baby can run and jump 10 hours after it is born, but it cannot outrun an enemy.

The mother hides the calf in tall grass. Then she goes to search for food. The baby is safe as long as it stays still. The cow returns to nurse the baby. The calf stays hidden for about a month.

After a month the mother and baby join a group of four or five other cows with their calves. The calves stay together while their mothers gather food. Sometimes one mother stays with them. The cows return at night to protect the calves. The calves stay in this group until they are about a year old.

By the time they are a year old, the giraffes are 10 to 12 feet tall. They can outrun all of their enemies except the cheetah. The giraffes rarely attack an animal larger than themselves. They continue to grow until they are 7 or 8 years old. Adults are between 14 and 18 feet tall.

5   **Which happens first in the story?**

     F   The mother joins a group.

     G   The mother hides the calf.

     H   The mother searches for a safe place.

     J   The mother searches for food.

     Hint: Look at the beginning.

6   **When does a female giraffe give birth?**

     A   after she joins a group of other cows

     B   every 15 months

     C   15 months after mating

     D   every year

     Hint: Look at paragraph 2.

7   **When are the mother and baby in greatest danger?**

     _____

     _____

     _____

     _____

     Hint: Look at paragraph 2.

8   **When do the cow and calf join a group?**

     F   about a month after the baby is born

     G   when the calf is a year old

     H   when the calf is 7 or 8 years old

     J   10 to 12 months after the baby is born

     Hint: Look at paragraph 5.

9   **When do giraffes stop growing?**

     A   when they are 10 or 12 years old

     B   when they are 7 or 8 years old

     C   when they join a group of other giraffes

     D   when they are 14 to 18 years old

     Hint: Look at the second to last sentence in the selection.

     GO ON ⇒

Answers

5 Ⓕ Ⓖ Ⓗ Ⓙ   **6** Ⓐ Ⓑ Ⓒ Ⓓ   **8** Ⓕ Ⓖ Ⓗ Ⓙ   **9** Ⓐ Ⓑ Ⓒ Ⓓ

Written directions tell you how to do something. To follow them means to do them in the same order in which they are given.

Linda left a note for her daughter, because school was starting the next day. In the note she said, "Erin, take the list of supplies you need down to the stationery store. I left $20 on the kitchen counter for you. Put the money and your house key in your pocket. Please walk so you don't have to worry about your bicycle while you shop. Get as many of the items on the list as you can. We'll get the rest after I get home from work. If you have any money left over, you can get a soda at the luncheonette next door. Please be careful, and don't buy candy!"

10   What is Erin to do after she puts the $20 in her pocket?

    F   ride her bicycle

    G   leave a note for her mother

    H   walk to the store

    J   put her house key in her pocket

Hint: Find the part of the directions about putting the money in her pocket and read what comes after that.

Peggy Johnson is a firefighter. When she arrived at midnight for her eight-hour shift, she found instructions from her new supervisor:

Sign in. Inspect engine 5 first. After making sure it is running well, be sure that it has plenty of gas. Inspect the hats, coats, and other firefighting equipment. If you have time before your 4:00 A.M. meal break, inspect engine 1 and check the gas tank on that engine as well. I hope that you will not be called out on any fire and can use the rest of your shift to fill out next week's work schedules for the rest of the crew. See you at 8:00 A.M.!

11   When should Peggy inspect engine 5?

_____

_____

_____

_____

Hint: Find the sentence that directs Peggy to inspect engine 5.

TEST TIP

Time order is also called *chronological order*. Pay close attention to dates and times, as well as signal words that tell about time, such as:

first	next
then	finally
before	after
since	lastly

You might circle these words in the test passage to help you decide the order of events.

GO ON

The setting of a story lets you know when and where it is taking place.

Chimney sweeps have been around for hundreds of years. Chimneys had to be cleaned or the fireplaces would not work properly. Dirty chimneys could cause fires. Many countries passed laws that required chimneys to be cleaned once or twice a year. Chimney sweeping became a regular profession.

Life was hard for chimney sweeps in England in the 1700s. Tall, narrow houses were built in the cities. Chimneys were designed to take up as little space as possible. They were too small for adults to climb into. So, many sweeps hired young boys as helpers, or apprentices. These boys were not treated well. They spent long hours climbing into dirty chimneys. Most of the time, they were not given enough warm food or warm clothing. In 1788 a law was passed that said sweeps could not be younger than eight.

12   What were houses like in English cities in the 1700s?

   A   They were dirty and rundown.

   B   They had no chimneys.

   C   They were tall and narrow with small chimneys.

   D   They were large with small chimneys.

   Hint: Find the description of the English houses.

13   What century is the passage about?

   F   16th century

   G   17th century

   H   18th century

   J   19th century

   Hint: Look for a date.

Would you like to step back in time? If so, you might enjoy a trip to Mesa Verde National Park. Mesa Verde is in southwestern Colorado. Spanish explorers gave this region its name. Mesa verde means "green plateau." It became a national park in 1906.

Scientists have studied the region and have learned a great deal about the people who lived there. They called them the Anasazi, or "old ones." We know that about the year 1200 the Anasazi built their homes in the caves of the canyon walls. They used stone blocks to build apartment-like dwellings. When you see them, it is easy to pretend you are one of the people who lived there centuries ago.

14   The Anasazi built their homes —

   A   about 1906.

   B   about 1200.

   C   about 1900.

   D   about 600 years ago.

   Hint: Read paragraph 2, sentence 3.

15   Where does the story take place?

   _____

   _____

   _____

   _____

   Hint: Read sentence 3.

STOP

Answers
12 Ⓐ Ⓑ Ⓒ Ⓓ   **13** Ⓕ Ⓖ Ⓗ Ⓙ   **14** Ⓐ Ⓑ Ⓒ Ⓓ

The main idea is the overall meaning of a piece of writing. Often the main idea is written in the passage.

When Millard Fillmore was nineteen, he could hardly read or write. He lived on a farm. He spent more time working than going to school. But later he decided to return to school. Abigail Powers was Fillmore's teacher. They fell in love, and later they were married. Fillmore went on to become a teacher, a lawyer, and the President of the United States!

1   What is the main idea of this story?

   A   Fillmore achieved great things after being educated.

   B   Fillmore went to school as a boy.

   C   Fillmore taught Abigail to read.

   D   Fillmore never married.

   Hint: What is the point of the story?

In 1692 some girls in Massachusetts decided that they did not like their neighbors. So the girls accused the neighbors of being witches. The girls said they were cut, pinched, and choked by strange visitors who looked like their neighbors. Many people were arrested, and twenty people were put to death. But one man accused of being a wizard said he would file a lawsuit against the girls. Then the girls took back their lies.

2   What is the main idea of the story?

   F   The girls disliked normal people.

   G   Some girls caused trouble in their town.

   H   A man threatening to file a lawsuit put an end to the girls' lies.

   J   Witchcraft trials were held in Massachusetts.

   Hint: What does the whole story talk about?

Frederic Bartholdi was the French sculptor of the Statue of Liberty. When Bartholdi was a student in France, a wall was built to keep out the enemy. One night a girl carrying a torch jumped over the wall and yelled, "Forward!" The enemy soldiers shot her. Years later Bartholdi remembered the girl with the torch in her hand. It gave him an idea. Bartholdi used his wife as the model for the shape of the statue. His mother served as the model for the statue's face.

3   What is this story mostly about?

   _____

   _____

   _____

   _____

   Hint: What is the whole story about?

In 1174 work began on the bell tower of a church in Pisa, Italy. Because the foundation of the tower was laid in soil that was too soft, it began to lean. Work on the tower stopped. For more than one hundred years, people suggested ways to prevent the tower from leaning. The building was finished in 1350, but it continued to sink. Each year the tower leans a little more. Tourists today still visit the famous Leaning Tower of Pisa.

4   The main idea of this story is that the Leaning Tower of Pisa —

   A   had been leaning from its beginning.

   B   was poorly built.

   C   is one of many bell towers.

   D   has many visitors.

   Hint: What is the whole story about?

GO ON

Answers
1 Ⓐ Ⓑ Ⓒ Ⓓ   2 Ⓕ Ⓖ Ⓗ Ⓙ   4 Ⓐ Ⓑ Ⓒ Ⓓ

Often the main idea is not given in the text. Sometimes you need to draw your own conclusion by putting the facts together.

Chip's family was at the beach. His grandmother had planned to come but couldn't because she was ill. Chip remembered how she would let him look at her shell collection when he was younger. He used to enjoy holding the big conch shell up to his ear to hear the sound of the sea. The day before his family planned to return home, Chip went out early in the morning and picked up several interesting shells for his grandmother.

5   What is the main idea of this passage?

F   Chip always enjoyed going to the beach with his family.

G   Chip's grandmother was always getting sick and disappointing Chip.

H   Chip wanted his grandmother to know he was thinking of her.

J   Chip's grandmother collected seashells.

Hint: What point does the story make?

The first pair of roller skates was made in 1760 by Joseph Merlin. Merlin tried to sell his skates in London, but he didn't have much success. One problem was that they didn't have brakes! That problem was soon solved, and more people began trying the new sport. But it wasn't until 1849 that the sport caught on. That year a play was held in which actors were supposed to ice skate. But they could not make ice on stage. So the actors used roller skates instead.

6   What is the implied main idea?

A   The sport of roller skating was made popular by a stage play.

B   Roller skating will never become a very popular sport.

C   Merlin made the first pair of skates.

D   Skates are dangerous without brakes.

Hint: Think about what the passage is about. Which choice best sums it up?

Martin loved dogs. He asked his parents for a golden retriever. His parents agreed to get him a dog for his birthday if he promised to take care of it. Martin quickly agreed. He named the dog Calvin. The first few weeks, Martin took Calvin out for a walk twice a day. He kept his bowl filled with water and fed him each evening. But after two months, Martin's parents noticed that the water bowl was often empty and that Calvin had not been fed.

7   What is the main idea of this passage?

_____

_____

_____

_____

Hint: What is the point of the story?

TEST TIP

When you want to find the main idea of a test passage, ask yourself, "What is this passage mostly about?" The *main idea* should describe the big idea of a passage, not specific details.

Sometimes the main idea is stated in a topic sentence, often at the beginning of a paragraph. Other times, you will need to figure out the main idea of a passage. Try to name the big idea supported by the paragraph's details.

GO ON

Answers
5 Ⓕ Ⓖ Ⓗ Ⓙ   **6** Ⓐ Ⓑ Ⓒ Ⓓ

A good summary contains the main idea of a passage. It is brief, yet it covers the most important points.

Do you ever wonder how games are invented? James Naismith was teaching a physical education class when he accidentally made up a new game. He combined the games of lacrosse and soccer. But the players neither used a stick as in lacrosse nor kicked a ball as in soccer. Instead they bounced, or dribbled, the ball and shot at a goal. The only thing Naismith had to use as a goal was a peach basket. This is why he decided to call his game basketball.

8   What is this story mostly about?

   F   Most people can learn lacrosse.

   G   Naismith taught physical education.

   H   New games can be invented by accident.

   J   Soccer and lacrosse are different.

Hint: Look at sentences 1 and 2.

It is possible to eat healthy food at a fast-food restaurant. You could drink orange juice or low-fat milk instead of a malt or a milk shake. You could try a whole-grain bun rather than the regular white one on your sandwich. A baked potato instead of fried potatoes would be a healthy choice. But you'll need to have the potato plain rather than with all the trimmings.

9   What is the best summary of this passage?

   A   The most popular fast foods are healthy foods.

   B   There are healthy ways to eat at fast-food restaurants.

   C   All fast food is junk food.

   D   Fried potatoes are a healthy choice.

Hint: Which choice tells you about the whole passage?

There are about 2,000 kinds of snakes in the world. They live on land, in the ground, in water, and in trees. About 120 types of snakes are found in the United States. But only four types are actually poisonous. These are the coral snake, rattlesnake, copperhead, and water moccasin. The coral snake lives mainly in the South. Rattlesnakes are found in most states. The copperhead lives mostly in the East, while the water moccasin can be found in the Southeast.

10   What is this story mostly about?

   _____

   _____

   _____

   _____

   _____

   _____

Hint: Which sentences tell you about the whole passage?

TEST TIP

When you read the answer choices for question 9, notice some of the signal words that make answers incorrect. Answer A includes the word *most* and answer C includes the word *all*. These strong adjectives often make a sentence false. The correct answer to this question tells about the whole passage and makes a less extreme statement.

GO ON

Answers
8 Ⓕ Ⓖ Ⓗ Ⓙ   9 Ⓐ Ⓑ Ⓒ Ⓓ

Colorblindness has to do with a person's lack of ability to see colors. But it doesn't affect a person's sight. People with full-color vision have three kinds of cone-shaped cells in their eyes. One kind of cone sees red, another sees green, and the third kind of cone sees blue. A person who is colorblind is missing one or more of these kinds of cones. Red-green colorblindness is the most common. People with this kind of colorblindness see red or green as gray-brown. They don't have red or green cones.

11   What is this story mostly about?

   F If people are missing certain cone-shaped cells in their eyes, they are colorblind.

   G There are a number of people who are colorblind.

   H Red-blue colorblindness is very common.

   J People who are colorblind wear glasses.

Hint: Read sentences 3 and 5.

Which kind of clam chowder do you prefer? In the United States, there are two kinds of clam chowder. Manhattan clam chowder is made with tomatoes. New England clam chowder is made with milk. People from Massachusetts take their clam chowder very seriously. They even passed a law that does not allow clam chowder with tomatoes in their state!

12   What is the best summary of this passage?

   A There is a difference between New Englanders and other people.

   B There are different kinds of clam chowders.

   C Clam chowder is a kind of soup.

   D There is only one way to make clam chowder.

Hint: Pick the choice that sums up the passage.

During the 1850s, Levi Strauss moved to San Francisco. He sold canvas material used for making tents and covered wagons. Gold miners and railroad workers complained that their pants tore easily or wore out too soon. So Strauss used his canvas to make a pair of pants. He named the pants after himself. They sold for 22 cents a pair. Later Strauss made a pair of denim pants, dyed them blue, and named them Levi's also.

13   What is this passage mostly about?

_____

_____

_____

_____

_____

Hint: Read sentences 4, 5, and 7.

TEST TIP

A good summary should give the main idea of a passage without focusing on specific details. A summary should not be too general, though. As you read the answer choices for question 12, you will notice that answer C is too general. It makes a true statement, but it does not really tell about the passage.

STOP

Answers
11 Ⓕ Ⓖ Ⓗ Ⓙ   **12** Ⓐ Ⓑ Ⓒ Ⓓ

Knowing what made something happen or why a character did something will help you to understand what you read.

The telephone rang sharply in the middle of the night. Missy sat upright in her bed, rubbing her eyes. Again the sharp ringing split the silence. Trying to pull herself together, Missy scrambled for the phone. She had no idea who could be calling at that time of night, but she hoped it was not an emergency. When she answered the phone, a voice at the other end asked for someone named Felix. Disgusted, Missy said that Felix did not live there. Then the person on the other end slammed down the phone.

1 Why did Missy rub her eyes?

_____

_____

_____

_____

_____

Hint: Rubbing her eyes is the effect. What made this happen?

2 What caused Missy to hope that it was not an emergency?

A   The sound of the telephone was sharp.

B   She associated the voice on the phone with trouble.

C   The call came in the middle of the night.

D   She tore her nightclothes trying to scramble for the phone.

Hint: The effect was hoping that it was not an emergency. What caused Missy to hope that?

3 Why was Missy disgusted?

F   She did not like the name Felix.

G   She did not like to be awakened by someone calling the wrong number.

H   The person calling slammed down the phone.

J   She did not know who was calling.

Hint: Being disgusted is the effect. What made this happen?

Emma Willard worked hard for women's rights. In the early nineteenth century, she came up with a plan to improve schools for women. She felt that a woman could master any subject that a man could. So she offered a wide range of subjects at her school. She trained many young women to be teachers.

4 Which of the following did not cause Emma Willard to want to improve schools for women?

A   She believed that women could master any subject men could.

B   She wanted women to have a wider range of subjects to choose from.

C   She wanted to train young women to be teachers.

D   She wanted to make women better than men.

Hint: Improving schools for women is the effect. What was NOT one of Emma's reasons for wanting to improve schools?

GO ON ▶

Answers
2 Ⓐ Ⓑ Ⓒ Ⓓ   **3** Ⓕ Ⓖ Ⓗ Ⓙ   **4** Ⓐ Ⓑ Ⓒ Ⓓ

Michael liked the cool, crisp fall weather so much that he actually enjoyed raking leaves. One day he noticed that Mr. Longly's yard down the road was full of leaves. Michael knew that Mr. Longly used a wheelchair to get around. That day after school, Michael picked up his rake and headed for Mr. Longly's house.

5 **Why did Michael go to Mr. Longly's house?**

    F He planned on raking Mr. Longly's leaves, since Mr. Longly couldn't do it himself.

    G He liked fall better than the other seasons.

    H He didn't want to go inside.

    J He enjoyed raking leaves so much that he went looking for some more.

Hint: Read each choice and decide which makes the most sense.

Patty and her mom were very excited about planting their first garden. They looked forward to growing their own vegetables. First they used a hoe to prepare the soil. Then they added peat moss to the soil. They planted tomatoes, lettuce, beans, and peas. Every week Patty spent at least an hour weeding and watering the plants. At the end of the summer, Patty shared the vegetables with her friends.

6 **Why was Patty excited about planting a garden?**

_____

_____

_____

_____

_____

_____

Hint: Getting excited about planting a garden is the effect. What caused Patty to get excited?

TEST TIP

When a question begins with the word *why*, you need to find a cause-and-effect relationship to answer it. The effect is what happens; the cause is the reason why it happens. You can use the word *because* to answer a question that asks *why*. Begin your response to question 6 by writing "Patty was excited about planting a garden because . . . "

GO ON

Answers
5 Ⓕ Ⓖ Ⓗ Ⓙ

Many times you can predict, or tell in advance, what is probably going to happen next. You must think about what would make sense if the story were to go on.

Ruth's hobby was making radio-controlled airplanes. But even more than making them, she enjoyed flying the planes. Once Ruth spent every weekend for an entire month working with her dad to build an airplane. The next Saturday Ruth decided to try out the plane. When Ruth set up the airplane for takeoff, she didn't notice the tall pine trees standing in its path.

7 What might happen next?

    A Ruth and her father will cut down the trees.

    B The airplane will crash into the trees.

    C Ruth's father will finish building the airplane.

    D Ruth will get a ticket for flying an airplane without a license.

Hint: You need to look at all the facts in the story. What choice makes the most sense?

James and Jenny wanted to give their mom a special birthday present. "I have an idea," James said. "We could clean the whole house from top to bottom." "You're right! Mom would never believe it!" Jenny said. The next Saturday they asked their dad to take their mom out all afternoon. They vacuumed, dusted, and washed floors and windows until the whole house sparkled.

8 What will happen when James' and Jenny's mom gets home?

_____

_____

_____

_____

_____

_____

Hint: You need to read the entire paragraph.

TEST TIP

When a test asks you to predict what will happen next, do not try to think of a creative or weird event that *could* happen. Your goal should be to answer with something that is likely to happen.

Look at question 8. The test writers want to know what is the most likely thing to happen, not the most unusual or funniest event. Think about the clues in the paragraph. How do you think their mom will react to the clean house?

GO ON ➡

Answers
7 Ⓐ Ⓑ Ⓒ Ⓓ

"A package came for you today," Greg's mother said as he walked into the house. "I think it's from Aunt Ginny." Greg peeled the tape from the box and ripped off the brown paper. He tore off the gift wrap to find a stuffed bear inside. Aunt Ginny never seemed to realize that he was no longer three years old and hadn't been for over seven years. But then, he thought about the trouble Aunt Ginny had gone through to select the present and mail it. Greg sat down at the kitchen table with a pen and paper.

9   What will Greg probably do next?

_____

_____

_____

_____

Hint: What is the paragraph mostly about? The answer will be about that, too.

Each summer Jackie visited her grandparents on their farm for two weeks. She loved feeding the ducks on the pond. In the early evening, after a hot day of working in the fields, she took some bread to the pond. The ducks swam quickly to gobble up the bread she threw in the water. She watched the clear water reflect the bright colors of the sun as it disappeared beyond the horizon.

10   What did Jackie probably do next?

F   camp out by the pond

G   start a campfire

H   go to the store for more bread

J   go back to the farmhouse

Hint: Which of the choices would most likely come next?

TEST TIP

Remember that the word *probably* is a clue that helps you pick an answer. In question 10, all of the answer choices are possible, but only one of them is the most likely thing to happen. Notice that there is nothing in the story about camping. Therefore, you have no reason to think that Jackie will decide to camp out. The story begins in the early evening, so what is she most likely to do after the sun sets?

STOP

Answers
10 Ⓕ Ⓖ Ⓗ Ⓙ

Sometimes a passage will have a graph or diagram with it. These are there to help you understand the passage.

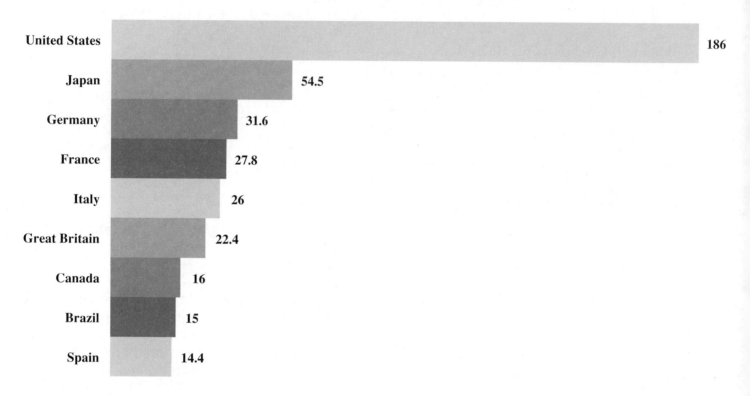

**NUMBER OF PASSENGER CARS
PER COUNTRY IN MILLIONS (1990)**

Country	Millions
United States	186
Japan	54.5
Germany	31.6
France	27.8
Italy	26
Great Britain	22.4
Canada	16
Brazil	15
Spain	14.4

France has an excellent railroad system. Despite this fine system, the French still prefer to travel by car. There are 27.8 million cars on the road in France. If all these vehicles were placed end to end, the line would stretch four times around the world. Only the United States, Japan, and Germany have more vehicles than France.

1 **According to the graph, which country has the most cars?**

A Japan

B Germany

C France

D United States

Hint: Which bar on the graph is the longest?

2 **How many cars were there in France in 1990?**

_____

_____

_____

_____

_____

_____

Hint: Look at the bar labeled "France."

GO ON ➡

Answers
1 Ⓐ Ⓑ Ⓒ Ⓓ

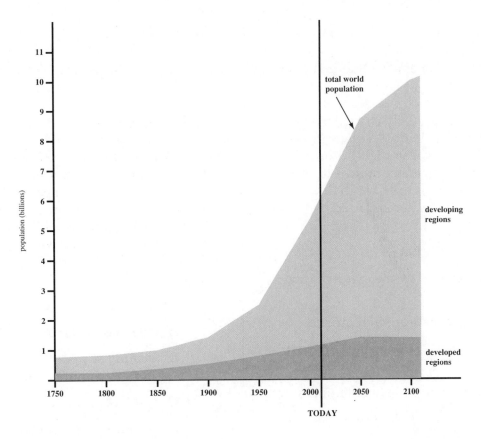

population (billions)

11 —
10 —
9 —
8 —
7 —
6 —
5 —
4 —
3 —
2 —
1 —

total world population

developing regions

developed regions

1750 1800 1850 1900 1950 2000 2050 2100

TODAY

There are more people in the world than ever before. This is because people all over the world are living longer. More people have clean water. We have medicine to fight many illnesses. People are eating better than ever before. However, scientists think that this population growth will slow down by the year 2050.

3   According to the graph, what is the total world population today?

_____

_____

_____

_____

_____

Hint: Find the place where the "today" line crosses with the "total world population."

4   According to the graph, what can be said about the world population?

F   The population of the developed regions is greater today than that of the developing regions.

G   The population of the developing regions is greater today than that of the developed regions.

H   The population of the developing regions today is equal to that of the developed regions.

J   The population of the developing regions is decreasing.

Hint: Check each choice against the graph.

GO ON ➡

Answers
4 Ⓕ Ⓖ Ⓗ Ⓙ

A logical conclusion is an ending that makes sense. Many times it can be proved by the information given in the paragraph.

Seashores experience a daily change in water level. This change is called tide. As the water is pulled from the shore, the water level drops. This is known as low tide. As the water returns to shore, the water level rises. This is called high tide. The coming and going of the water is caused by the pull of the moon's gravity.

5   **You can conclude that —**

   A   tides are caused by the gravity of the sun.

   B   the water level drops at high tide.

   C   the moon has a strong effect on Earth's seas.

   D   a tide is a change in water temperature.

Hint: Read the last sentence to draw the proper conclusion.

Carbon dioxide in the atmosphere acts as a blanket. It lets light pass through, but it traps heat. This occurrence is called the greenhouse effect. It is good, for without it the earth would be much colder. But as the carbon dioxide increases, the heat of the earth's surface rises. This isn't good. Carbon dioxide comes from the burning of oil, coal, and gasoline. If we do not limit this burning, the world may suffer as a result.

6   **From the passage you can tell that —**

   F   carbon dioxide traps light.

   G   the earth would be warmer without the greenhouse effect.

   H   the greenhouse effect is never good.

   J   too much carbon dioxide is bad.

Hint: You must read the entire paragraph, especially sentences 5 and 6.

Why do some dogs bark all the time? Some experts believe that dogs communicate through their barking. Other experts believe that dogs bark just to make noise. A new study supports this second view. The study suggests that dogs are wolves that just never grew up. Although dogs and wolves have the same ancestors, modern dogs behave in much the same ways as wolf pups, which bark all the time. However, older wolves seldom bark.

7   **From the passage you can tell that —**

   A   all experts agree on why dogs bark.

   B   a study supports the claim that dogs bark to communicate.

   C   old wolves bark all the time.

   D   a study suggests that dogs bark just to make noise

Hint: Pick the choice that can be proved true by what's in the passage.

TEST TIP

If you have trouble finding an answer, first cross off any answer choices you know are incorrect. Then keep the remaining answer choices in mind as you reread the paragraph. Look for clues in the paragraph to help you decide which answer makes the most sense.

GO ON

Answers
5 Ⓐ Ⓑ Ⓒ Ⓓ   6 Ⓕ Ⓖ Ⓗ Ⓙ   7 Ⓐ Ⓑ Ⓒ Ⓓ

By noting a person's physical changes, a lie detector machine shows whether someone is lying. The machine shows changes in heartbeat and breathing. These changes might take place when a person is lying. But these changes also take place when a person is nervous. Sometimes a person is lying but doesn't know it. In this case the machine doesn't note any change at all.

8 **From this selection, you cannot tell —**

    F what happens when a person lies.

    G what a lie detector shows.

    H which changes take place when a person is nervous.

    J how a lie detector is used in court.

Hint: You need to read the entire selection to see what you cannot tell.

The porcupine uses the quills on its tail to defend itself. When an animal comes too close, the porcupine slaps its tail at the enemy. The sharp quills come off easily. They stick into the other creature's skin. Each quill has a hook at the end. This makes the quills very painful to remove from the skin.

9 **If porcupines did not have quills, they would —**

    A use claws for defense.

    B be unable to defend themselves.

    C build dams with their tails.

    D find it painful.

Hint: First, cross out the choices that cannot be supported by the information in the passage.

Inventors record their inventions with the government. The inventors hope that someone will buy their bright ideas. But some inventions are so strange that no one wants them. Government files show inventions for odd things, such as flying fire escapes and eyeglasses for chickens. There is even an alarm clock that hits the sleeping person on the head.

10 **What type of inventions are described in this story?**

_____

_____

_____

_____

_____

Hint: Read the first three sentences to draw the proper conclusion.

TEST TIP

Always read a question carefully. Notice that question 10 asks, "What *type* of inventions is described in this story?" This is a very different question from "What inventions are described in this story?" You could answer the second question with a list of inventions. The first question, however, asks you to make a generalization. You need to explain what all of the inventions described in the story have in common.

GO ON

Answers
8 (F) (G) (H) (J)   **9** (A) (B) (C) (D)

The way a person acts tells you about the character's mood. Other clues may be what is said or how the character responds to what happens in the passage.

Alur had a beautiful wife and four cheerful children, and there were never any quarrels in his home. One day Alur visited his old friend Gungu. Gungu was smoking a pipe, which was an unusual thing for him to do. "Why are you smoking a pipe?" asked Alur. "Well, my friend," answered Gungu, "the smoke from this pipe carries my troubles away."

Alur asked, "What is trouble? I've never heard of it. It sounds exciting and interesting. I would like to obtain some of this trouble." Gungu was amazed. "You want trouble? No one wants that!" he said. Alur replied, "But I am curious! Please, Gungu, give me some of this trouble you've spoken of." Gungu frowned, but he said to Alur, "If you insist, I will present you with a little trouble. Send your children here tomorrow afternoon to get some trouble for you."

The next day Gungu put a hummingbird in a box and wrapped it up. When Alur's children arrived, Gungu said, "Take this present to your father. It is the trouble he asked for." The children had never heard of trouble either. As they walked home, they became curious about the contents of the box. They began to quarrel about whether they should open it. "I'll settle this!" said one child. He opened the box, and the hummingbird escaped. Now the children began to argue about whose fault it was that the bird had gotten away. When Alur came along to find his children, they were fighting and yelling.

Alur ran to Gungu's house and shouted, "What is this you have done, Gungu? My children never fought before!" Gungu replied, "Now you know what trouble is. And I hope you know something else now, too. Never think that something is wonderful just because you don't have it."

11 **How did Alur feel before he visited Gungu and asked for trouble?**

F happy and content

G nervous and unhappy

H poor and upset

J overwhelmed with four children

Hint: Read the first paragraph.

12 **Describe how Alur felt at the end of the story.**

_____

_____

_____

_____

_____

_____

Hint: Read what Alur says to Gungu.

GO ON

Answers
11 Ⓕ Ⓖ Ⓗ Ⓙ

Sometimes you need to generalize. This means to come up with a general statement about something in the text.

In the 1860s, two crews set out to build a railroad. It would cross the western United States. One crew started laying tracks in Nebraska. The other crew began its work in California. Building the railroad took four years. The two crews met at Promontory Point, Utah, in May 1869. A golden spike was driven into the ground. The spike honored the completion of the railroad.

13 **From this passage, you can make the generalization that —**

A the railroad crossed western Canada.

B the two crews worked in directions toward each other.

C the golden spike was driven in Nebraska.

D Promontory Point is in California.

Hint: Cross out the choices that can be proved untrue.

TEST TIP

Trick answers often contain just one incorrect word. Be an alert reader to avoid falling for this type of error. For example, in question 13, answer A sounds reasonable except that the country named is incorrect. The answer mentions Canada while the passage talks about the United States.

The Ghost Dance is a traditional dance among many Native American tribes. Legend claims that the dance was begun by a Paiute named Wovoka, who had spoken to the Great Spirit. The Great Spirit advised the Paiute people to be good and to live in peace. He presented Wovoka with the dance and told him that if the tribe danced for five nights, they would gain happiness. He also told him that the spirits of the dead would join the tribe.

14 **Why was the Ghost Dance performed?**

_____

_____

_____

_____

_____

_____

Hint: You need to read the entire paragraph.

STOP

Answers
13 Ⓐ Ⓑ Ⓒ Ⓓ

It is important to know the difference between fact and opinion. A fact is real and true. An opinion is a feeling or belief. Words that describe feelings or beliefs are used to offer opinions.

The wood for baseball bats comes from the ash tree forests of Pennsylvania. Ash wood is especially strong, so it makes good baseball bats. Ash trees are thin compared with other trees. In a high wind, an ash tree can break and fall. However, in the Pennsylvania forests, thicker kinds of trees grow all around the ash trees. These thick trees keep the ash trees from bending too far in a windstorm. Only a strong wooden bat can make a solid crack when it comes into contact with a baseball — and the fans love it!

1   **Which of the following is a FACT from the passage?**

A   Ash trees are the most beautiful trees.

B   Ash trees break in high winds.

C   The Pennsylvania forests have the best trees.

D   Baseball is the best sport for major league fans.

Hint: A fact is real and true.

The English word *robot* comes from another language. The Latin word *robota* means work that is dull because it has to be done over and over. This type of work is perfect for robots. Many robots are used in factories to do jobs that are hard or dangerous for people to do. They can be used to paint car parts and drill holes, make plastic food containers, and wrap ice cream bars.

2   **Which of the following is an OPINION?**

F   It is better for robots to do dull jobs than for people to do them.

G   Robots can do jobs that are dangerous.

H   The study of robots is called robotics.

J   Painting and making plastic containers are jobs that robots can do.

Hint: A fact is real and true. What is actually said in the passage? Words such as "it is better" are opinion words.

Ocean waves pound against the shore. Each wave leaves behind thousands of grains of sand. The grains of sand were once part of solid rocks. The rocks were worn down by water and weather into small grains. The wind blows the dry grains of sand into each other and into other objects. Over time the grains are molded into tiny balls. They keep this round shape for millions of years.

3   **Which of the following is an OPINION?**

A   Sand comes from rocks.

B   Water and weather wear rocks down.

C   Grains of sand stay round for millions of years.

D   It is good to have ocean waves so that we have shorelines.

Hint: Opinions describe feelings.

GO ON ➡

Answers
1 Ⓐ Ⓑ Ⓒ Ⓓ   2 Ⓕ Ⓖ Ⓗ Ⓙ   3 Ⓐ Ⓑ Ⓒ Ⓓ

Horses are specially trained to do stunts in movies. You have probably seen horses fall through walls, glass windows, or even barbed-wire fences. There is no need to worry about the horses. Moviemakers use special props for such stunts. The walls are made of soft wood. The wire in the fences is really rubber. And the glass in the windows is made from sugar. This is one reason that making movies is so expensive. Most special props can be used only once, and then new ones have to be built.

4 **Which of the following is an OPINION?**

F Only the best breeds of horses are used to do stunts in movies.

G Special props are used by moviemakers to do stunts.

H One of the high costs of making movies is special props.

J New props are usually built after the old ones have been used only once.

Hint: An opinion is a feeling or belief.

TEST TIP

Look for signal words that make a statement an opinion. Opinions often contain exaggerations, such as *most exciting* or *least interesting*. An opinion often names something as the *best* or *worst* or claims that one thing is *better* or *worse* than another.

The American Humane Association protects horses used in making movies. Members of the group stay on movie sets to see that the horses are taken care of properly and not mistreated. The horses are protected from being hurt during exciting scenes. Have you ever seen a horse run at a full gallop for miles and miles in a movie? The horse really ran for shorter distances and was filmed each time. When the film is shown, it looks as though the horse ran a long distance. If guns are fired in a scene, the horse may have cotton in its ears for protection.

5 **Which of the following is a FACT from the passage?**

A Horses make movies more exciting.

B Horses run for miles at full gallop in order to be filmed.

C Horses put cotton in their ears before firing guns.

D Members of the American Humane Association protect horses.

Hint: A fact is something real and true.

STOP

Answers
4 Ⓕ Ⓖ Ⓗ Ⓙ   **5** Ⓐ Ⓑ Ⓒ Ⓓ

Directions: Read each selection carefully. Then read each question. Darken the circle for the correct answer, or write the answers in the space provided.

| TRY THIS | More than one answer choice may seem correct. Choose the answer that goes best with the selection. |

Sample A   **The Lost Dog**

Mike and his father found a dog in the park. They brought it home. Mike placed an advertisement in the newspaper about finding the dog. Two days later the dog's owner came to get her dog.

How did the dog's owner find out that her dog was with Mike?

A She saw Mike with the dog.

B She read about it in the newspaper.

C Mike's father told her.

D She searched until she found her dog.

| THINK IT THROUGH | The correct answer is <u>B</u>. The third sentence tells you that Mike placed an advertisement in the newspaper. You can guess that the owner read about her dog. |

STOP

An Ancient Wonder

The Egyptians made statues of sphinxes to honor kings and queens. A sphinx has the head of a human and the body of a lion. The oldest and largest sphinx is the Great Sphinx. It was built in the desert near Giza, Egypt, thousands of years ago. At times the Great Sphinx has been buried by sand. Weather has worn away part of the stone. Today scientists are working on ways to save the Great Sphinx.

1   What is the land like where the Great Sphinx stands?

A snowy

B dry

C rainy

D full of trees

2   What is a sphinx?

_____

_____

_____

_____

_____

_____

GO ON

Answers
SA Ⓐ Ⓑ Ⓒ Ⓓ   1 Ⓐ Ⓑ Ⓒ Ⓓ

Camino and Mr. Mishima

Mr. Mishima has a true best friend. His name is Camino, and he is a dog. Camino always helped Mr. Mishima, but one day he saved his owner's life.

Mr. Mishima was about seventy years old. He lived all alone on a farm outside of town. Most people didn't know him well. He liked to be alone, and people thought he was unfriendly. He was very strong and worked very hard to grow and harvest his crops. He grew the largest tomatoes in the county. During a very busy season, he would hire me after school to help around the farm. He always told me that I was the son he never had. Camino helped, too. Mr. Mishima loved his pet.

One day Mr. Mishima decided he would start loading the truck before I got to the farm. Sometimes he was stubborn that way. He tried lifting a very heavy crate. He felt a sharp pain in his chest and fell to the ground. Camino ran to the gas station near the farm and barked. Rubén, the gas station worker, thought the dog had gone wild. The dog began pulling and biting at Rubén's pants. Camino then ran to Rubén's jeep and leaped into the back seat. Rubén finally understood that something was wrong. He drove back to the farm and found Mr. Mishima on the ground. Rubén immediately took Mr. Mishima to the hospital.

Mr. Mishima was lucky. He had suffered a heart attack, but thanks to Camino and Rubén, he would be all right.

After Mr. Mishima had fully *recuperated*, he had a big party and invited the entire town. Everyone came to honor Camino and Rubén. But something else happened at the party, too. People finally realized that Mr. Mishima was not unfriendly after all.

GO ON➡

3 From the story you can assume that the author—

   F thinks that Mr. Mishima should be more friendly.

   G thinks that Mr. Mishima should retire.

   H is fond of Mr. Mishima.

   J does not like farm work.

4 If the author added a sentence to the end of the fourth paragraph, which of the following would fit best?

   A I hope to work on Mr. Mishima's farm this summer, too.

   B Mr. Mishima learned how to farm from his father.

   C Mr. Mishima was able to return to farm work within a few weeks.

   D I am able to lift the heavy crates of tomatoes.

5 Why did Camino leap into the jeep?

   F He wanted Rubén to go with him to the farm.

   G He wanted to go for a ride.

   H He was crazy.

   J He was trying to get away from Rubén.

6 In this selection, the word "recuperated" probably means—

   A recovered.

   B made a profit.

   C doing things one's own way.

   D leave.

7 How many sons did Mr. Mishima have?

   F one

   G two

   H none

   J This information is not stated in the selection.

8 Who is the author of this story?

   A Mr. Mishima's son

   B Camino's owner

   C Rubén

   D someone who works for Mr. Mishima

9 Why was Camino a special dog?

   F He was excellent at farm work.

   G He saved his owner's life.

   H He liked to ride in automobiles.

   J He knew how to do many tricks.

10 Why was Mr. Mishima lucky?

_____

_____

_____

_____

_____

_____

GO ON ▶

Answers

3 Ⓕ Ⓖ Ⓗ Ⓙ   **5** Ⓕ Ⓖ Ⓗ Ⓙ   **7** Ⓕ Ⓖ Ⓗ Ⓙ   **9** Ⓕ Ⓖ Ⓗ Ⓙ

4 Ⓐ Ⓑ Ⓒ Ⓓ   **6** Ⓐ Ⓑ Ⓒ Ⓓ   **8** Ⓐ Ⓑ Ⓒ Ⓓ

Reggie Learns a Lesson

Once there was a terrible fire in a forest. The only way for a group of monkeys to survive was to escape into a river. The river had a fast current that swept the monkeys downstream. After several minutes all the monkeys were able to grab hold of a large branch. They floated on the branch for hours. The monkeys fell asleep from exhaustion. When they awoke, they found themselves *marooned* on the shore of an island.

The monkeys investigated the island and found that there were plenty of trees and generous amounts of food to eat. All the monkeys came to accept their new home, except one named Reggie. Reggie missed his old environment. He wanted to go back, but there was no way to do that.

As time passed, Reggie became lazy. He spent his days napping in the shade. The other monkeys would try to get Reggie to play with them.

"Reggie, come swing in the trees with us. Exercise. You'll feel better," they would shout to Reggie.

"Why should I? Life is uninteresting. Especially being stranded on this island. Just leave me alone. I'm tired. I'm also young. I have the rest of my life to do those kinds of things. Maybe I'll feel like doing that tomorrow," would be his reply.

One day while Reggie was napping, a trapper came to the island to capture animals for his small zoo in a nearby country. The other monkeys saw the trapper and warned Reggie. Reggie got up to run away, but he had grown fat and slow. The trapper easily imprisoned Reggie in a net. The other monkeys were strong and healthy and had no problem running away and climbing trees to escape capture.

11 **What is meant by the word "marooned" in the first paragraph?**

_____

_____

_____

_____

_____

_____

12 **Which of these proverbs best fits this selection?**

A Enjoy life as it is today; tomorrow may never come.

B A penny saved is a penny earned.

C If at first you don't succeed, try, try again.

D A stitch in time saves nine.

13 **This story most likely would be found in a book of—**

F fables.

G facts.

H biographies.

J myths.

14 **According to the selection, which of these events happened last?**

A The monkeys were in a forest fire.

B The monkeys were stranded on an island.

C Reggie was captured by an animal trapper.

D Reggie napped in the shade.

GO ON

Cats: Past to Present

Cats are so popular today that about 58 million of them are kept as pets in the United States alone. Even thousands of years ago, in ancient Egypt, cats were admired and loved.

The Egyptians began to tame wild cats around 3500 B.C. These cats protected the Egyptians' crops from mice, rats, and snakes. Thus they became pets.

Greek and Phoenician traders probably brought cats to Europe and the Middle East around 1000 B.C. From the Middle East, cats spread throughout Asia. There, cats protected silkworms and temple manuscripts from rats, so they were pampered and admired.

However, cats did not do so well in Europe during the Middle Ages (A.D. 400-1500). At that time, many people believed that cats were evil, and people killed thousands of cats. Some historians believe that the destruction of so many cats led to the spread of bubonic plague, called the Black Death. This disease was spread by rats, which were no longer being killed off by cats.

By the 1600s, cats were once again popular in Europe, and explorers brought them to America. Here, they have become one of the best-loved of household pets.

15 Which of the following expresses an opinion stated in the selection?

F Traders brought cats to Europe.

G Cats are evil.

H Cats became pets in ancient Egypt.

J Cats were tamed by the Egyptians.

16 When did cats come to Asia?

_____

_____

_____

_____

17 The selection is *mainly* about—

A how cats attack rats.

B cats in ancient Egypt.

C how cats came to America.

D the history of cats.

18 Cats in the Ancient Middle East and in Asia can be compared to today's—

F explorers.

G security guards.

H lions.

J historians.

GO ON

Answers
15 Ⓕ Ⓖ Ⓗ Ⓙ   **17** Ⓐ Ⓑ Ⓒ Ⓓ   **18** Ⓕ Ⓖ Ⓗ Ⓙ

Kites through the Ages

The oldest form of aircraft is the kite. However, no one knows where kites were first flown. Some people think the people of the South Sea Islands invented them. The people of the Solomon Islands still use kites to help with fishing. From their canoes, they fly a kite with a fishing line hanging from it. When the person in the canoe sees the line move, he or she pulls in the fish.

Some people think the art of flying kites spread to New Zealand next. The native people of New Zealand, the Maori, often made kites in the shapes of birds. They believed that birds carried messages from Earth to the gods. Some kites were designed with the bodies of birds and the heads of people. Feathers and shells were used to decorate these kites.

Most people think that the Chinese were the first to use kites. There is a story about a Chinese general who fought a battle in the year 202 B.C.

His army was surrounded by the enemy. He had his men build many kites. He told them to put a small piece of bamboo on each kite. Then he instructed the men to fly the kites over the enemy camp at night. When the wind whistled through the bamboo, the kites *shrieked*. The enemy feared they were being chased by evil spirits, and they ran away.

There is also a story about a famous Japanese thief who used a kite to reach the top of a castle. On the roof of the castle were statues of dolphins made of gold. The thief stole some of the gold from the dolphins. Then he used the kite to lower himself to the ground. Unfortunately for him, he was caught and put to death for stealing.

Kites have had many uses. In the past they have been used in scientific experiments. The National Weather Service used kites to measure the weather. Kites were also important to the development of the airplane.

Today kites are used mostly for recreation. Since the 1970s there has been renewed interest in kites. Kites come in many shapes, sizes, and colors. Kites can be flown and enjoyed the year round. There are even kite clubs and festivals in many parts of the world.

GO ON

19 In order to answer question 20, the best thing to do is—

  A reread the second question.

  B reread the third paragraph.

  C think about the selection's mood.

  D reread the entire selection.

20 The author included the third paragraph in order to—

  F describe the setting of the selection.

  G describe the actions of a character in the selection.

  H explain the likely origin of the kite.

  J summarize the main ideas in the selection.

21 Who were probably the first people to use kites?

  _____

  _____

  _____

  _____

  _____

22 According to the selection, in what country did a thief use a kite to steal gold?

  A China

  B the Solomon Islands

  C India

  D Japan

23 Where were kites invented?

  F No one knows for sure.

  G in New Zealand

  H in Japan

  J in China

24 According to the selection, the kite is the oldest form of—

  A toy.

  B aircraft.

  C communication.

  D art.

25 The Chinese general told his men to attach bamboo to the kites in order to—

  F balance the kites.

  G make the kites look better.

  H make the kites shriek.

  J make the kites fly higher.

26 Why did the Maori fashion kites in the shapes of birds?

  A In their culture, the Maori worshipped birds as gods.

  B They believed the bird shapes would make the kites fly high.

  C The Maori feared birds and made the kites in bird shapes for protection from the birds.

  D They believed that birds carried messages from the Maori to their gods.

27 According to the selection, kites were important to the development of the—

  F yo-yo.

  G submarine.

  H airplane.

  J gondola.

28 In line 4 of the fourth paragraph, the word "shrieked" means—

  A fished.

  B surrounded.

  C screamed.

  D fled.

GO ON ➡

Answers

| 19 Ⓐ Ⓑ Ⓒ Ⓓ | 22 Ⓐ Ⓑ Ⓒ Ⓓ | 24 Ⓐ Ⓑ Ⓒ Ⓓ | 26 Ⓐ Ⓑ Ⓒ Ⓓ | 28 Ⓐ Ⓑ Ⓒ Ⓓ |
| 20 Ⓕ Ⓖ Ⓗ Ⓙ | 23 Ⓕ Ⓖ Ⓗ Ⓙ | 25 Ⓕ Ⓖ Ⓗ Ⓙ | 27 Ⓕ Ⓖ Ⓗ Ⓙ | |

An Amazing Trick

    I learned a magic trick that will amaze people young and old. You will need the following supplies: a strip of paper about two inches wide by eight inches long, two paper clips, and a rubber band. Follow the steps and refer to the pictures to help you. The pictures are numbered according to the steps.

    First, bring one end of the paper to the middle. Secure it with a paper clip.

    Second, slip the rubber band through to the middle of the paper.

    Next, bring the other end of the paper around to the front to form a loop around the first paper clip and the rubber band. Hold the middle and the front of the paper together with the second paper clip.

    Fourth, say the word "Abracadabra." At the same time, pull the ends of the paper in opposite directions.

    The result of the trick should be that the two clips will hang together from the rubber band on the paper.

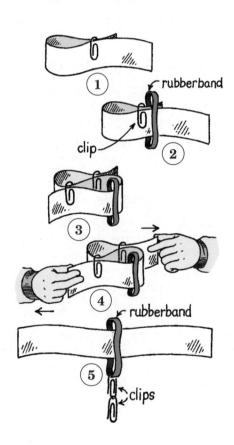

29 **If the trick is done correctly, what should happen when the ends of the strip of paper are pulled in opposite directions?**

  F The paper should rip.

  G The two paper clips should hang together from the rubber band on the paper.

  H The rubber band should stay on the paper, but the paper clips should fly off.

  J The rubber band should fly into the air, and the paper clips should remain on the paper.

30 **What should you do just before you use the strip of paper to form a loop around the first paper clip and the rubber band?**

_____

_____

_____

_____

_____

_____

_____

31 **The best title for this magic trick might be—**

  A "The Amazing Clip Link."

  B "Loop de Loop."

  C "Shooting Rubber Bands."

  D "The Disappearing Paper Clips."

STOP

A sample question helps you to understand the type of question you will be asked in the test that follows.

Sample A   **Buying a Reed**

Riley needed a new reed for his clarinet. He asked his teacher if he could purchase one from her. She replied, "Yes, you can buy one from me in the band room after school today."

What did Riley have to do in order to get a new reed for his clarinet?

A buy one from a music store after school

B borrow one from a band member

C buy one in the office during lunch time

D buy one in the band room after school

STOP

For questions 1–32 carefully read each selection and the questions that follow. Then darken the circle for the correct answer, or write the answer in the space provided.

A Neighborhood Ball Game

The children on Wisconsin Avenue played wiffle ball every day during the summer. One day they decided to hold a wiffle ball game to raise money to buy bats and balls. They passed out fliers to all the homes on the block. The fliers read:

> **Wiffle Ball Game**
>
> The Mighty Mites vs. The Fabulous Five
> When: Saturday, August 15
> Where: 721 S. Wisconsin
> Time: 6:00 P.M.
> Cost: Tickets $0.25 each or 5 for $1.00.
>
> Tickets are refundable if game is rained out.
>
> There will be a home-run hitting contest. The winner will receive an autographed baseball card.

1   **What was the prize for the contest?**

A a bat and ball

B a ticket to a ball game

C an autographed baseball card

D a baseball cap

2   **What would happen if it rained at game time?**

F The game would be played.

G The game would be played later.

H The game would be cancelled.

J Ticket money would be returned.

3   **Why did the children hold the game?**

_____

_____

_____

_____

_____

_____

GO ON

Answers
SA Ⓐ Ⓑ Ⓒ Ⓓ   **1** Ⓐ Ⓑ Ⓒ Ⓓ   **2** Ⓕ Ⓖ Ⓗ Ⓙ

A Great Woman

Marian Anderson was born in 1902 in Philadelphia. At the age of six, she was singing solos in front of the *congregation* of the Union Baptist Church. Her pure, soaring voice moved the audience, and everyone who heard her knew that the child had great talent.

Marian loved to sing. She hoped that she would be able to take singing lessons one day. But Marian's family was poor. When her father died, the family was overwhelmed with sadness and financial problems. Marian offered to quit school and go to work, but her mother refused to listen. She wanted her children to get an education.

The members of Marian's church started a collection and suggested that Marian perform at various events and make money from her singing. Marian was proud to be able to make enough money to help her family.

Marian even managed to save enough money for singing lessons. But when the music school refused to accept her because she was African-American, Marian was deeply hurt. Her mother continued to encourage her, and Marian decided to take private lessons. She had an appointment to sing for the well-known teacher Giuseppe Boghetti, who was very impressed. He said that after studying with him, Marian would be able to sing for kings and queens!

Mr. Boghetti taught Marian to sing opera. In 1925 he encouraged her to enter a contest. Although there were three hundred people entered in the contest, Marian won. She became a guest soloist with the New York Philharmonic Symphony Orchestra. She finally felt confident enough to sing anywhere. However, when Marian tried to sing at the best concert halls in the country, she was turned away because she was African-American.

Frustrated, Marian decided to go to Europe, where she hoped to be judged on her talent and not her race. During the two years she spent in Europe, Marian was made to feel very welcome. She won the admiration of Europeans in city after city. The famous conductor Arturo Toscanini told her, "A voice like yours is heard only once in a hundred years."

The overwhelming *acclamation* Marian received in Europe made new opportunities available to her in the United States. Following her return from Europe, she became the first African-American to be named a permanent member of the Metropolitan Opera Company. She also became the first African-American to perform at the White House. Through her perseverance and positive attitude, Marian Anderson was able to make the most of her talent and to open the door for other African-American performers.

GO ON ➡

4 When the author states, "Through her perseverance and positive attitude, Marian Anderson was able to make the most of her talent and to open the door for other African-American performers," the author is trying to convince the reader that—

A Marian succeeded only because her talent was so great.

B Marian's hard work and talent enabled her and others to break through the barriers of prejudice.

C Marian was only interested in making money and in furthering her own career.

D Marian probably would have been more successful if she had stayed in Europe.

5 Why did Marian offer to quit school?

_____

_____

_____

_____

_____

_____

6 To find out more about Marian Anderson you could look in the library under—

F Famous Europeans.

G Famous Opera Singers.

H Jazz Musicians.

J History of Art.

7 The author uses the word "acclamation" in line 1 of the last paragraph to mean—

A enthusiastic approval.

B singing appearances.

C salary.

D audiences.

8 Which of these is a fact stated in the selection?

F Marian Anderson sang duets with her mother.

G Marian felt lonely in Europe.

H Marian was very close to her father.

J The members of Marian's church helped her family.

9 In line 3 of the first paragraph, the word "congregation" means—

A fire.

B assembly.

C piano.

D stage.

10 Where was Marian Anderson born and raised?

F in New York

G in Europe

H in Boston

J in Philadelphia

11 What generalization can you make about the 1920s from this selection?

A Laws ensured equal rights for all citizens.

B There was less prejudice against African-Americans at that time than there is now.

C There was more prejudice against African-Americans in the United States than in Europe.

D African-Americans had more civil rights during the 1920s than they have today.

GO ON ⟹

Answers

4 Ⓐ Ⓑ Ⓒ Ⓓ   **7** Ⓐ Ⓑ Ⓒ Ⓓ   **9** Ⓐ Ⓑ Ⓒ Ⓓ   **11** Ⓐ Ⓑ Ⓒ Ⓓ

6 Ⓕ Ⓖ Ⓗ Ⓙ   **8** Ⓕ Ⓖ Ⓗ Ⓙ   **10** Ⓕ Ⓖ Ⓗ Ⓙ

A Tasty Mexican Treat

Tacos are among the most popular of all Mexican foods. They are easy and fun to make, and you can vary the ingredients depending upon your taste. For example, you can use hamburger or chicken for the meat. Some people even substitute shrimp for the hamburger. You can also add hot peppers, if your mouth can take the heat!

Tacos

Ingredients:

1 box taco shells

$\frac{1}{4}$ cup oil

1 onion, chopped

1 pound hamburger (or chicken)

1 pinch cumin

1 tomato, diced

1 cup lettuce

$\frac{1}{2}$ cup cheese, grated

Hot sauce to taste

Prepare the tomato, lettuce, and cheese. Set them aside. Next, in a large pan, heat the oil and brown the onions. Add the hamburger or chicken to the onions. Stir over medium heat until the meat is browned. Add a pinch of cumin. Heat the taco shells according to the package directions. Fill the taco shells with meat, tomato, lettuce, cheese, and hot sauce. Serve with plenty of napkins!

GO ON

12 Which meat can you use instead of hamburger?

_____

_____

_____

_____

_____

13 According to the recipe for tacos, how much cumin should you use?

F $\frac{1}{3}$ cup

G 1 cup

H a pinch

J 1 teaspoon

14 Which of these ingredients is *not* cooked?

A onion

B hamburger

C tomato

D oil

15 If you wanted to learn more about Mexican food, you should—

F locate Mexico on a map.

G ask a bookstore owner.

H read a book about Mexican cooking.

J study the history of Mexico.

TEST TIP

Use the letter groups ABCD and FGHJ to make sure you are filling in the circle for the right question.

16 The boxes show some directions for making tacos.

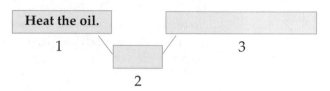

Heat the oil.		
1	2	3

Which of these belongs in Box 2?

A Add cumin to meat.

B Prepare the tomato, lettuce, and cheese.

C Brown the onions.

D Fill the taco shells with the ingredients.

17 How are the taco shells prepared?

F The shells are heated in oil.

G The shells are browned with the onions.

H This information is not stated in the selection.

J They are heated according to the package directions.

18 What is the last ingredient that is put into the taco shell?

A meat

B hot sauce

C cheese

D lettuce

19 The tacos are served with napkins because they—

F are filling.

G are messy.

H are hot.

J should be carried outside.

GO ON ⇨

The California Gold Rush of 1848

The California Gold Rush of 1848 began at John Sutter's sawmill in the Sacramento Valley. Sutter was a shopkeeper from Switzerland. He had come to California ten years before, hoping to find a new life. He probably never dreamed that gold would be found on his land.

One day one of Mr. Sutter's partners, John Marshall, found a shiny nugget in a ditch near the sawmill. It was the size of a dime. Marshall tested the nugget to see if it was in fact the precious metal, gold. He tried shattering it and tarnishing it. He put it in lye to see if it would melt or crack. It did none of these things. Marshall was very excited and rode all one night to show the nugget to Sutter. Sutter was *skeptical* at first. He couldn't believe that there might be gold on his land. Then he tried the ultimate test. He poured nitric acid on the metal to see if it would be eaten away. It was not.

When news of the discovery broke, California was changed forever. Sutter and Marshall could no longer operate the sawmill. Their workers abandoned their jobs to search for gold. People from all over the country came to California. Even people from Europe and China arrived in California to look for gold.

New trails were opened to the West. People seemed not to mind the hardships of pioneer living as long as they found gold. In 1848 the population of California grew from 20,000 to 107,000 people. San Francisco and Sacramento were transformed from sleepy towns into booming cities. Miners who found gold were eager to spend their money in the cities. Others who were not so lucky remained in the area and became farmers or ranchers. The Gold Rush lasted from 1848 until 1852. During that time the population continued to grow, and in 1850 California became a state.

Unfortunately, the Gold Rush was not very good for Sutter and Marshall. So many people were living on the land around the sawmill that Sutter was forced to give up his claim to the land. Marshall tried searching for gold but never had much luck after that first find.

GO ON ➡

20 This selection is *mainly* about—

    A John Sutter's sawmill.

    B early California history.

    C the life of James Marshall.

    D the Gold Rush.

21 Which of the following events happened *first*?

    F The population of California grew.

    G Marshall discovered gold near the sawmill.

    H New trails were opened to the West.

    J California became a state.

22 In line 6 of the second paragraph, the author uses the word "skeptical" to mean—

    A doubtful.

    B hopeful.

    C inspired.

    D puzzled.

23 Which word best describes California during the Gold Rush?

    F uneventful

    G pessimistic

    H prosperous

    J frightening

24 Why did so many people leave their homes and jobs to search for gold?

_____

_____

_____

_____

_____

25 According to the selection, why is gold considered a precious metal?

    A It is easily tarnished, and lye melts it.

    B It is very valuable.

    C People use it to make chains and other jewelry.

    D It is used only to make coins.

26 What are paragraphs 3 and 4 *mainly* about?

    F how California became a state

    G how the Gold Rush affected California

    H how people lived in California during the Gold Rush

    J how gold was discovered in California

27 The author included the first paragraph in order to—

    A introduce an important character.

    B describe the setting.

    C describe the mood.

    D explain the term "Gold Rush."

28 Why did the author write this selection?

_____

_____

_____

_____

_____

_____

_____

GO ON

Answers

20 Ⓐ Ⓑ Ⓒ Ⓓ   **22** Ⓐ Ⓑ Ⓒ Ⓓ   **25** Ⓐ Ⓑ Ⓒ Ⓓ   **27** Ⓐ Ⓑ Ⓒ Ⓓ

21 Ⓕ Ⓖ Ⓗ Ⓙ   **23** Ⓕ Ⓖ Ⓗ Ⓙ   **26** Ⓕ Ⓖ Ⓗ Ⓙ

Frontier Adventure

The February wind blew chill across the prairie. Mae and Milly huddled together in the wagon, trying to stay warm. Soon their father would stop to make camp for the night. Then they could build a fire to warm themselves. The sisters watched their mother. She was swaying with the motion of the wagon as she mended their clothes. When they reached their new home on the frontier, there would be no store nearby to buy things. They would have to make do with what they had. That seemed both scary and exciting to the girls. This move was really an adventure.

Suddenly the girls heard their father shout, "Quick, come up here and look at this!" The girls and their mother crawled to the front of the wagon, opened the flap, and looked out upon a large herd of buffalo. The powerful animals with their brown, shaggy coats moved slowly toward the south. They kept their backs to the wind, which seemed to blow colder as the day progressed.

"This might be a good stopping place. It looks like we might be in for some bad weather," their father said. Clouds were gathering on the northern horizon as the family prepared for the night. Mae helped her father look for dry brush to start a fire, while Milly and her mother made preparations for dinner. They all worked quickly, sensing that they had a long night ahead.

29 Why was the family expecting a long, hard night?

_____

_____

_____

_____

_____

30 The family was traveling in—

F a canoe.

G a railroad compartment.

H a covered wagon.

J a houseboat.

31 There is enough information in this selection to learn how—

A to mend clothes.

B pioneers traveled across the prairie.

C to make camp.

D buffalo crossed the prairie.

32 According to the selection, how many family members are making the journey?

F three

G four

H five

J seven

STOP

Answers
30 Ⓕ Ⓖ Ⓗ Ⓙ   **31** Ⓐ Ⓑ Ⓒ Ⓓ   **32** Ⓕ Ⓖ Ⓗ Ⓙ

READING VOCABULARY

===IDENTIFYING WORD MEANINGS===

Directions: Darken the circle for the word or group of words that has the same or almost the same meaning as the underlined word, or write in the answer.

| TRY THIS | Choose your answer carefully. The other choices may seem correct. Be sure to think about the meaning of the underlined word. |

Sample A

To <u>chat</u> is to—

A   agree   C   plan

B   laugh   D   talk

THINK IT THROUGH

The correct answer is <u>D</u>. To <u>chat</u> is to <u>talk</u>. To <u>chat</u> is not to agree, laugh, or plan.

STOP

1   A <u>drill</u> is—

   A   an engine   C   a fire

   B   an exit   D   an exercise

2   Something that is <u>brief</u> is—

   F   long   H   serious

   G   thin   J   short

3   To <u>admit</u> something is to—

   A   hide it   C   improve it

   B   confess it   D   change it

4   A person who is <u>idle</u> is—

   F   busy   H   loyal

   G   lazy   J   quick

5   A <u>festival</u> is a kind of—

   A   journey   C   song

   B   celebration   D   dessert

6   Something that is <u>urgent</u> is—

   F   confusing   H   important

   G   silly   J   simple

7   A walk that is <u>brisk</u> is—

   A   slow   C   fun

   B   quick   D   steady

8   If you are <u>chilly</u>, you are—

_____

_____

_____

_____

STOP

Answers

SA ⓐ ⓑ ⓒ ⓓ   2 ⓕ ⓖ ⓗ ⓙ   4 ⓕ ⓖ ⓗ ⓙ   6 ⓕ ⓖ ⓗ ⓙ

1 ⓐ ⓑ ⓒ ⓓ   3 ⓐ ⓑ ⓒ ⓓ   5 ⓐ ⓑ ⓒ ⓓ   7 ⓐ ⓑ ⓒ ⓓ

Directions: Darken the circle for the sentence in which the underlined word means the same as it does in the sentence in the box.

TRY THIS

Read the sentence in the box carefully. Decide what the underlined word means. Then look for the sentence in which the underlined word has the same meaning.

Sample A

> We saw the deer easily <u>clear</u> the fence.

In which sentence does <u>clear</u> have the same meaning as it does in the sentence above?

A Will that runner <u>clear</u> the hurdle?

B I need to <u>clear</u> this issue with the boss.

C It was a crisp, <u>clear</u> morning.

D Her speech was loud and <u>clear</u>.

THINK IT THROUGH

The correct answer is **A**. In this sentence and in the sentence in the box, <u>clear</u> means "to pass without touching."

STOP

1

> Miranda seems to <u>favor</u> the color purple.

In which sentence does <u>favor</u> have the same meaning as it does in the sentence above?

A I will do this as a <u>favor</u>.

B She has a puzzle as a party <u>favor</u>.

C The people <u>favor</u> keeping that law.

D Does the baby <u>favor</u> his mother?

2

> Judy placed a <u>fork</u> on the table.

In which sentence does <u>fork</u> have the same meaning as it does in the sentence above?

F Turn right at the <u>fork</u> in the road.

G The child is learning to eat with a <u>fork</u>.

H Jake used a tuning <u>fork</u> to fix the piano.

J Mary sat in the <u>fork</u> of the tree.

3

> First, <u>stir</u> the paint.

In which sentence does <u>stir</u> have the same meaning as it does in the sentence above?

A Ming didn't <u>stir</u> during the scary movie.

B The speech created quite a <u>stir</u>.

C You must <u>stir</u> the sauce until it thickens.

D See the wind <u>stir</u> the leaves.

4

> She didn't leave a <u>drop</u> of juice.

In which sentence does <u>drop</u> have the same meaning as it does in the sentence above?

F The price of the skates will <u>drop</u>.

G The baby was about to <u>drop</u> his toy.

H There was one <u>drop</u> of medicine left.

J Can we please <u>drop</u> the subject?

STOP

Answers
SA Ⓐ Ⓑ Ⓒ Ⓓ   1 Ⓐ Ⓑ Ⓒ Ⓓ   2 Ⓕ Ⓖ Ⓗ Ⓙ   3 Ⓐ Ⓑ Ⓒ Ⓓ   4 Ⓕ Ⓖ Ⓗ Ⓙ

Directions: Darken the circle for the word or words that give the meaning of the underlined word, or write in the answer.

> **TRY THIS**
> Read the first sentence carefully. Look for clue words in the sentence. Then use each answer choice in place of the underlined word. Remember that the underlined word and your answer must have the same meaning.

Sample A

Grandpa <u>recalled</u> the games he played as a child. <u>Recalled</u> means—

A remembered

B played

C forgot

D listed

> **THINK IT THROUGH**
> The correct answer is <u>A</u>. The clue words are "Grandpa" and "child." Grandpa would remember games he had played as a child.

1 The students were surprised by the principal's <u>startling</u> announcement. <u>Startling</u> means—

A unexpected

B daily

C brief

D usual

2 The <u>acute</u> ache in her side caused Minnie intense pain. <u>Acute</u> means—

F frequent

G occasional

H slight

J severe

3 Karen noticed items missing from the store's <u>inventory</u>. <u>Inventory</u> means—

A warehouse

B bill

C property

D truck

4 She didn't like the dance because it had <u>complicated</u> steps. <u>Complicated</u> means—

_____

_____

_____

_____

5 Jean has won <u>numerous</u> awards for all her paintings. <u>Numerous</u> means—

F many

G secret

H art

J foreign

6 The heavy rains <u>replenished</u> the empty well. <u>Replenished</u> means—

A refilled

B destroyed

C ruined

D poisoned

Answers
SA Ⓐ Ⓑ Ⓒ Ⓓ   2 Ⓕ Ⓖ Ⓗ Ⓙ   5 Ⓕ Ⓖ Ⓗ Ⓙ
1 Ⓐ Ⓑ Ⓒ Ⓓ   3 Ⓐ Ⓑ Ⓒ Ⓓ   6 Ⓐ Ⓑ Ⓒ Ⓓ

Sample A

To **investigate** is to—

A   plan

B   hide

C   mix

D   examine

STOP

For questions 1–8, darken the circle for the word or words that have the same or almost the same meaning as the underlined word.

1   Something that is **incomplete** is—

A   finished

B   excellent

C   unfinished

D   perfect

2   To **resume** is to—

F   end

G   begin

H   hide

J   continue

3   Something that is **brutal** is—

A   harsh

B   gentle

C   warm

D   soft

4   Someone who is **courageous** is—

F   brave

G   friendly

H   shy

J   afraid

5   A **solution** is—

A   a plan

B   an answer

C   a question

D   a trick

6   A **tradition** is the same as—

F   a sport

G   an activity

H   a barrier

J   a custom

7   An **error** is a—

A   game

B   race

C   mistake

D   visitor

8   An **academy** is a kind of—

F   school

G   family

H   channel

J   custom

Write your answer for the following:

9   Someone who is **weary** is—

_____

_____

_____

_____

_____

_____

STOP

Answers

SA Ⓐ Ⓑ Ⓒ Ⓓ   **2** Ⓕ Ⓖ Ⓗ Ⓙ   **4** Ⓕ Ⓖ Ⓗ Ⓙ   **6** Ⓕ Ⓖ Ⓗ Ⓙ   **8** Ⓕ Ⓖ Ⓗ Ⓙ

1 Ⓐ Ⓑ Ⓒ Ⓓ   **3** Ⓐ Ⓑ Ⓒ Ⓓ   **5** Ⓐ Ⓑ Ⓒ Ⓓ   **7** Ⓐ Ⓑ Ⓒ Ⓓ

Sample B

> Marissa tried to spare her sister's feelings.

In which sentence does spare have the same meaning as it does in the sentence above?

A   The spare tire was also flat.

B   Do you have any spare change?

C   The knight decided to spare the dragon.

D   We have a spare bedroom for guests.

 STOP

For questions 10–14, darken the circle for the sentence in which the underlined word means the same as it does in the sentence in the box.

10
> The steps to our porch are not level.

In which sentence does level have the same meaning as it does in the sentence above?

A   This recipe requires one level teaspoon of sugar.

B   We traveled high above sea level.

C   Manuel advanced to the next level of tennis.

D   She used a level to make sure the shelf was straight.

11
> She scored double the points of her friend.

In which sentence does double have the same meaning as it does in the sentence above?

F   The pilot lived a double life as a spy.

G   The twin was his double.

H   Zack hit a double in today's game.

J   Six is the double of three.

12
> Ben read the instructions on the computer monitor.

In which sentence does monitor have the same meaning as it does in the sentence above?

A   Her job is to be the playground monitor.

B   A radar device will monitor the traffic.

C   The monitor recorded the patient's heartbeat.

D   Who will monitor the players?

13
> Be sure to pound the nail in carefully.

In which sentence does pound have the same meaning as it does in the sentence above?

F   Ned had to pound the tent stakes into the ground.

G   This weighs little more than one pound.

H   His heart began to pound as he stepped up to the plate.

J   They went to a pound to find a new puppy.

14
> The soccer ball rolled past the foul line.

In which sentence does foul have the same meaning as it does in the sentence above?

A   Our plane was delayed due to foul weather.

B   The chemical gave off a foul odor.

C   That group was guilty of foul play.

D   The batter hit a foul ball.

STOP

Answers
SB Ⓐ Ⓑ Ⓒ Ⓓ   11 Ⓕ Ⓖ Ⓗ Ⓙ   13 Ⓕ Ⓖ Ⓗ Ⓙ
10 Ⓐ Ⓑ Ⓒ Ⓓ   12 Ⓐ Ⓑ Ⓒ Ⓓ   14 Ⓐ Ⓑ Ⓒ Ⓓ

Sample C

The celebration is about to <u>commence</u>. <u>Commence</u> means to—

A begin

B end

C continue

D close

STOP

For questions 15–21, darken the circle for the word or words that give the meaning of the underlined word.

15 They set up camp in a <u>remote</u> part of the forest. <u>Remote</u> means—

F small

G large

H distant

J woody

16 The two politicians <u>collided</u> over the new tax plans. <u>Collided</u> means—

A talked favorably

B agreed to discuss

C supported

D strongly disagreed

17 Make sure to <u>secure</u> the lock on the door. <u>Secure</u> means—

F fasten

G open

H measure

J insert

18 We laughed aloud at her <u>hilarious</u> tale. <u>Hilarious</u> means—

A obviously fictional

B very stupid

C extremely funny

D quite offensive

19 Be <u>specific</u> about what you need done. <u>Specific</u> means—

F unsure

G secretive

H vague

J definite

20 She <u>indicated</u> the route to take to the store. <u>Indicated</u> means—

A closed

B drove off

C pointed out

D left

21 The fast-running river flowed <u>rapidly</u> down the steep mountainside. <u>Rapidly</u> means—

F slowly

G swiftly

H lazily

J secretly

Write your answer for the following:

22 The novel has an interesting <u>plot</u>. What is the <u>plot</u> of a novel?

_____

_____

_____

_____

STOP

MATH PROBLEM-SOLVING PLAN

OVERVIEW

THE PROBLEM-SOLVING PLAN

When solving math problems follow these steps:

STEP 1: WHAT IS THE QUESTION/GOAL?

Decide what must be found. This information is usually presented in the form of a question.

STEP 2: FIND THE FACTS

Locate the factual information in three different ways:

    A. KEY FACTS are the facts you need to solve the problem.

    B. FACTS YOU DON'T NEED are those facts that are not necessary for solving the problem.

    C. ARE MORE FACTS NEEDED? Decide if you have enough information to solve the problem.

STEP 3: SELECT A STRATEGY

Decide what strategies you might use, how you will use them, and then estimate what your answer will be. If one strategy doesn't help you to solve the problem, try another.

STEP 4: SOLVE

Apply the strategy according to your plan. Use an operation if necessary, and clearly indicate your answer.

STEP 5: DOES YOUR RESPONSE MAKE SENSE?

Check to make sure that your answer makes sense. Use estimation or approximation strategies.

Directions: Use the problem-solving plan to solve this math problem.

PROBLEM/QUESTION:

Mr. Gonzalez is a salesman from Manorville. He drove 45 miles to visit his first customer in Boston. The drive took him 1 hour. On his return trip he drove an extra 30 minutes to visit a customer in Oaktown, which is 15 miles north of Boston. If Manorville is west of Boston, draw a map of the trip.

STEP 1: WHAT IS THE QUESTION/GOAL?

_____

_____

_____

STEP 2: FIND THE FACTS

_____

_____

_____

STEP 3: SELECT A STRATEGY

_____

_____

_____

STEP 4: SOLVE

STEP 5: DOES YOUR RESPONSE MAKE SENSE?

_____

_____

_____

_____

Directions: Use the problem-solving plan to solve this math problem.

PROBLEM/QUESTION:

Su Ling went to the bookstore to buy 5 books. Each of the books costs $4.95. Su Ling thought the total cost for the 5 books should be about $19.50. Is Su Ling correct? If she is wrong, what mistake did she make when she figured out the price.

STEP 1: WHAT IS THE QUESTION/GOAL?

_____

_____

_____

STEP 2: FIND THE FACTS

_____

_____

_____

STEP 3: SELECT A STRATEGY

_____

_____

_____

STEP 4: SOLVE

_____

_____

_____

STEP 5: DOES YOUR RESPONSE MAKE SENSE?

_____

_____

_____

UNDERSTANDING NUMBER RELATIONSHIPS

Directions: Darken the circle for the correct answer, or write in the answer.

> **TRY THIS**
> Read each question twice before choosing your answer. Be sure to think about which numbers stand for ones, tens, hundreds, and so on.

Sample A

The triangles represent what fraction of all the shapes shown?

> **THINK IT THROUGH**
> The correct answer is <u>A</u>. There are a total of 7 shapes in the picture. 3 of these shapes are triangles. This is expressed as the fraction $\frac{3}{7}$.

A $\frac{3}{7}$ C $\frac{4}{7}$

B $\frac{3}{4}$ D $\frac{1}{2}$

STOP

---

1 Jim's most recent recorded times for the 100-meter dash were: 12.2 seconds, 12.09 seconds, 12.225 seconds, and 12.53 seconds. List these times from fastest to slowest.

_____

_____

_____

_____

2 Vicky needs $2\frac{1}{4}$ yards of green ribbon, $1\frac{3}{4}$ yards of pink ribbon, $\frac{7}{8}$ yards of purple ribbon, and $2\frac{1}{2}$ yards of yellow ribbon for a spring basket. Which list shows the ribbons from least amount to greatest amount?

A green, yellow, pink, purple

B yellow, purple, green, pink

C purple, pink, green, yellow

D pink, purple, yellow, green

3 The new hockey team in town set a record selling 1,216,115 tickets to their third home game. How is 1,216,115 written in words?

F twelve million sixteen thousand one hundred fifteen

G one hundred twenty-one million six thousand fifteen

H one hundred thousand twenty-one thousand one hundred fifteen

J one million two hundred sixteen thousand one hundred fifteen

4 Which fraction means the same as $\frac{9}{12}$?

A $\frac{1}{3}$ C $\frac{1}{3}$

B $\frac{12}{9}$ D $\frac{3}{4}$

5 Which of these numbers is greater than 2,510 and less than 2,901?

F 2,505   H 2,888

G 2,911   J 2,910

STOP

Answers
SA Ⓐ Ⓑ Ⓒ Ⓓ   3 Ⓕ Ⓖ Ⓗ Ⓙ   5 Ⓕ Ⓖ Ⓗ Ⓙ
2 Ⓐ Ⓑ Ⓒ Ⓓ   4 Ⓐ Ⓑ Ⓒ Ⓓ

Directions: Darken the circle for the correct answer, or write in the answer.

> **TRY THIS**
>
> Work each problem on scratch paper. Try each answer choice in the problem before you choose your answer. Remember to think about which numbers stand for ones, tens, hundreds, and so on.

Sample A

What number is shown here in expanded form?

2,000 + 400 + 2

A   242

C   2,042

B   2,420

D   2,402

> **THINK IT THROUGH**
>
> The correct answer is D. First, place the numbers in a column:
> ```
>    2,000
>      400
> +      2
> ```
> and then add.

---

1 In which of the following numbers does the 6 stand for 6 hundreds?

A   246

B   468

C   637

D   6,052

2 Which number has an 8 in the ten thousands place and a 1 in the hundreds place?

F   982,135

G   153,982

H   298,351

J   581,293

3 Carlos wants a group of 27 girls and 18 boys to form into teams so that each team will have an equal number of boys and an equal number of girls. What is the greatest number of teams Carlos can form?

A   9

B   6

C   3

D   2

4 Laura will pay $50 more in rent on her apartment in two months. If she is paying $640 now, what will her monthly rent be in two months?

F $590

G $645

H $690

J $1,140

5 In the numeral 246,738, which digit is in the hundreds place?

_____

_____

_____

_____

6 What is the value of the 6 in 85.26?

A   6 tenths

B   6 hundredths

C   6 thousandths

D   6 tens

Answers

SA Ⓐ Ⓑ Ⓒ Ⓓ   2 Ⓕ Ⓖ Ⓗ Ⓙ   4 Ⓕ Ⓖ Ⓗ Ⓙ

1 Ⓐ Ⓑ Ⓒ Ⓓ   3 Ⓐ Ⓑ Ⓒ Ⓓ   6 Ⓐ Ⓑ Ⓒ Ⓓ

Directions: Darken the circle for the correct answer, or write in the answer.

> **TRY THIS**
> Check your work by making sure both sides of an equation are equal values. Try using all the answer choices in the problem.

Sample A

If $25 - y = 18$, what is the value of y?

A   4

B   7

C   18

D   43

THINK IT THROUGH   The correct answer is B. Subtract 18 from both sides of the equation, and $y = 25 - 18 = \underline{7}$.

STOP

---

1   Which expression could be used to find the number of inches there are in 5 yards 1 foot?

A $(36 + 5) - 12$

B $(36 - 12) \times 12$

C $(36 + 5) \times (12 \times 1)$

D $(36 \times 5) + (12 \times 1)$

2   Which of the following problems could be solved by using the equation $60 = t + 45$?

F   Wanda bought 60 cookies on Tuesday and 45 cookies on Wednesday. How many cookies did she buy?

G   Jim practiced the piano for 45 minutes today. He tries to practice 1 hour each day. How many minutes does he still have to practice?

H   The cab driver started the day with $60 and earned $45 more. How much does he have now?

J   The souvenir shop sells shells for 60 cents each. They sold 45 shells. How much money did the shop make from the sale of the shells?

3   If $y + 13 = 25$, then $y =$

A   6   C   15

B   12   D   38

4   What number makes the number sentence true?

$6 + (3 + 5) = (6 + \square) + 5$

F   3   H   11

G   8   J   13

5   Choose the number sentence that is in the same fact family as $8 + 3 = 11$.

A $8 \times 3 = 24$ C $11 - 3 = 8$

B $5 + 6 = 11$ D $8 - 11 = 3$

6   If $x = 7$, then $x + 4 =$

_____

_____

_____

_____

STOP

Answers

SA Ⓐ Ⓑ Ⓒ Ⓓ   2 Ⓕ Ⓖ Ⓗ Ⓙ   4 Ⓕ Ⓖ Ⓗ Ⓙ

1 Ⓐ Ⓑ Ⓒ Ⓓ   3 Ⓐ Ⓑ Ⓒ Ⓓ   5 Ⓐ Ⓑ Ⓒ Ⓓ

Directions: Darken the circle for the correct answer, or write in the answer.

| TRY THIS | Read each problem carefully. Study the graphs or other visual materials, and look for key words or numbers to help you choose your answer. |

Sample A

In a total of 10 spins, which number will the spinner probably point to the greatest number of times?

A 1
B 2
C 4
D 5

| THINK IT THROUGH | The correct answer is <u>B</u>. The number <u>2</u> appears 3 times on the spinner. This is more often than any other number. |

STOP

---

1 The graph shows the number of cans 3 classes collected for recycling. How many more cans did Grade 4 collect than Grade 6?

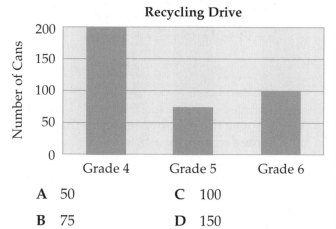

Recycling Drive

A 50   C 100

B 75   D 150

2 With his eyes closed, which card will Cal most likely pick?

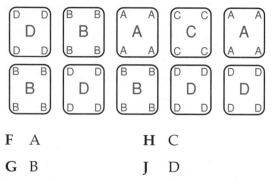

F A   H C

G B   J D

3 Lola has been saving money for her summer vacation. The last four deposits she made to her savings account were $17, $22, $34, and $26. What is the average of Lola's deposits?

_____

_____

_____

_____

_____

_____

4 The sports store sells shirts with long sleeves or short sleeves. They come in small, medium, large, and extra large sizes. They are available in blue with white letters, white with blue letters, and white with red letters. How many total choices of shirts are there?

A 9 choices   C 24 choices

B 12 choices   D 48 choices

GO ON

Answers
SA Ⓐ Ⓑ Ⓒ Ⓓ   1 Ⓐ Ⓑ Ⓒ Ⓓ   2 Ⓕ Ⓖ Ⓗ Ⓙ   4 Ⓐ Ⓑ Ⓒ Ⓓ

The graph shows the number of hours Lena baby-sat last week. Study the graph. Then answer questions 5–7.

Lena's Baby-sitting Record

5 How many hours did Lena baby-sit during this week?

F 16 hours   H 10 hours

G 13 hours   J 6 hours

6 On which day did Lena baby-sit the most hours?

A Sunday   C Saturday

B Thursday   D Monday

7 On which day did Lena baby-sit for 3 hours?

F Friday   H Thursday

G Sunday   J Saturday

8 Marcus bowled 113 the first game, 124 the second game, and 132 the third game. What was his bowling average?

_____

_____

_____

_____

9 Which tally chart was used to make the bar graph?

A
Carmen	⅃ℋℋ ⅃ℋℋ ⅃ℋℋ I
Lizzie	ℋℋ ℋℋ ℋℋ ℋℋ
Lauren	ℋℋ ℋℋ ℋℋ
Michiko	ℋℋ ℋℋ II

B
Carmen	ℋℋ III
Lizzie	ℋℋ ℋℋ
Lauren	ℋℋ II
Michiko	ℋℋ I

C
Carmen	ℋℋ ℋℋ II
Lizzie	ℋℋ ℋℋ ℋℋ
Lauren	ℋℋ ℋℋ ℋℋ ℋℋ
Michiko	ℋℋ ℋℋ ℋℋ I

D
Carmen	ℋℋ ℋℋ ℋℋ IIII
Lizzie	ℋℋ ℋℋ II
Lauren	ℋℋ ℋℋ IIII
Michiko	ℋℋ ℋℋ I

The bar graph shows the number of butterflies collected by four students during one week.

BUTTERFLY RECORD

Number Collected

10 How many more butterflies did Carmen collect than Michiko?

F 2   H 4

G 3   J 6

STOP

Answers

5 Ⓕ Ⓖ Ⓗ Ⓙ   **6** Ⓐ Ⓑ Ⓒ Ⓓ   **7** Ⓕ Ⓖ Ⓗ Ⓙ   **9** Ⓐ Ⓑ Ⓒ Ⓓ   **10** Ⓕ Ⓖ Ⓗ Ⓙ

Directions: Darken the circle for the correct answer, or write in the answer.

Read each problem carefully. Try using all the answer choices in the problem. Then choose the answer that you think best answers the question.

Sample A

A special machine multiplies any number entered into it by 6. The table shows how the numbers are changed. Which numbers are missing from the table?

Original number	5	7	10
New number	30		

A 13 and 16   C 36 and 42

B 42 and 52   D 42 and 60

THINK IT THROUGH

The correct answer is <u>D</u>. Multiply 7 × 6, which equals <u>42</u>. Next, multiply 10 × 6, which equals <u>60</u>.

STOP

---

1 Look at the pattern shown here. What number is missing from this number pattern?

101, 105, _____, 113, 117

A 107

B 110

C 109

D 112

2 Tim keeps a journal for his reading class. In it he records the number of hours and the number of pages he reads each week. Find the missing value in the table shown here.

Hours	3	6	18	36
Number of pages	40	80		480

_____

_____

_____

_____

3 Which piece of material is the one that has been cut out from the fabric?

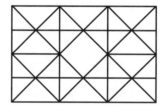

F

G

H

J

STOP

Answers

SA Ⓐ Ⓑ Ⓒ Ⓓ   **1** Ⓐ Ⓑ Ⓒ Ⓓ   **3** Ⓕ Ⓖ Ⓗ Ⓙ

Directions: Darken the circle for the correct answer, or write in the answer.

TRY THIS Round numbers when you estimate. For some problems, there are no exact answers. Then you should take your best guess. You can check your answer by using the numbers given in the problem.

Sample A

During the summer Arturo swims about 42 minutes every day. A reasonable amount of time in minutes that he would swim in 2 months is—

A 100 minutes   C 240 minutes

B 80 minutes   D 2,400 minutes

THINK IT THROUGH The correct answer is D. Start by rounding 42 to 40. There are about 60 days in 2 months. 60 × 40 = 2,400 minutes. The answer would not be 100, 80, or 240 minutes.

STOP

---

1 Mrs. Shriver's farm stand had 527 pumpkins. She sold 215 of them. Which is the best estimate of the number of pumpkins she has left?

A 100

B 200

C 300

D 400

2 Carmelo's Restaurant bought 32 boxes of napkins. There were 250 napkins in each box. *About* how many napkins did the restaurant buy?

_____

_____

_____

_____

_____

3 Use the table below to answer questions 3 and 4.

MENU	
Hamburger	$1.75
Hot dog	$1.25
Pizza	$2.00
Fruit	$0.50
Juice	$0.50
Milk	$0.40
Chips	$0.25

According to this menu, *about* how much does a hamburger and a carton of milk cost?

F $1.50   H $3.00

G $2.00   J $4.00

4 *About* how much change should Leon receive from $10.00 if he bought 2 hot dogs, a bag of chips, and a carton of milk?

A $3.00   C $5.00

B $4.75   D $7.00

STOP

Answers
SA (A) (B) (C) (D)   1 (A) (B) (C) (D)   3 (F) (G) (H) (J)   4 (A) (B) (C) (D)

Directions: Darken the circle for the correct answer, or write in the answer.

TRY THIS Use the objects shown to help you answer each question. Remember that perimeter is the measurement around the <u>outside</u>, while <u>area</u> is the measurement of the <u>inside</u> of a space.

Sample A

What is the area of the square shown here?

8 m

A   32 square meters

B   64 square meters

C   96 square meters

D   256 square meters

THINK IT THROUGH The correct answer is <u>B</u>. Each side of the square is 8m. To find the area, multiply 8m × 8m, which equals <u>64 square meters.</u>

STOP

Use the grid of a park shown here to answer questions 1 and 2.

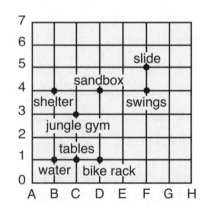

1   Which three items in the park are next to one another in a straight row?

_____

_____

_____

_____

2   More swings will be installed at F2. What will be closest to these swings?

A   slide   C   water

B   bike rack   D   other swings

3   What is the perimeter of the plot of land shown here?

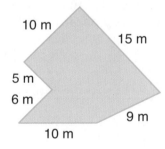

_____

_____

_____

_____

GO ON

Answers
SA Ⓐ Ⓑ Ⓒ Ⓓ   2 Ⓐ Ⓑ Ⓒ Ⓓ

4 The perimeter of a triangle measures 30 centimeters. Two sides of the triangle measure 8 centimeters and 14 centimeters. What is the length of the third side of this triangle?

F   6 centimeters   H   14 centimeters

G   8 centimeters   J   22 centimeters

5 Which transformation moves the figure from position A to position B?

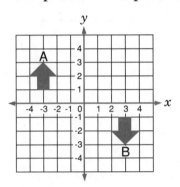

A   reflection   C   rotation

B   slide   D   translation

6 How many sides does a trapezoid have?

F   4   H   6

G   5   J   8

7 The quadrilaterals are grouped together. The other figures are not quadrilaterals.

Which shape below is a quadrilateral?

A   C

B   D

8 The length of Keiko's rectangular cookie sheet is 36 centimeters, and its width is 15 centimeters. What is the perimeter of the cookie sheet?

F   540 centimeters   H   51 centimeters

G   102 centimeters   J   21 centimeters

9 Which ordered pair is best represented by point S?

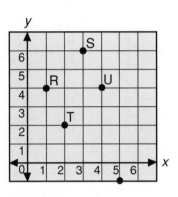

A   (1, 4)   C   (2, 2)

B   (4, 4)   D   (3, 6)

10 This is a diagram of the playground at Beth's school. What is its perimeter?

F   135 m

G   125 m

H   114 m

J   105 m

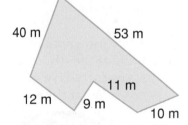

11 Which angle is a right angle?

A   C

B      D

STOP

Directions: Darken the circle for the correct answer, or write in the answer.

TRY THIS

Study the words in each problem carefully. Then decide what you have to do to find the answer.

Sample A

It was 9:00 P.M. when Sara went to bed. Which clock shows the time three and one-half hours later?

A [9:30 P.M.] C [12:30 A.M.]

B [1:30 A.M.] D [12:40 A.M.]

THINK IT THROUGH

The correct answer is <u>C</u>. Going ahead 3 hours from 9 P.M. moves the clock to 12 A.M. Another 30 minutes added brings the time to <u>12:30</u> A.M.

---

1 Which metric unit of measurement is best to use to describe the height of a tree?

A kilometers

B millimeters

C liters

D meters

2 Alice put some muffins into the oven to bake at the time shown on the clock. It takes forty-five minutes for the muffins to bake. What time will the muffins be done?

_____

_____

_____

_____

3 Which of these would hold a quart when full?

F

H

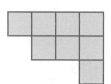

G

J

4 What is the area of this figure in square units?

= 1 square unit

A 14 square units   C 8 square units

B 12 square units   D 6 square units

GO ON ➡

Answers

SA Ⓐ Ⓑ Ⓒ Ⓓ   1 Ⓐ Ⓑ Ⓒ Ⓓ   3 Ⓕ Ⓖ Ⓗ Ⓙ   4 Ⓐ Ⓑ Ⓒ Ⓓ

5 Which of these equals the greatest amount of liquid?

F 1 gallon   H 3 pints

G 2 quarts   J 4 cups

6 Which unit of measurement is best to use to describe the weight of a bucket of sand?

A feet   C liters

B miles   D pounds

7 Use your inch ruler and the map to help you answer the question. What is the actual distance from Camp River Trails to State Park?

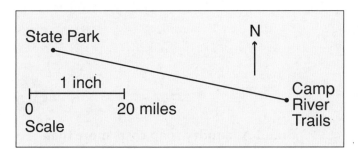

F 50 miles   H 40 miles

G 60 miles   J 45 miles

8 How many feet are there between the two trees?

A 27 feet   C 81 feet

B 9 feet   D 972 feet

9 What is the area of this figure?

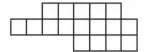

F 22 square units

G 17 square units

H 18 square units

J 12 square units

10 The length of an automobile would be best expressed in—

A centimeters.

B inches.

C feet.

D kilometers.

11 Use your centimeter ruler to answer this question.

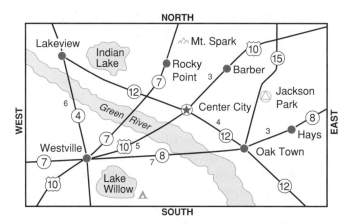

About how many centimeters longer is it from Lakeview to Oak Town on Highways 4 and 8 than on Highway 12?

_____

_____

_____

_____

STOP

Answers

5 Ⓕ Ⓖ Ⓗ Ⓙ   **7** Ⓕ Ⓖ Ⓗ Ⓙ   **9** Ⓕ Ⓖ Ⓗ Ⓙ

6 Ⓐ Ⓑ Ⓒ Ⓓ   **8** Ⓐ Ⓑ Ⓒ Ⓓ   **10** Ⓐ Ⓑ Ⓒ Ⓓ

Directions: Darken the circle for the correct answer, or write in the answer.

TRY THIS

Study the words in each problem carefully. Then decide what you have to do to find the answer.

Sample A

Henry has 50 pages in his stamp album. He needs 32 more stamps to complete his collection. What other information is needed to find the total number of stamps Henry will have in his collection?

A the number of stamps on each page

B the number of stamps he bought last week

C the cost of each stamp

D the size of each stamp

THINK IT THROUGH

The correct answer is A. The number of pages (50) in the stamp album is known. If we can find out how many stamps are on each page, we can find the total number of stamps in the completed collection.

STOP

1 There are 5 boxes of candles. Each box holds 25 candles. How many candles are there in all?

_____

_____

2 Juan needs some tiles similar to the one shown on the left. How many tiles like this one can he get from the large figure shown?

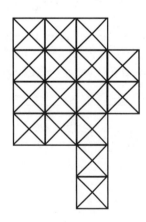

A 6   C 12

B 8   D 16

3 Brand A laundry soap costs more than Brand D laundry soap. Brand D costs less than Brand X. Brand Z costs more than Brand A. Which of the following is most reasonable?

F Brand Z costs more than Brand D.

G Brand X and Brand A cost the same.

H Brand Z costs less than Brand X.

J Brand A costs more than Brand X.

4 Which figure is made of all rectangles?

A   C

B 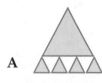   D

STOP

Answers
SA Ⓐ Ⓑ Ⓒ Ⓓ   2 Ⓐ Ⓑ Ⓒ Ⓓ   3 Ⓕ Ⓖ Ⓗ Ⓙ   4 Ⓐ Ⓑ Ⓒ Ⓓ

Directions: Darken the circle for the correct answer. Darken the circle for NH (Not Here) if the correct answer is not given. If no choices are given, write in the answer.

TRY THIS	When adding columns of digits, remember to rename when necessary. Write the sum and check it against the choices.

Sample A

$$\frac{2}{3}$$
$$+ \frac{1}{5}$$

A $\frac{1}{8}$

B $\frac{1}{8}$

C $\frac{7}{15}$

D $\frac{13}{15}$

E NH

THINK IT THROUGH	The correct answer is <u>D</u>. First, find the least common denominator, which is 15.

Convert each fraction to fifteenths: $\frac{2}{3} = \frac{10}{15}$

$$+ \frac{1}{5} = \frac{3}{15}$$

and add.

STOP

1

$17 + 2 =$

A 34
B 15
C 12
D 19
E NH

2

$4.35 \times 76.2 =$

F 331.470
G 80.55
H 303.70
J 3314.70
K NH

3

$$6\frac{3}{8}$$
$$+ 9\frac{5}{8}$$

A 17
B 15
C 16
D $15\frac{7}{8}$
E NH

4

$14 \times 23 =$

F 70
G 308
H 322
J 312
K NH

5

$$\$26.07$$
$$+ \$39.81$$

A $65.88
B $66.07
C $68.03
D $76.77
E NH

6

$62 \div 5 =$

_____

_____

_____

7

$650 \div 7 =$

F 88 R1
G 90 R2
H 92 R6
J 92 R3
K NH

8

$$\frac{7}{8}$$
$$- \frac{2}{8}$$

A $\frac{1}{8}$
B $\frac{1}{2}$
C $\frac{3}{8}$
D $\frac{5}{8}$
E NH

STOP

Answers

SA Ⓐ Ⓑ Ⓒ Ⓓ Ⓔ

1 Ⓐ Ⓑ Ⓒ Ⓓ Ⓔ

2 Ⓕ Ⓖ Ⓗ Ⓙ Ⓚ

3 Ⓐ Ⓑ Ⓒ Ⓓ Ⓔ

4 Ⓕ Ⓖ Ⓗ Ⓙ Ⓚ

5 Ⓐ Ⓑ Ⓒ Ⓓ Ⓔ

7 Ⓕ Ⓖ Ⓗ Ⓙ Ⓚ

8 Ⓐ Ⓑ Ⓒ Ⓓ Ⓔ

USING COMPUTATION IN CONTEXT

Directions: Darken the circle for the correct answer. Darken the circle for NH (Not Here) if the correct answer is not given. If no choices are given, write in the answer.

TRY THIS: Read the word problem carefully. Then set up the word problem as a numerical formula. Solve the formula and compare it to the answer choices.

Sample A

Sally mowed 2 lawns today and 3 lawns yesterday. She was paid $3 for each lawn.

How much money did she earn altogether?

A $5

B $10

C $12

D $15

E NH

THINK IT THROUGH: The correct answer is <u>D</u>. Add 2 lawns today and 3 lawns yesterday. This equals 5. Next, multiply $3 × 5. This gives the total of <u>$15</u> earned.

 STOP

---

1 A family of 8 wants to paddle in the canoes at the park. Each boat holds 2 people.

If they all want to ride at the same time, how many canoes will they need?

A 2

B 4

C 6

D 16

E NH

2 Mr. Klein drove his truck 17,234 miles.

What is that number rounded to the nearest thousand miles?

F 16,000

G 16,500

H 17,000

J 18,000

K NH

3 Suki took a trip. She drove 12 miles to the airport and flew 948 miles to Florida. How many miles did she travel in all?

A 747 miles

B 929 miles

C 960 miles

D 1,060 miles

E NH

4 Chairs for the office desks cost $8 each.

Find the total cost of 257 chairs.

_____

_____

_____

STOP

Answers
SA Ⓐ Ⓑ Ⓒ Ⓓ Ⓔ   **1** Ⓐ Ⓑ Ⓒ Ⓓ Ⓔ   **2** Ⓕ Ⓖ Ⓗ Ⓙ Ⓚ   **3** Ⓐ Ⓑ Ⓒ Ⓓ Ⓔ

Sample A

$$4\overline{)79}$$

A 19
B 19 R3
C 12 R1
D 17 R1
E NH

Sample B 🛑 STOP

Mr. Lyons used $2\frac{1}{2}$ cups of flour for one recipe and $4\frac{2}{3}$ cups of flour for another recipe. How much flour did he use altogether?

F $6\frac{2}{3}$ cups

G $6\frac{5}{8}$ cups

H $7\frac{1}{3}$ cups

J $7\frac{1}{2}$ cups

K NH

🛑 STOP

For questions 1–16, darken the circle for the correct answer. Darken the circle for NH (Not Here) if the correct answer is not given. If no choices are given, write in the answer.

1

$$\begin{array}{r} 5.872 \\ -\ 0.6821 \\ \hline \end{array}$$

A 5.191
B 5.211
C 4.190
D 1.552
E NH

2

$$\frac{7}{11} \times \frac{1}{2}$$

F
G $\frac{8}{13}$
H $\frac{7}{22}$
J $\frac{11}{14}$
K $\frac{3}{8}$NH

3

$$\begin{array}{r} \frac{1}{8} \\ +\ \frac{1}{4} \\ \hline \end{array}$$

A $\frac{1}{12}$
B $\frac{3}{8}$
C $\frac{1}{4}$
D $\frac{1}{6}$
E NH

4

$$\begin{array}{r} \frac{8}{21} \\ +\ \frac{9}{21} \\ \hline \end{array}$$

F $\frac{18}{21}$
G $\frac{17}{24}$
H $\frac{72}{21}$
J $\frac{1}{21}$
K NH

5

$$96 - 79 =$$

A 7
B 16
C 17
D 165
E NH

6

$$\frac{7}{8} - \frac{1}{8} =$$

F $\frac{5}{8}$
G $\frac{3}{4}$
H $\frac{8}{16}$
J $\frac{2}{4}$
K NH

7

$$600 \div 40 =$$

A 150
B 15
C 12
D 640
E NH

8

$$0.5 \times 8 =$$

F 40
G 4
H 0.04
J 0.004
K NH

9

$$85 \times 70 =$$

_____

_____

_____

GO ON ➡

Answers
SA Ⓐ Ⓑ Ⓒ Ⓓ Ⓔ
SB Ⓕ Ⓖ Ⓗ Ⓙ Ⓚ
1 Ⓐ Ⓑ Ⓒ Ⓓ Ⓔ

2 Ⓕ Ⓖ Ⓗ Ⓙ Ⓚ
3 Ⓐ Ⓑ Ⓒ Ⓓ Ⓔ
4 Ⓕ Ⓖ Ⓗ Ⓙ Ⓚ

5 Ⓐ Ⓑ Ⓒ Ⓓ Ⓔ
6 Ⓕ Ⓖ Ⓗ Ⓙ Ⓚ
7 Ⓐ Ⓑ Ⓒ Ⓓ Ⓔ

8 Ⓕ Ⓖ Ⓗ Ⓙ Ⓚ

10 Andy and Nate collect sports-team pennants. Andy has 18 and Nate has 13.

How many more pennants does Andy have than Nate?

A 5

B 21

C 15

D 31

E NH

11 Kenny wants to buy 4 hot dogs and 2 orders of french fries.

How much change will he get from a $20 bill?

hamburger $2

french fries $1

hot dog $1.50

Soda s- $1.00
L- $1.50

F $11

G $9

H $10

J $8

K NH

12 Sandra bought a package of 320 stickers for each of 15 friends she invited to her party. How many stickers did she buy?

A 4,800

B 3,812

C 1,920

D 4,700

E NH

13 Elizabeth plans to wrap 20 gifts. She needs 2 feet of ribbon for each gift.

How many feet of ribbon does she need?

F 10 feet

G 18 feet

H 40 feet

J 22 feet

K NH

14 Janet plants 20 varieties of flowers in the spring. She reports that 90% of the varieties of flowers she planted have bloomed.

How many varieties have bloomed?

A 19

B 18

C 17

D 9

E NH

15 The Fun Fair sold 1,839 food tickets.

What is this number rounded to the nearest thousand?

F 1,800

G 2,000

H 1,900

J 1,000

K NH

TEST TIP

Try circling key words in questions. In question 15, circle *thousand* to help you remember to round to the correct place.

STOP

Answers

10 Ⓐ Ⓑ Ⓒ Ⓓ Ⓔ   **12** Ⓐ Ⓑ Ⓒ Ⓓ Ⓔ   **14** Ⓐ Ⓑ Ⓒ Ⓓ Ⓔ

11 Ⓕ Ⓖ Ⓗ Ⓙ Ⓚ   **13** Ⓕ Ⓖ Ⓗ Ⓙ Ⓚ   **15** Ⓕ Ⓖ Ⓗ Ⓙ Ⓚ

Sample A

Which number sentence is in the same fact family as 3 × 8 = 24?

A   24 − 8 = 16

B   8 + 3 = 11

C   6 × 4 = 24

D   24 ÷ 8 = 3

STOP

For questions 1–50, darken the circle for the correct answer, or write in the answer.

1   Which decimal belongs in the box on the number line?

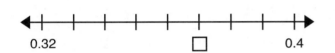

0.32   □   0.4

A   0.37

B   0.38

C   0.36

D   0.35

2   What number makes this number sentence true?

3 × (1 × 9) = (3 × □) × 9

F   27

G   13

H   9

J   1

3   What is another way to write 2,078?

A   20 + 70 + 80

B   20 + 78

C   2,000 + 70 + 8

D   2,000 + 7 + 80

4   Last year 567,290 people attended sporting events at the university. How is 567,290 written in words?

F   Fifty-six hundred thousand seven twenty-nine

G   Fifty-six thousand seven hundred twenty-nine

H   Five million sixty-seven thousand two hundred ninety

J   Five hundred sixty-seven thousand two hundred ninety

5   In the number 52,658, the 2 means—

A   200

B   20,000

C   2,000

D   20

6   $\frac{14}{18}$ means the same as—

F $\frac{3}{7}$ H $\frac{6}{8}$

G $\frac{5}{9}$ J $\frac{7}{9}$

7   The science class measured 2.56 inches of rain in September, 2.67 inches of rain in October, 2.43 inches of rain in November, and 2.13 inches of rain in December. During which month did it rain most?

A   September

B   October

C   November

D   December

8   What is the value of the 3 in 25.430?

_____

_____

_____

_____

GO ON

Answers

SA Ⓐ Ⓑ Ⓒ Ⓓ   2 Ⓕ Ⓖ Ⓗ Ⓙ   4 Ⓕ Ⓖ Ⓗ Ⓙ   6 Ⓕ Ⓖ Ⓗ Ⓙ

1 Ⓐ Ⓑ Ⓒ Ⓓ   3 Ⓐ Ⓑ Ⓒ Ⓓ   5 Ⓐ Ⓑ Ⓒ Ⓓ   7 Ⓐ Ⓑ Ⓒ Ⓓ

9 Mario works in a bakery. He made 90 more loaves of bread on Saturday than he did on Sunday. He made 70 more loaves of bread on Monday than he did on Sunday. If he made 340 loaves of bread on Monday, how many loaves of bread did he make on Saturday?

F   160

G   320

H   360

J   380

10 The school store sells paper with or without binder holes. It is available in white or in yellow. The paper comes in 3 sizes. How many choices of paper do students have when buying paper at the school store?

A   12 choices

B   7 choices

C   6 choices

D   3 choices

11 In which numeral does the 6 stand for 6 tens?

F   3,692

G   6,210

H   364

J   346

12 Carl has 36 fish in the first aquarium and 52 fish in the second aquarium. How many fish should he move to the first aquarium so that both aquariums have an equal number of fish?

A   24

B   16

C   12

D   8

13 Gerald bought 3 shirts for $8.40 each, 2 shirts for $12.89 each, and 1 shirt for $18.90. What was the average cost of the shirts?

F $13.40   H $10.45

G $11.65   J $10.24

14 Which equation could be used to find the number of seconds in a day?

A $60t = 60 + 60$

B $\frac{t}{24} = 60 \times 60$

C $t = (60 \times 60) \div 24$

D $24t = 60 + 60 + 60$

15 If x = 6, then x + 9 =

F   1   H   15

G   10   J   18

16 Heidi has a choice of 4 colors of paint, 3 kinds of curtains, and 2 colors of carpet to decorate her apartment. How many different combinations of paint, curtains, and carpets can she use?

_____

_____

_____

_____

17 Which problem could be solved by the equation x = 0.3 × 200

A   Three hamburgers cost $2.00. How much does one cost?

B   The theater holds 200 people. How many people would be able to attend 3 showings of a movie?

C   The regular fare of $200 for a plane ticket was just reduced by 30%. What would the savings be?

D   The temperature in an oven was 200 degrees. It was then increased by 0.3 degrees. What is the current oven temperature?

GO ON

Answers

9 Ⓕ Ⓖ Ⓗ Ⓙ   11 Ⓕ Ⓖ Ⓗ Ⓙ   13 Ⓕ Ⓖ Ⓗ Ⓙ   15 Ⓕ Ⓖ Ⓗ Ⓙ

10 Ⓐ Ⓑ Ⓒ Ⓓ   12 Ⓐ Ⓑ Ⓒ Ⓓ   14 Ⓐ Ⓑ Ⓒ Ⓓ   17 Ⓐ Ⓑ Ⓒ Ⓓ

This graph shows the number of students who eat certain kinds of snacks. Study the graph. Then answer questions 18–20.

STUDENTS' FAVORITE SNACKS

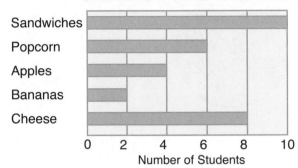

Number of Students

18 What two snacks together are eaten by the same number of students as the number of students who eat popcorn?

F apples and bananas

G bananas and cheese

H apples and sandwiches

J apples and cheese

19 Which of these questions cannot be answered using the information on the graph?

A How many students eat bananas?

B How many more students eat sandwiches than cheese?

C How many students eat two snacks?

D How many fewer students eat popcorn than cheese?

20 If 5 students switched from sandwiches to popcorn, how many students would then eat popcorn?

F 7

G 9

H 11

J 12

The graph below shows the number of students in each grade who ride the bus or walk to school. Study the graph. Then answer questions 21–23.

Methods of Transportation

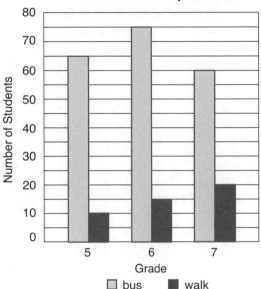

21 How many sixth-grade students ride the bus to school?

A 75   C 60

B 65   D 15

22 If half of the seventh-grade students who take the bus to school start walking to school, how many students would walk to school altogether?

F 55   H 75

G 60   J 80

23 How many students walk to school altogether?

_____

_____

_____

_____

GO ON ➡

Burnet School had a wrapping paper sale. The following graph shows how many rolls of wrapping paper were sold by each grade. Study the graph. Then answer questions 24–26.

WRAPPING PAPER SALES

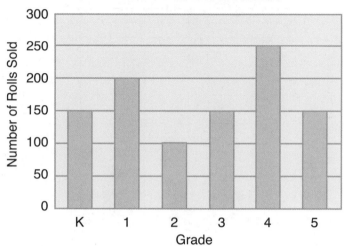

24 How many more rolls of wrapping paper did the fourth grade sell than kindergarten?

    A 100

    B 50

    C 150

    D 200

25 How many rolls of wrapping paper did the first grade sell?

    F 450

    G 200

    H 100

    J 250

26 Which grade sold the fewest rolls of wrapping paper?

    A K

    B 4

    C 2

    D 3

27 Kim's favorite word game uses the spinner shown here. What is the probability that the spinner will land on a vowel?

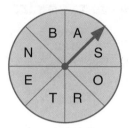

    F $\frac{2}{8}$

    G $\frac{3}{8}$

    H $\frac{4}{8}$

    J $\frac{5}{8}$

28 On four different days, Mrs. Scanlon's fifth-grade class collected 18, 26, 15, and 25 pounds of aluminum cans for recycling. What was the average number of pounds collected during the four days?

_____

_____

_____

_____

29 With his eyes closed, which card will Julio most likely pick?

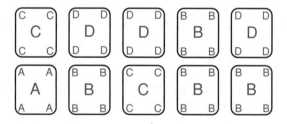

    A A

    B B

    C C

    D D

GO ON➡

30 A box of 10 computer diskettes costs $23. A reasonable price for a case of 136 of these boxes is —

F   less than $1,800.

G   between $2,000 and $2,500.

H   between $2,500 and $3,500.

J   between $3,500 and $4,500.

31 Each month Marty puts $17.00 in his savings account. What is the best estimate of Marty's total savings for 1 year?

A $100.00   C $200.00

B $150.00   D $300.00

32 The figure below shows the picture frame that Felix is making in art class. What is the perimeter of the picture frame?

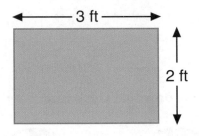

F   6 ft   H   12 ft
G   10 ft   J   20 ft

33 If the pattern formed by the dots continues, how many dots are needed to make the next shape?

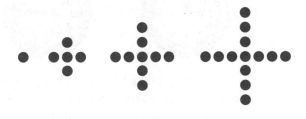

A   14   C   17
B   15   D   20

34 The table shown here represents the relationship between *x* and *y*. Based on the relationship shown here, what number belongs in the empty box in row x?

x	7	8	9	10	11	
y	21	24	27	30	33	48

F   12

G   16

H   24

J   30

35 Aunt Lila's rose garden is in the shape of a square. How many feet of edging does she need to go around the entire garden?

12 ft

_____

_____

_____

36 Juan can throw a football 42 yards. He can throw a baseball 109 yards. *About* how much farther can he throw a baseball than a football?

A   60 yards

B   80 yards

C   100 yards

D   150 yards

TEST TIP

The word *about* is a clue that tells you to estimate to find an answer.

GO ON

Answers
30 Ⓕ Ⓖ Ⓗ Ⓙ   **32** Ⓕ Ⓖ Ⓗ Ⓙ   **34** Ⓕ Ⓖ Ⓗ Ⓙ
31 Ⓐ Ⓑ Ⓒ Ⓓ   **33** Ⓐ Ⓑ Ⓒ Ⓓ   **36** Ⓐ Ⓑ Ⓒ Ⓓ

37 Choose the clock that shows the time 4 hours after 11:00 A.M.

F   H

G   J

38 What is the area of the rectangle shown?

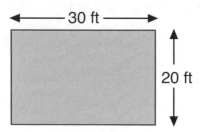

A   50 square feet

B   100 square feet

C   6,000 square feet

D   600 square feet

39 The area of figure A is 1 square unit. What is the area of figure B?

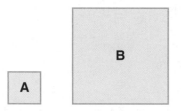

F   4 square units

G   6 square units

H   9 square units

J   12 square units

40 Marsha's soccer team starts its practice at 4:30. It ends at 5:15. How long does Marsha's soccer team practice?

A   15 minutes

B   30 minutes

C   40 minutes

D   45 minutes

41 How many right angles does this figure have?

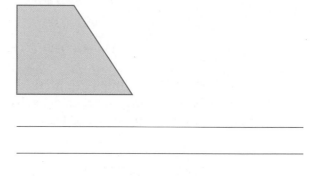

_____

_____

_____

_____

42 The hands of which clock form a right angle?

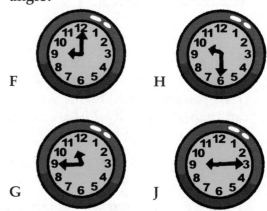

F   H

G   J

43 Mr. Lan has a greenhouse that is shaped like a rectangle. The length of one short side is 6 meters. The length of one long side is 12 meters. What is the perimeter of his greenhouse?

A   36 meters   C   24 meters

B   18 meters   D   12 meters

GO ON ➡

Answers

37 Ⓕ Ⓖ Ⓗ Ⓙ	**39** Ⓕ Ⓖ Ⓗ Ⓙ	**42** Ⓕ Ⓖ Ⓗ Ⓙ
38 Ⓐ Ⓑ Ⓒ Ⓓ	**40** Ⓐ Ⓑ Ⓒ Ⓓ	**43** Ⓐ Ⓑ Ⓒ Ⓓ

44 Yolanda's herb garden is shaped like a rectangle. How many feet of fencing does she need to go around the entire garden?

8 ft.

22 ft.

F 16 ft.   **H** 60 ft.

G 30 ft.   **J** 176 ft.

45 Which shows the piece missing from the figure?

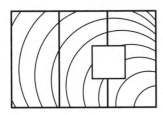

A   **C**

B   **D**

46 Tony's birthday is 20 days before Ann's. Ann's birthday is 7 days after Vic's. Vic's birthday is on the 20th. When is Tony's birthday?

_____

_____

47 Casey bought 3 small spools of string and 1 large spool that had 250 feet of string. What other information is needed to determine how much more string is on the large spool than on the 3 small ones combined?

F the number of inches in a foot

G the kind of string on each spool

H the number of feet of string on 3 large spools

J the number of feet of string on each small spool

48 The students in Longfellow School have decided to take part in their town's food drive. Their goal is to collect 600 cans of food. Each student plans to collect 5 cans. What do you need to know to find out whether the students will be able to reach their goal?

A how many people will provide food

B how many students there are at Longfellow School

C how many grocery stores there are

D how much each can costs

49 Bernie has a sheet of plastic that is 12 feet wide. Alex's sheet of plastic is also 12 feet wide, but it has an area that is 3 times as large as Bernie's. What additional information is needed to find the length of Alex's sheet of plastic?

F the thickness of Bernie's sheet

G the thickness of Alex's sheet

H the combined widths of the two sheets

J the length of Bernie's sheet

50 Marlene has 5 cats. Snowball is smaller than Sugar. Muffin is smaller than Pixy. Shadow is the smallest. Sugar is smaller than Muffin. Which of these is the most reasonable answer?

A Shadow is larger than Sugar.

B Pixy is the largest cat.

C Muffin is smaller than Snowball.

D Snowball is larger than Pixy.

> ### TEST TIP
>
> Try drawing a picture to answer question 50. Draw 5 cats and add their names.

STOP

Answers

44 Ⓕ Ⓖ Ⓗ Ⓙ   **47** Ⓕ Ⓖ Ⓗ Ⓙ   **49** Ⓕ Ⓖ Ⓗ Ⓙ

45 Ⓐ Ⓑ Ⓒ Ⓓ   **48** Ⓐ Ⓑ Ⓒ Ⓓ   **50** Ⓐ Ⓑ Ⓒ Ⓓ

LANGUAGE

Directions: Read each sentence carefully. Then darken the circle for the correct answer to each question, or write in the answer.

TRY THIS Pretend that you are writing each sentence. Use the rules you have learned for capitalization, punctuation, word usage, and sentence structure to choose the correct answer.

Sample A

Going Camping

Jeremy knows that many of his classmates are interested in camping. He has been camping many times and knows a lot about it. He wants to write an article for the school newspaper that will give students some camping tips.

Jeremy wants to find out if there is a camping supply store in his neighborhood. He should look in—

A   an encyclopedia.

B   a telephone directory.

C   an atlas.

D   a dictionary

THINK IT THROUGH   The correct answer is **B**. The telephone directory would have the address and telephone number of camping supply stores.

 STOP

The Hopi Indians

While Alexis was on vacation in Arizona, she learned about Native Americans who live there. She visited a museum that showed how the Hopi Indians lived. She wants to tell her grandmother about what she learned. She decides to write her a letter.

Dear Grandma,

Hopi Indians lived in the southwest part
(1)
of the United States. This part is now
                    (2)
Arizona. Hopi Indians were always growing
            (3)
their own crops for food.

1   **What is the best way to write sentence 3?**

A   Hopi Indians were planning to grow their own crops for food.

B   Hopi Indians grew their own crops for food.

C   Hopi Indians will be eating their own crops for food.

D   As it is written.

GO ON

Answers
SA Ⓐ Ⓑ Ⓒ Ⓓ   1 Ⓐ Ⓑ Ⓒ Ⓓ

Study the Table of Contents and Index from a book Jeremy found about camping. Then answer questions 2–6.

Table of Contents

Index

2   Which chapter should Jeremy read to find ideas for making tasty breakfasts when camping?

_____

_____

_____

_____

3   Which pages would have information about types of campgrounds available in national parks?

F   8–15

G   16–18

H   19–22

J   29–30

4   Which chapter should Jeremy read to help him explain about the kinds of sleeping bags used for camping?

A   Chapter 1

B   Chapter 2

C   Chapter 3

D   Chapter 4

5   Which page most likely would have information about how to deal with injuries on a camping trip?

F   36

G   37

H   53

J   70

6   Chapter 5 has information on all of the following except—

A   where to place the tent.

B   where to place the sleeping bags.

C   what to place in the cooking area.

D   what to do for poison ivy.

GO ON →

Answers

3 Ⓕ Ⓖ Ⓗ Ⓙ   4 Ⓐ Ⓑ Ⓒ Ⓓ   5 Ⓕ Ⓖ Ⓗ Ⓙ   6 Ⓐ Ⓑ Ⓒ Ⓓ

Here is a rough draft of the first part of Jeremy's article. Read the rough draft carefully. Then answer questions 7–14.

Going Camping

Have you ever been camping? I can tell you that camping can be fun
(1)   (2)

and exciting. It can be enjoyable. It gives you a chance to experience the
(3)   (4)

outdoors. For example, an example of this are smells, sights, and sounds
(5)

in the outdoors that you can never find in a town or a city. Yellowstone
(6)

National Park has some great campsites. You can enjoy swimming,
(7)

canoeing, and hiking. You can spend time and have fun with your family
(8)

and friends. And your pets.
(9)

Camping is also an affordable way to go on vacation. A campsite costs
(10)   (11)

about $15 and just as eating at home you can have meals for about the

same cost. You can cook these meals on an open fire or cook them on a
(12)

camp stove.

---

7 Which group of words is <u>not</u> a complete sentence?

  F 3

  G 9

  H 11

  J 12

8 What is the topic sentence of the second paragraph?

  A 12

  B 11

  C 10

  D 1

GO ON➡

Answers
7 Ⓕ Ⓖ Ⓗ Ⓙ   8 Ⓐ Ⓑ Ⓒ Ⓓ

9 Which of the following sentences best combines sentence 2 and sentence 3 without changing their meaning?

    F I can tell you a lot about camping, fun, exciting, enjoyable.

    G I can tell you that camping can be things such as fun, exciting, and enjoyable.

    H I can tell you that camping can be fun, exciting, and enjoyable.

    J Fun, exciting, and enjoyable is what I can tell you that camping is.

10 What is the best way to write sentence 5?

    A An example of an example are smells, sights, and sounds that you can never find in a town or a city.

    B There are smells, sights, and sounds in the outdoors that you can never find in a town or a city.

    C There are smell, sights, and sounds in the outdoors, for example, that are different than the smell, sights, and sounds in a city.

    D As it is written.

11 Which of the following sentences could be added before sentence 7?

    F My favorite part of camping is roasting marshmallows.

    G There are many activities you can enjoy.

    H While camping, everyone dresses comfortably.

    J My family usually goes camping four or five times a year.

12 The best way to write sentence 11 is—

    A A campsite costs $15 and for about as much as you eat at home will cost you camping.

    B A campsite is about $15 and meals are about the same as at home.

    C A campsite costs about $15, and meals cost about the same as eating at home.

    D As it is written.

13 What is the most colorful way to write sentence 12?

    F You can cook delicious meals on a crackling open fire or cook them on a camp stove.

    G You can cook meals on a fire or a stove.

    H You can cook some of the meals on a fire and some on a stove.

    J As it is written.

14 Which sentence contains information that does not belong in Jeremy's article? Write the number of the sentence.

_____

_____

_____

GO ON

Here is the next part of Jeremy's rough draft for his article. This part has certain words and phrases underlined. Read the draft carefully. Then answer questions 15–22.

To have the <u>best time camping plan ahead.</u> Choose a campground
(13)   (14)

carefully. <u>You needs to know</u> what you plan to do there and how to get
(15)

there. There are many different campgrounds available. Some
(16)   (17)

campgrounds may have a first-come, first-served policy, but at other

campgrounds you may have to make reservations.

<u>Once you chose</u> a campground, you need to have the right equipment.
(18)

The most important <u>equipment are the tent.</u> A tent keeps you dry, gave
(19)   (20)

<u>you shelter and protects</u> you from insects. The tent should be one that
(21)

you and your family can handle easily. <u>There is many kinds</u> of tents to
(22)

choose from. It <u>might be a good idea</u> to rent a tent for your first camping
(23)

trip. This <u>gave</u> you a chance to see how you like camping.
(24)

15   In sentence 13, <u>best time camping plan</u> is best written—

   A   best time camping, plan

   B   best, time camping plan

   C   best time, camping plan

   D   As it is written.

16   In sentence 15, <u>You needs to know</u> is best written—

   F   Yous need to know

   G   You need to know

   H   You needed to know

   J   As it is written.

GO ON

Answers
15 Ⓐ Ⓑ Ⓒ Ⓓ   16 Ⓕ Ⓖ Ⓗ Ⓙ

17 In sentence 18, <u>Once you chose</u> is best written—

   A Once you chooses

   B Once you chosen

   C Once you choose

   D As it is written.

18 In sentence 19, <u>equipment are the tent</u> is best written—

   F equipments are the tent

   G equipment is the tent

   H equipments is the tent

   J As it is written.

19 In sentence 20, <u>gave you shelter and protects</u> is best written—

   A gives you shelter, and protects

   B gives you shelter and, protects

   C gives you shelters and protects

   D As it is written.

20 In sentence 22, <u>There is many kinds</u> is best written—

   F There were many kinds

   G There is many kind

   H There are many kinds

   J As it is written.

21 In sentence 23, <u>might be a good idea</u> is best written—

   A was a good idea

   B might have been a good idea

   C might been a good idea

   D As it is written.

22 In sentence 24, <u>gave</u> is best written—

   F given

   G will give

   H gaves

   J As it is written.

STOP

Answers

17 Ⓐ Ⓑ Ⓒ Ⓓ   **19** Ⓐ Ⓑ Ⓒ Ⓓ   **21** Ⓐ Ⓑ Ⓒ Ⓓ

18 Ⓕ Ⓖ Ⓗ Ⓙ   **20** Ⓕ Ⓖ Ⓗ Ⓙ   **22** Ⓕ Ⓖ Ⓗ Ⓙ

Directions: Read each sentence carefully. If one of the words is misspelled, darken the circle for that word. If all the words are spelled correctly, then darken the circle for *No mistake.*

TRY THIS | Read each sentence carefully. If you are not sure of an answer, first decide which answer choices are spelled correctly. Then see if you can recognize the misspelled word from your reading experience.

Sample A

The <u>pair</u> Mother gave me was <u>ripe</u> and <u>juicy</u>. <u>No mistake</u>
A   B   C   D

THINK IT THROUGH | The correct answer is <u>A</u>. A piece of fruit is spelled <u>pear</u>.

STOP

1   Ms. Coe <u>clutched</u> her <u>purse</u> <u>tightly</u>. <u>No mistake</u>
              A   B   C   D

2   Jody took a long <u>trek</u> <u>through</u> the <u>meadows</u>. <u>No mistake</u>
                      F   G   H   J

3   The boys <u>observed</u> the <u>striped</u> <u>caterpiller</u> move along the leaf. <u>No mistake</u>
                   A   B   C   D

4   The <u>satelite</u> was <u>orbiting</u> the <u>earth</u>. <u>No mistake</u>
          F   G   H   J

5   The iron <u>filings</u> were <u>atracted</u> to the <u>magnet</u>. <u>No mistake</u>
              A   B   C   D

6   John <u>disliked</u> doing his <u>algabra</u> <u>homework</u>. <u>No mistake</u>
            F   G   H   J

7   Taki was <u>familier</u> with the <u>rules</u> of the <u>game</u>. <u>No mistake</u>
               A   B   C   D

8   Percy was <u>breathles</u> from <u>running</u> the <u>race</u>. <u>No mistake</u>
            F   G   H   J

STOP

Answers
SA Ⓐ Ⓑ Ⓒ Ⓓ   2 Ⓕ Ⓖ Ⓗ Ⓙ   4 Ⓕ Ⓖ Ⓗ Ⓙ   6 Ⓕ Ⓖ Ⓗ Ⓙ   8 Ⓕ Ⓖ Ⓗ Ⓙ
1 Ⓐ Ⓑ Ⓒ Ⓓ   3 Ⓐ Ⓑ Ⓒ Ⓓ   5 Ⓐ Ⓑ Ⓒ Ⓓ   7 Ⓐ Ⓑ Ⓒ Ⓓ

Save the Earth

Santina's school is celebrating Earth Day. She knows it is important to conserve resources. She wants to do a report about recycling. She hopes that the report will encourage everyone to recycle.

Santina wants to include a definition of the word <u>recycling</u>. Which guide words might mark the page on which she would find it?

A   recognize–recount

B   recess–recognize

C   recourse–red

D   rebound–reception

Here is a rough draft of the first part of Santina's report. Read the rough draft carefully. Then answer questions 1–7.

Save the Earth

(1) I think that Earth Day is a good time to think about our planet, our

(2) planet Earth. People who lived long ago enjoyed clean air, clean water,

(3) and open land. In the past couple of hundred years. (4) These things have

(5) changed. Our country was just starting two hundred years ago.

(6) Today, the air and water are polluted the land is filled with things

(7) that people throw away. Some of our garbage is loaded with dangerous

(8) chemicals. These chemicals are dangerous for both people and animals.

(9) To decrease this kind of pollution, we have to learn to care about our

(10) environment. We either have to find ways to properly dispose of dangerous

chemicals or stop making the products that produce the chemicals.

GO ON

Answers
SA Ⓐ Ⓑ Ⓒ Ⓓ

1 Which words are <u>not</u> a complete thought?

  A 3

  B 4

  C 5

  D 6

2 What is the best way to write sentence 1?

  F I think that Earth Day is a good time to think about Earth our planet.

  G I think that Earth Day is a good time to think about our planet.

  H I think that Earth Day is a good day to think about our Earth planet.

  J As it is written.

3 What is the most colorful way to write sentence 2?

  A People who lived long ago enjoyed clean air, water, and land.

  B People who lived long ago enjoyed clean-smelling air, pure water, and uncluttered land.

  C People enjoyed air, water, and land that was clean.

  D As it is written.

4 Which sentence needs to be made into more than one sentence? Write the number of the sentence.

_____

_____

_____

5 Which sentence does <u>not</u> belong in Santina's report?

  F 2

  G 3

  H 4

  J 5

6 Which of the following sentences best combines sentence 3 and sentence 4 without changing their meaning?

  A These things have been changed, in the past couple of hundred years.

  B In the past couple of hundred years, these things have changed.

  C In the couple of hundred years past these things have changed.

  D Things have changed these, in the past couple of hundred years.

7 What supporting information could be added after sentence 6?

  F Many trees have to be cut down to make paper for newspapers.

  G People in other countries also have problems with pollution.

  H The word *environment* means "the world around us."

  J More landfills are being built to hold this garbage.

GO ON

Answers

1 Ⓐ Ⓑ Ⓒ Ⓓ	**3** Ⓐ Ⓑ Ⓒ Ⓓ	**6** Ⓐ Ⓑ Ⓒ Ⓓ
2 Ⓕ Ⓖ Ⓗ Ⓙ	**5** Ⓕ Ⓖ Ⓗ Ⓙ	**7** Ⓕ Ⓖ Ⓗ Ⓙ

Here is the next part of Santina's rough draft for her report. This part has certain words and phrases underlined. Read the draft carefully. Then answer questions 8–16.

I think recycling is a great way to decrease garbage and save natural
(11)

resources. When items are recycled, they can be used again or made into
(12)

something new. Many items can be recycled. For example, aunt Jane's
(13)   (14)

aluminum cans the ones she saves, can be recycled. Plastic bottles
                                                   (15)

newspapers and jars are other things that can be recycled. By recycling
                                                             (16)

these things, we stop them from ending up as garbage.

How can we participate in recycling? There are a couple of ways. Our
(17)   (18)   (19)

towns recycling program makes recycling easy. Every house have a green
                                              (20)

box for collecting recyclable goods. Every week a recycling truck picked
                                                  (21)

up the materials that residents leave by the curb in the box. Other towns
                                                               (22)

have recycling centers. People can drop off recyclable goods at these
                          (23)

centers. Recycling is a sensible, easy solution to caring for our planet.
          (24)

---

8 In sentence 14, cans the ones she saves is best written—

A cans the ones, she saves,

B cans the, ones she saves,

C cans, the ones she saves,

D As it is written.

9 In sentence 14, aunt Jane's is best written—

F aunt janes

G Aunt Janes

H Aunt Jane's

J As it is written

Answers
8 Ⓐ Ⓑ Ⓒ Ⓓ   9 Ⓕ Ⓖ Ⓗ Ⓙ

10 In sentence 15, <u>Plastic bottles newspapers and jars</u> is best written—

A Plastic bottles, newspapers, and jars

B Plastic, bottles, newspapers and, jars

C Plastic, bottles, newspapers, and jars

D As it is written.

11 In sentence 19, <u>Our towns recycling program</u> is best written—

F Our towns' recycling program

G Our town's recycling program

H Our towns's recycling program

J As it is written.

12 In sentence 20, <u>Every house have</u> is best written—

A Every house having

B Every houses have

C Every house has

D As it is written.

13 In sentence 21, <u>that residents leave by the curb</u> is best written—

F that residents are leaving by the curb

G that residents left by the curb

H that, by the curb, residents leave

J As it is written.

14 In sentence 21, <u>recycling truck picked up is</u> best written—

A recycling truck picks up

B recycling truck picking up

C recycling truck had picked up

D As it is written.

15 In sentence 23, <u>can drop off recyclable goods</u> is best written—

F will drop off recyclable goods

G dropping off recyclable goods

H dropped off recyclable goods

J As it is written.

16 In sentence 24, <u>is a sensible, easy solution</u> is best written—

A is a sensible, easier solution

B is a sensible and easier solution

C is a sensible solution and easy

D As it is written.

GO ON ➡

Answers

10 Ⓐ Ⓑ Ⓒ Ⓓ   **12** Ⓐ Ⓑ Ⓒ Ⓓ   **14** Ⓐ Ⓑ Ⓒ Ⓓ   **16** Ⓐ Ⓑ Ⓒ Ⓓ

11 Ⓕ Ⓖ Ⓗ Ⓙ   **13** Ⓕ Ⓖ Ⓗ Ⓙ   **15** Ⓕ Ⓖ Ⓗ Ⓙ

For questions 17–28, read each sentence carefully. If one of the words is misspelled, darken the circle for that word. If all of the words are spelled correctly, then darken the circle for *No mistake.*

17   Marcus thought that Tim's piano resital was boring. No mistake
                               F   G   H   J

18   They were marooned on a dessert island. No mistake
                        A   B   C   D

19   My little sister Caroline was borne on Christmas. No mistake
          F   G   H   J

20   The sponge absorbed the liquid that she spilled. No mistake
              A   B   C   D

21   The adjective modifys the noun in that sentence. No mistake
              F   G   H   J

22   Veronica sprented to the finish line and won the race. No mistake
                   A   B   C   D

23   The conplete edition has ten volumes. No mistake
              F   G   H   J

24   Springfield is the capitol of Illinois. No mistake
          A   B   C   D

25   Jamal lived abroad when he was younger. No mistake
                F   G   H   J

26   Noriko spoke to the commisioner at the banquet. No mistake
                A   B   C   D

27   The vault door closed automatecally behind the bank guard. No mistake
              F   G   H   J

28   The otter sliped down the riverbank and splashed into the water. No mistake
          A   B   C   D

STOP

Answers
17 ⓕ ⓖ ⓗ ⓙ   20 Ⓐ Ⓑ Ⓒ Ⓓ   23 ⓕ ⓖ ⓗ ⓙ   26 Ⓐ Ⓑ Ⓒ Ⓓ
18 Ⓐ Ⓑ Ⓒ Ⓓ   21 ⓕ ⓖ ⓗ ⓙ   24 Ⓐ Ⓑ Ⓒ Ⓓ   27 ⓕ ⓖ ⓗ ⓙ
19 ⓕ ⓖ ⓗ ⓙ   22 Ⓐ Ⓑ Ⓒ Ⓓ   25 ⓕ ⓖ ⓗ ⓙ   28 Ⓐ Ⓑ Ⓒ Ⓓ

READING COMPREHENSION

Use the removable answer sheet on page 763 to record your answers for the practice tests.

Sample A

Polar Bears

Polar bears are sometimes called ice bears or snow bears. These huge bears live in the icy lands near the North Pole. They sometimes weigh more than 1,000 pounds. Their thick, white fur and layers of fat help them stay warm in freezing winters. Polar bears live by themselves except when a mother has cubs.

Why can polar bears live near the North Pole?

A They build fires.

B They huddle close together.

C They stay in caves all winter.

D They have thick fur and layers of fat.

STOP

For questions 1–40, carefully read each selection and the questions that follow. Then darken the circle for the correct answer, or write in the answer.

Fishing

David and Fumio take their canoe out after supper to fish for bass. As the sun starts to go down, a symphony rises from the lake. Insects buzz, frogs croak, and birds chirp a chorus. The boys give up fishing and enjoy the *natural wonders* around them. A snapping turtle glides near the boat. It submerges and resurfaces, then submerges again, a natural submarine. Its periscope neck sticks up through the surface of the water. Then with a splash, the turtle's head disappears.

"I think it's time for us to leave, too." David says. Both boys are smiling.

1 **"A symphony rises from the lake" means—**

A some musicians have come to play.

B birds, insects, and frogs make many different noises as night falls.

C lakes are musical places.

D Fumio is playing his portable radio.

2 **Why do David and Fumio go to the lake?**

_____

_____

_____

_____

3 **The snapping turtle was like a submarine because—**

F it had the shape of a submarine.

G it went under the water and had a "periscope" neck.

H it was the color of a submarine.

J submarines make a snapping sound.

4 **What are the natural wonders?**

_____

_____

_____

GO ON➤

An Interesting Collection

Erica's grandfather, Max, was a sailor. He traveled all over the world. When he traveled, he collected shells. Now he has shells from many different places.

Erica always admired her grandfather's shells. When she was nine years old, she started her own shell collection. She hopes to have a collection like her grandfather's someday. She knows it will take a long time.

Erica collects shells from the shores of rivers, seas, lakes, and streams. Sometimes she finds shells in dry places that used to be underwater. Most of the shells that she collects belong to a group of animals known as mollusks. Snails, clams, and oysters are all mollusks.

Each animal's shell differs in shape as well as in size and color. A snail's shell is one piece. It is like a tube that winds around itself as it grows. Clams and oysters have shells made of two parts joined together at one spot. Clams and oysters can keep their shells open when they are resting. Other mollusks have shells called tooth shells. These shells look like long needles.

Erica has been collecting shells for three years. She has almost one hundred shells. Max told her it was time to learn how to care for her collection properly. He taught Erica how to clean her shells. She boils them in water for five to ten minutes. Then she washes the shells in soap and water. Finally she puts the shells on pieces of cardboard. On each piece of cardboard, she writes down the name of the shell and when and where she found it.

Now Erica and her grandfather go looking for shells together. Erica even has one or two shells that her grandfather doesn't have. There are so many kinds of shells that both of their collections will keep growing for a long time.

GO ON

5 All of the following are facts that Erica records on the pieces of cardboard *except*—

   A the kind of shell.

   B where the shell was found.

   C the date the shell was found.

   D the shape of the shell.

6 Erica probably would find shells near all of the following *except*—

   F the shore of a lake.

   G an ocean beach.

   H a swimming pool.

   J a stream.

7 This selection is *mainly* about—

   A Erica's hobby of collecting shells.

   B Erica's grandfather's travels.

   C Erica's search for shells.

   D the benefits of collecting shells.

8 Which shells can open and close?

   _____

   _____

   _____

   _____

   _____

9 How old is Erica now?

   F nine years old

   G ten years old

   H twelve years old

   J six years old

10 According to the selection, Erica's grandfather taught her—

   A where to find shells.

   B the names of the animals that live in the shells.

   C how to avoid tooth shells.

   D how to clean shells.

11 According to the selection, why did Erica want a shell collection?

   F She liked her grandfather's collection.

   G She liked shells.

   H She wanted to travel around the world.

   J She liked to eat clams and oysters.

12 Which of the following could be another title for this selection?

   A "Erica's Grandfather Max"

   B "Erica's Hobby"

   C "All About Mollusks"

   D "Taking Care of a Shell Collection"

13 According to the selection, how are snail shells and clam shells different?

   F Snail shells are found only by lakes.

   G Clam shells are produced by mollusks.

   H Clam shells cannot be preserved.

   J Snail shells are one-piece shells.

14 What is the *next* thing Erica does with her shells after she gathers them?

   _____

   _____

   _____

   _____

   _____

GO ON➡

Making a Snow Cave

For those who enjoy cross-country skiing and hiking during the winter months, the following information on building a snow cave may prove *invaluable*.

Directions
1. First, find a deep snowdrift.
2. Next, dig a tunnel into the drift, angling it upward several feet.
3. Then, *excavate* a dome-shaped room at the top of the tunnel, judging the thickness of the roof by watching from the inside for the snow to turn a light blue color. This color tells you that the wall is the correct thickness.
4. Smooth the curved ceiling to remove sharp edges that could cause moisture to drip onto your gear.
5. Next, carve little shelves or spaces in the walls for candles.
6. Then, use a ski pole or a sharp stick to punch holes in the roof at a 45° angle to the floor. Holes made at this angle will allow fresh air in without allowing moisture to enter the dome.
7. Finally, fashion a door by piling snow on a ground cloth, gathering up the four corners, and tying them with a cord. Allow the snow to crystallize into a hard ball that can be pulled with the cloth into the entranceway to block the wind and trap warm air inside the cave.

The cave will probably take two people about two hours to build. Be sure to have a shovel included in your gear, in case a snowdrift blocks the entrance to your snow cave. You can use the shovel to dig an emergency exit.

GO ON ➤

15 If you wanted to learn more about winter camping, you should—

 A   visit a ski resort.

 B   look for books on this subject in your library.

 C   take a winter vacation.

 D   visit a sporting goods store.

16 The word "excavate" in this selection means to—

 F   hollow out.

 G   exclude.

 H   discover.

 J   calculate.

17 What does the word "invaluable" mean in this selection?

_____

_____

_____

_____

18 Besides serving as a door to block the cave entryway, the crystallized snow on the cloth—

 A   can be used as a freezer for food supplies.

 B   stores drinking water.

 C   traps warm air in the cave.

 D   supports the roof of the cave.

19 According to the selection, a shovel can be an important tool to have in a snow cave if you—

 F   need to dig an emergency exit.

 G   fight off a wild animal.

 H   need a support for the ceiling of the snow cave.

 J   have to dig for food.

20 Shelves are carved into the walls of the snow cave to—

 A   let in fresh air.

 B   make windows in the cave.

 C   support the roof.

 D   hold candles for lighting the cave.

21 How do you know when the cave walls are the correct thickness?

 F   Look for a blue color on the walls.

 G   Test the wall with your shovel.

 H   Try to punch a hole in the wall.

 J   This information is not stated in the selection.

22 The directions for making a snow cave help the reader to—

 A   realize that a snow cave is a permanent shelter.

 B   see that the author is very well read.

 C   survive in the winter.

 D   understand the steps involved in making a snow cave.

GO ON➡

Tepees: Native American Homes

The Great Plains stretch from Texas to Canada and from the Rocky Mountains to the Missouri River valley. For many years this huge area was nothing but flat grassland. Hawks, elk, deer, coyotes, and bears lived there. Of the many animals on the Great Plains, the most plentiful was the buffalo. One herd might have several million buffaloes.

The Native Americans who lived on the Great Plains followed the buffaloes. They used them for food, clothing, tools, and fuel. For this reason, they needed homes that were light and easy to move. The Sioux, Dakota, Crow, Cheyenne, and Blackfoot peoples all lived in tepees.

No one knows when tepees were first used, but the Spanish explorer Coronado saw them in 1541. Tepees were made from wooden poles tied together in a cone shape. Buffalo hides were sewn together as a covering for the poles. The tepees were warm in winter, dry in rainstorms, and sturdy enough to withstand heavy winds.

Because there were very few trees on the Great Plains, it was difficult to get the long straight poles needed for the tepees. The Cheyenne sometimes traveled from Oklahoma to Montana to get lodge poles. These poles were highly valued. Sometimes a horse would be traded for five poles. The average tepee needed about fifteen poles. The largest tepees used more than thirty.

The women owned the tepees and did most of the work in building them. They took the bark off the poles and let them dry for about three weeks. Meanwhile the cover was made. Twelve to fourteen buffalo hides usually were needed. First, all the fat was scraped off the hides. Then they were left out in the sun to dry for a few days. Next, the hides had to be tanned with a special mixture made from bark, grease, and water. Then they were dried again. Later, the skins were stretched and rubbed to soften them.

Often the woman who owned a tepee held a feast. This was her way of asking the other women to help her. Some women would prepare the buffalo *sinew*, or tissue, that was used as thread. Others cut the hides and then sewed them together.

When it was finished, the new cover was soft, smooth, and white. Then the women hung the cover over the tepee poles and built a fire inside. The smoke would waterproof the cover. The Native Americans usually decorated the tepees with meaningful symbols and designs. Often they recorded the history of an earlier family member on the tepee. The Native Americans used colorful paints made from plants and roots found in their surroundings.

GO ON➡

23 You would most likely find this selection in a—

   F history book.

   G travel magazine.

   H literature textbook.

   J health magazine.

24 What was the *first* step in preparing the buffalo hides as tepee covers?

   A The hides were sewn together.

   B The fat was scraped off the hides.

   C The hides were left in the sun to dry.

   D The hides were tanned with a special mixture.

25 In line 3 of the sixth paragraph, the word "sinew" means—

   F the lodge poles used to build tepees.

   G bark removed from lodge poles.

   H plants and roots used for paint.

   J buffalo tissue used as thread to sew hides together.

26 Which of these statements expresses an *opinion* from the selection?

   A Tepees were the best homes ever invented.

   B Tepees were often decorated with meaningful symbols and designs.

   C Tepees were first used in the 1600s.

   D Tepees were used for many different purposes.

27 There is enough information in the selection to suggest that—

   F tepees were not practical on the Great Plains.

   G Native Americans respected and made good use of their environment.

   H most Native Americans made their living by farming.

   J Native Americans held many colorful celebrations.

28 The Great Plains are located from—

   A the Cascade to the Rocky Mountains.

   B Oregon to California.

   C the Rocky Mountains to the Missouri River valley.

   D Maine to Florida.

29 The web shows some important ideas in the selection.

Tepees	
Materials	**Advantages**
1 Poles	1 Warm in winter
2 Buffalo hides	2

Which belongs in the empty box?

   F Wet in rainstorms

   G Difficult to make

   H Easy to move

   J Owned by women

30 Why was it hard to find poles for tepees?

_____

_____

_____

_____

GO ON ➡

Carnival Fun!

Mercer School is having a Spring Carnival on Saturday and Sunday, April 20 and 21. The carnival will take place on the school playground. It will begin at 11:00 A.M. and end at 5:00 P.M. each day.

Dozens of booths will feature food and handmade items for sale. Everyone will enjoy the entertainment. A children's comedy show will be provided. There will also be live music. All children can enjoy a pony ride. There will be many games, including a three-legged race and a ring toss. All money raised at the carnival will help to fund the Children's Summer Day Camp.

For more information or to buy tickets, call Ms. Díaz, the carnival chairperson, at the school between 8:00 A.M. and 1:00 P.M on school days.

31 If the author added a sentence to the end of the second paragraph, which of these would fit best?

A No one will be allowed on the school playground the day before the carnival.

B For information about selling tickets, call the chairperson.

C This camp is open to all students at Mercer School.

D Mercer School teaches students in grades 5 through 8.

32 There is enough information in this selection to show that—

F the carnival is for senior citizens only.

G the carnival events will especially interest teen-agers.

H there will be events to interest people of all ages.

J the carnival is for small children only.

33 Which of these states an *opinion?*

A The carnival will take place on the school playground.

B Everyone will enjoy the entertainment.

C The carnival will begin at 11:00 A.M. each day.

D Dozens of booths will feature food and handmade items for sale.

34 Where would this selection most likely be found?

F in a public library

G in a national magazine

H in a school bulletin

J in a science textbook

35 When will the carnival take place?

_____

_____

_____

_____

_____

_____

36 According to the announcement, the carnival is being held to raise money for—

A the children's comedy show.

B the Children's Summer Day Camp.

C the Mercer School PTA.

D winners of the three-legged race.

GO ON

A Terrible Flood

The newspaper headlines claimed that the recent flood was a once-in-a-lifetime event. People in the soggy farm town in Iowa certainly hoped that was true. The Mississippi River knew no banks for two weeks in August. The mess that was left behind would take an incredible amount of time, money, and energy to clean.

When Dawn and Greg arrived on the bus at their grandmother's farm town, they didn't recognize much. They saw a lot of rubbish, including parts of homes, pieces of furniture, piles of sandbags, and acres of slimy mud. Here and there they could even see dead fish that had been left behind when the waters *receded*.

Grandmother was anxious to greet Dawn and Greg and get back to the house to start their discouraging clean-up chores. Her car had been ruined in the flood, so they walked the mile to the house.

"Grandma, how badly damaged was your house?" asked Dawn as they slopped through the mud.

"Well, the house is still standing, but it is covered with the same kind of slimy mud we're walking in," replied Grandma.

"You mean this mud came through the doors and windows?" asked Greg incredulously.

"I'm afraid the force of the water and mud broke the basement windows and filled the house up to the second story with river water, silt, and fish," said Grandma sadly.

---

37 Why did Grandma, Dawn, and Greg walk the mile to Grandma's house?

_____

_____

_____

_____

_____

38 The author included the sixth paragraph to show the reader that—

F Greg wasn't surprised about the damage to Grandma's house.

G Greg couldn't believe what his grandmother told him about the damage to her house.

H Greg wasn't listening to his grandmother.

J Greg couldn't hear what his grandmother was saying.

39 According to the selection, why didn't Dawn and Greg recognize their grandmother's town?

A They had never been there before.

B They hadn't visited there in many years.

C The flood had severely damaged the town.

D The town had been remodeled after the flood.

40 In line 5 of the second paragraph, the word "receded" means—

F advanced.

G rose.

H flooded.

J withdrew.

STOP

READING VOCABULARY

Sample A

Fabric is a kind of—

A cloth   C package

B box   D factory

🛑 STOP

For questions 1–8, darken the circle for the word or group of words that has the same or almost the same meaning as the underlined word.

1 To pursue is to—

A lead

B stop

C find

D follow

2 Perpetual means—

F fades in sunlight

G lasts forever

H foreign

J priceless

3 Something that is meager is—

A hearty

B fattening

C skimpy

D silly

4 Something that is trivial is—

F important

G large

H unimportant

J confusing

5 Something that is wrinkled is—

A dirty

B creased

C pretty

D closed

6 To combine means to—

F separate

G blend

H package

J spend

7 Something that is dismal is—

A gloomy

B bright

C windy

D happy

8 Elderly means—

F old

G young

H new

J friendly

Write your answer to the following:

9 Absurd means—

_____

_____

_____

_____

GO ON ➡

Sample B

> The gardeners will <u>deposit</u> the soil in the backyard.

In which sentence does <u>deposit</u> have the same meaning as it does in the sentence above?

A Zoe put a <u>deposit</u> down on the dress.

B I will <u>deposit</u> the stack of books on your porch.

C Rachel wanted to <u>deposit</u> her earnings in her bank.

D The miners found a <u>deposit</u> of gold.

🛑 **STOP**

For questions 10–14, darken the circle for the sentence in which the underlined word means the same as it does in the sentence in the box.

10

> Jamie had to <u>force</u> his way through the crowd.

In which sentence does <u>force</u> have the same meaning as it does in the sentence above?

A The <u>force</u> of the explosion blew out the windows in the building.

B Don't <u>force</u> the child to play.

C The <u>force</u> of gravity keeps things in place on Earth.

D We had to <u>force</u> the puppy through the hole in the fence.

11

> We studied the <u>culture</u> of the ancient Egyptians.

In which sentence does <u>culture</u> have the same meaning as it does in the sentence above?

F Her family's customs are influenced by the Spanish <u>culture</u>.

G The scientist grew the <u>culture</u> overnight.

H She is a person with <u>culture</u>, who writes poetry and plays the piano.

J The doctor took a throat <u>culture</u> from Stella and her brother.

12

> The <u>key</u> to good health is exercise.

In which sentence does <u>key</u> have the same meaning as it does in the sentence above?

A Make sure you don't lose your <u>key</u>.

B The choir was singing off <u>key</u>.

C Max found the <u>key</u> to the mystery.

D She needed to get the piano <u>key</u> fixed.

13

> To start the machine, <u>press</u> the red button.

In which sentence does <u>press</u> have the same meaning as it does in the sentence above?

F Can you <u>press</u> this shirt for me?

G The governor's speech was reported by the <u>press</u>.

H The chef needed to use a garlic <u>press</u> .

J <u>Press</u> the elevator button for the third floor.

14

> Grandpa showed us how to <u>pitch</u> horseshoes.

In which sentence does <u>pitch</u> have the same meaning as it does in the sentence above?

A The campers had to <u>pitch</u> their tents before nightfall.

B Mandy's instrument was off <u>pitch</u>.

C Mary's sister learned to <u>pitch</u> at baseball practice.

D The heavy storm caused the sailboat to <u>pitch</u>.

GO ON ➡

Sample C

She gave a feeble excuse for not completing her homework. **Feeble means—**

A good

B strong

C believable

D weak

🛑 STOP

For questions 15–20, darken the circle for the word or words that give the meaning of the underlined word.

15 The teacher perceived that the confused students did not grasp the lesson. **Perceived means—**

F understood

G remembered

H begged

J expected

16 Nate soon tired of the tedious work he had been assigned. **Tedious means—**

A exciting

B computer

C boring

D complicated

17 The little boy cried when the tower he was building collapsed. **Collapsed means—**

F blew up

G sold out

H fell down

J went up

18 The fierce storm terrified the children. **Terrified means—**

A entertained

B delighted

C confused

D frightened

19 It was difficult for Alexander to drive through the dense fog. **Dense means—**

F dirty

G smoky

H thick

J dangerous

20 Mother wanted to paint the dingy room. **Dingy means—**

A dull

B small

C bright

D damp

Write your answer to the following:

21 The authentic fort had been demolished years earlier. **Authentic means—**

_____

_____

_____

_____

🛑 STOP

PART 1: MATH PROBLEM SOLVING

Sample A

Which fraction means the same as $\frac{10}{16}$?

A $\frac{1}{8}$ C $\frac{6}{16}$

B $\frac{5}{8}$ D $\frac{2}{3}$

STOP

For questions 1–50, darken the circle for the correct answer, or write in the answer.

1 Which list shows the colleges in order from the earliest date founded?

Year Founded	Name of School
1636	Harvard
1701	Yale
1754	Columbia University
1764	Brown University

A Columbia, Harvard, Brown, Yale

B Harvard, Yale, Columbia, Brown

C Harvard, Yale, Brown, Columbia

D Yale, Brown, Columbia, Harvard

2 The space shuttle *Atlantis* can travel as many as 452,384 miles in one day while in orbit. How would this number be written in words?

F forty-five thousand twenty-three hundred forty-eight

G four hundred fifty-two thousand three hundred eighty-four

H four million fifty-two thousand three hundred eighty-four

J four million five hundred twenty-three thousand eighteen four

3 Which number has a 3 in the tens place?

A 463

B 4,371

C 398

D 830

4 Patti needs $3\frac{1}{2}$ yards of white fabric, $2\frac{1}{3}$ yards of green fabric, $1\frac{1}{2}$ yards of black fabric, and $2\frac{3}{4}$ yards of brown fabric. Choose the list that shows the fabrics from least to greatest amounts.

F white, green, black, brown

G black, green, brown, white

H green, black, white, brown

J brown, black, white, green

5 What fraction of the set of shapes are squares?

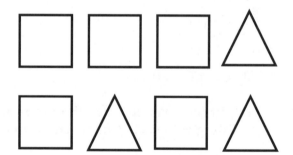

A $\frac{3}{8}$

B $\frac{3}{5}$

C $\frac{5}{8}$

D $\frac{8}{5}$

GO ON ▶

6 If $130 + x = 420$, then $x =$

    F 550   **H** 290

    G 390   **J** 210

7 Which number is in the same fact family as

$3 \times 8 = \square$?

    A $\square \times 8 = 16$

    B $8 + 3 = \square$

    C $6 \times 4 = \square$

    D $\square \div 8 = 3$

8 What number is shown here in expanded form?

$5,000,000 + 500 + 4$

    F 50,540

    G 550,400

    H 5,005,400

    J 5,000,504

9 At Wendy's school, the students are selling boxes of candles to raise funds. Wendy has been selling 5 boxes an hour at the mall. Which equation could be used to find x, the number of boxes Wendy sells in 6 hours at this rate?

    A $6 \div 5 = x$

    B $6 + 5 = x$

    C $5x \times 5 = x$

    D $6 \times 5 = x$

10 What number would replace the $\square$ to make the number sentence true?

$73 + (68 + 31) = (68 + 31) + \square$

    F 99

    G 73

    H 68

    J 31

11 Suzanne's monthly insurance payments will increase by \$45 per month. Her current payment is \$84. What will her new monthly payment be?

_____

_____

_____

12 There are 13 students in one lunch line and 29 students in another line. How many students would need to move from the second line in order to have the same number of students in both lines?

    A 24

    B 16

    C 8

    D 4

13 What is the value of the 9 in 75.09?

    F 9 ones

    G 9 thousandths

    H 9 tenths

    J 9 hundredths

14 Which decimal belongs in the box on the number line?

_____

_____

_____

_____

GO ON➡

15 Wanda is choosing what to wear to school. She has 3 pairs of jeans, 4 tops, and 2 pairs of shoes to choose from. How many different clothing combinations does Wanda have?

A 9

B 12

C 14

D 24

16 If Larry picked one of the cards shown here without looking, which of the cards would he most likely pick?

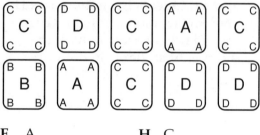

F A

G B

H C

J D

17 It is Carmela's turn in a board game she is playing with her family. What is the probability that Carmela will lose a turn on this spin?

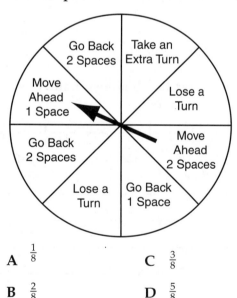

A $\frac{1}{8}$

B $\frac{2}{8}$

C $\frac{3}{8}$

D $\frac{5}{8}$

18 Every morning Sam takes his two dogs, Rocket and Jackpot, for a 35-minute walk. Which equation could be used to find t, the total number of minutes Sam walks his dogs each week?

F $7 + 2 + 35 = t$

G $7 \times 35 = t$

H $7 (2 + 35) = t$

J $7 \times \frac{35}{60} = t$

19 Which equation means the same as $9 \times 6 = 54$?

A $54 \times 6 = 9$

B $54 \div 9 = 6$

C $9 \div 6 = 54$

D $54 - 9 = 6$

20 A special machine multiplies any number entered into it by 8. The table shows how the numbers are changed. Which numbers complete the table? Write them in the boxes.

Original number	4	6	9
New number	32		

GO ON➡

21 The table shows Wyatt's earnings over a 5-week period last summer.

Wyatt's Earnings

Week 1	$12
Week 2	$20
Week 3	$15
Week 4	$25
Week 5	$13

Wyatt wanted to earn $40 to buy a remote-controlled car. During which week did he reach his goal?

F   week 2

G   week 3

H   week 4

J   week 5

22 The graph shows the population changes in Smithville over the years.

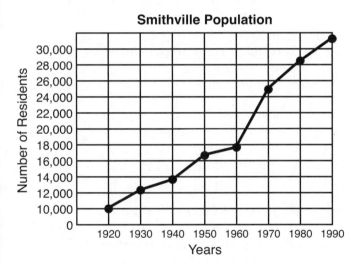

When did Smithville's population grow the most?

A   from 1950 to 1960

B   from 1960 to 1970

C   from 1970 to 1980

D   from 1980 to 1990

23 One piece of the puzzle is missing. Which piece is the missing one?

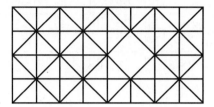

F

G

H

J

24 Jean likes 2 shirts and 3 skirts at a local department store. She can afford to buy only 1 shirt and 1 skirt. How many different combinations are available to Jean?

A   12   **C**   6

B   8   **D**   5

25 How many dots would form the sixth figure if this pattern continues?

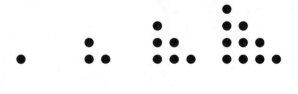

_____

_____

_____

_____

GO ON➡

26 Which tally chart shows the data used in the bar graph?

	Cake	卌 卌 卌 卌 卌 卌
F	Cookies	卌 卌 |||
	Pie	卌 卌
	Ice Cream	卌 卌 卌 卌 |||

	Cake	卌 卌 卌
G	Cookies	卌 卌
	Pie	卌 ||
	Ice Cream	卌 卌 卌

	Cake	卌 卌 卌 卌 卌 卌
H	Cookies	卌 卌 卌 卌 卌
	Pie	卌 卌 卌
	Ice Cream	卌 卌 卌 卌 卌 卌 卌

	Cake	卌 卌 卌 卌 卌 卌
J	Cookies	卌 卌 卌 卌 ||
	Pie	卌 卌 卌
	Ice Cream	卌 卌 卌 卌 卌 卌 卌

27 The graph shows the results of a survey taken at the mall.

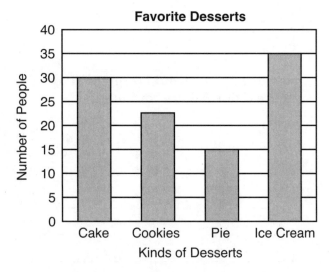

Favorite Desserts

What is the total number of people who liked cake and pie?

A 15   C 45

B 30   D 112

28 The octagons are grouped together in the oval. The other figures are not octagons.

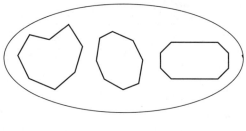

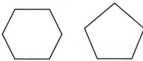

Which shape below is an octagon?

F   H

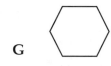

G   J

29 How many right angles does this figure have?

A 1

B 2

C 4

D none

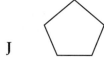

30 Mick delivered 26, 19, 23, and 20 newspapers on the blocks of his route. What was the average number of newspapers Mick delivered?

_____

_____

_____

_____

GO ON➡

This graph shows the number of videotapes purchased by the public library each month from January through May. Study the graph. Then answer questions 31 and 32.

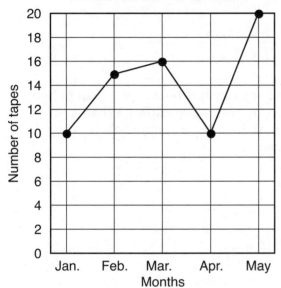

VIDEOTAPES PURCHASED

31 How many more tapes were purchased in May than in January?

F 10   H 30

G 20   J 4

32 How many tapes were purchased altogether?

_____

_____

_____

_____

33 The Jordan Middle School held a car wash to raise funds to buy computers. During the first 4 hours, the following number of cars were washed: 46, 59, 64, and 63. What was the average number of cars washed in an hour?

A 64   C 232

B 46   D 58

34 Find the area of a rectangle that is 4 meters by 8 meters.

F 12 square meters   H 36 square meters

G 24 square meters   J 32 square meters

35 Which figure does not show a line of symmetry?

A   C

B   D

36 If the pattern formed by the blocks continues, how many blocks will be needed to make the next shape?

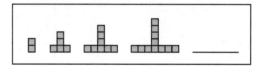

F 12   H 17

G 14   J 20

37 Which transformation moves the figure from position A to position B?

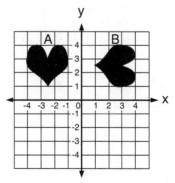

A rotation

B reflection

C translation

D rotation and translation

GO ON➡

38 What is the area of the shaded part of the figure shown here?

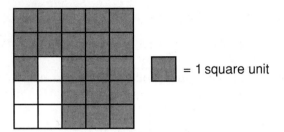

☐ = 1 square unit

F   5 square units

G   11 square units

H   18 square units

J   20 square units

39 Amir drew a picture of the sandbox at his neighborhood playground. What is the perimeter of the sandbox?

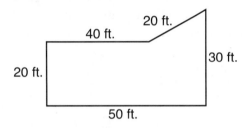

20 ft.
40 ft.
20 ft.
30 ft.
50 ft.

A   100 ft.

B   160 ft.

C   140 ft.

D   80 ft.

40 What is the perimeter of this figure?

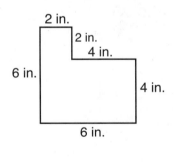

2 in.
2 in.
4 in.
6 in.
4 in.
6 in.

_____

_____

_____

_____

41 Which of the following units of metric measurement is best to use to measure the length of a bike path?

F   meter

G   kiloliter

H   milligram

J   kilometer

42 Use your inch ruler and the map to help you answer the question. What is the actual distance from the beach to the airport?

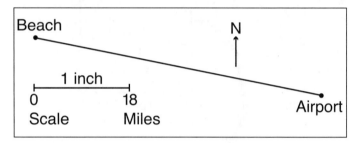

Beach
N
1 inch
0   18
Scale   Miles
Airport

A   36 miles   C   54 miles

B   72 miles   D   62 miles

43 Which best represents the coordinates of the location of 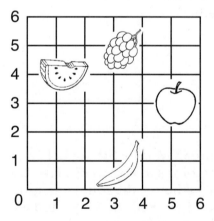 on the map?

F   (4, 3)

G   (1, 3)

H   (1, 4)

J   (3, 5)

GO ON➡

44 Yugi was keeping track of how many times each team in his baseball league won a game. The Rangers had more wins than the Tigers. The Bullets had more wins than the Pirates. The Bullets had fewer wins than the Tigers. Which team had the most wins?

_____

_____

_____

_____

45 Which figure is made of all triangles?

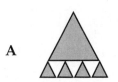

A

C

B

D

46 Barry ordered a ham sandwich for $2.89, a small salad for $1.25, and iced tea for $0.89. What is the *best estimate* of the total cost of his bill?

F $5.00   H $7.00

G $6.00   J $8.00

47 What time will it be in 35 minutes?

A 6:00

B 6:05

C 5:55

D 7:05

48 Maria makes decorative pillows. She can sew a pillow in 25 minutes. What additional information is needed to find out how long it takes Maria to sew an entire set of pillows?

F the length of each pillow

G the number of pillows in a set

H the weight of each pillow

J the number of sets Maria has made

49 Meili needs to have pieces of fabric that are the same shape and size as the small figure shown here.

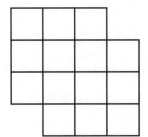

What is the greatest number of these fabric pieces Meili could cut from this large piece of fabric?

A 12

B 14

C 16

D 18

50 The House of Flowers bought 72 flats of seedlings from their wholesaler. There were 96 seedlings per flat. What is the *best estimate* of the number of seedlings that the House of Flowers bought?

F 6,000

G 7,000

H 7,500

J 12,500

STOP

Sample A

$$7\frac{2}{3}$$
$$+10\frac{1}{4}$$

A $17\frac{11}{12}$

B $17\frac{10}{12}$

C $17\frac{3}{7}$

D $18\frac{1}{2}$

E NH

STOP

For questions 1–14, darken the circle for the correct answer. Darken the circle for NH (Not Here) if the correct answer is not given. If no choices are given, write in your answer.

1 $0.17 \times 0.05 =$

_____

_____

_____

_____

2 $878 - 69 =$

A 809

B 701

C 398

D 947

E NH

3 $67 \times 53 =$

F 3,551

G 3,531

H 3,421

J 3,651

K NH

4

$$\frac{7}{16}$$
$$-\frac{5}{16}$$

A $\frac{3}{4}$

B $\frac{7}{8}$

C $\frac{5}{6}$

D 12

E NH

5 $0.23 \times 0.09 =$

F 0.0207

G 0.2007

H 0.207

J 0.27

K NH

6 $\frac{1}{2} \times \frac{1}{8} =$

A $\frac{1}{16}$

B $\frac{1}{6}$

C $\frac{1}{8}$

D $\frac{1}{4}$

E NH

7 $17\overline{)238}$

F 13 R 7

G 7 R 13

H 13

J 14

K NH

8

$$\$4.18$$
$$+ \$2.31$$

A $1.87

B $4.39

C $6.49

D $6.59

E NH

9 The grocery store received a shipment of 120 cases of milk yesterday. If 75 of the cases were whole milk, and the rest were skim milk, then how many of the cases were skim milk?

F 92 cases

G 75 cases

H 60 cases

J 195 cases

K NH

GO ON

Sample B

Mr. Mendoza uses his own truck at work. If he drove 128 miles last week, and 62 of those miles were for his personal use, how many miles did he drive on the job?

A 190 miles

B 55 miles

C 58 miles

D 66 miles

E NH

STOP

10 Kelly worked $9\frac{1}{3}$ hours at the shoe store last week. She worked $14\frac{1}{3}$ hours this week.

How many more hours did Kelly work this week?

A 5

B $5\frac{1}{3}$

C $5\frac{2}{3}$

D $6\frac{1}{3}$

E NH

11 Leland went to his grandfather's apple orchard to help pick apples. One day he picked 8 baskets of Winesap apples and 13 baskets of Granny Smith apples.

How many baskets of apples did he pick altogether?

F 19 baskets

G 21 baskets

H 23 baskets

J 5 baskets

K NH

12 Mr. Ralston has 420 coins in his collection. Of those coins, 70% are very valuable.

How many of the coins are very valuable?

A 168

B 210

C 252

D 294

E NH

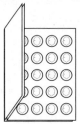

13 The diameter of the sun measures 1,392,000 kilometers.

What is that number rounded to the nearest hundred thousand miles?

F 1,300,000

G 1,390,000

H 1,395,000

J 1,400,000

K NH

14 Ms. Nakamura's class has only 1 computer. She lets each student use it for 10 minutes at a time.

How many students can use the computer during the 60 minutes before school?

_____

_____

_____

_____

STOP

LANGUAGE

Hawaii

The students in Rachel's class are preparing travel guides for places that they have visited. Rachel wants to do a travel guide about Hawaii, where she went on vacation with her family. She wants to let others know what Hawaii is like. She wants to inform everyone about the great places she visited in Hawaii.

Sample A

What would Rachel <u>not</u> want to include in her travel guide?

A the names of beaches she visited

B a description of Hawaii's climate

C the names of the counties in Hawaii

D the names of national parks in Hawaii

STOP

For questions 1–5, darken the circle for the correct answer.

1 **Rachel wants to know the meaning of the word *dormant*. Where should she look?**

A a dictionary   C an atlas

B a thesaurus   D a history book

2 **Rachel wants to read some travel brochures about Hawaii. To find the nearest travel bureau, she should look in—**

F a dictionary.

G a thesaurus.

H an atlas.

J a telephone directory.

3 **Rachel has found a book called *The Hawaiian Islands*. She wants information about the climate of Hawaii. What part of the book would help her find her topic quickly?**

A the copyright page

B the introduction

C the index

D the title page

4 **Which guide words might mark the page on which Rachel would find the word *volcanic*?**

F void–volume   H volunteer–vote

G vivid–voice   J visual–vitamin

5 **In which part of *The Hawaiian Islands* would Rachel find the author's name?**

_____

_____

GO ON

Here are the Table of Contents and Index from *The Hawaiian Islands*, the book Rachel found in the library. Study them carefully. Then answer questions 6–11.

Table of Contents

Index

6   Which chapter should Rachel read to learn about the lakes and rivers in Hawaii?

   A   Chapter 1

   B   Chapter 2

   C   Chapter 3

   D   Chapter 4

7   Which pages would have information about where active volcanoes are found in Hawaii?

   F   6–7

   G   9–11

   H   15–16

   J   37–38

8   Which pages would have information about the Polynesians, the first Hawaiians?

   A   6–7

   B   15–16

   C   35–36

   D   56–57

9   Chapter 4 contains information on all of these except—

   F   national parks to visit.

   G   the best places for surfing.

   H   the government of Hawaii.

   J   harbor towns along the coasts.

10   Which chapter should Rachel read to find out about the way the land in Hawaii was formed?

   _____

   _____

   _____

11   Which pages would have information about the daily temperatures in Hawaii?

   A   6–7

   B   9–11

   C   12–13

   D   37–38

GO ON➡

Here is a rough draft of the first part of Rachel's travel guide. Read the rough draft carefully. Then answer questions 12–19.

Hawaii

Do you want to have the greatest time in the world? If you do, and
(1)   (2)

you do then Hawaii is the vacation spot for you.

Hawaii is one of the 50 states of the United States. It is the only
(3)   (4)

state that is not part of the mainland of North America. Hawaii is our
(5)

southernmost state.

Hawaii has many beautiful and interesting sights to see. The
(6)   (7)

islands are a wonderful place to experience volcanoes. You can
(8)

experience magnificent waterfalls and beautiful beaches. The weather
(9)

is warm year–round, so every day is a good day for any outdoor plans.

The people of Hawaii have many colorful customs. You can enjoy
(10)   (11)

interesting food and music. You can also watch folk dancing, parades, and
(12)

special events. You can travel from island to island. By boat or by plane.
(13)   (14)

---

12 Which sentence does <u>not</u> belong in Rachel's travel guide? Write the number.

_____

_____

_____

_____

13 What is the best way to write sentence 2?

F If you do, then Hawaii is the vacation spot for you.

G If you do, then you do know that Hawaii is the vacation spot for you.

H If you do want to, then you do want to have Hawaii as a vacation spot for you.

J If you want to, then you want to visit Hawaii for vacation.

GO ON➤

14 Which of the following sentences best combines sentences 4 and 5 without changing their meaning?

   A Hawaii is the only state that is not part of the mainland of North America, and is our southernmost state.

   B Hawaii is our southernmost state and Hawaii is the only state that is not part of the mainland of North America.

   C It is the only state that is not part of the mainland of North America, and is our southernmost state.

   D Hawaii is our southernmost state, and the only state that is not part of the mainland of North America.

15 Which of the following sentences best combines sentences 7 and 8 without changing their meaning?

   F The islands are a wonderful place to experience volcanoes and a wonderful place to experience magnificent waterfalls and beaches.

   G The islands are a wonderful place to experience volcanoes and to experience magnificent waterfalls and beautiful beaches.

   H Volcanoes, waterfalls, and beautiful beaches in the islands are wonderful places to experience.

   J The islands are a wonderful place to experience volcanoes, magnificent waterfalls, and beautiful beaches.

16 Which of these sentences could be added before sentence 9?

   A Hawaii has several active volcanoes.

   B Hawaii has a very pleasant climate.

   C The original natives of Hawaii were Polynesians.

   D Hawaii has eight major islands.

17 What supporting information could be added after sentence 11?

   F For example, poi is a favorite native Hawaiian delicacy made from cooked, fermented taro root.

   G There are many things to do in Hawaii.

   H Hawaii is in the Pacific Ocean.

   J There are other interesting vacation spots.

18 What is the most colorful way to write sentence 11?

   A You can enjoy some food and some music.

   B You can eat food and listen to music.

   C You can enjoy native Hawaiian food and music.

   D As it is written.

19 Which group of words in Rachel's travel guide is <u>not</u> a complete sentence? Write the number of the group of words.

_____

_____

_____

GO ON ➤

Here is the next part of Rachel's rough draft for her travel guide. This part has certain words and phrases underlined. Read the draft carefully. Then answer questions 20–29.

Hawaii is made up of eight major islands. The state capital,
(15)   (16)

Honolulu, is located at the island of Oahu. All the islands was formed by
                                      (17)

volcanoes. Today these volcanoes are the islands mountains. Mauna Loa
          (18)   (19)

and Kilauea are Hawaiis' only active volcanoes.

Hawaii has more than 1,000 miles of coastline. Much of the coastline
(20)   (21)

is covered with white sand beaches. Some of the coastline is covered with
                                      (22)

black sand sand made from lava. On the island of Kauai, there is a beach
                              (23)

called "Barking Sands." When walked upon in dry weather, the sand
                  (24)

makes a crunching noise that sounds like dogs barking.

Hawaii has mildest temperatures all year. The cool ocean breezes
(25)   (26)

help created a wonderful climate. For this reason people sometimes call
                              (27)

Hawaii "Paradise."

---

20 In sentence 16, is located at the island of Oahu is best written—

F   is located upon the island of Oahu

G   is located in the island of Oahu

H   is located on the island of Oahu

J   As it is written.

21 In sentence 17, All the islands was formed is best written—

A   All the island is formed

B   All the islands is forming

C   All the islands were formed

D   As it is written.

22 In sentence 18, <u>volcanoes are the islands mountains</u> is best written—

   F volcanoes are the islands' mountains

   G volcano's are the islands mountains

   H volcanoes are the island's mountains

   J As it is written.

23 In sentence 19, <u>Hawaiis' only active volcanoes</u> is best written—

   A Hawaiis only active volcanoes

   B Hawaii's only active volcanoes

   C Hawaiis' only, active volcanoes

   D As it is written.

24 In sentence 21, <u>is covered</u> is best written—

   F will be covered

   G was covered

   H were covered

   J As it is written.

25 In sentence 22, <u>black sand sand made</u> is best written—

   A black, sand sand made

   B black sand, sand made

   C black sand made

   D As it is written.

26 In sentence 23, <u>a beach</u> is best written—

   F the beach

   G an beach

   H the beaches

   J As it is written.

27 In sentence 25, <u>has mildest temperatures</u> is best written—

   A has mild temperatures

   B has most mild temperatures

   C has milder temperatures

   D As it is written.

28 In sentence 26, <u>breezes help created</u> is best written—

   F breezes help creates

   G breezes help create

   H breezes help creating

   J As it is written.

29 In sentence 27, <u>For this reason people</u> is best written—

   A For this, reason people

   B For, this reason people

   C For this reason, people

   D As it is written.

GO ON➡

For questions 30–41, read each sentence carefully. If one of the words is misspelled, darken the circle for that word. If all of the words are spelled correctly, then darken the circle for *No mistake.*

30   He was positive his homework was corect. No mistake
            F   G   H   J

31   The wooden shingel fell off the roof during the thunderstorm. No mistake
            A   B   C   D

32   Teofila injered herself when she fell at the skating rink. No mistake
            F   G   H   J

33   Miriam had a wonderfull time at the party. No mistake
                        A   B   C   D

34   The freighter crossed the Pacific Ocean in two weeks. No mistake
            F   G   H   J

35   Edward shoped around to get the best price on a new stereo. No mistake
               A   B   C   D

36   The collie wagged its tale as it approached us. No mistake
            F   G   H   J

37   His automobile accident was caused by a leak in the break line. No mistake
                        A   B   C   D

38   The new golf coarse is located west of town. No mistake
                     F   G   H   J

39   The view from the mountain was spectaculer. No mistake
            A   B   C   D

40   Sam complimented Lynn on her rousing speech. No mistake
               F   G   H   J

41   Every year Hector donates money to several charitys. No mistake
                        A   B   C   D

STOP

Answer Sheet

Fill in the circle for each multiple-choice answer. Write the answers to the open-ended questions on a separate sheet of paper.

TEST 1   Reading Comprehension

SA Ⓐ Ⓑ Ⓒ Ⓓ
1 Ⓐ Ⓑ Ⓒ Ⓓ
2 OPEN ENDED
3 Ⓕ Ⓖ Ⓗ Ⓙ
4 OPEN ENDED
5 Ⓐ Ⓑ Ⓒ Ⓓ
6 Ⓕ Ⓖ Ⓗ Ⓙ
7 Ⓐ Ⓑ Ⓒ Ⓓ
8 OPEN ENDED
9 Ⓕ Ⓖ Ⓗ Ⓙ
10 Ⓐ Ⓑ Ⓒ Ⓓ
11 Ⓕ Ⓖ Ⓗ Ⓙ
12 Ⓐ Ⓑ Ⓒ Ⓓ
13 Ⓕ Ⓖ Ⓗ Ⓙ
14 OPEN ENDED
15 Ⓐ Ⓑ Ⓒ Ⓓ
16 Ⓕ Ⓖ Ⓗ Ⓙ
17 OPEN ENDED
18 Ⓐ Ⓑ Ⓒ Ⓓ
19 Ⓕ Ⓖ Ⓗ Ⓙ
20 Ⓐ Ⓑ Ⓒ Ⓓ
21 Ⓕ Ⓖ Ⓗ Ⓙ
22 Ⓐ Ⓑ Ⓒ Ⓓ
23 Ⓕ Ⓖ Ⓗ Ⓙ
24 Ⓐ Ⓑ Ⓒ Ⓓ
25 Ⓕ Ⓖ Ⓗ Ⓙ
26 Ⓐ Ⓑ Ⓒ Ⓓ
27 Ⓕ Ⓖ Ⓗ Ⓙ
28 Ⓐ Ⓑ Ⓒ Ⓓ
29 Ⓕ Ⓖ Ⓗ Ⓙ
30 OPEN ENDED
31 Ⓐ Ⓑ Ⓒ Ⓓ
32 Ⓕ Ⓖ Ⓗ Ⓙ
33 Ⓐ Ⓑ Ⓒ Ⓓ
34 Ⓕ Ⓖ Ⓗ Ⓙ
35 OPEN ENDED
36 Ⓐ Ⓑ Ⓒ Ⓓ
37 OPEN ENDED
38 Ⓕ Ⓖ Ⓗ Ⓙ
39 Ⓐ Ⓑ Ⓒ Ⓓ
40 Ⓕ Ⓖ Ⓗ Ⓙ

TEST 2   Reading Vocabulary

SA Ⓐ Ⓑ Ⓒ Ⓓ
1 Ⓐ Ⓑ Ⓒ Ⓓ
2 Ⓕ Ⓖ Ⓗ Ⓙ
3 Ⓐ Ⓑ Ⓒ Ⓓ
4 Ⓕ Ⓖ Ⓗ Ⓙ
5 Ⓐ Ⓑ Ⓒ Ⓓ
6 Ⓕ Ⓖ Ⓗ Ⓙ
7 Ⓐ Ⓑ Ⓒ Ⓓ
8 Ⓕ Ⓖ Ⓗ Ⓙ
9 OPEN ENDED
10 Ⓐ Ⓑ Ⓒ Ⓓ
SB Ⓐ Ⓑ Ⓒ Ⓓ
11 Ⓕ Ⓖ Ⓗ Ⓙ
12 Ⓐ Ⓑ Ⓒ Ⓓ
13 Ⓕ Ⓖ Ⓗ Ⓙ
14 Ⓐ Ⓑ Ⓒ Ⓓ
SC Ⓐ Ⓑ Ⓒ Ⓓ
15 Ⓕ Ⓖ Ⓗ Ⓙ
16 Ⓐ Ⓑ Ⓒ Ⓓ
17 Ⓕ Ⓖ Ⓗ Ⓙ
18 Ⓐ Ⓑ Ⓒ Ⓓ
19 Ⓕ Ⓖ Ⓗ Ⓙ
20 Ⓐ Ⓑ Ⓒ Ⓓ
21 OPEN ENDED

TEST 3   Part 1: Math Problem Solving

SA Ⓐ Ⓑ Ⓒ Ⓓ	9 Ⓐ Ⓑ Ⓒ Ⓓ	17 Ⓐ Ⓑ Ⓒ Ⓓ	26 Ⓕ Ⓖ Ⓗ Ⓙ	34 Ⓕ Ⓖ Ⓗ Ⓙ	43 Ⓕ Ⓖ Ⓗ Ⓙ
1 Ⓐ Ⓑ Ⓒ Ⓓ	10 Ⓕ Ⓖ Ⓗ Ⓙ	18 Ⓕ Ⓖ Ⓗ Ⓙ	27 Ⓐ Ⓑ Ⓒ Ⓓ	35 Ⓐ Ⓑ Ⓒ Ⓓ	44 OPEN ENDED
2 Ⓕ Ⓖ Ⓗ Ⓙ	11 OPEN ENDED	19 Ⓐ Ⓑ Ⓒ Ⓓ	28 Ⓕ Ⓖ Ⓗ Ⓙ	36 Ⓕ Ⓖ Ⓗ Ⓙ	45 Ⓐ Ⓑ Ⓒ Ⓓ
3 Ⓐ Ⓑ Ⓒ Ⓓ	12 Ⓐ Ⓑ Ⓒ Ⓓ	20 OPEN ENDED	29 Ⓐ Ⓑ Ⓒ Ⓓ	37 Ⓐ Ⓑ Ⓒ Ⓓ	46 Ⓕ Ⓖ Ⓗ Ⓙ
4 Ⓕ Ⓖ Ⓗ Ⓙ	13 Ⓕ Ⓖ Ⓗ Ⓙ	21 Ⓕ Ⓖ Ⓗ Ⓙ	30 OPEN ENDED	38 Ⓕ Ⓖ Ⓗ Ⓙ	47 Ⓐ Ⓑ Ⓒ Ⓓ
5 Ⓐ Ⓑ Ⓒ Ⓓ	14 OPEN ENDED	22 Ⓐ Ⓑ Ⓒ Ⓓ	31 Ⓕ Ⓖ Ⓗ Ⓙ	39 Ⓐ Ⓑ Ⓒ Ⓓ	48 Ⓕ Ⓖ Ⓗ Ⓙ
6 Ⓕ Ⓖ Ⓗ Ⓙ	15 Ⓐ Ⓑ Ⓒ Ⓓ	23 Ⓕ Ⓖ Ⓗ Ⓙ	32 OPEN ENDED	40 OPEN ENDED	49 Ⓐ Ⓑ Ⓒ Ⓓ
7 Ⓐ Ⓑ Ⓒ Ⓓ	16 Ⓕ Ⓖ Ⓗ Ⓙ	24 Ⓐ Ⓑ Ⓒ Ⓓ	33 Ⓐ Ⓑ Ⓒ Ⓓ	41 Ⓕ Ⓖ Ⓗ Ⓙ	50 Ⓕ Ⓖ Ⓗ Ⓙ
8 Ⓕ Ⓖ Ⓗ Ⓙ		25 OPEN ENDED		42 Ⓐ Ⓑ Ⓒ Ⓓ	

Part 2: Math Procedures

SA Ⓐ Ⓑ Ⓒ Ⓓ Ⓔ	3 Ⓕ Ⓖ Ⓗ Ⓙ Ⓚ	6 Ⓐ Ⓑ Ⓒ Ⓓ Ⓔ	9 Ⓕ Ⓖ Ⓗ Ⓙ Ⓚ	11 Ⓕ Ⓖ Ⓗ Ⓙ Ⓚ	14 OPEN ENDED
1 OPEN ENDED	4 Ⓐ Ⓑ Ⓒ Ⓓ Ⓔ	7 Ⓕ Ⓖ Ⓗ Ⓙ Ⓚ	SB Ⓐ Ⓑ Ⓒ Ⓓ Ⓔ	12 Ⓐ Ⓑ Ⓒ Ⓓ Ⓔ	
2 Ⓐ Ⓑ Ⓒ Ⓓ Ⓔ	5 Ⓕ Ⓖ Ⓗ Ⓙ Ⓚ	8 Ⓐ Ⓑ Ⓒ Ⓓ Ⓔ	10 Ⓐ Ⓑ Ⓒ Ⓓ Ⓔ	13 Ⓕ Ⓖ Ⓗ Ⓙ Ⓚ	

TEST 4   Language

SA Ⓐ Ⓑ Ⓒ Ⓓ	7 Ⓕ Ⓖ Ⓗ Ⓙ	14 Ⓐ Ⓑ Ⓒ Ⓓ	21 Ⓐ Ⓑ Ⓒ Ⓓ	28 Ⓕ Ⓖ Ⓗ Ⓙ	35 Ⓐ Ⓑ Ⓒ Ⓓ
1 Ⓐ Ⓑ Ⓒ Ⓓ	8 Ⓐ Ⓑ Ⓒ Ⓓ	15 Ⓕ Ⓖ Ⓗ Ⓙ	22 Ⓕ Ⓖ Ⓗ Ⓙ	29 Ⓐ Ⓑ Ⓒ Ⓓ	36 Ⓕ Ⓖ Ⓗ Ⓙ
2 Ⓕ Ⓖ Ⓗ Ⓙ	9 Ⓕ Ⓖ Ⓗ Ⓙ	16 Ⓐ Ⓑ Ⓒ Ⓓ	23 Ⓐ Ⓑ Ⓒ Ⓓ	30 Ⓕ Ⓖ Ⓗ Ⓙ	37 Ⓐ Ⓑ Ⓒ Ⓓ
3 Ⓐ Ⓑ Ⓒ Ⓓ	10 OPEN ENDED	17 Ⓕ Ⓖ Ⓗ Ⓙ	24 Ⓕ Ⓖ Ⓗ Ⓙ	31 Ⓐ Ⓑ Ⓒ Ⓓ	38 Ⓕ Ⓖ Ⓗ Ⓙ
4 Ⓕ Ⓖ Ⓗ Ⓙ	11 Ⓐ Ⓑ Ⓒ Ⓓ	18 Ⓐ Ⓑ Ⓒ Ⓓ	25 Ⓐ Ⓑ Ⓒ Ⓓ	32 Ⓕ Ⓖ Ⓗ Ⓙ	39 Ⓐ Ⓑ Ⓒ Ⓓ
5 OPEN ENDED	12 OPEN ENDED	19 OPEN ENDED	26 Ⓕ Ⓖ Ⓗ Ⓙ	33 Ⓐ Ⓑ Ⓒ Ⓓ	40 Ⓕ Ⓖ Ⓗ Ⓙ
6 Ⓐ Ⓑ Ⓒ Ⓓ	13 Ⓕ Ⓖ Ⓗ Ⓙ	20 Ⓕ Ⓖ Ⓗ Ⓙ	27 Ⓐ Ⓑ Ⓒ Ⓓ	34 Ⓕ Ⓖ Ⓗ Ⓙ	41 Ⓐ Ⓑ Ⓒ Ⓓ

Answer Key

Reading Skills

p. 8
Fact: There are more than 2,400 different kinds of snakes.
Fact: One of the smallest snakes is the thread snake.

p. 9
3. A

p. 10-11
1. C
2. B
3. A
4. C
5. B
6. D
7. B
8. A
9. C
10. B

p. 12-13
1. C
2. A
3. D
4. B
5. D
6. C
7. D
8. A
9. B
10. A

p. 14-15
1. C
2. D
3. A
4. B
5. D
6. D
7. C
8. A
9. D
10. A

p. 16-17
1. C
2. B
3. D
4. A
5. C
6. A
7. C
8. B
9. C
10. C

p. 18-19
1. C
2. A
3. D
4. A
5. B
6. C
7. A
8. B
9. C
10. D

p. 20-21
1. B
2. C
3. D
4. B
5. C
6. D
7. A
8. B
9. B
10. B

p. 22-23
1. B
2. C
3. C
4. A
5. B
6. B
7. A
8. D
9. C
10. C

p. 24-25
1. A
2. B
3. C
4. B
5. C
6. D
7. C
8. D
9. A
10. B

p. 26
Possible answers include:
1. In ancient times salt was often traded for gold.
2. "You are worth your salt" means you are worth the money you are being paid.
3. Salty water is called brine.

p. 27
Check that you have four facts in your paragraph.

p. 28
2, 3, 1

p. 29
3. B

p. 30-31
1. 3, 1, 2
2. B
3. A
4. C
5. B

p. 32-33
1. 2, 3, 1
2. B
3. A
4. C
5. C

p. 34-35
1. 3, 2, 1
2. C
3. B
4. A
5. B

p. 36-37
1. 3, 2, 1
2. A
3. C
4. C
5. C

p. 38-39
1. 1, 2, 3
2. C
3. B
4. A
5. C

p. 40-41
1. 1, 3, 2
2. C
3. A
4. B
5. C

p. 42-43
1. 2, 1, 3
2. B
3. B
4. C
5. A

p. 44-45
1. 3, 2, 1
2. C
3. A
4. B
5. C

p. 46
Possible answers include:
1. Chris challenged Andrew after Andrew talked about how well he could shoot free throws.
2. The ball bounced off the backboard.
3. Chris took his first shot after Andrew's first shot.
4. Andrew decided to get tips after Chris shot two free throws.

p. 47
Check that your paragraph is written in sequence.
Check that you have used time order words, such as first, next, and last.

p. 49
2. C
3. C

p. 50-51
1. B
2. C
3. D
4. A
5. B

p. 34-35 (continued)
6. D
7. C
8. D
9. A
10. C
11. A
12. C
13. D
14. B
15. B
16. C

p. 52-53
1. D
2. B
3. C
4. D
5. A
6. D
7. C
8. A
9. B
10. D
11. D
12. A
13. D
14. A
15. D
16. C

p. 54-55
1. C
2. B
3. C
4. A
5. A
6. C
7. C
8. B
9. D
10. A
11. B
12. D
13. B
14. C
15. A
16. C

p. 56-57
1. D
2. C
3. C
4. D
5. B
6. A
7. A
8. C
9. A
10. B
11. A
12. D
13. B
14. D
15. C
16. D

p. 58–59
1. C
2. D
3. C
4. D
5. C
6. B
7. C
8. D

p. 60–61
1. C
2. C
3. A
4. A
5. C
6. A
7. C
8. D

p. 62–63
1. A
2. B
3. C
4. B
5. D
6. D
7. A
8. B

p. 64–65
1. B
2. B
3. D
4. A
5. D
6. A
7. D
8. C

p. 66
Possible answers include:
1. exciting or realistic
2. boring or silly
3. nervous or uncertain
4. performance or music
5. electricity or power
6. candles or flashlights

p. 67
Possible answers include
1. They could use rocks.
They could use shell-shaped macaroni
2. They could draw fish.
They could use fish crackers.
3. They could paint the box.
They could put sand in the box.
4. It might be horses. It might be the mayor's car.
5. It was a marching band. It was a group of clowns.
6. It was the circus animals. It was a float.

p. 69
The correct answer is C.
The paragraph tells about the front, sports, and comics sections of the newspaper.

p. 70–71
1. B
2. B
3. C
4. C
5. A

p. 72–73
1. C
2. A
3. B
4. B
5. A

p. 74–75
1. D
2. B
3. A
4. C
5. B

p. 76–77
1. C
2. C
3. A
4. A
5. B

p. 78–79
1. B
2. C
3. A
4. A
5. D

p. 80–81
1. D
2. B
3. B
4. C
5. A

p. 82–83
1. B
2. D
3. B
4. A
5. A

p. 84–85
1. D
2. B
3. C
4. A
5. D

p. 86
Possible answers include:
1. Birds never forget a food that made them sick.
2. A dead rattlesnake can be as dangerous as a live one.
3. A Comanche tribe in New Mexico provided the idea for semaphore.

p. 87
Check that you have underlined your main idea.
Check that you have used four details in your story.

p. 89
geography, physical education, language, art

p. 90–91
1. C
2. C
3. B
4. A
5. D

p. 92–93
1. C
2. D
3. B
4. A
5. D

p. 94–95
1. C
2. B
3. B
4. C
5. A

p. 96–97
1. D
2. A
3. B
4. C
5. A

p. 98–99
1. B
2. A
3. C
4. D
5. A

p. 100–101
1. C
2. B
3. B
4. D
5. D

p. 102–103
1. D
2. D
3. A
4. A
5. B

p. 104–105
1. C
2. B
3. A
4. B
5. D

p. 106
Possible answers include:
1. Georgia Broadwick was a daring woman.
2. There probably aren't any $100,000 bills in use now.
3. Amalia likes listening to birds.

p. 107
Possible answers include:
1. No African American played in the major leagues in 1946. Jackie Robinson was the first African American to play in the major leagues in 1947.
2. Robinson was the only African American in the major leagues when he played his first game with the Dodgers. Dan Bankhead joined the Dodgers later in the year.
3. Bankhead was not a star with the Dodgers. He pitched in four games, and he was not with the Dodgers until the following year.
4. Robinson was a baseball star. He is in the Baseball Hall of Fame.

p. 109
2. A. F   B. F   C. I   D. I

p. 110–111
1. A. F   B. I   C. I   D. I
2. A. I   B. F   C. F   D. F
3. A. F   B. I   C. F   D. I
4. A. I   B. F   C. I   D. F
5. A. I   B. I   C. F   D. F

p. 112–113
1. A. F   B. F   C. I   D. F
2. A. F   B. I   C. F   D. F
3. A. I   B. F   C. I   D. F
4. A. I   B. F   C. F   D. F
5. A. F   B. F   C. I   D. I

p. 114–115
1. A. F   B. F   C. I   D. F
2. A. I   B. I   C. F   D. I
3. A. F   B. F   C. F   D. I
4. A. F   B. F   C. I   D. I
5. A. F   B. F   C. F   D. I

p. 116–117
1. A. F   B. F   C. I   D. I
2. A. F   B. I   C. F   D. I
3. A. I   B. F   C. I   D. F
4. A. F   B. I   C. I   D. F
5. A. F   B. F   C. I   D. F

p. 118–119
1. A. F   B. I   C. I   D. I
2. A. I   B. F   C. I   D. I
3. A. I   B. F   C. I   D. F
4. A. F   B. I   C. F   D. F
5. A. I   B. F   C. F   D. F

p. 120–121
1. A. I   B. I   C. I   D. F
2. A. F   B. F   C. I   D. I
3. A. F   B. F   C. I   D. I
4. A. F   B. F   C. I   D. I
5. A. F   B. F   C. I   D. F

p. 122–123
1. A. I   B. F   C. I   D. F
2. A. F   B. I   C. I   D. F
3. A. I   B. F   C. F   D. I
4. A. F   B. F   C. I   D. I
5. A. I   B. I   C. F   D. F

p. 124–125
1. A. F   B. I   C. F   D. I
2. A. I   B. I   C. F   D. I
3. A. I   B. F   C. I   D. I
4. A. I   B. I   C. I   D. F
5. A. I   B. F   C. F   D. I

p. 126
Possible answers include:
1. Carmela was wrapping a gift for her mother.
2. The tree needed water.
3. Yoko was in a post office or a store for mailing letters and packages.

p. 127
Possible answers include:
1. Bernardo is almost 70 years old.
2. Bernardo needed a ladder to reach cherries that he could not reach from the ground.
3. Bernardo is hard-working, weary, and lonely.
4. Keeping up the farm was too much work for one person.

SPELLING SKILLS

P. 132
1. act, sandwich, traffic, magic, chapter, rabbit, snack, rapid, plastic, calf, program, planet, crash, salad, factory, magnet, half, crack
2. laughter, aunt

P. 133
1. planet
2. factory
3. traffic
4. calf
5. laughter
6. program
7. plastic
8. act
9. rapid
10. half
11. magnet
12. snack
13. crash
14. crack
15. aunt
16. salad
17. rabbit
18. chapter
19. magic

P. 134
Spell correctly: rapid, crash, sandwich, snack, laughter
Capitalize: Andy, I, It
Add period: after "my dad"; after "plastic wrapper"

P. 135
1. half, plastic, rabbit, traffic
2. act, aunt, planet, program
3. calf, chapter, crack, factory
4. magic, magnet, salad, sandwich
5. laughter, length, library, loose
6. rabbit, raccoon, rapid, raw

P. 136
1. scale, parade, escape, snake, male, female
2. bakery
3. paid, brain, raise, explain, holiday, remain, complain, container, delay
4. weigh, weight, neighbor
5. break

P. 137
1. snake
2. weigh
3. break
4. explain
5. remain
6. parade
7. container
8. raise
9. complain
10. holiday
11. brain
12. paid
13. scale
14. weight
15. female
16. neighbor
17. bakery
18. male
19. delay

P. 138
Spell correctly: neighbor, male, container, remain, escape
Capitalize: Pete, He, Having
Add period: after "snake Toby"; after "at Pete's house"

P. 139
1. Our class planned a holiday vacation.
2. Mr. Peterson bought fresh bread at the bakery.
3. Watch out for that snake by your foot!
4. What did you do on your break from school?

P. 140
1. bench, intend, invent, sentence, self, questions, address, checkers, depth
2. healthy, thread, wealth, weather, instead, measure, breath, pleasure, sweater, treasure
3. friendly

P. 141
1. sweater
2. thread
3. address
4. treasure
5. depth
6. healthy
7. friendly
8. questions
9. checkers
10. measure
11. bench
12. wealth
13. weather
14. breath
15. self
16. intend
17. invent
18. instead
19. pleasure

P. 142
Spell correctly: checkers, weather, instead, friendly, questions
Capitalize: Because, Beth
Add: the (between "for" and "annual"); in (between "meet" and "Memphis"); a (between "home" and "trophy")

P. 143
Guide words will vary according to dictionary.
1. address
2. bench
3. intend
4. measure
5. sentence
6. wealth

P. 144
1. century, extra, selfish, petal, length, metal, metric, wreck, special
2. else, remember, pledge, exercise, elephant, energy, desert, expert, excellent, vegetable, gentle

P. 145
1. vegetable
2. desert
3. selfish

4. excellent
5. petal
6. wreck
7. century
8. length
9. remember
10. metal
11. metric
12. gentle
13. extra
14. else
15. special
16. exercise
17. energy
18. pledge
19. expert

P. 146
Spell correctly: expert, remember, exercise, energy, excellent
Add period: after "her work"; after "555–6262"
Take out: extra "is" in first sentence; extra "of" in fourth sentence; unnecessary "a" between "give" and "an"

P. 147
1. We drove through the (desert) last (week.)
2. The (divers) swam down to the (wreck.)
3. (Elephants) are large (animals) from (Africa.)
4. (Andy) ran the (length) of the (field.)
5. (Jill) ate every (vegetable) on her (plate.)
6. I can't remember where I put my (pen) and (paper.)
7. (Explorers) began to circle the (globe) in the seventeenth (century.)

P. 148
1. March, June, May
2. Thursday, Monday, April, Wednesday, August, Tuesday, Sunday, July, Friday
3. October, November, September, December, Saturday
4. January, February
5. St.

P. 149
1. March
2. June
3. May
4. September
5. Monday
6. Tuesday
7. Sunday
8. St.
9. January
10. Friday
11. November
12. Thursday
13. October
14. April
15. Saturday
16. Wednesday
17. February
18. December
19. July

P. 150
Spell correctly: St., Monday, October, Tuesday, November
Capitalize: Dear, Mr., Han's
Add period: after "sounds great"; after "November 11"

P. 151
1. recede
2. ailment
3. easel
4. built
5. mystery
6. laughter
7. lunar
8. comet
9. cousin
10. breath
11. friendly
12. busy
13. bridge
14. relax
15. ski
16. guide

P. 152–153
1. half
2. factory
3. sandwich
4. laughter
5. parade
6. bakery
7. neighbor
8. holiday
9. escape
10. break
11. container
12. friendly
13. breath
14. treasure
15. wealth
16. depth
17. vegetable
18. excellent
19. length
20. special
21. exercise
22. February
23. Tuesday
24. Saturday
25. January

P. 154
1. hobby, delivery, angry, tardy, fancy, merry, pretty, penalty, ugly, liberty, empty, shady, busy
2. complete, evening, trapeze, athlete, theme, complete
3. believe

P. 155
1. trapeze
2. theme
3. ugly
4. empty
5. hobby
6. believe
7. shady
8. evening
9. penalty
10. delivery
11. liberty
12. pretty
13. angry
14. tardy

15. fancy
16. merry
17. busy
18. complete
19. compete

p. 156
Spell correctly: evening, busy,
  empty, ugly, believe
Capitalize: Friday, To
Add: on (between "life" and
  "other"); a (between "surprise"
  and "Martian")

p. 157
1. adjective; fully equipped
2. verb; to remove the contents of
3. verb; to finish
4. adjective; containing nothing
5. adjective; whole
6. adjective; without meaning

p. 158
1. weak, breathe, increase, peace,
defeat, reason, wheat, beneath
2. greet, freeze, speech, asleep,
needle, steep, sheet, agree, degree
3. pizza, piano, ski

p. 159
1. needle
2. ski
3. breathe
4. increase
5. defeat
6. beneath
7. wheat
8. pizza
9. degree
10. piano
11. sheet
12. peace
13. speech
14. weak
15. steep
16. reason
17. greet
18. freeze
19. asleep

p. 160
Spell correctly: breathe, reason,
  wheat, pizza, sheet
Capitalize: I, That, A
Take out: to (between "his" and
  "bakery"); am (between "I" and
  "want")

p. 161
Phrases below indicate the complete
predicate and should be circled.
1. is difficult to <u>defeat</u>
2. will <u>ski</u> down these snowy
mountains every winter
3. listened to the principal's farewell
<u>speech</u>
4. is much too <u>steep</u> to climb
5. began to <u>freeze</u> at midnight
6. <u>agree</u> on the date for Maria's
surprise party
7. can <u>greet</u> him at the door

p. 162
1. wrist, chimney, riddle, bridge,
since, disease, quit, quickly,
different, discuss, divide
2. expect, enough, except, relax,
review
3. equipment
4. guitar, guilty, built

p. 163
1. bridge
2. wrist
3. divide
4. guilty
5. chimney
6. quit
7. quickly
8. different
9. relax
10. review
11. enough
12. built
13. equipment
14. guitar
15. riddle
16. since
17. expect
18. discuss
19. except

p. 164
Spell correctly: since, different,
  quickly, relax, quit
Capitalize: You, I, Ted
Add period: after "the keyboard";
  after "started lessons"

p. 165
1. I broke my wrist last April. *or*
Last April I broke my wrist.
2. We've had our trampoline since
February.
3. Let's discuss where we'll go on
our field trip in June.
4. Dad built a new chimney on our
house last September.
5. We can expect really hot weather
in July and August.
6. I need to review my notes before
our test on Tuesday.
7. We'll go to a different movie
theater next Saturday.

p. 166
1. skill, chicken, arithmetic, film,
picnic, kitchen, sixth, pitch, insect,
insist, timid
2. system, mystery
3. package, message, damage,
garbage, cottage
4. village
5. business

p. 167
1. chicken
2. pitch
3. film
4. arithmetic
5. kitchen
6. package
7. system
8. picnic
9. village
10. garbage

11. cottage
12. sixth
13. timid
14. message
15. damage
16. skill
17. insist
18. insect
19. business

p. 168
Spell correctly: kitchen, timid,
  insect, garbage, picnic
Capitalize: Our, He, I
Add period: after "the glass"; after
  "scared me"

p. 169
1. I need a pencil, an eraser, and
some paper to do my arithmetic.
2. Chicken can be fried, broiled, or
baked.
3. We saw tulips, roses, and daisies
outside the cottage.
4. The village had a bakery, a post
office, and a town hall.
5. Lynn wanted to study history,
business, and medicine.
6. The timid elephant was afraid of
mice, snakes, and his own shadow!

p. 170
1. skis, athletes, neighbors, exercises,
degrees, vegetables
2. benches, sandwiches, branches,
speeches, crashes, wishes, businesses
3. stories, wives, calves, parties,
companies, hobbies, penalties

p. 171
1. vegetables
2. skis
3. sandwiches
4. calves
5. neighbors
6. wives
7. branches
8. benches
9. crashes
10. hobbies
11. exercises
12. athletes
13. stories
14. penalties
15. companies
16. benches
17. degrees
18. speeches
19. parties

p. 172
Spell correctly: neighbors, benches,
  sandwiches, stories, hobbies
Capitalize: Melinda, I, Now
Add period: after "and Melinda";
  after "each one"

p. 173
1. My neighbor was upset about
losing her parrot.
2. The vegetables in our garden are
ready to be picked.
3. The mayor's speech seems too
long and too serious.
4. These cucumber sandwiches
really do taste good.

5. Our calves spend most of the day
playing.
6. The benches at the city park need
to be replaced.
7. His father's company builds parts
for computers.

p. 174–175
1. athlete
2. evening
3. believe
4. delivery
5. empty
6. piano
7. weak
8. breathe
9. reason
10. speech
11. chimney
12. guilty
13. except
14. different
15. enough
16. garbage
17. business
18. message
19. mystery
20. kitchen
21. calves
22. companies
23. skis
24. wives
25. businesses

p. 176
1. quiet, awhile, polite, decide,
revise, knife, invite
2. mild, library, science, idea, ninth,
pirate, remind, island, grind, climb,
blind
3. tried
4. guide

p. 177
1. science
2. guide
3. pirate
4. grind
5. revise
6. knife
7. tried
8. idea
9. mild
10. ninth
11. climb
12. decide
13. blind
14. quite
15. invite
16. awhile
17. library
18. remind
19. island

p. 178
Spell correctly: guide, idea, decide,
  awhile, pirate
Add question mark: after "awhile";
  after "attack"
Take out: a (between "and" and
  "covered"); it (between "drop"
  and "the"); the (between
  "would" and "that")

p. 179

1. Mr. Perry said, "My workload is easing up quite a bit."
2. "Why don't you decide to take a vacation?" asked Mrs. Perry.
3. Mr. Perry answered, "I'd like to climb a high mountain."
4. "We should take a guide so that we won't get lost," added Mr. Perry.

p. 180

1. dollar, honor, collar, closet, common, lobster, hospital, solid, copper, problem, object, comma, bother, bottom, shock, honest, promise
2. quantity, wander, watch

p. 181

1. hospital
2. bother
3. problem
4. common
5. solid
6. bottom
7. object
8. honor
9. quantity
10. promise
11. wander
12. honest
13. copper
14. shock
15. dollar
16. lobster
17. collar
18. closet
19. watch

p. 182

Spell correctly: promise, object, wander, collar, problem
Capitalize: Do, I, The
Take out: a (between "your" and "catalog"); and (between "and" and "my")

p. 183

1. hospital
2. lobster
3. comma
4. closet
5. dollar
6. watch
7. promise
8. bottom
9. honor
10. Copper
11. object
12. Dina
13. collar
14. problem

p. 184

1. vote, zone, alone, microscope, telephone, code, suppose, chose, owe
2. known, follow, arrow, grown, borrow, swallow, tomorrow, throw, bowl, elbow
3. sew

p. 185

1. throw
2. bowl
3. tomorrow
4. grown
5. sew
6. suppose
7. known
8. zone
9. arrow
10. microscope
11. chose
12. code
13. alone
14. telephone
15. Follow
16. swallow
17. owe
18. borrow
19. vote

p. 186

Spell correctly: Tomorrow, chose, grown, known, suppose
Capitalize: April, Microscope, Without
Trade places: give/will, have/I

p. 187

1. I owe Jo Anne a dollar.
2. Noah can borrow my bike.
3. I sew my own clothes.
4. Tyler and Cody follow directions well.
5. Zoey answered the telephone.
6. Rosie put the slide under the microscope.

p. 188

1. hotel, notice, yolk, poem, echo, control, tornado, hero, clothing, scold
2. oak, coach, boast, groan, float, coast, throat, roast
3. dough, though

p. 189

1. clothing
2. yolk
3. echo
4. oak
5. throat
6. though
7. control
8. scold
9. dough
10. coach
11. hotel
12. notice
13. float
14. hero
15. poem
16. coast
17. groan
18. boast
19. roast

p. 190

Spell correctly: tornado, groan, control, hotel, oak
Make lowercase: town, midnight, we
Add period: after "the hall"; after "all unharmed"

p. 191

1. control/verb
2. coast/verb
3. coast/noun
4. control/noun
5. control/noun
6. coast/noun

p. 192

1. graph-ics
by-line
ear-phones
net-work
head-line
mast-head
broad-cast
2. col-um-nist
stu-di-o
pro-duc-er
com-mer-cial
re-cord-er
vid-e-o
cam-er-a
news-pa-per
di-rec-tor
mu-si-cian
3. an-i-ma-tion
tel-e-vi-sion
ed-i-tor-i-al

p. 193

1. earphones
2. headline
3. byline
4. broadcast
5. masthead
6. network
7. newspaper
8. commercial
9. musician
10. columnist
11. editorial
12. video
13. camera
14. animation
15. director
16. studio
17. producer
18. recorder
19. graphics

p. 194

Spell correctly: producer, television, columnist, camera, studio
Capitalize: The, Job, If
Trade places: about/is, are/you

p. 195

1. The broadcast came from New York.
2. The commercial was filmed in the Rocky Mountains.
3. The headline mentioned Virginia and Washington, D.C.
4. The newspaper article was about the Arctic Ocean.
5. We visited a Hollywood studio.
6. The director of that film lives in Paris.
7. The television show was about the Atlantic Ocean.

p. 196–197

1. island
2. decide
3. ninth
4. science
5. guide
6. library
7. collar
8. hospital
9. common
10. promise
11. wander
12. telephone
13. borrow
14. sew
15. owe
16. echo
17. throat
18. though
19. notice
20. groan
21. yolk
22. musician
23. graphics
24. camera
25. commercial

p. 198

1. crush, judge, husband, pumpkin, hundred, jungle, knuckle, instruct
2. tongue, monkey, onion, compass, among, dozen, wonderful
3. rough, touch, country
4. blood, flood

p. 199

1. judge
2. onion
3. jungle
4. tongue
5. compass
6. knuckle
7. crush
8. blood
9. husband
10. dozen
11. wonderful
12. rough
13. instruct
14. hundred
15. country
16. flood
17. among
18. touch
19. monkey

p. 200

Spell correctly: onion, tongue, country, dozen, wonderful
Add question mark after: "peel an onion"; "your eyes"
Add: you (between "when" and "peel"); that (between "one" and "does"); are (between "They" and "wonderful")

p. 201

1. bowl, 1
2. bowl, 2
3. bowl, 2
4. desert, 1
5. bowl, 2
6. desert, 2

p. 202
1. all right, already
2. wrong, often
3. autumn, fault, automobile
4. dawn, raw, crawl, lawn, straw, awful
5. thought, fought, daughter, caught, bought, brought, taught

p. 203
1. dawn
2. bought
3. wrong
4. often
5. awful
6. raw
7. all right
8. taught
9. autumn
10. caught
11. lawn
12. crawl
13. fought
14. Already
15. thought
16. daughter
17. straw
18. brought
19. fault

p. 204
Spell correctly, lawn, autumn, taught, wrong, awful
Capitalize: Sylvia, Mrs., He
Add period: after "was wrong"; after "was fine"

p. 205
1. Mom: I've brought you a surprise.
2. Stuart: I thought you'd forgotten my birthday.
3. Mom: It's all boys' favorite means of transportation.
4. Stuart: You bought me a car like Dad's!
5. Mom: You're wrong, silly boy. It's a bicycle.

p. 206
1. choose, loose, rooster, balloon, shampoo, kangaroo, proof, foolish, raccoon
2. clue, fruit, truth, juice, glue
3. lose, improve, prove, shoe, whom, whose

p. 207
1. glue
2. raccoon
3. juice
4. loose
5. truth
6. shoe
7. whom
8. fruit
9. prove
10. whose
11. shampoo
12. proof
13. foolish
14. rooster
15. balloon

p. 208
16. lose
17. choose
18. improve
19. clue

p. 208
Spell correctly: whose, clue, shoe, fruit, prove
Make lowercase: story, missing, smashed
Add period: after "Anna Heglin"; after "the floor"

p. 209
1. raccoon
2. juice
3. balloon
4. truth
5. improve
6. proof
7. loose
8. rooster
9. shampoo
10. foolish
11. lose
12. glue

p. 210
1. destroy, annoy, enjoy, employment, oyster, loyal, loyalty, voyage, royal, employ
2. noise, choice, appoint, moisture, boiler, coin, avoid, voice, broil, appointment

p. 211
1. voice
2. oyster
3. appointment
4. employment
5. moisture
6. voyage
7. boiler
8. appoint
9. royal
10. destroy
11. choice
12. broil
13. loyal
14. annoy
15. employ
16. loyalty
17. avoid
18. noise
19. enjoy

p. 212
Spell correctly: enjoy, choice, voice, noise, employ
Capitalize: Maria, I
Take out: a (between "a" and "ballet"); to (between "to" and "avoid"); with (between "with" and "them")

p. 213
1. di (stroi)
2. (roi) əl
3. (mois) chər
4. ə (point)
5. (oi) stər
6. ə (void)
7. (loi) əl tē
8. (voi) ĭj
9. ə (noi)

p. 214
10. ĕn (joi)
11. ĕm (ploi) mənt
12. (boi) lər
13. ə (point) mənt
14. ĕm (ploi)

p. 214
1. skin diving
2. track, golf
3. cycling, soccer, football, skiing, bowling, skating, baseball, swimming, tennis, hockey
4. basketball, Olympics, champion, volleyball, amateur
5. professional, competition

p. 215
1. skating
2. baseball
3. skiing
4. golf
5. hockey
6. tennis
7. skin diving
8. bowling
9. cycling
10. soccer
11. basketball
12. track
13. volleyball
14. football
15. amateur
16. professional
17. swimming
18. champion
19. competition

p. 216
Spell correctly: golf, baseball, skiing, soccer, track
Capitalize: Trail, Louisiana, Ana
Add: is (between "Ana" and "the"); to (between "like" and "do")

p. 217
Add a comma after: Chicago, May 5, Alicia, Sincerely
Spell correctly: Swimming, skating, professional, basketball, amateur

p. 218–219
1. rough
2. judge
3. flood
4. tongue
5. fault
6. daughter
7. awful
8. all right
9. often
10. fought
11. shoe
12. raccoon
13. truth
14. whose
15. juice
16. clue
17. whom
18. choice
19. annoy
20. destroy
21. avoid
22. appointment
23. amateur
24. cycling
25. champion

p. 220
1. score, adore, shore, before, wore, tore
2. export, perform, fortunate, orchard, import, important
3. quarrel, reward, warn, toward
4. court, course
5. roar, board

p. 221
1. perform
2. adore
3. board
4. warn
5. course
6. tore
7. quarrel
8. before
9. toward
10. wore
11. court
12. reward
13. score
14. shore
15. fortunate
16. orchard
17. important
18. roar
19. export

p. 222
Spell correctly: important, before, wore, quarrel, fortunate
Capitalize: Thursday, According, He
Add period: after "discovery"; after "one another"

p. 223
Answers will vary.

p. 224
1. certain, service, perfect, permit, perfume, personal
2. skirt, dirty, thirteen, firm, third
3. purpose, furnish, hurt, furniture
4. earn, early, learning, heard, pearl

p. 225
1. perfume
2. certain
3. perfect
4. thirteen
5. personal
6. early
7. learning
8. furniture
9. furnish
10. permit
11. service
12. purpose
13. firm
14. dirty
15. earn
16. heard
17. skirt
18. pearl
19. third

p. 226
Spell correctly: thirteen, purpose, certain, perfume, skirt
Add period: after "for money"; after "Grandma's skirt"
Take out: to (between "to" and "buy"); you (between "you" and "bought"); you (between "you" and "have")

p. 227
1. We made <u>new</u> furniture for the treehouse.
2. I heard there is a <u>fantastic</u> movie downtown.
3. The <u>early</u> bird catches the worm.
4. I'd like to furnish my room with <u>large green</u> plants.
5. I hurt my foot when I dropped the <u>heavy</u> suitcase.
6. Jennifer wants a <u>pearl</u> necklace for her birthday.

p. 228
1. sh<u>are</u>, aw<u>are</u>, prep<u>are</u>, f<u>are</u>, st<u>are</u>, c<u>are</u>fully, decl<u>are</u>, comp<u>are</u>, squ<u>are</u>, b<u>are</u>
2. ch<u>ar</u>ge, disch<u>ar</u>ge, h<u>ar</u>vest, al<u>ar</u>m, f<u>ar</u>ther, st<u>ar</u>ve, m<u>ar</u>gin, dep<u>ar</u>t, m<u>ar</u>bles, ap<u>ar</u>tment

p. 229
1. alarm
2. marbles
3. discharge
4. fare
5. square
6. bare
7. stare
8. starve
9. prepare
10. carefully
11. compare
12. margin
13. share
14. farther
15. aware
16. apartment
17. charge
18. depart
19. declare

p. 230
Spell correctly: aware, compare, farther, bare, prepare
Capitalize: A, Arizona, Although
Take out: to (between "to" and "the"); the (between "the" and "flat")

p. 231
1. noun
2. noun
3. noun
4. verb
5. noun
6. verb
The number of the definition will vary.

p. 232
1. birthday, sailboat, hallway, nightmare, notebook, upset, cartwheel, flashlight, chalkboard, suitcase, sawdust, uproar, weekend, homework, breakfast
2. thunderstorm, strawberry, cheeseburger, grasshopper, blueberry

p. 233
1. breakfast
2. chalkboard
3. cheeseburger
4. uproar
5. sawdust
6. hallway
7. strawberry
8. thunderstorm
9. sailboat
10. upset
11. homework
12. blueberry
13. notebook
14. suitcase
15. grasshopper
16. birthday
17. weekend
18. nightmare
19. cartwheel

p. 234
Spell correctly: blueberry, weekend, breakfast, strawberry, notebook
Capitalize: Drop, Just, Birthday
Add period: after "to eat"; after "to me"

p. 235
1. Ling's flashlight was lying by the door.
2. The men's cheeseburgers came quickly.
3. The children's pet grasshopper was in a cage.
4. Mrs. Sperry's chalkboard was clean.
5. The six performers' cartwheels were magnificent.

p. 236
1. shuttle, comet, axis, orbit, motion, light-year, solar, eclipse, lunar
2. celestial, galaxy, meteors, universe, rotation, telescope, asteroids, satellite
3. astronomy, revolution, constellation

p. 237
1. comet
2. astronomy
3. revolution
4. shuttle
5. telescope
6. rotation
7. light-year
8. axis
9. solar
10. lunar
11. constellation
12. orbit
13. satellite
14. meteors
15. celestial
16. galaxy
17. universe
18. eclipse
19. motion

p. 238
Spell correctly: solar, light-year, shuttle, asteroids, galaxy
Capitalize: Travel, A, It
Add question mark: after "solar systems"; after "we make"

p. 239
1. universe
2. unicorn
3. unicycle
4. uniform
5. unify, unite
6. asteroids
7. astronomy
8. astronaut
9. aster

p. 240–241
1. board
2. fortunate
3. course
4. perform
5. quarrel
6. orchard
7. furniture
8. certain
9. firm
10. pearl
11. perfect
12. service
13. prepare
14. carefully
15. declare
16. marbles
17. starve
18. margin
19. apartment
20. compare
21. nightmare
22. suitcase
23. meteors
24. celestial
25. astronomy

p. 242
1. government, dangerous, banana, beautiful
2. ocean, again, approve, against, canoe
3. perhaps
4. qualify, cousin
5. season, memory, mosquito, comfort
6. citrus, chorus, industry, surprise

p. 243
1. chorus
2. perhaps
3. dangerous
4. surprise
5. beautiful
6. comfort
7. approve
8. ocean
9. again
10. government
11. banana
12. qualify
13. memory
14. mosquito
15. season
16. cousin
17. citrus
18. against
19. industry

p. 244
Spell correctly: beautiful, season, wonder, ocean, against
Trade places: a/is, the/of
Take out: the (between "the" and "jewel")

p. 245
1. "A Beautiful Memory"
2. <u>Highlights</u>
3. <u>Chicago Tribune</u>
4. <u>The Canoe</u>
5. "Computer Tips for Kids"
6. <u>Industry and the Canadian Government</u>
7. "Stopping by Woods on a Snowy Evening"

p. 246
1. general, animal, final, natural, musical, signal
2. nickel, barrel
3. whistle, simple, pickles, trouble, double, puzzle, tumble, tremble, example, sample, wrinkle, couple

p. 247
1. pickles
2. example
3. signal
4. double
5. puzzle
6. sample
7. whistle
8. musical
9. general
10. natural
11. nickel
12. tumble
13. animal
14. final
15. barrel
16. couple
17. simple
18. trouble
19. tremble

p. 248
Spell correctly: general, puzzle, trouble, whistle, simple
Capitalize: October, Bank, Marvin
Trade places: the/at, things/of

p. 249
1. We tremble <u>excitedly</u>.
2. All of the animals wait <u>obediently</u>.
3. A couple of people <u>busily</u> sell souvenirs.
4. <u>Suddenly</u> the signal is given.
5. Each animal steps <u>quickly</u>.
6. The circus parade marches <u>noisily</u>.
7. Two tall clowns dance <u>happily</u>.

p. 250
1. teacher, center, toaster, rather, character, whether, discover, answer, another, silver, gather, member, master
2. actor, humor
3. similar, calendar, cellar, polar, sugar

p. 251
1. sugar
2. similar
3. humor
4. silver
5. center
6. another
7. answer
8. character
9. cellar
10. teacher
11. actor
12. master

13. whether
14. polar
15. member
16. toaster
17. discover
18. rather
19. gather

p. 252
Spell correctly: whether, similar, rather, master, center
Capitalize: Hi, My, I
Add period: after "dancer"; after "ballet center"

p. 253
Answers may vary slightly.
1. trying hard to solve something
2. not feeling well; ill
3. immediately
4. to be a model worthy of imitation

p. 254
1. action, inspection, invention, section, election, direction, collection, instruction, fraction, selection, mention
2. information, education, location, nation, vacation, pollution, population, transportation, station

p. 255
1. station
2. vacation
3. population
4. nation
5. fraction
6. mention
7. selection
8. information
9. section
10. transportation
11. invention
12. education
13. collection
14. pollution
15. inspection
16. action
17. instruction
18. location
19. direction

p. 256
Spell correctly: pollution, mention, education, population, action
Capitalize: Mayor, The, The
Take out: in (between "in" and "out"); to (between "to" and "speak")

p. 257
1. 6:30
2. 12:10
3. 2:45
4. 9:05
5. Some of the world's best inventions include the following: the wheel, the gasoline engine, the telephone, and pizza.
6. Three candidates are running for election: Mayor Hibbs, Mrs. Gold, and Mr. Santos.
7. Three topics will be covered on our test: pollution, transportation, and population.

p. 258
1. road, rode, waist, waste, right, write, its, it's, hole, whole, plain, plane, threw, through
2. their, there, they're, to, too, two

p. 259
1. hole
2. road
3. threw
4. its
5. write
6. right
7. too
8. two
9. they're
10. their
11. waist
12. plain
13. it's
14. plane
15. whole
16. through
17. rode
18. to
19. there

p. 260
Spell correctly: their, write, whole, waste, there
Capitalize: Late, Emily, For
Trade places: the/of, our/on

p. 261
1. golf
2. clue
3. destroy
4. earn
5. polite
6. siege
7. pecan
8. easel
9. feud
10. code

p. 262–263
1. beautiful
2. surprise
3. dangerous
4. mosquito
5. ocean
6. against
7. barrel
8. natural
9. couple
10. general
11. example
12. similar
13. humor
14. calendar
15. character
16. whether
17. collection
18. education
19. direction
20. invention
21. they're
22. it's
23. their
24. its
25. there

Math Skills

p. 268

1.	3	6	6,7	8	9,3	0	2
2.			2,3	0	4,3	6	1
3.		1	9,0	7	6,5	4	1
4.			8,8	5	4,6	3	2
5.					9	7,0 6 5	
6.			8,0	0	5,0	0	2

7. **a:** tens, **b:** ten thousands
8. **a:** hundred thousands, **b:** millions
9. **a:** hundreds, **b:** ones
10. **a:** thousands, **b:** ten millions
11. **a:** 0 thousands, **b:** 8 tens
12. **a:** 8 ten millions, **b:** 4 millions
13. **a:** 4 hundred thousands, **b:** 5 ones
14. **a:** 1 hundred million, **b:** 0 hundreds

p. 269

	a	b	c
1.	758,493	6,473,829	868,582
2.	2,030,200	5,000,400	6,050,407
3.	30,782	406,702	3,908,454

4. 720,462
5. 25,201
6. 184,039
7. 100,243,000
8. sixteen thousand, three hundred forty-nine
9. seven hundred seventy-six
10. one hundred twenty-three thousand, four hundred fifty-six

p. 270

	a	b	c	d
1.	844	617	1,203	1,390
2.	1,153	1,160	1,118	1,697
3.	721	613	905	841
4.	441	551	661	521

p. 271

	a	b	c	d	e
5.	8,033	6,413	7,520	9,229	2,638
6.	9,552	9,179	8,692	9,225	8,369
7.	8,898	8,340	7,204	2,110	9,489
8.	4,537	9,529	8,356		
9.	8,322	8,981	5,223		

p. 273
1.

2.
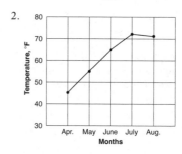

p. 274

	a	b	c	d	e
1.	662	1,350	511	323	174
2.	1,089	1,266	1,342	1,619	1,700
3.	1,433	756			

p. 275

	a	b	c	d
1.	546	574	247	403
2.	709	309	359	103
3.	165	431	874	252
4.	89	99	422	469

p. 276

	a	b	c	d	e
5.	3,259	2,553	1,594	1,579	688
6.	3,490	6,145	8,518	3,883	1,357
7.	1,524	2,762	5,964	112	3,537
8.	2,857	1,081	7,606		
9.	2,094	7,763	945		

p. 277

	a	b	c	d
1.	100,114	103,013	158,441	70,042
2.	20,008	94,976	19,000	19,000
3.	28,467	28,888	27,788	35,389
4.	64,909	26,000	52,379	63,776
5.	13,153	76,000		

p. 278

	a	b	c	d
1.	600	700	600	500
2.	900	900	700	700
3.	100	500	400	400
4.	600	300	600	900

p. 279

	a	b	c	d
5.	600	600	700	900
6.	300	500	500	1,000
7.	1,100	6,800	4,600	4,400
8.	3,700	9,100	7,000	6,900
9.	6,000	8,000	1,000	9,000

p. 281
1. 45 acres of corn
2. $112
3. 20 hamsters
4. 4:30
5. $56

p. 282
1. 787 feet
2. 412 Nobel Prizes
3. 4,250,000 miles
4. 83,861 square miles
5. about 400 miles
6. about 700 species

p. 283
1. **a:** hundred thousands, **b:** thousands
2. **a:** millions, **b:** ten thousands
3. **a:** tens, **b:** hundreds
4. **a:** 0 hundreds, **b:** 3 ones
5. **a:** 9 hundred thousands, **b:** 5 tens
6. **a:** 6 thousands, **b:** 1 hundred million
7. 72,085
8. 2,040,506
9. 17,500,018
10. twenty-one hundred, one hundred six
11. four hundred three thousand, eight hundred seventy-two
12. one million, seven hundred twenty thousand, five hundred sixty-four

p. 323

	a	b	c	d
7.	$1\frac{1}{5}$	$1\frac{2}{3}$	$5\frac{1}{3}$	$1\frac{1}{2}$
8.	$2\frac{2}{5}$	$5\frac{1}{3}$	$1\frac{1}{3}$	$4\frac{1}{3}$
9.	$1\frac{3}{4}$	$3\frac{5}{6}$	$6\frac{1}{2}$	$2\frac{1}{2}$
10.	4	1	2	9
11.	$\frac{17}{4}$	$\frac{11}{3}$	$\frac{9}{2}$	$\frac{7}{6}$
12.	$\frac{9}{4}$	$\frac{15}{3}$	$\frac{13}{3}$	$\frac{16}{9}$
13.	$\frac{14}{3}$	$\frac{11}{3}$	$\frac{13}{3}$	$\frac{19}{7}$
14.	$\frac{20}{9}$	$\frac{22}{5}$	$\frac{5}{2}$	$\frac{11}{2}$

p. 324

	a	b	c	d	e
1.	$\frac{2}{3}$	$\frac{2}{3}$	$\frac{4}{7}$	$\frac{1}{2}$	$\frac{7}{9}$
2.	$1\frac{1}{5}$	$1\frac{2}{5}$	$1\frac{1}{8}$	$1\frac{1}{3}$	1
3.	$\frac{1}{2}$	$\frac{1}{3}$	$\frac{1}{4}$	$\frac{1}{2}$	$\frac{1}{3}$

p. 325

	a	b	c	d	e
1.	$5\frac{1}{2}$	$9\frac{3}{4}$	$14\frac{4}{5}$	$9\frac{1}{4}$	$9\frac{3}{5}$
2.	$17\frac{4}{5}$	$15\frac{3}{4}$	$11\frac{1}{3}$	$21\frac{3}{5}$	$16\frac{2}{3}$
3.	$2\frac{5}{6}$	$1\frac{1}{4}$	$4\frac{1}{3}$	$2\frac{1}{5}$	$5\frac{2}{3}$
4.	$3\frac{1}{4}$	$5\frac{1}{4}$	$5\frac{2}{5}$	$1\frac{1}{3}$	$4\frac{2}{5}$

p. 327

1. New York: $\frac{7}{10}$; Cleveland: $\frac{1}{2}$; Boston: $\frac{5}{9}$
2. petroleum: $\frac{2}{5}$; natural gas: $\frac{1}{4}$; coal: $\frac{1}{5}$
3. Kitti's hognosed bat: $\frac{7}{10}$ ounce; proboscis bat: $\frac{11}{10}$ ounce; banana bat: $\frac{9}{10}$ ounce

p. 328

	a	b
1.	about $\frac{1}{2}$	about 1
2.	about 0	about 0
3.	about 1	about $\frac{1}{2}$

	a	b	c
4.	1	1	1
5.	0	1	$\frac{1}{2}$
6.	1	$\frac{1}{2}$	1

p. 329

1. a: 1; 2; $\frac{1}{2}$, b: 3; 5; $\frac{4}{5}$, c: 1; 6; $\frac{7}{8}$, d: 3; 1; $\frac{2}{3}$
2. a: 6; 7; $1\frac{3}{10}$, b: 12; 5; $1\frac{3}{14}$, c: 8; 6; $1\frac{5}{9}$, d: 10; 9; $1\frac{7}{12}$
3. a: $\frac{3}{8}$, b: $\frac{1}{2}$, c: $\frac{4}{5}$, d: $\frac{7}{8}$

p. 330

	a	b	c	d
1.	4; 1; $\frac{3}{4}$	2; 1; $\frac{1}{2}$	3; 2; $\frac{1}{4}$	5; 4; $\frac{1}{6}$
2.	13; 6; $\frac{1}{2}$	3; 1; $\frac{1}{3}$	8; 3; $\frac{1}{2}$	7; 5; $\frac{1}{10}$

p. 331

	a	b	c	d
1.	$9\frac{7}{8}$	4; $10\frac{5}{6}$	6; $5\frac{11}{12}$	2; $8\frac{7}{8}$
2.	$16\frac{7}{8}$	$20\frac{7}{8}$	$11\frac{7}{9}$	$13\frac{7}{10}$
3.	$9\frac{7}{8}$	$23\frac{3}{4}$	$16\frac{1}{2}$	$17\frac{8}{9}$

p. 332

	a	b	c	d
1.	$4\frac{2}{3}$	$7\frac{3}{10}$	$10\frac{1}{8}$	$13\frac{3}{4}$
2.	$5\frac{1}{3}$	$9\frac{1}{4}$	$8\frac{1}{2}$	$11\frac{3}{4}$
3.	$4\frac{1}{4}$	$7\frac{3}{8}$	$9\frac{7}{10}$	
4.	$13\frac{1}{4}$	$7\frac{1}{2}$	$9\frac{1}{6}$	

p. 333

	a	b	c	d
1.	2; $6\frac{1}{2}$	2; $2\frac{1}{4}$	2; $6\frac{3}{8}$	5; $7\frac{1}{5}$
2.	$7\frac{3}{8}$	$6\frac{1}{3}$	$3\frac{1}{6}$	$5\frac{3}{8}$
3.	$2\frac{1}{9}$	$3\frac{11}{14}$	$1\frac{1}{6}$	$3\frac{1}{6}$

p. 334

	a	b	c	d
1.	6; $3\frac{6}{6}$	8; $5\frac{8}{6}$	3; $1\frac{3}{6}$	
2.	5; $9\frac{5}{6}$	3; $13\frac{3}{3}$	6; $8\frac{9}{6}$	
3.	4; $6\frac{4}{4}$	3; $6\frac{2}{3}$	4; $5\frac{3}{4}$	10; $16\frac{3}{10}$
4.	$11\frac{3}{8}$	$4\frac{5}{6}$	$12\frac{5}{9}$	$8\frac{4}{7}$

p. 335

	a	b	c
1.	$5\frac{4}{3}$	$7\frac{15}{8}$	$8\frac{7}{6}$
2.	$2\frac{14}{8}$	$4\frac{21}{12}$	$13\frac{18}{10}$
3.	$4\frac{5}{8}$	$4\frac{1}{2}$	$6\frac{9}{10}$
4.	$1\frac{9}{10}$	$6\frac{5}{8}$	$4\frac{3}{4}$

p. 337

1. $\frac{11}{12}$ mile
2. $\frac{9}{10}$ inch
3. $\frac{5}{8}$ inch
4. $\frac{7}{12}$ yard
5. $\frac{3}{4}$ cup

p. 338.

1. $15\frac{2}{3}$ miles
2. $3\frac{1}{4}$ inches
3. $4\frac{1}{2}$ cups
4. $14\frac{1}{16}$ pounds
5. $4\frac{1}{2}$ inches
6. $3\frac{1}{5}$ ounces
7. $7\frac{3}{4}$ pounds

p. 339

	a	b	c
1.	$\frac{3}{5}$	$\frac{4}{9}$	$\frac{1}{6}$

	a	b
2.	$\frac{1}{9}\ \frac{3}{9}\ \frac{2}{9}$	$\frac{3}{10}\ \frac{3}{5}\ \frac{4}{5}$

	a	b	c	d
3.	$\frac{3}{4}$	$\frac{3}{5}$	$\frac{2}{3}$	$\frac{1}{2}$
4.	6	2	9	5
5.	$\frac{7}{9}$	1	$\frac{5}{8}$	$\frac{3}{5}$
6.	$2\frac{5}{8}$	$1\frac{1}{9}$	$2\frac{9}{10}$	$2\frac{9}{16}$
7.	$10\frac{7}{9}$	$11\frac{1}{6}$	$10\frac{7}{8}$	$7\frac{7}{15}$

p. 340

	a	b	c	d
8.	$3\frac{7}{8}$	$2\frac{1}{6}$	5	$4\frac{3}{4}$
9.	$\frac{13}{3}$	$\frac{42}{4}$	$\frac{17}{2}$	$\frac{53}{10}$
10.	2; $4\frac{2}{2}$	5; $7\frac{5}{5}$	9; $11\frac{9}{2}$	7; $15\frac{7}{7}$
11.	$\frac{2}{5}$	$\frac{2}{7}$	$\frac{1}{3}$	$\frac{1}{2}$
12.	$5\frac{1}{3}$	$2\frac{2}{3}$	$4\frac{3}{8}$	$8\frac{3}{4}$
13.	$5\frac{1}{3}$	$1\frac{3}{4}$	$3\frac{9}{10}$	$4\frac{5}{9}$
14.	$\frac{1}{2}$	1	1	

p. 341

15. Atlanta: $\frac{2}{3}$; Philadelphia: $\frac{4}{9}$; New York: $\frac{5}{9}$
16. Goliath: $8\frac{3}{10}$ in.; Queen Alexandra: 11 in.; African swallowtail: $9\frac{1}{10}$ in.
17. $\frac{5}{12}$ mile
18. $\frac{5}{8}$ gallon

p. 342

	a	b	c
1.	0.3	0.8	2.4
2.	0.32	0.68	1.21

	a	b
3.	$1.00	$0.10
4.	$12.00	$0.30

p. 343

1.		2	9	•	0	1	
2.			0	•	4	8	5
3.			3	•	7	8	2
4.		6	7	•	5	6	7
5.			1	•	0	0	
6.	1	4	2	•	0	4	

7. a: tenths, b: hundredths, c: thousandths
8. a: thousandths, b: ones, c: thousandths
9. a: hundredths, b: tens, c: tenths
10. a: 3 thousandths, b: 9 hundredths, c: 4 thousandths
11. a: 5 hundredths, b: 3 ones, c: 8 hundredths
12. a: 4 ones, b: 8 thousands, c: 6 hundredths

p. 344

1. a: hundredths, b: thousandths, c: tenths
2. a: tenths, b: hundredths, c: thousandths
3. a: tenths, b: thousandths, c: hundredths

4.	0.4	0.04
5.	0.004	0.504
6.	0.016	0.16
7.	10.13	54.01

8. forty-eight thousandths
9. sixty-four hundredths
10. nine and four tenths

p. 345

	a	b
11.	0.5	0.89
12.	3.004	0.63
13.	4.7	8.05
14.	0.31	0.028
15.	0.017	8.009
16.	9.09	0.23
17.	70.1	0.71

18. twenty-three hundredths
19. eight tenths
20. four and fifty-three hundredths
21. six and nine thousandths
22. nine and eight hundred two thousandths
23. eighteen and four hundredths
24. eighteen hundredths

p. 346

	a	b	c
1.	<	<	>
2.	<	<	>
3.	=	>	<

	a	b
4.	1.4 14.0 140	0.007 0.07 0.7
5.	3.45 34.5 345	0.79 0.80 0.81

p. 347

	a	b	c
6.	>	<	<
7.	<	<	=
8.	=	>	>
9.	>	>	<
10.	=	>	=
11.	>	>	<

12. a: $1.70 $17.0 $170, b: 0.06 0.066 0.60
13. a: 5.06 5.6 5.602, b: 0.003 0.03 0.3
14. a: 1.2 2.1 21, b: 0.007 0.090 0.8

p. 348

	a	b	c	d
1.	$\frac{3}{10}$	$\frac{7}{10}$	$\frac{9}{10}$	$\frac{1}{10}$
2.	$\frac{3}{100}$	$\frac{7}{100}$	$\frac{9}{100}$	$\frac{1}{100}$
3.	$2\frac{3}{10}$	$6\frac{9}{10}$	$3\frac{7}{10}$	$8\frac{1}{10}$
4.	$9\frac{88}{100}$	$5\frac{7}{100}$	$4\frac{90}{100}$	$2\frac{5}{100}$
5.	0.4	0.8	0.6	0.2
6.	0.23	0.97	0.246	0.810
7.	3.06	9.01	8.825	6.975

p. 349

	a	b	c
1.	0.75	0.2	0.96
2.	0.8	0.35	0.15
3.	0.24	0.5	0.52
4.	3.4	4.5	2.55
5.	2.72	8.25	
6.	4.15	20.2	
7.	3.08	5.88	

p. 351

1. 18 inches
2. Subtract $\frac{1}{10}$; $\frac{3}{5}$
3. Subtract 0.2; 8.12
4. Add 3; 13 toothpicks
5. Add 11; 66

p. 352

	a	b	c	d
1.	4	3	2	7
2.	40	82	79	51
3.	$9.00	$4.00	$1.00	$73.00
4.	$1.00	$3.00	$10.00	$26.00
5.	0.4	0.7	0.8	0.5
6.	82.8	29.9	85.5	60.0

p. 353

	a	b	c	d
1.	26.5	76.8	91.5	77.2
2.	8.813	5.882	9.991	64.190
3.	10.15	9.59	15.69	13.75

p. 354

	a	b	c
4.	5.9	7.2	76.4
5.	7.33	4.28	37.91
6.	$51.26	$9.74	$79.51
7.	294.2	98.67	1.25
8.	1.5	4.5	95.8
9.	$10.58	$8.99	$90.00
10.	8.988	14.197	4.405
11.	11.5	17.2	16.6

p. 355

	a	b	c	d
1.	9	$13	$109	$86
2.	17	119	8	39
3.	1.2	6.8	17.3	$99.50
4.	53.1	1.2	4.7	6.6

p. 356

	a	b	c	d
1.	48.5	8.4	$43.71	$7.91
2.	1.88	4.31	10.94	32.28
3.	8.363	2.236	1.226	4.505

p. 357

	a	b	c	d
4.	1.8	2.6	6.5	3.4
5.	5.29	0.58	10.89	5.22
6.	$3.64	$2.64	$4.18	$10.75
7.	5.9	5.16	1.379	
8.	1.71	7.796	4.775	

p. 358

	a	b	c	d
1.	3	$4	5	$15
2.	1	3	5	25
3.	0.4	2.5	8.8	12.3
4.	7.7	0.8	53.7	1.6

p. 360
1. about $72.00
2. about 28 meters
3. about 486 inches
4. about 22 tons
5. about 30 years

p. 361
1. **a:** hundredths, **b:** thousandths, **c:** tenths
2. **a:** 3 tenths, **b:** 0 hundredths, **c:** 9 thousandths
3. **a:** 0.014, **b:** 0.07
4. eight and fifty-two hundredths
5. twelve and twenty-three thousandths

	a	b	c
6.	<	>	<

	a	b
7.	0.32 0.42 053	0.033 0.303 0.33

	a	b	c	d
8.	0.7	0.82	0.4	14.5
9.	2.7	12.8	8.35	

p. 362

	a	b	c	d
10.	$\frac{41}{100}$	$\frac{63}{1,000}$	$\frac{8}{10}$	$3\frac{17}{100}$
11.	0.4	0.8	0.9	1.0
12.	15	7	20	$13

	a	b	c	d	e
13.	12.5	7.56	88.295	13.2	9.01
14.	1.6	1.589	9.63	0.61	2.235

	a	b	c	d
15.	13	$5	94	7
16.	1.6	32.4	3.3	39.9

p. 363
17. $1\frac{1}{4}$ in. a week
18. 4.2 miles
19. about 27 years
20. about 0 meters
21. about 248 years

p. 364

	a	b
1.	in.	ft.
2.	1	1
3.	1	36
4.	84	45
5.	216	10,560
6.	$3\frac{1}{2}$	2
7.	$2\frac{11}{12}$	$5\frac{2}{3}$

p. 365

	a	b
1.	lb.	T.
1.	oz.	lb.

	a	b	c
3.	1	1	16
4.	80	4,000	32
5.	$1\frac{1}{2}$	3	$1\frac{1}{2}$
6.	$2\frac{1}{4}$	$5\frac{3}{4}$	$3\frac{1}{8}$

p. 366

	a	b
1.	c.	gal. or qt.

	a	b	c
2.	1	1	1
3.	28	48	16
4.	32	100	800
5.	$1\frac{1}{2}$	3	1
6.	$2\frac{1}{2}$	$1\frac{7}{8}$	$1\frac{3}{4}$

p. 367

	a	b
1.	=	>
2.	>	=
3.	>	>
4.	>	<
5.	<	>
6.	>	=

p. 368

	a	b
1.	km	m
2.	km	km

	a	b
3.	125 km	2.8 m
4.	30 m	5 km

	a	b	c
5.	7,000	3,000	57,000
6.	2	6	10

p. 369

	a	b
1.	cm	cm or mm
2.	mm	cm
3.	m	mm
4.	1 cm	100 m
5.	3 m	25 cm
6.	50	1,200
7.	2	5

p. 370

	a	b
1.	kg	g
2.	kg	kg
3.	9 kg	1 g
4.	500 g	18 kg

	a	b	c
5.	9,000	7,000	13,000
6.	4	2	15

p. 371

	a	b
1.	mL	L
2.	L	mL
3.	5,000 L	4 L
4.	700 mL	180 mL

	a	b	c
5.	10,000	4,000	250,000
6.	5	6	30

p. 372

	a	b	c
1.	>	>	<
2.	<	<	<
3.	>	<	<
4.	1,000	0.01	0.01
5.	0.01	0.001	0.001
6.	>	<	<
7.	<	>	>

p. 373

	a	b
1.	=	>
2.	>	>
3.	=	=
4.	=	>
5.	>	<
6.	>	<

p. 375
1. Kendra: 8 years old; Tim: 4 years old
2. 2 dimes, 2 nickels, 1 penny
3. gray whale: 36 tons; Baird's whale: 12 tons
4. Vatican City: 0.5 square kilometers; Monaco: 1.8 square kilometers
5. 20 grams

p. 376

	a	b
1.	ft.	gal.
2.	lb.	in.
3.	200 mL	1 L
4.	25 mm	1 kg

	a	b	c
5.	16	5,000	6,000
6.	70	1	4
7.	<	>	
8.	<	<	
9.	<	>	

p. 377
10. 3 dimes, 2 nickels, 93 pennies
11. basketballs: 9 footballs: 15
12. one box: 24 cards one box: 12 cards
13. Ron: 4 goldfish Caroline: 7 goldfish
14. ostrich: 100 inches

p. 378

	a	b	c	d
1.	∠LMN	∠EFG	∠PQR	∠K
2.	obtuse angle	acute angle	right angle	obtuse angle

p. 379

	a	b	c
1.	8 units	8 units	10 units
2.	12 units	10 units	12 units
3.	16 units	12 units	14 units

p. 380

	a	b
1.	12 feet	14 meters
2.	18 yards	32 inches
3.	40 inches	17.8 meters

p. 381

	a	b
1.	5 square units	4 square units
2.	8 square units	15 square units
3.	9 square units	6 square units

p. 382
1. **a:** 16 sq. yards, **b:** 3 sq. feet
2. **a:** 4 sq. centimeters, **b:** 12 sq. inches
3. **a:** 40 sq. meters, **b:** 144 sq. millimeters

p. 384
1. 20 yards
2. 143 sq. feet
3. 12 feet
4. 1 acre
5. 370 meters

p. 385

	a	b	c	d
1.	∠EFG	∠LMN	∠ABC	∠P
2.	right angle	acute angle	obtuse angle	obtuse angle

3. 10 units 16 units 14 units
4. **a:** 5 square units, **b:** 15 square units, **c:** 4 square units

p. 386
5. 20 feet
6. 138 yards
7. 20 miles
8. 1,508 square meters
9. $1,296.00

Language Arts

p. 388
Descriptions of what the nouns name may vary.
1. sense, thing; smell, thing; nose, thing; 2. people, person; smell, thing; food, thing; grass, thing; rain, thing; 3. People, person; lot, thing; enjoyment, thing; odors, thing; 4. eggs, thing; odor, thing; 5. sense, thing; smell, thing; person, person; danger, thing; 6.–7. Sentences will vary.

p. 389
1. common: scientist; proper: Maryland, 2. common: friends; proper: Benjamin Banneker, 3. common: People, accomplishments; proper: United States, 4. proper: Banneker, Washington, D.C., 5. common: man, memory, 6. common: astronomer, nights, stars, planets, 7. common: scientists, planets; proper: Mars, Jupiter, 8. common: changes, country; proper: Banneker, 1.–8. Rewritten sentences will vary.

p. 390
1. tornado, singular; hurricane, singular; 2. minutes, plural; hours, plural; 3. winds, plural; 4. air, singular; fire, singular; 5. conditions, plural; signs, plural; 6. The girls ate their lunches on the school benches., 7. The young ladies looked at the dark clouds overhead., 8. Strong winds picked up boxes of books by the library doors.

p. 391
1. trout, 2. fish or fishes, 3. heroes, 4. women, 5. men, 6. mice, 7. beliefs, 8. wolves, 9. oxen, 10. calves, 11. children, 12. feet, 13. lives

p. 392
1. My friend's mother had a baby yesterday., 2. The baby's teeth are not in yet., 3. The child's head is still soft., 4. The bib's tie is torn., 5. The crib's sheets are pink., 6. The uncle's smile is happy., 7. The grandmother's gift is a new blanket., 8. The father's pleasure is easy to see., 9. The infant's eyes are blue., 10. My friend's life will be different now.

p. 393

1. Imagine the children's surprise!,
2. They found the robins' baby on the sidewalk., 3. They returned it to the parents' nest., 4. They watched the adult birds' activities for a while., 5. The birds' fear was apparent., 6. The humans' odor was on the baby bird., 7. The bird was now the young people's responsibility., 8. The students' job was to find a shoe box., 9. The parents' job was to find some soft lining.

p. 394

1. They, Explorers; 2. It, animal; 3. them, animals or kangaroos; 4. They, birds; 5. It, platypus; 6. They, Scientists; 7. It, coolabah or tree; 8. It, flower or kangaroo paw

p. 395

1. We read about the Wrights last week., 2. It was he who found the book., 3. They grew up in Dayton, Ohio., 4. He was a bishop there., 5. She helped care for them., 6. It was a gift from their father., 7. He was four years older than Orville., 8. On December 17, 1903, it took place., 9. It lasted 12 seconds., 10. They were 13 seconds, 15 seconds, and 59 seconds.

p. 396

1. Darkness covered them., 2. The game wardens noticed it., 3. Then, the game wardens saw them., 4. Two men and a woman were searching it for alligators., 5. The game wardens pushed it out of the brush., 6. The wardens raced toward them., 7. The powerful engine moved it quickly over the water., 8. The poachers quickly dumped them back into the water., 9. The wardens searched the inside of it.

p. 397

1. He, subject pronoun; 2. him, object pronoun; 3. We, subject pronoun; 4. them, object pronoun; 5. She, subject pronoun; 6. her, object pronoun; 7. They, subject pronoun; 8. them, object pronoun; 9. She, subject pronoun; 10. them, object pronoun

p. 398

1. myself, 2. himself, 3. itself, 4. herself, 5. yourselves, 6. ourselves, 7. yourself, 8. ourselves, 9. herself, 10. myself, 11. herself, 12. himself

p. 399

1. their, before a noun; 2. Its, before a noun; 3. hers, stands alone; 4. Her, before a noun; 5. theirs, stands alone; 6. our, before a noun; 7. her; 8. hers; 9. their; 10. your

p. 400

1. He, Mr. Les Harsten; 2. them, plants; 3. He, Les; 4. It, sound; 5. it, plant; 6. them, sounds; 7. It, recording; 8. They, plants; 9. It, music; 10. They, plants

p. 401

1. spectacular, what kind; 2. superb, what kind; beautiful, what kind; 3. winter, what kind; 4. many, how many; different, what kind; 5. red, what kind; pink, what kind; violet, what kind; white, what kind; 6. spongy, what kind; acid, what kind; 7. three, how many; four, how many; flowering, what kind; 8. bright, what kind; colorful, what kind; special, what kind

p. 402

1. Greek, Greece; 2. Spartan, Sparta; 3. Athenian, Athens; 4. Roman, Rome; 5. Korean, Korea; 6. Romanian, Romania; 7. English; 8. Norwegian; 9. Canadian; 10. American

p. 403

1. crunchy, peanuts; 2. salty, They; 3. red, skin; 4. delicious, seeds; 5. inedible, seeds; 6. popular, They; 7. healthful, snacks; 8. sour, apples; 9. crisp and juicy, fruit; 10. noisy, vegetable; 11.–15. Adjectives will vary.

p. 404

1. a, 2. These, 3. the, 4. this, 5. a, 6. the, 7. a, 8. this, 9. these, 10. those

p. 405

1. more wonderful, 2. most beautiful, 3. highest, 4. deeper, 5. biggest, 6. largest, 7. easiest, 8. most unusual, 9. stranger, 10. more excited, 11. most interesting, 12. oldest

p. 406

1. better, 2. less, 3. worst, 4. more, 5. worse, 6. more, 7. Many, 8. most

p. 407

1. linking: felt, 2. action: left, 3. action: needed, 4. action: looked, 5. action: saw, 6. action: ran; studied, 7. linking: appeared, 8. action: pulled; action: moved, 9. action: slid, 10. action: hurried, 11. action: bowed, 12. linking: was

p. 408

1. told, main verb; 2. looking, main verb; 3. tell, main verb; 4. was, helping verb; 5. leaned, main verb; 6. was, helping verb; 7. fallen, main verb; 8. was, helping verb

p. 409

1. likes, 2. visits, 3. comes, 4. fix, 5. mixes, 6. takes, 7. show, 8. wishes, 9. worries, 10. watches, 11. makes, 12. needs

p. 410

1. walked, 2. sampled, 3. seemed, 4. described, 5. served, 6. sipped, 7. fried, 8. tried, 9. passed, 10. pinned, 11. featured, 12. tasted

p. 411

1. will happen, 2. will hunt, 3. will gather, 4. Will Sam miss, 5. Will they search, 6. will not find, 7. will remember, 8. will cook, 9. will float, 10. will hide, 11. will notice, 12. Will Sam leave

p. 412

1. look, present; 2. have, present; 3. climbs, present; 4. make, present; 5. climbed, past; 6. jumps, present; 7. will see, future; 8. will go, future; 9. will ride, future; 10. will tell, future; 11. Sam will see ten lizards.; 12. I will see only four.; 13. Some lizards will change colors.

p. 413

1. done, 2. rode, 3. gave, 4. ran, 5. come, 6. ate, 7. saw, 8. said, 9. took, 10. thought, 11. written, 12. went

p. 414

1. her, 2. immigrants, 3. torch, 4. hope, freedom, 5. statue, 6.–16. Sentences will vary. Be sure each sentence contains an appropriate direct object.

p. 415

1. carefully, how; 2. First, when; 3. Next, when; 4. Then, when; 5. Finally, when; 6. firmly, how; 7. surely, how; 8. joyfully, how; 9. higher, where; 10. Soon, when; 11. down, where; 12.–13. Sentences will vary. Be sure each sentence contains an adverb.

p. 416

1. more eagerly, 2. more strongly, 3. most courageously, 4. more completely, 5. more often, 6. most convincingly, 7. better, 8. worse, 9. better, 10. well

p. 417

1. very, 2. extremely, 3. carefully, 4. quite, 5. too, 6. fairly, 7. certainly, 8. rather, 9. much, 10. charming, 11. suggests, 12. uses, 13. work, 14. decided, 15. less

p. 418

1. gently, 2. great, 3. carefully, 4. completely, 5. firmly, 6. serious, 7. fairly, 8. entire, 9. good, 10. well, 11. well, 12. good

p. 419

1. to her island, island; 2. below the waves, waves; 3. without any means, means; of navigation, navigation; except the stars, stars; 4. For many centuries, centuries; by the stars, stars; 5. in the 1700s, 1700s; 6. on the sea, sea; of celestial navigation, navigation; 7. of a star, star; 8. above the horizon, horizon; 9. from that reading, reading; 10. Without this information, information

p. 420

1. in a car, in; 2. from the sea, from; 3. from the motion, from; of the waves, of; 4. In this same way, In; in the back, in; of a car, of; 5. of balance, of; 6. inside your ears, inside; 7. with a fluid, with; with special hairs, with; 8. of movement, of; 9. in the bottom, in; of the canals, of; 10. around the canals, around; 11. in your stomach, in; 12.–14. Sentences will vary. Be sure that each sentence contains a prepositional phrase.

p. 421

1. preposition, 2. adverb, 3. preposition, 4. adverb, 5. preposition, 6. adverb, 7. preposition, 8. preposition, 9. preposition, 10.–13. Sentences will vary. Be sure that each sentence contains a prepositional phrase.

p. 422

1. and, 2. but, 3. and, 4. or, 5. but, 6. or, 7. and, 8. and, 9. or, 10. and, 11. and, 12. but

p. 423

1. Gee!, 2. Wow!, 3. Oh, dear!, 4. Oh, my!, 5. Good grief!, 6. Oops!, 7. Great!, 8. Alas!, 9. Of course! 10.–18. Sentences will vary. Be sure that each sentence contains an interjection.

p. 424

1.–9. Sentences will vary. Be sure each sentence contains a subject or predicate as needed.

p. 425

1. We memorized the capitals of all of the states., 2. Everyone knew the capital of Arkansas., 3. The capital is not always the largest city in the state., 4. You should picture the map in your mind., 5. The left side is the west side., 6. not a sentence, 7. That river empties into the Gulf of Mexico., 8. not a sentence, 9. Three people found Delaware right away., 10. not a sentence

p. 426

1. predicate, 2. predicate, 3. subject, 4. subject, 5. predicate; 6. subject: The eye; predicate: is made of many parts., 7. subject: The pupil; predicate: is the round, black center of the eye., 8. subject: The outer, colored part; predicate: is called the iris., 9. subject: The iris; predicate: is made of a ring of muscle., 10. subject: Too much light; predicate: can damage the eye., 11. subject: The iris; predicate: closes up in bright light.,

12. subject: Some people; predicate: are colorblind., 13. subject: They; predicate: cannot see shades of red and green., 14. subject: A nearsighted person; predicate: cannot see distant things well., 15. subject: Close objects; predicate: are blurry to a farsighted person., 16. subject: People who need glasses to read; predicate: are farsighted.

P. 427
1. Two young men, men; 2. A raging tornado, tornado; 3. Two square miles of the city, miles; 4. An odd roaring noise, noise; 5 The strong wind, wind; 6. Giant walls, walls; 7. One side of a street side; 8. The other side, side; 9. Some people; people; 10. A tornado, tornado; 11. This lucky person, person; 12. Unlucky people, people; 13. Dorothy, Dorothy; 14. She, She; 15. A ride in a tornado, ride

P. 428
1. Sally and John; 2. Roses, daisies, and violets; 3. Jim and Meg, 4. Sally, John, Jim, and Meg; 5. A picnic basket and a jug of lemonade; 6. The four friends and their two dogs; 7. Apples, peaches, and plums; 8. Frankie and Joanne, 9. The six friends, the two dogs, and a few cats

P. 429
1. can be very interesting, can be; 2. have found almost a million different types of insects, have found; 3. live almost everywhere on Earth's surface, live; 4. can study insects in the woods, streams, parks, and your own yard, can study; 5. has no backbone, has; 6. makes insects different from many animals, makes; 7. have six legs, have; 8. appeared about 400 million years age, appeared; 9. live together in large groups, live; 10. capture insects and other small animals, capture; 11. use the insects for food, use; 12. attracts insects with its sweet nectar, attracts; 13. snaps its leaves shut on insects, snaps; 14. traps insects with a sticky liquid, traps

P. 430
1. planned and prepared; 2. shopped, cleaned, and cooked; 3. hired and bought; 4. ordered and borrowed; 5. wore and played; 6. laughed and danced; 7. cleared and helped; 8. walked, ran, or rode; 9. sat and rested

P. 431
1. subject: Our favorite coach, coach; predicate: cheers during the race, cheers; 2. subject: My youngest sister, sister; predicate: swims ahead of the others, swims;

3. subject: Her strokes, strokes; predicate: cut through the water, cut; 4. subject: Ripples, Ripples; predicate: splash at the edge of the pool, splash; 5. subject: The exciting race, race; predicate: ends with a surprise, ends; 6. subject: My sister's team, team; predicate: finishes first, finishes; 7. subject: The people in the bleachers, people; predicate: cheer wildly, cheer; 8. subject: The team, team; predicate: holds the silver trophy for a school photograph, holds; 9. subject: The team members, members; predicate: hug each other happily, hug; 10. subject: Everyone in my family, Everyone; predicate: goes for an ice-cream cone, goes

P. 432
1. subject: house, it; predicate: was, had; compound; 2. subject: Railroad; predicate: brought; simple; 3. subject: wagons; predicate: were; simple; 4. subject: rides; predicate: were; simple; 5. subject: slaves, they; predicate: stopped, stayed; compound; 6. subject: home; predicate: was; simple; 7. subject: Levi Coffin, he; predicate: was, earned; compound; 8. subject: Dies Drear, he; predicate: was, lived; compound; 9. subject: Allan Pinkerton, he; predicate: made, hid; compound; 10. subject: Harriet Tubman, she; predicate: led, took; compound

P. 433
Sentence types may vary.
1. ., declarative; 2. ., declarative; 3. ?, interrogative; 4. !, exclamatory; 5. ., imperative; 6. ., declarative; 7. ?, interrogative; 8. !, exclamatory; 9. ., declarative; 10. ., imperative, 11. ?, interrogative; 12. ., imperative

P. 434
Students should circle sentences 2, 3, 4, 6, and 7.
1. Trash, 2. (You), 3. (You), 4. (You), 5. problem, 6. (You), 7. (You), 8. Pieces, 9.–12. Sentences may vary slightly. 9. Avoid packages with too much wrapping., 10. Buy the largest sizes of products., 11. Use old T-shirts as wiping rags., 12. Use both sides of writing paper.

P. 435
1. Chad and his friends, look; 2. Chad, finds; 3. He, pulls; 4. rug, takes; 5. friends, come; 6. They, stand; 7. Chad, explains; 8. rug, tells; 9. Chad and his friends, go; 10. They, fly; 11. Chad, wishes; 12. he, hears; 13. She, says; 14. Chad; thanks, thinks

P. 436
Possible response: Each year, King Minos demanded a human sacrifice from the people of Athens. Seven boys and seven girls would enter the Labyrinth. The Labyrinth was the

home of the Minotaur. The Minotaur was half man and half beast.

P. 437
1. Joanie waited patiently and quietly., adverbs; 2. She had felt disappointed and rejected before., adjectives; 3. She really and truly wanted to be a scientist., adverbs; 4. Joanie read the letter slowly and calmly., adverbs

P. 438
Patrick studied the wall, and he found a hidden button., 2. Patrick pushed the button, and the bookcase moved., 3. Patrick could wait, or he could explore the path., 4. He wasn't afraid, but he wasn't comfortable either.

P. 439
1. The sunlight shone on the little door., 2. Into the shack walked Margaret and Danny., 3. A large wooden table was inside the shack., 4. A black cat lay on the table., 5. Cannot be changed; inverting would change meaning., 6. A witch's magic was at work in the shack!, 7. Cannot be changed; inverting would change meaning.

P. 440
Corrections of sentences may vary.
1. A box turtle is a reptile. It lives in woods and fields., 2. Simple sentence, 3. It can pull its legs, head, and tail inside its shell and get "boxed in.", 4. Many kinds of turtles live on land and in the water., 5. Turtles belong to the same family as lizards, snakes, alligators, and crocodiles., 6. Simple sentence, 7. Painted turtles eat meal worms, earthworms, minnows, and insects. The musk turtle finds food along the bottoms of ponds or streams., 8. Painted turtles get their name from the red and yellow patterns on their shells. They also have yellow lines on their heads.

P. 441
Corrections of sentences may vary.
1a. You'll need 101 index cards. You'll need a colored marker.
1b. You'll need 101 index cards, and you'll need a colored marker.
2a. Print the name of a state or a state capital on each index card. Print the rules on the last index card.
2b. Print the name of a state or a state capital on each index card, and print the rules on the last index card.
3a. Put the marker away. Put all the cards in an envelope.
3b. Put the marker away, and put all the cards in an envelope.
4a. This game is for small groups. Up to three students may play.

4b. This game is for small groups, and up to three students may play.
5a. Players mix up the cards. They lay the cards face down.
5b. Players mix up the cards, and then they lay the cards face down.

P. 442
1. I was going camping with my friend Michael., 2. We met Mr. Carl G. Carbur at the camping supply store., 3. Michael and I decided that we needed a new tent., 4. Mrs. Albright showed us many different tents., 5. We chose one just like Dr. Pelky's., 6. Michael's mother, Mrs. Mixx, gave us a ride to the campsite., 7. After we set up the ten, I walked down the road., 8. Dr. Pelky was at the next site!, 9. Dr. Pelky was camping with Mario J. Moreno., 10. Mario showed Michael and me a great place to fish., 11. I caught some trout, and Michael caught a bass., 12. Michael and I ate supper at Dr. Pelky's camp.

P. 443
1. My best friends and I plan to tour the United States., 2. My friend Sandy is very excited because she has never been to California., 3. She has never tasted any Mexican food, either., 4. She will be coming from New York and meeting Jane in Philadelphia., 5. Then, the two of them will pick up Roxanne in Phoenix, Arizona., 6. When they get to San Francisco, I plan to take them out for Chinese food., 7. If we go to Green's Restaurant for vegetarian food, even Jane will like the brussels sprouts., 8. Sometimes I think that July will never get here., 9. I received a letter from Sandy last Tuesday.

P. 444
1. I found a book of rhymes at the library in Milwaukee., 2. The book was published in London, England., 3. The book contained rhymes from the countries of Kenya, Ecuador, and even New Zealand., 4. My favorite poem told of a crocodile that lived at the corner of Cricket Court and Bee Boulevard., 5. We started driving across the Painted Desert Wednesday., 6. Thursday morning we saw a beautiful sunrise., 7. We decided to drive to the Rocky Mountains on Sunday., 8. We finally reached El Paso, Texas, on Tuesday.

P. 445
Period placement: 1. end of sentence, 2. end of sentence, 3. end of sentence, 4. after Ms., end of sentence, 5. after Dr., after B., 6. after Dr., 7. after T., R., end of sentence, 8. after J., B., 9. after N., after St., 10. After I., A., B.

p. 446
1. My name is C. M. Dooley. I live at 4338 Market Blvd. in Alabaster, Alabama. My birthday is on Oct. 27., 2. Suzy E. Ziegler requests the pleasure of your company at a party in honor of her friend, Maryanne M. Marbles. Please come to the country club at 23 Country Club Dr. at 4:00 on Tues., Apr. 14., 3. The J. Harold Calabases take great pride in announcing the birth of their twins, Heather H. Calabas and J. Harold Calabas, Jr. This happy event took place on Mon., Aug. 23, at 3:00, 4. F. A. Jones has been appointed assistant to the president of Bags and Boxes, Inc. This store is located at 45 Ninety-ninth Ave.

p. 447
1. Three plants to avoid are poison ivy, poison, oak, and poison sumac., 2. "Steven, I see that you have some poison oak growing in your yard.", 3. "Your dog, cat, or rabbit can pick it up on its fur and rub against you," Wesley said., 4. Yes, it will make your skin burn, itch, and swell., 5. Dana put his clothes in a hamper, and his mother got a rash from touching the clothes., 6. Poison ivy looks like a shrub, a vine, or a small plant., 7. Poison ivy has green leaves in clusters of three, and so does poison oak.

p. 448
Comma placement: 1. after interesting, 2. after upstairs, 3. after open, 4. after room, 5. after First, 6. after Next, 7. after while, 8. after addition, 9. after lived, after played, 10. after footsteps, after whispers, 11. after cellar, 12. after Soon

p. 449
Comma placement: First letter: after Albuquerque, after April 22, after Dear Ernest, after Your friend,; Second letter: after Albuquerque, after May 3, after Dear David, after Sincerely

p. 450
1. ?, 2. !, 3. !, 4. ?, 5. ?, 6. ?, 7. !, 8. !, 9. !, 10. ?, 11. !, 12. ?, 13. !, 14. ?, 15. !, 16. ?, 17. !, 18. !

p. 451
Apostrophe placement: 1. Chen's, 2. children's, 3. boys', 4. can't, 5. Won't, Colon placement: 6. 3:30, 7. 6:00, 8. 7:15, 9. Dear Ms. Parker:

p. 452
1. You're, you'd, 3. You'll, 4. It's, 5. won't, 6. aren't, 7. mustn't, 8. don't, 9. shouldn't, 10. mustn't

p. 453
1. "Have you heard of the Nobel Peace Prize?" asked Emi., 2. "Yes. Mother Teresa and Nelson Mandela have won it," replied Jan.,

3. "But do you know who Nobel was?" Emi asked., 4. Jan responded, "No, I guess I don't.", 5. "He invented dynamite," stated Emi., 6. "It seems weird," said Jan, "to name a peace prize for the inventor of dynamite.", 7. "In fact," Emi said, "dynamite was once called Nobel's Safety Blasting Powder.", 8. "Nobel patented the blasting powder in 1867," Emi continued., 9. "He did not want dynamite used for war," he said., 10. He added, "Nobel once said that war is the horror of horrors and the greatest of all crimes.", 11. "How did the Nobel Prizes get started?" asked Jan., 12. Emi said, "In his will, Nobel said that his money should be used to establish prizes in five areas: physics, chemistry, medicine, literature, and peace.", 13. "Sometimes a prize is shared by two or three people," he continued., 14. "I'd like to know more about some of the winners," Jan said., 15. "Jimmy Carter, the 39th president of the United States, won the Nobel Peace Prize in 2002," replied Emi.

p. 454
1. A Wrinkle in Time, 2. "Camping in the Mountains", 3. "It's Not Easy Being Green", 4. Sounder, 5. The New York Times, 6. Humpty Dumpty, 7. "The Little House", 8. "Why I Like Gymnastics", 9. The Little Prince, 10. "The Owl and the Pussycat", 11. The sixth chapter in that book is called "Animal Language", 12. A book I really like is If I Were in Charge of the World by Judith Viorst.

p. 455
1. wisdom teeth, 2. armchair, sunshine, 3. ten-year-old, 4. sky-high, birthplace, 5. slave driver, bloodhounds, 6. storm cellar, smokehouse, 7. hand-to-mouth, run-ins, 8. folksinger, notebook, 9. run-of-the mill, wallpaper, 10. family tree, best-selling

p. 456
1. synonyms, 2. antonyms, 3. antonyms, 4. synonyms, 5. antonyms, 6. synonyms, 7. antonyms, 8. antonyms, 9. antonyms

p. 457
1. success, failure; 2. left back, promoted; 3. solution, problem; 4. burning, ice-cold; Answers in chart may vary. end: finish, begin; fast: quick, slow; simple: easy, complicated; gloomy: sad, upbeat; concealed: hidden, open; unsure: undecided, convinced

p. 458
Definitions may vary. 1. unearthed, uncovered; 2. nonexistent, does not exist; 3. unable, incapable; 4. discontinued, stopped; 5. improbable, unlikely; 6. inability, failure; 7. resell, 8. insincere, 9. discomfort, 10. mislead, 11. prepay, 12. unorganized or disorganized

p. 459
1.–12. Sentences will vary. New words: 1. sailor, 2. fearless or fearful, 3. kindness, 4. mighty, 5. happiness, 6. lighten, 7. cloudy, 8. suddenly, 9. quietly, 10. player, playful, 11. wonderful, 12. teacher

p. 460
1. air, 2. you, 3. course, 4. would, 5. need, 6. main, 7. mist, 8. can, can; 9. object, object; 10. present, present; 11. spring, spring

p. 461
1. week, 2. way, 3. find, 4. know, 5. do, 6. through, 7. see, 8. beat, 9. one; 10.–21. Sentences will vary. Suggested homophones: 10. pale, 11. sun, 12. flee, 13. straight, 14. too or to, 15. meat, 16. lead, 17. side, 18. blue, 19. him, 20. pain, 21. horse

p. 462
1. to move in a boat; 2. a ship, boat, or aircraft; 3. something a person sets out to do; 4. moved past or went by; 5. gave a name to; 6. arrived at or came to; 7. ended or finished

p. 463
1. to, 2. well, 3. It's, 4. your, 5. Two, there, 6. its, 7. You're, 8. too, 9. good, 10. They're, 11. well, 12. their, 13. it's, 14. two, 15. They're

p. 464
1. will, 2. a, 3. are, 4. anything, 5. anybody, 6. ever, 7. any, 8. There are no more than four kinds of poisonous snakes in North America., 9. It won't do any good to try to run away from a rattlesnake.

p. 465
Sentences will vary. 1. Our family was packing suitcases., 2. Everyone was looking forward to our annual vacation., 3. When all the suitcases were packed, Mom loaded the trunk., 4. We left at noon on Saturday., 5. We drove to the freeway., 6. We stopped often because my little brother was ill., 7. The first day of travel seemed fine, though., 8. The second day we visited historical places., 9. Everyone enjoyed the rest of the trip, too., 10. Everyone welcomed us back.

p. 466
Senses may vary. 1. blue, sight; 2. cool, touch; 3. large, sight; 4. loud, hearing; 5. chlorine, smell; 6. jagged, touch or sight; 7. rough, touch; 8. soft, touch; 9. warm, touch; 10. delicious, taste

p. 467
1. wonderful, 2. Brave, 3. fascinating, 4. hilarious, 5. smile, 6. cheap, 7. soggy, 8. nagged, 9. stubborn, 10. silly, 11. A disaster is more serious than a problem., 12. An antique is worth more than something old.

p. 468
Answers may vary. 1. neutral, 2. positive, 3. neutral, 4. negative, 5. negative, 6. negative, 7. negative, 8. positive, 9. negative, 10. positive, 11.–13. Sentences may vary.

p. 469
Answers will vary. Possible responses are given. 1. I was very nervous., 2. As I looked out over the audience, my heart felt heavy., 3. I touched the piano keys, and my fingers were stiff., 4. Luckily for me, the performance went very well., 5. As I played the last notes, I knew that I had done well., 6.–7. Responses will vary.

p. 470
1. as fast as the wind, 2. They were able to whisper, "Hurry! Hurry!", 3. It rode beside him like a good friend., 4. They were enemies that caught at his sleeves., 5.–7. Sentences will vary.

p. 471
Possible responses: Main Idea: how optical illusions occur; Detail: brain compares images you see to images in memory; Detail: brain cannot choose between possible interpretations; Detail: bending of light creates mirages that fool eyes

p. 472
1. b, 2. a, 3. b, 4. a; Students should draw a line through these sentences: My mother went to India last year., Cinnamon and ginger come from India., The Ganges is a river in India.

p. 473
1. M, 2. D, 3. D, 4. D; Paragraph: Main Idea: Many large factories have been built in southern Brazil., Detail: Some of these manufacturing plants produce cars, trucks, and farm equipment., Detail: Other products of these new factories include shoes, textiles, construction equipment, and leather products., Detail: Many of the goods produced in the factories of southern Brazil are shipped to the United States.

P. 474
1. He had a slow and serious nature.
2. He was already an expert rider.,
3. The Crow Indians had stolen some Sioux horses., 4. It was considered braver to push an enemy off a horse than to shoot an arrow from far away., 5. Slow had jabbed the Crow with his stick., 6. They had won the battle.

P. 476
1. Marc is sad because his friend Thomas is leaving., 2. Marc finds a valuable coin that gives him an adventure and makes him happy., 3. Marc and Mr. Ortiz have dialogue.

P. 478
Answers will vary.

P. 479
1. Thanksgiving, 2. Thanksgiving has to be my favorite holiday., 3. delicious aromas of turkey roasting and pumpkin pies baking; lovely autumn colors of orange, gold, red, and brown; sound of children laughing; music being played

P. 482
1. soft-drink machines in the park; 2. The writer is against having soft-drink machines in the park.; 3. Soft drinks have too much sugar in them, and they have no nutritional value. With soft-drink machines, the city has the problem of cleaning up the empty cans that are sometimes left in the park.; 4. polite but firm

P. 485
1. pop popcorn in a microwave oven; 2. Two items are listed, special microwave popcorn and a microwave oven.; 3. Remove the plastic overwrap from the bag, and set it in the center of the microwave.; 4. Set the microwave to full power.; 5. Set the timer and start the oven.; 6. Shake the bag before opening.

P. 488
1. Storing food in cans was developed in England in 1810.; 2. Details may vary. Possible response: A British merchant named Peter Durchand came up with the idea. No one invented a can opener until 50 years later.; 3. The can opener that we use today was invented about 1870.; 4. Details may vary. Possible response: It was invented by an American named William W. Lyman. It has only been changed once since it was invented.

P. 491
1. The Tasady tribe and the Ik tribe are two examples of people still living in the Stone Age.; 2. the Tasady and the Ik; 3. Both are still primitive. Neither tribe knew about the outside world until recently. Both live in mountain areas.; 4. The Tasady live in caves, but the Ik live in grass huts. The Tasady have plenty of food, but the Ik are always struggling to find food. The Tasady have a good chance of surviving, but the Ik do not.; 5. contrast

P. 494
1. a girl named Katharine goes back in time; 2. Merlin reversed Katharine's wish in the story.; 3. Katharine would have won the jousting tournament instead of Sir Lancelot. Sir Lancelot would have been dismissed from the Queen's order of knights. King Arthur's Round Table would have been dissolved and never heard of again.

P. 496
Order of reasons will vary.

P. 497
1. how Mr. and Mrs. Hak-Tak made doubles of themselves; 2. It was a very clever thing to do.; 3. Keeping the doubles nearby was a clever way of protecting themselves.; 4. Building a house next door for their doubles gave Mr. and Mrs. Hak-Tak extra help around the farm.; 5. Their doubles became Mr. and Mrs. Hak-Tak's best friends.

P. 500
1. Wisconsin should have a "Caddie Woodlawn Day" to celebrate the trust between Caddie and her Indian friends.; 2. "Caddie Woodlawn Day" would remind people to settle problems by peaceful means. Such a holiday would give people a reason to practice their ancestors' customs.; 3. The state legislature should vote in favor of this idea.

P. 504
1. five, 2. verb, 3. noun, 4. The balloon . . . 3, Have you . . . 5

P. 505
Sentences will vary. 1. optical, 2. reflection, 3. magician, 4. nature

P. 506
1.–9. Synonyms will vary.
10.–12. Sentences will vary.

P. 507
1. Anthony, 2. water, 3. New, 4. Scotland, 5. Rio, 6. United, 7. literature, 8. horses, 9. Gila, 10. Frost, 11. Industrial, 12. Victoria

P. 508
1. four, 2. T 232, 3. United States History, 4. United States History, 5. Origins, 6. Black Americans

P. 509
Answers may vary. 1. Sports, 2. Reference Materials, 3. Arts and Entertainment, 4. Shopping, 5. Games, 6. Arts and Entertainment, 7. Science or Reference Materials, 8. Reference Materials

P. 510
1. Giants: In Myth and Legend, 2. King Press, Inc., 3. 1983, United States of America, 4. 6, 5. 2, 6. 51, 7. 73, 8. 17

P. 511
1. two; hurricanes and tornadoes, 2. causes of the storms, 3. when and where the storms strike, 4. tie it down securely, 5. They could be broken by flying objects., 6. when the authorities announce that it's safe.

P. 512
Zeus's symbols were king's scepter, thunderbolt, oak tree, eagle.

P. 513
Notes will vary but should focus on main ideas and include abbreviations whenever possible. 1. Responses will vary but should include a reference to key points or main ideas., 2. Responses will vary but should include abbreviations for North America and California., 3. Responses will vary but should include that good notes help the reader to remember key ideas.

P. 514
Answers may vary. Who: people from the northern United States; What: visit warmer places; Where: Florida's beaches; When: during the winter; Why: escape the cold; beaches and tourist attractions; Summary: Many Americans living in the north travel to Florida during the winter to escape the cold climate. They like to visit the beaches and many tourist attractions the state has to offer.

P. 515
1. Greg was angry because his mother had made him miss a movie with friends. 2. Greg was glad that he had not gone to the movies and gotten into trouble.

P. 516
1. c, 2. e, 3. a, 4. d, 5. b, 6. f

P. 517
The Job of a Mother Bird; I. Find a Good Place for a Nest, A. correct, B. Warm enough, C. Out of reach of cats; II. Make the Nest, A. Big enough, B. correct, C. Sides tall enough, D. Inside soft enough; III. Take Care of Eggs, A. Sit on them, B. Keep them warm

P. 518
p. I. Cells, A. Smallest living parts of body, B. Building blocks, C. Many different kinds, 1. Bone cells, 2. Skin cells; II. Tissues, A. Groups of cells that work together, B. Many different kinds, 1. Fat tissue, 2. Muscle tissue, C. Each kind has a different function; III. Organs, A. Tissues that work together, B. Each has its own job, C. Need to work with other organs

P. 519
Topic and detail sentences will vary but should be related to the chosen outline.

P. 520
1. Elizabeth Dixon, 2. Volume 18, 3. Owl, November 1986, 4. www.owltime.net, 5. 24 March 2005

P. 521
Answers will vary. Possible responses are given. 1. Our Old Superstitions, 2. the superstition of knocking on wood, 3. the superstition of opening umbrellas indoors, 4. The custom is 4,000 years old. It began with some Native American tribes of North America. The oak tree was believed to be the home of the sky god.

WRITING SKILLS

Answers to the practice paper exercises questions may vary, but examples are provided here to give you an idea of how your child may respond.

P. 524
Possible responses: 1. Susie's sister 2. the preparations for the party 3. She was surprised and happy. 4. They wore polka-dot party hats, ate, laughed, danced.

P. 525
Possible responses: 1. what happens when the writer gets a Mohawk haircut 2. getting the haircut 3. the reaction of his mother 4. the reaction of his teacher 5. what happens during the school play

P. 526
1. none 2. cause: Two grizzly bears suddenly appeared, effect: The men were immediately frightened. 3. cause: The men fired, effect: One bear was wounded. 4. cause: The other bear was not hurt, effect: It ran away. 5. cause: The wounded bear was very angry, effect: It charged Captain Lewis. 6. cause: Because Lewis still had time to reload, effect: He lived to tell the tale. 7. none 8. cause: If you bother or frighten a grizzly, effect: It will attack. 9. cause: It goes its own way, effect: A person avoids trouble. 10. cause: Because these bears do not climb trees, effect: Many people have escaped angry grizzlies.

p. 527

1. He had a slow and serious nature.
2. He was already an expert rider.
3. The Crow Indians had stolen some Sioux horses. 4. It was considered braver to push an enemy off a horse than to shoot an arrow from far away. 5. Slow had jabbed the Crow with his stick. 6. They had won the battle.

p. 528

Be sure that answers are synonyms for the underlined words. Possible responses: 1. huge 2. approximately 3. raising 4. labored diligently 5. farmed 6. The situation; difficult 7. stores 8. enterprising 9. Three decades; nation
10, 11, 12. Responses will vary. Be sure that synonyms are vivid.

p. 529–530

Last weekend I traveled more
hundred
than a ⟨hunderd⟩ years back in time.

No, I didn't find a time machine—I

went to the Dickens Fair in San
fair
Francisco. The ⟨fare⟩ was held on Pier
famous
45 at the ⟨famuos⟩ Fisherman's

Wharf. The whole wharf was

crowded with people, and everyone
great
seemed to be having a ⟨grate⟩ time!

The people who worked at the

Dickens Fair were all dressed the
England
way people dressed in ⟨Engaland⟩

when Charles Dickens was alive.

The women wore long dresses, and

most of the men had fancy hats.

These people all spoke with English

accents and used special phrases. My

parents especially liked being greeted

by people who said, "Hello fair

lady" and "Good day, kind, sir."

there were some special booths at

the dickens Fair. My older sister
hours   *jewelry*
spent ⟨ours⟩ looking at the ⟨jewlry⟩
pair
Finally, she chose a ⟨pare⟩ of earrings.

I had fun looking at all the booths,
buy
but I didn't ⟨by⟩ anything.

p. 538

1. Benny wrote "The Mysterious Atlantic Ocean Fish" to tell his story in his own words and to explain how he became friends with Sammy. The very first sentence says, "I'm Benny, and here's my story."
2. Benny begins by explaining why he doesn't want to be friends with Sammy. He says Sammy is too young to be included in games with his other friends. 3. Benny says that he and Sammy have grown close. He goes on to say that they like to trade books and play video games together. 4. Be sure your child correctly summarizes the significant events of the story, paraphrasing as needed.

p. 539

1. Benny uses words such as *I, me,* and *my* to show that he is writing about his personal experiences. 2. A younger kid, Sammy, lives across the hall and wants to be Benny's friend. Benny thinks Sammy is too young to be his friend. Then Benny's dad invites Sammy to the beach. With Benny's help, Sammy brings home an ocean fish. Sammy asks Benny for help when the fish gets sick. 3. Benny adds fresh water to the fish bowl. He saves the fish, and in the process, he and Sammy become friends. 4. Benny shares his funny inner thoughts with us by talking directly to us. When the fish gets sick, he says something really funny: "I start making funeral plans." Also, Benny keeps our interest by telling us about the fish. We want to find out what happens to it. 5. In the first paragraph, Benny tells us why he and Sammy cannot be friends and why he doesn't want to introduce Sammy to his other friends. In the last paragraph, Benny ties up the loose ends of the story and tells us that he and Sammy are now friends and that they play ball with Benny's friends.

p. 544

Time-order words and phrases may vary. First, pick out your favorite color of balloon. Stretch the balloon several times. Then, blow it up slowly. The next thing you do is tie a knot in the balloon. Then, tie a ribbon around the knot. Last, hang it from the ribbon. 1. how to blow up a balloon 2. Pick out your favorite color of balloon.

p. 545

1. two items—a microwave oven and popcorn 2. Take the plastic overwrap off and place the bag in the microwave. 3. Set the timer and start the microwave. 4. Stop the microwave when the popping slows down. 5. Remove the bag from the microwave and shake it.

p. 546

Time-order words and phrases may vary. To wash your family car, there are six steps you should follow. First, get a bucket. Then, fill the bucket with soapy water. Next, hose down the car to get it wet. After that, wash the car, using the soapy water and a soft cloth or sponge. The next thing you do is dry the car. Finally, shine the windows and any chrome trim.

p. 547

Possible responses: 1. the first one— It gives very detailed directions, as if this were the first time the reader had ever chopped an onion. 2. the second one—It assumes that the reader has done this before; and therefore, it leaves out some of the details. 3. how to peel the onion; directions on being very careful not to cut fingers; an explanation of what a cutting board is; more explanation of what "lengthwise" and "crosswise" mean

p. 548

1. a. You'll need 101 index cards. You'll need a colored marker.
b. You'll need 101 index cards, and you'll need a colored marker.
2. a. Print the name of a state or a state capital on each index card. Print the rules on the last index card. b. Print the name of a state or a state capital on each index card, and print the rules on the last index card. 3. a. Put the marker away. Put all the cards in an envelope. b. Put the marker away, and put all the cards in an envelope. 4. a. This game is for small groups. Up to three students may play. b. This game is for small groups, and up to three students may play. 5. a. Players mix up the cards. They lay the cards face down. b. Players mix up the cards, and they lay the cards face down.

p. 549–550

Do you have a little brother or
sister? Do you sometimes help take

care of little children? If so, you

might want to make a set of special

building blocks. These blocks are

large and light enough for even a
easily
two-year-old to handle ⟨easaly⟩ They

are sturdy and colorful, and they

can be lots of fun ⊙

To make a set of blocks, you

need as many half-gallon milk
as
cartons ∧ you can collect. you also
  =
need sheets of colorful paper and

some glue.

For each block, use two of your

milk cartons ⊙ Cut the tops off both

cartons ⊙ Then wash them thoroughly
         ∧
and let them dry ⊙ Be sure your

cartons are completely clean.

When both cartons are dry, push
                          carton
the open end of one ⟨cartoon⟩ into

the other carton ⊙ Press the two

cartons together as far as possible.

You should end up with a block that

is the size of a single carton, with

both ends closed and with

extra-long sides. Then cover each

block, using glue and the paper you

have chosen ⊙

p. 558

1. This how-to paper teaches you how to decorate a T-shirt. 2. The materials needed to decorate a T-shirt include 1 white T-shirt, an 8 in. x 8 in. piece of drawing paper, pen or pencil, 2 safety pins, transfer paper, and 3 or 4 felt-tipped pens in different colors. 3. The first thing to think about is where to wear the T-shirt. 4. The second thing to think about is what to put on the T-shirt. 5. The third thing to think about is the T-shirt's colors.
6. Answers will vary, but look for indications of understanding, such as a clear description of the T-shirt and a corresponding illustration.

p. 559

1. The writer states the purpose of the paper clearly, lists materials, gives clear step-by-step instructions, and gives helpful hints and details. 2. Sequence words such as now, first, and second help the reader understand the order of the steps. 3. The writer lists the materials so they can be collected before starting the project. That saves time and makes the project easier to do.

4. The numbered steps make the complicated process easier to understand. It shows that each step builds on a previous step and that each needs to be done in order.
5. Pictures and answers may vary. Check pictures to determine if your child understood the instructions.

P. 564
1. Paul Bunyan and Juan 2. They discuss solving the problem of cold food in the big dining hall. 3. a. He is Paul Bunyan's helper. b. He is smaller than Paul.

P. 565–566
1. the wife, the husband, and the baby 2. their home and field. 3. A husband who thinks his wife can't do anything right trades jobs with her. 4. The husband and the wife agree to trade jobs. 5. The baby's diaper ends up on the baby's head.

P. 567
Possible responses: 1. a. "You know I'll be sure to do it later." b. "This is the best time of day for a swim." 2. a. Sal ran out, wearing his bathing suit. b. After his swim, Sal fell asleep. 3. a. "He's always into some mischief, but I know he's a good boy deep down." b. "Where are you going in such a hurry. You know you have chores to do."

P. 568
Possible responses: 1. Gabrielle had a bad toothache on the right side of her mouth. 2. Her mother drove her to the dentist's office on the other side of town. 3. Gabrielle did not have to wait for very long. 4. The dentist's assistant had her sit in the big chair in the first room. 5. The assistant took an X-ray of Gabrielle's mouth. 6. The dentist looked at the X-ray on the light table.

P. 569–570

One of Paul Bunyan's helpers stared up at Paul and shook his head. "How will we ever get all this hot food (two)to the tables?" he asked. The dining hall is so big that the food gets cold before we can serve it⊙" ¶ "Why, that's easy," answered Paul⊙ ¶ "We'll just put roller skates on the ponies. Then the ponies can skate in quickly and deliver the food before it gets cold." ¶ "What a great

idea!" cried Paul Bunyan's helpers.

¶ The next night, however, Paul and his helpers discovered that his idea wasn't great after all. The ponies weren't good roller-skaters. They spilled most of the food, and then they stopped to eat the spilled food.

¶ "What a mess!" exclaimed Paul.

¶ "What will we do?" asked his helpers. ˇ "Well ˇ" said Paul, "first, we'll have to clean up the dining hall. Then, I think we should build tracks between the (rose)rows of tables. We can use freight trains to deliver the food."

P. 577
1. Tanisha and Jemma live in a future time when students take field trips to Mars and have clones. Also, kids play in anti-gravity chambers and can download experiences from and into their clones. 2. In the beginning of the story, Tanisha is helping Jemma put on her leg brace. Later, Jemma smooths her school uniform. These are clues that the girls are in Jemma's bedroom getting ready for school. Other clues in the story, such as the clone, suggest that the time is in the future. 3. Jemma hurt her leg in the anti-gravity chamber and won't be able to pass her physical fitness test. If she doesn't take and pass the test, she won't be able to go on the class trip to Mars. 4. Tanisha suggests that Jemma let her clone practice for the physical fitness test. Then Jemma can download the experience. 5. Be sure that your child correctly summarizes the significant events of the story, paraphrasing as needed.

P. 578
1. The writer uses dialogue to make the story seem like a typical school day for two good friends. 2. The writer includes fantastic details about the future. There is an anti-gravity chamber, a class trip to Mars, and clones that can go to school with their owners. 3. The writer uses dialogue to make the unbelievable seem believable. The story is told through a conversation between the girls. 4. The mood of the story is playful. First, Tanisha

teases Jemma about playing in the anti-gravity chamber. Both girls laugh about the time Jemma sent her clone to take her French test and the clone had a meltdown and caught on fire. Finally, Tanisha teases Jemma again, saying that if the clone passes the fitness test, the clone can go on the school trip.

P. 583
1. The first time LeAnn went to visit her friend Vanessa, she noticed how much Vanessa's furniture was like her own. 2. both are made of pine, both were chosen by an aunt 3. one is a rolltop and one has a flat surface.

P. 584
1. the Tasady and the Ik tribes. 2. Neither tribe knew about the outside world until recently, both still live in the Stone Age, both live in the mountains. 3. The Tasady live in caves, and the Ilk live in grass huts. The Tasady have plenty of food, but the Ik do not. The Tasady have a good chance of surviving, but the Ik may not. 4. contrasts

P. 585
Responses will vary. Be sure that likenesses and differences are appropriate.

P. 586
1. formal 2. informal 3. informal 4. formal 5. formal 6. informal 7. formal 8. formal 9. formal 10. informal 11. formal

P. 587
1. The Pygmies live in the forest in Africa, and they hunt there. 2. Pygmy men are about four and a half feet tall, and the women are even smaller. 3. They are the smallest people in the world, and their small size helps them to hide. 4. Children the same age call boys "brother," and they call girls "sister." 5. Pygmies look at a broken branch, and they can tell which animal has been there. 6. Pygmies know a lot about plants, and they can tell which are good to eat.

P. 588–589

The first time Lee went ˄to visit his Vladimir, he noticed how much Vlad's furniture was like his own. He saw that the desk in Vlad's room was made of pine, just like Lee's desk. Vlad's mom had chosen the

desk, just as lee's Lee's mom had chosen Lee's. Lee also noticed the bed in Vlad's room. Vlad explained that it had been his grandfather's bed. Lee remembered that the bed in his own room had once belonged to his dad's dad⊙

As Lee looked at Vlad's bed, he pictured his own bed in his mind. Lee's bed was made of brass and steel. It had been made in England more (then)than 100 years ago. Vlad's desk, on the other hand, was dark wood with a tall (hedboard)headboard⊙ It had been made in Russia about 60 years ago. Lee realized that he would rather have a bed like Vlad's. The headboard was good for holding books.

P. 596
Guide your child in organizing the information in a clear manner. How American Black Bears and Polar Bears Are Alike: Both are large, smart bears.; Both can be found in Canada.; Both have heavy fur coats.; Both have a good sense of smell.; Both use their sense of smell to find food.; Both eat small animals.; Both sometimes eat dead animals.; Both hibernate.; Both have young that are born blind.; Both commonly give birth to twins.; Both have young that grow quickly.; Both are endangered.; Both are models for stuffed toy bears.
How American Black Bears and Polar Bears Are Different: American black bears live in most of the United States; polar bears live along the coasts of Canada, Greenland, and Siberia, and on islands in the Arctic Ocean.; American black bears live in forests; polar bears live where there is ice.; The adult male black bear is between 3 and 4 feet tall and weighs between 135 and 350 lbs.; the adult male polar bear stands 8 to 11 feet tall and weighs more than 1,000 lbs.; Black bears like berries, nuts, grass, and other plants; polar bears are meat-eaters that feed mainly on seals.; Black bears are

chocolate brown, cinnamon, blond, and silver gray; polar bears have fur that looks white or yellow.; Black bears hibernate in the winter; only pregnant female polar bears hibernate.; Black bears are usually born in January or February; polar bears are often born in December.; Black bear cubs weigh less than 1 pound at birth; new born polar bear cubs weigh 1½ pounds.

p. 597

1. The writer gets out attention by linking the subject of the paper to something we know and love, namely, teddy bears. 2. The writer tells us a story about how President Roosevelt's meeting with a real bear ended and how teddy bears were named as a result. 3. The color of the bears' fur is discussed. 4. The writer uses the bears' powerful sense of smell to introduce the topic of what bears eat. 5. In the last paragraph, the writer summarizes how American black bears and polar bears are alike. The writer ties the last paragraph to the first paragraph by saying that both kinds of bears are "wonderful models for the stuffed bears we love so much."

p. 603

1. a box turtle 2. a. hinged lower shell b. can pull its legs, head, and tail inside its shell c. eats earthworms, insects, berries, and green leafy vegetables 3. smooth—touch, hard—touch 4. rustle—hearing, loud—hearing

p. 604–605

1. Thanksgiving 2. Thanksgiving has to be my favorite holiday.
3. a. aromas of turkey roasting and pumpkin pies baking b. autumn colors of orange, gold, red, and brown flowers c. the sound of children laughing and music playing
4. a kitchen just before a special feast 5. Did you ever walk into the kitchen of a good cook just before a special feast?

p. 606

A. 1. left to right 2. top to bottom
B. Responses will vary. Be sure that the organization is appropriate.

p. 607

1. blue—sight; suit—sight 2. cool—touch; water—sight 3. large—sight; black—sight 4. loud—hearing 5. hair—sight; chlorine—smell 6. rough—touch, sight; jagged—touch, sight 7. foot—sight, touch; yelled—hearing 8. soft—touch, sight; bandage—sight, touch 9. warm—touch; soft—touch 10. delicious—taste; sandwich—taste, sight, smell

p. 608

Possible responses: 1. Young Soren rolled in the grass under a tree and watched the sailboats. 2. The ships were going to Baltimore or sailing out to sea. 3. Young Soren did not know what geography and arithmetic books were. 4. He had never been to school or learned how to read. 5. The hill was a good place to stand and watch the boats. 6. Soren visited his grandmother in the summer and his uncle in the winter.

p. 609–610

Aunt jane said she would have a surprise for us last saturday, but she refused to give us any hints. Just after breakfast, we heard a low humming sound in our driveway. It was followed by an unusual, squeaky car horn. "A car! A car!" my sister shouted. "Aunt Jane's surprise is a Car!"

We all rushed out to see Aunt Jane's new car, and what a surprise it was! Her "new" car was more than 50 years old. It was a beautiful 1938 whippet. Its bright green surface shimmered in the sunlight. Its long hood stretched forward elegantly, and its whitewall tires gleamed on our dusty driveway.

"Oh, jane," said mom. "What a great car! May we get in?"

"Of course," laughed Aunt Jane, and she clicked the front door open for us. The inside of the car was dark and cool and filled with the soft smell of old (leather).

"Let's go for a drive," suggested dad. "Who wants to ride out to Lake barton?"

p. 618

1. The writer describes the Gonzalez family's "vacation" experience at a museum.
2. Everyone in the family wants to go to a different place on the family vacation. 3. Miguel wants to see the ocean. Angela wants to visit the White House. Mrs. Gonzalez wants to go to Arizona to see a rodeo. Mr. Gonzalez wants to visit Yellowstone National Park. 4. Mrs. Gonzalez solves her family's problem by taking them to a museum where they can see paintings of all the places they want to go. 5. Be sure that your child correctly summarizes the significant events of the story, paraphrasing as needed.

p. 619

1. The writer uses descriptive action words, such as "soared," "swooped," "squirming," "gripped," "steaming," and "shimmered." 2. The writer uses descriptive phrases, such as "blue-green water looked as smooth as silk," "a net filled with slick, squirming fish," and "the White House shimmered in the light." 3. Possible answer: The seagulls' feathers combed through the strands of fiery sunlight like soft, white fingers. 4. Possible answer: The spouting geyser made a mighty mountain of steam and water. 5. Another surprise ending might be that Mrs. Gonzalez entered a travel contest on the Internet and won! The grand prize was an all-expense-paid family trip around the United States.

p. 624

Possible responses:
1. Protection from Ultraviolet Rays
2. how ultraviolet rays are harmful
3. how to make your own suntan lotion 4. b, c, d

p. 625

Possible responses: 1. Some Superstitions and Their Origins
2. knocking on wood for good luck
3. opening umbrellas indoors is bad luck 4. Response should include one of the following: The custom is four thousand years old. The Indians thought the oak was the dwelling place of a sky god. They thought that knocking on an oak tree was a way of contacting the sky god and being forgiven for boasting.

p. 626

1. a 2. b 3. a 4. a 5. c 6. b 7. c 8. In 1980 Reinhold Messner climbed Mt. Everest alone, without bottled oxygen, a ladder, a rope, or a radio.

p. 627

1. c 2. e 3. a 4. d 5. b 6. f

p. 628

Possible responses: 1. For homework, did you read about the Boston Tea Party? 2. On December 16, 1773, patriots threw tea into Boston Harbor. 3. When the dumping occurred, the tide was going out. 4. Lead lined the chests. 5. Painted with Chinese lacquer, they looked beautiful. 6. Except for about 50 of the crates, these were all simple wooden boxes. 7. Of an ornate Chinese design, these 50 were large boxes. 8. In Boston Harbor an explorer plans to look for the boxes. 9. Probably the tide has moved the chests farther out into the harbor.

p. 629–630

The Dead Sea is the world's saltyest body of water. Usually, sea water has a salt content of 3.5 percent. The Dead sea is 28 percent salt, or eight times as salty as the oceans. By comparison, the Great Salt Lake in utah is six times as salty as Sea water. The water of the Dead Sea is so salty that salt columns come up out of the water in strange formations. Many people say these salt formations look like oddly formed, discolored icebergs.

the salt in the Dead Sea helped give the huge lake its name. The salt in the water kills almost every form of life that is swept into the Dead Sea. The salt is also the cause of the Dead Sea's most well-known quality: its buoyancy. According to Rupert o. Matthews in his book The atlas of natural Wonders, "Sinking and diving are impossible, but it is far easier to swim here than in any other stretch of water."

p. 637

1. The problem is that there aren't enough left-handed desks or other specially designed items available to left-handers. 2. Scientists are not sure if left-handedness relates to genes because research shows that if both parents are left-handed, about half of their children are right-handed. Also, identical twins have the same genes, but almost 20 percent of them have different handedness. 3. Tools made by Stone Age people show scientists that the number of left-handed and right-handed people used to be about equal. 4. Be sure that your child identifies the report's main ideas and include significant details.

p. 638

1. The writer gives an example of what it is like to be left-handed in a right-handed world. This example makes us want to read more. 2. The writer invites the reader in the puzzle and grabs the reader's attention by asking that short question. 3. The writer uses simpler words to define each word that the reader might not know. 4. The writer includes facts from scientists' work to show that he or she did research for this report. The facts also give interesting information about the kinds of questions scientists are asking, what they know, and what they don't know. 5. The last paragraph repeats the subject of the first paragraph. That helps tie the beginning of the report to the ending. The conclusion also brings the reader into the report. The writer says, "Next year you might want to join them."

Test Prep

p. 650-653

1. B 2. The balloon will get smaller since the air escapes when it deflates. 3. J 4. B 5. G 6. C 7. The fuel reservoir holds gasoline. It is the tank. 8. H 9. B 10. An epidemic is when many people, animals, or plants get sick. 11. H 12. A 13. F 14. to travel

p. 654-657

1. B 2. H 3. C 4. The Arctic ice rests on the ocean. 5. H 6. C 7. They are in greatest danger right after the baby's birth. 8. F 9. B 10. J 11. Peggy should inspect engine 5 first, after she signs in. 12. C 13. H 14. B 15. The story takes place in southwestern Colorado.

p. 658-661

1. A 2. G 3. The story is mostly about how Bartholdi got his idea from a girl he once saw. 4. A 5. H 6. A 7. The main idea is that Martin did not realize how hard it is to take care of a dog. 8. H 9. B 10. This story is mostly about the four types of poisonous snakes found in the United States. 11. F 12. B 13. This passage is mostly about how Levi Strauss invented the first pair of blue jeans.

p. 662-665

1. Missy rubbed her eyes because she was trying to wake up. 2. C 3. G 4. D 5. F 6. She was excited because she looked forward to growing her own vegetables. 7. B 8. She will be pleasantly surprised. 9. He will probably write a thank-you note to his aunt. 10. J

p. 666-671

1. D 2. There were 27.8 million cars. 3. It is about 6 billion. 4. G 5. C 6. J 7. D 8. J 9. B 10. Inventions that did not make money. 11. F 12. Alur felt angry. 13. B 14. It was performed to bring happiness and a feeling of connection with those who died.

p. 672-673

1. B 2. F 3. D 4. F 5. D

p. 674-681

SA. B 1. B 2. A sphinx is an imaginary animal with a human head and the body of a lion. 3. H 4. C 5. F 6. A 7. H 8. D 9. G 10. He arrived at the hospital in time. 11. stranded 12. A 13. F 14. C 15. G 16. after they came to Europe or before they came to America 17. D 18. G 19. B 20. H 21. the Chinese 22. D 23. F 24. B 25. H 26. D 27. H 28. C 29. G 30. Slip the rubber band through to the middle of the paper. 31. A

p. 682-689

SA: D 1. C 2. J 3. to raise money to buy bats and balls 4. B 5. To take a job, as her family needed money following her father's death. 6. G 7. A 8. J 9. B 10. J 11. C 12. chicken 13. H 14. C 15. H 16. C 17. J 18. B 19. G 20. D 21. G 22. A 23. H 24. They hoped to become rich quickly. 25. B 26. G 27. A 28. to tell the history of the California Gold Rush 29. The weather was threatening. 30. H 31. B 32. G

p. 690

SA. D 1. D 2. J 3. B 4. G 5. B 6. H 7. B 8. cold

p. 691

SA. A 1. C 2. G 3. C 4. H

p. 692

SA. A 1. A 2. J 3. C 4. difficult 5. F 6. A

p. 693-695

SA. D 1. C 2. J 3. A 4. F 5. B 6. J 7. C 8. F 9. tired SB. C 10. A 11. J 12. C 13. F 14. D SC. A 15. H 16. D 17. F 18. C 19. J 20. C 21. G 22. the story

p. 697

Step 1. to draw a map illustrating Mr. Gonzalez's trip Step 2. He drove 45 miles to Boston from Manorville. From Boston he drove 15 miles north to Oaktown. Manorville is west of Boston. Step 3. Draw a map and label it. Step 4. Step 5. Yes, because the diagram drawn shows the information included in the problem.

p. 698

Step 1. Is $19.50 the approximated cost for 5 books? If not, indicate what error Su Ling may have made. Step 2. Each book costs $4.95. Su Ling bought 5 books. Su Link estimated the total cost to be $19.50. Step 3. Calculate: Multiply $4.95 x 5 Step 4. $4.95 x 5 = $24.75. Su Ling's estimate of $19.50 was wrong. Her mistake may have been that she rounded off $4.95 to be $4.00. Then she estimated the total cost to be just under $20 instead of just under $25. Step 5. Yes, because Su Ling did estimate incorrectly and the explanation offered is one possible explanation.

p. 699

SA. A 1. 12.09, 12.2, 12.25, 12.53 2. C 3. J 4. D 5. H

p. 700

SA. D 1. C 2. F 3. A 4. H 5. 7 6. B

p. 701

SA. B 1. D 2. G 3. B 4. F 5. C 6. 11

p. 702-703

SA. B 1. C 2. J 3. $24.75 4. C 5. G 6. C 7. F 8. 123 9. A 10. H

p. 704

SA. D 1. C 2. 240 3. G

p. 705

SA. D 1. C 2. 9,000 3. G 4. D

p. 706-707

SA. B 1. bike rack, tables, water 2. D 3. 55 m 4. G 5. C 6. F 7. C 8. G 9. D 10. F 11. B

p. 708-709

SA. C 1. D 2. 12:15 3. F 4. C 5. F 6. D 7. F 8. C 9. G 10. C. 11. 2 cm

p. 710

SA. A 1. 125 2. B 3. F 4. D

p. 711

SA. D 1. D 2. F 3. C 4. H 5. A 6. 12 R4 7. H 8. D

p. 712

SA. D 1. B 2. H 3. C 4. $2,056

p. 713-714

SA. B SB. K 1. E 2. G 3. B 4. K 5. C 6. G 7. B 8. G 9. 5,950 10. A 11. K 12. A 13. H 14. B 15. G

p. 715-721

SA. D 1. A 2. J 3. C 4. J 5. C 6. J 7. B 8. 3 hundredths 9. H 10. A 11. H 12. D 13. G 14. B 15. H 16. 24 17. C 18. F 19. C 20. H 21. A 22. H 23. 45 24. A 25. G 26. C 27. G 28. 21 29. B 30. H 31. C 32. G 33. C 34. G 35. 48 ft. 36. A 37. H 38. D 39. H 40. D 41. 2 42. F 43. A 44. H 45. C 46. on the 7th 47. J 48. B 49. J 50. B

p. 722-727

SA. B 1. B 2. Chapter 6 3. G 4. D 5. J 6. D 7. G 8. C 9. H 10. B 11. G 12. C 13. F 14. 6 15. A 16. G 17. C 18. G 19. A 20. H 21. D 22. G

p. 728

SA. A 1. D 2. J 3. C 4. F 5. B 6. G 7. A 8. F

p. 729-733

SA. C 1. A 2. G 3. B 4. Sentence 6 5. J 6. B 7. J 8. C 9. H 10. A 11. G 12. C 13. J 14. A 15. J 16. D 17. G 18. B 19. H 20. D 21. G 22. A 23. F 24. B 25. J 26. B 27. H 28. B

p. 734-742

SA. D 1. B 2. to fish for bass 3. G 4. the sunset, the animal sounds, and the snapping turtle 5. D 6. H 7. A 8. clams and oyster shells 9. H 10. D 11. F 12. B 13. J 14. She boils them in water for five to ten minutes. 15. B 16. F 17. extremely important 18. C 19. F 20. D 21. F 22. D 23. F 24. B 25. J 26. A 27. H 28. C 29. H 30. There were very few trees growing on the Great Plains. 31. C 32. H 33. B 34. H 35. Saturday and Sunday, April 20 and 21 36. B 37. Grandma's car had been ruined in the flood. 38. G 39. C 40. J

p. 743-745

SA. A 1. D 2. G 3. C 4. H 5. B 6. G 7. A 8. F 9. ridiculous SB. B 10. D 11. F 12. C 13. J 14. C SC. D 15. F 16. C 17. H 18. D 19. H 20. A 21. real

p. 746-753

SA. B 1. B 2. G 3. D 4. G 5. C
6. H 7. D 8. J 9. D 10. G 11. $129
12. C 13. J 14. 0.7 15. D 16. H
17. B 18. G 19. B 20. 48 and 72
21. G 22. B 23. J 24. C 25. 21
26. J 27. C 28. H 29. D 30. 22
31. F 32. 71 33. D 34. J 35. B
36. G 37. A 38. J 39. B 40. 24 in.
41. J 42. C 43. H 44. The Rangers
had the most wins. 45. A 46. F
47. B 48. G 49. B 50. G

p. 754-755

SA. A 1. 0.0085 2. A 3. F 4. E 5. F
6. A 7. J 8. C 9. K SB. D 10. A
11. G 12. D 13. J 14. 6

p. 756-762

SA. C 1. A 2. J 3. C 4. F 5. the title
page 6. A 7. F 8. B 9. H 10.
Chapter 1 11. B 12. 3 13. F 14. D
15. J 16. B 17. F 18. C 19. 14
20. H 21. C 22. F 23. B 24. J
25. C 26. J 27. A 28. G 29. C
30. H 31. B 32. F 33. A 34. J
35. A 36. H 37. C 38. F 39. C
40. J 41. C